FERTILITY TRANSITION IN SOUTH ASIA

The International Union for the Scientific Study of Population Problems was set up in 1928, with Dr Raymond Pearl as President. At that time the Union's main purpose was to promote international scientific co-operation to study the various aspects of population problems, through national committees and through its members themselves. In 1947 the International Union for the Scientific Study of Population (IUSSP) was reconstituted into its present form.

It expanded its activities to:
- stimulate research on population
- develop interest in demographic matters among governments, national and international organizations, scientific bodies, and the general public
- foster relations between people involved in population studies
- disseminate scientific knowledge on population.

The principal ways through which the IUSSP currently achieves its aims are:
- organization of worldwide or regional conferences
- operations of Scientific Committees under the auspices of the Council
- organization of training courses
- publication of conference proceedings and committee reports.

Demography can be defined by its field of study and its analytical methods. Accordingly, it can be regarded as the scientific study of human populations primarily with respect to their size, their structure, and their development. For reasons which are related to the history of the discipline, the demographic method is essentially inductive: progress in knowledge results from the improvement of observation, the sophistication of measurement methods, and the search for regularities and stable factors leading to the formulation of explanatory models. In conclusion, the three objectives of demographic analysis are to describe, measure, and analyse.

International Studies in Demography is the outcome of an agreement concluded by the IUSSP and the Oxford University Press. The joint series reflects the broad range of the Union's activities; it is based on the seminars organized by the Union and important international meetings in the field of population and development. The Editorial Board of the series is comprised of:

FERTILITY TRANSITION IN SOUTH ASIA

Edited by

Zeba Ayesa Sathar
and
James F. Phillips

OXFORD
UNIVERSITY PRESS

OXFORD

UNIVERSITY PRESS

Great Clarendon Street, Oxford OX2 6DP

Oxford University Press is a department of the University of Oxford.
It furthers the University's objective of excellence in research, scholarship,
and education by publishing worldwide in

Oxford New York

Athens Auckland Bangkok Bogotá Buenos Aires Cape Town
Chennai Dar es Salaam Delhi Florence Hong Kong Istanbul Karachi
Kolkata Kuala Lumpur Madrid Melbourne Mexico City Mumbai Nairobi
Paris São Paulo Shanghai Singapore Taipei Tokyo Toronto Warsaw
with associated companies in Berlin Ibadan

Oxford is a registered trade mark of Oxford University Press
in the UK and in certain other countries

Published in the United States
by Oxford University Press Inc., New York

© IUSSP, 2001

British Library Cataloguing in Publication Data

Data available

Library of Congress Cataloging in Publication Data

Data available

ISBN 0-19-924185-6

10 9 8 7 6 5 4 3 2 1

Typeset by Newgen Imaging Systems Pvt. Ltd. Chennai, India.
Printed in Great Britain
on acid-free paper by
Biddles Ltd., *www.biddles.co.uk*

Preface

South Asia's population totals over 1.2 billion people, more than one-fifth of humankind, and its countries contribute more than those of any other geographic subregion to the growth of the world's population. With the bulk of the world's poor in its midst, South Asia is rightly an area of major concern to all of us, and a highly relevant focus for this IUSSP seminar.

The demographic landscape of Asia has seen unprecedented changes in the post-World War II era. Population policies, and, through them, public-sector family planning programmes, have had a major influence in shaping these changes. In fact, national family planning programmes had their birth in South Asia.

The East Asia Experience

Just as the family planning programmes in South Asia were slowly gaining momentum, those in East Asia were beginning. In the 1950s and early 1960s, the demographic situation of East Asia was much the same as that of South Asia. Fertility levels were high but death rates were declining. In other words, the countries in both regions were at the first stage of the demographic transition. However, the post-World War II modernization of East Asia's mortality was more spectacular than that in South Asia, and it was South Asia that continued to experience rapid population growth rates, as East Asia's fertility declined dramatically.

By the mid-1980s, most of the countries of East Asia had, or had nearly, completed the demographic transition. This transformation transcended political, economic, cultural and religious boundaries, and its speed and magnitude were historically unprecedented. What were the reasons behind it, and are there lessons to be learnt for South Asia?

Supply-side factors, in particular population policy and family planning programmes, played a major part in the East Asian fertility transition. In sharp contrast with the earlier fertility decline in the West, the role played by government leadership—through population policy, and particularly government-led family planning programmes—was highly significant. However, the role and importance of policies and programmes was by no means the same throughout East Asia.

In East Asia, the rapid decline in infant and child mortality reinforced the demand for smaller families, and could itself have been an outcome of family planning. But the major factor affecting the demand for children was undoubtedly the spread and upgrading of schooling and the associated decline in levels of illiteracy among women of reproductive ages. Throughout East Asia, governments adopted people-centred development strategies and made major investments in education, particularly in primary education, as well as in rural health programmes.

The South Asia Experience

In general, the economic and social conditions of the countries of South Asia stand in sharp contrast to those of East Asia. Economic growth in South Asia has been much less pronounced, and all the countries under consideration at this meeting are very low-income economies. Their populations remain predominantly rural, and rates of unemployment and underemployment are high. Rapid population growth has clearly put pressures on the governments' budgets, and has lessened their ability to increase social investments in education and health. Social progress has been relatively modest, with substantial gender differences remaining in schooling and, as a consequence, in levels of female literacy. Thus, for example, just one-quarter of all adult females in Bangladesh and Pakistan are literate, and just over one-third in India—figures that are substantially lower than among adult males in these countries.

Both the persistence of strong patterns of son preference and discrimination against girls reflect attitudes and values deeply rooted in traditional agrarian modes of organization in patriarchal societies. While in most countries of the world, female life expectancy at birth exceeds that of males, this is not generally so in South Asia.

In many countries of South Asia, differentials also exist during the reproductive ages, when maternal mortality remains very high. High maternal mortality reflects weaknesses in the coverage and quality of reproductive health services, including family planning, particularly in rural areas. Significant proportions of mothers in all countries except Sri Lanka give birth without the presence of, or even having seen, a trained birth attendant, and most women at the time of childbirth are out of reach of emergency care to deal with obstetric complications. The lack of services, both human and physical, results in many readily avoidable maternal deaths. This unmet need, which is most concentrated in areas of extreme poverty, requires both the extension of services and improvements in the quality of delivery. It more generally reflects the inadequacy of the overall health infrastructure throughout most rural parts of South Asia.

Fertility Change

While fertility reductions have been much slower in South Asia than in East Asia, there have been some impressive recent changes. Sri Lanka is the only South Asian country that has completed the transition to replacement level fertility. Its decline began in the 1950s, largely as a result of the rise in the age at marriage, and, subsequently, through a fall in marital fertility as a result of increased contraceptive use.

In the mid-1990s, women in Bangladesh and India were having between three and four children. The relatively recent, remarkable and largely unexpected rapid fertility decline seen in Bangladesh since the early 1980s contrasts with the much steadier change that has occurred in India. Initial doubts about the magnitude of fertility decline in Bangladesh have been swept aside by evidence from recent surveys showing increasing use of modern methods of contraception, with the oral pill now accounting for 60 per cent of all methods.

In India, trends in aggregate fertility levels conceal marked state variations. Thus, for example, whereas fertility in the southern states of Kerala and Tamil Nadu is around replacement level, women in the poor states, such as Bihar and Uttar Pradesh, are still bearing just under five children. The areas where fertility has declined most are those where social progress has been greatest.

In the mid-1990s, women in Pakistan and Nepal were having between five and six children. Although higher than the fertility levels prevailing in the other South Asian countries, the evidence of some recent declines is promising and is consistent with a small rise in the age of women at first marriage. A key factor in the persistence of high fertility in both countries appears to be the neglect of women's education and their generally low social and economic status.

The lesson from Sri Lanka, and even more spectacularly from Bangladesh, is that fertility can decline in low-income countries, so long as investments are made in social-sector programmes, and with strong political commitment.

Family Planning Programme Experiences in South Asia

The evidence from successive surveys in South Asia has shown a secular increase in the knowledge and, to a lesser extent, the use of modern contraceptive methods, although levels vary sharply between the countries. By the mid-1990s, knowledge of contraception was very widespread among women in Bangladesh, India and Sri Lanka, but somewhat less so among the populations of Nepal and Pakistan, where the family planning programmes have had less impact.

As might be expected from trends in levels of fertility, the spread of the use of contraception has been very uneven. Sri Lanka has long been, and remains, significantly ahead of the other countries in its level of contraceptive use. However, levels in Bangladesh are now much the same as in India, where contraceptive prevalence rates are currently around 50 per cent. Both Nepal and Pakistan remain well below these levels, consistent with their higher fertility.

Although ostensibly offering a cafeteria approach, South Asian family planning programmes have traditionally placed more emphasis on long-term and permanent, rather than reversible, methods, particularly female sterilization—but less so recently, especially in Bangladesh and Nepal. The emphasis on one-time methods was based on the consideration that they required little followup with acceptors, are not user-dependent for success, and are logistically convenient to deliver.

In general, female sterilization seems to have become culturally acceptable and is often the method of choice of service providers, if not of their clients. This has led to less attention given to women's need to space their births. Consequently, maternal mortality rates have declined much more slowly than might have been possible in South Asian countries if a wider choice of contraceptive methods for spacing and higher quality family planning services had been offered.

Meeting Unmet Need Throughout South Asia

There is considerable evidence of high levels of unmet need for family planning services in this region. Successive series of demographic and health surveys tend to show that women have an increasing preference for a moderate number of children—although with at least one son. The survey findings also reveal that substantial proportions of women with three or more living children want to stop childbearing altogether. Unmet need for family planning is also reflected in other ways. For example, among older women, a significant proportion report that their last pregnancy was unwanted. Moreover, and in addition to unwanted births, survey evidence also shows that there is considerable unmet demand for reversible methods to improve the spacing between births.

The challenge for the governments and non-governmental organizations of this region remains translating this unmet need for contraception into effective demand by minimizing the constraints on family planning use. This may be done by improving the coverage and quality of delivery systems, and the provision of appropriate counselling to reduce non-use due to side effects. Further, social constraints can be reduced through culturally sensitive IEC campaigns.

Research Needs

Before concluding, I would like to allude to a few areas in which policy-relevant research is needed:

- *Education*: It is now abundantly clear that education has a major impact on population dynamics. Yet through the developing world, and particularly in South Asia, there are still high levels of dropouts at all educational grades. In that respect it would be helpful if research could focus on the transaction costs of attending school, from the perspective of poor rural parents, so that more can be done to promote higher school enrolment and continuation rates, especially for girls.

- *Gender discrimination against girls*: The value of girl children to both their family and society must be expanded beyond their definition as potential childbearers and caretakers, and must be reinforced through the implementation of expanded educational and social policies aimed at this neglected group. Further research is needed to discover the extent of discriminatory practices, and to identify appropriate public education and information campaigns that could be launched to promote the equal treatment of boys and girls.
- *Status of women*: There is still an overwhelming lack of information on the linkages between the status and rights of girls and women and their reproductive behaviour. Research on this important topic is much needed.

Nafis Sadik

Contents

Contributors

LAXMI ACHARYA, London School of Hygiene and Tropical Medicine, UK
SHAMEEM AHMED, International Centre for Diarrhoeal Disease Research, Bangladesh
SAJEDA AMIN, Population Council, USA
FRED ARNOLD, Macro International, USA
JOHN BONGAARTS, Population Council, USA
JOHN C. CALDWELL, Australian National University, Australia
BRUCE K. CALDWELL, Australian National University, Australia
PAT CALDWELL, Australian National University, Australia
A. M. R. CHOWDHURY, Bangladesh Rural Advancement Committee, Bangladesh
MARTINE COLLUMBIEN, London School of Hygiene and Tropical Medicine, UK
MONICA DAS GUPTA, World Bank, USA
PAUL DEMENY, Population Council, USA
IAN DIAMOND, University of Southampton, UK
TIM DYSON, London School of Economics and Political Science, UK
ABDULLAHEL HADI, Bangladesh Rural Advancement Committee, Bangladesh
ABDUL HAKIM, National Institute of Population Studies, Pakistan
SHI-JEN HE, East-West Center, USA
ANRUDH JAIN, Population Council, USA
SHIREEN J. JEJEEBHOY, World Health Organization, Switzerland
SHAHNAZ KAZI, Pakistan Institute of Development Economics/World Bank, Pakistan
ANDREW KANTNER, East-West Center, USA
BARKAT-E-KHUDA, International Centre for Diarrhoeal Disease Research, Bangladesh
C. M. LANGFORD, London School of Economics and Political Science, UK
JULIET MCEACHRAN, University of Southampton, UK
PETER C. MILLER, Population Council, Pakistan
VINOD MISHRA, East-West Center, USA
R. L. NARASIMHAN, Ministry of Health and Family Welfare, India
SAMIR R. NATH, Bangladesh Rural Advancement Committee, Bangladesh
JAMES F. PHILLIPS (Editor), Population Council, USA
INDRANI PIERIS, Australian Institute of Health and Welfare, Australia
B. M. RAMESH, J.S.S. Institute of Economic Research, India
ROBERT D. RETHERFORD, East-West Center, USA

WARREN C. ROBINSON, Professor Emeritus, Pennsylvania State University, USA
T. K. ROY, International Institute for Population Sciences, India
ZEBA A. SATHAR (Editor and Contributor), Population Council, Pakistan
SHARON STASH, David and Lucile Packard Foundation, USA
IAN M. TIMÆUS, London School of Hygiene and Tropical Medicine, UK

Introduction

ZEBA A. SATHAR AND JAMES F. PHILLIPS

Introduction

As recently as a decade ago, experts continued to write about the demographic homogeneity of South Asia. Few would have predicted the demographic diversity that has emerged in recent years. Given the common history, cultural affinity, and shared geography of South Asian populations, authors often overlooked the possible demographic implications of linguistic, religious, and political diversity. But evidence of profound demographic change is now unmistakable.

All countries of South Asia have now entered the fertility transition; fertility levels, which were once consistently high, now evince pronounced areal variance within countries, profound differences between countries, and substantial variance within cultural zones that span international borders. Although the origins and determinants of this variation are poorly understood, and the precise onset of fertility decline is still subject to discussion and debate, fertility transition in combination with demographic heterogeneity in South Asia is now an established fact.

This new era of demographic heterogeneity has inspired the present volume. The South Asian demographic transition requires documentation because new demographic regimes and circumstances challenge conventional views on the determinants of fertility and the rationale for existing policies. Although rapid population growth will continue well into the next century, alarmist views of past circumstances are no longer helpful in guiding contemporary policy. Evidence of a South Asian fertility transition gives rise to renewed questions about fertility determinants, the causes of differences in the timing and pace of reproductive change, and the role of policies in influencing the trends observed and explaining the contrasting demographic results achieved. It is appropriate to determine whether a major demographic transition is in progress, whether observed changes represent a departure from past expectations, and whether conventional explanations of demographic determinants still apply or require modification.

Geographic variance represents a resource for testing the relevance of social theory to explaining a current scenario[1] and for examining the relative roles of population programmes and secular socioeconomic trends as determinants of

---

[1] The role of policy as envisaged in earlier seminal work of Coale and Hoover (1958), UN reviews, and field experiments merits reappraisal in light of evidence of rapid reproductive change in the region.

demographic change. While there is little doubt that health policy played a major role in the process of fertility decline by reducing mortality, the role of family planning programmes and other policies continues to be debated. As demographic transitions progress, the rationale for public investment in large-scale programmes has re-emerged as an issue for discussion and debate.

While the demographic transition in South Asia is assumed to be well under way, the fact remains that fertility in the region is high by global standards, and that the onset of the transition there was late, relative to that of East Asia. While the global total fertility rate is now below 3, and near replacement level in East Asia, the South Asia total fertility rate remains above 4 (United Nations 1998). Nonetheless, the fact that the region's population now exceeds one billion means that the weight of the sheer numbers associated with the South Asian fertility decline has already had a substantial impact on global population size and the pace of demographic trends.

This volume focuses on the fertility changes in South Asia that have occurred in the past five decades. The first few chapters review evidence of the timing and pace of reproductive change. Data are described, their deficiencies are reviewed, and contemporary trends are compared with the historical record. Authors agree that fertility transition has begun throughout the region, but controversy about the timing of the transitions persists, because of data deficiencies. A subsequent section presents general explanations for fertility change in the region and interpretations of change in particular countries or subregions. Comparative perspectives are utilized to explore the importance of alternative explanations for the special features of the fertility transition in this region. A final section examines the role of population policy in the past and issues for population policy in the future. Particular attention is directed to discussion of the role of family planning programmes as the first 'social engineering' effort ever to have had an arguably demonstrable influence on mass behaviour. The implications for future population policy of current demographic circumstances and of population momentum are addressed. The volume concludes with an examination of the policy implications of the 1994 Cairo International Conference of Population and Development, emerging research gaps, and issues to be addressed by population programmes in the future.

The Fertility Transition in South Asia

Levels and trends in total fertility rates and in life expectancy for the countries of South Asia are presented in Figs. 1 and 2, respectively.[2] Figure 1 illustrates the pace of fertility transition in South Asia and the transformation of the South Asian fertility regime from homogeneously high fertility in the period before 1960 to heterogeneously declining fertility in the 1990s. The figure shows that the onset

---

[2] Figures 1 and 2 are derived from United Nations demographic estimates (United Nations 1998).

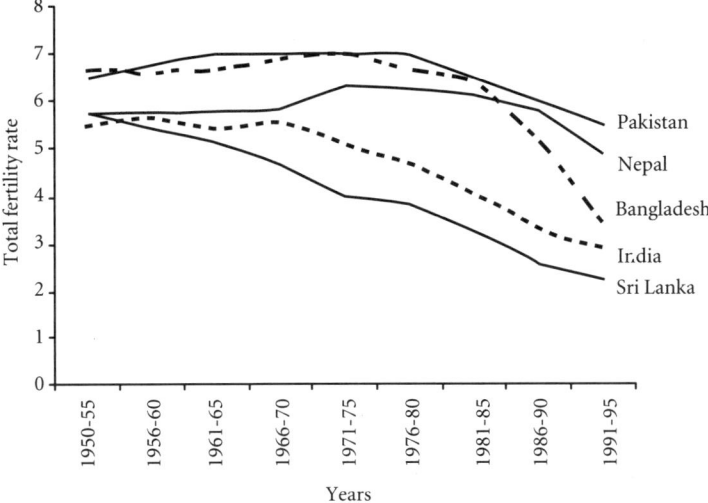

Figure 1. Fertility transition in South Asia.

of fertility decline in Sri Lanka dates to the 1960s. Evidence of fertility decline in India emerged in the 1970s, a rapid transformation of fertility was under way in Bangladesh in the early 1980s, and a less pronounced, but substantial fertility decline was evident soon after in Pakistan and Nepal. Thus, by the end of the century, fertility was declining throughout the region.

As Fig. 2 shows, throughout the region, mortality declines preceded fertility declines by several decades, although the health transition is still under way in each South Asian country. The immediate cause of general mortality declines in the post-Independence period was the successful eradication of smallpox, the control of cholera, improved treatment of other diarrhoeal diseases, and mass campaigns against other major infectious diseases such as measles, malaria, and acute respiratory infections. The overall burden of disease has been most substantially reduced by advances in the coverage of immunization programmes, the availability of antibiotic therapy, and promotion of other low-cost interventions that can be administered by paramedics.

As Dyson notes, however (Chapter 2 in this volume), the onset of mortality decline in the region was not uniform. In Sri Lanka and Kerala, mortality decline commenced in the 1940s, while Pakistan and South India witnessed the onset of decline in the 1950s, and North India somewhat later. In the 1970s, Bangladesh and Nepal were the last countries in the region to enter the mortality transition. Infant mortality rates have generally lagged behind declines in adult mortality. This is reflected in the United Nations South Asia model life tables, which portray high infant mortality rates relative to mortality rates for other ages. While infant

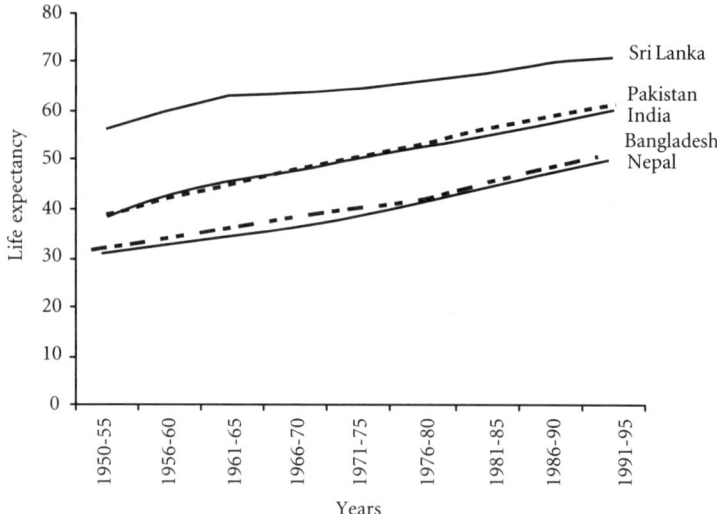

Figure 2. Life expectancy in South Asia.

mortality declined rapidly throughout the 1960s and 1970s and then more gradually in the 1980s and 1990s (Kantner and He, Chapter 1 in this volume), it remains high in most of South Asia. Infant mortality in the mid-1990s ranges from 17 per 1,000 live births in Sri Lanka to about 80 in Nepal, India, and Bangladesh and 90 in Pakistan (Kantner and He, Chapter 1).

While the broad outlines of the timing and sequence of mortality and fertility trends are consistent with conventional demographic transition theory, the precise link between mortality trends and fertility change in South Asia is often unclear, since mortality decline is not a strong predictor of fertility decline in localities of the region.[3] In general, however, major improvements in survival in one generation were followed by subsequent fertility decline in the next. In Sri Lanka, for example, mortality declined earlier than in the rest of the region, and fertility decline ensued. Most other countries experienced mortality declines in the 1950s and 1960s somewhat in unison; however, the timing of the fertility decline is relatively varied. Thus, mortality decline tends to predate fertility decline, but the lag in adjusting to lower levels of mortality and the duration of the demographic transition vary across the region.

In Sri Lanka the decline in fertility seems to have closely followed mortality declines in earlier decades, while the decline in Bangladesh occurred while mortality levels were relatively much higher. However, equivalent levels of mortality in Pakistan (as in Bangladesh) in earlier decades of the 1970s did not seem to be a

---

[3] Similar conclusions have been reached about the demographic transition in Western Europe. While aggregate trends suggest that mortality declines were antecedent to fertility declines, areal analysis of small geographic units fails to substantiate this hypothesis.

trigger to fertility change. It is necessary to find the missing link in the lag between mortality and fertility change and a possible correlation of the two phases of the traditional demographic transition.

Interpreting current trends requires a long-term historical perspective on the relationship of contemporary fertility to fertility levels and cycles in the distant past (Dyson, Chapter 2; Collumbien *et al.*, Chapter 4). Where data permit a historical appraisal (e.g. India and Nepal), comparative analyses suggest a much earlier onset of declines than do judgements based on data from recent decades alone. In comparison to demographic transitions observed in other regions, South Asian transitions suggest that couples have taken longer than in other regions to 'adjust' to mortality declines in altering their reproductive intentions and behaviour in response to changes in mortality.

A dominant theme in South Asian demography, and one echoed loudly in this volume, is that of the problems and limitations of data. The authors of many of the chapters in Part I challenge the validity of data from various sources, including vital registration, surveys, and censuses (Kantner and He, Chapter 1; Collumbien *et al.*, Chapter 4; Narasimhan *et al.*, Chapter 3). It is difficult to draw firm conclusions about demographic trends in South Asia when the demographic data are marred by a long history of problems of age misreporting, birth and death omissions, and errors in the timing of events. The errors are not uniform, however, which makes establishing exact levels of fertility and mortality impossible. The papers in this volume review both data sources that are weak and sources that are relatively robust and reliable.

Some major controversies arise out of the papers included in this volume. For example, the findings of Dyson (Chapter 2) seem to be in direct contradiction with those of Narasimhan *et al.* (Chapter 3). Data, as we well know, are interpretable in many ways. These differences demonstrate the importance of incorporating different interpretations before reaching any conclusions. Moreover, researchers engaged in the interpretation and analysis of demographic trends in South Asia continued in the 1990s, as they did decades earlier, to reflect on the fundamental question of what inferences can be drawn from existing data.

In general there is a greater reliance on cross-sectional surveys, with some adjustment made for age-reporting errors, through own-children techniques, adjusted parity progression ratios, etc. The techniques used to correct for data have been applied most extensively to data from South Asia precisely because a lot of data are available and there are large deficiencies. Censuses are another major source of information, especially in the construction of time trends. Vital registration is a particularly weak base of information in this region, which attaches very little importance to the registration of births and deaths. With a few exceptional trial sites, vital registration systems cover only a small proportion of the population of South Asia.

This compiled documentation of reproductive change in the 1990s locates individual countries and subregions (within India especially) at different stages of the fertility transition. While 15 years ago very little change in fertility was documented, with the exception of Sri Lanka, Kerala, and Tamil Nadu (Dyson and Crook 1984), most of the region is now experiencing declines in fertility (Kantner and He, Chapter 1). Although there is unequivocal evidence of a fertility transition in all localities of South Asia, Dyson presents historical evidence from vital registration systems suggesting that fertility and mortality declines were already under way much earlier in the 1950s and 1960s. If, indeed, reproductive change began much earlier than has been previously documented, this conclusion has some important ramifications for interpretation of the demographic transition in South Asia. Dyson's main sources in support of his argument of earlier reproductive change are vital registration rates reconstructed to produce time trends. Cross-sectional data do not support this argument, however, and secular deterioration in data quality may have compromised his analysis by producing spurious trends. Moreover, he argues that population laboratory data from Bangladesh suggests earlier declines than were previously acknowledged, when in fact these declines have been noted and attributed to the effects of economic shocks, war, famine, and the early impact of the introduction of family planning.[4]

Sri Lanka, the forerunner of the South Asian region, has completed its demographic transition, reaching fertility below replacement level (Langford, Chapter 5 in this volume). Kerala and Tamil Nadu within southern India are following closely behind, with fertility close to replacement levels. Bangladesh experienced the most rapid transition in the region. Contraceptive prevalence rates rose from 19 to 45 per cent, and total fertility rates declined from 6.6 to 3.3 in the brief period between 1982 and 1994 (McEachran and Diamond, Chapter 7). Until recently, Nepal was widely believed to be a pretransitional setting, but evidence of reproductive change in that country is now unmistakable (Collumbien et al., Chapter 4). Pakistan is the last country in the region to experience reproductive change, following even the northern Indian states of Uttar Pradesh and Rajasthan, which are known to be slower than other Indian states to enter the transition. Although a decline in fertility is being witnessed in Pakistan in the early 1990s, fertility remains above five births per woman (Hakim and Miller, Chapter 6), a level that is fully 60 per cent higher than that in Bangladesh and more than double prevailing rates in Kerala and Sri Lanka.

Analyses reported in this volume demonstrate that the relatively earlier fertility transitions in the region have not necessarily been the most rapid. In fact, the speed of fertility decline has been more dramatic in Bangladesh than in Sri Lanka, which

---

[4] The demographic effect of the Bangladesh War of Independence has been analysed by Curlin et al. (1975), and the demographic effects of economic crises and famine have been reviewed in Chen (1973), Chen and Chowdhury (1975), and Arthur and McNicoll (1978). The Independence conflict and the crisis that preceded it were associated with reduced fertility and elevated mortality; a famine in 1976 and 1977 was associated with marked fertility decline. In Matlab, a family planning experiment that began in 1975 reduced fertility over the 1976–78 period by about 9 per cent (Phillips et al. 1982; Stinson et al. 1982).

led in its fertility transition by two decades. Furthermore, Kerala and Sri Lanka, both with fairly parallel declines in death rates, experienced birth rate declines that shared a common point of onset but then followed contrasting trajectories over time (Dyson, Chapter 2). The onset of the fertility decline has been relatively late in Nepal and Pakistan, but even these transitions may have occurred earlier than has been generally believed (Collumbien *et al.*, Chapter 4). On the other hand, the onset appears to have been later than some authors had predicted for Pakistan (Retherford *et al.* 1987).

Furthermore, Sri Lanka began its fertility transition in the early 1960s, Bangladesh in the early 1980s, India in the mid-to-late 1980s (with the exceptions of Tamil Nadu and Kerala at least a decade earlier), and Pakistan, probably in the early 1990s. Thus, the South Asian fertility transition spans over almost 30 years, and remains incomplete in all countries except Sri Lanka. While Sri Lanka is close to completing its transition, having reached replacement fertility (Langford, Chapter 5), even the most optimistic appraisal for Pakistan suggests that it will take that country another 20 years to reach replacement fertility (United Nations 1998; Government of Pakistan 1965).

The varied pace of transition in the region raises several important issues about the future of reproductive change. If a country is late to experience fertility decline, will it be more likely to experience a relatively rapid transition? Is there a diffusion effect, whereby neighbouring countries eventually converge towards lower fertility in sequence? Thus, will the contemporary demographic heterogeneity of South Asia eventually coalesce at homogeneously low fertility levels throughout the region? While the South Asian experience appears to demonstrate that there is little under-lying commonality in the countries involved, it may be more of an historical aberration than an accurate portrayal of underlying circumstances. The South Asia transition began at similar points, and countries and localities are following differ-ent paths of reproductive change, but the process may produce similar end points in a manner that raises the ante of what theories of fertility decline have to offer.

Comparative Perspectives

The most widely studied of the demographic transitions is certainly the European transition. Studies of the European transition and demographic transition theory are the only guiding frameworks available to us from the past as to how and when to expect the demographic transition in South Asia. But because the South Asian region seemed to diverge from 'expected' patterns, speculation has arisen about the contextual theoretical basis and explanations for demographic change based on the European model. The main features of the European transition were unprecedented industrialization, followed by increasing educational and living standards that improved survival and well-being, leading to changes in family forms and to a rise in the age at marriage and in the use of fertility control within marriage. The broad outlines of the events associated with the European transition were framed by the pioneering work of Frank Notestein (1945), and subsequently examined in a series of important appraisals (Coale and Watkins 1986).

Contemporary transitions in East Asia and Latin America have followed patterns somewhat different from the European model. First, Asian and Latin American transitions occurred in settings in which families were larger and pronatalist institutions more entrenched in society than was the case at the beginning of the European demographic transition. Moreover, the onset and pace of the Latin American transition seem to have been much more uniform across the region than was the case in Europe, East Asia, and South Asia (Guzman *et al.* 1996).

No region has presented a greater challenge to the notion of a unified theory of fertility transition than South Asia. South Asia could not have been predicted to have such a varied fertility transition in terms of disparate onsets and speed of reproductive change. Furthermore, there is sparse commonality in the conditions leading up to a decline across countries within the region. Rapid industrialization and economic development is not an appealing explanation of the changes that occurred. Most of South Asia seems to have experienced the onset of fertility transition in the context of relatively low per capita income, with most of its labour force still involved largely in agricultural occupations, of continuing strong family ties, and of the predominance—or at least a substantial continuation—of extended family systems throughout the region.

The disparate conditions setting the stage for South Asian fertility transitions challenge conventional wisdom about the role of economic development in fostering reproductive change. In Bangladesh and the South Indian states of Kerala and Tamil Nadu, for example, much 'earlier' declines ensued than in relatively wealthy and advanced states such as the Punjab. Pakistan, with its relatively high economic growth in the 1980s and its relatively high per capita income, would also have been expected to experience concomitant demographic change earlier than the early 1990s. In fact, an early and rapid fertility decline in places such as Bangladesh often suggests that poverty is more of a cause or catalyst for fertility change than a factor inhibiting transition. Urbanization is also a factor producing counter-conventional trends. For example, of the countries in the region, the rate of urbanization is highest in Pakistan, the country that is last to experience the fertility transition. In general, urban areas across the South Asian region have experienced fertility change before it proliferated to rural areas. However, the lag has been quite short in settings such as Bangladesh.

The role of social structure also challenges conventional views of the determinants of transition. In Europe and Latin America, which tend to be more stratified than East Asia, transition began in the higher social strata and subsequently diffused to other groups. This pattern is also evident in highly stratified South Asian settings, where affluent, educated, urban élites first controlled their fertility, and this behaviour then spread to other segments of society. In Bangladesh and Sri Lanka, however, rapid reproductive change occurred in all segments of society with equal force—the wealthy and the poor, the educated and the less educated, the rural and the urban; all experienced rapid reproductive change once transition began. These contrasts suggest that a diffusion or contagion process plays a crucial catalytic role in South Asian transitions. The process accelerates transition in settings where the lack of social stratification fosters the communication of ideational change, and constrains it where caste structures, inequalities in educational or income levels, and cultural institutions isolate people and limit social interaction. South Asian élites in India and Pakistan espoused smaller family sizes even at the time of Independence, and certainly soon after. The fissure between their behaviour and that of the larger groups of uneducated and rural South Asians has always been vast. Fertility transitions have to reflect the final bridging of the gap between the smaller population of élites and the larger population.

The papers dealing with possible explanations of reproductive change in South Asia explore the relative importance of all these issues. The role of the state does seem to be important in determining the timing and speed of reproductive change. The clear differences noted across the two Punjabs (in Pakistan and in India), and the slighter but significant differences across the two Bengals, demonstrate that state boundaries are important. Forms of government and the strength and popularity of the state must determine factors such as major institutional arrangements, which ultimately impact on the social values surrounding reproduction. Examples of these are the educational system, for one, the power of the citizenry, and the effectiveness of civil society in influencing public opinions, morality, and values. Democratic values and the breakdown of feudalism in parts of India, in particular, are forcefully argued to be transmitted particularly through the media, thus leading to some social and demographic change (Das Gupta, Chapter 9). Bangladesh, Sri Lanka, Tamil Nadu, and Kerala are examples of more equitable societies, with class hierarchies that appear to be less strictly defined and more amenable to penetration. This may be a strong reason for the earlier onset of social change in these settings, when compared to the highly stratified and feudalistic class structures found in Pakistan and in some northern states of India.

Comparisons between the two Punjabs and the two Bengals demonstrate that demographic trends differ across political boundaries despite common historical, cultural, and linguistic identities. This conclusion suggests that different policy environments have influenced demographic trends (as noted by papers in this volume by Ramesh, Chapter 8; Das Gupta, Chapter 9; and Dyson, Chapter 2). Other authors in this volume reflect on linguistic and cultural heritage and argue that the diffusion of reproductive change should be affected by cultural boundaries, as was the case in Europe and East Asia (Coale and Watkins 1986; Leete and Alam 1993; Ramesh, Chapter 8). The absence of a common transition across borders challenges established theory, which emphasizes the importance of linguistic affiliation in sustaining simultaneous demographic trends. In Europe and East Asia, populations that shared a common language transcending political boundaries also shared a common transition. This does not appear to be the case for South Asia.

Common linguistic boundaries do not seem to predict simultaneous change in South Asia, as demonstrated by differences in the two Punjabs (Ramesh, Chapter 8) and Bengals (Das Gupta, Chapter 9). On the contrary, political boundaries representing genuinely different political, economic, and social institutions do have bearings on reproductive behaviour that far outweigh the role of language.

Political boundaries in South Asia define natural experiments for testing the hypothesis that policies have an impact. Political boundaries in South Asia are far less porous than borders of contiguous modern-day states, because of current hostile political relationships in the region. Social interactions believed to be so important in the European context—and presumably in Latin America—do not seem to be as effective a means of conveying changes in reproductive intentions and behaviour across South Asia. Differences, rather than similarities between the classes, limit the influence of social interactions, which might explain some of the diversity of the timing of reproductive change within countries of this region.

On the other hand, religion, which is often cited as a personal hindrance to the adoption of any form of fertility control throughout South Asia, does not appear to be a binding factor across the subcontinent. Hinduism and Islam are the major religions of this region. And yet religious differences in India are apparent but not as striking as regional differences (Jejeebhoy, Chapter 10) and populations bonded by common religions—such as the Muslims of Bangladesh (the former East Pakistan) and Pakistan—do not share much in common in terms of the timing and nature of reproductive change. Thus, religion does not seem to contribute to the explanation for other common affinities across South Asia that influence familial and other value systems.

Perhaps the most important social institutions and value systems are those surrounding gender relations and the role of families and intergenerational power-sharing. South Asia has been studied extensively in the search for gender-based explanations of reproductive change, or perhaps more aptly, stagnation (Dyson and Moore 1983). Caldwell, who has written extensively on South Asian demography, posited that mass education was a predictor of fertility decline, that major wealth flows from the young to the old depict high fertility regimes, and flows from the old to the young signify a change in fertility from high to low (Caldwell 1978). He also argues elsewhere that countries that over-invest in the social sectors (Costa Rica and Sri Lanka) have reaped benefits in terms of more rapid demographic change (Caldwell 1986). Other significant contributions explaining resistance to changes in fertility are by Cain (1979), who bases his explanation for Bangladesh on risk aversion through ensuring the survival of several sons, and on the importance of the value of children's net labour to family survival.

Some of the earliest explanations for demographic variation in South Asia, particularly India, rested on differences in the position of women and gender-based comparisons. In her book on the 'Endangered Sex', Miller first emphasized the differential in the 'worth' of women of South and North India (Miller 1981). The work of Dyson and Moore contributed further explanations for differences between the demographic regimes of the northern and southern states of India, based on different levels of female autonomy and other social differences (Dyson and Moore 1983). The research of Caldwell, Cain, and others has reinforced the dominance of gender-related behaviour in shaping demographic outcomes in South Asia. Most analysts are struck by the limited mobility, constrained autonomy, reliance on children (particularly sons in old age), the outstanding preference for male progeny, and the differences in the access of South Asian women to resources such as livelihood sources, education, and public space. However, it has been difficult to marshal definitive evidence demonstrating that these factors influence demographic behaviour.

Several papers in this volume specifically address issues relating gender to reproductive behaviour, while several others allude to these issues indirectly. The former set of papers illustrates the complexity of studying gender and demographic change. The importance of female education, but more importantly, of other indicators of female autonomy, is explored for two states in India. The findings throw into question the 'accepted' role of women's education (Jejeebhoy, Chapter 10). Women's empowerment, with its multiple facets, seems to have a strong regional basis, and religion has a minor influence. While women's autonomy indicators are generally related to socioeconomic status and, in particular, to education, the influence of education on reproductive behaviour is mitigated when other more direct indicators of women's ability to execute decisions and to move freely are included in the explanation (Jejeebhoy, Chapter 10). The difference between North and South is clearly indicated through these measures, thereby upholding the importance of region rather than religion, or even political boundaries, as the circumscribing characteristic.

Using similar data and parallel measures of women's status for the Punjab regions of Pakistan another set of authors argue that the role of gender is being mediated through the role of migration and increasing urbanization. Both these social and economically driven phenomena are having direct impacts on family structure and gender hierarchies and roles, including the levels of education of women. These factors, in conjunction with women's autonomy and mobility, are explored as reasons for differences in reproductive behaviour in rural Pakistan. There, paid employment outside the home emerges as a strong influence on reproductive behaviour (Kazi and Sathar, Chapter 11). This finding leads us to expect a strong lesson in terms of 'social engineering' designed to empower women to make critical decisions. Another paper in this section looks at the role of women's empowerment through credit schemes in generally poor settings. The engineering of social change through programmes is explored for the relative impact of such an approach in Bangladesh, where such schemes as the Grameen Bank and BRAC micro-credit programmes seem to have had unprecedented success (Hadi *et al.*, Chapter 12). This is a particularly important paper in the context of exploring the role of women's empowerment as a determinant of rapid reproductive change in Bangladesh.

The findings of these studies lend support to the framework of gender and family systems proposed by Mason and Bulatao (1998). In their view, family systems are important as a conditioning factor that determines the readiness of society for fertility decline and the potential for gender systems to be 'undermined' by development. Multiple-generation hierarchies would be oppositely positioned against more egalitarian conjugal family units, in which decisions are made and resources distributed more equally across family members—including women. This process, the authors argue, would also lead to greater diffusion of information and new ideas, in other words, to better communication between spouses and greater convergence in reproductive intentions and behaviour.

Another set of papers addresses the role of son preference in structuring high fertility. Preference for sons in the region is often seen as a consequence of the low status of women, as well as a cause of resistance to changes in the demand for children. This resistance, which is based on strong patriarchal systems and an unchanging lower status for women—two factors that are particularly characteristic of this region—impedes fertility change. Two papers explore this particular source of resistance to fertility change in South Asia (Arnold, Chapter 13; Stash, Chapter 14). Arnold concludes that son preference does not constrain fertility change, while Stash, in an analysis of data from Nepal, concludes that the number of living sons influences use of permanent methods.[5]

Social structure, in summary, sets the stage for transition in two ways: First, family structure and systems of partiarchy define the influences on women's ability to implement their childbearing preferences. In a strongly patriarchal male-dominated society, women may have reproductive preferences oriented to fertility regulation, but these are irrelevant, since they lack behavioural implications. Second, social structure can define the openness of society to the flow of new ideas, impeding or facilitating change through institutions that structure norms about social interaction. Authors in this volume have argued that both sets of structures had eroded, to some degree, prior to the onset of fertility decline.

For the duration of its colonial history, South Asia has witnessed economic shocks and famine; and despite some progress in recent decades, stringent economic circumstances still prevail. Nepal and Bangladesh rank among the world's poorest countries, and the large North Indian states are similarly disadvantaged. Some analyses of economic–demographic relationships have posited links between the economics of poverty and factors that catalyse demographic change.

This awareness leads directly into papers in this volume that examine the role of economics in explaining the diversity of fertility change in South Asia, both within the region and within countries. The tradeoff between fewer children of 'high quality' and a large number of children in whom parents do not invest is at the crux

---

[5] The Stash analysis is corroborated by research in Bangladesh by Rahman (1992) showing that the gender composition of children ever born affects contraceptive adoption, method choice, and continuity of use.

of most fertility explanations beyond the transition theory. The work of Becker (1991), Easterlin (1975), and others promotes this as the point of change in societies. However, since the point of transition is difficult to define, let alone pinpoint definitively, and because household or family decisions are in fact more complex—involving different household members and gender concerns—this type of explanation has been severely contested (Casterline 1998).

Micro-level explanations are usually quite different from macro-level explanations based on such considerations as increasing levels of poverty, or improved standards of health. Within a group, the timing of fertility change in Pakistan would no doubt be influenced by the costs of bearing and rearing children, and by aspirations regarding their futures (Sathar and Casterline 1998). However, other mechanisms that impact at a societal level are harder to gauge. It has been strongly argued that economic factors had little influence on fertility change in Bangladesh (Cleland *et al.* 1994). The view of Caldwell and others has been quite different. They emphasize the importance of factors that created higher levels of employment among young women, as well as of landlessness, migration, and the growing realization that a large family is untenable (Caldwell *et al.* 1999). Macro factors interact with micro factors in a more complex set of interactions than are evident in the constrained time- and society-bound explanations being sought to prove and disprove the importance of economic factors.

In summary, contextual differences in gender and family hierarchies are often proposed as determinants of demographic regimes in South Asia. Economic explanations, based on assumptions about the impact of development on fertility, are less robust in the South Asian context, particularly in Pakistan, where a relatively high per capita income has not led to a relatively early or precipitous fertility decline. However, factors such as women's position, social equity, and social betterment may in fact be as—if not more—important as other factors (e.g. in Kerala and Sri Lanka), and the role of policy in the mere provision of family planning services is a much less prominent factor.

The Role of Policy

At the time of the partition of the Indian subcontinent in 1947, most respected analysts portrayed the demographic future of South Asia in the language of impending doom. Alarmed by evidence that rates of growth had increased from zero at the turn of the century to 2 per cent by 1950, and by the doubling of the region's population in the corresponding period, the policy community opted for the creation of large public-sector family planning programmes to solve the population problem. By the 1960s, centralized state bureaucracies had been created throughout the region for the purpose of promulgating national programmes. An army of workers was hired, assigned targets, and equipped with contraceptive supplies to support the practice of family planning. Underpinning this commitment was the consensus that high fertility threatened future economic development and human welfare (e.g. Coale and Hoover 1958) and that, if left unaddressed, rapid population growth would soon generate nonsustainable requirements for land, food, and other resources (e.g. Ehrlich 1978). The apparent homogeneity of demographic circumstances and economic consequences fostered portrayals of South Asia as a regional demographic monolith, where diverse peoples shared common underlying demographic regimes, fertility determinants, population problems, and policy options.

The role of population policies in the South Asian region is perhaps the most critical issue surrounding the study of fertility transition. South Asia is the region with the oldest family planning programmes, those of India and Pakistan. Yet other countries, like Korea and Indonesia, using similar models, have far surpassed the achievements of these two South Asian countries. In fact, with the glaring exception of Bangladesh, the bulk of South Asia demonstrates resilience to policy interventions. In Sri Lanka, most reproductive change occurred in the absence of any aggressive state family planning programme. Most of the changes in fertility happened first as a result of a rising age at marriage and increasing proportions of women never marrying—a situation akin to what had happened in Europe. Control of marital fertility was largely through access to the services of a privately run family planning programme. Changes in mortality, in social factors leading up to the greater involvement of women in education and employment and eventually in migration, were more prominent determinants of Sri Lanka's fertility transition.

Demeny explores post-World War II policy in a much broader perspective, that is, from a more theoretical or moral standpoint. Can the State be expected to play a role in bringing about transition, and does it? India is an extremely interesting case at hand. As Demeny (Chapter 15) points out, as early as the 1950s Nehru was the first national leader to relate population to development and to highlight population policy. Several experiments to implement the nationally declared population policy were carried out in the 1950s and 1960s, by which time an official programme was eventually in place and functioning. Yet, this programme did not produce results—at least in terms of a decline in fertility.

India as well as Pakistan and Nepal (and to a much lesser degree, Bangladesh) were part of a UNFPA-funded South Asia study to investigate factors behind the lack of success of family planning programmes. Donors, including UNFPA, were concerned (just as the World Bank was encouraged in the case of Bangladesh) about the effectiveness of huge amounts of resources being channelled into family planning programmes with little commensurate changes in reproductive behaviour (UNFPA 1989, 1990a–c; Cleland et al. 1994).

A comparison based on the Indian experience found the same policies to be 'effective' in some states like Tamil Nadu and Kerala, and not in others, like Uttar Pradesh, Rajasthan, and Bihar (Satia and Jejeebhoy 1991). While fertility began declining almost synchronously with the onset of the family planning programme in the former states, it became effective in the latter states at least two decades after the official programme was initiated. Several questions remain unanswered. Was

India's official population programme—the main instrument of its population policy—effective in initiating fertility change? Would fertility transition have taken its course (state by state) anyway, with the southern states that had the necessary societal ingredients (high literacy, higher women's autonomy and mobility, more equitable access to resources, including income distribution) preceding the North Indian states in fertility decline, regardless of the introduction of any population policy?

When evaluating the success of policy in engineering reproductive change, comparisons between Pakistan and Bangladesh are illuminating. Several papers tackle these issues (Robinson, Chapter 16; Hakim and Miller, Chapter 6; Barkat-e-Khuda et al., Chapter 17). Clearly, policy—in the form of an effective family planning programme—has worked in Bangladesh (Barkat-e-Khuda, Chapter 17), while Pakistan's weak family planning programme did not work until recently (Hakim and Miller, Chapter 6). The two countries started out similarly in the 1970s, but have taken very different paths since then. Islam was clearly not enough of a commonality (Robinson, Chapter 16).

Pakistan and Bangladesh have other distinguishing characteristics based on land tenure systems, type of crop dependence, and stability of economy, to name a few. The role of the government in its outright commitment to curb high fertility in Bangladesh is not paralleled by a similar effort in Pakistan. Yet, it is questionable whether greater effort in terms of a voluntary family planning programme in Pakistan—similar in nature to the one in Bangladesh—would have met with equal success before the onset of fertility transition. That is to say, it is likely that the 'demand' factors were just not as fermented in the case of Pakistan as they were in Bangladesh. Conditions may not have been ripe for a programme (regardless of its nature) to be effective in a setting like Pakistan until the 1990s, when, in fact, all the factors came into play and produced a decline in fertility (Sathar and Casterline 1998).

Population policy is generally more effective in settings in which society is amenable to change, particularly if factors surrounding the economics and value of children and the costs of contraception change. If demand-related factors were of negligible importance, the earlier instituted family planning programmes (which reduced the social and political obstacles to the use of modern contraception and increased the availability of actual methods) would have produced results more uniformly, and in a synchronous manner. However, this has not been the case, as was pointed out earlier in the chapter: the timing of the approach to fertility transition in South Asia has been rather erratic. Yet, it can justifiably be argued that more effective policy is the key catalyst (Cleland et al. 1994).

This argument may certainly be true in Bangladesh, even though Robinson (Chapter 16), who seems to strongly endorse the view that most of the success in reducing fertility can be attributed to the family planning programme in Bangladesh, also acknowledges the role of other social and economic factors in supporting reproductive change in the 1980s. Caldwell's fresh look at the Bangladesh debate, in which he argues for almost an even balance of strength assigned to all factors in the Bangladesh fertility decline, perhaps brings this discussion to a more agreeable close.

We ... believe the activities of the family planning programme to have been important, probably in the timing of the fertility decline and certainly in the pace of that decline. But we strongly doubt whether a total fertility rate little above three would have been reached had the society of the early 1970s remained largely unchanged. It was a society that offered fewer opportunities and demanded fewer economic decisions from parents. (Caldwell *et al.* 1999)

While the countries of this region have all experienced the onset of fertility transition, only one has completed it. The factors driving population growth have shifted from marital fertility to momentum represented by the fact of younger cohorts approaching their reproductive period. In their analysis of this phenomenon, Bongaarts and Amin (Chapter 19) show the potential demographic role for policies directed to the determinants of momentum, and the large differences in population growth that arise if momentum is abated in the region. While the role of rising age at marriage is rarely addressed as an issue for population policy, the potential impact of an increase in the age of marriage is quite large. Nonetheless, marital age changes have not yet contributed significantly to fertility decline in the region. For example, Pakistan has experienced a dramatic rise in the age at marriage of females and has the highest singulate mean age at marriage in South Asia— 22 years—alongside the highest total fertility rate in the region, an indication that this shift has not been associated with corresponding decline in fertility. Bongaarts and Amin, nevertheless, show that raising the age at first birth through the delay in marriage could curtail that part of population growth that arises from population momentum.

With time, large-scale programmes to promote contraceptive practice become less important than other determinants in sustaining the demographic transition. Thus, with the arrival of the new millennium, deliberations about population policy have shifted to a new generation of themes, issues, and debates. These concern the need for policies to adapt to the emerging climate of demand. While the focus of earlier policy was almost entirely directed at reducing population growth through the reduction of fertility, this can no longer be the sole aim. At best, policies will be aimed at sustaining the fertility transition in the large countries of South Asia. But above all, the debate has shifted towards giving a much broader responsibility to population programmes identified in the International Conference on Population and Development (ICPD) agenda as involving education, the empowerment of women, the environment, and other major areas of reproductive health. Jain (Chapter 18) offers an exploration of the recent ICPD agenda and its potential to shape policy in India.

Qualitative and quantitative change is required to focus on a wider range of policy instruments than family planning programmes alone. Individual countries will need to prioritize their needs and match them to their own resources. Thus far, in

1999, most developing countries have invested a relatively greater part of their budgets on ICPD agenda implementation, when compared to the share of the total that was originally pledged by the developed world. Resources for population are also much more constrained in the beginning of the twenty-first century than they were in the 1960s and 1970s, and donors want to invest more strategically.

Conclusion

The authors participating in the present volume have addressed questions about the onset, pace, and determinants of reproductive change in South Asia. In the first section, the change is documented, and its onset and speed are discussed for all countries of the region. While the fragility and limitations of some of the data leads to some disagreement on these issues, there is general consensus that fertility transition is under way in the entire region. While Sri Lanka has completed its transition—reaching replacement fertility—Pakistan has at last reached a turning point in its contentious demographic history.

Most of the remaining papers concentrate on the determinants of change. Some authors present evidence of factors that impede reproductive change—high mortality, social institutions based on gender stratification and patriarchy, and social characteristics that impede the diffusion of reproductive change. Others in this volume have examined factors that set the stage for transition. These factors alter society to create circumstances in which women prefer fewer children than they actually bear. Mortality decline in the post-war period has ensured families that the desired number of children—particularly sons—would actually survive. Institutional changes lead to a lessening of the perceived social costs of fertility regulation and the perceived benefits of bearing many children. Such changes may have been linked to changes in the agrarian economy, which in turn may have been precipitated by diminishing land holdings and concomitant pressures on families to develop new economic survival strategies. While such phenomena have contributed to fertility transition, they are not sufficient to cause fertility change.

The South Asia experience demonstrates that demand for fertility regulation does not necessarily cause reproductive behaviour to change. Nonetheless, economic and social changes can shift the dynamics of reproductive decision-making from the extended family to individual couples, and alter the perceived value of children from quantity needs and security considerations to quality aspirations. Throughout South Asia, aspirations for children's schooling have changed, and literacy has increased, particularly among women. While such changes may not immediately cause fertility to decline, they weaken the influence of pronatalist institutions and empower couples to pursue their individual reproductive aspirations. Thus, as fertility transitions are completed, the culture of family planning is established, and demand for contraception becomes the norm.

Factors that catalyse rapid reproductive change are critical to transition once conditions are suited to change. Among these factors are mechanisms that foster the diffusion of ideational change: open communication and trade, improved govern-ance, travel, etc. Factors that reduce the costs of fertility regulation also have a catalytic role, for example, family planning programmes that foster new ideas and behaviour and diminish contraceptive costs. Also important in the South Asia context are mechanisms that rapidly alter the demand for children. Temporary adversity caused by wars, economic and political shocks, or famine can foster the spread of new ideas, instil normative changes and foster unconventional economic behaviour.

Finally, the authors in this volume make note of factors that sustain and acceler-ate the momentum of reproductive change, once transition begins. These are demand-side factors affecting individual aspirations and behaviour, such as changes in educational attainment, women's status, and the economy that lead to later marriage, reduced exposure to marriage, the desire to limit children, and the need for greater child spacing within marriage. Yet supply-side determinants are also critical to the momentum of reproductive change: improvements in the intensity, quality and scope of population, development, and health policies exert consider-able influence on the pace of fertility decline.

References

Arthur, W. B., and McNicoll, G. (1978), 'An Analytical Survey of Population and Develop-ment in Bangladesh', *Population and Development Review*, 4(1): 23–80.

Becker, Gary S. (1991), *A Treatise on the Family* (2nd edition), Cambridge: Harvard Univer-sity Press.

Cain, M. (1979), 'Risk and Insurance: Perspectives on Fertility and Agrarian Change in India and Bangladesh', *Population and Development Review*, 7(3): 435–74.

—— Khanam, S. R., and Nahar, S. (1979), 'Class, Patriarchy, and Women's Work in Bangladesh', *Population and Development Review*, 5(3): 405–38.

Caldwell, John C. (1978), 'A Theory of Fertility: From High Plateau to Destabilization', *Population and Development Review*, 4(4): 553–77.

—— (1986), 'Routes to Low Mortality in Poor Countries', *Population and Development Review*, 12(2): 171–220.

—— Barkat-e-Khuda, Caldwell, Bruce, Pieris, Indrani, Caldwell, Pat. (1999), 'The Bangladesh Fertility Decline: An Interpretation', *Population and Development Review*, 25(1): 67–84.

Casterline, John B. (1998), 'The Onset and Pace of Fertility Transition: National Patterns in the Second Half of the Twentieth Century', Paper prepared for the Conference on Global Fertility Transition, Bellagio, Italy, May.

Chen, L. C. (1973), 'Nutrition and Fertility', *Lancet*, 1(7793): 47–8.

—— and Chowdhury, R. H. (1975), 'Demographic Change and Trends of Food Production and Availabilities in Bangladesh (1960–1974)', Dacca, Bangladesh: Ford Foundation.

Cleland, J., Phillips, James F., Amin, S., and Kamal, G. M. (1994), *The Determinants of Reproductive Change in Bangladesh: Success in a Challenging Environment*, Washington, DC: World Bank.

Coale, Ansley J., and Hoover, Edgar M. (1958), *Population Growth and Economic Development in Low-Income Countries: A Case Study of India's Prospects*, Princeton, NJ: Princeton University Press.

—— and Watkins, Susan Cotts (1986), *The Decline of Fertility in Europe*, Princeton: Princeton University Press.

Curlin, G. T., Chen, L. C., and Hussain, S. B. (1975), 'Demographic Crisis: The Impact of the Bangladesh Civil War (1971) on Births and Deaths in a Rural Area of Bangladesh', Dacca: Ford Foundation.

Dyson, Tim, and Moore, Mick (1983), 'On Kinship Structure, Female Autonomy, and Demographic Behaviour in India', *Population and Development* Review, 9(1): 35–60.

—— and Crook, Nigel (1984), 'Issues in India's Demography', in *India's Demography: Essays on the Contemporary Population*, Atlantic Highlands, NJ: Humanities Press, 1–12.

Easterlin, Richard (1975), 'An Economic Framework for Fertility Analysis', *Studies in Family Planning*, 6(1): 54–63.

Erlich, P. R. (1978), *The Population Bomb*, New York: Ballantine.

Government of Pakistan (1965), *Third Five Year Plan*, Karachi: Planning Commission.

Guzman, Jose Miguel, Singh, Susheela, Rodriguez, German, and Pantelides, Edith A. (1996), *The Fertility Transition in Latin America*, Oxford: Oxford University Press.

Leete, Richard, and Alam, Iqbal (1993), *The Revolution in Asian Fertility: Dimensions, Causes, and Implications*, Oxford: Clarendon Press.

Mason, Karen O., and Bulatao, Rodolfo A. (1998), 'Gender and Family Systems in the Fertility Transition', Paper presented at the Rockefeller Foundation's Conference on the Global Fertility Transition, Bellagio, Italy, 18–22 May.

Miller, Barbara D. (1948), *The Endangered Sex: Neglect of Female Children in Rural North India*, Ithaca: Cornell University Press.

Notestein, Frank W. (1945), 'Population: The Long View', in T. W. Schultz (ed.), *Food for the World*, Chicago: University of Chicago Press, 36–57.

Phillips, James F., Stinson, W. S., Bhatia, S., Rahman, M., and Chakraborty, J. (1985), 'The Demographic Impact of the Family Planning Health Services Project in Matlab, Bangladesh', *Studies in Family Planning*, 13(5): 131–40.

Rahman, M., Akbar, J., and Phillips; James F. (1992), 'Contraceptive Use in Matlab, Bangladesh: The Role of Gender Preference', *Studies in Family Planning*, 23(4): 229–42.

Retherford, Robert, Mirza, G. M., Ifran, M., and Alam, Iqbal (1987), 'Fertility Trends in Pakistan: The Decline That Wasn't', *Asia and Pacific Forum*, 1(1): 3–10.

Sathar, Zeba, and Casterline, John (1998), 'The Onset of Fertility Transition in Pakistan', *Population and Development Review*, 24(4): 773–96.

Satia, J. K., and Jejeebhoy, Shireen J. (1991), *The Demographic Challenge: A Study of Four Large Indian States*, Bombay: Oxford University Press.

Stinson, W. S., Phillips, James F., Rahman, M., and Chakraborty, J. (1982), 'The Demographic Impact of the Contraceptive Distribution Project in Matlab, Bangladesh', *Studies in Family Planning*, 13(5): 141–8.

United Nations Population Fund (UNFPA) (1989), 'South Asia Study on Population Policies and Programmes: Nepal'.

United Nations Population Fund (UNFPA) (1990*a*), 'South Asia Study on Population Policies and Programmes: Bangladesh', Dhaka: UNFPA.

—— (1990*b*), 'South Asia Study of Population Policies and Programmes: India', New Delhi: UNFPA.

—— (1990*c*), 'South Asia Study on Population Policies and Programmes: Pakistan', Islamabad, Pakistan.

United Nations, Department of Economic and Social Affairs, Population Division (1998), 'World Population Prospects: The 1998 Revision: Volume I: Comprehensive Tables'.

Part I

Fertility Levels and Trends

1 Levels and Trends in Fertility and Mortality in South Asia: A Review of Recent Evidence

ANDREW KANTNER AND SHI-JEN HE

Introduction

In recent years, there has been an emerging perception that the countries of South Asia are undergoing a process of rapid transition to conditions of low fertility and low mortality. The most spectacular decline in fertility appears to have occurred in Bangladesh, a country generally not considered to have experienced a socioeconomic transformation of similar dimensions. However, substantial declines in birth and death rates have also been recorded in India and Nepal over the past 10–15 years, and some evidence of recent fertility decline has been noted in Pakistan. In addition, since the early 1980s, there have been reports of impressive reductions in infant and child mortality from the region. For example, current estimates indicate that infant mortality rates have now fallen to well below 100 infant deaths per 1,000 births in all South Asian countries.

The statistical information that is currently available provides encouraging evidence that a demographic transition is well under way in South Asia. Much of the evidence for this conclusion comes from surveys (primarily national demographic and health surveys (DHSs)) and from sample registration data. Unlike in earlier periods (e.g. the 1960s and 1970s), in recent years population censuses have been somewhat neglected as a source of information on demographic trends.

The following brief review of the evidence from a broad range of data sources seeks to present more definitive conclusions about demographic trends in this region and to confirm the consistency and reliability of the demographic information available in South Asia.

The Current Demographic Situation in South Asia

While there is evidence that the rate of population growth has recently slowed down in South Asia, there is little doubt that growth over the previous four decades had been unprecedented. Population estimates compiled by the United Nations Population Division (based largely upon official country statistics) indicate that, with the exception of Sri Lanka, all major countries in South Asia have seen their populations grow by approximately 300 per cent since 1951. As a result, by mid-year 1997, India was estimated to have a population of 960.1 million (the region's largest), followed by Pakistan (144.2 million), Bangladesh (122.3 million), Nepal (22.6 million), and Sri Lanka (18.3 million) (United Nations 1996).

These rapid gains in population size were driven by high fertility and declining mortality, and by the momentum that is associated with very young age structures. During the 1960s and 1970s, annual rates of natural increase were well above 2 per cent throughout the region. United Nations estimates suggest that annual population growth only began to fall below 2 per cent in India and Bangladesh during the 1990s. The populations of Nepal and Pakistan were still growing at a rate substantially above 2 per cent a year over the period 1990–95. The issue that requires further study is whether the fertility and mortality data reported by the United Nations are actually very reliable.

As can be seen in Table 1.1, there is some inconsistency between the vital rate estimates and total population projections compiled by the United Nations and those of the International Population Center of the United States Bureau of the Census—differences that are particularly notable in the cases of Bangladesh and Pakistan. Such discrepancies naturally lead one to inquire about the range of data sources available in each country, whether they are consistent, and whether diagnostic measures give one confidence in the reliability of vital rate estimates. More critically, is there any evidence that contrarian evidence raising possible doubts about the direction and tempo of South Asia's demographic transition is being ignored? To address these questions, it is necessary to review critically the primary

Table 1.1. Comparison of US Bureau of the Census and United Nations Population Division demographic estimates and projections for South Asia (1995 and 2000)

Country	US Bureau of the Census, international database	United Nations Population Division
Bangladesh		
TFR 1995	3.7	3.4
IMR 1995	105	91
Life expectancy 1995	55.5	55.5
Annual growth rate 1990–95	1.85	1.49
Mid-year population 1995	120.8	118.2
Mid-year population 2000	132.1	128.3
India		
TFR 1995	3.3	3.4
IMR 1995	73	78
Life expectancy 1995	59.3	60.5
Annual growth rate 1990–95	1.81	1.76

Country	US Bureau of the Census, international database	United Nations Population Division
Mid-year population 1995	936.5	929
Mid-year population 2000	1012.9	1006.8
Nepal		
TFR 1995	5.2	5.4
IMR 1995	81	96
Life expectancy 1995	53.1	54.6
Annual growth rate 1990–95	2.46	2.67
Mid-year population 1995	21.6	21.5
Mid-year population 2000	24.4	24.3
Pakistan		
TFR 1995	5.4	5.5
IMR 1995	99	85
Life expectancy 1995	58.1	61.5
Annual growth rate 1990-95	2.08	2.69
Mid-year population 1995	126.4	136.3
Mid-year population 2000	141.1	156
Sri Lanka		
TFR 1995	2.1	2.2
IMR 1995	21	18
Life expectancy 1995	72.1	71.9
Annual growth rate 1990-95	1.24	1
Mid-year population 1995	18.3	17.9
Mid-year population 2000	19.4	18.8

data sources available in each of the major countries in South Asia, rather than having to rely on secondary data compilations and national projections.

Estimates of Fertility and Infant Mortality from Recent Census, Survey, and Sample Registration Data

Given the broad array of data sources available (see the Appendix), what can be concluded about recent levels and trends in fertility and mortality in these countries, and how much faith should be placed in the numbers currently being cited? We start with a brief assessment of each country's estimated total fertility rate (TFR) and estimated infant mortality rate (IMR), for the years in which these are

Table 1.2. Total fertility rates from recent census, survey, and sample registration data in Bangladesh, India, Nepal, Pakistan, and Sri Lanka, 1981–1996

Country	81	82	83	84	85	86	87	88	89	90	91	92	93	94	95	96
Bangladesh																
1989 Bangladesh Fertility Survey	7.0	6.1	6.1	5.9	5.6	5.0	4.9	4.6								
1989 Contraceptive Prevalence Survey				5.6	5.5	5.0	4.6	4.9								
1991 Contraceptive Prevalence Survey					7	5.2	4.9									
1991 Population Census[a]			7.7													
1993/94 Demographic and Health Survey								5.0	4.5	4.2	4.2	3.2	3.2			
1995 Health and Demographic Survey								6.1		5.7	4.7			3.6	3.6	
1996/97 Demographic and Health Survey[b]								5.1	4.8	4.5	3.7					3.3
Sample Vital Statistics Registration (SRS)	5.0	5.2	5.1	4.8	4.7	4.7	4.4	4.4	4.4	4.3	4.2	4.2	3.8	3.6		
India																
Sample Vital Statistics Registration (SRS)	4.5	4.5	4.5	4.5	4.3	4.2	4.1	4.0	3.9	3.8	3.6	3.4				
1992/93 National Family Health Survey[c]												3.4				
Nepal																
1986 Nepal Fertility Survey						6.0										
1991 Family Health Survey											5.1					
1991 Population Census[d]			7.8					6.0		4.6	4.3					
1996 Nepal Family Health Survey[e]																4.6

Pakistan

1981 Population Census	6.5				
1984/85 Contraceptive Prevalence Survey		6.0			
1988 Demographic Survey [f]			6.9		
1990/91 Demographic and Heath Survey [g]				6.1	
1994/95 Contraceptive Prevalence Survey [h]					5.7

Sri Lanka

1982 Contraceptive Prevalence Survey [i]	3.7										
1987 Demographic and Health Survey [j]		2.8									
1993 Demographic Health Survey [k]										2.3	
Sample Vital Registration [l]	3.4	3.0	3.0	2.7	2.6	2.5	2.5	2.3	2.3	2.3	

---

[a] Bangladesh census estimates for 1983 = (average for 1981–86); 1988 = (average for 1986–91); 1990 = (average for 1988–91); and 1991 = 1991.

[b] The preliminary TFR from the 1996/97 Bangladesh Demographic and Health Survey is a three-year average for the period 1994–1996.

[c] India National Family Health Survey estimate is a three-year average covering the period 1990/91–1992/93.

[d] Nepal census estimates for 1983 = (average for 1981–86); 1988 = (average for 1986–91); 1990 = (average for 1988–91); and 1991 = 1991.

[e] 1996 Nepal Family Health Survey estimate is a three-year average covering the period 1994–96.

[f] 1988 Pakistan Demographic Survey estimate is a five-year average for the period 1984–88.

[g] 1990/91 Pakistan Demographic and Health Survey estimate is a six-year average for the period 1986–91. This estimate was adjusted upward from 5.4 based upon a post-enumeration check of the original survey.

[h] 1993/94 Pakistan Contraceptive Prevalence Survey estimate is for the three-year period 1991/92–1993/94.

[i] 1982 Sri Lanka Contraceptive Prevalence Survey is a single-year estimate based upon 1982 data.

[j] 1987 Sri Lanka Demographic and Health Survey estimate is a five-year average for the period 1982–87.

[k] 1993 Sri Lanka Demographic and Health Survey is a five-year average for the period 1988–93.

[l] Registration estimate for 1981 is a two-year average combining data from 1980–81.

available, and then attempt to construct a regional synthesis based on the accumu-lated evidence at hand.

Bangladesh

In Bangladesh, the most consistent evidence of a rapid fall in fertility since 1981 comes from data provided by national surveys. A linking of the 1989 Bangladesh Fertility Survey (BFS), the 1993/94 Bangladesh Demographic and Health Survey (BDHS), and preliminary results from the 1996/97 BDHS indicates that fertility appears to have declined in this country, from a TFR of around 6.7 in 1981 to 3.4 in 1993/94 and 3.3 in 1996–97 (see Table 1.2). These numbers illustrate an unprece-dented rate of decline, not just for South Asia, but for any region of the world.

However, it is somewhat disquieting to note that the fertility estimates for the three-year (1991–93) period before the 1993/94 BDHS survey actually drop below estimates from the Bangladesh Bureau of Statistics (BBS) Sample Registration System (SRS) for the same years. In Bangladesh, demographers have tended to view SRS estimates as 'lower bound' estimates, so that some observers initially tended to dismiss the BDHS figures as falling outside a plausible range. However, a validation study of the Bangladesh DHS conducted in Matlab thana in April 1994 found that, when compared with data from the International Centre for Diarrhoeal Disease Research (ICDDR,B) Demographic Surveillance System, the DHS birth history questionnaire appeared to be generating remarkably accurate fertility estimates. On the other hand, there was some evidence that infant deaths were underreported, especially for periods more than five years prior to the date of interview (see Bairagi *et al.* 1997).

Adding more uncertainty to the Bangladesh picture are the results of the 1991 Population Census. The age–sex distribution from the census produced a surpris-ingly high count in the 0–4 age group and pronounced deficits among 10–14- and 15–19-year-olds. Fertility estimates derived by reverse-surviving the census age–sex distribution, using various mortality assumptions, are consistently well above the survey and sample registration estimates. For example, the average three-year TFR for the period from mid-1988 to mid-1991 is 5.7—compared with survey results of between 4.3 and 4.5 for the same period (see Kantner *et al.* 1995). These results obviously produced considerable consternation among demographers and family planning programme managers alike.

At present, it is not clear what implications can be drawn from the 1991 census. The quality of age reporting is not very good in this enumeration, and comparisons with age–sex distributions from survey household listings suggest substantial coverage error in the census. In addition, when age information was missing from census forms, or illegible, the attribution procedures employed by BBS were never adequately clarified. While it is not possible to have great confidence in the reliabil-ity of the 1991 census age–sex distribution (or the fertility estimates it generates), it is also not possible to dismiss the message the census may have been trying to send completely; namely, that fertility, while declining, may still be significantly higher than current survey and sample registration data suggest. Only time and a reasonably reliable census will be able to completely dispel this demographic uncertainty.

Survey-based estimates of infant mortality suggest a decline from approximately 120 deaths per 1,000 births in 1981 to around 80 by 1996 (see Table 1.3). The 1991 Contraceptive Prevalence Survey is the only data source that appears to have produced mortality estimates substantially lower than those coming from other sources of information. It is also interesting to note that the 1993/94 and 1996/97 BDHS, when compared to the BBS sample registration data, produce reasonably consistent infant mortality levels and trends over the period 1981–91. However, since the validation study in Matlab did find some evidence that the DHS birth history was underreporting infant deaths, the BDHS may be producing infant mortality rates that are a little low, especially for periods more than five years prior to the survey date.

India

Since 1984, the Indian Sample Registration System has reported a significant decline in fertility. Between 1984 and the three-year period 1990–92, the TFR apparently fell from 4.5 to 3.6 births (see Table 1.2). The 1992/93 NFHS reports a TFR of 3.4 for the 1990–92 period, a figure very similar to SRS estimates for the same period. National Family Health Survey (NFHS) fertility rates for earlier periods suggest that the SRS may have underestimated fertility during the 1970s and 1980s (Narasimhan *et al.* 1997). However, the magnitude of this possible underreporting is difficult to assess. There may have been some tendency to overstate the ages of children in the NFHS birth history, a feature that might produce underestimates of current fertility and slightly inflated estimates for earlier years. On the other hand, in retrospective birth histories, respondents may tend to omit births occurring during earlier periods (a problem commonly identified as recall lapse), which could produce underestimates in more distant time periods.

Unlike Bangladesh, with its multitude of national surveys providing the possibility of independent consistency checks, India must rely primarily on only two national data sources—the SRS and 1992/93 NFHS—for measuring national levels and trends in vital rates. A survey conducted in 1994 by the National Council of Applied Economic Research also produced preliminary rural fertility estimates. These tend to be somewhat higher than the NFHS estimates and those derived from the rural SRS, especially in the states of Bihar, Uttar Pradesh, Rajasthan, and West Bengal (Shariff 1996). However, little is currently known about the quality of the survey. An earlier all-India family planning survey conducted in 1988–89 by the Operations Research Group (ORG) in Baroda did not report conventional fertility or infant mortality rates, so findings from this effort are not included in this review.

Table 1.3. Infant mortality rates from survey and sample registration data in Bangladesh, India, Nepal, Pakistan, and Sri Lanka, 1981–1996

Country	81	82	83	84	85	86	87	88	89	90	91	92	93	94	95	96
Bangladesh																
1989 Bangladesh Fertility Survey	128	129	136	134	111	113	84									
1989 Contraceptive Prevalence Survey					107	99	90	102								
1991 Contraceptive Prevalence Survey							73	88	88	75						
1993/94 Demographic and Health Survey[a]			116													
1995 Health and Demographic Survey								112					87			
1996/97 Demographic and Health Survey[b]						117					96				78	
Sample Vital Statistics Registration (SRS)	112	122	118	122	112	116	113	116	98	94	91	88	84			82
India																
Sample Vital Statistics Registration (SRS)		115					99					85				
1992/93 National Family Health Survey[c]		101					94					79				
Nepal																
1986 Nepal Fertility Survey[d]	123			83												
1991 Family Health Survey[e]				115					80							
1996 Nepal Family Health Survey[f]				127					108							79
Pakistan																
1984/85 Contraceptive Prevalence Survey				106												
1988 Pakistan Demographic Survey								112								
1990/91 Demographic and Heath Survey[g]				97							91					
Sri Lanka																
1987 Demographic and Health Survey[h]	39.2						25.4									
Sample Vital Statistics Registration	29.5	30.5	28.4	27.2	24.2	23.2	22.6	20.2	18.4	19.3	17.2					

[a] 1993/94 Bangladesh Demographic and Health Survey IMR estimates are five-year averages for the period 1979–83, 1984–88, and 1989–93/94.

[b] 1996/97 Bangladesh Demographic and Health Survey IMR estimates are five-year averages for the period 1982–86, 1987–91, and 1992–96.

[c] Indian IMR estimates from the SRS and the 1992/93 National Family Health Survey are five-year averages for the periods 1978–82, 1983–87, and 1988–92.

[d] Indirect IMR estimate from the 1986 Nepal Fertility Survey was 110 deaths per 1,000 births.

[e] 1991 Nepal Family Health Survey IMR estimates are five-year averages for 1977–81, 1982–86, and 1987–91.

[f] 1996 Nepal Family Health Survey IMR estimates are five-year averages for 1982–86, 1987–91, and 1992–96.

[g] 1990/91 Pakistan Demographic and Health Survey IMR estimates are six-year averages for the periods 1978–84 and 1985–91.

[h] 1987 Sri Lanka Demographic and Health Survey estimates are five-year averages for the periods 1977–81 and 1982–87.

Table 1.4. Percentage of currently married women using contraception in Bangladesh, India, Nepal, Pakistan, and Sri Lanka compiled from survey data (1975–1996)

Country	75	76	77	78	79	80	81	82	83	84	85	86	87	88	89	90	91	92	93	94	95	96
All methods																						
Bangladesh	7.9				12.6	19.6	19.6		19.1		25.3				31.4		39.9		44.6	46.3		49.2
India	21.0		8.9			32.4								42.9		44.9		40.7				
Nepal		2.9										15.1					25.1					28.5
Pakistan	4.0						6.8			9.1						11.8				17.8		
Sri Lanka	32.0		41.0					54.9					61.7						66.1			
Modern temporary																						
Bangladesh	4.0				6.0		6.5		6.3		9.0				13.3		20.8		27.1	34.0		32.7
India	4.5					5.2								7.8		8.6		5.5				
Nepal		0.9					1.7					2.2					4.5					8.5
Pakistan	2.1					1.7					4.9					5.5				7.5		
Sri Lanka	8.5							8.4					10.8						16.5			
Sterilization																						
Bangladesh	1.0				3.4		5.0		7.4		9.4				10.0		10.3		9.2	5.3		8.7
India	13.0					20.6								30.8		31.3		30.9				
Nepal		2.0					5.2					13.0					19.6					17.5
Pakistan	0.7					0.6					2.6					3.5				5.0		
Sri Lanka	9.9		18.0					20.6					29.8						27.2			
Traditional methods																						
Bangladesh	3.1				3.2		8.0		5.4		6.9				8.1		8.7		8.4	6.9		7.7
India	5.0					6.6								4.3		5.0		4.3				
Nepal		0.1					0.0										1.0					2.5
Pakistan	1.3					4.2					1.5					2.8				5.2		
Sri Lanka	13.6		23.0					25.9					21.2						22.4			

The 1991 Indian Population Census should also be a national resource for evaluating results reported by the SRS and NFHS. Unfortunately, as of December 1996, the single-year age–sex distribution from the 1991 census, as well as vital rate estimates from a census sample enumeration (CSE), had not been released. It is therefore not possible to determine whether the census provides confirmation that India's fertility transition is well under way. Five-year census age distributions, released in 1997, suggest a 1990–91 TFR ranging between 3.6 and 4.2, depending upon what assumptions are made about the level of mortality, age misreporting, and coverage errors (underenumeration) affecting the 0–1 age group (estimates computed by the authors). Without a more thorough examination of the 1991 Population Census, one cannot be totally confident about the reliability of the demographic scenarios depicted by the SRS and NFHS. In addition, there do not appear to have been any systematic evaluations of SRS data quality in recent years.

Both the SRS and the NFHS report a drop in India's infant mortality rate between the early 1980s and 1988–92 (see Table 1.3). However, the NFHS estimates are slightly lower than the SRS results, especially for periods more than five years prior to interview. This pattern is not unexpected, since recall problems in birth histories tend to undermine the accuracy of birth and death reporting in more distant time periods. On the other hand, this traditional source of error may be somewhat compensated for by the tendency in many South Asian demographic surveys to overstate children's ages. In any event, both the SRS and the NFHS show clear evidence of falling infant mortality, probably from around 115 deaths per 1,000 live births in 1981 to about 86 during the period 1988–92.

Nepal

According to the Nepal Central Bureau of Statistics, fertility remained unchanged throughout the 1970s, at around 6.3 births per woman. As can be seen in Table 1.2, results from the 1986 Nepal Fertility Survey (NFS) and the 1991 Nepal Fertility, Family Planning, and Health Survey (1991 NFHS) indicate that fertility declined to 6.0 in 1986 and to 5.1 in 1991. Reverse-survival estimates based upon the 1991 Nepal Population Census suggest an even more rapid rate of decline, with the TFR falling to around 4.7 for the three-year period from mid-1988 to mid-1991. However, possible underenumeration in the 0–4 age group may be biasing this estimate to the low side. Preliminary findings from the 1996 Nepal Demographic and Health Survey (1996 NDHS) show that the TFR may have declined to 4.6 over the three-year period from 1994 to 1996.

The 1991 NFHS reports that infant mortality fell from 123 per 1,000 live births in 1981 to 80 as of 1987–91 (see Table 1.3). This is one of the more rapid declines reported in South Asia since 1981. Unfortunately, preliminary results from the 1996 NFHS confuse rather than clarify the picture, since they indicate a decline similar to that found in the 1991 NFHS. These new results imply serious underestimates for the five-year period prior to the survey (from 1987 to 1991). Between 1987 and

1991, the 1996 NFHS reports an IMR of 108 rather than 80. If one compares 1991 and 1996 NFHS estimates for the five-year period prior to each survey (1987–91 for the 1991 NFHS and 1992–96 for the 1996 NFHS), then both surveys generate an estimate of 80, implying that there was no change in infant mortality between the late 1980s and the mid-1990s. However, this depiction is speculative, and must await further diagnostic assessment before firm conclusions can be reached. If the apparent declines in the IMR revealed in both surveys are due in part to the over-statement of children's ages, then it may prove very difficult to make definitive judgements about the course of infant mortality in Nepal.

Pakistan

National surveys provide the principal evidence of recent fertility and mortality change in Pakistan. The 1984–85 Contraceptive Prevalence Surveys and the 1990/91 Pakistan Demographic and Health Survey (PDHS) report a decline in the TFR from 6.0 in 1984 to 5.4 over the six-year period between 1985 and 1991 (Table 1.2). However, following a postenumeration check of the original survey, the 1990/91 PDHS estimate was later adjusted up to 6.1. In addition, the 1988 Pakistan Demographic Survey produced a far higher estimate; namely, 6.9 for the period 1984–88. Therefore, through the early 1990s, the picture for Pakistan is somewhat confused. The 1994/95 Contraceptive Prevalence Survey has produced a provisional TFR estimate of 5.7 for the period 1991–93/94, which appears to be consistent with the recent rise in contraceptive prevalence reported by the same source.

The 1990/91 PDHS suggests that infant mortality appears to have fallen, from 97.4 per 1,000 live births in 1978–84 to 90.5 in 1985–89, a rather modest decline in comparison with those of other countries in the South Asian region. However, these figures are called into question by a 1984 estimate of an IMR of 107 from the 1986 Contraceptive Prevalence Survey (a figure lying outside the range provided by the PDHS). There is apparently no additional national survey information available on infant mortality levels and trends since the release of the 1991 PDHS.

Sri Lanka

As Table 1.2 indicates, the principal national vital rate data available for Sri Lanka comes from the vital statistics registration system. This data series reports a slow gradual decline in fertility during the 1980s, resulting in a TFR of 2.3 by 1991 (the last year available to this review). The last national survey to be carried out was the 1993 Sri Lanka Demographic and Health Survey (SLDHS), which reported an average TFR of 2.3 for the period 1988–93, a figure consistent with vital statistics registration data. However, this is not a nationally representative estimate since the survey was not able to operate in the northeast of the country because of the ongoing civil war. A previous DHS in 1987 also produced a TFR estimate that was closely consistent with registration data for the same time period.

Infant mortality appears to be quite low in Sri Lanka. The last available estimate from the vital statistics registration system is 17.9 per 1,000 live births for the year 1991, a level considerably below all other countries in the region. It is not clear to what extent adult mortality may have been affected by the civil disturbances that have plagued Sri Lanka for the past two decades. At the very least, there has probably been a stall in the improvement of adult mortality in recent years.

The fertility and mortality data described above provide much of the evidence supporting conclusions about the speed and the direction of the demographic transition in South Asia. The picture to emerge is that fertility is falling throughout South Asia. Bangladesh and India appear to have experienced the most rapid declines in fertility since 1981, but preliminary results from the 1996 Nepal DHS suggest that the pace of fertility decline may now be accelerating there as well. Fertility decline may also have begun in Pakistan, but the speed and direction of this change is far from clear.

Most countries in South Asia appear to have achieved reductions in infant mortality—on average, from levels around 110–130 in the early 1980s to between 70 and 90 in the early 1990s. However, time series across surveys do not always provide consistent evidence of a decline in the IMR (a recent example being the situation in Nepal). An analysis of infant and child mortality in Bangladesh (see Hill *et al.* 1996) also noted considerable variation in survey results, but was nevertheless able to discern definitive declines over 10- to 15-year time horizons.

Nevertheless, the timing of fertility and mortality change in South Asia is difficult to document definitively. For example, it could be the case that recent fertility decline in some South Asian countries may actually be in response to an apparent drop in infant and child mortality that started during the immediate post-World War II period. As more children survived to adulthood during the 1950s and 1960s, women were able to have fewer children in order to attain the number of surviving offspring they wanted (around three children in most South Asian settings). This adjustment was finally made possible with the widespread introduction of modern contraception over the past two decades. While possibly valid, it is difficult to have total confidence in this scenario, given the paucity and poor quality of vital rate information in South Asia over the period from 1940 to 1980.

Actually, since 1980, one could argue that despite persistently high levels of infant and child mortality by international standards, fertility still appears to have fallen substantially in Bangladesh, and to a lesser extent in Nepal. In fact, fertility decline in these two countries may have largely preceded or coincided with declines in infant and child mortality, rather than being a response to earlier reductions in mortality. Cleland *et al.* (1994: 4), writing on the Bangladesh fertility transition, conclude that the 'modest' changes in infant and child mortality thought to have occurred during the 1950s and 1960s 'are unlikely to have altered parental perceptions of child survival or to have induced recent changes in reproductive behavior'.

Seeking greater confidence in the levels and trends reported in the South Asia region, it might be instructive to assess some additional demographic determinants of these rates. We begin by examining family planning programme performance. Does the use of contraception appear to be highly correlated with the declines in fertility reported in national survey and registration data in this region?

Family Planning Programme Performance

Of all the countries of South Asia, Sri Lanka has achieved the highest contraceptive prevalence rate (CPR) during the past 20 years. However, over this same period, it is Bangladesh that has experienced the most rapid rise in contraceptive prevalence. As can be seen in Table 1.4, only 7.9 per cent of currently married women were using any method of contraception in 1975. Two decades later, based upon preliminary results from the 1996/97 BDHS, the CPR had risen to 49.2 per cent. Levels of use in India nearly doubled during this period, from 21.0 per cent in 1975 to 40.7 per cent in 1992/93 (the latter figure being based upon 1992/93 NFHS findings). Nepal and, more recently, Pakistan have also recorded some gains in use, but levels are still considerably lower than in Sri Lanka, Bangladesh, and India.

Most patterns of family planning practice in South Asia (Sri Lanka, India, and Nepal, in particular) are typified by considerable reliance on sterilization by older women. Since the early 1980s, Bangladesh is the only country in South Asia to have demonstrated major gains in the use of modern temporary methods of family planning (pills, IUDs, injectables, implants, and condoms). As a result, Bangladesh provides far higher levels of contraceptive protection for women under the age of

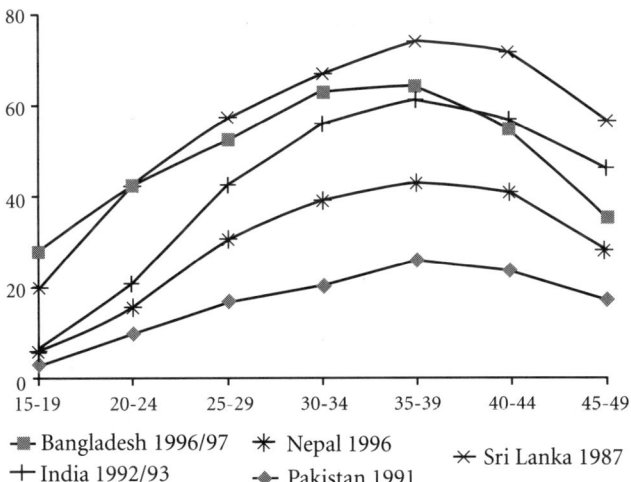

Figure 1.1. Age composition of contraceptive use, all methods.

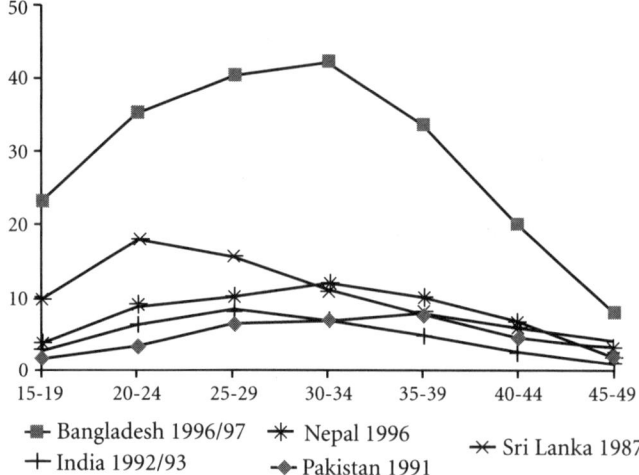

Figure 1.2. Age composition of contraceptive use, modern temporary methods.

30 than do other countries in the region (see Figs 1.1–1.4). However, the Bangladesh programme is also dominated by the use of contraceptive methods with typically higher levels of discontinuation and failure (primarily the oral pill). So, while Bangladesh may have attained higher levels of overall use than India, Bangladeshi women may be more likely than Indian women to discontinue the use of a method and to experience accidental pregnancies.[1]

A curious feature of the situation in South Asia is that fertility rates appear to have declined below levels that might be anticipated from the level of contraceptive use. This anomaly is especially apparent in India and Pakistan. In an assessment of global fertility trends and family planning performance, Ross and Frankenberg (1993: 6) concluded that the average relationship between fertility and the contraceptive prevalence rate could be best captured by the following equation: TFR = $7.2931 - (0.0700{*}CPR)$. Yet, based upon the average international experience summarized by this equation, every country and region of South Asia reports a lower fertility rate than is implied by its level of contraceptive use. In other words, family planning programmes appear to be even more effective than anticipated in reducing fertility in South Asia.

[1] There is currently considerable controversy about the true level of user failure in the Bangladesh family planning programme. The 1993/94 BDHS reported exceptionally low levels of user failure after one year of use despite also recording poor levels of use compliance. For example, only 1.7 per cent of women using pills reported an accidental pregnancy following 12 months of use. Use failure for modern temporary methods in Matlab appears to be considerably higher (e.g. the 12-month pill user failure rate is reported to be 15 per cent), which raises serious questions about how effective the Bangladesh programme actually is in preventing unwanted pregnancies (see Bairagi and Rahman 1996).

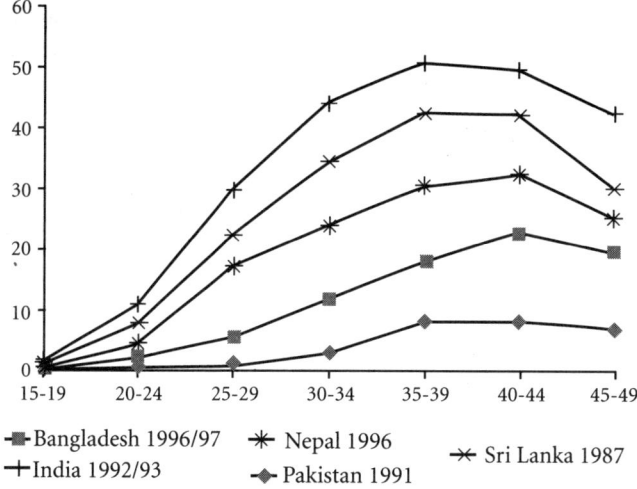

Figure 1.3. Age composition of contraceptive use, sterilization.

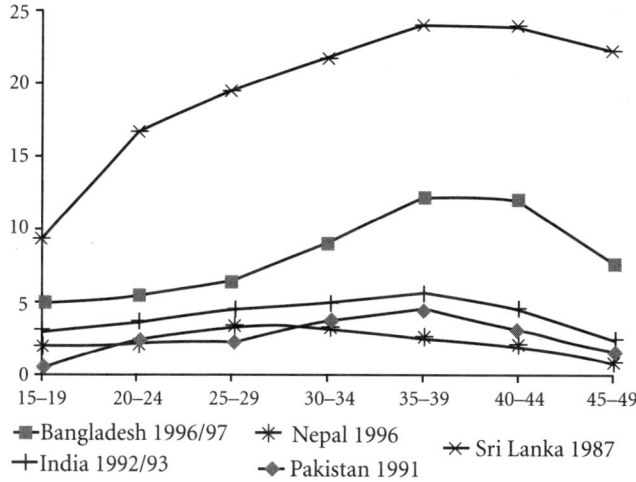

Figure 1.4. Age composition of contraceptive use, traditional methods.

Can this be the case? Are family planning programmes in South Asia actually more effective (distinguished by higher use compliance, lower discontinuation, lower user failure) in reducing fertility than they are in other parts of the world? Could other proximate determinants (lengthy breastfeeding durations, abortion, and infecundity) be behind this apparent discrepancy? Is the Ross–Frankenberg

Table 1.5. Implied TFR levels based upon estimates of the contraceptive prevalence rate (CPR) in Bangladesh, India, Nepal, Pakistan and Sri Lanka and in major subregions with high TFR differences (implied versus reported)

Country/region	Reported CPR	Implied TFR[a]	Reported TFR	TFR difference[b]
Bangladesh (1991)	39.9	4.5	4.3	0.2
Bangladesh (1993/94)	44.6	4.2	3.4	0.8
Chittagong	29.3	5.2	4.0	*1.2*
Bangladesh (1996/97)[c]	49.2	3.9	3.3	0.6
India (1992/93)	40.6	4.5	3.4	*1.1*
Andhra Pradesh	47.0	4.0	2.6	*1.4*
Bihar	23.1	5.7	4.0	*1.7*
Goa	47.8	3.9	1.9	*2.0*
Karnataka	49.1	3.9	2.9	*1.0*
Rajasthan	31.8	5.1	3.6	*1.4*
Tamil Nadu	49.8	3.8	2.5	*1.3*
Uttar Pradesh	19.8	5.9	4.8	*1.1*
Nepal (1991)	25.1	5.5	5.1	0.4
Nepal (1996)	28.9	5.3	4.6	0.7
Pakistan (1990/91)	11.8	6.5	5.4	*1.1*
Balochistan	2.0	7.2	5.8	*1.3*
Punjab	13.0	6.4	5.4	*1.0*
Sindh	12.4	6.4	5.1	*1.3*
NWFP	8.6	6.7	5.5	*1.2*
Sri Lanka (1987)	61.7	3.0	2.7	0.3
Sri Lanka (1993)	66.1	2.7	2.3	0.4

[a] Computed using the formula TFR = 7.2931 − (0.0700*CPR); see Ross and Frankenberg (1994: 6).
[b] Italic type indicates that the difference between the reported and implied TFR (derived from the CPR) is 1.0 or more births.
[c] Division-level breakdowns are not yet available from the 1996/97 BDHS.

equation a reliable approximation? Or do the results in Table 1.5 simply mean that fertility rates are substantially underestimated?

It is not possible, within the bounds of this review, to provide definitive answers to all of these questions. However, the differences between reported and CPR-implied TFRs are certainly considerable in many South Asian settings. Regions where this discrepancy is equal to or greater than one full birth include such highly populous areas as Chittagong Division in Bangladesh, the states of Rajasthan, Uttar Pradesh, Bihar, Orissa, Andhra Pradesh, Karnataka and Tamil Nadu in India, and all of the provinces of Pakistan. Only Nepal and Sri Lanka do not appear to be significantly out of range (i.e. indicating less than one full birth between the reported and the CPR-based TFR).

To evaluate the possibility of substantial underreporting of fertility in South Asian survey data, it is necessary to probe somewhat deeper into the issue of data quality. In the regions of South Asia pointing to much lower fertility than would be

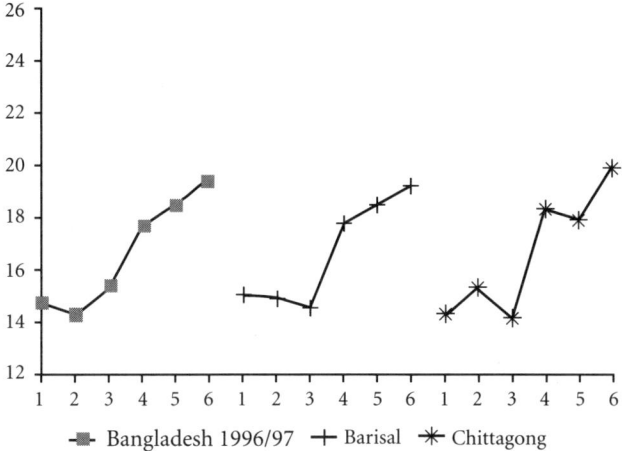

Figure 1.5. Percentage distribution of total births by the number of years preceding the date of interview in Bangladesh and subregions with evidence of age shifting.

expected, given the level of family planning programme performance, is it possible to identify systematic error patterns that may be producing serious underestimates in vital rates?

Diagnostic Measures from Recent Surveys in Bangladesh, India, and Pakistan

Especially in regions with lower than anticipated fertility rates, it is important to consider whether there is evidence of distortion that may undermine confidence in the reliability of survey findings. Traditionally, demographic censuses and surveys in South Asia have been plagued by serious age misreporting and omission of births (especially among infants and children who subsequently died).

In addition, there has arisen a new concern, which results from the structure of the DHS questionnaires: Could the interviewers intentionally be transferring children to older ages in order to avoid having to ask a lengthy array of child health questions, thereby significantly shortening the interview time and reducing their work loads? This type of age transfer could be causing deficits in the number of young children, thereby generating underestimates of current fertility and mortality levels and producing rates farther back in time that are too high—thereby exaggerating the actual pace of fertility and mortality decline.

Most demographic data sources in South Asia suffer from age misreporting (with age heaping most commonly occurring on digits 0 and 5). The 1991 Bangladesh Population Census had highly unreliable age misreporting; namely, a Myers index

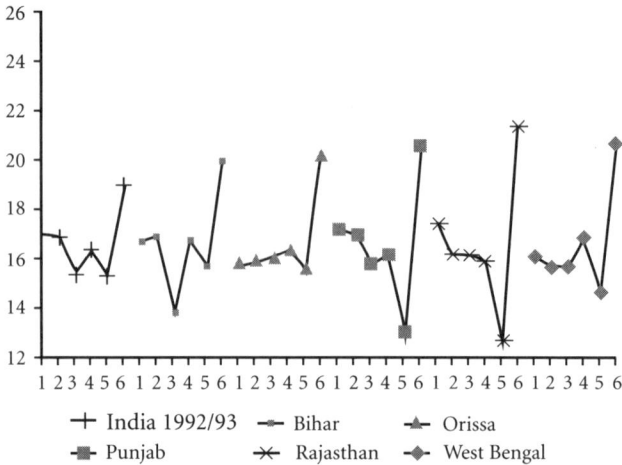

Figure 1.6. Percentage distribution of total births by the number of years preceding the date of interview in India and subregions with evidence of age shifting.

of 74.0.[2] However, the quality of recent survey data appears to be considerably better. The 1993/94 BDHS has reasonably good-quality age data (Myers index 16.2). The 1992/93 India NFHS and the 1991 PDHS have greater age misreporting (the Myers index was 35.9 for the 1992/93 NFHS, and 44.3 for the 1991 PDHS). It is interesting to note that data quality in the 1992/93 NFHS appears to be somewhat better in the southern states of India. Northern states with poorer-quality age data include Delhi, Haryana, Punjab, Rajasthan, Orissa, and Assam.

Evidence concerning the quality of age reporting does not get one very far. There does not seem to be any strong correlation between regions with less reliable age reporting and lower-than-anticipated fertility rates. However, further clarification could possibly come from an examination of the annual distribution of births and deaths reported from survey birth histories.

As noted previously, South Asian demographic surveys have shown a tendency to overstate children's ages, thereby creating the effect of fertility decline when in fact there was little change occurring. This clearly happened during earlier periods in Bangladesh. Surveys conducted during the 1960s and 1970s (e.g. the 1961–62 Demographic Survey of East Pakistan, the 1968–69 National Impact Survey, and the 1975 Bangladesh Fertility Survey) reported substantial falls in fertility. Unfortunately, considerable underreporting of births, combined with age misreporting (especially the overstatement of children's ages), produced fertility estimates that

[2] For a technical description of the Myers index and other age heaping/digit preference summary measures, see Shryock *et al.* (1976: 116–8).

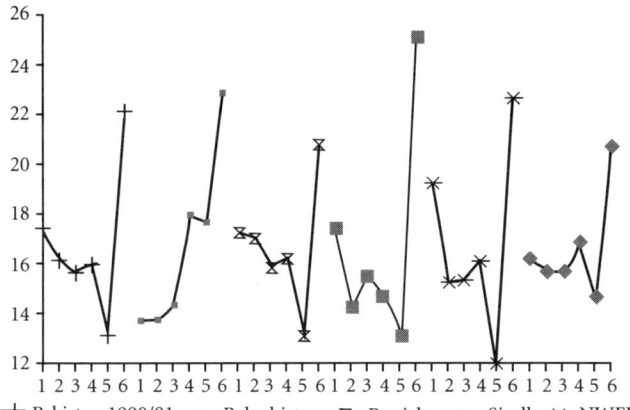

Figure 1.7. Percentage distribution of total births by the number of years preceding the date of interview in Pakistan and subregions with evidence of age shifting.

were too low and fertility trends that proved largely nonexistent (National Academy of Sciences 1981: 2). Could similar error patterns be distorting our current view of reality?

Figures 1.5–1.7 provide information on the annual distribution of births and deaths by the number of years prior to interview, as reported by birth histories in the 1993/94 BDHS, the 1992/93 NFHS, and the 1990/91 PDHS. The distribution of births and deaths by year prior to interview is computed from century–month codes for children's ages and the date of interview in each region. If the reporting of births and deaths in these surveys is reasonably accurate, one should not expect to see pronounced fluctuations in the number of vital events by single year of occurrence. More critically, one should not see clear evidence of age shifting at the cutoff date for the health sections of DHS-type surveys. In other words, in Bangladesh, one should not expect to see a jump in the distribution of births between years 3 and 4 (all health questions were asked of children aged 0–3) and in India and Pakistan between years 5 and 6 (all health questions were asked of children aged 0–5).

While one must be cautious in interpreting the figures in Table 1.5 owing to variations in sample size, it may still be possible to draw some tentative conclusions from these diagnostics. In Bangladesh, the annual distribution of births and deaths at the national level appears unremarkable for a country reporting declines in fertility and mortality. However, by region, a different picture emerges. In Barisal and Chittagong Divisions, there is a jump in the number of births and deaths between years 3 and 4 prior to the survey (the cutoff point for implementing the health component of the 1992/93 BDHS). While the size of the Barisal sample is too small to draw any definitive conclusions, it appears that Chittagong may have experienced some shifting of children aged 0–3 to ages 4 and above. Chittagong is also the one division in Bangladesh that reports a fertility rate (based on births three years prior to interview) that is more than a full birth below what one would anticipate from a CPR of 29.3 per cent. Since Chittagong is one of the largest divisions in Bangladesh and accounts for approximately one-third of all births in the 1993/94 BDHS, a poorly functioning birth history in this region could produce some downward bias in the national TFR.

In the 1992/93 India NFHS, several states present clear evidence of age shifting and, as hypothesized, this age transference is most pronounced between years 5 and 6 (the cutoff point for the health questions). States that appear to have experienced systematic age shifting are Bihar, Orissa, Punjab, Rajasthan, and West Bengal. Other states have annual percentage distributions of births and deaths symptomatic of age overstatement (e.g. Andhra Pradesh, Gujarat, Jammu, and Madhya Pradesh), but the patterns are not sufficiently pronounced (or, in the case of Jammu, not based upon enough cases) to reach definitive conclusions. On the other hand, some of India's largest states (e.g. Uttar Pradesh and Maharashtra) do not show evidence of substantial age displacement.

In the India NFHS, estimates of current fertility were derived from births three years prior to the date of interview. Since much of the age displacement noted in Fig. 1.6 appears to be occurring between years 5 and 6, it is possible to argue that current fertility estimates may not have been seriously compromised by the tendency to overstate children's ages. However, in states with very pronounced age shifting (e.g. Rajasthan), this assumption seems a little tenuous.

There is little correlation between Indian states with lower-than-expected TFRs (based upon the CPR) and suspected age displacement. Among the states judged to have pronounced age shifting, only Orissa and Rajasthan have fertility rates substantially below what might be anticipated from the level of family planning programme performance.

The 1990/91 Pakistan DHS demonstrates more evidence of age shifting than do the Bangladesh and India surveys. Children born five years prior to the survey date are clearly being moved back to year 6—and probably to higher ages as well. It is doubtful whether birth histories with such distortion can be used to generate reliable estimates of current fertility and infant mortality. The strategy adopted in the 1990/91 PDHS was to average all births over the six-year period from 1985 to 1991 to produce an estimate of current fertility. However, with such extreme age displacement, it is likely that children may have been shifted to 7, 8, 9, or even 10 years prior to the survey, rather than just to year 6. Therefore, even taking a six-year average for the 'current' TFR may have resulted in a sizable underestimate. In conclusion, error patterns in the 1990/91 PDHS raise serious concerns about the reliability of fertility and mortality estimates in Pakistan.

In Bangladesh, Chittagong Division may have fallen victim to some age shifting between years 0–3 and 4 and above, producing a regional underestimate in fertility that could have biased the national TFR to the low side. Since Chittagong is the only major region in Bangladesh with evidence of age displacement, it is unlikely that national estimates of the TFR have been badly compromised from this source of error (probably by not more than 0.5 births).

In India, it seems that Orissa, Punjab, Rajasthan, and West Bengal experienced significant age displacement, but most of the remaining states are not badly distorted. Therefore, as in Bangladesh, the problem of overstating children's ages was probably not a major factor affecting the quality of national estimates from the 1992/93 NFHS. However, other traditional sources of error (e.g. omission of births, especially children born alive who subsequently died) could still be plaguing the quality of national and regional estimates.

While patterns of error in survey data may partially account for national and regional differentials in fertility and mortality, other factors may, of course, be responsible for generating levels and trends in the vital rates identified by survey data. This review of recent demographic evidence from South Asia concludes with a decomposition analysis of fertility, using recent survey data from Bangladesh, India, and Pakistan.[3]

National and Regional Fertility Determinants in Bangladesh, India, and Pakistan

In an analysis of provincial fertility patterns in Indonesia, Suyono and Palmore (1995) developed a novel procedure for summarizing the determinants of fertility in demographic and health surveys. Their analysis attempted to explain why TFRs and CPRs are not highly correlated across provinces in Indonesia. A subsequent analysis of regional fertility in the Philippines utilized the same methodology (see Go *et al.* 1995).

This decomposition approach deals with the fact that the TFR and CPR are different types of indicators. The TFR is an age-standardized measure and is a 'true' rate in the sense that the numerator is a demographic event (births) and the denominator is a measure of women exposed to the risk of experiencing that event. The TFR also has a useful interpretation—it summarizes the fertility experience for a synthetic or hypothetical cohort of women. More precisely, it shows the total number of live births a woman would have if she were subject to a fixed set of age-specific fertility rates and lived throughout the 15–49 age range. On the other hand, the CPR is not age standardized and does not have a synthetic cohort interpretation. However, Suyono and Palmore were able to calculate age-standardized CPRs (computed in the same manner as a TFR) that measure the number of person-years lived by a synthetic cohort in the state of 'currently using contraception'. This synthetic-cohort definition of contraceptive use is directly comparable to a standard TFR.

---

[3] Recent data files from Nepal and Sri Lanka (the 1996 NDHS and the 1993 SLDHS) were not available for use in this analysis.

Table 1.6. Exposure status to the risk of pregnancy by the percentage of person-years lived by synthetic cohorts in recent surveys from Bangladesh, India, and Pakistan (national decompositions)

Country/region	Never married	Not currently married	In-fecund	Modern temporary methods	Steriliza-tion	Traditi-onal	Pregnant or amen.	Women exposed to risk of pregnancy	Total
Bangladesh (1993/94)	20.2	7.0	12.5	18.1	8.5	6.7	6.8	20.2	100.0
India (1992/93)	12.9	6.1	14.8	4.1	28.9	3.5	12.3	17.4	100.0
Pakistan (1990/91)	20.0	3.5	19.3	4.1	3.5	2.2	19.5	27.9	100.0

Other determinants of fertility can be computed in much the same fashion as an age-standardized CPR. In this analysis of regional fertility, 'synthetic cohorts' are constructed that classify women by their exposure and nonexposure to the risk of having children. It is possible to estimate the total percentage of time that women spend in various 'exposed' or 'nonexposed' states (e.g. as never married, not currently married, infecund, using contraception, and currently pregnant or amenorrhoeic) if they all live through their reproductive periods (ages 15–49) and are subject to a given (and unchanging) set of exposed and nonexposed states. This decomposition may allow for the identification of demographic, programmatic, and behavioural factors that determine national and regional patterns of fertility in South Asia.

Comparisons of Proximate Determinant Measures in Bangladesh, India, and Pakistan

Decomposition profiles for Bangladesh (1993/94), India (1992/93), and Pakistan (1990/91) are presented in Table 1.6 and shown graphically in Fig. 1.8. Results indicate that the percentage of person-years lived by women as never married is 20.2 per cent in Bangladesh, 12.9 per cent in India, and 20.0 per cent in Pakistan. This finding suggests that the age at marriage may be considerably lower in India than in Bangladesh and Pakistan. Women in Bangladesh and India are more likely to be widowed or divorced (6.9 per cent and 6.1 per cent, respectively) than are women in Pakistan (3.5 per cent). Therefore, when considering both never-married and not currently married categories, a higher percentage of Bangladeshi women are protected from the risk of childbearing than in India and Pakistan. In other words, based upon current marital status, Bangladesh could be expected to have lower fertility than India and Pakistan.

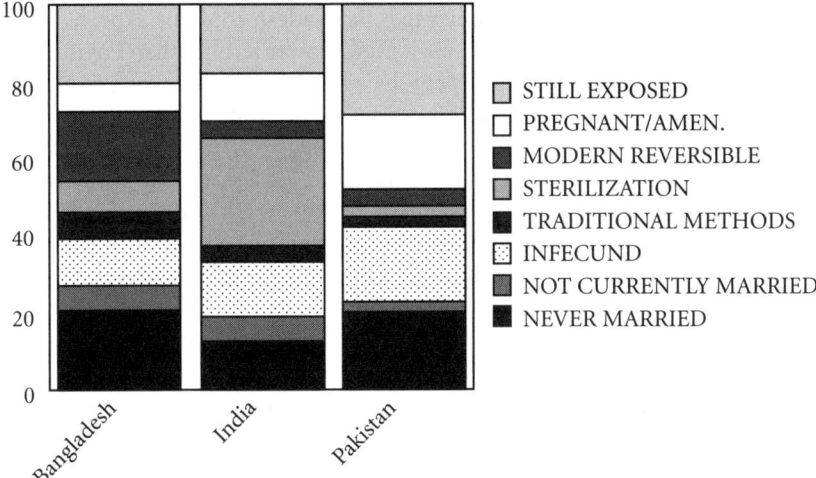

Figure 1.8. Exposure status to the risk of pregnancy by the percentage of person-years lived for synthetic cohorts in Bangladesh (1993/94), India (1992/93), and Pakistan (1990/91).

Infecund women are defined as those who were (1) currently married, (2) not using contraception, and (3) without a live birth over the five-year period prior to interview. The percentage of person-years spent as infecund is 19.3 per cent in Pakistan, compared to 12.5 per cent in Bangladesh and 14.8 per cent in India. Therefore, more women in Pakistan than in Bangladesh and India are protected from the risk of pregnancy because of infecundity. It is important to note that infecundity as measured here could be capturing actual sterility, abortion, or underreporting of fertility. With the data currently available, it is not possible to distinguish between these components.

Much of the regional variation in fertility in South Asia appears to result from differences in contraceptive use. There are also considerable variations in patterns of method use throughout the region. The percentage of person-years lived by women who are using modern temporary contraception is considerably higher in Bangladesh (18.1 per cent) than in India (4.1 per cent) and Pakistan (4.1 per cent). However, sterilization is much more common in India and Pakistan, while Bangladeshi women are more likely to be using traditional methods.

When all contraceptive methods are considered together (as the percentage of person-years lived using pills, IUDs, injectables, condoms, sterilization, and traditional methods) and are added to the person-years that women spend as never married, not currently married, or infecund, one can see that more women in Bangladesh than in India or Pakistan fall into one of these categories. In other words, fewer Bangladeshi women are still exposed to the risk of childbearing than in

India and Pakistan. This finding implies that Bangladesh could be expected to have slightly lower fertility than India and substantially lower fertility than Pakistan.

The percentage of person-years spent by women in a state of pregnancy or amenorrhoea is higher in Pakistan (19.5 per cent) and India (12.3 per cent) than in Bangladesh (6.8 per cent). In addition, the percentage of person-years lived as still exposed to the risk of pregnancy (i.e. women who are fecund, currently married, not using contraception, and not pregnant or amenorrhoeic) is also higher in Pakistan than in Bangladesh and India. These findings also suggest that India and Pakistan may have higher fertility than Bangladesh, especially when one takes into account that Bangladeshi women tend to breastfeed for long periods and have extended periods of postpartum infecundity. This finding again calls into question whether Bangladesh and India could have identical fertility rates during the early 1990s; namely TFRs of 3.4 as reported by the 1993/94 BDHS and 1992/93 NFHS.

Summary and Conclusions

This review of demographic data, focusing primarily upon fertility and infant mortality, finds impressive evidence of fertility and mortality decline in South Asia. While Sri Lanka has attained the lowest levels of fertility and mortality in the region, the most rapid decline in fertility over the past 20 years appears to have occurred in Bangladesh. All major countries in South Asia have registered reductions in mortality, particularly infant mortality, over the past two decades. By the early 1990s, infant mortality had probably dropped below 100 in Bangladesh, India, Nepal and Pakistan (although this level may still be exceeded in certain regions within each country), and life expectancy had probably risen to around 58 years or more throughout the South Asian region.

Most of the current evidence on fertility and mortality decline in South Asia comes from survey and sample registration data. Unfortunately, population censuses have been neglected in recent years as a source of information on vital rates, most conspicuously in India, Pakistan, and Sri Lanka. Age misreporting is still a problem in South Asian censuses and surveys. However, at least in Bangladesh, the quality of age data in surveys appears to be superior to comparable census information. There is also some evidence of age shifting (overstatement of children's ages) in birth history data from DHS-type surveys. This problem was noted in Chittagong Division in Bangladesh; Orissa, Punjab, Rajasthan, and West Bengal in India; and in all provinces of Pakistan.

It is difficult to say to what extent the problem of birth history age displacement may have affected national vital rate estimates. Since the other three large divisions in Bangladesh (Dhaka, Khulna, and Rajshahi) did not produce any clear evidence of age shifting, it is unlikely that problems in Chittagong Division alone could have produced substantial underreporting of national vital rates (e.g. more than half a birth in the national TFR estimate). In India, the problem of age shifting in birth history data also appears to be localized in a minority of states. While it is more difficult to judge the case of India, one could reasonably argue that national-level estimates have been seriously compromised. Fertility estimates from DHS-type surveys in Bangladesh and India probably constitute plausible lower-bound estimates of current fertility, with actual levels possibly being as much as 0.5 births above published point estimates (e.g. TFRs of 3.3–3.8 in Bangladesh and of 3.4–3.9 in India). However, in the 1990/91 PDHS, birth history age displacement is a far larger problem. Vital rate estimates from this survey are probably not reliable, even when based upon a six-year average.

An analysis of national fertility levels using a synthetic cohort approach developed by Suyono and Palmore confirms that Pakistan has higher fertility than India and Bangladesh. However, these results also suggest that Bangladesh might be expected to have somewhat lower fertility than India, since the percentage of person-years lived by women not exposed to the risk of childbearing is higher in Bangladesh than in India. However, if women in Bangladesh are more likely to use methods ineffectively (e.g. if they have poor use compliance and high levels of discontinuation) compared to women in India (where the main contraceptive method is sterilization), then it would still be possible to argue that the two countries should have comparable levels of fertility.

Obviously, the national decomposition profiles presented in this review do not arrest all concerns about the quality of survey data. Variations in respondent age misreporting, the omission of vital events, and the temporal displacement of vital events in survey birth histories inevitably make cross-national comparisons in South Asia problematic. Confidence in DHS and DHS-type surveys would be considerably enhanced if more sources of demographic data were routinely available (population census age distributions) to corroborate survey results. In addition, greater efforts should be made to evaluate and upgrade the reliability of alternative sources of information, especially the sample vital statistics registration systems in the South Asian region.

If nothing else, this review of demographic estimates in South Asia should clearly underscore the importance of investing resources in different sources of demographic and programme performance information (including KAP and rapid survey approaches) rather than placing the burden of proof for demographic analysis on data from increasingly expensive and unwieldy demographic and health survey operations.

Appendix

There are many different data sources measuring fertility and mortality in the South Asian region. Since 1981, Bangladesh has probably developed the most extensive variety of such data sources. At the present time, the BBS conducts both decennial population censuses and a nationally representative sample vital statistics registration system. In addition, since 1981, the National Institute of Population Research and Training (NIPORT) of the Ministry of Health and Family Welfare has carried out an extensive array of national surveys. These include biennial contraceptive prevalence surveys conducted between 1981 and 1991, the 1989 BFS, and the 1993/94 and 1996/97 BDHS, which collect information on morbidity and mortality, disease incidence and coverage and treatment patterns relating to major health interventions.

In 1983, responsibility for conducting the BDHS was handed over to private-sector research firms. Since then, this approach has come to constitute an unusually successful collaboration in data collection and programme evaluation between public- and private-sector agencies. In addition, for the past two decades the International Centre for Diarrhoeal Disease Research (ICDDR,B) has maintained a complete registration system of births and deaths in Matlab thana (the Demographic Surveillance System—DSS) as well as an SRS in areas maintained by ICDDR,B to extend the reach of the original demonstration project.

In India, the Office of the Registrar General (ORG)/Census Office implements national population censuses every ten years and conducts an annual national SRS that provides the only national vital rate time series for the country. Recently, a second major resource became available with the release of results from the 1992/93 India National Family Health Survey (NFHS). This survey, implemented by the International Institute for Population Sciences in Bombay in collaboration with 18 regional Population Research Centres, provides information very similar in content and style to that produced by demographic and health surveys conducted by Macro International in other countries (e.g. Bangladesh, Nepal, Pakistan, and Sri Lanka). A follow-on NFHS had been planned for 1999. In addition, the ORG in Baroda implemented three rounds of an all-India family planning survey—the latest round taking place in 1988–89. In 1994, the National Council of Applied Economic Research in Delhi also carried out a national demographic and health survey. At the time of this writing, the only results to have been publicly released were those pertaining to the country's rural areas.

Nepal is also reasonably rich in data. The country has conducted three national surveys over the past decade—the 1986 National Fertility Survey (NFS), the 1991 Fertility, Family Planning, and Health Survey (NFHS) and the 1996 (NDHS). In addition, Nepal has kept to schedule in conducting 1981 and 1991 decennial population censuses and in disseminating the results. However, Nepal's efforts to develop a vital statistics registration system have not been successful. This is partly owing to an early decision to design a logistically more onerous total, rather than sample, registration system for the country.

In Pakistan, data sources appear to be somewhat less plentiful. Pakistan has not generated any census data since 1981. Pakistan does have a little-noticed SRS, but it is not clear whether the information it yields is very reliable. Much of the available information on demographic and health conditions comes from national contraceptive prevalence surveys (the 1984–85 and the 1994–95 Pakistan Contraceptive Prevalence Surveys), the 1988 Pakistan Demographic Survey and the 1990/91 Pakistan Demographic and Health Survey (PDHS).

In recent years, Sri Lanka also appears to have become deficient in data resources. This is no doubt a reflection of the political turmoil that has engulfed the country over the past decade. The latest available census is from 1981, and the last survey on population and health conditions was carried out in 1993. However, this survey was not nationally representative because of the civil war going on in the northeast of the country. Nevertheless, Sri Lanka is generally considered to have a reasonably reliable vital statistics registration system, although it does not appear to have been evaluated in recent years.

References

Bairagi, Radheshyam and Rahman, Mizanur (1996), 'Contraceptive Failure in Matlab, Bangladesh', *International Family Planning Perspectives*, 22(1): 21–5.

Becker, Stan, Kantner, Andrew, Allen, Karen, Datta, Ashish, and Purvis, Keith (1997), *An Evaluation of the 1993–94 Bangladesh Demographic Survey within the Matlab Area*, Asia-Pacific Population Research Reports, Honolulu: East-West Center.

Cleland, John, Phillips, James F., Amin, Sajeda, and Kamal, G. M. (1994), *The Determinants of Reproductive Change in Bangladesh: Success in a Challenging Environment*, Washington, DC: The World Bank.

Department of Census and Statistics, Ministry of Plan Implementation, and Institute for Resource Development/Westinghouse (1988), *Sri Lanka Demographic and Health Survey, 1987*, Colombo: Department of Census and Statistics, Government of Sri Lanka.

—— Ministry of Plan Implementation, and Institute for Resource Development/ Westinghouse (1995), *Sri Lanka Demographic and Health Survey, 1993: Preliminary Report*, Colombo: Department of Census and Statistics, Government of Sri Lanka.

—— Ministry of Finance, Planning, Ethnic Affairs and National Integration (1994), *Statistical Abstract of the Democratic Socialist Republic of Sri Lanka, 1994*, Colombo: Department of Census and Statistics, Government of Sri Lanka.

—— Ministry of Finance, Planning, Ethnic Affairs and National Integration (1995), *Statistical Pocket Book of the Democratic Socialist Republic of Sri Lanka–1995*, Colombo: Department of Census and Statistics, Government of Sri Lanka.

Go, Elizabeth, Palmore, James, Tabije, Tita L., and Reolalas, Aurora (1995), *Regional Variations in Philippine Fertility: An Exposure Analysis for 1993*, Manila: National Statistics Office and Honolulu: Program on Population, East-West Center.

Hill, Ken, Baqui, A. H., Jamil, K., Mozumder, A. B. M., and Sabir, A. (1996), 'Infant and Child Mortality in Bangladesh', *Bangladesh Demographic and Health Survey 1993/94: Extended Analysis*, Dhaka: National Institute of Population Research and Training and Honolulu: East-West Center.

International Institute for Population Sciences (IIPS) (1995), *National Family Health Survey, 1993–93: India*, Bombay: IIPS.

Kantner, Andrew, Lerman, Charles, and Yusuf, Mohammed (1995), *What can We Say About Fertility Trends in Bangladesh? An Evaluation of the 1991 Population Census*, Honolulu: East-West Center, Asia Pacific Population Research Reports, No. 5.

Ministry of Population Welfare and the Population Council (1995), *Pakistan Contraceptive Prevalence Survey, 1994–95: Basic Findings*, Islamabad: Ministry of Population Welfare, Government of Pakistan.

Narasimhan, R. L., Retherford, Robert, Mishra, Vinod, Arnold, Fred, and Roy, T. K. (1997), 'Measuring the Speed of India's Fertility Decline', *National Family Health Survey Bulletin*, Mumbai: International Institute for Population Sciences and Honolulu: East-West Center.

National Academy of Sciences (1981), *Estimation of Recent Trends in Fertility and Mortality in Bangladesh*, Washington, DC: National Academy Press.

National Institute of Population Research and Training (NIPORT), Mitra and Associates, and Macro International (1995), *Bangladesh Demographic and Health Survey 1996–97: Preliminary Report*, Dhaka: Mitra and Associates and NIPORT, and Calverton, Maryland: Macro International.

National Institute of Population Research and Training (NIPORT), Mitra and Associates, and Macro International (1995), *Bangladesh Demographic and Health Survey, 1993–94*, Dhaka: Mitra and Associates and NIPORT, and Calverton, Maryland: Macro International.

National Institute of Population Studies (NIPS) and Macro International (1992), *Pakistan Demographic and Health Survey, 1990/1991*, Islamabad: NIPS and Columbia, Maryland: Macro International.

New Era (1986), *Fertility and Mortality Rates in Nepal*, Kathmandu: National Commission on Population.

—— and Macro International (1996), *Nepal Family Health Survey, 1996: Preliminary Report*, Kathmandu: New Era and Calverton, Maryland: Macro International.

—— IIDS, and VaRG (1993), *Nepal Fertility, Family Planning, and Health Survey, 1991: Main Report*, Kathmandu: Ministry of Health, His Majesty's Government.

Ross, John A., and Frankenberg, Elizabeth (1993), *Findings from Two Decades of Family Planning Research*, New York: Population Council.

Shariff, Abusaleh (1996), 'Determinants of Fertility Differentials in Indian States: New Evidence from Cross-Sectional Data', Paper prepared for the IUSSP Seminar on Comparative Perspectives on Fertility Transition in South Asia, Islamabad, Pakistan. 17–20 December 1996.

Shryock, Henry S., Siegel, Jacob S., and Associates (1976), The Methods and Materials of Demography, New York: Academic Press.

Suyono, Haryono, and Palmore, James (1995), *Indonesian Fertility, the Proximate Determinants, and Unmet Need for Family Planning*, Jakarta: National Family Planning Coordinating Board (BKKBN) and Honolulu: Program on Population, East-West Center.

United Nations (1996), *World Population Prospects: The 1996 Revision, Annex II and III: Demographic Indicators by Major Area, Region and Country*, New York: United Nations Population Division, Department for Economic and Social Information and Policy Analysis.

2 Birth Rate Trends in India, Sri Lanka, Bangladesh, and Pakistan: A Long Comparative View

TIM DYSON

[W]e can fully understand the present only in the light of the past.
History is movement; and movement implies comparison.

(E. H. Carr 1968)

Introduction

This chapter presents time series of annual crude birth rates (CBRs) for selected populations in South Asia. It argues that birth rates throughout the region were declining from the 1950s and early 1960s. In Sri Lanka, the CBR decline dates from about 1950. The turning point in Kerala's birth rate may have happened slightly earlier, in the late 1940s. For West Bengal we present fairly convincing evidence that the CBR has been falling since about 1956. And the data strongly suggest that the turning point in Bangladesh's birth rate probably occurred only slightly later. The CBR on the Indian side of former Punjab too was falling from about 1955. It seems reasonable to speculate that a similar trend was happening only a little later in core parts of Punjab province in Pakistan. In contrast, in much of India it is the early 1960s that marks the onset of sustained birth rate decline.

Differences of historical experience and geographical location are crucial to an understanding of different South Asian fertility transitions. And, ultimately, the latter have to be seen in the context of mortality decline. There is convincing evidence that fertility often rose substantially before it fell.

Of course, the CBR is only one measure of fertility, and the timing of the onset of its decline is not necessarily indicative of the speed of its subsequent fall. Nevertheless, the very early dates of these birth rate falls, their historical contexts and interactions, and, most certainly, their detailed courses, have generally been unrecognized. But, then, demographers have a poor record of detecting fertility declines throughout the developing world (Dyson and Murphy 1985; Eberstadt 1981). Moreover, it is clear that the ultimate causes of fertility decline in South Asia lie in historical developments long before the 1950s.

Background

If the present study has one message it is that there has been much too little history, and much too little geographical comparison in the study of South Asia's demography. Populations live through time. But a disproportionate share of the research on this region's demographic evolution has relied upon the deficient data yielded by cross-sectional censuses and surveys. Policymakers and administrators certainly need both these tools. Sometimes data from censuses and surveys can provide valuable insights regarding the internal dynamics of fertility change. But the use of these sources to draw inferences about fertility (and mortality) *trends* has often been extremely crude—for example, because the resulting estimates often pertain to substantial and diffuse periods of time (as in intercensal analysis). At worst, particularly in the early stages of fertility decline, use of these data often produced misleading results, because the conclusions about trends derived from comparing the results of one piece of questionable estimation with those of another.

This verdict may seem harsh. Moreover, recent decades in South Asia have seen the establishment of some good data collection systems that have produced demographic time series capable of providing better insights on trends (see below). Furthermore, the problem of insufficient spatial comparison itself derives partly from history. Things are better now. But during recent decades, many of the region's demographers found themselves working in rather discrete geographical domains.

However the basic charge—essentially, that of insufficient regard to both geography and history—still stands. Thus, when considering fertility and mortality in Sri Lanka and Kerala, there has often been scant attention given to the geographical proximity of these two areas. Similarly, fertility trends in the countries of South Asia are usually described in very broad terms. True, Sri Lanka is something of an exception, because its annual time series of registered vital rates enables fairly detailed discussion of fertility change (see Langford 1996). But trends and turning points for the region's other countries are commonly depicted with little precision. India's birth rate is often described as having started to decline from sometime in the 1970s. In the case of Bangladesh we are told that fertility began to decline in the late 1970s (Cleland and Streatfield 1992). Similarly, for Pakistan, there is a long and complicated history of claim and counterclaim as to whether fertility decline has or has not started—although now most agree that it has (see Juarez and Sathar 1996).

Data and Aims

The present paper is an attempt to address some of the shortcomings of earlier analyses by simultaneously providing some historical and geographical perspective on the fertility transitions of South Asia. We will examine recent birth rate trends in their longer-term context, and with reference to trends in neighbouring countries. This is a huge task, which will probably raise more questions than can be answered.

The major form of data to be used are *annual* time series of crude vital rates—stemming from several different types of registration systems. All of these registration data have problems. The problems relating to data derived from the region's general system of vital registration (VR)—which, in most areas, was instigated soon after the middle of the nineteenth century—can be considerable. For example, not only are birth and death coverage deficient, but the extent of the deficiency changes through time; the territorial jurisdiction to which time series relate can also change, sometimes quite substantially; and several series have gaps and abrupt endings. The Appendix summarizes how the various time series have been compiled, and provides more information on these problems.

However, whatever their undoubted deficiencies, in the context of trends these time series data still have very considerable value. Our prime interest here is with *trend* rather than *level*. Unfortunately, demographers have too often been transfixed by the latter at the expense of the former. Moreover, in 1946 the population covered by general birth and death registration in South Asia was at least 320 million—equivalent to nearly 14 per cent of all humanity alive at that time. These data, therefore, have precious and significant historical value.

The analysis will make some reference to total fertility rates (TFRs), but the main focus is on CBRs. This is because only during the relatively recent past (in fact, since the early 1950s in Sri Lanka) have *some* registration systems in South Asia collected information on age of mother at time of birth. Although CBRs are influenced by changes in population age composition, as well as by alterations in marriage patterns and levels of marital fertility, it is this rate that directly influences the rate of population growth. It is unfortunate that the sample sizes of many cross-sectional demographic surveys—like those of the WFS and DHS—provide a rather weak basis from which to produce robust estimates of the CBR.

The approach of our analysis is to draw conclusions and raise questions from comparisons of time series. On occasion, time series are interpreted and adjusted, partly as a result of these comparisons. The comparisons will reveal some significant trend similarities. It will also detect some differences—no doubt, partly reflecting South Asia's linguistic, cultural and religious diversity.

The map in Fig. 2.1 serves to illustrate the geographical progression of the analysis, which, inevitably, has had to be highly selective. The analysis starts with India—the trunk, and parts of which also feature in the subsequent comparisons—then moves east to Bengal, both its western part (West Bengal) and Bangladesh. It then moves to South Asia's southern littoral, which has been exposed to outside influences for long. Here we compare Sri Lanka and Kerala (or, more specifically, Malabar). Next, we move north to Punjab, to both its Pakistani and its Indian parts. The final section of the chapter provides some thoughts regarding matters of explanation. In particular, we highlight some neglected aspects and agents of birth rate declines in South Asia, and argue that family planning programmes have mostly acted as important facilitators—rather than ultimate causal forces—of the region's fairly varied birth rate declines.

Figure 2.1. Principal study locations.

Note: Boundaries shown are mostly modern and are not authoritative. They do not always correspond to the precise territorial jurisdictions used in the text and figures.

India

First, we consider recent birth rate trends derived from India's Sample Registration System (SRS). We then compare these with birth rate trends from the general VR system from 1947 onwards. Finally, we draw inferences about longer-run fertility dynamics from a brief examination of estimates for the Berar region of central India.

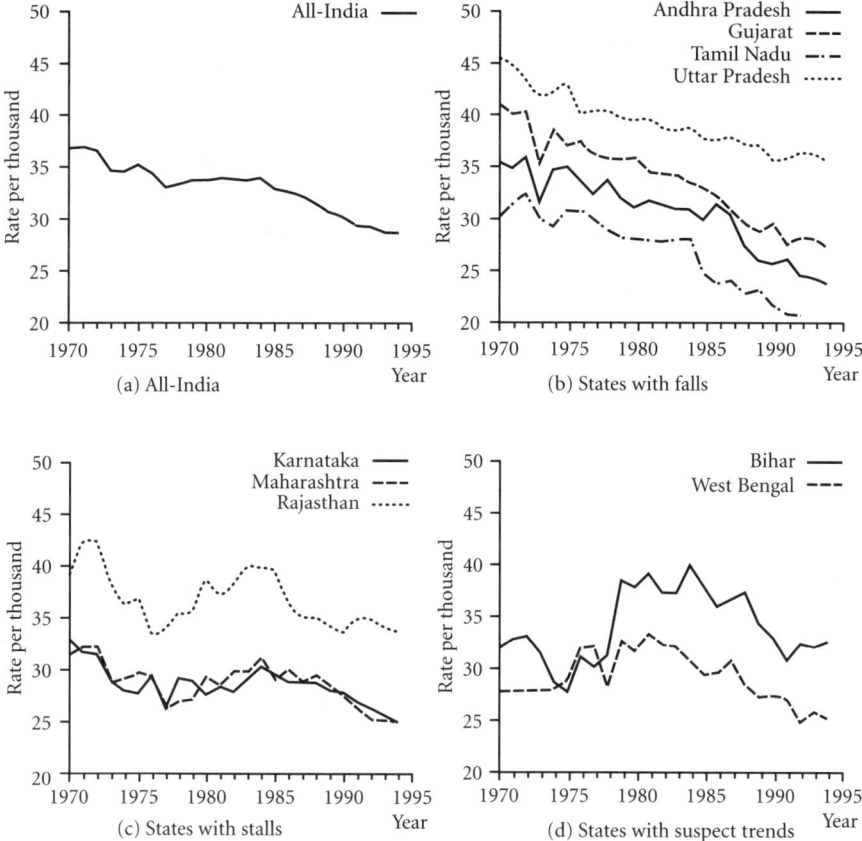

Figure 2.2. Unadjusted crude birth rates from the Sample Registration System, all-India and selected states.

Trends from the SRS

From about 1970 onwards, as the four charts in Fig. 2.2 indicate, CBR trends constructed from India's SRS are generally credible, even though levels of birth rates may be underestimates (see Dyson 1984; Dyson and Moore 1983). Figure 2.2(a) shows that the all-India CBR derived from the SRS data fell from about 36.8 births per 1,000 population in 1970–72 (this rate excludes Bihar and West Bengal) to 29.0 in 1990–93—a decline of about 21 per cent. Over the period 1970–72 to 1990–93, the SRS all-India TFR (not shown) fell from about 5.2 to 3.6 live births per woman—a decline of 31 per cent. So, due to age-structural changes, fertility per woman in India has been declining somewhat faster than the CBR. Indeed, the true declines for both measures may be marginally greater if the level of SRS birth coverage improved slightly over the course of time. Without doubt, control of marital fertility is the chief reason for these declines.

Another notable feature of Fig. 2.2(a) is the fairly lengthy period from 1977 to 1984 in which the decline in the SRS CBR stalled at around 33–34 births per 1,000 population. Explanations to account for this stall have included the setback to the family planning programme following Mrs Gandhi's Emergency measures of 1975–77, and upward pressures on fertility linked to various aspects of modernization—such as reductions in breastfeeding (see the contributions to Singh *et al.* 1989). But adverse age-structural change—specifically, an increase in the proportion of women in the reproductive ages, stemming from earlier changes in fertility and mortality—is probably the most important single explanation (see below). Moreover, we will see that stalls have not been restricted to India.

If state-level CBRs are examined, three broad patterns of time trend emerge: First, several states have experienced a fairly steady decline in the CBR since at least 1970—although sometimes with echoes of stall. Figure 2.2(b) shows that Andhra Pradesh, Gujarat, Tamil Nadu, and Uttar Pradesh (UP) fall in this category, as probably does Kerala (see below). Interestingly, this pattern of trend characterizes states with both relatively high and relatively low birth rates.

Second, Fig. 2.2(c) shows that several states (e.g. Karnataka, Maharashtra, and Rajasthan) experienced falling CBRs between the early and mid-1970s, followed by a period of rise lasting until the mid-1980s, since when the CBRs have resumed their decline. Clearly, here is the locus of much of the national stall.

Third, Fig. 2.2(d) shows two states (Bihar and West Bengal) with particularly suspect CBR trends. In these states, the birth rate rises shown between the early and late 1970s certainly partly reflect improvements in registration coverage (another conceivable, though probably minor, explanation for state stalls). Because of this rather obvious early coverage deficiency, data for Bihar and West Bengal were only included in the official all-India SRS birth rates from 1979 on.

It is worth highlighting two subperiods of relatively pronounced CBR decline shared by most Indian states. The first is the rather abrupt drop in the CBR between 1972 and 1973. Although budgetary-induced restrictions on SRS data collection procedures in late 1973 probably contributed to this decline, it also reflected genuine fertility reduction consequent upon the conditions of near-famine that prevailed in large parts of India during 1972 (Dyson and Maharatna 1992). The second subperiod relates to 1976 and 1977. The sharply lower all-India birth rate for 1977 certainly reflects the family planning programme's heightened emphasis on sterilization during 1976, which, significantly, was the only full calendar year of the Emergency period.

Trends from Vital Registration

The main conclusion from Fig. 2.2 is that India's birth rate has been falling since about 1970. This is an important but limited result. Accordingly, it is worth looking

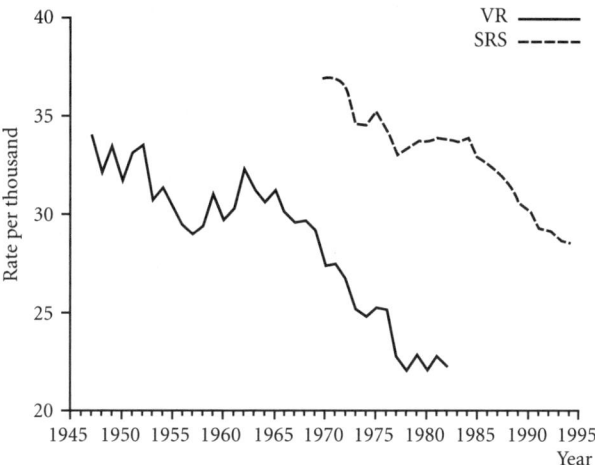

Figure 2.3. Vital registration (five states) and all-India SRS crude birth rates.

at CBRs produced by the general VR system—because they extend much further back in time. Figure 2.3 compares the all-India CBR derived from the SRS with a composite weighted-average CBR derived from VR for five major Indian states— Maharashtra, Gujarat, Tamil Nadu, Punjab and Haryana—known to have somewhat better general VR coverage (Dyson 1987). Together, these states contained a quarter of India's population in 1991.

Assembling a time series of composite population-weighted vital registration CBRs is a complex and lengthy task. It is all but impossible to list every single minor assumption and inexactitude that could be involved. Precise territorial jurisdictions of numerators and denominators often change through time. The registration CBRs used to compile the series in Fig. 2.3 are mostly the official state CBRs published by the Registrar General's office. Unfortunately, it has usually been impossible to work directly with the raw numbers of vital events registered since 1947, or with corresponding census population totals for areas under registration (as is usually possible for earlier times). Nevertheless, the main judgements likely to influence the comparisons significantly can be reasonably precisely specified. Thus, the CBR of 36.5 per 1,000 derived from the 1955 VR was clearly relatively much too high (probably in some way related to the major state reorganization then under way within India). The figure for that year has therefore been replaced by the average of the CBRs derived for 1954 and 1956. Also, the VR time series ends in 1982, partly because of a similar sudden birth rate discontinuity in 1983.

Nevertheless, several interesting points arise from Fig. 2.3. Perhaps most importantly, the VR CBR confirms the general fall in the birth rate. However, comparing averages for 1970–72 and 1980–82, the VR CBR fell by 18 per cent, compared to a decline of only 8 per cent in the SRS CBR. Despite their different geographical jurisdictions, it is certain that most of the widening discrepancy shown between the two time series in Fig. 2.3 reflects a continuing deterioration in general birth registration coverage—a consideration that will recur below. However, several other features of the SRS series are confirmed by the VR time series. Thus, both 1972–73 and 1976–77 show sharp declines in the CBR, and there is even a hint of a stall in the birth rate in the years after 1977.

Interestingly, the VR CBR in Fig. 2.3 declines from 34.0 in 1947 to a minimum of 29.0 per 1,000 in 1957; it then rises to a secondary peak of 32.3 in 1962—before falling again. Fertility transition is a complex evolutionary process. And selecting an onset year for birth rate decline is rarely straightforward. However, if a three-year moving average is used, the year of the final turning point in Fig. 2.3 would be 1963. During the 1950s the proportion of women of childbearing age in India's population was falling. This development occurred throughout South Asia, mainly because of considerable mortality decline. It probably contributed substantially to the limited fall in the birth rate in the decade immediately after Independence in 1947, although there was probably some deterioration in birth registration coverage too. However, given these considerations, the indication of a minor CBR rise between about 1957 and the early 1960s is highly suggestive of an increase in total fertility throughout much of India at this time.

Fertility Trends in Berar

Further light on these issues comes from the very long run registration-based time series compiled for the four of Maharashtra's 30 districts once known collectively as Berar. The great value of the Berar series derives from: (i) the generally very high coverage level of the region's VR since 1881; (ii) the absence of any change in the region's territorial jurisdiction over this period; (iii) the region's considerable geographical area (45,871 sq. km, about the size of Switzerland or Greece), which helps to minimize the effects of migration; (iv) the ability to simulate and *independently* cross-check (by comparing registration-based estimates and census data) alterations in the population's age structure, thus permitting the calculation of annual TFRs through indirect standardization; and (v) the territory's location right in the middle of India (see Fig. 2.1).

The complete time series for Berar, including sex-specific infant mortality rates and life expectancies, are available elsewhere (see especially Dyson 1989*a*; also Dyson 1989*b*). So Fig. 2.4 shows only the ratios of three-year moving averages of the CVRs and the TFR, compared to their respective long-run average values during 1881–1980. These long-run average values are: 40.7 for the CBR; 30.0 for the crude death rate (CDR); and 5.25 for the TFR. Three points of probable wider significance for past fertility trends in South Asia deserve comment.

First, prior to 1947 mortality movements had a very strong influence on fertility trends. Major rises in the CDR—such as occurred with the famines of the late nineteenth century and the influenza epidemic of 1918—produced lagged

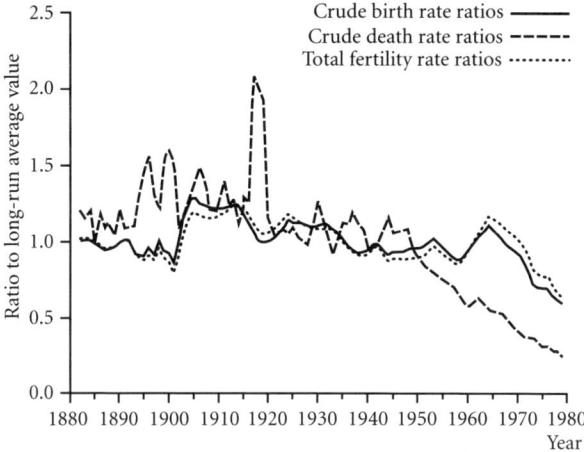

Figure 2.4. Indices of crude birth rate, crude death rate and total fertility rate variation in Berar, 1881–1980.

short-term declines in the CBR. This pattern of inverse variation between the CBR and CDR persisted, albeit on a reduced scale, until 1947—the year in which the CDR really began its sustained decline. Such inverse variation was by no means the only way in which mortality influenced fertility. For example, mortality crises affected population structures in ways that influenced subsequent birth rate trends. Thus, major famines throughout South Asia tended to kill males slightly more than females, and they also resulted in an increased proportion of the population being in the reproductive years. Therefore, in much of South Asia, the major famines of 1896–97 and 1899–1900 induced a fairly extended period of unusually high CBRs until about 1917—an effect very clearly seen in Berar (Fig. 2.4).

Also, high death rates contributed to high levels of widowhood, which, in turn, considerably limited levels of fertility (Davis 1951). Averaging across the four censuses from 1901 to 1931 in Berar, women classified as current widows constituted, respectively, 6, 18 and 41 per cent of the age groups 20–29, 30–39, and 40–49 (Dyson 1989a).

Second, and despite these caveats, variation in Berar's CBR mainly reflected variation in the TFR. The chief explanation is that mortality crises depressed total fertility, and conversely better times were free of this effect. Periods of minor divergence included the early years of the twentieth century, following the major famines.

Finally, Fig. 2.4 shows that Berar experienced a sharp *pre-decline rise* in total fertility immediately prior to the onset of sustained fertility decline. The turning-point year is 1964. Here again there was a minor divergence between the CBR and TFR movements—because the mortality improvement after 1947 reduced the proportion of the population in the reproductive years. Therefore, a rise in total fertility—probably partly itself reflecting improvements in health, declines in widowhood (and reductions in traditional practices of sexual abstinence)—was the cause of the CBR rise. And the main explanation for Berar's falling birth rate after 1964 is declining total fertility.

Concluding this section on India, over the longer run we see a progressive weakening of the extent to which the death rate determined fertility trends. Effectively, this mortality/fertility connection snapped around 1947—when, following earlier modest mortality improvements, there was a sudden sharp mortality reduction, and the sustained CDR decline began (a trend experienced throughout the whole of South Asia). In addition, it seems inescapable that the modern fall in India's CBR probably preceded the establishment of the SRS by several years. And this fall started in much of central and peninsular India around 1963–64. Furthermore, the 1950s and early 1960s probably witnessed some increase in birth rates and total fertility. Data from districts with better registration coverage strongly imply that it is this basic description, more than any other, that has characterized India's fertility transition since 1947 (Padalia 1988).

However, analysis in the following sections will suggest that certain outlying populations within South Asia experienced rather different specific birth rate histories in the modern era—linked to the experience by these populations of particular events and, sometimes, to their special susceptibility to external influences.

Bangladesh and West Bengal

Two main CBR time series exist for the former territory of Bengal. We have already mentioned that, on the Indian side, the SRS birth rates for West Bengal were exceptionally deficient before about 1979. In Bangladesh, of course, there is the well-known Matlab demographic surveillance system (DSS), which is maintained by the International Centre for Diarrhoeal Disease Research, Bangladesh (ICDDR,B). The Matlab registration system has been providing CBRs of comparatively good quality since about 1966. However, these data pertain to a fairly small rural population (about 205,000 in 1991) inhabiting an area approximately 55 km southeast of Dhaka (see Fig. 2.1). Moreover, the size and nature of the surveillance area has changed over time (perhaps most notably around 1977, when the number of villages covered was reduced, and those remaining were split into two groups—one being subject to an MCH-Family Planning programme, and the other being used for comparison). So, for many reasons, there is understandable reluctance to generalize from Matlab to broader developments for Bangladesh as a whole. Nevertheless, Fig. 2.5(a) presents a simple comparison of the CBRs from the West Bengal SRS and the Matlab DSS. Several suggestions emerge.

First, the deficiency of the SRS prior to about 1979 is very apparent. However, since that time, the CBR for West Bengal might, for many reasons, be expected to be lower than that prevailing in Matlab. Indeed, from about 1979 onwards, there is nothing

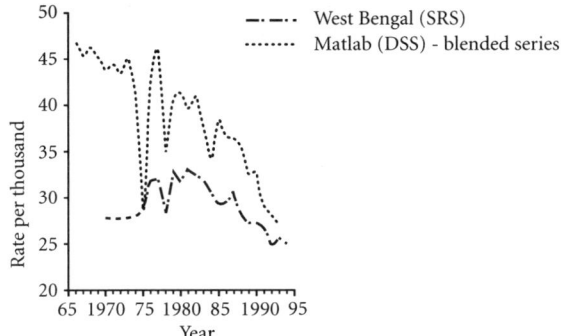

(a) West Bengal (SRS) compared to Matlab series

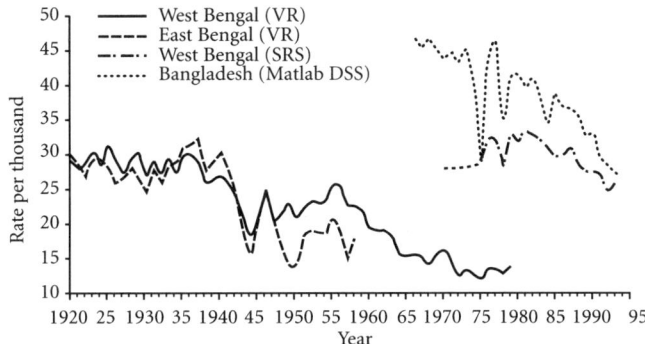

(b) Unadjusted series, West Bengal (VR and SRS), East Bengal (VR) and Matlab series

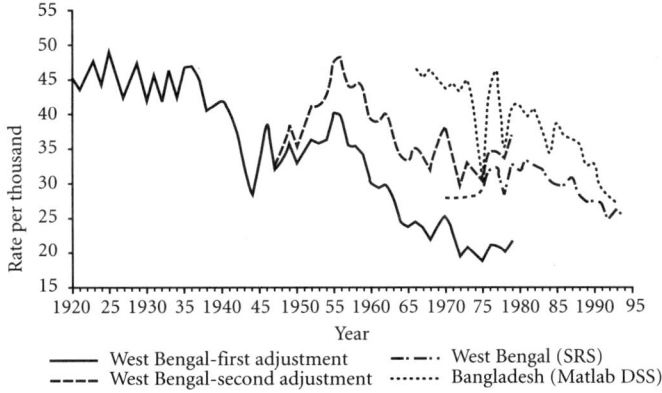

(c) Adjusted VR and SRS series for West Bengal, and Matlab series

Figure 2.5. Crude birth rates for West Bengal and Bangladesh.

obviously implausible about either the level or the trend in these two time series. They both convey a broadly similar pace of birth rate decline, although, very plausibly, with a somewhat lower birth rate in West Bengal than in Bangladesh, which is fully consistent with generally slower post-1947 population growth in West Bengal.

Second, despite the deficiency of the early SRS birth rates for West Bengal, the fact that population movements between Bangladesh and West Bengal have never been easy, and the fact that Matlab lies nearly 200 km away from West Bengal (see Fig. 2.1), it is clear that some short-term influences have simultaneously affected CBR movements in both populations. Perhaps this conclusion is most evident in the data from the late 1970s—particularly the drop in the CBR in 1978, following the very hard year of 1977. But the CBR recovery in Matlab in 1976–77, following the extraordinary fall in 1975 (a consequence of the Bangladesh famine of 1974–75), also had probable echoes in West Bengal.

Third, the CBR in Matlab appears to have been declining—albeit slightly—from the very first years in which it was recorded. Except for the rebound year of 1977, no subsequent CBR has attained the levels of 45–46 per 1,000 registered during each of the years during 1966–69. So, however circumscribed the Matlab data may be, the one birth rate time series we have for Bangladesh suggests that the CBR was falling there from the mid-1960s. Moreover, the fact that we find credible echoes of Matlab birth rate trends in the SRS rates for West Bengal strongly indicates that the Matlab data do indeed also convey the resonance of wider developments within Bangladesh.

Figure 2.5(b) replicates the time series of Fig. 2.5(a) and also shows for a much longer earlier time frame (starting in 1920) all the annual CBRs separately derived for East and West Bengal from the general system of VR. The registered CBRs before 1947 are obviously much too low. However, a similar trend in the birth rate is revealed in these two parts of Bengal before Partition—perhaps the most notable feature of which is the sharp CBR decline between 1940 and 1944. Undoubtedly, this decline reflected mounting economic stress, which culminated in the latter half of 1943. Interestingly, the decline was appreciably sharper in the eastern part of Bengal—arguably reflecting a greater intensity of stress there. Immediately after the 1943–44 famine, the registered CBR recovered somewhat—peaking in 1946, and then falling in 1947.

When considering the registered birth rate trends in Bengal for years after 1947, shown in Fig. 2.5(b), it should be recognized that both the eastern and western parts experienced major changes in population composition. That is, they became somewhat different entities after Partition. Governments on both sides of the new border—particularly to the east—certainly attached lesser importance to VR. Thus the extremely low CBRs registered for the eastern part of Bengal in each of the years 1948, 1949, and 1950 probably reflect numerator problems; specifically, in those years there was probably a failure to assemble data on *all* the registered births—and deaths. Also, in both 1949 and 1950, a suspiciously similar number of births (57,000) was registered for the then East

Pakistan. In addition, we have been unable to find any registered CBRs for eastern Bengal after 1958. However, the time series for West Bengal after Partition obviously has greater integrity. This series suggests that there was a rise in the birth rate until the mid-1950s—followed by a sustained decline. Note that even in this undoubtedly highly deficient VR series, the birth rate indicated for 1975 was especially low.

Finally, it is worth considering whether anything more constructive can be done with these data. A first attempt at cut-and-paste template demography is summarized in Fig. 2.5(c). Studies conducted earlier this century by Porter and Chowdhury provide similar estimates of the level of birth registration coverage in Bengal during 1921–40 (see Maharatna 1996: 140–1). The result of averaging these estimates suggests that the registered birth rates need to be adjusted upwards by a correction factor (CF) of 1.575. This CF was therefore applied to all the available registered birth rates for the western part of Bengal. However, as previously noted, the already deficient level of birth registration coverage in West Bengal certainly deteriorated considerably after Partition—although we have no detailed knowledge as to the timing of this deterioration. Nevertheless, we can use the CBRs from the SRS to gain an idea of its extent. Comparison of the adjusted registered birth rates for 1975–79 with the general level of CBRs implied by the linear trend of the SRS birth rates after 1979 suggests that, by that year, the already adjusted VR CBR needs to be pro-rated upwards by a further 71 per cent. For simplicity, this proportional pro-ration was introduced in constant increments over the period 1947–79; the outcome is shown in the second adjustment series in Fig. 2.5(c). It should be noted that the adjusted VR CBRs for the brief period of overlap (1975–79) are higher than those for the SRS (as is appropriate because the latter are too low), but the *pattern* of annual inflections within this quinquennium is almost identical. There is no claim here that the results of these adjustments—summarized in Fig. 2.5(c)—might not be improved. But we would be surprised if there currently exists a better representation of CBR trends in West Bengal or, by implication, and with qualification, in Bangladesh.

In summary, Fig. 2.5(c) strongly suggests that the CBR in both West and East Bengal fluctuated around 45 in the 1920s and 1930s, with little trend. It then fell sharply from 1939 to 1944. This was followed by a very brief recovery to 1946, and then, no doubt consequent upon the commotion of the impending Partition, there was another lesser decline in 1947. After 1947 the birth rate rose very substantially to the mid-1950s. For West Bengal this rising birth rate is powerfully and directly supported by the registration data; and if the CBRs for Matlab have any representativeness at all, then a similar—perhaps slightly greater—rise in birth rate must have occurred in Bangladesh. But this period of recovery was quite brief. Figure 2.5(c) indicates that the CBR in West Bengal has been falling fairly regularly since the mid-1950s. Combined with the data for Matlab, it seems virtually certain that the birth rate in Bangladesh was falling slowly from the early 1960s, and perhaps even from the late 1950s.

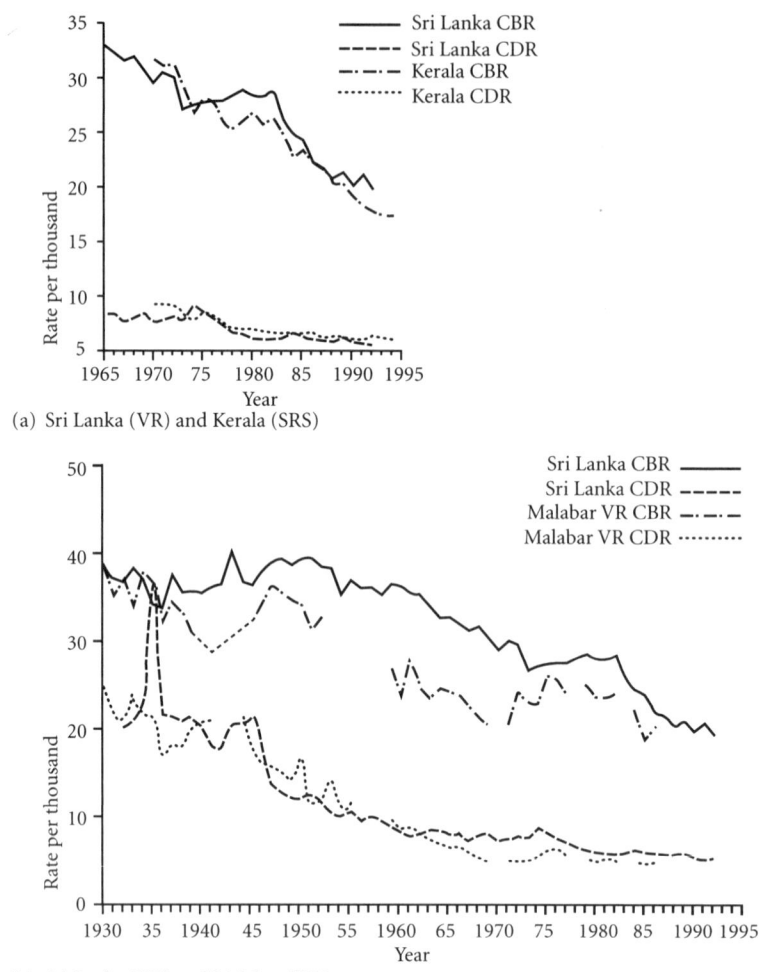

Figure 2.6. Crude birth rates and death rates for Sri Lanka and Kerala (Malabar).

Sri Lanka and Kerala

Sri Lanka and Kerala are usually considered as demographically the most advanced populations in South Asia. But their time series of vital rates are seldom, if ever, compared. Figure 2.6 provides such comparison, and because the information is relatively straightforward, CDRs are also shown.

Again, we start by considering the more recent past. Figure 2.6(a) focuses on the period for which SRS data are available for Kerala. The most obvious point illus trated is that birth and death rate trends in these two populations have been very similar. In other words, trends in the registered vital rates for Sri Lanka have been good, though not precise, proxies for the corresponding trends in Kerala.

A second interesting feature is that Sri Lanka also experienced something of a stall in its CBR decline. This occurred between 1973 and 1982—when the registered CBR rose slightly from 27.0 to 28.8 per 1,000. This was somewhat earlier than in India as a whole—where the stall was located between 1977 and 1984. Kerala may also have experienced a lesser stall at this comparatively early time: between 1974 and 1982, the SRS CBR fell only from 26.8 to 26.2 per 1,000.

Figure 2.6(b) shows an analogous comparison, but for a much longer period. Kerala mainly comprises two former units—Travancore-Cochin (itself formed from two princely states united in 1949) and Malabar. Malabar was the most populous district of former Madras state and, with state reorganization around 1956, it was divided into the three main districts (Cannanore, Kozhikode, and Palghat), which together then formed the northern half of Kerala. Unfortunately, only an extremely patchy registration time series for Travancore-Cochin can be constructed during the 1930s and 1940s; there are also other difficulties with the data. Accordingly, Fig. 2.6(b) relates only to the Malabar (i.e. *northern*) half of Kerala. We have been more successful in piecing together the registered death rate series although, because of further territorial changes in 1959, Fig. 2.6(b) excludes data for Palghat after that year.

Despite these deficiencies, the figure shows some interesting points and raises some intriguing questions. The birth rate in Sri Lanka fell slightly during the 1930s, before rising in the late 1940s. Langford (1996) has linked these movements to annual fluctuations in the island's marriage rate. If we apply a three-year moving average to the rates in Fig. 2.6(b) then Sri Lanka's CBR peaked in 1950, before falling to the stall of 1973–82.

Although the time series shown for Malabar are certainly less satisfactory than those for Sri Lanka—particularly given the gaps—they convey a strong suggestion that Malabar's birth rate also increased in the 1940s and then began to decline, perhaps from as early as the late 1940s. The relatively low registered CBRs in Malabar during the period from the 1940s to the 1970s could partly reflect poorer registration coverage. Nevertheless, an upward adjustment of Malabar's time series would be unlikely to alter the general conclusion that the birth rate was probably falling from the 1950s.

Moreover, comparison of the more satisfactory CDR time series lends further support to the suggestion that the onset of Malabar's birth rate decline may have slightly preceded that of Sri Lanka. First, comparison of the CDRs suggests that there may actually have been no major deficiency in Malabar's registration coverage before the 1960s (incidentally, Malabar did not experience the malaria outbreak of 1935). Second, it is intriguing that Malabar's sharp CDR drop in the 1940s also appears to have occurred marginally ahead of that in Sri Lanka: in Malabar the drop was between 1944 and 1946; in Sri Lanka it was between 1945 and 1947.

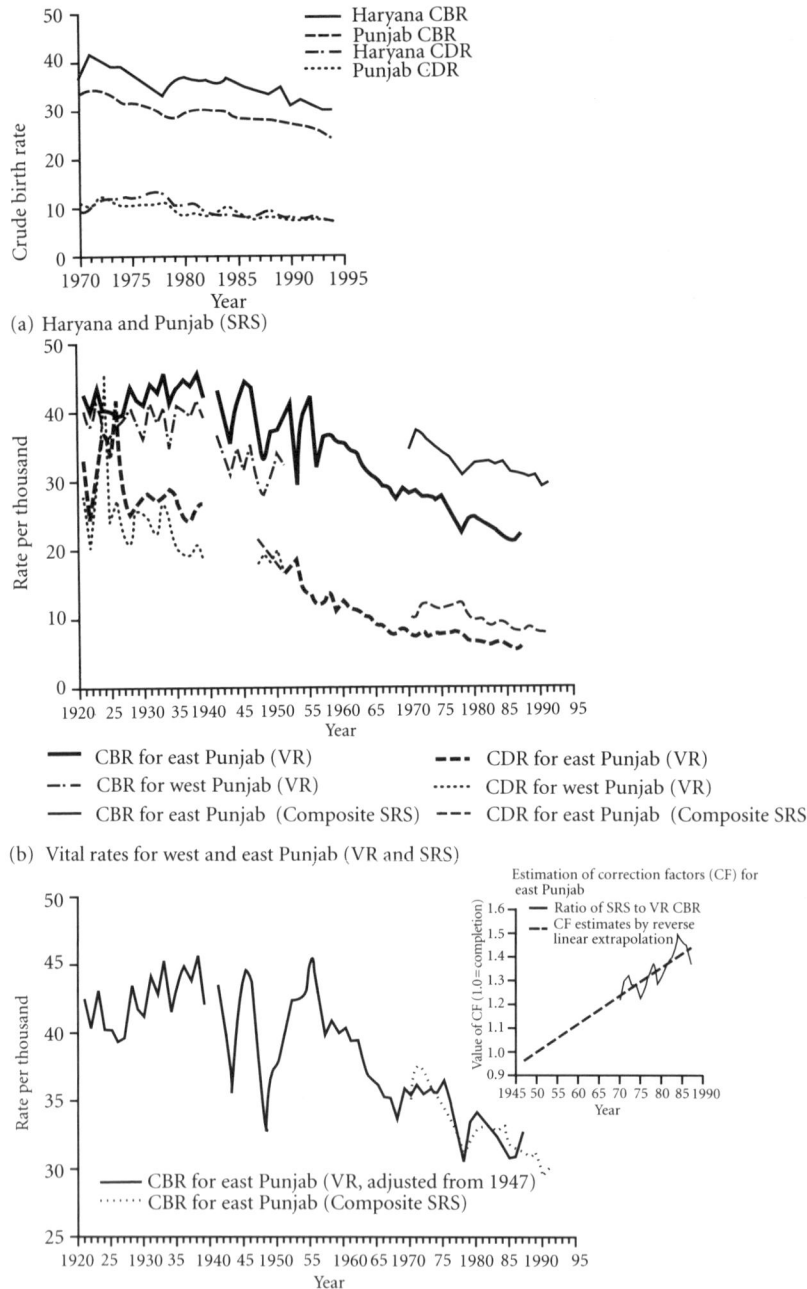

(a) Haryana and Punjab (SRS)

(b) Vital rates for west and east Punjab (VR and SRS)

(c) Adjusted VR CBR time series for east Punjab compared to SRS

Figure 2.7. Crude birth and death rates for Pakistani and Indian Punjab.

Of course, it is important not to push these registration data too far. Nevertheless, it seems entirely reasonable to conclude that many of the details of Kerala's birth and death rate trends since the 1930s have been similar to those in Sri Lanka. Indeed, the turning point of Kerala's birth rate may have very slightly preceded Sri Lanka's. There can be little doubt that the changing mix of factors behind these two birth rate declines was also similar. Initially, changes in age structure and rising female age at marriage were the predominant factors. However, by the early to mid-1960s, marital fertility in Sri Lanka was falling because of the deliberate practice of birth control (Langford 1981). Almost certainly, this was true for Kerala too. The 1951 census report for Travancore-Cochin remarks that '[t]he number of people who have broken away from the traditional patterns of family life and reproductive behaviour remains as yet infinitesimally small' (Census of India 1953b: 19). But it may be significant that this remark was made at all. The onset of some deliberate way of limiting fertility in a population must precede the time when it becomes apparent to demographers.

Punjab: Pakistan and India

Few comparisons of birth rates for neighbouring populations seem likely to provide greater contrast than that of Pakistani (west) and Indian (east) Punjab. Over half (56 per cent in 1981) of Pakistan's total population now resides in Punjab province. Although the 1990–91 PDHS survey suggests that national fertility decline began sometime in the 1980s, hitherto, Pakistan's fertility has usually been characterized as high, unchanging, and relatively homogeneous. Official estimates of the birth rate—from a variety of surveys—for the period 1962–90 all fall in the range 40–44 births per 1,000 population (see Pakistan Federal Bureau of Statistics, various years). And estimates of total fertility for Pakistan—from still more surveys—have ranged between five and seven live births per woman, with no clear trend observable (Juarez and Sathar 1996).

In contrast, Indian Punjab appears as a remarkable case of fertility decline—compared even with much of the rest of northern India. That fertility has been declining in east Punjab has been apparent for a long time (Visaria and Jain 1976). By 1991–93 the SRS put the state's CBR at 27.0, with a corresponding TFR of 3.1 live births.

However, this contrast between fertility in Pakistani and Indian Punjab—territories joined by history, although separated by a far from impermeable border—may not be nearly as stark as the preceding paragraphs suggest. This can be elaborated using the registration time series shown in Fig. 2.7. Again, since they are both straightforward and informative, CDRs are shown as well.

It is important to recall that despite its numerical predominance in Pakistan, the fertility characteristics of west Punjab may differ somewhat from those of the country as a whole. Much more significant is the fact that contemporary Pakistani

Punjab is a larger entity than Rawalpindi, Multan and (parts of) Lahore—divisions that used to form most of the west Punjab with which we are concerned here. Similarly, it is important to recall that Indian Punjab today is a very different entity to the areas of Punjab that became part of India in 1947 (Partition being accompanied by huge migrations). Small parts of the former British territory of Punjab are now in Himachal Pradesh state. By far, the most significant change came with the territorial subdivision of the then Indian Punjab in 1966—creating the new states of Punjab and Haryana.

Figure 2.7(a) plots the SRS vital rates for these two Indian states. It shows that any initial idea of much greater fertility decline in Indian than in Pakistani Punjab is in large part because the birth rate in the contemporary Indian state of Punjab (which, significantly, is contiguous to Pakistani Punjab and the major urban centre of Lahore) is appreciably lower than the birth rate in Haryana. Indeed, during the period 1970–92 the average SRS birth rate for Indian Punjab was 5.9 births per 1,000 lower than the corresponding rate for Haryana. And, plausibly, Haryana's SRS death rate is generally slightly higher too.

Therefore, when Haryana is duly taken into account, the Indian side of former Punjab is evidently not quite as advanced in terms of fertility decline. Moreover—apart from a probable rogue SRS birth rate estimate for Haryana in 1970—Fig. 2.7(a) shows that both Indian states have experienced similar birth (and death) rate declines during recent decades. There is some suggestion that the CBR in both parts of east Punjab (Punjab *and* Haryana) may have been falling from before 1970, which is entirely consistent with census-based studies (Visaria and Jain 1976). However, given Haryana's higher CBR, it may be reasonable to conclude that Haryana's birth rate decline started somewhat later than that in contemporary Punjab state—a consideration that may also be relevant for west Punjab.

Figure 2.7(b) broadens these comparisons in space and time. For most of the period 1920–51 inclusive, registered vital rates are shown separately for west Punjab and east Punjab—that is, on both sides of the contemporary international border. Unfortunately, we have been unable to extend the Pakistani series beyond 1951 (though, hopefully, some limited extension may prove possible). However, for the Indian side it is possible to compile the series until the late 1980s. Essentially what is shown for east Punjab from 1966 onwards are population-weighted averages of the registered vital rates for the Indian states of Punjab and Haryana plus, from 1970 onwards, the similarly weighted composite SRS rates. Several interesting points arise.

First—and not for the first time—we see evidence that birth and death rates may have moved in broadly similar ways in neighbouring populations. Before 1947 this correspondence may be less surprising. But the snippets of data available for west Punjab for 1947–51 also tentatively suggest some continuing similarity of trend, again despite alterations in population composition. With Partition portending, it is plausible that in both parts of former Punjab the birth rate really did fall sharply in 1947 (as in Bengal), and further still in 1948, before some recovery in 1949–50. It is suggested that registration coverage in west Punjab before 1940 may have been somewhat less complete than in east Punjab, although the registered birth rate in both areas was high.

A second interesting point arising from Fig. 2.7(b) is the marked degree of similarity between the composite SRS and registration CBR (and CDR) trends in the years for which both series exist. This similarity includes an abrupt (presumably Emergency-related) CBR dip in 1978. It is obvious that the VR system has been under-reporting the level of the birth (and death) rate in Indian east Punjab. But here we are chiefly concerned with the trend, not the level. And if it is reasonable to assume that the trend in the registered birth rate is also accurate for the years before about 1970 then, clearly, the birth rate in east Punjab has been falling since about 1960. Furthermore, if, again we disregard the suspect registration CBRs for the years 1953 and 1956 (see the Appendix) then the onset of the CBR decline in east Punjab actually dates from the *mid*-1950s, following the recovery after Partition.

At this juncture, the question arises as to whether the CBR in the previously mentioned core divisions of Pakistani Punjab might also have been declining—albeit slowly—from about 1960, or perhaps earlier still. We have already proposed a similar conclusion in our discussion of west and east Bengal. But this does not mean that any CBR decline in west Punjab has been nearly as great as in east Punjab. Indeed, we have already seen that there is significant regional variation in birth rate level within east Punjab. Unfortunately, because we have so few registration data on trends in west Punjab for the period after 1947, this question is not really directly answerable here. Nevertheless, it is inviting to employ the template approach used in Fig. 2.5(c) to the VR time series for east Punjab.

Figure 2.7(c) shows an attempt at this for east Punjab. Comparison of the VR and SRS CBRs for the years for which both are available indicates that birth registration coverage has been steadily declining and, therefore, that any CF for birth registration coverage has been increasing with time. The inset to Fig. 2.7(c) shows this, and, using a simple linear extrapolation, it gives the CFs implied for earlier years. Interestingly, and conveniently, these factors approach unity (i.e. registration completeness) around 1947. The registered CBRs before 1947 are probably slight underestimates (indeed, the same may apply to the SRS rates used to derive the post-1947 CFs). Nevertheless, before 1940, almost all the registered CBRs for east Punjab were in the range 40–45. So any CBR underestimation was fairly minor. Accordingly, Fig. 2.7(c) simply replicates the unadjusted VR CBRs for years prior to 1947. It also replaces the observations for 1953 and 1956 with the average figures for the adjacent years.

Figure 2.7(c) presents a very detailed and highly plausible annual birth rate time series for the eastern part of former Punjab for most of the present century. The CBR dipped somewhat during World War II, no doubt related to famine stress in certain districts (notably Gurgaon, Rohtak, and Hisar). There was then a brief recovery, before a second, greater, Partition-related dip in the birth rate. The CBR recovered in the early 1950s, before starting its fairly sustained decline.

In view of their close proximity to the modern Indian state of Punjab—with its especially low level of fertility—it is not difficult to believe that at least neighbouring districts of Pakistani Punjab, especially those in Lahore division, may have experienced a broadly similar CBR trend to that shown in Fig. 2.7(c) after Partition. True, any birth rate decline from the mid-1950s may not have been nearly as great on the Pakistani side. Of course, historical demography furnishes examples of neighbouring populations with dissimilar fertility trends. However, it is worth noting that, by 1981, over 38 per cent of the people in Pakistani Punjab lived in urban areas. Unfortunately, the plethora of cross-sectional surveys for Pakistan constitutes a flimsy basis from which to evaluate this issue. Only a time series of registered CBRs for the former Rawalpindi, Multan, and (parts of) Lahore divisions for years after 1951 would really suffice.

Towards an Alternative Theoretical Approach

In summary, the evidence reviewed here suggests that fertility declines started significantly earlier in most of South Asia than has hitherto generally been supposed. In the late 1940s and 1950s, changes in age-structure were probably the main—though probably not the sole—factor behind declining CBRs. However, by the early 1960s this age-structural factor had largely played out; indeed, in India, the proportion of females aged 15–44 actually increased slightly between the censuses of 1961 and 1971. And, as we noted above for Berar and Sri Lanka, there is fairly firm evidence that total fertility was falling from the mid-1960s. The sharp and sustained nature of some of the other birth rate declines—for example, those for West Bengal and east Punjab shown in Figs 2.5(c) and 2.7(c)—is indicative of a broadly similar deduction.

In turn, the conclusion that fertility was probably beginning to fall from such comparatively early times has major implications for matters of explanation. Contemporary accounts of the fertility transition in South Asia have often focused too readily upon the role of family planning programmes—to the neglect of other considerations. While we would not wish to deny that these programmes have played an important part in facilitating the region's fertility declines, taken together they have largely been a consequence—a manifestation—of a more fundamental and complex nexus of historical causal processes.

Without doubt, the most important engine of fertility decline in South Asia has been mortality decline. The massive quantity of detailed registration data available for the region shows widespread mortality improvement starting from around 1920 (earlier in some locations). Virtually everywhere, mortality became much less variable during the 1920s and 1930s—as major epidemics and famines became comparatively rare events. Greater stability in the death rate led directly to greater stability in the birth rate (see Dyson 1989b). And, in some areas—Bengal is an excellent illustration—the underlying level of mortality also improved considerably (Chowdhury 1989).

The upshot was very considerable population growth in much of South Asia long before 1947. For example, Sri Lanka's population grew at an average annual rate of 1.9 per cent between 1931 and 1953. The population of India as a whole grew at about 1.3 per cent per year in the 1930s and the 1940s. But in Malabar and Punjab, the corresponding growth rates were, respectively, 1.5 and 1.8 per cent. Similarly, following major mortality improvement during the 1920s, the population of Bengal expanded at nearly 1.9 per cent a year between 1931 and 1941.

On top of this, and in common with much of the rest of the world (see Dyson and Murphy 1991), most parts of the region then experienced extremely rapid mortality improvement in the few years immediately following World War II. Indeed, it may well be that about one-third of all mortality improvement in South Asia between 1947 and 1990 happened in the brief period between about 1947 and 1952. Accordingly, the initial period following political independence saw a significant further increase in the rate of population growth.

It was in this context that both India and Pakistan took the pioneering step of instigating official government family planning programmes around 1951–52. However changeable may have been the subsequent nature and level of support of family planning offered by governments in South Asia, it is highly significant that such steps were taken at all at such an early time. Regardless of the difficulties of articulating the subject of birth control, there can be no doubt that the concept was in the air. The stresses and strains engendered by growing populations meant that there had to be the murmurs of a fertility response as an adjustment to mortality decline. But then, of course, the history of the birth control movement in the region goes back at least to the 1920s. By the early 1950s, modern methods of contraception were certainly being used by many among the elite, and many more people—especially in urban areas—were undoubtedly aware of their existence. Bearing Fig. 2.7(c) in mind, another quotation from a census report can be used to illustrate the point.[1]

This view should not detract from the existence of traditional adjustment mechanisms for maintaining some degree of balance between a population and its resource base. In South Asia, these certainly included both marriage regulation (Das Gupta 1995) and birth control. The former probably included some degree of variation in the quantum and tempo of marriage; and the latter probably embraced withdrawal, abortion, and straightforward sexual abstinence. In short, the means

---

[1] There are references to the importance attached to the topic of family limitation in the 1951 census report for Indian Punjab. The report states: 'Recently, the subject of family limitation has begun to receive serious consideration in the towns, and at Ferozepur in a Women's College, while delivering his convocation address, an eminent public leader emphasized the importance of family limitation to the girl students. The adoption of birth control and other measures which go to reduce unwanted births are to figure more and more when the married couples begin to seriously think that they should ensure a suitable future for their children.' (Census of India 1953a: 47.)

required for the start of fertility declines in the 1950s and 1960s were most certainly in place.

Nor is it necessary to deny the operation of social, cultural, and institutional factors in conditioning the timing and speed of the fertility response to the changed circumstances that were increasingly brought about by mortality decline. It is obvious, for example, that populations situated in southern and eastern parts of South Asia generally reacted earlier and faster than those in the north and west of the region. Ultimately, it is probably this consideration that largely explains the earlier fertility transition of Bangladesh compared to Pakistan. However, as we have repeatedly stressed, differences of historical experience have also been crucially important in conditioning the speed and tempo of the fertility response. This brings us to some concluding comments on the particular fertility transitions considered in this paper.

With hindsight it is now clear that, after an initial period of fertility increase, large areas of contemporary India experienced declines in their birth rates (and probably TFRs) starting from around 1963–64. This time trend probably occurred throughout the most important populations of peninsular India (although detailed investigation for the north-central heartland, including UP, is required before generalization to India as a whole). We have shown elsewhere that the forgoing time trend also occurred in Egypt and, indeed, that in many ways the longer-run CBR trends in that country have paralleled those in much of India during this century (Dyson and Murphy 1985). This is not surprising, since both countries have been linked closely by shipping, and their experiences of many things (epidemics, wars, economic down-turns and, perhaps, policy ideas) have been connected in time. Such developments probably affected vital rates in both countries in similar ways and, through their effects on age structures, lent further similarity to subsequent birth rate trends. In this connection the CBR stall in India between the mid-1970s and mid-1980s finds parallel with the experience of Egypt—again, adverse age structural change being the principal cause (Bucht and El-Badry 1984).

The comparison for Sri Lanka and Kerala (Malabar) reveals the earliest and greatest fertility declines. And, from relatively early in the twentieth century, both these populations enjoyed comparatively favourable death rates (a fact that is often neglected when considering the progress of these two regions since 1947). Therefore, because ultimately fertility decline is an adjustment to mortality decline, the early timing of the fertility transitions in Sri Lanka and Kerala is perhaps only to be expected. A similar rationale probably applies to the explanation of the relatively early birth rate stalls there.

Bengal and Punjab provide us with the most intriguing comparisons. In both cases there are good reasons to believe that birth rates were declining on both sides of the international border from the early 1960s at the latest. Moreover, these comparisons are much more informative within Bengal and Punjab, when compared with the over-simple contrast between Bangladesh and Pakistan so often entertained by demographers (the latter may both be Muslim countries, but most of any similarity ends there).

Additionally, a key feature of any comparison between trends in these two parts of South Asia is the much greater impact that the events of the 1940s had in Bengal, which, like the southern littoral, was exposed to external forces—although in an entirely different way. Our adjusted time series for east Punjab in Fig. 2.7(c) certainly reveals the impact of World War II and Partition. But both events had comparatively constrained effects there. However, for West Bengal, Fig. 2.5(c) indicates that the combined influence of the war (which directly affected Bengal), the major famine (for which there was no real counterpart in Punjab), and Partition created a huge trough in the birth rate. Its brims stretched for nearly 20 years. Surely no account of the fertility transition in either part of Bengal can be complete without attention both to the substantial mortality decline of the 1920s and 1930s and the truly momentous upheavals of the 1940s.

More generally, we have tried to show that the usually neglected bodies of registration data for South Asia can provide essential perspective on the contemporary fertility transitions. It is misleading to consider national experiences either in isolation, or apart from their historical experience. Doing so misses the early origins of these transitions and their interactions with broader historical developments.

Unfortunately, demographic analysis of much cross-sectional survey data has probably been a significant impediment in this respect. Surveys are often ahistorical. By themselves, they generally provide a weak basis from which to estimate birth rates; and they are generally poor, and late, at detecting small, but significant, changes in fertility.

These criticisms of cross-sectional survey analysis can be extended. Increasingly, it is being recognized that such data cannot really provide conclusions about the underlying causes of fertility decline. To claim that this is possible, as analysts sometimes do, has rightly been compared to trying to explain the phenomenon of gravity with reference to the characteristics of objects as they fall outside a vacuum (see Lieberson 1985; Ní Bhrolcháin 1997). But it simply cannot be done. Hopefully, future research on South Asia's fertility transitions will avoid these pitfalls and adopt a more historical approach. Older forms of data must be revisited and revived.

Appendix

Sources for the Fertility Time Series Shown in the Figures

The Indian SRS rates for 1970–79 used in Figs 2.2, 2.3 and 2.5–2.7 are taken from Bhat *et al.* (1984); and the rates for later years are from the *Sample Registration Bulletin* (Office of the Registrar General, various years). For 1957 and subsequent years, the composite VR birth rate shown for five states in Fig. 2.3 is based on data from *Vital Statistics of India* (Office of the Registrar General, various years). For earlier years, it is based on data from *Health Statistics of India* (Director General of Health Services, various years). The originally derived rate for 1955 in Fig. 2.3 has been replaced, since the constituent rate published for former Bombay state was very probably biased upwards—in some way linked to state reorganization. Likewise, this composite CBR series ends in 1982 because the published official CBR for Gujarat falls abruptly from 28.7 (in 1982) to 20.7 in (1983). The rates for Berar that form the basis for Fig. 4 are available in Dyson (1989*a*). The Sri Lankan rates in Fig. 2.6 for years before 1976 are taken from Mitchell (1982), and those for later years are taken from the *Demographic Yearbook* (United Nations, various years).

For the years 1966–71, the Matlab blended CBR series in Fig. 2.5 are taken from Chen and Chowdhury (1977); these CBRs run from May to April and, for simplicity, they are plotted against their principal calendar-year counterparts (1966 in the case of the rate for 1966–67). The Matlab series for 1976 and subsequent years are from *Demographic Surveillance System— Matlab, Registration of Demographic Events* (ICDDR,B, various years). For the years 1972–75 inclusive, somewhat different CBRs are available from both sources. For simplicity, we have used the arithmetic averages—hence the term blended. For Fig. 2.5(b), for 1920–47 the CBRs for West and East Bengal were derived directly from data in *Annual Report of the Sanitary Commissioner for Bengal* (Sanitary Commissioner for Bengal, various years). The West Bengal series is based on registered births in Burdwan division, plus 24-Parganas, Calcutta, Murshidabad, and Darjeeling districts, plus the following proportions of births in the divided districts of Nadia (0.5), Malda (0.7), Dinajpur (0.3) and Jalpaiguri (0.7); for these proportions see Census of India (1952). The data used to calculate the East Bengal series were obtained by subtracting the West Bengal data from the totals for Bengal as a whole. As is the case with almost all the vital rates before 1947 presented in this paper, these West and East Bengal rates were calculated directly from the raw published data—with appropriate adjustments to denominators for population growth. However, after 1947, the CBRs for both parts of Bengal are largely taken from official published sources (these make adjustments too, although they are not always easy to appraise). For West Bengal, these sources are Census of India (1952), Government of West Bengal (1966) and *Vital Statistics of India*; and for East Bengal see *Statistical Abstract for East Pakistan* (Government of East Pakistan, various years).

For Malabar (Fig. 2.6(b)) the principal data source for 1952 and earlier years is *Report on the Health Conditions in Madras State* (Director of Public Health, Madras, various years). The CDR series covers more years than the CBR series—mainly because of additional data on annual registered deaths during 1944–55, published in Census of India (1961). From 1956 onwards, the main data source is *Vital Statistics of India*. The vital rates from the mid-1950s onwards are obviously very patchy, and for some years they are either missing or, as in 1970, so out of line as to be omitted altogether. After 1959, the unweighted average CBRs for the then reorganized Kozhikode and Cannanore districts are shown.

For Fig. 2.7, the vital rates for east Punjab from 1921 to 1939 were reconstituted directly from the published data found in the *Report on the Public Health Administration of the Punjab* (Punjab Public Health Department, various years). East Punjab was taken as Ambala and Jullundar divisions, plus Amritsar and Gurdaspur districts. As in the case of Bengal above, the corresponding rates for west Punjab were then obtained by subtraction. We have been unable to derive any rates for 1940. For 1941–50, registered births in east Punjab are available in Census of India (1953*a*), and birth data for total Punjab for 1940–46 are available in the *Annual Report of the Public Health Commissioner with the Government of India* (Government of India, various years); together these sources enable the derivation of CBRs for east Punjab for 1941–50 and (by subtraction) for west Punjab for 1941–46. All these data pertain to areas formerly under British administration. They do not cover the small minority Punjab States. For east Punjab in the period 1951–87, the main source of data on mortality is *Vital Statistics of India*; beginning from 1966, the registered death rates for Punjab and Haryana were population-weighted, using proportions of 0.559 and 0.441, respectively (these weights were also used to produce the composite SRS rates in Fig. 2.7). As noted in the text, for east Punjab the official CBRs for 1953 and 1956 again seem very suspect—probably reflecting some kind of administrative changes. For west Punjab the vital rates shown for 1947–51 are the official published rates contained in *Statistical Abstract of the Punjab* (Board of Economic Inquiry 1954).

The precise titles of many of the annual publications mentioned above vary from year to year. In all cases, copies of the numerical VR series used are available from the author upon request. Finally, the straight dashed lines shown in some of the time series in Figs 2.2(d), 2.5(a)–(c), 2.6(a), and 2.7(b) all bridge gaps in the series.

References

Bhat, P. N., Preston, S., and Dyson, T. (1984), *Vital Rates in India, 1961–1981*, Washington, DC: National Academy Press.

Board of Economic Inquiry (1954), *Statistical Abstract of the Punjab 1947 to 1953*, Lahore: Board of Economic Inquiry.

Bucht, B., and El-Badry, M. A. (1984), 'Reflections on Recent Levels and Trends of Fertility and Mortality in Egypt', CDC Working Paper No. 8, Cairo Demographic Centre, Cairo.

Carr, E. H. (1968), *What is History?*, Harmondsworth: Penguin Books.

—— (1952), *Vital Statistics, West Bengal 1941–50*, Delhi: Manager of Publications.

—— (1953a), *Census of India, 1951, Punjab, Pepsu, Himachal Pradesh, Bilaspur and Delhi, Report*, Vol. VIII, Part 1-A, Simla: Army Press.

—— (1953b), *Census of India, 1951, Travancore-Cochin*, Part 1-A, Report, Delhi: Manager of Publications.

—— (1961), *Census of India, 1961, Kerala, General Report*, Vol. VII, Part 1 A(i), Delhi: Manager of Publications.

Chen, L. C., and Chowdhury, A. K. M. (1977), 'The Dynamics of Contemporary Famine', *Mexico International Population Conference*, Vol. 1, Liège: International Union for the Scientific Study of Population.

Chowdhury, S. R. (1989), 'The Unprecedented Growth of Population in Bengal in the 1930s: An Effort to Find Out the Real Mechanism', M.Sc. Demography Dissertation, London School of Economics, London.

Cleland, J., and Streatfield, K. (1992), 'The Demographic Transition: Bangladesh Staff Reference Series 1/92, Programme Planning Unit', UNICEF Dhaka.

Das Gupta, M. (1995), 'Fertility Decline in Punjab, India: Parallels with Historical Europe', *Population Studies*, 49(3): 481–500.

Davis, K. (1951), *The Population of India and Pakistan*, Princeton: Princeton University Press.

Director General of Health Services (various years), *Health Statistics of India*, Delhi: Ministry of Health.

Director of Public Health, Madras (various years), *Report on the Health Conditions of Madras State*, Madras: Government Press.

Dyson, T. (1984), 'India's Regional Demography', *World Health Statistics Quarterly*, 37(2): 200–31.

—— (1987), 'An Assessment of Fertility Trends in India', in P. Padmanabha, Leejay Cho and R. Retherford (eds.), *Recent Population Trends in South Asia*, New Delhi: Government of India Press, 67–81.

—— (1989*a*), 'The Historical Demography of Berar', in T. Dyson (ed.), *India's Historical Demography: Studies in Famine, Disease and Society*, London: Curzon Press, 150–96.

—— (1989*b*), 'The Population History of Berar Since 1881 and its Potential Wider Significance', *The Indian Economic and Social History Review*, 26(2): 167–201.

—— and Moore, M. (1983), 'On Kinship Structure, Female Autonomy and Demographic Behavior in India', *Population and Development Review*, 9(1): 35–60.

—— and Murphy, M. (1985), 'The Onset of Fertility Transition', *Population and Development Review*, 11(3): 399–440.

—— and Murphy, M. (1991), Macro-Level Study of Socioeconomic Development and Mortality: Adequacy of Indicators and Methods of Statistical Analysis', in J. Cleland and A. G. Hill (eds.), *The Health Transition: Methods and Measures*, Canberra: Health Transition Centre.

—— and Maharatna, A. (1992), 'On the Demographic Consequences of the Bihar Famine of 1966–67 and the Maharashtra Drought of 1970–73', *Economic and Political Weekly*, XXVII(26): 1325–32.

Eberstadt, N. (1981), 'Recent Declines in Fertility in Less Developed Countries and What Population Planners May Learn From Them', in N. Eberstadt (ed.), *Fertility Decline in the Less Developed Countries*, New York: Praeger.

Government of East Pakistan (various years), *Statistical Abstract for East Pakistan*, Dacca: The Provincial Statistical Board and Bureau of Industrial Intelligence.

Government of India (various years), *Annual Report of the Public Health Commissioner with the Government of India*, Delhi: Manager of Publications.

Government of West Bengal (1966), *Statistical Abstract for West Bengal, 1962*, Alipore: West Bengal Government Press.

ICDDR,B (various years), *Demographic Surveillance System—Matlab, Registration of Demographic Events*, Dhaka: International Centre for Diarrhoeal Disease Research.

Juarez, F., and Sathar, Z. (1996), 'Emerging Evidence of Fertility Change in Pakistan?', Research Paper, London School of Hygiene and Tropical Medicine, London.

Langford, C. M. (1981), 'Fertility Change in Sri Lanka Since the War: An Analysis of the Experience of Different Districts', *Population Studies*, 35(2): 285–306.

—— (1996), 'Trends and Fluctuations in Fertility in Sri Lanka During the First Half of the Twentieth Century', Paper presented to the IUSSP Conference on Asian Population History, January 1996, Taipei.

Lieberson, S. (1985), *Making it Count. The Improvement of Social Science Research and Theory*, London: University of California Press.

Maharatna, A. (1996), *The Demography of Famines*, Delhi: Oxford University Press.

Mitchell, B. R. (1982), *International Historical Statistics: Africa and Asia*, London and Basingstoke: Macmillan.

Ní Bhrolcháin, M. (1997), 'Future Prospects for Population Research in the United Kingdom', in J. Chasteland and L. Roussel (eds.), *1945–1995: Un Demi-Siècle de Démographie, Bilan et Perspectives,* Paris: INED/Presses Universitaires de France.

Office of the Registrar General (various years), *Vital Statistics of India*, New Delhi: Government of India Press.

—— (various years), *Sample Registration Bulletin*, New Delhi: Ministry of Home Affairs.

Padalia, M. C. (1988), 'Long-run Demographic Trends in India', M.Sc. Demography Dissertation, London School of Economics, London.

Pakistan Federal Bureau of Statistics (various years), *Pakistan Statistical Yearbook*, Karachi: Manager of Publications.

Punjab Public Health Department (various years), *Report on the Public Health Administration of the Punjab*, Lahore: Superintendent of Government Printing.

Sanitary Commissioner for Bengal (various years), *Annual Report of the Sanitary Commissioner for Bengal*, Alipore: Bengal Government Press.

Singh, S. N., Premi, M. K., Bhatia, P. S., and Bose, A. (eds.) (1989), *Population Transition in India*, Vol. 1, Delhi: B.R. Publishing Corporation.

United Nations (various years), *Demographic Yearbook*, New York: United Nations.

Visaria, P., and Jain, A. K. (1976), *India, Country Profiles*, New York: The Population Council.

3   Comparison of Fertility Estimates from India's Sample Registration System and the 1992–1993 National Family Health Survey

R. L. NARASIMHAN, ROBERT D. RETHERFORD,
VINOD MISHRA, FRED ARNOLD, AND T. K. ROY

Introduction

Fertility has certainly been declining in India, but there is some question as to how fast the decline has been. Answering this question is important because accurate estimates of the speed of fertility decline are needed for monitoring the progress of India's national family planning programme and for formulating India's five-year development plans, which require population projections.

This article addresses the question of the rate of fertility decline by comparing fertility estimates derived alternatively from India's Sample Registration System (SRS) and the 1992–93 National Family Health Survey (NFHS). Both sources indicate a fertility decline, but they differ in their estimates of fertility levels and the speed of fertility decline. Our analysis attempts to explain how these discrepancies are accounted for by age misreporting, underregistration of births in the SRS and displacement and omission of births in the NFHS. The objective is to arrive at an improved assessment of the true trend in fertility in India during the 15-year period immediately preceding the NFHS. The basic NFHS reports already include some comparisons of fertility estimates from the SRS with those of the NFHS for the three-year period immediately preceding the NFHS. In addition, Arnold (1993), Bhat (1995), and Swamy (1995) have investigated discrepancies between the two sources. Our conclusions differ somewhat from those of these earlier studies.

We begin with brief descriptions of data sources and methodology. The own-children method is our preferred method of fertility estimation, and the general

We thank P. N. Mari Bhat, Norman Y. Luther, K. S. Natarajan, K. B. Pathak, B. M. Ramesh, O. P. Sharma, S. K. Sinha, and V. S. Swamy for their helpful comments. We also thank Judy Tom for computer programming assistance. The United States Agency for International Development (USAID) provided support for this research. The views presented in this article are our own and do not necessarily reflect the views of those who provided comments, of USAID, or of the organizations with which we are affiliated.

fertility rate is our preferred measure of fertility, for reasons that we explain. Following a discussion of comparisons between the SRS and the NFHS that were made before in the basic NFHS reports, we compare fertility trends estimated from the two sources. As part of this comparison, we examine evidence of birth underregistration in the SRS and evidence of displacement and omission of births in the NFHS. We also compare fertility trends estimated from the SRS and the NFHS with fertility trends implied by contraceptive use rates.

Data

The principal data sources for this analysis are India's SRS and the 1992–93 NFHS. A third data source is the family planning service statistics compiled by the Ministry of Health and Family Welfare. The first two of these data sources are described below.

Sample Registration System

In the absence of a complete and reliable civil registration system, the Office of the Registrar General, India, established the SRS in 1964–65 on a pilot basis. This was expanded into a full-scale system in 1969–70. Since the early 1970s the SRS has been the authoritative source of fertility estimates for the country.

The SRS is, in essence, a demographic sample survey based on a dual-record system, designed to provide national and state-level estimates of fertility and mortality on an annual basis. The system, which involves both continuous registration and a survey every six months to catch missed events, is based on a nationally representative sample of villages and urban blocks. The SRS sample currently includes 4,149 villages (or segments of villages in the case of large villages) and 2,151 urban blocks, comprising a population of about 6 million. The dual-record method for estimating fertility is described in more detail in the section on methods.

National Family Health Survey

India's NFHS, conducted during 1992–93, is our second source of information for estimating fertility trends. It is a nationally representative survey that includes both a household sample, covering everyone in the sampled households, and an individual sample, covering all ever-married women aged 13–49 within those households. Corresponding to these two samples are a household questionnaire and an individual questionnaire. The household sample comprises 88,562 households, and the individual sample, 89,777 ever-married women aged 13–49 within those households. The survey covers a range of topics in the areas of fertility, family planning, and maternal and child health.

The NFHS was designed to provide not only national estimates but also state-level estimates. In some states the sample was self-weighting, and in others it was weighted. There are two sets of weights, one set for each state and the other for the nation. The national weights take into account the state-level weights, as well as the fact that overall sampling fractions vary from state to state. Results reported here are based on the weighted data for all India.

Methods

The SRS uses a dual-record method for estimating fertility and mortality. We use two methods to derive estimates of fertility from the NFHS: the birth-history method and the own-children method.

Dual-Record Method

To understand how the dual-record method works, it is useful to consider the following basic characteristics of the SRS:

- Sample units are villages or urban blocks. Each unit has a local part-time enumerator.
- When a unit is first included in the system, a baseline survey is conducted. The baseline survey is a complete census of the sample unit conducted by staff from the state or district census directorate, with assistance from the local part-time enumerator. In principle, the baseline surveys are taken on January 1. In practice, most occur in January and February, and a few take place in March. The household informant is asked to provide the ages of household members as of January 1, even if the baseline survey is taken later. Ages in the household register are subsequently updated once a year on January 1.
- The local part-time enumerator is responsible for continuously enumerating births and deaths as they occur in the sample unit. In the case of births, the recorded age of the mother at childbirth is her age as of the last update on January 1.
- Every six months an independent survey is taken in the unit for purposes of recording births and deaths in the previous six months. This survey is scheduled for January 1 and July 1.
- After the half-yearly survey takes place, events from the two sources (the continuous register and the half-yearly survey) are matched at state or district headquarters. Matching is done using information on house number, name of household head, name of mother (for births), name of deceased (for deaths), residence status (usual resident present, usual resident absent, inmigrant present, inmigrant absent, visitor), sex, and month of occurrence. All unmatched and partially matched events are verified in the field by a third person or by the supervisor and enumerator together, after which personnel from the Census Directorate prepare a final list of births and deaths.
- At the time of the half-yearly survey, the supervisor updates the house listing in the sample unit and the household registers.

• Crude birth rates are calculated by pooling births from the final list of births for two half-yearly surveys covering January through December and then dividing this estimated number of births by the estimated mid-year population as obtained from the updated household registers. Crude death rates, age-specific fertility rates, and age-specific mortality rates are calculated similarly.

The half-yearly survey mentioned above is conducted in each sample unit by a full-time supervisor from state or district headquarters, who collects information about births and deaths occurring not only to usual residents but also to visitors. However, the information about visitors is not used in the calculation of fertility and mortality rates. The supervisor records age in the half-yearly survey, simply transferring updated ages from the household register to the survey schedule. When conducting the half-yearly survey at the start of the year, the supervisor simultaneously updates the household register, including updating of the ages of household members. Ages are updated in the household register by incrementing age by one year as of January 1 (RGI 1996; personal communication from Deputy Registrar General S. K. Sinha).

As the above description of the SRS estimation procedures makes clear, age-specific fertility rates (ASFRs) in the SRS are tabulated by age at the beginning of the year. This means that a reported ASFR for a given five-year age group actually pertains to a five-year age group that is on average six months older. In tabulations of ASFRs in the SRS reports, the age groups 15–19, 20–24, … , 45–49 actually pertain to age groups 15.5–20.4, 20.5–25.4, … , 45.5–50.4. We shall return to this point when discussing discrepancies between the NFHS and the SRS in estimated patterns of fertility by age.

Birth-History Method

The birth-history method, one of two methods by which we derive fertility estimates from the NFHS, is straightforward. One simply counts births by age of mother as reported in the birth histories for each year up to the fifteenth year before the survey. One similarly counts woman-years of exposure to the risk of birth by woman's age. One then divides births (by age of mother) by woman-years of exposure in each age group to obtain estimates of ASFRs and general fertility rates. To derive total fertility rates (TFRs) from the ASFRs, one sums the ASFRs in five-year age groups from 15–19 to 45–49 and multiplies the sum by five. In calculating these various fertility rates, which pertain to all women, not just ever-married women, it is assumed that never-married women have had no births. Base calculations are done in months. Rates are converted to a yearly basis only at the end of the calculations.

Because the NFHS collected birth histories only from ever-married women aged 13–49, we cannot calculate a complete set of ASFRs for each of the 15 years before the survey. For example, the oldest women in the individual sample, who were 49 at the time of the survey, were only 44, five years earlier. Therefore, one cannot calculate an ASFR for women aged 45–49 for years earlier than five years before the survey. Fifteen years ago, the oldest woman in the sample was 34 years old. If we want comparable fertility measures for each of the 15 years before the survey, we cannot make use of fertility at ages 35 and over. A suitable summary measure of fertility that is comparable over the entire period is the cumulative fertility rate up to age 35, or CFR(35). This measure is calculated by adding ASFRs in five-year age groups from 15–19 to 30–34 and multiplying the sum by five.

Own-Children Method

The own-children method is a reverse-survival method for estimating ASFRs and other fertility measures for years prior to a census or household survey. In the present instance we apply the method to the NFHS household sample. The NFHS household sample includes women of all ages, which means that it is possible to calculate a full set of ASFRs out to the age group 45–49 for each of the 15 years before the survey.

In the own-children method, one first matches enumerated children to mothers within households, on the basis of respondents' answers to questions about age, sex, marital status, and relation to head of household. A computer algorithm is used for the matching. One then reverse-survives the matched (i.e. own) children, classified by their own age and mother's age, to estimate numbers of births by age of mother in previous years. Similarly, one uses reverse-survival to estimate numbers of women by age in previous years. After making adjustments for unmatched (i.e. non-own) children, one calculates ASFRs by dividing the number of reverse-survived births by the number of reverse-survived women.

Estimates are normally computed for each of the 15 years before the survey. Estimates are not usually computed further back than 15 years because births must then be based on children aged 15 or more at enumeration, a large proportion of whom do not reside in the same household as their mother and hence cannot be matched. All calculations are done initially by single years of age and time. One obtains estimates for grouped ages or grouped calendar years by appropriately aggregating single-year numerators (births) and denominators (women) and then dividing the aggregated numerator by the aggregated denominator. Such aggregation is useful for minimizing the distorting effects of age misreporting on the fertility estimates (Cho *et al.* 1986).

Reverse-survival requires life tables, which we obtained from publications of the Registrar General, India (RGI 1986, 1990, 1995). We used separate life tables for urban areas, rural areas, and both areas combined. We obtained published life tables for the two time periods 1976–80 and 1988–92. We considered the life tables for these two periods to be located at the mid-points, 1978 and 1990. We then obtained life tables for years other than 1978 and 1990 by linearly interpolating or extrapolating age-specific probabilities of dying from the observed life tables for those two years, and then aggregating the interpolated age-specific probabilities of dying to complete life tables. In the end, for each geographic unit considered, we obtained a set of 15 life tables, one for each year within the 15-year estimation period 1978–92. We used these life tables for reverse-surviving women and children when applying the own-children method.

It should be noted that the own-children fertility estimates are not affected much by errors in the mortality estimates used for reverse-survival. One reason is that the reverse-survival ratios used to back-project children and women are both fairly close to 1.00. The other reason is that errors in the reverse-survival ratios used to back-project births based on children in the numerators of ASFRs cancel to some extent errors in the reverse-survival ratios used to back-project women in the denominators of ASFRs (Cho *et al.* 1986).

The own-children method is our preferred method, because, unlike the birth-history method, it yields a complete set of ASFRs between ages 15–19 and 45–49 for each of the 15 years before the NFHS.

Choosing an Appropriate Measure of Fertility

As will be seen later, both the SRS and the NFHS are characterized by considerable age misreporting, which produces systematic biases in estimates of ASFRs and in summary fertility measures, such as the TFR, that are calculated from ASFRs. It is therefore desirable to choose a summary measure of fertility that is less affected by age misreporting. A suitable measure is the general fertility rate (GFR), which is calculated as the number of annual births divided by the mid-year number of women between ages 15 and 49. In both the SRS and the NFHS, the total number of women aged 15–49 in the denominator of the GFR is biased by age misreporting only to the extent that women are moved across the age boundaries at ages 15 and 50. It is unaffected by age misreporting within the age range of 15–49. Moreover, the number of women transferred across the boundaries at either end of this range is small, compared with the total number of women within the age range, and this further minimizes the distorting effects of transfers across the age boundaries.

In the NFHS, but not in the SRS, misreporting of children's ages affects the numerator of the GFR. In the SRS, annual births in the numerator are obtained simply as registered births, which age misreporting does not affect. In the NFHS, annual births are derived by reverse-surviving children of each single year of age. If children's ages are incorrectly reported, the estimates of annual births are biased, unless there are compensating errors stemming from children erroneously moved into an age group being balanced by children erroneously moved out of that age group.

In sum, age misreporting has little effect on GFRs estimated from the SRS. GFRs estimated from the NFHS are somewhat affected by the misreporting of children's ages but affected very little by the misreporting of women's ages. One can reduce the bias from the misreporting of children's ages by calculating the GFR for time periods longer than one year, which entails grouping children's ages.

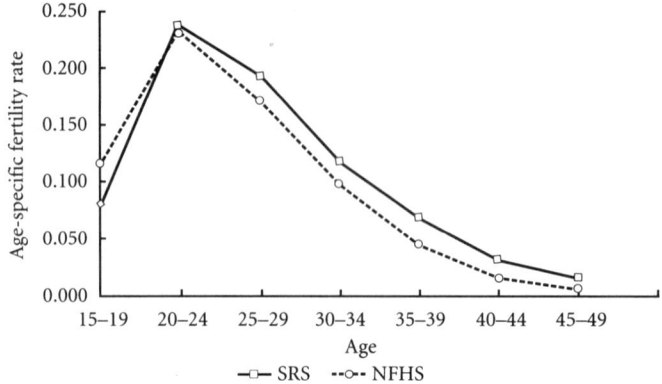

Figure 3.1. Age-specific fertility rates from the NFHS and the SRS: India, 1990–1992.

Source: IIPS (1995), Fig. 5.2.

Earlier Comparisons of Fertility Estimates from the SRS and the NFHS

It is useful to re-examine comparisons of SRS and NFHS fertility estimates that were done for the three-year period immediately preceding the survey and reported in the basic NFHS report for all India (IIPS 1995: 89). That three-year period, which varied somewhat in timing from state to state because not all states were surveyed at the same time, coincides approximately with calendar years 1990–92. Accordingly, comparisons at the national level are made with an average of SRS fertility estimates over this three-year period.

Table 3.1, drawn from the NFHS report for all India, shows comparisons of NFHS and SRS fertility estimates for the three-year period, and indicates fairly close agreement between the two sources. The last column shows that the agreement is better for the GFR and the crude birth rate (CBR) than for the TFR. This difference may occur in part because the GFR and the CBR are population-weighted averages of ASFRs, whereas in the calculation of the TFR, ASFRs are weighted equally. If errors in estimating ASFRs vary by age, those errors will affect the CBR and the GFR differently from the way they affect the TFR.

The NFHS report for all India additionally compares the age pattern of fertility derived from the NFHS and the SRS, as shown in Fig. 3.1 for the three-year period immediately preceding the survey. The figure shows that ASFRs from the NFHS are higher than those from the SRS at ages below the peak age of fertility, and lower at ages above the peak age of fertility. In effect, the age curve of fertility is shifted to the right in the SRS, relative to the NFHS. Presumably the peak of the curve also shifts to the right, but any shift in the peak is obscured by the grouping of ages into five-year age groups. The presumed shift in the peak might be revealed by a graph of

Table 3.1. Total fertility rates, general fertility rates, and crude birth rates from the NFHS and the SRS, by urban–rural residence: India, 1990–1992

Fertility measure	NFHS			SRS			NFHS/SRS		
	Urban	Rural	Total	Urban	Rural	Total	Urban	Rural	Total
TFR	2.70	3.67	3.39	2.71	3.99	3.67	1.00	0.92	0.92
GFR	98	133	123	93	129	121	1.05	1.03	1.02
CBR	24.1	30.4	28.7	24.0	32.2	29.6	1.00	0.94	0.97

Source: IIPS (1995), Table 5.1.
TFRs are expressed as births per woman. GFRs are expressed as births per 1,000 women (age 15–49) per year, and CBRs are expressed as births per 1,000 population per year. The NFHS estimate of the CBR pertains to the period 1–24 months before interview.

ASFRs for single-year age groups, but it is not possible to produce such a graph, because ASFRs for single-year age groups are not published by the SRS.

The NFHS report for all India hypothesizes that the higher NFHS estimate at ages 15–19 in Fig. 3.1 may be due to the fact that the NFHS estimates are based on the *de facto* population (the population actually in the household at the time of the survey), whereas the SRS estimates are based on the *de jure* population (defined in terms of usual place of residence). The NFHS report suggests that because births often occur away from the mother's usual place of residence, the SRS may not be able to obtain complete information about recent births to usual residents who are temporarily absent. Most, but not all, of the births initially missed in this way would probably be picked up in the next half-yearly survey. This effect could produce a downward bias in the SRS estimate of fertility at ages 15–19, when women are more likely, than at older ages, to return to their parents' home for delivery. In the NFHS, the percentage of births that occurred in the home of the mother's parents during the four years immediately preceding the survey was 21 per cent for women below age 20, 10 per cent for women aged 20–34, and 2 per cent for women 35 and above (IIPS 1995: 238). Such women typically spend an extended period away from their usual place of residence. Beyond age 20, however, the percentages are small and probably do not significantly bias the SRS estimates of fertility. In any case, after ages 20–24 the SRS estimates of fertility are higher than the NFHS estimates, not lower.

It is likely that a considerably more important cause of the observed pattern of discrepancies in Fig. 3.1—one that can explain discrepancies at both younger and older reproductive ages—is differences between the NFHS and the SRS in the extent and pattern of age misreporting. For example, ages might be reported as either somewhat too young in the NFHS or somewhat too old in the SRS. In the first case, the age curve of fertility from the NFHS would be shifted to the left, so that fertility below the peak age of fertility would be too high and fertility above the peak age of fertility would be too low. In the second case, the age curve of fertility from the SRS

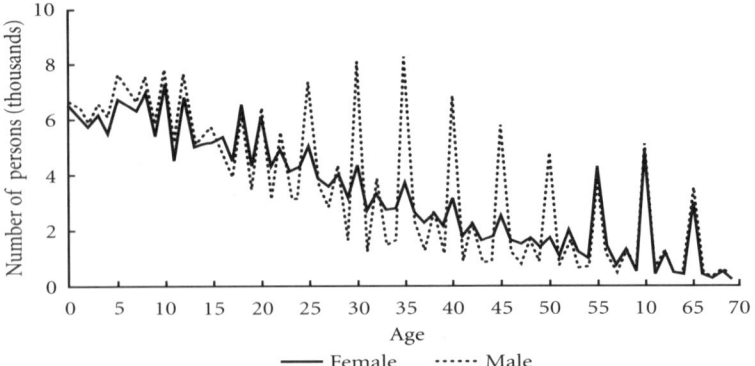

Figure 3.2. Number of persons by age and sex in the NFHS: India, 1992–1993.

Source: IIPS (1995), Fig. 3.1.

would be shifted to the right, so that fertility below the peak age of fertility would be too low and fertility above the peak age of fertility would be too high.

Which case is more likely? In the NFHS, the training of field staff lasted for a minimum of 20 days in each state, and a considerable amount of the training focused on how to collect accurate age data. Moreover, the NFHS asked questions on age as well as the month and year of birth, which were extensively probed. Despite the fact that only 16 per cent of ever-married women were able to report both the month and the year of their birth (which, when missing, were imputed from reported age or estimated by the interviewer after probing), the training appears to have had the desired effect. Figure 3.2, which graphs the single-year age distribution by sex for all India, as derived from the NFHS, shows that in the 15–49 age range, but not outside this range, heaping on ages ending in 0 and 5 is much less marked for women than for men. Outside this range the extent of heaping is about the same for both sexes. The ages of men, unmarried persons, and persons below age 15 or over age 50 were obtained from the household schedule. The informant in that case was the household head or, in the absence of the head, any other presumably knowledgeable adult in the household. The ages of ever-married women between ages 15 and 49, on the other hand, were obtained from the individual sample, in which the women themselves reported their ages and the interviewers carefully probed them for accurate responses. We believe that women are more likely than household heads or other household informants to have accurate knowledge of their own age. Moreover, women—especially younger women—are less likely than household heads or other household informants to report themselves as older than they really are.

The SRS baseline surveys collect information on age in completed years but not on month and year of birth, and interviewer training on how to collect accurate age data is less intensive than in the NFHS. Moreover, the SRS typically obtains information from the household head, who reports for the entire household. It is therefore likely that age reporting for women in the reproductive ages is less accurate in the SRS than in the NFHS. We hypothesize that the pattern of discrepancy between the NFHS-derived age curve of fertility and the SRS-derived age curve of fertility shown in Fig. 3.1 is due in part to a greater extent of misreporting of women's ages in the SRS. This could result from a net upward bias in reported ages of women who are young but married, and of women who have a higher than average number of children relative to their true age. For example, in the case of brides, the father-in-law might report the bride as somewhat older by virtue of her being married, and in some cases also because she is under the minimum legal age of marriage for women, which is 18 in India. There may also be some downward bias in reported ages of older single women and of women who have a lower than average number of children relative to their true age. For example, women who remain unmarried in their early twenties may be reported as younger than their true age because of the anxiety their parents may feel over not having already arranged a suitable match for them.

If this age-misreporting hypothesis is valid, proportions currently married at ages 15–19 and ages 20–24 should be lower in the SRS than in the NFHS. This is indeed the case. The proportion currently married at 15–19 is 38 per cent in the 1992–93 NFHS, compared with 30 per cent in the 1992 SRS. Comparable figures for the 20–24 age group are 80 per cent in the NFHS and 75 per cent in the SRS (IIPS 1995: 45; RGI 1994: 12). If our hypothesis is valid, mean parity (i.e. the mean number of children ever born to a woman) at the younger reproductive ages should also be lower in the SRS than in the NFHS. However, a direct comparison cannot be made in this case because the SRS does not tabulate mean parity by age. In sum, the available data on proportions married tend to support the hypothesis that greater age misreporting in the SRS than in the NFHS accounts for most of the rightward shift of the age curve of fertility in the SRS, relative to the NFHS.

As mentioned earlier, in the SRS a baseline survey is conducted when a village or urban block is first included in the SRS sample. Once this happens, the ages of children born after the baseline survey should be accurate. Their year of birth is obviously correctly recorded when they are born, and subsequently their ages are updated annually. However, there is scope for age misreporting for persons whose ages were obtained at the time of the baseline survey and for immigrants (including brides) who subsequently moved into the sample unit. The SRS sample of villages and urban blocks was completely replaced with a new sample of villages and urban blocks during 1982–84. None of the births that occurred after 1982–84 had reached reproductive age by the time the NFHS was conducted in 1992–93. Therefore, the ages of women for whom birth rates were calculated after 1982–84 are all subject to age misreporting in the SRS baseline surveys. A similar mechanism operated between 1978 and 1982–84, inasmuch as the SRS sample was expanded by about half during 1978–79. In this regard, it should be noted that when ages are updated in the half-yearly survey at the start of the year, age-reporting errors in the baseline survey are preserved. For example, if a woman's age is exaggerated by one year in the baseline survey, it will also be exaggerated by one year in every subsequent calendar year for as long as she remains in the SRS sample.

Further indirect evidence in support of the hypothesis that age misreporting tends to shift the age curve of fertility to the right in the SRS is provided by graphs similar to Fig. 3.1 for the states of India. The graphs for individual states, which are contained in the NFHS state reports but not reproduced here, show a pattern similar to that for all India in Fig. 3.1: a rightward shift in the SRS curve that tends to be more marked for states with lower rates of female literacy. In Kerala, the most literate state, a rightward shift is not observed at all. Inasmuch as literacy is inversely correlated with age misreporting, the inverse correlation of percentage literate with rightward shift supports the hypothesis that age misreporting accounts for most of this shift.

To examine the state-level pattern, we grouped 16 major states into three groups: those with low literacy (below 40 per cent literate among females aged 6+), medium literacy (40–55 per cent), and high literacy (above 55 per cent). Low-literacy states (by ascending level of literacy) are Rajasthan, Bihar, Uttar Pradesh, Madhya Pradesh, and Andhra Pradesh. Medium-literacy states are Orissa, Haryana, Karnataka, Assam, Gujarat, and Punjab. High-literacy states are West Bengal, Maharashtra, Tamil Nadu, Himachal Pradesh, and Kerala. All the low-literacy states show a large shift, and three out of five high-literacy states (Tamil Nadu, Himachal Pradesh, and Kerala) show a small shift or no shift. The pattern in the middle group is variable. These state comparisons also reveal that the association between literacy and extent of rightward shift is stronger at ages above the peak age of fertility than at ages below the peak, suggesting that age misreporting is a more predominant source of distortion at ages above the peak than below the peak. This is consistent with our earlier observation that fertility at ages 15–19 may be distorted not only by age misreporting but also (in the SRS) by unreported births to women who gave birth in their parental village.

Earlier we noted that, in the SRS published reports, age groups 15–19, 20–24, ... , 45–49 actually pertain to age groups 15.5–20.4, 20.5–25.4, ... , 45.5–50.4. Fertility in the age group 15–19 is lower than fertility in the age group 15.5–20.4, and the differential goes the other way at ages above the peak age of fertility. Thus the six-month offset tends to bias the SRS estimates of ASFRs in the direction of being too high at ages below the peak age of fertility and too low at ages above the peak age of fertility. This pattern is the reverse of what we observe in the comparison of SRS estimates of ASFRs with parallel estimates from the NFHS. Thus the six-month offset cannot explain the pattern of discrepancies shown in Fig. 3.1. Evidently, the bias caused by the six-month offset is more than compensated by the other sources of bias (mainly age misreporting) that act in the opposite direction.

This evidence on how age misreporting distorts the age curve of fertility justifies our choice of the general fertility rate as our preferred measure of fertility.

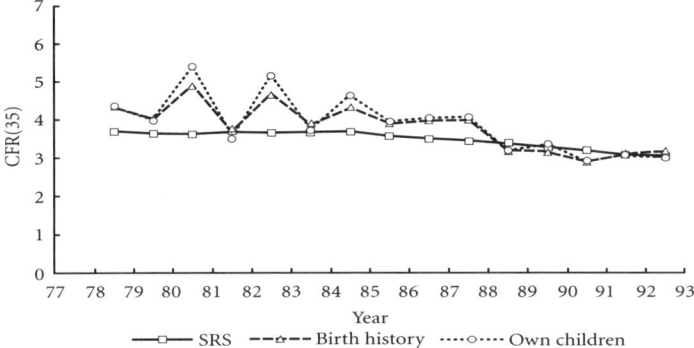

Figure 3.3. Cumulative fertility rates, CFR(35), from the NFHS (birth-history and own-children estimates) and the SRS: India, 1978–1992.

Comparing Birth-History Estimates with Own-Children Estimates of Fertility Trends

Next we compare fertility trends estimated by the birth-history method with fertility trends estimated by the own-children method in order to validate the use of the own-children method. If the two methods give similar results, we shall consider that the own-children method may be used in place of the birth-history method. As discussed earlier, estimating a 15-year trend restricts the birth-history estimates of fertility to ages below 35, so that the GFR cannot be used for this comparison. We therefore use the cumulative fertility rate up to age 35, CFR(35), for this purpose.

Figures 3.3–3.5 show birth-history and own-children estimates of the trend in CFR(35) for all India and for urban and rural areas. They also show SRS estimates of CFR(35). Several features are immediately evident from the graphs. The SRS trend is smooth, whereas the birth-history and own-children trends show systematic fluctuations. The fluctuations in the birth-history and own-children trends are similar, but those in the own-children trends are somewhat greater. This greater exaggeration occurs because interviewers in the NFHS were not required to probe extensively for age in the initial household interview. In addition, they were instructed not to correct ages in the household questionnaire on the basis of probed information obtained in the individual questionnaire unless a woman's reported age in the individual interview was outside the eligible age range of 13–49. Ages of children from the household questionnaire therefore do not necessarily agree with ages of children implied by birth dates in the birth histories obtained from the individual questionnaire. Consequently, ages of children in the NFHS suffer from misreporting to a greater extent in the household data used to obtain the own-children estimates than in the individual data used to obtain the birth-history

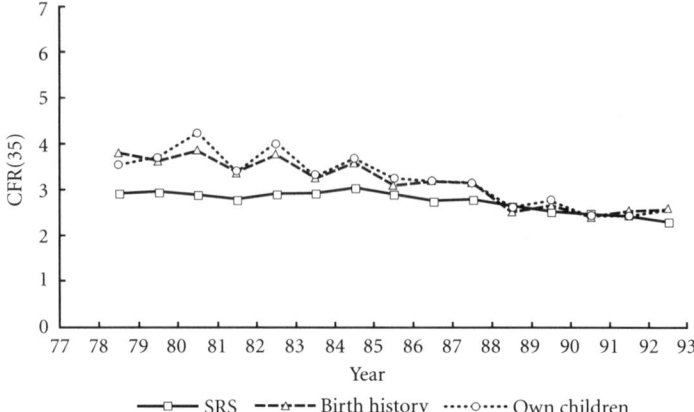

Figure 3.4. Cumulative fertility rates, CFR(35), from the NFHS (birth-history and own-children estimates) and the SRS: urban areas, 1978–1992.

estimates. (As discussed earlier, ages of ever-married women aged 13–49 are identical in the household data and the individual data used in our analysis. An additional age variable was created in the household data set, which is the same as the original age variable in the household data set except that ages of ever-married women aged 13–49 are replaced with corresponding ages collected for these women in the individual questionnaire. We have used this additional age variable in place of the original age variable obtained from the household questionnaire.)

The own-children estimates of CFR(35) tend to exceed slightly the birth-history estimates of CFR(35) during the earlier half of the estimation period. On the whole, however, there is quite close agreement between the birth-history and own-children trends in CFR(35), in both urban and rural areas.

The fluctuations in the trends derived from birth histories and those derived from the own-children method reflect patterns of misreporting of children's ages in the NFHS. Births in the first year before the survey, whether obtained from the birth histories or by reverse-survival of children, are based on children aged 0 (i.e. under age 1) at the time of the survey. Similarly, births in the second year before the survey are based on children aged 1 at the time of the survey, and so on. The upward jump in the sixth year before the survey may be due to a tendency of NFHS interviewers to shift some children under five years of age to age 5 or older in order to avoid having to ask a large block of questions pertaining only to children born since January 1 of the fourth full calendar year before the start of the survey in any given state. It is also possible that interviewers sometimes omitted children under age 5 and the births corresponding to them in the birth histories in order to avoid having to ask this same block of questions. Some of the upward jump in the sixth year before the survey may also be due to heaping on age 5.

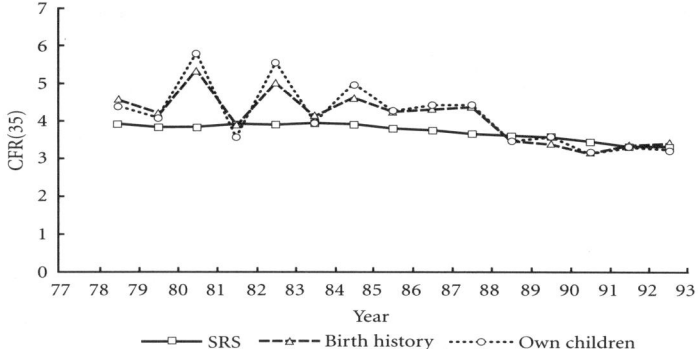

Figure 3.5. Cumulative fertility rates, CFR(35), from the NFHS (birth-history and own-children estimates) and the SRS: rural areas, 1978–1992.

The peaks in the trends derived from birth-history and own-children methods in the 9th, 11th, and 13th years before the survey reflect heaping of children's ages, respectively on 8, 10, and 12 at the time of survey. This pattern of heaping is found in many developing countries, including other countries of South Asia (Cho *et al.* 1986; Retherford and Alam 1985). The effects of heaping are slightly more evident in the own-children estimates than in the birth-history estimates because, as already mentioned, the children's ages on which the own-children estimates are based are taken from the household schedule, whereas the children's ages implicit in the birth histories were obtained by a more involved process of dating birth events that has no parallel in the household sample. In the individual sample, a mother reported a child's month and year of birth, whereas in the household sample the household head or another household informant reported a child's age only in completed years.

Graphs similar to Figs 3.3–3.5 for age-specific fertility rates (not shown) indicate that the ASFRs primarily responsible for raising the CFR(35) based on the NFHS above the CFR(35) based on the SRS are those at 15–19 and, to a lesser extent, at 20–24.

In sum, the close agreement between the birth-history estimates and the own-children estimates of CFR(35) validates our use of the own-children method for generating trends in the GFR from the NFHS. These we present in the next section.

Comparing Trends in SRS and NFHS Estimates of the General Fertility Rate

Earlier we mentioned that the problem of misreported children's ages can be reduced by calculating fertility estimates for periods longer than one year, which entails grouping children's ages. This problem can be minimized further by calcu-

Table 3.2. Estimates of the GFR from the NFHS and the SRS, by urban–rural residence: India, 1978–1992

Time period	NFHS			SRS			NFHS/SRS		
	Urban	Rural	Total	Urban	Rural	Total	Urban	Rural	Total
1978–92	122	158	148	107	143	134	1.14	1.11	1.10
1978–82	143	174	167	111	147	140	1.28	1.18	1.19
1983–87	128	171	159	113	148	140	1.14	1.16	1.14
1988–92	101	134	124	96	133	124	1.05	1.01	1.00

Note: GFRs are expressed as births per 1,000 women (age 15–49) per year.

lating a single general fertility rate for the entire 15-year estimation period from 1978 to 1992 (1977 to 1991 for some states and 1979 to 1993 for one state). In the case of the NFHS, we do this by calculating, first, the total number of births over the 15-year time period and, second, the number of person-years of exposure of women aged 15–49 over this same period, and then dividing the number of births by the person-years of exposure to obtain an estimate of the GFR for the entire 15-year period. Births in this aggregated GFR are derived from children aged 0–14. The number of net transfers across the boundary at age 15 is probably quite small in percentage terms, inasmuch as there is almost no heaping on age 15, as shown earlier in Fig. 3.2. Thus the estimated number of births in the numerator of this aggregated GFR, and hence the estimate of the GFR itself, should be quite accurate, except for births corresponding to children who are missed or intentionally omitted by interviewers to lighten their workload.

In the case of the SRS, we were not able to aggregate numerators and denominators separately over the 15-year period, because the SRS does not publish estimates of the numerators and denominators separately—only the rates. Therefore, for the SRS we simply calculated a 15-year average of GFRs for single calendar years.

Table 3.2 shows estimates of the GFR derived alternatively from the SRS and the NFHS, by urban–rural residence, for the 15-year period 1978–92 as a whole and also for three component five-year periods, 1978–82, 1983–87, and 1988–92. For all India, the SRS estimate of the GFR for the entire 15-year estimation period is 134, and the NFHS (own-children) estimate is 148. The NFHS/SRS ratio of GFRs is 1.10. Thus the NFHS estimate is 10 per cent higher than the SRS estimate. How shall we interpret this?

Evidence of Birth Underregistration in the SRS

We can think of no reason why the NFHS estimate of the GFR for 1978–92 in Table 3.2 should be biased upward. On the contrary, the NFHS estimate may be too low

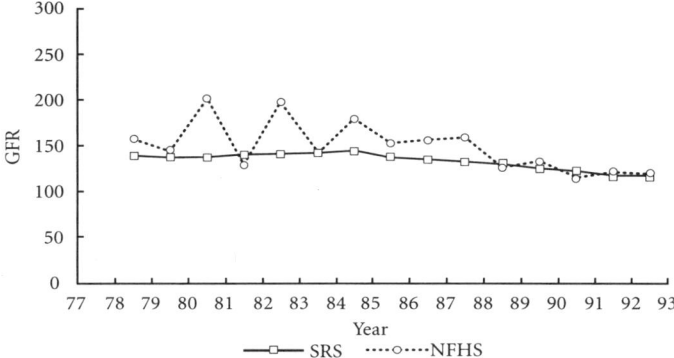

Figure 3.6. General fertility rates from the NFHS and the SRS: India, 1978–1992.

because of omission of births during the first five years before the survey. The SRS estimate may also be too low because of underregistration of births. The results therefore suggest that, for the period 1978–92 as a whole, SRS births are underregistered by at least 10 per cent. This minimal figure of 10 per cent appears robust, given the negligible effects of age misreporting on the underlying calculations.

If the discrepancies in the GFR between the SRS and the NFHS stem from greater underregistration of births in the SRS than undercoverage of births in the NFHS, we would expect the magnitude of the discrepancy to be greater in earlier years, when the SRS did not cover events as completely as it does today. Table 3.2 shows that this is indeed the case. The NFHS/SRS ratio of GFRs is 1.19 for 1978–82, 1.14 for 1983–87, and 1.00 for 1988–92. The value of 1.00 for 1988–92 indicates that in this most recent period, registration of births in the SRS is as complete as birth coverage in the NFHS. However, the precipitous drop from 1.14 to 1.00 between 1983–87 and 1988–92 seems too large to be caused by more complete birth registration in the SRS alone. It suggests that omission of births in the NFHS during the five years before the survey and displacement of births in the NFHS from the first five years to earlier periods may also have played a role. This possibility is consistent with evidence discussed earlier that there was some omission and displacement of births in the first five years before the NFHS on the part of some NFHS interviewers. We shall discuss omission and displacement of births in the NFHS in more detail later.

Several previous studies that evaluated the completeness of registration in the SRS also indicate that birth registration in the SRS has improved over time. All of these studies were based on special surveys conducted by the Office of the Registrar General in a subsample of SRS sample units. One such study, based on the 1972 Fertility Survey conducted in a 25 per cent subsample of the SRS for 1971–72, concluded that the SRS underregistered births in 1972 by about 8 per cent (Mishra

1988; see also RGI 1976, 1983). Two subsequent inquiries concluded that the SRS underregistered births by 3.2 per cent in 1980–81 and by 1.8 per cent in 1985 (RGI 1984, 1988). Taken together, these studies also indicate that completeness of birth registration in the SRS has been improving, although not nearly as much as our own analysis indicates.

If underregistration in the SRS was a problem in earlier years, we would expect the problem to be somewhat worse in urban areas than in rural areas, because of well-known difficulties of completely enumerating persons and events in urban areas. Table 3.2 confirms this expectation. The urban–rural differences are not large, however, perhaps because the registration difficulties posed by the population's greater anonymity in urban areas tend to be offset by higher levels of education and a greater need for a birth certificate (e.g. for entering school). For the entire estimation period 1978–92, urban births appear to be underregistered by 14 per cent and rural births, by 11 per cent, relative to the NFHS. (It may seem odd that 14 per cent and 11 per cent do not bracket the overall figure of 10 per cent for urban and rural combined, but this can happen computationally.) The picture is similar, but not entirely consistent, when we look at component five-year time periods. The urban ratio exceeds the rural ratio for the first and third periods, but not for the second period.

The Registrar General, India, has recently reported sex ratios at birth in the SRS for the period 1981–90 as a whole (RGI 1997). For all India the reported sex ratio at birth is 110. Among 15 major states, the sex ratio at birth is 105 in Andhra Pradesh and Tamil Nadu; 106 in Assam, Orissa, Kerala, and West Bengal; 107 in Karnataka; 108 in Madhya Pradesh; 109 in Maharashtra; and 110 or higher in Bihar, Gujarat, Haryana, Punjab, Rajasthan, and Uttar Pradesh. Sex ratios are highest in the northern states: 112 in Bihar and Uttar Pradesh, 113 in Punjab, 114 in Rajasthan, and 115 in Haryana. The high sex ratios in these northern states indicate substantial underregistration of female births in the SRS during the period 1981–90. If birth registration in the SRS were becoming more complete over time, one would expect the SRS estimates of the sex ratio at birth to be moving in the direction of 105. However, it is not possible to ascertain whether this has been happening because the SRS has not published annual estimates of the sex ratio at birth. The high sex ratio at birth in the SRS for the period 1981–90 constitutes additional evidence of substantial underregistration of births in the SRS in the past.

Evidence of Displacement and Omission of Births in the NFHS

At several points in earlier sections, we noted an apparent deficit of births in the first five years before the NFHS. This deficit could be due to displacement of births from the first to the second five years before the survey, or to omission of births during the first five years before the survey. Some interviewers were undoubtedly motivated to displace or omit births in order to avoid having to ask a large block of questions about children under a cutoff age (approximately age 5).

If interviewers consciously displace births from time to time to avoid having to ask a block of questions, an obvious way to do it would be to report a child of age 4 as age 5, and to do this on both the household interview and the individual interview, to be consistent and thus avoid detection. The result would be a noticeable deficit of children at age 4 and a noticeable surplus at age 5. It would show up in the age distribution as a downward spike at age four and an upward spike at age 5, as is indeed indicated by Fig. 3.2. It would also show up in the fertility trend estimates as a downward spike in the fifth year before the survey and as an upward spike in the sixth year before the survey, as is indeed indicated by Figs. 3.4–3.6. Overall, these results suggest that some intentional displacement occurred. As mentioned earlier, however, some of the surplus at age 5 may, instead, be due to a simple digit preference for age 5 on the part of respondents.

There may also be some unintended displacement. Children about to reach a birthday in one or two months may tend to be rounded up to the next age in completed years, especially by persons who do not recall the exact birth dates and ages of their children. For example, children whose true ages are 2 years and 11 months might be reported as age 3 in a substantial percentage of cases. If this kind of upward rounding of ages occurred, there would be displacement of births from the first five years into the second five years before the survey, but without downward and upward spikes in the fifth and sixth years before the survey.

It is also likely that another kind of unintentional displacement, resulting from heaping on age 10 but not on age 15 (as seen in Fig. 3.2), has tended to inflate fertility estimates in the third five years before the survey. In effect, this pattern of age heaping shifts births from the second five years before the survey to the third five years before the survey, but not from the third five years before the survey to the fourth five years before the survey. The result is a bunching of births in the third five years before the survey.

In Table 3.2, moving backward over time, the NFHS/SRS ratios of GFRs increase from 1.00 to 1.14 to 1.19 over three five-year periods before the survey. The value of 1.14 for the second period seems too large to be explained only by displacement of births, inasmuch as displacement from the first five years to the second five years is balanced to some extent by displacement from the second five years to the third five years. This is additional evidence that some interviewers omitted a birth from time to time in the first five years before the survey to lighten their workload. The ratio of 1.00 for the first five years before the survey indicates that the combined effects of displacement and omission in the NFHS are balanced by an equal extent of under-registration of births in the SRS during the same period.

In the NFHS there appears to be little omission of births by respondents (as opposed to interviewers). This is indicated by an examination of the trend in the estimated sex ratio at birth during the 20 years preceding the survey. If respondents were omitting births, female births would be more likely to be omitted than male births, given the high degree of preference for sons in India, and the distortion would become worse further back in time. But in the NFHS the sex ratio at birth is virtually constant over this 20-year period. It becomes heavily male only when one goes back more than 20 years. In the absence of large-scale sex-selective abortion, the sex ratio at birth is biologically determined and should be in the range of 105–107 male births per 100 female births. In the NFHS the sex ratio at birth is 106.3 males per 100 females in 1987–91, 106.3 in 1982–86, 106.6 in 1977–81, 106.6 in 1972–76, and 112.0 in 1971 or earlier (IIPS 1995: 325). These results indicate that, if significant numbers of births were missed in the NFHS during the 20 years before the survey, it is not because respondents did not report them. It is because interviewers who wanted to lighten their workload intentionally omitted some births during the first five years before the survey. The results also indicate that such intentional omissions, to the extent that they occurred, were random with regard to sex. That is, an interviewer was no more likely to omit a female birth intentionally than a male birth.

What Do the Comparisons Tell Us?

Taken together, the various pieces of evidence indicate three main reasons why the fertility estimates from the NFHS are progressively higher than those from the SRS, as one moves backward in time over the period 1978–92. They are: first, a higher rate of underregistration of births in earlier years of the SRS; second, backward displacement of births in the NFHS; and, third, omission of births in the NFHS in the first, but not in the second or third, five-year period before the survey.

If these explanations are correct, the fertility decline estimated from the NFHS is too steep, and the fertility decline estimated from the SRS is not steep enough. The fertility trend predicted by the trend in contraceptive use provides further evidence that the speed of fertility decline is underestimated by the SRS but overestimated by the NFHS.

The general fertility rate estimated from the NFHS for 1988–92 appears to be too low, yet it is identical to the GFR estimated from the SRS for the same period. This result suggests that the SRS underregistered births during this most recent period to the same extent that the NFHS displaced and omitted births. The true level of fertility during 1988–92 was probably somewhat higher than indicated by either the SRS or the NFHS.

The NFHS estimated the general fertility rate for the period 1978–92 at 148 births per 1,000 women aged 15–49. We estimated the number of births used to calculate this rate by reverse-surviving children aged 0–14 at the time of the survey back to births. We found no heaping of children's ages on age 15, which suggests that few births were shifted from those 15 years back to an earlier period. This result means that the general fertility rate estimated for the full 15-year period should be affected little, if at all, by displacement of births. The rate is undoubtedly somewhat too low, however, because of the omission of births during the most recent five-year period.

Nevertheless, the NFHS estimate of the general fertility rate for the full 15-year period is 10 per cent higher than the SRS estimate. This suggests that the SRS underregistered births during that period by at least 10 per cent. This level of underregistration is considerably higher than indicated by earlier evaluation studies conducted by the Office of the Registrar General. This finding, together with the finding that the NFHS/SRS ratio of GFRs converges to unity in the most recent five-year period, suggests that birth-registration completeness in the SRS has improved much more sharply over time than previously thought.

References

Arnold, F. (1993), *National Family Health Survey: Data Quality*, Unpublished paper, Calverton, Maryland: Macro International.

Bhat, P. N. Mari (1995), 'On the Quality of Birth History Data Collected in National Family Health Survey, 1992–93', *Demography India*, 24(1): 245–58.

Cho, Lee-Jay, Retherford, R. D., and Choe, M. K. (1986), *The Own-Children Method of Fertility Estimation*, Honolulu: East-West Center.

IIPS (International Institute for Population Sciences) (1995), *National Family Health Survey (MCH and Family Planning): India 1992–93*, Bombay: International Institute for Population Sciences.

Jain, A. (1996), *Consistency Between Contraceptive Use and Fertility Estimates for India*, Paper presented at the annual meeting of the Population Association of America, New Orleans, 9–11 May.

Mauldin, W. P., and Ross, J. A. (1991), 'Family Planning Programs: Efforts and Results', 1982–89, *Studies in Family Planning*, 22(6): 350–67.

Mishra, V. (1988), *India's Stagnated Birth Rate: A Matter of Serious Concern*, Unpublished paper, Delhi: Institute of Economic Growth.

MOHFW (Ministry of Health and Family Welfare) (1994), *Family Welfare Programme in India, 1992–93*, New Delhi: Department of Family Welfare, Ministry of Health and Family Welfare.

Ramesh, B. M., Gulati, S. C., and Retherford, R. D. (1996), *Contraceptive Use in India, 1992–93*, National Family Health Survey Subject Reports, No. 2, Mumbai: International Institute for Population Sciences; and Honolulu: East-West Center.

Retherford, R. D., and Alam, I. (1985), *Comparison of Fertility Trends Estimated Alternatively from Birth Histories and Own Children*, Papers of the East-West Population Institute, No. 94, Honolulu: East-West Center.

RGI (Registrar General, India) (1976), *Fertility Differentials in India, 1972: Results of the Fertility Survey in a Subsample of SRS (1972)*, New Delhi: Office of the Registrar General.

—— (1983), *Sample Registration System, 1976–78*, New Delhi: Office of the Registrar General.

—— (1984), *Report on the Intensive Enquiry Conducted in a Subsample of Sample Registration System Units (1980–81)*, Occasional Paper No. 2 of 1983, New Delhi: Office of the Registrar General.

RGI (Registrar General, India) (1986), *SRS-Based Abridged Lifetables, 1976–80,* Occasional Paper No. 1 of 1985, New Delhi: Office of the Registrar General.

—— (1988), *Report on the Intensive Enquiry Conducted in a Subsample of Sample Registration System Units (1985),* Occasional Paper No. 1 of 1988, New Delhi: Office of the Registrar General.

—— (1990), *SRS-Based Abridged Lifetables, 1981–85,* Occasional Paper No. 1 of 1989, New Delhi: Office of the Registrar General.

—— (1994), *Sample Registration System: Fertility and Mortality Indicators, 1992,* New Delhi: Office of the Registrar General.

—— (1995), *SRS-Based Abridged Lifetables, 1988–92,* Occasional Paper No. 4 of 1995, New Delhi: Office of the Registrar General.

—— (1996), *Sample Registration System: Fertility and Mortality Indicators, 1993,* New Delhi: Office of the Registrar General.

—— (1997), *Report of the Technical Group on Population Projections,* New Delhi: Office of the Registrar General.

Ross, J. A., and Frankenberg, E. (1993), *Findings from Two Decades of Family Planning Research,* New York: The Population Council.

Swamy, V. S. (1995), 'Age Pattern and Current Fertility From National Family Health Survey vis-à-vis Sample Registration System', *Demography India,* 24(2): 195–209.

Westoff, C. F. (1990), 'Reproductive Intentions and Fertility Rates', *International Family Planning Perspectives,* 16(3): 84–96.

4 Fertility Decline in Nepal

MARTINE COLLUMBIEN, IAN M. TIMÆUS, AND
LAXMI ACHARYA

Introduction

Secular reductions in fertility are now a well-established feature of the demography of South Asia. Fertility began to decrease in parts of India in the 1960s (Preston and Mari Bhat 1984; Rele 1987). By the late 1970s, a downward trend was apparent throughout nearly the entire country. In Bangladesh, the onset of fertility decline dates back to the end of the 1970s (Cleland *et al.* 1994). Moreover, while claims that fertility is falling in Pakistan have repeatedly been discredited (Retherford *et al.* 1987), detailed analysis of the most recent surveys suggests that some decline in fertility has now occurred (Juarez and Sathar, 2001).

Until the late 1980s, most experts were in agreement that no reduction in fertility had occurred in Nepal. The 1986 Nepal Fertility and Family Planning Survey (NFFPS) showed that current use of a modern method of contraception by non-pregnant married women had risen to 15 per cent. Some analysts felt that the results of the survey provided evidence of the onset of fertility decline (Tuladhar 1989). Others who examined the data were more sceptical and argued that fertility remained persistently high (Nepal 1987; Shah and Cleland 1993). The results of the 1991 Nepal Fertility, Family Planning and Health Survey (NFFPHS 1993) revealed that the contraceptive prevalence rate had risen to 24 per cent, however, and suggested that total fertility had fallen by perhaps as much as one child per woman. For example, total fertility in 1991 has been estimated to be 5.3 children per woman (Karki 1992), 5.7 (Joshi 1993), and 5.6 (Chhetry 1995). In response, a new consensus has emerged that the onset of fertility decline in Nepal occurred in the 1980s (see, e.g. Nepal 1995). The latest United Nations' population forecasts incorporate this view (UN 1995).

In this chapter we attempt to rewrite the fertility history of Nepal. We believe that fertility in Nepal has fallen further than most previous analysts have concluded. More controversially, based on a detailed analysis of the 1991 NFFPHS and supported by evidence from other enquiries, we argue that fertility decline dates back not to the mid-1980s but to the beginning of the 1970s. The chapter discusses briefly the implications of this suggestion for efforts to explain fertility change in Nepal and for the prediction of future fertility trends. For the benefit of readers who are not familiar with the demography of Nepal, the chapter begins with a short description of some salient facts about the country. It then discusses briefly fertility estimates from other censuses and surveys conducted during the last two decades before focusing on the analysis of the 1991 NFFPHS data.

Nepal is one of the world's poorest countries. It has a predominantly agricultural economy with less than 10 per cent of the population living in urban areas (World Bank 1993). Depending on how much allowance is made for an undercount in the census, the population in 1991 was a little over or under 19 million (Karki 1995). In recent decades, it has been growing at nearly 2 per cent a year. The population is differentiated by ethnicity, language, religion, and caste. While Nepali is the mother tongue of about half the population, ten other languages are spoken by at least 250,000 of the country's inhabitants (Kumar 1995). Hindus comprise about 86 per cent of the population, Buddhists 8 per cent, and Muslims 4 per cent.

Nepal is divided into three contrasting ecological zones. The Mountain zone is lightly settled and is home to only 8 per cent of the population (Singh 1995). The Hill zone lies between 5,000 and 15,000 feet in altitude. It incorporates a number of fertile and densely settled valleys, most notably Kathmandu Valley, and is home to about 45 per cent of the country's population. The Terai zone is a low-altitude and fertile region. Formerly, it was densely forested and malarious. Since 1951, however, there has been large-scale migration into the area, which is now the most densely settled part of Nepal, with about 47 per cent of the national population. For administrative purposes, the 75 districts are divided into five development regions. These divide the country from east to west, cross-cutting the ecological zones.

Despite its poverty, Nepal has achieved some success in improving the education and health of the population. School enrolments have risen rapidly during the last few decades, and nearly all boys and the majority of girls now attend primary school (Manandhar 1995). On the other hand, less than a fifth of children in the relevant age group attend secondary school. While the level of mortality is still high, the under-five mortality rate has probably fallen from over 250 per 1,000 in the 1960s to about 120 per 1,000 in the early 1990s (Nepal 1996).

Demographic Data on Nepal

The 1991 NFFPHS is the main source of data analysed here to assess recent trends in fertility. This survey used a modified version of the Demographic and Health Surveys (DHS) Model B questionnaire (Nepal 1993). A household survey was conducted to identify all ever-married women aged 15–49 years, who were eligible to answer the individual questionnaire, that is, women who had started living with their husbands and slept in the sample household the night before the interview. A total of 25,384 questionnaires with full reproductive histories were completed. This sample is large enough to allow analysis at the subnational level.

Table 4.1. Average parity by age of women, 1971–1991

Age	1971 Census	1976 survey	1981 Census	1986 survey	1991 Census	1991 survey	1996 survey
15–19	0.160	0.200	0.222	0.174	0.158	0.148	0.226
20–24	1.025	1.348	1.031	1.350	1.121	1.280	1.434
25–29	2.135	2.853	1.990	2.703	2.317	2.721	2.848
30–34	3.051	4.047	2.796	3.740	3.249	3.912	3.924
35–39	3.688	5.083	3.309	4.502	3.929	4.860	4.670
40–44	3.950	5.536	3.569	4.613	4.315	5.455	5.571
45–49	3.977	5.767	3.582	4.679	4.388	5.880	5.838

Nepal has completed four other national, single-round demographic surveys: the Nepal Fertility Survey (NFS) in 1976, the Nepal Contraceptive Prevalence Survey (NCPS) in 1981, the Nepal Fertility and Family Planning Survey (NFFPS) in 1986, and the Nepal Family Health Survey (NFHS) in 1996. Only preliminary results are available from the last of these surveys, which was undertaken within the DHS programme (Nepal 1996). As the 1976 NFS (Nepal 1977) was part of the World Fertility Survey programme, its methods and coverage were comparable with those of the 1991 and 1996 surveys. In contrast, the two surveys in the 1980s interviewed only currently married women. The 1981 NCPS did not include a full birth history, and the 1986 NFFPS (Nepal 1987) used male interviewers. This may have resulted in more serious underreporting of births than in the more recent surveys, although the 1976 NFS enumerators were also men.

We begin by examining the most simple measure of fertility, average parities by age of women according to the three censuses and four single-round surveys since the beginning of the 1970s. The mean parities in Table 4.1 reveal more about data quality than about fertility trends. Parity has been underreported to a greater extent in the censuses than in the surveys that included full birth histories. This is probably because all the censuses had high levels of proxy reporting: the fertility questions were often answered by the head of household rather than the women concerned.

Figure 4.1 shows the reported parity distributions of women aged 45–49 years. This age group has almost completed childbearing. It compares the 1981 and 1991 Census data with those on women interviewed in the 1991 survey. The mode of the parity distribution obtained from the survey data is six children, whereas the census-based distributions have a mode of four children. The most conspicuous features of the latter, however, are the high proportions of women at parity zero: 22 per cent of women were recorded as childless in 1981 and 14 per cent in 1991, compared with 2.5 per cent in the 1991 survey. The high levels of childlessness reported in the censuses are implausible, given that marriage is universal in Nepal and there is no other evidence of a high prevalence of primary sterility in the country.

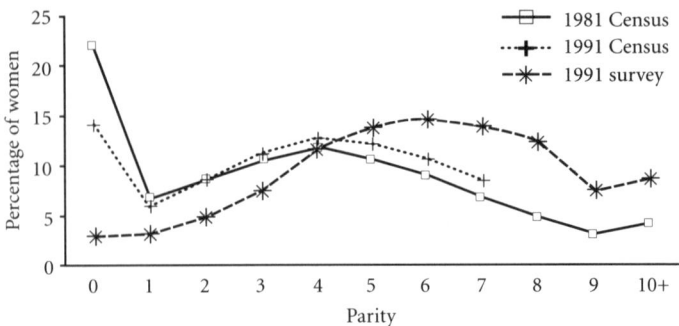

Figure 4.1. Parity distribution of women aged 45–49, Nepal 1981 and 1991 Censuses and 1991 survey.

The 1986 survey also yielded relatively poor quality fertility data. Comparison of the results with those from the 1976 survey for the same cohorts reveals that women aged 35–39 years in 1976 reported ,5.1 children in the first survey but only 4.7 children ten years later. Omission of births on this scale again suggests that little is to be gained from detailed analysis of the fertility data collected in 1986. Data quality in the 1976 NFS has been discussed at length by Goldman *et al.* (1979). They conclude that omission and misdating of births have an increasingly serious effect on fertility estimates for five and more years before the survey. However, they argue that recent events were reported fairly accurately in the NFS.

Comparisons of the mean children ever born, according to the 1991 survey and Census from the 20–24-year age group onward, emphasize that underreporting of lifetime fertility in the census increases with the age of the women. On the other hand, the very close agreement between the 1991 and 1996 survey data suggests that reporting of births may have been reasonably complete in both of these enquiries. What is surprising is that, on average, 15- to 19-year-old women reported fewer children in the 1991 survey than in the 1991 Census or 1996 survey. Moreover, according to the Census, 47 per cent of women aged 15–19 years had married, compared with only 33 per cent of such women according to the 1991 survey. The proportions of women ever-married in older cohorts are similar in the two sources.

While a fall in ages at first birth might account for part of the rise in the mean parity of teenage women between 1991 and 1996, the discrepancies between the two 1991 enquiries for the youngest age group are difficult to explain. In part, they may reflect the use of different definitions of marriage (Collumbien *et al.* 1997), but this cannot explain why teenage women reported more live births in the Census than in the NFFPHS. By evaluating age-group ratios and sex ratios for the age groups immediately above and below the age eligibility boundaries for individual interview, Collumbien *et al.* (1997) detect evidence of systematic exclusion of eligible women from the survey. Deliberate fertility-related underreporting of ages of young women

Table 4.2. P/F ratios and estimates of total fertility based on births in the last year

Age	1976 NFS	1986 NFFPS	1991 NFFPHS	1991 Census	1996 NFHS[a]
15–19	0.86	1.10	1.12	2.72	1.10
20–24	0.98	1.12	1.08	2.33	1.11
25–29	0.95	1.07	1.07	2.19	1.11
30–34	0.92	1.04	1.09	2.13	1.10
35–39	0.93	0.98	1.11	2.08	1.16
40–44	0.93	0.93	1.13	2.07	1.25
45–49	0.94	0.93	1.14	2.06	1.28
Unadjusted TFR	6.33	5.12	5.09	2.22	4.64
Adjusted TFR	6.21	5.72	5.48	5.17	5.13

[a] Based on births in the three years preceding the survey.

by the interviewers during the household questionnaire in order to reduce their workload could explain the lower fertility and proportions married reported for the 15- to 19-year-old age group in the survey compared with the Census.

To summarize the findings of this section, the 1991 and 1996 survey data seem more complete than those from the 1991 Census. However, there seems to be a downward bias in the estimate of the mean parity of the first age group in the 1991 survey. Although the parity distribution of women reported in the 1991 Census differs from the equivalent distribution reported in the 1991 survey, studying trends in parity-specific measures across cohorts from both sources may prove useful. The most appropriate baseline with which to compare the data collected in the 1990s is the 1976 NFS. Because the earlier censuses and 1981 and 1986 surveys collected poorer-quality data than the enquiries in the mid-1970s and 1990s, estimates based on them are more likely to obscure than elucidate fertility trends.

Trends in Total Fertility

P/F ratio methods provide a useful tool for comparison of information on the age pattern of fertility derived from reports of recent births, F, with information on the lifetime fertility, P (UN 1983). The pattern, by age, of the ratios not only enables one to detect if fertility has been changing but also to assess the quality of the data on lifetime and current fertility. If fertility has been constant, one can use information on the parities of women in their twenties to adjust the current fertility data for underreporting or overreporting of births in the last year. If fertility has been falling, however, these parities reflect the higher fertility of the past few years and so such adjustments produce overestimates of current fertility.

Table 4.3. Cohort-period fertility rates and P/F ratios, 1976 and 1991 surveys

Age	Years prior to survey						
	0—4	5—9	10—14	15—19	20—24	25—29	30—34
Cohort-period fertility rates – 1976 NFS							
15—19	0.037	0.043	0.048	0.043	0.046	0.031	0.029
20—24	0.223	0.225	0.210	0.194	0.181	0.174	
25—29	0.296	0.285	0.283	0.270	0.267		
30—34	0.271	0.280	0.267	0.259			
35—39	0.213	0.224	0.221				
40—44	0.129	0.151					
45—49	0.053						
P/F ratios – 1976 NFS							
20—24	1.03	1.02	0.98	1.01	0.94	0.99	
25—29	1.02	0.97	0.97	0.95	0.95		
30—34	0.98	0.96	0.93	0.95			
35—39	0.98	0.92	0.92				
40—44	0.94	0.91					
45—49	0.94						
Cohort-period fertility rates – 1991 NFFPHS							
15—19	0.029	0.055	0.056	0.051	0.049	0.040	0.045
20—24	0.201	0.244	0.241	0.212	0.207	0.183	
25—29	0.244	0.293	0.311	0.282	0.281		
30—34	0.197	0.257	0.282	0.270			
35—39	0.142	0.197	0.230				
40—44	0.083	0.130					
45—49	0.036						
P/F ratios – 1991 NFFPHS							
20—24	1.11	1.00	0.98	1.00	0.96	1.02	
25—29	1.15	0.99	0.94	0.97	0.95		
30—34	1.17	0.98	0.91	0.96			
35—39	1.20	0.96	0.90				
40—44	1.22	0.97					
45—49	1.26						

Source: Estimates for 1976 are taken from Goldman and Hobcraft (1982).

Table 4.2 shows the P/F ratios derived from data collected in 1976, 1986, 1991 and 1996, unadjusted total fertility rates based on births in the year before the enquiry, and total fertility rates obtained by multiplying up by the P/F ratio for women aged 20–24. There seems little wrong with the current fertility data collected in 1976. The unadjusted total fertility rate is similar to that of 6.26 yielded by the multiround Demographic Sample Survey conducted in 1974–75 (Bourini 1976). The fertility rates reported in 1986 seem somewhat too low. Nevertheless, even the adjusted total fertility rate is more than half a child smaller than that for ten years earlier. Fertility fell in the 1976–86 decade. This implies that using the P/F ratios to produce an adjusted rate will overstate fertility. Thus, it is unlikely that total fertility at this time was more than 5.5 children per woman.

The rise in the P/F ratios with age apparent in the 1991 and 1996 survey data represents strong evidence that fertility is falling. The adjusted rates are certainly too high. In addition, the P/F ratio for the 20- to 24-year-olds in the 1991 survey may be inflated by parity-related age misstatement. In the 1991 Census, current fertility was underreported by over 50 per cent. The question used was, 'During the last 12 months, how many children were born alive by the woman?' This question tends to be subject to larger reference-period errors than a question about the date of the last live birth (Karki 1995). If fertility is declining, an adjustment factor of 2.3 is probably too large, but the adjustment of such incomplete data is an imprecise process anyway. Nevertheless, the adjusted rate agrees fairly well with those obtained from the survey in the same year. Considering the two 1991 enquiries together, it is likely that the total fertility rate was about 5 children per woman, not 5.5 or more.

While inconclusive, the P/F analysis suggests that reporting of current fertility in the 1976, 1991, and 1996 surveys was fairly accurate. Fertility may have been declining continuously in Nepal since the 1970s. The full birth-history data collected in 1976 and 1991 are a further source of evidence as to trends in fertility. P/F ratio methods can also be used to evaluate these data (Hobcraft et al. 1982). In Table 4.3 we present age cohort-period fertility rates and the P/F ratios calculated by summing these rates down the diagonals and columns of the table. One striking feature of the 1976 data is the low P/F ratios for the two oldest cohorts, which suggest that these women may have omitted up to 7 per cent of their births. All the other P/F ratios fall in the range 0.96–1.03. Second, the fertility of women aged more than 30 years appears to have been slightly lower in the five years before the survey than previously. It is unclear from these data whether this apparent decline in the fertility of older women immediately before the survey could result from heaping of births in the period 5–9 years before the survey.

In 1991, the ratios for the most recent period are much higher than one and rise with age. Since the ratios for the preceding periods are only slightly below one, exaggeration of the ages of young children could not account for all the apparent fall in fertility, at least part of which must be genuine. The ratios for cohorts of women in their forties tend to be higher than they were 15 years earlier. Nevertheless, if one compares the information about their early fertility with the information collected from the same cohorts of women in 1976, it becomes clear that they are omitting some births. In particular, while women born in 1941–51 reported slightly more births before age 20 in 1991 than in 1976, they reported fewer births in total before age 30 than were reported by the same cohorts 15 years earlier.

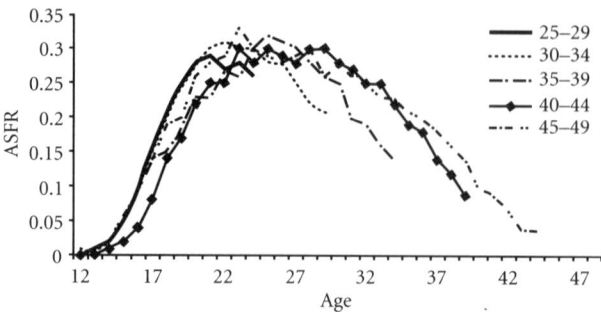

Figure 4.2. Age-specific fertility by birth cohort, 1991 survey.

Evidence of omission and event displacement was found in an earlier study of the 1976 NFS birth-history data (Goldman *et al.* 1979). This concluded that older women overstated the ages at which their early births occurred. The same pattern of errors becomes evident in the 1991 data if one looks at the age pattern of fertility of different cohorts in more detail. Figure 4.2 presents data on fertility by age for different cohorts in 1991. Focusing on the four oldest cohorts, the distributions shift to the right for older cohorts. This pattern is inconsistent with what one would expect in a population where ages at marriage have risen. Thus, older women have moved the dates at which their children were born toward the time of the survey.

When one examines age-specific measures of fertility, bunching of dates of birth several years before a survey produces an exaggerated impression of fertility decline in the recent past (Potter 1977). While the amount of bias revealed by Fig. 4.2 is fairly small, in combination with the omission of births by older women it makes it difficult to determine from Table 4.3 either when fertility decline began in Nepal or exactly how far it has progressed. To validate the *prima facie* evidence of fertility decline provided by the current fertility data, other ways of analysing the 1976 and 1991 birth histories are required. These should yield indicators of fertility that are both more sensitive to change and more robust in the face of errors in the data. Such methods exist in the form of measures of parity progression.

Trends in Family Formation

Trends in total fertility reflect changes in both the pace and the quantum of reproduction. Aggregate measures of period fertility do not distinguish the impact of limitation of family sizes from the temporary impacts of changes in ages at marriage and the length of birth intervals. To detect a drop in family sizes resulting from the adoption of birth control, fertility is best examined using parity-specific measures. The truncated parity progression ratio approach (Brass and Juarez 1983) uses life

Table 4.4. Parity progression (adjusted B_{60}'s) for Nepal, 1976 and 1991[a]

Age cohort	Parity progression to:									
	1st	2nd	3rd	4th	5th	6th	7th	8th	9th	10th
1976 NFS survey										
20–24	0.6738	0.8862	0.8991							
25–29	0.6670	0.8636	0.8449	0.7837	0.7435	0.8167				
30–34	0.6277	0.8696	0.8587	0.7974	0.7730	0.7299	0.6406	0.6892	0.5111	
35–39	0.6415	0.8712	0.8551	0.8183	0.7415	0.7865	0.6903	0.6942	0.6411	0.4434
40–44	0.5655	0.8531	0.8336	0.8309	0.7712	0.7814	0.7120	0.7126	0.6074	0.4196
45–49	0.5673	0.8215	0.8001	0.8006	0.7829	0.7844	0.7772	0.6857	0.5762	0.5926
1991 NFFPHS survey										
20–24	0.8424	0.8562	0.7355	0.6186	0.5453					
25–29	0.7965	0.8857	0.7974	0.6528	0.5778	0.5257	0.5499			
30–34	0.7210	0.8939	0.8306	0.7488	0.6311	0.5783	0.4812	0.5321		
35–39	0.6551	0.8818	0.8655	0.7964	0.7006	0.6207	0.5860	0.5349	0.4280	0.5215
40–44	0.6136	0.8760	0.8508	0.8234	0.7392	0.6960	0.6212	0.5823	0.4723	0.4696
45–49	0.5280	0.8597	0.8464	0.8225	0.7797	0.7257	0.6915	0.6246	0.5372	0.5134

[a] B_{60} is the proportion of women having a further birth within 60 months (see text for details).

Source: Estimates for 1976 are taken from Brass and Jaurez (1983).

table estimates of parity progression to detect which cohorts have limited their family sizes and the parities at which stopping occurs.

The measure used is B_{60}, the proportion of women having a birth within 60 months of their previous birth. In societies with low rates of divorce and remarriage, few women have birth intervals that are longer than five years and B_{60} is only slightly less than the parity progression ratio (PPR). The truncation approach adjusts for bias introduced by selection for speed of reproduction in the younger cohorts. Indices of relative change are derived by comparing the B_{60}'s for successive pairs of age cohorts after truncating the fertility experience of the older cohort by five years to render it comparable with the younger one. Adjusted B_{60}'s are produced by multiplying the B_{60} of the oldest cohort by the index of relative change from 45–49 to 40–44 and repeating this multiplication process to produce a B_{60} for each younger age cohort. These adjusted indices are projected final values of B_{60} by the age group 45–49 years if the current pattern of progression by age continues to prevail.

A simpler measure of parity progression, P_n, the proportion of women with an nth birth who have gone on to another birth, can be adjusted by the same truncation procedure as for the B_{60}'s. Unadjusted P_n's are dominated by bias due to censoring of young women at short open birth intervals. The adjusted P_n's may still

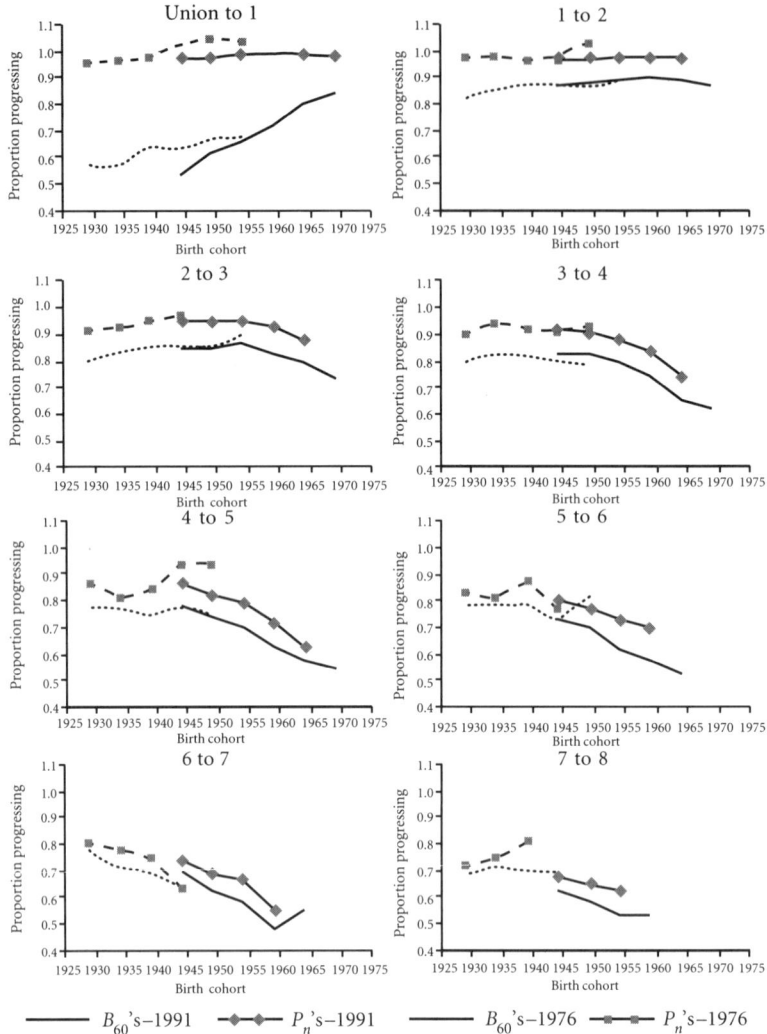

Figure 4.3. Parity progression according to birth cohort, 1976 and 1991 surveys.

be affected by censoring and changes in the distribution of birth intervals and the values for the younger cohorts should be treated with caution. In our analysis, however, they yield plausible and consistent trends.

Table 4.4 presents adjusted B_{60}'s calculated from both the 1976 NFS and the 1991 NFFPHS. Figure 4.3 portrays trends in progression to parities one to eight, according to the adjusted B_{60}'s and the adjusted P_n's calculated from both surveys. The indices are plotted against the mid-year of the birth cohort, so that cohorts aged 20–34 years in 1976 are lined up with the same women, aged 35–49 years in 1991. It is immediately obvious that, except for the transition to motherhood, the estimates of parity progression from the two surveys agree remarkably well, and the B_{60}'s and the P_n's suggest similar and consistent trends, especially for the 1991 survey.

Focusing first on the progression from union to first birth, it appears that the proportion of women having a first birth within five years of marriage has risen from a very low level. In Nepal, B_{60} is a poor proxy for the first progression ratio because many marriage-to-first-birth intervals are longer than 60 months. In contrast, the P_n indices for women interviewed in 1991 and those for older women in 1976 indicate that a high and unchanging proportion of women have become mothers. Although marriage was defined as the start of cohabitation in the 1991 NFFPHS survey, nearly 25 per cent of intervals to the first birth are longer than 60 months. This proportion drops from 45 per cent for the oldest cohort to 10 per cent for the 20- to 24-year-old age group. This trend could stem in part from a rise in ages at marriage, since fecundity is lower and foetal loss more common among very young women (Rindfuss and Morgan 1983). However, the adjusted B_{60}'s for progression to the first birth reported in 1991 are consistently lower than those reported by the same cohorts of women 15 years earlier. The discrepancy increases with the age of the cohort. Thus, at least part of the rise in the B_{60}'s for union to first birth is spurious due to understatement, by older women, of their ages at marriage.

Turning to progression to second- and higher-order births, a substantial trend toward lower progression for successively younger age cohorts is manifest in the 1991 data for third-and higher-order births. The 1976 B_{60} estimates of progression to the seventh and perhaps fourth births show some sign of declining across cohorts. In addition, progression to the fifth birth for the 25- to 29-year-old age group and progression to the sixth birth for the 30- to 34-year-old age group fluctuate downward. Considered alone, such fluctuations would never be regarded as indicative of the onset of a decline. With the benefit of hindsight, however, these declines seem to have been real. The close agreement of the B_{60}'s from the 1991 NFFPHS with those from the NFS suggests that the 1976 survey successfully picked up the initial stages of a decline in progression to births of order five to seven in the early 1970s. This decline continued in the late-1970s and 1980s and spread to progression to the fourth, eighth, and then third birth.

An alternative tabulation of the parity progression estimates allows one to examine trends by time periods rather than cohorts. Brass *et al.* (1998) suggest that one can estimate the approximate time location of the B_{60}'s by organizing the indices by diagonals of the age–cohort table. Table 4.5 presents these measures of parity progression for two-year intervals preceding the time of the survey. The B_{60} of the 20–24 age group indicates transition to the second birth at the time of the survey. Assuming birth intervals close to two years, the corresponding transition for the 25–29 cohort will have occurred five years preceding the survey and the transition for the 30–34 cohort, ten years before the survey. Estimates of transition 2, 7, etc., years before the survey are obtained by interpolation. The 25–29 cohort is assumed

Table 4.5. Trends in parity progression (adjusted B_{60}'s) by time period[a]

Progression to:	Years preceding survey										
	0	2.5	5	7.5	10	12.5	15	17.5	20	22.5	25
1976 NFS survey											
2nd	0.886	0.875	0.864	0.867	0.870	0.870	0.871	0.862	0.853	0.837	0.822
3rd	0.872	0.845	0.852	0.859	0.857	0.855	0.844	0.834	0.817	0.800	
4th	0.784	0.791	0.797	0.808	0.818	0.825	0.831	0.816	0.801		
5th	0.758	0.773	0.757	0.742	0.756	0.771	0.777	0.783			
6th	0.730	0.758	0.787	0.784	0.781	0.783	0.784				
7th	0.665	0.690	0.701	0.712	0.745	0.777					
8th	0.694	0.703	0.713	0.699	0.686						
9th	0.624	0.607	0.592	0.576							
10th	0.420	0.506	0.593								
1991 NFFPHS survey											
2nd	0.856	0.871	0.886	0.890	0.894	0.888	0.882	0.879	0.876	0.868	0.860
3rd	0.766	0.797	0.814	0.831	0.848	0.865	0.858	0.851	0.849	0.846	
4th	0.653	0.701	0.749	0.773	0.796	0.810	0.823	0.823	0.823		
5th	0.604	0.631	0.666	0.701	0.720	0.739	0.759	0.780			
6th	0.578	0.599	0.621	0.658	0.696	0.711	0.726				
7th	0.534	0.586	0.604	0.621	0.656	0.692					
8th	0.535	0.559	0.582	0.603	0.625						
9th	0.450	0.472	0.505	0.537							
10th	0.470	0.491	0.513								

[a] B_{60} is the proportion of women having a further birth within 60 months (see text for details).

to have been having its third births about two years before the survey, and the corresponding transition for the 30–34 cohort to have occurred around seven years before the survey. Values for 0, 5, etc. years before the survey can again be interpolated.

The consistency between the two surveys permits us to synthesize their results to produce a full set of estimates for the 1971–91 period. The B_{60}'s for 1976 are obtained by averaging the progression ratios from the two surveys. The values for the early 1970s are taken from the 1976 survey. Table 4.6 shows the proportional reductions in parity progression during the 20 years up to 1991, indexed to a value of 1,000 in 1971. It confirms that Nepalese women started to limit their families to sizes of five, six and seven children in the early 1970s. Indeed, progression to the seventh birth started to decline in the 1960s (see Table 4.5). The drop in progression to the fifth birth started in the late 1970s. By the 1980s the fertility decline was affecting transitions to third and fourth births. Progression from the first to second birth within five years rose in the 1970s but declined to its initial level in the 1980s (this trend, also

Table 4.6. Proportional reductions in parity progression in Nepal, 1971–1991

Progression to:	Years preceding 1991 survey								
	0	2.5	5	7.5	10	12.5	15	17.5	20
2nd	991	1009	1026	1030	1035	1028	1024	1013	1000
3rd	900	936	956	975	996	1016	1016	992	1000
4th	819	879	939	969	999	1016	1008	991	1000
5th	798	833	879	925	951	976	1002	1021	1000
6th	735	762	789	837	885	904	925	964	1000
7th	761	836	861	886	936	986	949	985	1000
8th	751	784	817	847	877	925	974	987	1000

evident in Fig. 4.3, may be spurious and due to event displacement). Thus, there is neither a clear cohort nor period pattern of decline across all parities. In the 20 years up to 1991, progression to third births has fallen by 10 per cent, progression to fourth and fifth births by about 20 per cent, and progression to sixth to eighth births by about 25 per cent. The extent of this decline suggests that a well-established and irrevocable fertility transition is under way in Nepal.

Alternative Estimates of Parity Progression

Projected parity progression ratios for cohorts with incomplete fertility can also be calculated from census data, provided that births in the last year are tabulated by age of mother and birth order, and that the parity distribution is tabulated for each five-year age group. The P/F synthesis method (Brass 1985) uses current age-order-specific fertility rates (AOSFRs) to calculate additional proportions of women expected to reach parity n or more. By adding these proportions to the current proportions of women with $n+$ children, one obtains the final proportions of women expected to reach parity n or more. The large sample size of the 1991 NFFPHS also allows the application of the P/F synthesis method. To obtain more stable AOSFRs, these were calculated from births in the last five years.

Figure 4.4 summarizes trends in the quantum of reproduction, using an index of progression from the first to the sixth birth. Indices obtained by applying the P/F synthesis method to the 1991 Census and survey data are compared with indices based on adjusted P_n's, adjusted B_{60}'s, and adjusted B_{72}'s (proportions progressing within six years of the preceding birth). The summary index is calculated simply by multiplying together the progression ratios to the second, third, fourth, fifth and sixth births (these more detailed statistics are presented in Collumbien et al. 1997). The first interval is not considered because of its unusual characteristics. Thus, Fig. 4.4 depicts the relative change in the proportion of mothers attaining a family

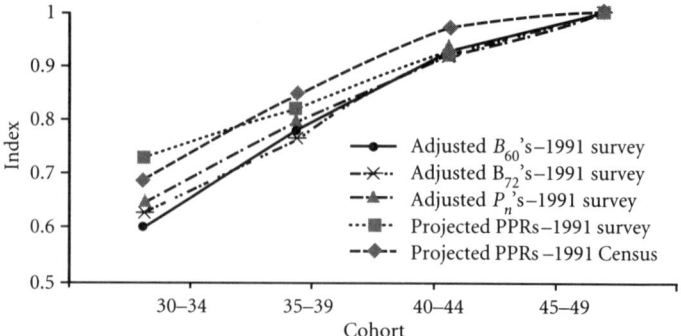

Figure 4.4. Progression from first to sixth birth according to different indices, 1991 survey.

size of six or over, using four different ways of measuring parity progression and two sources of data. While the other measures yield slightly more conservative estimates of progression to the sixth birth than the adjusted B_{60}'s, all five series of indices indicate a very similar downward trend in the proportion of women bearing large families. This decline in the proportion of mothers reaching a family size of at least six accelerated across the cohorts aged 30–49 in 1991, dropping by about 35 per cent in total.

Average Completed Family Size

One can calculate a projected order-standardized total fertility ratio for each age cohort by adjusting the B_{60}'s by the ratio P_n/B_{60} for the oldest cohort, to convert them into parity progression ratios (Aoun 1989). Total fertility is then computed by reconstructing the equivalent parity distribution from the progression ratios and summing births per woman for each parity. Future progression to higher parities by younger women is estimated from data on the last cohort that provides a stable estimate. If fertility is falling, this procedure yields a conservative estimate of total fertility since it assumes no further decline at higher parities. For transition to first birth we replace the B_{60}'s by the P_n's, which indicate a constant and consistently high transition to first births. The resulting completed family sizes for ever-married women are shown in Table 4.7.

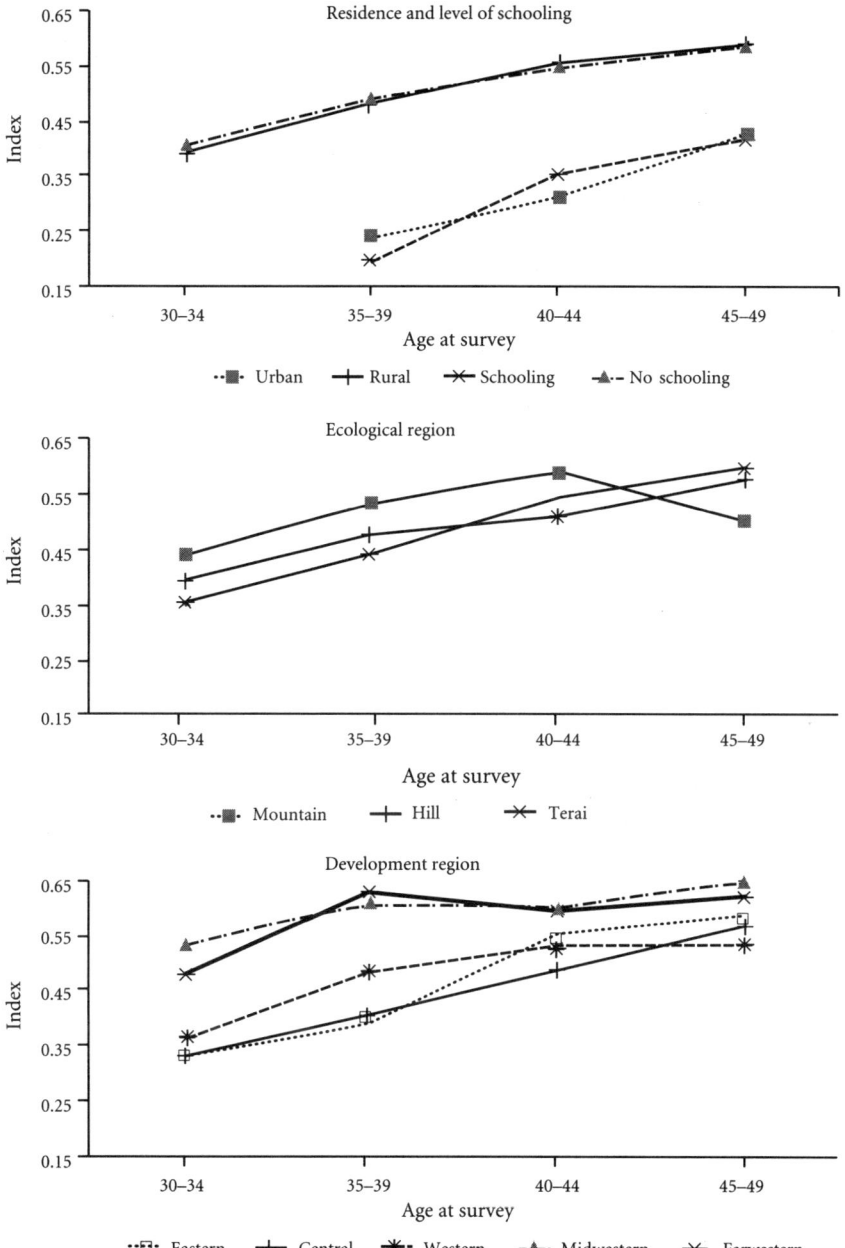

Figure 4.5. Differential progression from the first to sixth birth by cohort, 1991 survey.

Table 4.7. Projected
completed family sizes,
1991 survey

Age cohort	Projected completed family size
20–24	4.05
25–29	4.36
30–34	4.89
35–39	5.39
40–44	5.69
45–49	5.97

This measure makes it easier to assess the magnitude of reduction that has occurred in fertility. This appears to be about one-third. However, the B_{60}'s indicate a slightly greater fall in parity progression than the other indices presented in Fig. 4.4. Bearing this in mind, we conclude that fertility in Nepal has fallen by at least one-quarter. Omission of births by women in their late forties implies that all the estimates of total fertility in Table 4.7 are a little low. The current fertility data collected in 1976 suggest that mothers aged 45–49 in 1991 may have had closer to 6.5 than 6.0 children. Allowing for all these considerations, women aged 20–24 years in 1991 will probably have about 4.6 children. This agrees very closely with the 1996 NFHS estimate of total fertility, which refers to the time when this cohort were in their peak childbearing years.

Differential Fertility Decline

In order to assess whether the entire country is participating in the fertility decline, this section looks briefly at differential parity progression. The ecological and development regions are considered and we also examine urban–rural and educational differentials. The small size of the urban population and of the female population who have attended school limits the scope of the analysis. However, if we concentrate on progression to low- and middle-order parities, some clear trends are evident. As a proxy for the quantum of fertility, we use the probability of progressing from the first to sixth birth. The trends in proportions of mothers attaining a family size of six or above have been calculated using both adjusted P_n's and B_{60}'s. The two approaches give very similar results, but the P_n's are somewhat more stable and are presented in Fig. 4.5. This portrays the trend in progression from first to sixth birth by place of residence, school attendance, ecological zone, and development region.

These indices of parity progression show that rural residents as well as urban residents, and the uneducated as well as those who have attended school, are contributing to the fertility decline. Residential and educational differentials are similar in size, and both appear to have widened slightly as fertility has fallen. (Too few school attendees exist in the oldest cohort to derive estimates, and not enough urban women in the 30–34 group have reached parities four and five to derive P_n's and B_{60}'s.)

The level and trend in fertility are similar in all three ecological zones. The low estimate for the oldest cohort in the Mountain region may suggest that omission of births is particularly common in this zone. For the other cohorts, progression is somewhat higher than in the Hills and Terai, but a steady decline is under way. Whereas the fertility of 40- to 44-year-old women fell by as much in the Hills as in the Terai, parity progression in younger cohorts has fallen slightly faster in the Terai. Finally, differentials in the quantum of fertility between the development regions have widened over time. Fertility decline seems to have begun first in the eastern and central regions and to have spread to the three western regions only in the cohort ages 30–34 years in 1991.

Discussion

The main aim of this paper has been to present a detailed justification of the assertion that fertility began to fall in Nepal at least 25 years ago. Our claim is based on measures of parity progression calculated by pairwise comparison of truncated and untruncated cohorts. These show consistent evidence of decline since the beginning of the 1970s. The first signs of family limitation appeared among women with five or six live births, but this development spread rapidly to higher-order births and fifth births during the second half of the 1970s, and to fourth and then third births in the 1980s. The excellent agreement between the measures of parity progression calculated from the 1991 fertility survey and those derived from the 1976 fertility survey represents strong evidence that these indices are more or less accurate. Evidence that the decline in parity progression has come to affect all parts of the population, spreading between subgroups in a plausible way, provides further support for our conclusion. While a small part of the reduction in total fertility may be a temporary effect stemming from a rise in women's ages at marriage (Acharya 1993), the drop in parity progression clearly indicates that quantum of fertility has been falling since the early 1970s.

The failure of other analysts of Nepalese fertility to detect the early onset of fertility transition is rooted in the poor quality of the fertility data collected in the censuses and in the national surveys conducted in the 1980s, in over-eagerness to adjust fertility rates upward using P/F ratios, and in over-reliance on conventional age-specific measures rather than the more robust parity-specific approach adopted here. Faced with ambiguous evidence and knowing that Nepal is one of the world's least developed countries with a low level of use of modern methods of contraception, analysts have tended to adopt a conservative interpretation of their results. Goldman *et al.* (1979) did point out that the fertility rates of women aged 30–44 appeared to have declined during the ten years prior to the 1976 NFS. In the absence of the confirmatory evidence from later surveys available to us, however, they attribute this to the displacement of dates of birth. Similarly, Brass and Juarez (1983) note some evidence of decline in the B_{60}'s for younger cohorts obtained from the NFS data, but, lacking the evidence that we now possess showing that this was the beginning of a long-term trend, ascribe this to instability in the estimates.

If the onset of the decline in marital fertility in Nepal dates back to the early 1970s, rather than to the mid-1980s, it preceded widespread provision of access to modern methods of contraception by the family planning services. The contraceptive prevalence rate among currently married women was just 4 per cent in 1976 (Nepal 1993). At that time, only 21 per cent of women reported knowledge of even one method of contraception. By 1981, the contraceptive prevalence rate had only risen to 8 per cent. The increase in the use of modern methods of contraception to 29 per cent of currently married non-pregnant women in 1996 (Nepal 1996) indicates that the services provided by the family planning programme are now the main means by which couples limit their family sizes. Nevertheless, the initial drop in fertility in Nepal must be accounted for in other ways.

One factor contributing to the initial fall in fertility was an increase in the temporary separation of spouses. During the early 1970s, growth occurred in the seasonal migration of men in the developing Terai region to work in urban Nepal and India, and on the construction of the Kathmandu–Pokhara and the East–West highways. Labour migration from the Hill zone was probably more common than migration from the Terai. This, as well as the more patriarchal culture of the Terai (Morgan and Niraula 1995), may explain why the fertility decline began first in the Hill zone. On the other hand, despite the growing importance of spousal separation, it is clear that marital fertility in the 1970s was not determined solely by proximate behaviours directed at other ends. The 1976 NFS documents that the sex composition of couples' living children was associated with large differentials in marital fertility (Cleland *et al.* 1983). This is unequivocal evidence that couples were controlling fertility within marriage at the time when fertility began to fall.

We believe that demand to limit family size is well established in Nepal. This accords with what women report in fertility surveys. By 1991, women aged less than 25 years had ideal family sizes of less than three children (Hayes 1993). Even in 1976, women aged less than 30 years reported an ideal family size of about 3.7 children, and older women, one of about 4.3 children. Moreover, only just over a quarter of women favoured family sizes of five or more children. The overall impression gained from the series of family size preference measures considered in a comparative study of World Fertility Survey data for the 1970s is that those for Nepal are only slightly higher than those for Sri Lanka and Thailand (Lightbourne and MacDonald 1982).

They are lower than those for Bangladesh, Malaysia, Pakistan, and the Philippines. Thus, to at least some extent, small family size preferences in Nepal seem to predate both IEC programmes intended to promote birth control and any impact that the provision of services has had on the demand for children.

Many experts would accept that substantial latent demand to limit family size existed in many developing countries prior to the inception of state-sponsored family planning programmes. Moreover, the comparison of Nepal with countries other than its immediate neighbours reminds us that the fertility decline also occurred before the initiation of major government family planning programmes in many other parts of Asia. Fertility began to fall between the late 1950s and late 1960s in Taiwan, Malaysia, Korea, Sri Lanka, Thailand, and the Philippines. In each instance, an effective national family planning programme was not established until at least five years later. The population in Nepal was and remains poor, poorly educated, and largely rural, compared with these middle-income Asian countries: equally, its fertility transition began last. Moreover, fertility began to fall somewhat later in the 1970s in very poor Asian countries other than Nepal, most notably Bangladesh (Cleland *et al.* 1994). Thus, the early onset of fertility transition in Nepal does not mark the country out as exceptional within Asia. Rather, the country lies at one end of the spectrum of experience observed across the continent.

It is difficult to establish so long after the event how Nepalese couples began to control their fertility in the 1970s without access to modern methods of contraception. However, the data do provide clues as to two factors that may have been of importance. First, among older women the very long intervals between marriage and the birth of the first child in Nepal must originate in low coital frequency within marriage. Recent evidence of low coital frequency early in marriage exists for some groups of the population (Fricke and Teachman 1993). For Confucian populations, Rindfuss and Morgan (1983) have observed that, as marriages move away from the most traditional form of arranged marriage towards ones where the woman has greater individual choice of partner, the level of coital frequency increases.

Similar developments may explain the decrease in the length of the union to first birth interval in Nepal. Women denied knowing about or practising abstinence in the 1976 survey. Nevertheless, abstinence was common early in marriage. Thus, reducing coital frequency could have been one means by which parous women began to limit their fertility. Second, in 1976, while women who wanted another child breastfed their babies for 28 months on average, other women breastfed for 40 months (Smith and Ferry 1984). This differential is accounted for only to a small extent by the differing parity distributions of the two groups of women. It appears that extended breastfeeding was being used to try to avoid conception. This fact probably reveals more about the strength of women's motivation to avoid childbearing than about how they did so but it could have had some impact on fertility. Third, although there is no direct evidence of this in Nepal in the 1970s, recent qualitative research in other Asian countries has revealed evidence of the wide-spread use of withdrawal as a method of contraception (Miller *et al.* 1997).

The early adoption of birth control in Nepal probably reflects a combination of factors rather than a single unique characteristic of the country (see also Dangol *et al.* 1997). The desperate economic plight of the growing landless population in a society living in an evidently marginal environment may be one factor. Increasing poverty is not a factor among the urban and educated elites who led the decline but could be one reason for the rapid spread of fertility control into the rural population. Two triggers that were probably more important, however, are the decline from very high levels of infant and child mortality during the 1960s and the rapid growth in school enrolments. In addition, the fact that the sex composition of families influenced marital fertility at the onset of fertility decline suggests that the idea of managing biological and social reproduction was not innovatory in Nepal. Moreover, the scale of international labour migration from Nepal and the growth of a substantial tourist industry suggest that, by the 1970s, exposure of the Nepalese to the ideas that fertility could and should be limited was far more widespread than in most very poor countries. As a result, fertility decline in Nepal followed more rapidly than is usual on the heels of social, economic and other demographic changes.

According to the 1991 survey, the middle-order parity progression ratios of younger Nepalese women have fallen dramatically. Mothers aged 30–34 in 1991 were at least one-third less likely to progress to a sixth birth than were women aged 45–49. Moreover, progression to the third birth began to drop in the late 1980s. The NFHS estimate of total fertility for the mid-1990s, of 4.6 children per woman seems very plausible and the government's 1992 objective to reduce total fertility to 4 children per woman by 2001 seems attainable.

References

Acharya, L. B., (1993), 'Nuptiality Levels and Trends in Nepal', in B. Kumar KC (ed.), *Population Dynamics in Nepal and Related Issues of Sustainable Development*, Vol. 2, Central Department of Population Studies, Kathmandu: Tribhuvan University.

Aoun, S. (1989), *An Assessment of the Paired Comparison Procedure for Measuring Early Changes in Fertility in Syria, Tunisia and Yemen Arab Republic*, CPS Research Paper 89-2, London: London School of Hygiene & Tropical Medicine.

Bourini, A. K. (1976), *The Demographic Sample Survey of Nepal 1974–1975*, Kathmandu: UN Office of Technical Co-operation and UN Fund for Population Activities.

Brass, W. (1985), 'P-F Synthesis and Parity Progression Ratios', in W. Brass (ed.), *Advances in Methods for Estimating Fertility and Mortality from Limited and Defective Data*, CPS Occasional Publication, London: London School of Hygiene & Tropical Medicine.

——— and Juarez, F. (1983), 'Censored Cohort Parity Progression Ratios from Birth Historics, *Asian and Pacific Census Forum*, 10(1): 5–12.

Brass, W., Juarez, F., and Scott, A. (1998), 'An Analysis of Parity Dependent Fertility Falls in Tropical Africa', in G. W. Jones, R. M. Douglas, J. C. Caldwell, and R. M. D'Souza (eds.), *The Continuing Demographic Transition*, Oxford: Clarendon Press.

Chhetry, R. K. G. (1995), 'Fertility Levels, Patterns and Trends', *Population Monograph of Nepal*, Kathmandu: Central Bureau of Statistics.

Cleland, J., Phillips, J. S., Amin, S., and Kamal, G. M. (1994), *The Determinants of Reproductive Change in Bangladesh*, Washington, DC: The World Bank.

—— Verral, J., and Vaessen, M. (1983), *Preferences for the Sex of Children and their Influences on Reproductive Behaviour*. WFS Comparative Studies, 27, Voorburg, Netherlands: International Statistical Institute.

Collumbien, M., Timæus, I., and Acharya, L. (1997), *The Onset of Fertility Decline in Nepal: A Reinterpretation*, CPS Research Paper 97-2, London: London School of Hygiene & Tropical Medicine.

Dangol, B. S., Retherford, R. D., and Thapa, S. (1997), 'Declining Fertility in Nepal', *Asia-Pacific Population Journal*, 12: 33–54.

Fricke, T., and Teachman, J. D. (1993), 'Writing the Names: Marriage Style, Living Arrangements and the First Birth Interval in a Nepali Society', *Demography*, 30: 175–88.

Goldman, N., Coale, A. J., and Weinstein, M. (1979), *The Quality of Data in the Nepal Fertility Survey*, WFS Scientific Reports, 6, Voorburg, Netherlands: International Statistical Institute.

—— and Hobcraft, J. (1982), *Birth Histories*, WFS Comparative Study 17, Voorburg Netherlands: International Statistical Institute.

Hayes, A. C. (1993), 'The Changing Demand for Children and Socioeconomic Development in Nepal', in B. Kumar K. C. (ed.), *Population Dynamics in Nepal and Related Issues of Sustainable Development*, Vol. 2, Central Department of Population Studies, Kathmandu: Tribhuvan University.

Hobcraft, J. N., Goldman, N., and Chidambaram, V. C. (1982), 'Advances in the P/F Ratio Method for the Analysis of Birth Histories', *Population Studies*, 36: 291–316.

Joshi, P. L. (1993), 'Estimation of Fertility Levels', *The Analysis of the 1991 Population Census (Based on Advance Tables)*, Kanthmandu: Central Bureau of Statistics.

Juarez, F., and Sathar, Z. (2001), 'Changing Patterns of Family Limitation: Evidence of Fertility Fall in Pakistan', in J. Blacker and B. Zaba (eds.), *Brass Tacks: Essays in Medical Demography*, London: Athlone Press.

Karki, Y. B. (1992), 'Estimates and Projections of Population, Nepal: 1981–2031', in B. Kumar KC (ed.), *Population Dynamics in Nepal and Related Issues of Sustainable Development*, Vol. 1, Central Department of Population Studies, Kathmandu: Tribhuvan University.

—— (1995), 'Organization, Design and Quality Aspects of the 1991 Population Census of Nepal', *Population Monograph of Nepal*, Kathmandu: Central Bureau of Statistics.

Kumar KC, B. (1995), 'Social Composition of Population', *Population Monograph of Nepal*, Kathmandu: Central Bureau of Statistics.

Lightbourne, R. E., and MacDonald, A. L. (1982), *Family Size Preferences*, WFS Comparative Studies 14, Voorburg, Netherlands: International Statistical Institute.

Manandhar, T. B. (1995), 'Educational Development, Population and Literacy', *Population Monograph of Nepal*, Kathmandu: Central Bureau of Statistics.

Miller, P., Douthwaite, M., ul-Haque, M., Kayani, A., and Sathar, Z. (1997), *Withdrawal in Pakistan: Men as Partners*, Population Council Working Paper No. 3, Islamabad: Population Council.

Morgan, S. P., and Niraula, B. B. (1995), 'Gender Inequality and Fertility in Two Nepali Villages', *Population and Development Review*, 21: 541–61.

Nepal, Central Bureau of Statistics (1995), *Population Monograph of Nepal*, Kathmandu: Central Bureau of Statistics.

Nepal, Family Planning and MCH Project, (1977), *Nepal Fertility Survey 1976: First Report*, Kathmandu: Ministry of Health.

—— (1987), *Nepal Fertility and Family Planning Survey Report*, Kathmandu: Central Bureau of Statistics.

—— (1993), *Nepal Fertility and Family Planning and Health Survey: Main Report*, Kathmandu: Central Bureau of Statistics.

Nepal, Family Health Division (1996), *Nepal Family Health Survey 1996: Preliminary Report*, Kathmandu: Ministry of Health.

Potter, J. E. (1977), 'Problems in Using Birth History Analysis to Estimate Trends in Fertility', *Population Studies*, 31: 335–64.

Preston, S. H., and Mari Bhat, P. N. (1984), 'New Evidence on Fertility and Mortality Trends in India', *Population and Development Review*, 10: 481–503.

Rele, J. R. (1987), 'Fertility Levels and Trends in India, 1951–58', *Population and Development Review*, 13: 513–30.

Retherford, R. H., Mirza, G. M., Irfan, M., and Alam, I. (1987), 'Fertility Trends in Pakistan: The Decline that Wasn't', *Asian and Pacific Population Forum*, 1(2): 1–10.

Rindfuss, R. R., and Morgan, S. P. (1983), 'Marriage, Sex, and the First Birth Interval: the Quiet Revolution in Asia', *Population and Development Review*, 9: 259–78.

Shah, I. H., and Cleland, J. C. (1993), 'High Fertility in Bangladesh, Nepal, and Pakistan: Motives vs Means', in R. Leete, and I. Alam (eds.), *The Revolution in Asian Fertility*, Oxford: Clarendon Press.

Singh, M. L. (1995) 'Population Distribution and Growth', *Population Monograph of Nepal*, Kathmandu: Central Bureau of Statistics.

Smith, D. P., and Ferry, B. (1984), *Correlates of Breastfeeding*, WFS Comparative Studies 41, Voorburg, Netherlands: International Statistical Institute.

Tuladhar, J. M. (1989), 'The Onset of a Fertility Decline in Nepal', *Asian-Pacific Population Journal*, 4(3): 15–30.

UN (1983), *Indirect techniques for Demographic Estimation*, New York: United Nations.

—— (1995), *World Population Prospects as Assessed in 1994*, New York: United Nations.

World Bank (1993), *World Development Report 1993*, New York: Oxford University Press.

5 Fertility Decline in Sri Lanka: Could Fertility Now Be at about Replacement Level?

C. M. LANGFORD

Introduction

On the face of it, fertility in Sri Lanka—a very poor country, though with a good record in terms of literacy, education, and health (Caldwell 1986)—has now fallen to extremely low levels. According to the 1993 Demographic and Health Survey of Sri Lanka, the total fertility rate (TFR) for the five-year period before the survey was 2.3 children per woman (Department of Census and Statistics 1995: 26). The main object of this chapter is to assess the likelihood that fertility in Sri Lanka has indeed fallen to around replacement level. A wide range of fertility estimates, based upon census and registration data, and on the data provided by a number of sample surveys, are considered, and checked against each other for consistency. Changes in fertility over the entire period since World War II are examined, to see if apparent recent developments seem plausible. Changes in nuptiality are also considered, and information on recent birth control practice is examined.

Fertility Estimates

Figure 5.1 shows estimates of the TFR for Sri Lanka for various years from 1946 to 1991. TFRs were calculated as five times the sum of age-specific fertility rates per woman for five-year age groups from 15–19 to 45–49. Most of the TFRs refer to a three-year period centred on the year for which they are shown; some are based on a longer period; and one TFR, that from the 1982 Contraceptive Prevalence Survey (CPS), is based upon data for a single year.

Censuses of Sri Lanka were carried out in 1946, 1953, 1963, 1971, and 1981. Regrettably, the census scheduled for 1991 had to be cancelled because of the civil war that had broken out by then and was seriously disrupting parts of the north and east of the island. Numbers of births by age of mother at birth, from birth registration, are available for 1952 and later years (before that, only total number of births). The TFRs shown in Fig. 5.1, as based on 'census plus registration' for the years 1953, 1963, 1971, and 1981, were calculated from age-specific fertility rates derived from census and registration data. Each age-specific fertility rate was calculated by dividing

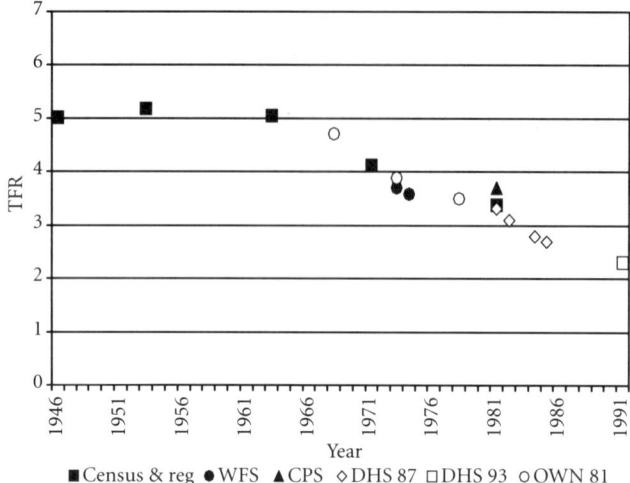

Figure 5.1. TFR per woman for Sri Lanka, various years 1946–1991.

one-third of the number of births to women of the age group in question during the three years centred on the census year by the census count of women in that age group. The few births to women under age 15 were assigned to women aged 15–19. All births to women over the age of 45 were assigned to women aged 45–49. The census-plus-registration-based TFR for 1946 shown in Fig. 5.1 was obtained by multiplying the 1953 TFR by the ratio of the actual number of births in 1946 (in fact, one-third of the number during 1945–47) to the number of births there would have been if women in 1946 had experienced the age-specific fertility rates of 1953. Numbers of registered births and births by age of mother were taken from the annual *Reports of the Registrar General of Ceylon on Vital Statistics* or later *Bulletins on Vital Statistics*. Numbers of women by age group come from the census reports.

All the other TFRs presented in Fig. 5.1 have been taken from, or calculated from, measures provided in previously published work, rather than computed from basic data. A number of TFRs estimated from 1981 census data by Ratnayake *et al.* (1984) using the own-children method are shown (these are labelled as OWN81 in Fig. 5.1), as well as a whole range of estimates derived from the analysis of birth history data from surveys. The surveys in question are the Sri Lanka round of the World Fertility Survey (WFS) in 1975, the Contraceptive Prevalence Survey (CPS) in 1982 and the Demographic and Health Survey (DHS) of 1987 and again in 1993. Estimates for 12-month periods are not presented where figures based on longer periods of time are available from the same source. Thus, single-year estimates produced by Ratnayake *et al.* and one single-year estimate from the WFS are omitted.

Sources of data and the periods to which TFRs refer are indicated in the Appendix. It should be noted that many of the measures presented in Fig. 5.1 refer, on average, to a point in time other than the mid-point of the year. The data from the

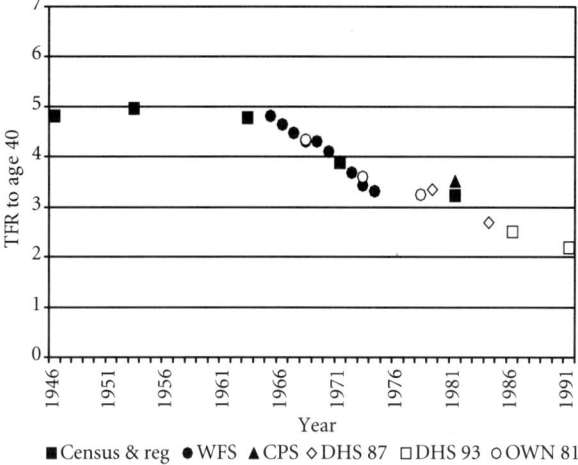

Figure 5.2. TFR to age 40 per woman for Sri Lanka, various years 1946–1991.

two DHS enquiries are not strictly comparable with the earlier material, since these two surveys had to exclude parts of the north and east of the island because of the military situation. The civil war began, effectively, in 1983. However, the effect of this exclusion on the figures is almost certainly slight, and the overwhelming majority of the Sri Lankan population was still covered by the DHS enquiries. According to the report on the 1987 survey, only about 14 per cent were not (Department of Census and Statistics 1988: 7). Moreover, as noted later, data from the DHS enquiries are consistent with, and run on plausibly from, data collected earlier for the whole country. If anything, one might guess that the exclusion of northern and eastern areas from the DHS enquiries would lead to some *underestimation* of the extent of the national fertility decline recently, since conditions in these areas have hardly been conducive to childbearing in recent years.

The data shown in Fig. 5.1 suggest that fertility in Sri Lanka rose slightly between 1946 and 1953. It has been proposed that this increase may have been a response to the near disappearance of malaria in that period (Langford 1981). Fertility then fell just a little between 1953 and 1963, but rather more noticeably subsequently. The TFR for Sri Lanka was 5.18 children per woman in 1953 and 5.04 in 1963. By 1971 it had fallen to 4.12 and, as already noted, according to the 1993 DHS enquiry, it was about 2.3 children per woman by around 1991.

Most of the TFRs presented in Fig. 5.1, although derived from various sources, seem to fit together plausibly as a sequence. However, the TFR for 1981, estimated from the 1982 CPS, is clearly discrepant from both the estimate for that year based on census-plus-registration data and that from the 1987 DHS. These latter two, moreover, more or less agree with each other. Another discrepancy apparent in Fig. 5.1 is

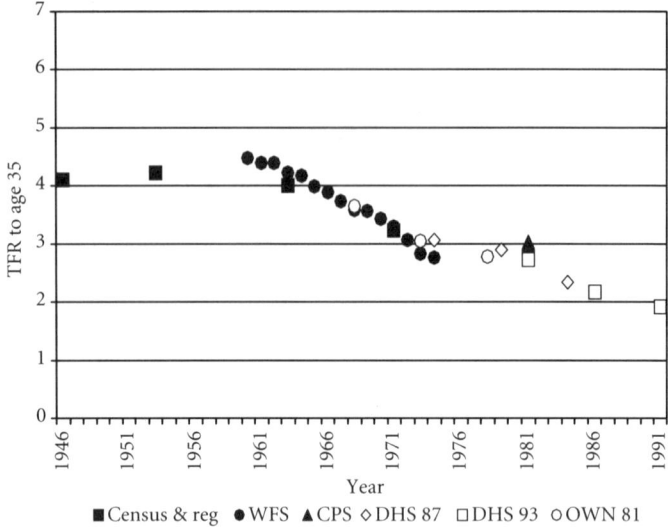

■Census & reg ●WFS ▲CPS ◊DHS 87 □DHS 93 ○OWN 81

Figure 5.3. TFR to age 35 per woman for Sri Lanka, various years 1946–1991.

that between the WFS-based TFR for 1973 and the own-children estimate for that year made from 1981 census data. Indeed, both of the WFS-based TFRs shown, for 1973 and 1974, seem to be a little out of line, on the low side, compared with other figures.

Figure 5.2 shows measures based on the same sources of data as Fig. 5.1 and calculated in exactly the same way as the TFRs, except that they cover only fertility before age 40. Figures 5.3 and 5.4 show TFR-style measures truncated at ages 35 and 30, respectively. An important advantage of these statistics is that they can be calculated from survey data for more points in the past than can TFRs as such. All the surveys drawn on here covered only women under age 50 so that TFRs are only calculable for periods close to these surveys.[1] However, a TFR to age 40, for example, is calculable for points up to ten years before any such survey.

A number of points emerge from these data. Almost all estimates from both the 1993 DHS and the 1987 DHS tie in well with figures from other sources, and with each other. An exception is that the TFR to age 35 for 1981, based on the 1993 DHS, tallies well with the estimate based on registration-plus-census data, but differs from that derived from the 1982 CPS. Moreover, both the TFR to age 35 and the TFR to age 30 for 1974, based on the 1987 DHS, exceed the corresponding WFS-based estimate. Just as the TFR based on the own-children method for 1973 is higher than the WFS-based TFR for that year,

[1] Strictly, TFRs are not calculable even for periods close to these surveys since there is incomplete exposure in the 45–49 age group. This fact has been ignored here, and estimated TFRs for periods close to the surveys were accepted. Since there is little childbearing by women in their late forties in Sri Lanka, errors should be negligible.

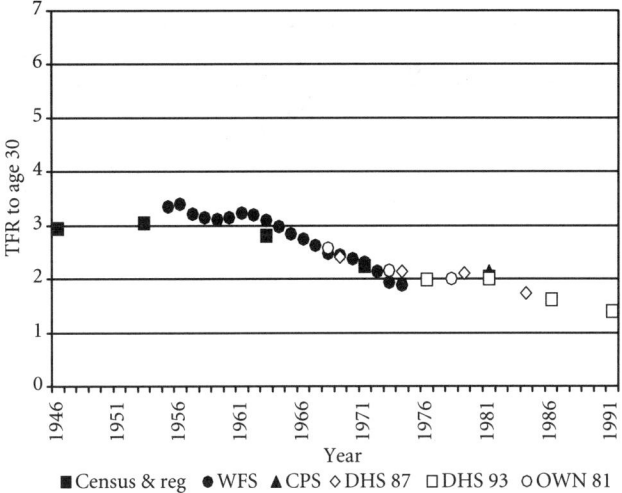

Figure 5.4. TFR to age 30 per woman for Sri Lanka, various years 1946–1991.

so also own-children estimates of the TFR to ages 40, 35, and 30 for that year exceed the WFS values. Although WFS-based estimates of fertility for the years between about 1965 and 1972 fit well with figures from other sources, WFS-based estimates of fertility in the late 1950s and early 1960s (i.e. fertility at relatively young ages) are somewhat higher than other (i.e. census-plus-registration) estimates.

All in all, the data on fertility in Sri Lanka from different sources fit together reasonably well. The exceptions are: that estimates for 1981 based on the 1982 CPS tend to exceed those from other sources (the discrepancies stem from different levels of fertility over age 30); that WFS-based figures for 1973 and 1974 are lower than the other estimates available; and that WFS-based estimates for the late 1950s and early 1960s (that means, of relatively youthful fertility) exceed the corresponding figures based on census and registration data. The most likely explanation for these discrepancies is simply that the CPS and WFS figures in question are incorrect. Both the CPS-based figures for 1981 and the WFS-based figures for around 1973–74 are contradicted by data from more than one source, which are, however, consistent with each other. In the case of the other discrepancy, it seems reasonable to prefer the figures based upon current, complete coverage—that is, the census-plus-registration estimates—to those derived from retrospective data collected in a sample survey. Moreover, the census-plus-registration estimates for 1971 and 1981 do match the other data available.

On the basis of these comparisons of total fertility rates, the following picture of changing fertility in Sri Lanka over the period since World War II seems to emerge: the TFR rose slightly between 1946 and 1953 but fell a little between 1953 and 1963; the decline in fertility then speeded up and was apparently especially marked

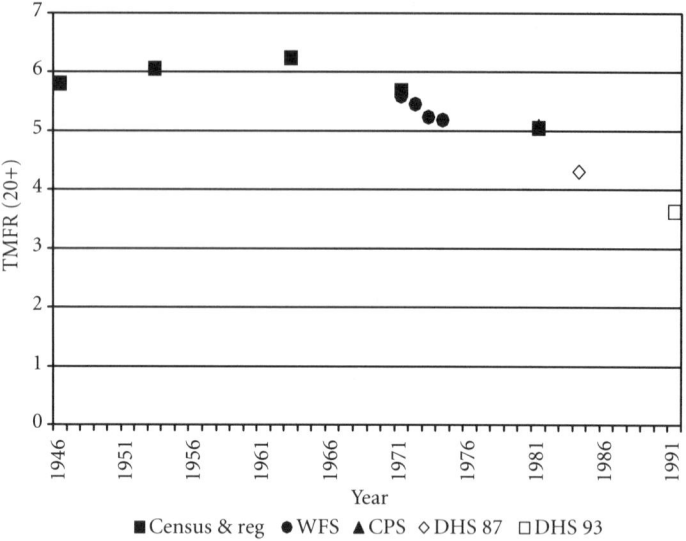

Figure 5.5. TMFR(20+) per woman for Sri Lanka, various years 1946–1991.

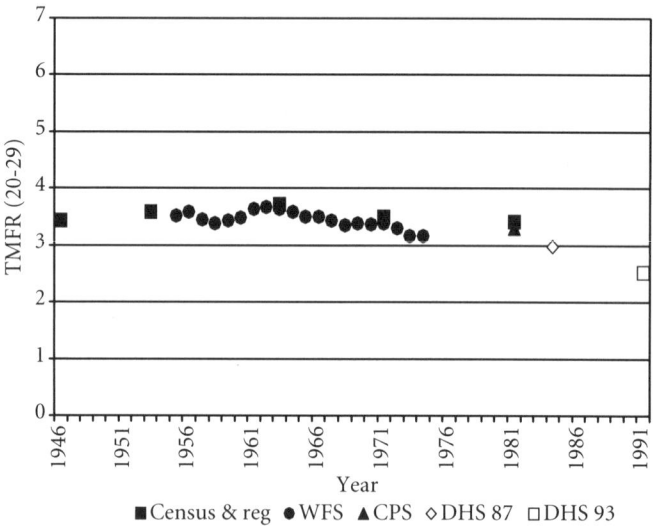

Figure 5.6. TMFR(20–29) per woman for Sri Lanka, various years 1946–1991.

in the late 1960s; the TFR continued to fall after this, though there seems to have been some slackening of the rate of decline during the 1970s; and in the early 1980s, there was apparently a further period of fairly rapid fertility decline, which was then followed by a period of more gradual fertility decline in the late 1980s and into the 1990s (see Fig. 5.1).

Table 5.1. Singulate mean ages at marriage (SMAMs) for women and percentage never-married women aged 45–49

Year and source	SMAM	Per cent single 45–49
1946 Census	20.7	3
1953 Census	21.0	4
1963 Census	22.1	4
1971 Census	23.5	4
1975 WFS	25.1	2
1981 Census	24.4	4
1987 DHS	24.8	4
1993 DHS	25.3	5

Note: Census-based estimates calculated from data provided in the census reports; other values calculated from data provided in Department of Census and Statistics (1978, 1988, 1995).

The Role of Nuptiality

Table 5.1 shows estimates of the mean age at first marriage for females in Sri Lanka at various points since World War II, as well as the proportions of women still single at the end of the reproductive period in these years. Mean age at first marriage was computed from proportions never married by age group, using the Hajnal (1953) method—that is, they are singulate mean ages at marriage (SMAMs). Proportions of women never married by age group come from the censuses and surveys already referred to. These data indicate, with a single exception, a steadily increasing mean age at first marriage for females in Sri Lanka over the period since World War II: the singulate mean age at marriage for females in 1946 was 20.7 years; the 1993 figure was 25.3 years. The data suggest also—with the same single exception—that there was only a slight change over this period in the proportion of women who never married: some 3 per cent of women aged 45–49 were still unmarried in 1946; the corresponding estimate from the 1993 DHS is 5 per cent.

It may be seen from Table 5.1 that the WFS-based female SMAM for 1975 was 25.1 years, higher than either the earlier 1971 figure or the later 1981 value. Could it have been the case that there was indeed a fairly marked but temporary further depression in the marriage rate in Sri Lanka in the early 1970s, which then showed up as a higher SMAM in 1975? This seems rather unlikely, though it is true that the early 1970s was economically a difficult time in Sri Lanka (Langford 1982: 24). There was certainly no sign of a dip in the registered crude marriage rate in this

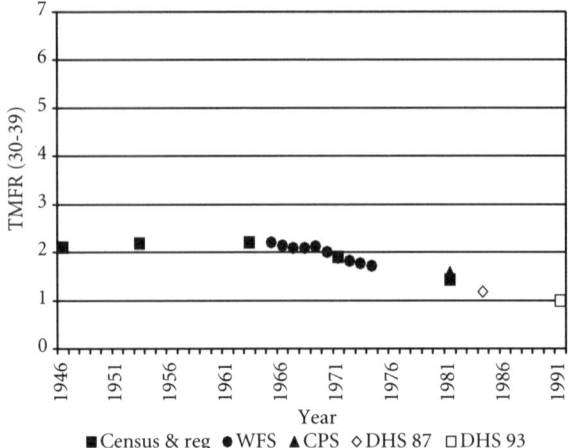

Figure 5.7. TMFR(30–39) per woman for Sri Lanka, various years 1946–1991.

period.[2] The most likely explanation is simply that the WFS misrepresented the situation in this respect, either because of sampling variability or because of reporting or coverage errors. It may be seen that the proportion of women aged 45–49 who were recorded as never married in the 1975 WFS (2 per cent) is also out of line with the figures from other sources.

Marital Fertility

Has the decline in overall fertility in Sri Lanka simply been a reflection of changes in nuptiality, or has there also been a change in the rate of childbearing within marriage? Figure 5.5 shows total marital fertility rates for Sri Lanka at various points since World War II. These have been calculated as five times the sum of age-specific marital fertility rates per woman for five-year age groups from 20–24 to 45–49 (the abbreviation TMFR(20+) has been used). The age group 15–19 has been omitted since the marital fertility of this group is often found to exert a disproportionate and distorting influence on the total rate. Age-specific marital fertility rates were calculated from basic data, or obtained from previously published work, in exactly the same way and drawing on exactly the same sources as detailed earlier in

[2] According to official statistics, the annual marriage rate between 1971 and 1975 varied between 6.8 and 7.0 per 1,000 population, with no trend over time. The average annual marriage rate over the period 1961–70 was 6.2 per 1,000 and the highest rate for any year in this period was 6.8 (Department of Census and Statistics 1987: 4).

connection with age-specific fertility rates (see the Appendix). However, the denominators used in calculations were married women rather than all women. The census-plus-registration TMFR(20+) for 1946 was obtained by multiplying the 1953 value by the ratio of one-third of the actual number of births during 1945–47 to the number of births that would have been if married women in 1946 had experienced the age-specific marital fertility rates of 1953.

Further data based upon age-specific marital fertility rates are presented in Figs 5.6 and 5.7. Figure 5.6 shows measures calculated as five times the sum of age-specific marital fertility rates per woman for the age groups 20–24 and 25–29 (denoted TMFR (20–29)); and Fig. 5.7 shows measures calculated as five times the sum of age-specific marital fertility rates for women aged 30–34 and 35–39 (denoted TMFR (30–39)).

Figure 5.5 suggests that marital fertility in Sri Lanka actually rose to some extent, not only between 1946 and 1953, when, as already noted, overall fertility rose, but also between 1953 and 1963, when overall fertility fell slightly. In other words, without the changes in nuptiality that occurred, overall fertility would have risen between 1953 and 1963. After 1963, however, marital fertility seems to have declined in Sri Lanka. The decline was apparently fairly gradual between 1963 and 1981. (It is being assumed here that the WFS-based figures for 1973 and 1974 are probably incorrect, just as were the WFS-based TFRs for those years.) However, marital fertility seems to have declined at a faster pace in the 1980s, especially in the early years of the decade. These changes may be examined in greater detail using the data presented in Figs 5.6 and 5.7. It may be seen that whereas the fertility of married women in their thirties seems to have declined fairly steadily over the entire period since the early 1960s (disregarding the CPS-based figure as probably incorrect), the fertility of married women in their twenties seems to have fallen only very slightly before the 1980s, when a distinctly sharper decline set in (disregarding WFS and CPS figures).

The Role of Contraception

Does the evidence on birth control practice in Sri Lanka tie in with the suggestion that there may have been some acceleration in the rate of decline of marital fertility in recent years? Table 5.2 shows the percentage of currently married women aged 15–49 using various methods of contraception in 1975 (according to the WFS), 1982 (CPS), 1987 (DHS), and 1993 (DHS).

Table 5.3 shows the percentage of currently married women, by age group, who reported using any method of contraception and the percentage who used a modern method, that is, the pill, IUD, injectable, condom, male or female sterilization, a female barrier method or a spermicide.

Table 5.2. Percentage of currently married women aged 15–49 using particular contraceptive methods at different surveys

Year and source	WFS 1975	CPS 1982	DHS 1987	DHS 1993
Pill	1.7	2.7	4.1	5.5
IUD	5.2	2.9	2.1	3.0
Injection	0.4	1.0	2.7	4.6
Condom	2.3	3.3	1.9	3.3
Sterilization (male or female)	10.6	22.0	29.8	27.2
Norplant®	—	—	0.0	0.1
Any 'modern' method (any of the above plus diaphragm and spermicides)	20.2	31.9	40.6	43.7
Safe period	8.9	14.2	14.9	15.2
Withdrawal	1.6	5.1	3.4	5.0
Other	3.7	6.7	2.8	2.2
Any method	34.4	57.8	61.7	66.1

Note: Data refer to the geographic area covered by the DHS enquiries; data taken from Department of Census and Statistics (1995: 54).

Table 5.3. Percentage of currently married women in different age groups using any method of contraception and (in brackets) a 'modern' method of contraception at different surveys

Age group	WFS 1975	CPS 1982	DHS 1987	DHS 1993
15–19	14 (10)	28 (7)	20 (11)	30 (18)
20–24	19 (12)	41 (17)	42 (26)	54 (36)
25–29	30 (18)	52 (29)	57 (38)	61 (40)
30–34	43 (27)	64 (37)	67 (45)	67 (45)
35–39	41 (26)	71 (44)	74 (50)	77 (52)
40–44	35 (19)	65 (37)	72 (48)	74 (48)
45–49	20 (8)	36 (18)	56 (34)	62 (42)

Note: 'Modern' contraception as defined in Table 5.2; data taken or calculated from Carrasco (1981: 46); Department of Census and Statistics (1983: 76, 1995: 57).

It cannot be claimed that the changes in contraceptive practice revealed by these data correspond in any detailed way with the changes in fertility that appear to have occurred since the mid-1970s. This same point was noted by Gajanayake and Caldwell (1990)—in relation to the period between the 1975 WFS and the 1987 DHS—who believe that an important part of the explanation is that these surveys, and especially the 1975 WFS, tended to under-record the true extent of reliance on non-'modern' methods. Nevertheless, the data do very clearly show a considerable increase in the use of modern methods of contraception in Sri Lanka between 1975 and 1982 and between 1982 and 1987, with some further increase, though much smaller, between 1987 and 1993 (see Table 5.2). Moreover, between 1987 and 1993, reliance on modern methods of contraception continued to grow among married women under the age of 25 (Table 5.3). And even though abortion is formally proscribed in Sri Lanka, there is also good reason to believe that there has been a considerable increase in the number of induced abortions carried out in Sri Lanka in recent years.[3]

Conclusion

All in all, it seems reasonable to accept that fertility in Sri Lanka is by now at about replacement level. The available data on fertility are remarkably consistent with each other (only the CPS and a few elements of the WFS need to be discarded) and point very clearly to a pattern of declining fertility in Sri Lanka over 30 or more years. This picture is reinforced by the available data on nuptiality, which show a rising mean age at first marriage for females in Sri Lanka over the entire period since World War II. There is also evidence, at least in relation to the period since the mid-1970s, of increasing reliance on the more effective methods of birth control.

Can an explanation be offered for why a country as little developed economically as Sri Lanka seems to have achieved such a low level of fertility? According to Gajanayake and Caldwell (1990: 97), 'the decline in Sri Lanka's marital fertility may well be explained by social and demographic factors such as high female literacy and mass education, decreasing infant mortality, high social welfare standards and high aspirations in the face of a worsening economy and increasing unemployment'. My own sense of the situation is not unlike theirs, even though I am conscious, as I am sure they were, that such statements are easier to make than demonstrate. One or two other points might be added, however. In recent years, the increasing financial burden of the civil war has undoubtedly exacerbated the economic situation, and the war has led to a fairly general sense of difficulty and insecurity. These difficulties were added to in the late 1980s by a very serious and damaging youth insurrection in the south of the country.[4]

In addition, in recent years, very large numbers of Sri Lankans have gone overseas as temporary migrant workers, mostly to the Middle East. Most of these migrant workers were women (according to the Sri Lanka Bureau of Foreign Employment, at least 72 per cent of those who went to work overseas each year

---

[3] Information I have collected convinces me that an absolute minimum of 55,000 induced abortions were carried out under modern conditions in Sri Lanka during 1995. The number of live births in Sri Lanka in 1993 was about 350,000.

[4] The civil war involves fighting between government forces and Ceylon Tamil separatists in the north and east of the island. The insurrection involved Sinhalese youth in the south.

from 1991 to 1995[5]), most were married women (79 per cent of female migrants in 1994), and virtually all were under age 50. In fact, most were 35 or younger (over 70 per cent in 1994). These factors seem virtually certain to have acted as a restraining influence on fertility, both by reducing exposure to the risk of pregnancy through absence overseas (the DHS samples of 1987 and 1993 must have included women who had spent some time abroad) and by providing couples with an incentive to control their family size. Some idea of the possible importance of this phenomenon may be gained from the fact that the Sri Lanka Bureau of Foreign Employment has estimated that, by 1996, there were 378,500 Sri Lankan female contract workers overseas. As a ratio, this number represents over 8 per cent of the estimated mid-year population of females aged 15–49 in Sri Lanka in 1994 (estimated mid-year population taken from Department of Census and Statistics 1996: 34).

It may be worth noting, finally, that some of the suggestions that have been made in relation to the decline of fertility in Sri Lanka seem to have arisen also in discussions about fertility decline in the state of Kerala in South India, where, according to Zachariah and Rajan 1997: 18), the TFR had fallen to about 1.7 by 1993. Zachariah and Rajan (1997) observe that in Kerala, '... rapid changes in fertility and mortality took place in the context of very rapid developments in the social sector and very little movement in the productive sector' (p. 19). They speak of Kerala's 'success in several key areas including education, health and family planning', alongside its 'dismal record in industrial and agricultural production and in employment generation' (p. 17). They refer to 'the catalytic role of literacy and female education' in Kerala in connection with family planning and maternal and child health (p. 19). In the light of such remarks, it really is tempting to wonder whether there might not be common factors behind the fertility declines in Kerala and Sri Lanka.

---

[5] These and subsequent figures relating to overseas employment were made available by the Sri Lanka Bureau of Foreign Employment.

Appendix

Source of data and length of time period to which they refer, where previously published
material has been used

Enquiry	Source of data	Period on which rates are based
WFS 1975	Alam and Cleland (1981: 28, table 9; 50, table B5)	3 years
CPS 1982	D of C and S (1983: 42, table 4.8)	1 year
DHS 1987	D of C and S (1988: 40, table 3.3)	5 years
	D of C and S (1988: 33, table 3.1)	3 years
	Freedman and Blanc (1992: 48, table 3)	4 years
DHS 1993	D of C and S (1995: 26, table 2.1; 28, table 2.2)	5 years
1981 Census (own children)	Ratnayake *et al.* (1984, 9, table 2)	5 years

Note: D of C and S = Department of Census and Statistics; the Freedman and Blanc estimate for up to four years prior to the survey has not been used because essentially the same figure is provided by another source; marital rates provided by Ratnayake *et al.* have not been used because of possible inaccuracy in the denominators; marital rates based on the 1987 DHS and the 1993 DHS are approximate in that they have been calculated (by the author) by modifying overall rates for the five-year period prior to the survey by the marital status distribution at the survey.

References

Alam, I., and Cleland, J. (1981), *Illustrative Analysis: Recent Fertility Trends in Sri Lanka*, WFS Scientific Reports No. 25, London: World Fertility Survey.

Caldwell, J. C. (1986), 'Routes to Low Mortality in Poor Countries', *Population and Development Review*, 12(2): 171–220.

Carrasco, E. (1981), *Contraceptive Practice*, WFS Cross National Summaries No. 9, London: World Fertility Survey.

Department of Census and Statistics (1978), *World Fertility Survey, Sri Lanka 1975: First Report*, Colombo: Government Printer.

—— (1983), *Sri Lanka Contraceptive Prevalence Survey Report 1982*, Colombo: Government Printer.

—— (1987), *Vital Statistics 1967–1980 for Sri Lanka, Vol. 1*, Colombo: Government Printer.

—— (1988), *Sri Lanka Demographic and Health Survey 1987*, Columbia, Maryland: IRD/Westinghouse.

—— (1995), *Sri Lanka Demographic and Health Survey 1993*, Colombo: Government Printer.

—— (1996), *Statistical Abstract of Sri Lanka 1995*, Colombo: Government Printer.

Freedman, R., and Blanc, A. K. (1992), 'Fertility Transition: An Update', *International Family Planning Perspectives*, 18 (2): 44–50.

Gajanayake, I., and Caldwell, J. (1990), 'Fertility and its Control: The Puzzle of Sri Lanka', *International Family Planning Perspectives*, 16(3): 97–102.

Hajnal, J. (1953), 'Age at Marriage and Proportions Marrying', *Population Studies*, 7(2): 111–136.

Langford, C. M. (1981), 'Fertility Change in Sri Lanka Since the War: An Analysis of the Experience of Different Districts', *Population Studies*, 35 (2): 285–306.

—— (1982), *The Fertility of Tamil Estate Workers in Sri Lanka*, WFS Scientific Reports No. 31, London: World Fertility Survey.

Ratnayake, K., Retherford, R. D., and Sivasubramaniam, S. (1984), *Fertility Estimates for Sri Lanka*, Colombo: Aitken Spence and Co.

Zachariah, K. C. and Rajan, S. I. (1997), *Kerala's Demographic Transition*, New Delhi: Sage Publications.

6   Family Planning in Pakistan: A Turning Point

ABDUL HAKIM AND PETER C. MILLER

Introduction

In the five decades that have elapsed since independence, the population of Pakistan has doubled twice, going from 32.5 million in 1947 to 128 million in 1997 (Table 6.1). The immediate determinants of this growth are well known. Annual rates of natural increase accelerated in the post-independence era, from 2 per cent in 1947 to 3 per cent in the 1960s. The growing rate of natural increase was the direct outcome of reductions in child mortality in the 1950s and 1960s, and of sustained high fertility throughout the post-independence era (Sathar and Casterline 1998).

Pakistan's growth was anticipated early in the independence period—by both the policy community and international experts, leading to official expressions of concern about its possible consequences for the country. In fact, many of the consequences feared in the late 1940s have actually occurred. Urban population growth has accelerated to 4 per cent a year, straining the infrastructure, housing, employment opportunities, and social services. The consequences of rapid population growth in rural areas have been no less graphic. Land fragmentation[1] and attendant productivity problems were direct outcomes of rapid population growth. For five decades, development planners have consistently recognized the gravity of Pakistan's population problem and the need for sustained policies to address it.

In response to these concerns, Pakistan became one of the first countries to launch a population programme. In the 1950s, organized efforts were limited to family planning service delivery in a few urban clinics. By the 1960s, however, a more comprehensive public programme was launched, consisting of promotional campaigns, organizational efforts, and expanded service accessibility. Over the three decades that followed, strategic changes were introduced, often involving considerable public investment and, typically, attracting substantial foreign assistance. Although modest gains in contraceptive prevalence were registered, most respected observers portray family planning programme effort in Pakistan as a failure. As of 1990, contraceptive prevalence had increased to 11.8 per cent (from 5.5 per cent in 1968), while total fertility remained unchanged at about six. Few

[1] Declining farm size represents a serious constraint to agricultural development. In the decade of the 1980s alone, the number of farms that are under 3 acres increased from 2.1 million (51 per cent of all farms) to 3.3 million (64 per cent).

other countries have devoted so many resources to family planning for so long with so little success.[2]

This chapter reviews the legacy of family planning failure in Pakistan, notes certain features of both the setting and the programme that explain this failure, and argues that new circumstances have recently emerged, which suggest a demographic and policy turning point.[3] The data sources used in the analysis are: the 1975 Pakistan Fertility Survey (PFS); the 1984–85 Pakistan Contraceptive Prevalence Survey (PCPS); the 1990–91 Pakistan Demographic and Health Survey (PDHS); the 1994–95 Pakistan Contraceptive Prevalence Survey (PCPS); and the 1996–97 Pakistan Fertility and Family Planning Survey (PFFPS); the censuses of 1951, 1961, 1972 and 1981; and a 1996 evaluation of the Population Welfare Programme's IEC components, carried out by the National Institute of Population Studies (NIPS). In addition, the authors had access to a number of government documents and reports.

Sources of Past Programme Failure

Political Commitment

Open political commitment to family planning on the part of the highest government officials has at least three types of effects. First, it tends to result in the mobilization of increased resources for the programme. Second, it empowers and mandates bureaucrats both in the family planning programme and in related sectors. And third, it helps legitimize family planning among the general population and to neutralize cultural and ideological opposition.

The inconsistency of political support for family planning in Pakistan has been widely noted (Hakim 1992; Rukanuddin and Hardee-Cleaveland 1992). For about 20 years (1969–88) heads of state or government rarely, if ever, spoke openly in favour of family planning. Moreover, even when positive words were spoken, the subsequent actions did not always match the words.

Before 1958, little attention had been given to family planning at any level of government. The ascent of President Ayub in that year greatly changed the official approach to the population problem. In many of his major speeches, President Ayub referred to the problem of rapid population growth and to the need for family planning. The subject was also given a much higher priority in government programmes (Stamper 1979). For the first time, a significant budget was allocated to the

---

[2] Useful discussions of the apparent failure of the Pakistan programme appear in Robinson *et al.* (1981) and Rukanuddin and Hardee-Cleaveland (1992).

[3] On several occasions in the past, observers have claimed that a turning point on the road to success in family planning was at hand (Robinson 1978), only to be refuted by subsequent evidence. The present situation, with apparently substantial recent increases in contraceptive prevalence, is another such moment in the history of Pakistan's family planning programme.

Table 6.1. Population size and rate of growth, Pakistan, 1901–97

Year	Population (thousands)	Annual growth rate (%)
1901	16,576	—
1911	19,382	0.6
1921	21,109	0.8
1931	23,542	1.1
1941	28,282	1.9
1947	32,500	1.8
1951	33,740	1.8
1961	42,880	2.4
1972	65,309	3.6
1981	84,254	3.1
1991 (est.)	115,000	3.1
1997 (est.)	137,000	2.7

Note: Data from 1901 through 1981 are census figures, while 1991 and 1997 data are estimated.

Source: NIPS (1997).

family planning programme, and religious objections were met openly. President Ayub's lead set the tone for official public attitudes on the subject.

After the end of President Ayub's presidency in 1969, however, few leaders spoke openly in favour of the programme. Neither President Yahya Khan (1969–71) nor Prime Minister Zulfikar Ali Bhutto (1972–77) showed much public interest in the programme, although during the latter period, the programme was reactivated to some extent. The Islamization process of President Zia-ul-Haq had a strong adverse effect on public support for family planning, but the programme did continue in modified form.

After President Zia's death in 1988, the political climate gradually became more positive. In 1988, President Ghulam Ishaque affirmed Pakistan's need of a family planning programme in speeches to parliamentarians, and governments under Prime Ministers Benazir Bhutto (1988–90 and 1993–96) and Mian Nawaz Sharif (1990–93 and 1997–99) have shown increasingly positive public support for family planning.

Table 6.2 shows the results of this increased support in terms of budgetary support for family planning from 1965 to the present, in constant 1966–67 rupees. President Ayub's initial allocations in the Third Five-Year Plan were augmented in the 1970s to ensure full development of the programme's service structures. With the ascent of President Zia and the termination of the Continuous Motivation System, expenses for family planning were cut sharply, to levels from which

Table 6.2. Annual expenditures on the government family planning programme, including foreign assistance, 1965–1998

Five-year plan period	Mid-period	Rupee index	Annual nominal outlay (mil. rupees)	Annual outlay in 1967–68[a] (mil. rupees)
1965–70	1967–68	1000	34	34
1970–78[b]	1974	528.5	104	55
1978–83	1980–81	264.9	123	33
1983–88	1985–86	192.6	337	65
1988–93	1990–91	132.6	609	81
1993–98[c]	1995–96	79.9	1820	145

[a] Rupee index is derived from annual consumer price indices published in annual Economic Surveys.
[b] Includes the non-plan period 1975–78.
[c] Allocation rather than expenditure.
Source: Planning Commission (1988, 1993).

they have only gradually recovered. Even so, expenditures never reached more than 1 per cent of total non-military public sector expenditure (Hakim 1992). Moreover, foreign assistance accounted for about 44 per cent of total expenditure for family planning between 1965 and 1989 (Hakim 1992), and provincial governments provide no financial support to the programme.

Measuring the enthusiasm of a bureaucracy is difficult, but from the general view of people involved in the programme from the beginning, as well as from periodic reviews, it seems clear that the commitment of programme officials has greatly decreased. After a climate of hope and enthusiasm under Enver Adil in the 1960s, programme effort by the 1980s was generally characterized by lethargy and cynicism (Robinson *et al.* 1981), leaving a difficult legacy for programme managers in the 1990s.

Finally, the lack of open public support for family planning after President Ayub doubtless was a factor in the absence of major changes in demand for family planning by 1990 (see below). It is hardly surprising that a brief period of exhortation by a single government in the 1960s could not change so fundamental an aspect of Pakistani culture. However, a continuation of that support in the 1970s and 1980s could have made a substantial difference in the way Pakistanis responded to economic growth and modernization. Hence the absence of political commitment for family planning after 1969 must be considered a major factor in inhibiting the acceptance of family planning and in delaying the onset of the demographic transition in Pakistan.

Programmatic Action

Positive government policy towards family planning in Pakistan goes back as far as economic planning itself (Robinson 1978). Pakistan was one of the first developing countries to recognize the problem of rapid population growth and to attempt to control it through family planning. The family planning programme of Pakistan has operated under various structural forms, generally coinciding with successive five-year development plans, and these structures have been placed in several different locations within the government. In this process, each phase has tended to subsume the earlier phase, rather than replacing it (Population Welfare Division 1983).

Family planning was included in the First and Second Five-Year Plans, but the programmes were limited in scope and did not produce any major impact (Family Planning Division 1969). During the Third Five-Year Plan (1965–70), a comprehensive national family planning programme was designed as an integral part of overall development strategy. The scheme drawn up for this period emphasized that family planning was essentially an administrative, not a clinical, programme (Government of Pakistan 1965; Robinson 1978). An administrative structure for the programme was established at federal, provincial and district levels. Clients were approached through part-time *dais* (indigenous midwives), who motivated them to practice family planning and distributed contraceptives to eligible couples.

The speed with which the programme was launched was impressive, but it did not ensure that the practice of family planning would be adopted widely (Robinson *et al.* 1981). Among the important problems in this period were pressure to achieve unrealistic targets and the indiscriminate spreading of resources, irrespective of likely public response, which led to services of low quality (World Bank 1983).

In 1970, a new strategy, the Continuous Motivation System (CMS), was introduced, with *dais* being replaced as grass-roots workers by a team of men and women working in pairs as field motivators. CMS was a logical approach, and it had several well-conceived elements. However, it required recruiting male and female workers who were supposed to be local residents, educated and related to each other, and these criteria proved impossible to implement.

During 1975 the CMS programme was abandoned in favour of a multisectoral approach, and the programme was transferred from the Ministry of Health to the Ministry of Planning and Development. The multisectoral approach was implemented through Family Welfare Centres (FWCs), as well as the health outlets of governmental and non-governmental agencies (Population Welfare Division 1981). As the key institutions providing family planning services, the FWCs were supposed to cover 25,000–65,000 population, a goal that resulted in inadequate coverage.

Thus the failure of each model, combined with fluctuating government commitment, led to its replacement by another, with negative consequences for staff morale and for the orderly development of skills and careers. This contributed to problems of management, which have been increasingly serious throughout the life of the programme. Moreover, the models themselves were seriously flawed, notably in their failure to provide outreach to a population characterized by limited demand and mobility. In retrospect, only the CMS, given time and suitable modification, might have succeeded.

Sources of Resistance

The lack of sustained political commitment and the weaknesses in programme implementation did not exist in a vacuum. To a considerable extent, the weaknesses represent the success of several sources of opposition to the existence of a family planning programme. For convenience, we categorize these as either ideological or religious.

In the realm of ideology, one source of opposition to family planning came from a rejection of the need to control population growth. Among the élite of Pakistan were many who felt that a large population was a source of national power. This argument gained strength from comparison with Pakistan's populous neighbour and arch-rival, India, which was itself growing rapidly. Many felt that allowing the disparity in population size to continue would put Pakistan at a further disadvantage, even in danger of being swallowed up. The example of China was sometimes cited to show the military advantage of a large population. On the other hand, until the 1980s there were few examples of developing countries becoming powerful through economic growth strategies that incorporated population control.

A related idea claimed that family planning was a foreign plot to keep Pakistan weak and helpless. This view was advocated mainly by religious parties, who criticized the implementation of the programme. These two views served to inhibit the Information, Education and Communication (IEC) campaigns, and to the extent that they gained credence among the bureaucracy, they adversely affected the programme's ability to gain support from other sectors.

The 1974 Bucharest conference on population and development lent credence to the view that family planning could not succeed in Pakistan unless development progresses first. To many senior officials, this implied that family planning should be integrated into other development activities, a view that had strong intellectual backing at the time, but a view that also undermined direct commitment to population and family planning activities. Hence, the 'multisectoral' approach during the period of President Zia (1977–88) resulted in family planning neither receiving adequate support on its own, nor being effectively incorporated into other development sectors.

In terms of religious influences, there is no monolithic leadership for Muslims in Pakistan, and no clear statement in the *Quran* and *Hadith* to guide religious leaders on family planning matters. For this reason, religious leaders voice a wide range of attitudes towards family planning. However, one fact is uniform; none of the religious leaders or preachers in Pakistan have openly supported the view that the family planning programme is religiously acceptable. Moreover, the view of the late Maulana Maudoodi in the 1940s that family planning is unacceptable in Islam, has been quoted widely and accepted (Abedin 1977; Maudoodi 1982). On one occasion, the Islami Nazariati Council of Pakistan also based its opposition to the family planning programme as a national policy on religious grounds (Islami Nazariati Council 1984).

Other religious leaders neither favour nor oppose the ideas of Maudoodi and the Islami Nazariati Council on family planning. However, using the analogy of *azal* (withdrawal), a few scholars not belonging to religious organizations argue that the use of modern contraception is not contrary to the laws of Islam (Hussain 1987; Inayatullah 1992; Khan 1967). However, regardless of their general political stance, the hostility of many religious leaders and scholars has had a strongly inhibiting effect on political leaders. The planners of the family planning programme have generally tried to avoid religious controversy rather than convince religious leaders to support the programme.

At another level, the *maulvis*, local community religious leaders, influence family planning policy and implementation. Although influenced by Islamic scholars, their views are varied and governed less by theology than by tradition and by other local leaders. The widespread belief among Pakistanis that family planning goes against their religion probably owes much to the *maulvis*, although this possible influence has not been studied well.

Societal Institutions

The various sources of opposition, whether ideological or religious, have owed their strength in Pakistan less to their intellectual cogency than to their consonance with the cultural roots of the nation. Large families are traditionally believed to be a good thing, both because of their central place in the economic and social life of the society, and because Pakistanis love children. To say that children are a bad thing, either for the country or for the welfare of the family, cuts against a very strong grain in Pakistani culture.

Reproductive Preferences and Demand for Family Planning

The demand for children (and the demand for family planning, which is a different but related matter) is always a balance between factors encouraging more children (and less family planning) and those encouraging fewer children (and more family planning). Here we examine some of the main factors influencing such demand in Pakistan.

Demand for children remained high in Pakistan through the 1980s. Table 6.3 shows the average ideal family size among currently married women of reproductive age in the national surveys of 1975, 1984–85, and 1990–91 (1975 PFS; 1984–85 PCPS; 1990–91 PDHS; 1994–95 PCPS; 1996–97 PFFPS). Despite some significant fluctuation, the three surveys show a mean ideal size of more than four children. This figure is corroborated by relatively unchanging level of women who say they want no more children, which is also shown in Table 6.3. The table also shows little perceptible trend in the total demand for family planning (defined as the sum of contraceptive prevalence and unmet need for family planning). Total demand fell

Table 6.3. Trends in mean ideal family size, percentage of married women who want no more children, and total demand for family planning, national surveys, 1975–1997

Survey and year	Mean ideal family size	Overall proportion wanting no more children (%)
PFS 1975	4.2	49.0
PCPS 1984–85	4.9	43.4
PDHS 1990–91	4.1	36.4
PCPS 1994–95	3.4	52.0
PFFPS 1996–97	3.5	45.9

Sources: PFS 1975; PCPS 1984–85; PDHS 1990–91; PCPS 1994–95; PFFPS 1996–97.

from 66 per cent in 1984–85 to 40 per cent in 1990–91, and rose rapidly thereafter. However, the 1984–85 total demand figure includes an estimate of 35 per cent unmet need for spacing, based on data that are radically different from any published before or since. In general, the definitions of unmet need used in these studies are not consistent.

A related issue is the age at marriage. Table 6.4 indicates a monotonically increasing singulate mean age at marriage over the 1951 to 1990–97 period. The increase is comparable for men and for women, even though men consistently marry when they are 4–5 years older than women. The increase in age at marriage is probably somehow related to changes in expectations of what is required before a couple can marry. Nowadays, many families anticipate that before they marry, couples should have the wherewithal to establish an independent household, and should have obtained some higher education, for example.

Typically, traditional economies are understood to encourage large families. From the standpoint of the parent, children become a net economic asset at an early age, and remain so through the parent's old age. The contribution of children can take such forms as agricultural work, manufacturing labour, or services. When sons reach adulthood, they are expected to contribute to the wealth of the extended family, and to provide direct support to their parents. Because a married couple is expected to support the husband's parents rather than the wife's, there is a demand for sons, which is partially independent of the overall demand for children.

Demand for children can change if parents begin to perceive advantages in producing 'high-quality' children, that is, children whose educational background and other characteristics allow the prospect of far greater income in adulthood than their traditional labour can yield. Furthermore, the climate of demand may change if household aspirations change in ways that lead parents to make substantial outlays for schooling, clothing, medicines, toys, and other expenses. In such a situation, the

Table 6.4. Singulate mean age at marriage, by sex, Pakistan, 1951–1997

Source and year	Male	Female
Census, 1951	22.3	16.9
Census, 1961	23.6	18.1
Census, 1972	24.9	19.8
Census, 1981	25.0	20.7
PCPS, 1984–85	25.3	20.7
PDHS, 1990–91	26.3	21.6
PCPS, 1994–95[a]	26.1	22.0
PFFPS, 1996–97[a]	26.5	22.0

[a] Provisional.

Source: PFFPS 1996–97.

parents' calculus changes: a large number of children becomes unaffordable, and the future earning power of the children is no longer satisfactory.

Pakistan's economic picture changed substantially between 1965 and 1990, but not always in ways that would have created a demand for fewer children. In rural areas, decreases in average farm sizes were largely offset by increasing crop yields as a result of the 'green revolution'. In urban areas, much of the economic growth was in low-wage manufacturing and service sectors. Although the proportion of children attending school rose gradually, by 1990, education, even of boys, was still not considered an essential investment for children.

Educational attainment and economic conditions changed during the period in question. Table 6.5 shows increases in radio and television exposure and Table 6.6 indicates moderate increases in the proportion of men and women with some schooling. Similarly, rural electrification became more common, the proportions living in cities increased, and in general the influence of traditional culture may have eroded somewhat in response to changing economic conditions.

The demand for children and/or family planning can also change as a result of deliberate education or propaganda, either extolling small-family norms or providing information about the benefits and availability of family planning. The IEC approach was tried in Pakistan during 1965–90, but with little discernible influence on attitudes or behaviour. At least partly, this was due to lack of accessibility to media, which, although increasing during the period, was still low even by 1990–91. For example, the PDHS (1990–91) found that 35 per cent of households owned a radio, 27 per cent a television, 21 per cent of women and 50 per cent of their husbands had some schooling (and hence could potentially be reached by print media). The proportion who had discussed family planning with a fieldworker was not given but, throughout the period, it appears that only a small minority of

Table 6.5. Access to mass media and exposure to family planning messages, national surveys, 1975–1997

Study and year	% ownership of radio	% ownership of television	% heard mass media message	% knowing at least one FP message
PCPS, 1984–85	n.a.	n.a.	n.a.	61.5
PDHS, 1990–91	35.4	27.0	21.3[a]	77.9
IEC, 1994	32.2	47.5	88.3	83.7
PCPS, 1994–95	45.5	43.9	62.7	90.7
PFFPS, 1996–97	36.1	37.7	n.a.	94.3

n.a.: not available.
[a] Exposed to message in past month.
Sources: PCPS 1984–85; Hakim 1996; PCPS 1994–95; PFFPS 1996–97.

couples were reached through interpersonal communication. Only 21 per cent of women had heard any message about family planning during the month prior to the survey. Given this finding, coupled with the economic and cultural rationale for large families, it is perhaps not surprising that the IEC campaign did not have an important impact in this earlier period.

Uncertainty about how many children will survive leads couples to adopt an 'insurance' strategy of having more children than they want in order to ensure the survival of a sufficient number. Changing mortality conditions may therefore improve the climate for family planning. The infant mortality rate (IMR) did indeed fall between 1965 and 1990.[4]

Education—especially the education of women—is associated with reductions in fertility in nearly all societies. In addition, schooling is considered to be an essential element in producing 'quality' children. Although the proportion of children attending school rose gradually, by 1990, education, even of boys, was still not considered an essential investment for children. The proportion of married women 15–49 with some schooling rose from 11 per cent in 1975 to 21 per cent in 1990–91, while that of their husbands went from 41 per cent to 50 per cent in the same period (Table 6.6). Thus, while there was movement towards greater education during the period, levels of schooling remained low by almost any standard, and did not apparently contribute in any important way to an increased demand for fertility control.

These factors combined resulted in a fairly high demand for children. In three national surveys conducted between 1975 and 1990–91, we have seen that mean ideal

---

[4] For the period 1965–70, the IMR may have been as high as 137 (Population Planning Council of Pakistan 1976) or as low as 113 (Training Research and Evaluation Centre, n.d.); for the period 1985–1990, the PDHS (1990–91) estimates the IMR at 90.5. Trends for the utilization of health services are not readily available, but at the time of the PDHS in 1990–91, 85 per cent of all deliveries took place in the home, and 35 per cent of all children 12–23 months of age had been fully vaccinated.

Table 6.6. Percentage with some schooling: married women of reproductive age and their husbands, national surveys, 1975–1997

Study and year	% with some schooling	
	Wives	Husbands
PFS, 1975	10.7	41.2
PCPS, 1984–85	15.5	48.0
PDHS, 1990–91	20.8	49.8
PCPS, 1994–95	24.8	56.5
PFFPS, 1996–97	25.2	58.5

Sources: PFS 1995; PCPS 1984–85; PDHS 1990–91; PCPS 1994–95; PFFPS 1996–97.

family size was between 4.1 and 4.9 children (Table 6.3). This range, however, was substantially below actual fertility, which was consistently over 6 children per woman (Table 6.7). As a result, between 36 per cent and 49 per cent of all married women of reproductive age wanted no more children than they already had (Table 6.3). While measures of unmet need for family planning for the period are not comparable or unavailable, it is clear that the discrepancy between desired and actual fertility resulted in substantial unmet need for family planning during the period.

Evidence of Change in the 1990s

Various types of change occurring in the 1990s improved the climate for reproductive change. The relative importance of these background factors will never be known, but the emergence of a demographic transition in Pakistan is likely to be attributable to a combination of the following factors and influences.

Political Change

During the 1990s, the priority assigned to population and family planning increased visibly. In 1990, the Population Welfare Division, at the federal level, achieved the status of an independent ministry. And under the Pakistan Muslim League government of Nawaz Sharif, important enhancements of the family planning programme—such as the establishment of the Village Based Family Planning Worker Scheme—were incorporated into the Eighth Five-Year Plan (1993–98).

During the second Bhutto regime (1993–96), the social sector in general was given increased priority, both in rhetoric and in budgetary terms. The government assigned a high priority to family planning programme in its agenda for change, and family planning became a major component of the Social Action Programme.

Table 6.7. Trends in the total fertility rate and in contraceptive prevalence, national surveys, 1968–1997

Study and year	Total fertility rate	Contraceptive prevalence rate (%)
NIS, 1968	n.a.	5.5
PGS, 1968–71	6.0	n.a.
PFS, 1975	6.3	5.2
PCPS, 1984–85	6.0	9.1
PDHS, 1990–91	5.4–6.4[a]	11.8
IEC, 1994	n.a.	24.4
PCPS, 1994–95	5.62[b]	17.8
PFFPS, 1996–97	5.32[b]	23.9

[a] We have also taken the liberty of using the estimate of 6.4 for the TFR in the 1990–91 DHS, along with the published figure of 5.4, following the results of the PDHS's own Post Enumeration Survey (Curtis and Arnold 1994), and in keeping with criticism of the published rate.
[b] Provisional estimate.

Sources: Training Research and Evaluation Centre, n.d.; PFS 1975; PCPS 1984–85; PDHS 1990–91; Hakim, 1996; PCPS 1994–95; and PFFPS 1996–97.

The establishment, within the cabinet, of the Social Sectors Coordinating Committee, chaired by the Prime Minister, gave added impetus to the programme.

Under the second Bhutto government, bold and open political support for family planning—in the form of statements, interviews, discussions in cabinet meetings, and participation in international conferences at a high level—became the norm. Pakistan's contribution to the International Conference on Population and Development in Cairo in 1994, including the personal participation of Mrs Bhutto, was widely publicized. From 1994 through 1997, celebration of World Population Day became a regular July activity of the cabinet. The event is used to highlight the consequences of rapid population growth and to improve awareness of the issues involved. Likewise, federal and provincial parliamentary action has increased, including resolutions and the setting up of a parliamentary group on Population and Development and a Standing Committee on Planning and Development and Population Welfare in the National Assembly. These activities were supported by the main political opposition.

When the second Nawaz government took power in 1997, population activities were continued and strengthened.[5] It seems likely that maintaining a democratic form of government, whatever political problems this may generate, will be conducive to increasing priority to the social sector. Underlying all these developments is

[5] For example, a strong parliamentary resolution on population was passed, a cabinet group on population has met under the chairmanship of the Prime Minister, the Planning Commission has established an interministerial Working Group on Reproductive Health, and, in general, interministerial coordination has markedly increased.

a visible decline in opposition to family planning. The overall effect of the sustained development of population policy and programmes during this period has been to insulate commitment to population from the vagaries of political change. Pakistan has reached the point in its history when commitment to population policy is increasingly a matter of political consensus.

Programmatic Developments

The current family planning programme under the Eighth Five-Year Plan (1993–98) is designed to raise CPR from an estimated 14 per cent to 24 per cent, by expanding coverage from 20 per cent to 80 per cent—giving special attention to rural areas. The major new initiatives through which this expansion is to be accomplished are two new systems of community-based contraceptive distribution: the Village-Based Family Planning Workers (VBFPW) Scheme under the Ministry of Population Welfare; and the Prime Minister's Programme for Family Planning and Primary Health Care (also known as the LHW Scheme) in the Ministry of Health. These programmes, ultimately designed to place, respectively, 12,000 and 100,000 family planning and health workers in communities throughout Pakistan, are new, and their full impact remains to be seen. Preliminary indications indicate, however, that these programmes are effective.[6]

Another potentially important new service development is the expansion of social marketing activities. Through the existing programme, condoms are distributed through thousands of sale points throughout the country. A new initiative is being developed and expanded to include hormonal contraceptives and IUDs. Table 6.8 shows the development of the social marketing programme infrastructure between 1987 and 1996. As the table shows, accessibility to contraceptives has been greatly expanded by the social marketing programme.

The mass media campaign has also been somewhat strengthened in recent years, both through MPW and through massive advertising for the LHW Scheme. Messages have been somewhat more informative, and a national IEC strategy has recently been completed. Use of IEC materials in interpersonal communication, however, remains weak.

Knowledge of Contraception

As Table 6.5 shows, there has been a continuing increase in the proportion of women who have heard of at least one method of family planning; by 1995 that

---

[6] Preliminary evaluation of the VBFPW Scheme indicates that the VBFPWs have generally been properly recruited and placed, and that their relations with the community are satisfactory (MPW and Population Council 1996). Implementation of the programme has been associated with rapid increases in the CPR as documented in six VBFPW districts in Punjab and NWFP (MPW and Population Council 1997). However, there remain substantial problems in management and administration, and visitation rates appear low. Comparable evaluation of the newer LHW Scheme has not been undertaken, but early analysis indicates effective training and placement of the Lady Health Workers.

Table 6.8. Number of family planning service outlets by type, 1987–1996

Outlet type	1987	1996
Family Welfare Centres	1,275	1,344
Reproductive Health Service 'A' Centres	48	90
Mobile Service Units	7	131
Village Based Family Planning Workers	0	6,500
Health Department Outlets	1,390	5,910
Lady Health Workers	0	30,000
Health Outlets of other Line Departments	n.a.	433
Target Group Institutions	174	339
Registered Medical Practitioners	n.a.	14,152
Hakeems	156	7,694
Homeopaths	n.a.	3,544
Non-Governmental Organizations	393	582
Social Marketing Programme Sale Outlets	50,000	72,000

n.a.: not available.

Source: Planning Commission 1988 and 1993; personal communications from Ministry of Population Welfare and Ministry of Health.

figure had passed 90 per cent (Ministry of Population Welfare and Population Council 1995, hereinafter cited as PCPS 1994–95), and by 1997 had reached a level of 94 per cent (Hakim *et al.* 1998, hereinafter cited as PFFPS 1996–97).

Service Accessibility and Quality

Service availability increased during the 1990s, primarily through the placement of community family planning workers. Rural coverage, in particular, is rising rapidly, with now more than 40,000 VBFPWs and LHWs combined serving in rural communities. Expansion of the social marketing system has not yet taken full effect, but should provide another option, particularly for the urban population.[7]

Reduction in Opposition

While family planning is still not accepted in all quarters in Pakistan, there is clearly diminished opposition to programme activities. Although there is still little open

[7] Progress in service system development leaves considerable room for further improvement. Both the availability and quality of services remain deficient. In significant numbers of cases, centres are not open as scheduled, or personnel are not available, or supplies are not in place. When facilities are available, the quality of care provided has significant limitations (Cernada *et al.* 1993; MPW and Population Council 1996). Moreover, the programme is overwhelmingly oriented towards women. Neither services nor motivation are effectively targeted towards men and, despite the active cooperation of many husbands in family planning, male opposition sometimes prevents women who wish to use family planning from doing so (Bhatti and Hakim 1996; Population Council 1997).

support for family planning from religious leaders, whether among religious scholars or *imams*, there is clearly a visible reduction in opposition compared to the past.

Similarly, ideological opposition to family planning has decreased. The visible effects of population growth, coupled with disappointing progress in development, have made the equation of a large population with a strong country less tenable, and the end of the cold war, along with the acceptance of family planning through-out most of the Islamic world, has weakened the perception of family planning as an unwelcome innovation from outside. The 'population in development' position has been largely supplanted by the post-Cairo formulation of family planning within the framework of reproductive health and gender equity; but in arguing this case, its proponents are careful to stress the central position of family planning in service delivery.

Perhaps as a result of these trends, political élites and parties no longer criticize family planning. Political blackmailing of opponents for supporting the family planning programme has become a thing of the past. Recent years have also witnessed greater tolerance to the open advertisements and talks about family planning in the mass media (Hakim 1996). For example, a recently televised drama, *Jangal Pura,* is based around the activities of a Family Welfare Centre and discusses family planning issues with a breadth and openness that could not have been possible in the past.

Barring unanticipated changes in the balance of political power, it is unlikely that important political opposition will resurface in the foreseeable future. The plans for strengthening family planning in the Eighth Five-Year Plan were drawn up under a Pakistan Muslim League government, and were largely implemented under a People's Party government. The draft Ninth Five-Year Plan, under the new Pakistan Muslim League government, envisions further substantial expansion and strengthe-ning. The only significant opposition within the political system now comes from the Jamaat-i-Islami, which has been unable to gain significant parliamentary strength.

Emerging Demand for Family Planning

Levels of Demand

Earlier, we reviewed the demand for children and/or family planning, and found that, on the whole, most factors seemed to be operating to maintain a large-family norm. While change could be observed in some of these factors, it appears that by 1990, the changes were not sufficiently profound to have led to significantly increased demand for family planning. Has this situation changed in any essential way?

The series of national surveys suggests some change. Mean ideal family size, which was between 4.1 and 4.9 in the four surveys prior to 1994–95, was estimated at 3.4 children in the PCPS of 1994–95, and 3.5 in the PFFPS 1996–97. The propor-tion wanting no more children was measured at 52 per cent in the PCPS 1994–95 and 46 per cent in the PFFPS 1996–97, both substantially higher than the 36 per cent found in the PDHS of 1990–91.

It is more difficult to trace demand for family planning separately from demand for children. Since surveys have varied in the ways they dealt with interest in or approval of family planning, we were unable to obtain a consistent time series on this topic. Certainly, opposition to family planning has not disappeared.[8] Nonetheless, interviewers in recent national studies involving field research report a favourable change in interest in many communities in family planning.

Factors Explaining Increased Demand for Family Planning

What might account for a change in demand for children and/or family planning? We consider recent information on the demand factors cited previously.

The Growing Cost of Childbearing

After a long period of robust growth in the gross domestic product between 1965 and 1990, the 1990s have witnessed slowing growth accompanied by rising inflation. Field staff from NIPS and the Population Council are reporting a growing sense that rising prices have convinced a growing number of households that they cannot afford large families. This might be explained by changes in the perceived cost of children. Some signs suggest a fairly rapid increase in consumerism in forms that might be related to the demand for children, although in this regard the PCPS 1994–95 shows greater change than do the preliminary data from the 1996–97 PFFPS. For example, the proportion of households with electricity changed from 61 per cent in 1990–91 to 79 per cent in 1994–95, and to 70 per cent in 1996–97. Reported television ownership increased from 27 per cent in 1990–91 to 44 per cent in 1994–95, but declined to 38 per cent in 1996–97. (However, access to television increased considerably between the 1994–95 and 1996–97 surveys.) The proportion of primary school age children who are in school has risen from 14 per cent in 1961 to 75 per cent in 1996 (Hakim *et al.* 1998).

Social Change

This change in parents' understanding of the requirements of child rearing can be regarded as a cultural change as much as an economic one. In our view, two factors have been particularly important recently in facilitating this change. One is the

---

[8] Survey data consistently demonstrate significant reservations about family planning on religious grounds. For example, in the 1994–95 PCPS, 21 per cent of all never-users (who were 72 per cent of the whole sample) did not approve of family planning. When asked why they had never used, 20 per cent said family planning was contrary to their religion, and 12 per cent said it was because their husbands disapprove.

worldwide communications revolution. The rapid increase in access to television is augmented by the wider fare made available as a result of satellite dishes, as well as by the ready availability of foreign films on VCR. These have made a different view of life available, particularly in rural areas. Second, the replacement of the Zia regime by democratic forms of government has effectively reduced the government's support for traditional Islamic ways, and allowed for greater exposure to outside ideas. All Pakistani governments are Islamic according to the nature of the state, but recent governments have taken a broader view of what is permissible under Islam.

Exposure to Outside Ideas

Despite recent increases in access to media—television ownership and literacy, for example—it is not clear whether official IEC campaigns have had more effect in recent years than previously. Time series data on exposure to family planning messages are inadequate, but the proportion of women who have heard at least one family planning message through mass media seems about the same in 1994–95 as in 1975, and the proportion who have been contacted by a family planning worker has declined significantly. Moreover, the content of the mass media messages has always been limited to very general messages such as 'small family, happy family'. This may have begun to change, but too recently for any impact to be known. If the messages during the early 1990s were more effective, it is likely that this was because people were more ready to hear them than that they were more attractive or efficient.

Improved Health

While national morbidity data for the 1990s are not yet available, it is likely that the gradual increases in health utilization and declines in infant and child mortality have continued. Perceptions often lag behind reality, so perhaps there is a delayed response to the cumulative mortality declines in the past. However, those changes have not yet been so dramatic as to have been a major determinant of desired family size.

Increasing Educational Attainment

The 1994–95 PCPS and 1996–97 PFFPS show a continuing trend towards higher proportions of women and men with schooling. The proportion of married women of reproductive age with some education rose from 21 per cent in 1990–91 to 25 per cent in 1994–95 and 1996–97, and that of their husbands from 50 per cent to 57 and 59 per cent. This trend undoubtedly has had some effect on desired family size. However, similar increases between previous surveys were not associated with large effects on desired family size.

Thus, many of the trends expected to facilitate smaller family norms have continued to evolve in the 1990s in much the same way as in previous decades, without much effect on desired family size. It is our hypothesis that the shift in demand during the 1990s is primarily the result of a change in parents' perception of the costs of raising children properly. The reduction in desired family size, however, is far from revolutionary; small families have not yet become the norm in Pakistan.

Change in Behaviour

Contraceptive Prevalence

Table 6.7 shows contraceptive prevalence rates measured in national surveys between 1994–95 and 1996–97. Although the rates differ significantly (24.4 per cent in IEC 1994, 17.8 per cent for PCPS 1994–95, 23.9 per cent for the PFFPS in 1996–97), they all show major gains in contraceptive use since the PDHS of 1990–91, in all provinces and residence categories. Moreover, other surveys by both NIPS and the Population Council, although not conducted using national probability samples, have shown prevalence rates in the mid to high twenties. The impression in both organizations, whose staff are constantly involved in field research, is that the middle 1990s are seeing a rapid increase in the use of family planning in Pakistan (Hakim 1996; Hashmi *et al.* 1994; MPW and Population Council 1997; Population Council 1997). The preliminary estimates of the 1996–97 Pakistan Fertility and Family Planning Survey provide clear confirmation of this impression.

A substantial part of the growth of CPR in recent years has been in the use of withdrawal (MPW and Population Council 1996; PCPS 1994–95; PFFPS 1996–97; Population Council 1997). This suggests an increase in demand that is not being met with quality services for modern methods. Whether contraceptive use is contributing substantially to fertility limitation is not clear, but preliminary evidence is that use of withdrawal in Pakistan is fairly effective (MPW and Population Council 1997).

Despite the increase in contraceptive prevalence, there does not appear to be a reduction in unmet need for family planning. Although definitions used in different studies vary, unmet need during the 1990s does not appear to have fallen below 30 per cent, a high figure by international standards (PCPS 1994–95; PFFPS 1996–97; Population Council 1997). There remain many married women of reproductive age who want to know more about family planning and also would consider use of family planning methods if services were provided at their doorsteps (Hakim 1996).

Fertility

There is also some evidence of a clear decline in marital fertility. The Population and Family Planning Indicators (PFPI) survey of 1993, in a non-probability cluster sample, measured a TFR of 5.4, the PCPS 1994–95 estimates a TFR of 5.6, and the

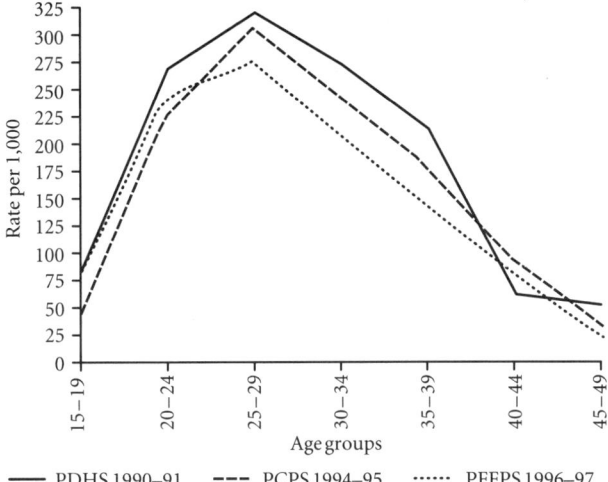

Figure 6.1. Age-specific fertility rates in Pakistan, PDHS 1990–91, PCPS 1994–95, and PFFPS 1996–97.

preliminary estimate from the PFFPS 1996–97 is 5.3. Analysis of the pattern of age-specific fertility rates from the major national surveys of 1990–91, 1994–95, and 1996–97, shown in Fig. 6.1, indicates a definite downward trend, concentrated in the ages 25–39, which is consistent with the increases in family planning use measured in the same surveys. Clear urban–rural differences in fertility, largely absent prior to 1990 (Hakim 1994), have begun to appear (Sathar 1993). However, difficulties in measuring fertility in Pakistan have not been solved in these surveys, and these fertility data cannot be taken to be definitive.

Whatever increases in family planning use or modest declines in fertility may be occurring, these changes are as yet of modest dimensions. A TFR of 5.3 in Pakistan remains much higher, for example, than the average of 3.7 for developing regions, or of 4.2 for South Asia. A CPR in the mid-twenties is still far below the levels achieved by Sri Lanka, Bangladesh, or India, or by other major Islamic countries (Hashmi 1993). Nevertheless, in the context of Pakistani history, even modest changes are noteworthy.

Continuing Constraints on Reproductive Change

While there have been changes in both the supply of and demand for family planning, which have led to significant recent increases in use, it is not clear that a momentum has been achieved, or that, once gained, it will automatically result in

small-family norms and universal family planning behaviour. Several major constraints to reproductive change must first be overcome:

- The demand for children remains high. Even with recent changes, at least half of
  women with three children want more, and only one-fourth of women with two
  children are ready to stop (MPW and Population Council 1995). Ideal family
  size is still well above three children with at least two sons
  (Hakim 1993, 1995; MPW and Population Council 1995). While spacing of children is practised to some degree, most couples start using family planning only
  when they already have a large number of children (Hakim 1993).
- The management of family planning programmes in the public sector remains
  weak, resulting in unnecessary limitations in coverage and poor quality of care.
  As yet, the contributions of NGOs, social marketing and the private sector have
  been limited. Until these new strategies are successfully implemented, effective
  access to quality family planning services will be limited.
- Even where services are available, public knowledge of methods is low, distrust
  is high, and service quality is suboptimal. Even current users of family planning
  have inadequate knowledge of the methods they are using (Cernada *et al.* 1993;
  MPW and Population Council 1996). Side effects are the main reason for dis-
  continuing modern temporary methods (PCPS 1994–1995) and are a major reason for continuing unmet need (Population Council 1997).

Conclusion

Between 1965 and 1990, family planning efforts in Pakistan were trapped in a
vicious cycle. Political constraints, fuelled by strong opposition from several quarters, led to inconsistent and often half-hearted family planning programme
implementation. Ineffective programmes coupled with weak demand led to low use
of family planning, which further encouraged opposition and demoralized programme workers. Although economic and social progress undoubtedly occurred,
little demographic change occurred.

During the 1990s, this vicious cycle appears to have been decisively broken. The
cumulative effect of past economic and social changes, coupled with the restoration
of democratic civilian government, has led to a substantial reduction in opposition
to family planning as well as to a clear, if as yet modest, reduction in desired family
size and an increase in the demand for family planning. Although improvements
in family planning service availability have yet to meet expectations, some such
improvement has occurred. Use of contraception, albeit still at modest levels,
doubled between 1990–91 and 1996–97. Finally, there is now evidence that marital
fertility has begun to fall as a direct result of voluntary use of family planning.

Pakistan's earlier family planning failure occurred not because of programmatic
inadequacies alone, or because of weak demand alone, but because of the concomitant effects of fragile demand and weak programme effort. Strong opposition to

family planning among the élite, coupled with weak demand for family planning among the population, convinced leaders that stronger efforts were not worthwhile.

By the 1990s, however, this dynamic was decisively broken. First, demand for family planning increased, as a result of economic and social changes that occurred in the late 1970s and 1980s. These changes fostered a latent demand for family planning, but, because of constraints on the programme that arose from the policies of the Zia-ul-Haq regime over the 1977–88 period, they led to little change in contraceptive practice.

Following President Zia's death in 1988, government commitment to family planning improved noticeably. Mass communication campaigns were launched, and substantial increases in financial allocations were instituted. These actions were undertaken in conjunction with new initiatives in family planning services. It is not clear, however, whether these initiatives have yet resulted in major improvements in family planning services; it appears that the changed dynamic of the 1990s is primarily demand-led rather than supply-led.

In any case, data from the 1996–97 PFFPS confirm earlier findings of substantially increased family planning demand and contraceptive use, along with a modest but definite reduction in fertility. Social and economic changes in Pakistan have generated a new and robust climate of demand for family planning; and political and administrative commitments have generated a new climate for sustained action. Taken together, the changed demand and changed supply context may foster rapid reproductive change in the coming decade.

This is not equivalent to saying that success is assured. However, an important change is taking place, even if we still do not know its full dimensions or its future. Family planning and fertility are starting to change, regardless of government programmes; but programmes may greatly speed up the process. At present, the demand for small families is not widespread, so we can expect, as in other countries, a gradual process rather than an explosion. But it is now clear that the process of reproductive change in Pakistan has at last begun, if only tentatively.

References

Abedin, Saleha Mahmood (1977), 'Islam and Muslim Fertility: Sociological Dimensions of a Demographic Dilemma', Ph.D. thesis, University of Pennsylvania.

Bhatti, Mansoor ul Hassan, and Hakim, Abdul (1986), 'Males' Attitudes and Motivation for Family Planning in Pakistan (first report)', Islamabad: National Institute of Population Studies.

Cernada, G. P., Rob, A. K. U., Ameen, S. I., and Ahmed, M. S. (1993), 'A Situation Analysis of Family Welfares Centres', ANEOR/TA Working Papers No. 4, Islamabad: The Population Council.

Curtis, Sian L., and Arnold, Fred (1994), 'An Evaluation of the Pakistan DHS Survey Based on the Reinterview Survey', Calverton, MD: Macro International Inc.

Family Planning Division (1969), 'Proposal of the Family Planning Division for Family Planning Sector During the Fourth Five Year Plan 1970–75', Islamabad: Family Planning Division.

Government of Pakistan (1965), 'Family Planning Scheme for Pakistan During the Third Five Year Plan Period 1965–70', Rawalpindi: Ministry of Health, Labour and Social Welfare.

Hakim, Abdul (1992), 'Fertility Control in the Context of the Family and Society in Pakistan', Ph.D. thesis, Australia National University.

—— (1993), 'Contraceptive Use in Pakistan: Variations and Determinants', *Pakistan Population Review*, Vol. 4, No. 1, Islamabad: National Institute of Population Studies.

—— (1994), 'Factors Affecting Fertility in Pakistan', *Pakistan Development Review*, Vol. 33, No. 4, Islamabad: Pakistan Institute of Development Economics.

—— (1995), 'Desire for More Children and Contraceptive Use in Pakistan', *Proceedings of the Eleventh Annual General Meeting*, Islamabad: Pakistan Institute of Development Economics.

—— (1996), 'Evaluation of IEC Components of the Population Welfare Programme of Pakistan', Islamabad: National Institute of Population Studies.

—— *et al.* (1998), 'Pakistan Fertility and Family Planning Survey', Islamabad: National Institute of Population Studies.

Hashmi, Sultan S. (1993), 'Fertility Trends and Family Planning in Selected Islamic Countries and Pakistan', *Pakistan Population Review*, Vol. 4, No. 1, Islamabad: National Institute of Population Studies.

Hashmi, S. S., Farouqui, M. N. I., and Hakim, Abdul (1994), 'Pakistan Family Planning Indicators: Results of the PCPS 1993', Islamabad: National Institute of Population Studies.

Hussain, Aftab (1987), *Status of Women in Islam*, Lahore: Law Publishing Company.

Inayatullah, Attiya (1992), 'Pakistan Population Explosion', *The Pakistan Times*, 15 May, p. 4.

Islami Nazariati Council (1984) (Islamic Ideological Council), Report: Khandani Mansuba-bandi (Family Planning), pp. 1–88, Islamabad: Islamic Nazariati Council.

Khan, Hameed Akhtar (1967), 'Islamic Opinion on Contraception: In Muslim Attitudes Towards Family Planning', pp. 62–71, New York: Population Council.

Maududi, S. Abu A'La (1982), Birth Control—Its Social, Political, Economic, Moral and Religious Aspects', Lahore: Islamic Publications.

Ministry of Population Welfare and Population Council (1995), 'Pakistan Contraceptive Prevalence Survey 1994–95: Basic Findings', Islamabad: Population Council.

—— (1996), 'A Situation Analysis of Village Based Family Planning Workers in Pakistan, 1995', Research Report No. 3, Islamabad: Population Council.

—— (1997), 'Initial Performance and Impact of Village Based Family Planning Workers in Four Districts of Punjab', Research Report No. 5, Islamabad: Population Council.

National Institute of Population Studies (1997), 'Population Growth and its Implications on Socio-Economic Development in Pakistan', Islamabad: National Institute of Population Studies.

National Institute of Population Studies and IRD/Macro International, Inc. (1992), *Pakistan Demographic and Health Survey 1990/91*, Columbia, MD: IRD/Macro International.

Planning Commission (1988), '7th Five Year Plan, 1988–93 and Prospective Plan 1988–2003', Vol. 2, Islamabad.

—— (1993), 'Eighth Five-Year Plan', Islamabad.

Population Council (1997), 'The Gap between Reproductive Intentions and Behaviour: A Study of Punjabi Men and Women', Islamabad: Population Council.

Population Planning Council of Pakistan (1976), Pakistan Fertility Survey: First Report, Islamabad.

Population Welfare Division (1981), 'Fifth Five-Year Plan: Population Welfare Planning Plan 1980–83', Islamabad: Population Division.

—— (1983), 'Population Welfare Programme: A Document on Sixth Five-Year Population Welfare Plan 1983–88', Islamabad: Population Welfare Division.

—— (1986), 'Pakistan Contraceptive Prevalence Survey 1984–85', Islamabad: Ministry of Planning and Development.

Robinson, W. C. (1978), 'Family Planning in Pakistan, 1955–77: A Review', *The Pakistan Development Review*, XVII: 233–47.

—— Shah, Makhdoom A., and Shah, Nasra M. (1981), 'Family Planning Programme in Pakistan: What Went Wrong?', *International Family Planning Perspectives*, 7(3): 85–92.

Rukanuddin, A. R., and Hardee-Cleaveland, K. (1992), 'Can Family Planning Succeed in Pakistan?', *International Family Planning Perspectives*, 18(3): 109–15.

Sathar, Zeba A. (1993), 'The Much-Awaited Fertility Decline in Pakistan: Wishful Thinking or Reality?', *International Family Planning Perspectives*, 19(4): 142–6.

—— and Casterline, John B. (1998), 'The Onset of Fertility Transition in Pakistan', *Population and Development Review*, 24(4): 773–96.

Stamper, Bruce Frederick Maxwell (1979), 'Demographic Consideration and Population Policies in Developing Countries: A Survey of Third World Countries with Case Studies of Bangladesh and Pakistan', Ph. D thesis, The London School of Economics and Political Science, London: University of London.

Training, Research, and Evaluation Centre (n.d) 'National Impact Survey Report', Lahore: Pakistan Population Planning Council.

World Bank (1983), Staff Appraisal Report, Pakistan Population Sector, Document of the World Bank, Report No. 4166-Pak., Washington, DC.

7 Trends in Fertility and Contraceptive Use in Bangladesh

JULIET MCEACHRAN AND IAN DIAMOND

Despite differing opinions about fertility levels in the past, there is now broad agreement that a major fertility decline has now occurred in Bangladesh. Because it lacked evidence of any of the traditional precursors of fertility transition, Bangladesh has become a country of increasing interest to demographers and to the managers of reproductive health programmes. This chapter examines trends in fertility and contraceptive use in Bangladesh over the last 20 years, and describes how these changes have been brought about.

Fertility Trends

Although Dyson, in this volume, provides fascinating indirect evidence of fertility trends in the early part of this century, the first direct evidence on fertility trends comes from the 1974 Bangladesh retrospective survey of fertility and mortality. The 1974 study found serious reporting errors and differential omissions of information by respondents. The omission of data on young children was particularly widespread, and the under-reporting of recent births gave a misleading impression of fertility decline.

This particular type of omission, which is not uncommon in retrospective surveys, makes the verification of recent fertility trends difficult. In the case of the 1974 survey, it was possible to reduce the effects of poor data quality by using Coale–Trussell models of fertility distribution. The results from the adjusted data led the report to conclude that there had been little fertility reduction as a result of family limitation within marriage, and that the corrected total fertility rate (TFR) in 1974 was around seven births per woman (Population Bureau, Ministry of Overseas Development, and Census Commission 1977).

Subsequent surveys in Bangladesh have suffered from similar problems of data quality. However, these problems have progressively diminished, and by 1990 there appears to be solid evidence of a fertility decline, which had begun in the early 1980s. In fact, the 1989 Bangladesh Fertility Survey (BFS) reported a TFR of under five births per woman. Because of data problems in this survey, the evidence it provided of a seemingly rapid decline in fertility in Bangladesh was initially accepted only with great caution, and with a certain disbelief in the speed at which

Table 7.1. Trends in annual total fertility rates, Bangladesh 1980–1993

Year	BFS 1989	CPS 1989	CPS 1991	BDHS 1993–94
1980	6.8	—	—	—
1981	6.7	—	—	—
1982	6.4	—	—	6.6
1983	6.1	—	—	6.2
1984	5.9	—	—	6.6
1985	5.5	—	5.1	6.3
1986	5.1	5.2	5.0	6.1
1987	4.8	5.0	4.9	5.6
1988	—	4.9	4.6	5.2
1989	—	—	4.3	4.9
1990	—	—	4.2	4.4
1991	—	—	—	3.8
1992	—	—	—	3.4
1993	—	—	—	3.3

— indicates data not available.

Source: BDHS 1993–94.

Note: Rates from the surveys are three-year moving averages except the most recent rate, which is based on a two-year average.

the decline appeared to have taken place. One reason for this was that few commentators believed that conditions in Bangladesh were conducive to fertility transition, given that, in most societies, fertility decline has usually been associated with changes in the economic and social value of children, increased literacy and a certain degree of socioeconomic development. Many commentators argued that such changes had not been apparent in Bangladesh.

Cleland *et al.* (1994) addressed the problems of data quality by embarking on a rigorous examination of data from a variety of sources—the 1989 BFS, the 1989 and 1991 Contraceptive Prevalence Surveys (CPS), and the 1993–94 Bangladesh Demographic and Health Survey (BDHS). The authors' conclusion, using a variety of demographic methods, was that a fertility decline had indeed occurred in Bangladesh. Table 7.1 provides a variety of estimates of trends in the TFR derived from these surveys. The total fertility rates are calculated from birth histories in the case of the BFS and from full birth histories in the BDHS. The 1989 CPS and 1991 CPS collected five- and seven-year truncated histories, respectively. There has been some discussion on the relative accuracy of birth as opposed to pregnancy histories. In general, one might expect less reliability in pregnancy histories. However, as Cleland (1996) points out, there is little evidence of any systematic bias, the more important considerations being the 'skills, training and supervision or field staff' (Cleland 1996: 446).

Table 7.2. Per cent of currently married women who were pregnant at the time of the survey

Age group	1975 BFS	1989 BFS	1991 CPS	1993–94 BDHS
15–19	15.2[a]	14.7[a]	19.6	17.1
20–24	15.5	13.3	16.2	13.0
25–29	14.9	10.4	11.2	9.0
30–34	11.2	8.3	7.1	7.0
35–39	10.7	4.8	4.2	2.7
40–44	u	u	1.5	0.8
45–49	u	u	0.2	0.0
Total	12.5	9.3	10.7	8.7

u = unknown (not available).
[a] Currently married women less than 20 years old.
Source: BDHS 1993–94.

The age-specific data in Table 7.1 are sensitive to recall error and to the omission or displacement of births. Examination of the BDHS did not find any evidence of the systematic omission or displacement of births, although the authors admit that the existence of such problems in a random manner would be difficult to detect. However, if under-reporting is culturally widespread, while current TFRs may be underestimates, if it is assumed that under-reporting in previous surveys was of a similar degree, a rapid decline in fertility can be seen (BDHS 1993–94).

Table 7.1 clearly illustrates the difficulty in obtaining an absolute figure for a TFR, rather than a range in which it is believed to fall. For the years in which it is possible to calculate more than one TFR, measures from different sources vary considerably. For example, Cleland *et al.* (1994) concluded that fertility in Bangladesh in 1988 lay somewhere between 4.6 and 5.5 births per woman, and the TFR from the 1993–94 BDHS for this year is within that range. Despite the problems of data quality, Table 7.1 shows a marked decline in fertility between 1980 and 1993, with an acceleration of the decline in the more recent years, as the rate dropped from 4.4 in 1990 to 3.3 in 1993. These figures are annual rates, even though the three-year moving averages of 4.3 in 1989–91 and 3.4 in 1991–93 are the rates more commonly quoted in the literature.

Another indicator that is not prone to the type of data recall errors observed in fertility rates, is the proportion of women pregnant at the time of the survey. This measure has the additional advantage of being totally independent of other conventional fertility measures in terms of data requirements. Although it is likely that this measure may also be somewhat under-reported, due to women's shyness or a possible lack of awareness that they are pregnant, these biases are unlikely to vary a great deal over time.

Table 7.3. Total fertility rate among women aged 15–49, by education and residence

Category	TFR	% of women in each category
Total	*3.4*	*100.0*
Residence		
Urban	2.7	11.5
Rural	3.5	88.5
Education		
None	3.8	58.1
Primary incomplete	3.4	17.4
Primary complete	3.3	9.6
Secondary/higher	2.6	14.9

Source: BDHS 1993–94.

Table 7.2 indicates a decline over time in the proportion of women who are pregnant at the time of the survey, going from 12.5 per cent in 1975 to 8.7 per cent in 1993–94 among all women aged 15–49. However, there are fluctuations in this measure, and it is unclear whether these are real or due to misreporting. One consistent trend observable in Table 7.2 is the decline in the proportion of women in the older age ranges who are currently pregnant: 11.2 per cent of those aged 30–34 in 1975 compared to 7.0 per cent in 1993–94; and 10.7 and 2.7 per cent, respectively, among women aged 35–39. This evidence is consistent with the theory of fertility decline that older women are the first to reduce their fertility.

Table 7.3 illustrates variations in fertility among women resident in different areas and from different educational backgrounds. Lower fertility levels can be seen to be related to urban residence and increased education. While current fertility rates for women with secondary education are 33 per cent lower than those for women with no education, relative to rates in the 1970s, the measures for 1993–94 indicate that the fertility decline in Bangladesh has occurred across all residential and education divisions.

Proximate Determinants of Fertility

The evidence presented above indicates that a fertility decline has taken place in Bangladesh in the past 20 years. How did it occur? The Bongaarts framework (Bongaarts 1982) argues that socioeconomic factors influence fertility through a set of intermediate (or proximate) determinants: exposure to sexual intercourse,

Table 7.4. Trends in the proportion of women never married

Age group	BFS 1975	CPS 1983	CPS 1985	BFS 1989	CPS 1989	CPS 1991	BDHS 1993–94
10–14	91.2	98.0	98.7	96.2	96.4	98.5	95.2
15–19	29.8	34.2	47.5	49.0	45.8	46.7	50.5
20–24	4.6	4.0	7.1	12.0	9.3	12.3	12.4
25–29	1.0	0.7	1.0	2.3	1.6	2.8	2.2
30–34	0.2	0.4	0.1	0.3	0.5	0.5	0.3
35–39	0.4	—	—	0.1	0.5	0.1	0.3
40–44	0.1	0.1	—	0.2	0.2	0.3	0.7
45–49	0.0	0.1	—	0.1	0.1	—	0.2

— indicates less than 0.1%.
Source: BDHS 1993–94.

postpartum infecundity, induced abortion and contraception. Each of these are considered in turn.

Exposure to Sexual Intercourse

In the case of Bangladesh, the proxy for exposure to sexual relations is marriage. Data from the 1993–94 BDHS indicate the universality of marriage, among women aged 30 and over (99 per cent currently or previously married). However, it is early marriage that has had a major impact on childbearing. Table 7.4 indicates that there has been little change over time in the proportion of women getting married— 99 per cent among women aged 30–34 in both 1975 and 1993–94. However, there is evidence of an increase in age at marriage, as indicated by increases in the proportion of women who have never married. For example, only 4.6 per cent of women aged 20–24 in 1975 had never been married, compared to 12.4 per cent in 1993–94.

Postpartum Infecundity (Lactational Amenorrhoea)

The proxy for the measurement of postpartum infecundity is duration of breast-feeding. Breastfeeding has been found to postpone the resumption of menses and ovulation in the postpartum period. The relationship between the two is robust, and breastfeeding is much easier to measure than the resumption of ovulation. Bangladesh has a history of prolonged breastfeeding and there is little evidence of a substantial decline in recent years (see Table 7.5). However, although the duration of breastfeeding has changed little since 1975, there is evidence of a decline in the duration of postpartum amenorrhoea during this time (Weis 1993). The impact of breastfeeding on the suppression of fecundity has been found to be closely associated with suckling behaviour—the frequency, duration and intensity of suckling

Table 7.5. Duration of breastfeeding and postpartum amenorrhoea (months)

	Mean duration of breastfeeding[a]	Mean duration of postpartum amenorrhoea
1975 BFS[b]	28.9	14.6
1989 BFS[b]	28.6	12.4
1993–94 BDHS[c]	27.6	11.5

[a] The prevalence–incidence mean is borrowed from epidemiology, and is defined as the number of children whose mothers are breastfeeding (prevalence) divided by the average number of births per month (incidence).
[b] *Source*: Cleland *et al.* (1994).
[c] *Source*: BDHS 1993–94.

impacting on the maintenance of, or reduction in, postpartum amenorrhoea. The reduction in the duration of postpartum amenorrhoea in Bangladesh is likely to be due to changes in infant feeding practices, specifically, the earlier introduction of breastfeeding supplements.

While it may be true to say that the impact of lactational amenorrhoea on fertility levels in Bangladesh is declining, this factor still exerts a major impact on the fertility levels.

Abortion

Accurate data on abortion are notoriously difficult to obtain, especially in countries where the procedure is illegal. In Bangladesh, menstrual regulation up to eight weeks gestation has been available since the mid-1970s, despite the fact that abortion is illegal.

Cleland *et al.* (1994) examined the effect of abortion on fertility decline in Bangladesh in 1989, and concluded, based on the available evidence, that it reduced the TFR by around 5 per cent—a relatively small effect. Our analysis of the effect of abortion on fertility, shown in Table 7.6, is based on data from the 1993–94 BDHS.[1]

The specific purpose of the Abortion Frequency Survey (AFS) in Matlab was to obtain a more accurate estimate of induced abortion in Bangladesh. Using these data, Johnston (1998) compared the AFS results with data from two other studies covering similar time periods. The AFS found a relatively high annual rate—23.6 abortions per 1,000 women aged 15–49 in 1997—a level over five times higher than

[1] The 1993–94 figures are calculated using the same method as Cleland *et al.* (1994). The calculation of the impact of contraception uses the method-effectiveness rates listed in Johnston and Hill (1996), and the 1993–94 abortion values are calculated from the values for the other determinants. For additional discussion of this method, see Johnston and Hill (1996).

Table 7.6. Percentage reduction in fertility attributable to proximate determinants

	1975[a]	1989[a]	1993–94
Marriage	19	14	12.9
Lactational infecundity			
Definition A	51	51	48.5
Definition B	40	35	33
Abortion	2	5	
Definition A			19.8
Definition B			39.4
Contraception	7	29	38.2
Implied TFR			3.4
Definition A	5.5	4.3	
Definition B	6.8	5.8	

[a] Cleland *et al.* (1994).

Note: In the case of the 1993–94 data, two different figures are given for the impact of abortion. This is due to the fact that the measure is derived from the Bongaarts equation, a single estimate is given for each of the C_i values.

that obtained from the prospective Demographic Longitudinal Surveillance System in Matlab. Johnston also compared the AFS rate to the national rates of countries with provider registration systems,[2] and concluded that while the AFS value is high, it is not unusual when compared to those of other developing countries.

Provider-based figures for Bangladesh give an annual abortion rate of only 3.4 per 1,000 women (Johnston 1998). Exploring this large gap between the AFS results and the data from the providers of menstrual regulation, Johnston (1997) concludes that many Bangladeshi women go to non-authorized providers, who often perform unsafe abortions, despite the fact that they can obtain free and safe menstrual regulation services from authorized government providers. The main reasons for their not using government services were the poor quality of care, especially in terms of personal privacy, and the high fees charged for the operation.

Although more reliable data on abortion in Bangladesh are certainly needed, even from current estimates it nevertheless appears that abortion exerts a significant impact on national fertility levels. However, a cautionary note is necessary concerning these estimates. The calculations assume that the effects of fecundability, natural sterility and intrauterine mortality are minimal. In addition, the estimates are very

---

[2] Provider registration systems are available from countries where legal services are available. In the case of Bangladesh, menstrual regulation is available up to eight weeks gestation.

Figure 7.1. Trends in current contraceptive use, Bangladesh, 1975–93.

sensitive to the values of the other proximate determinants. However, similar estimates based on data from 1993–94 appear to show that abortion has an increasingly large impact on fertility levels.

Contraception

Between 1975 and 1993–94, the use of any method of contraception increased from 7.7 per cent of ever-married women aged 10–49, to 44.6 per cent. Most of this increase is accounted for by the use of modern methods of contraception, an increase from 5.0 per cent in 1975 to 36.2 per cent in 1993–94 (see Fig. 7.1). The fertility-reducing effect of contraceptive use was found by Cleland *et al.* (1994) to be 29 per cent in 1989, an increase from 7 per cent in 1975. We found that by 1993–94, this proportion had risen even higher—to 38 per cent (see Table 7.6).

Two key features of the Bangladesh family planning programme can probably account for its relatively strong impact on the fertility level: a high degree of government commitment; and an acute awareness of potential barriers to contraceptive use combined with attempts to lower these obstacles (see also Hakim and Miller, Chapter 6; and Robinson, Chapter 16 in this volume). Strong government commitment has been successful in maintaining the momentum and motivation of the family planning programme. Barriers to use, especially in a society in which many women live under conditions of purdah, have been lowered by providing women with family planning services where they are most convenient for the user. Most couples live within five miles of a service delivery point, and a network of village workers also visit women and men in their homes. Pills and condoms are available

Table 7.7. Knowledge of contraceptive methods among currently married women aged 10–49

	District					Residence	
	Barisal	Chittagong	Dhaka	Khulna	Rajshahi	Urban	Rural
Knows any method	100	99.3	100	100	99.8	99.9	99.7
Mean no. of methods known	7.2	6.4	7.0	7.2	7.1	7.2	6.9
Mean no. of modern methods known	5.8	5.3	5.6	5.8	5.7	5.7	5.6
Knows source for a modern method	99.4	94.8	99.0	99.7	99.1	99.2	97.9
% of women visited by fieldworker in previous six months[a]	41.1	29.3	34.9	49.2	43.9	41.8	37.3

[a] Fieldworker visited either to give a talk about family planning or to give a method.

Source: BDHS 1993–94.

free through the village workers and subsidized pills and condoms are available through the commercial sector. In addition, societal and cultural barriers to use have been minimized by the active inclusion of community and religious leaders by the family planning programme.

The impact of the Bangladesh family planning programme can also be seen in the high level of knowledge of contraceptive methods that exists, and the relatively frequent contact women report having with fieldworkers (see Table 7.7). Knowledge of methods varies little among districts, or by urban or rural residence. The success of the programme can be seen in the high number of contraceptive methods known by the various population groups. Many women know where to obtain a modern method, and more than one-third in every district except Chittagong had had contact with a fieldworker in the six months before the survey. Added to the TFRs of 2.7 and 3.5 in urban and rural areas, respectively, shown in Table 7.3, the data in Table 7.7 provide further evidence that the family planning programme of Bangladesh has not simply limited its services to the more accessible urban areas.

Contraceptive Trends

Since 1983 the use of any method of contraception has more than doubled and the use of modern methods has increased by nearly three times (see Table 7.8). Modern methods currently account for 80 per cent of total method use in Bangladesh, with the pill accounting for a total of 40 per cent. The pill has increased steadily in prevalence, becoming the most commonly used method at the end of the 1980s. Although

Table 7.8. Trends in current use of family planning methods among currently married women aged 10–49

Method	1975 BFS	1983 CPS	1985 CPS	1989 CPS	1989 BFS	1991 CPS	1993–94 BDHS
Any method	7.7	19.1	25.3	31.4	30.8	39.9	44.6
Any modern method	5.0	13.8	18.4	24.4	23.2	31.2	36.2
Pill	2.7	3.3	5.1	9.1	9.6	13.9	17.4
IUD	0.5	1.0	1.4	1.7	1.4	1.8	2.2
Injection	u	0.2	0.5	1.1	0.6	2.6	4.5
Vaginal methods	0.0	0.3	0.2	0.2	0.1	u	u
Condom	0.7	1.5	1.8	1.9	1.8	2.5	3.0
Female sterilization	0.6	6.2	7.9	9.0	8.5	9.1	8.1
Male sterilization	0.5	1.2	1.5	1.5	1.2	1.2	1.1
Any traditional method	2.7	5.4	6.9	7.0	7.6	8.7	8.4
Periodic abstinence	0.9	2.4	3.8	3.8	4.0	4.7	4.8
Withdrawal	0.5	1.3	0.9	1.2	1.8	2.0	2.5
Other traditional methods	1.3	1.8	2.2	2.0	1.8	2.0	1.1
N	u	7,662	7,822	9,318	10,907	9,745	8,980

u = unknown (no information).

Source: 1993–94 DHS.

initially popular, reliance on female sterilization declined in the late 1980s, due to a reduction in outside donor support for a programme that was then offering women remuneration for undergoing sterilization. Because few female sterilizations were carried out in the 1990s, the current level of prevalence consists primarily of women who underwent the procedure in the past (Steele and Diamond 1999).

The use of traditional methods has also increased over time, from 2.7 per cent in 1975 to 8.4 per cent in 1993–94. Periodic abstinence is the most commonly used traditional method, and appears to be the second most popular contraceptive method, in Bangladesh at the present time (that is, if female sterilization is excluded for the reasons described above). However, relative to the pill, all other contraceptive methods, including periodic abstinence, represent only a small proportion of total contraceptive use.

Despite widespread knowledge of contraceptive methods and near universal access to methods, rates of current contraceptive use vary quite widely across the country (see Table 7.9). Current use of any method ranges from 23.4 per cent in Chittagong to 54.8 per cent in Rajshahi, and variation in the use of modern methods is even greater. Contraceptive use among urban women is 10 per cent higher than among rural women. The use of the pill increases with increasing education, while injectable use appears to have an inverse relationship with education.

Table 7.9. Current use of family planning among currently married women aged 10–49, by background characteristics (1993–1994)

	Urban	Rural	None	Primary incomplete	Primary complete	Secondary/ higher	Barisal	Chittagong	Dhaka	Khulna	Rajshahi
Any method	54.4	44.6	41.0	45.5	45.6	56.1	47.7	29.3	44.3	55.3	54.8
Modern method	44.6	35.1	34.3	36.8	34.1	43.9	37.8	23.4	36.3	42.8	45.9
Pill	20.9	16.9	14.7	19.0	19.8	23.8	18.2	9.1	18.2	20.1	23.5
IUD	3.7	2.0	1.5	2.6	2.5	3.9	2.4	2.0	1.9	3.1	2.1
Injection	4.4	4.5	5.0	4.9	3.6	2.7	4.7	4.4	4.4	5.4	4.2
Condom	8.3	2.3	1.2	2.4	4.0	9.7	2.8	2.1	3.0	4.4	3.3
Female sterilization	6.4	8.3	10.4	6.9	4.0	3.5	8.2	5.5	8.2	8.5	10.4
Male sterilization	0.7	1.1	1.5	0.9	0.3	0.4	1.4	0.3	0.7	1.3	2.3
Traditional method	9.8	8.2	6.7	8.7	11.4	12.1	10.0	5.9	8.0	12.5	8.9
Periodic abstinence	5.5	4.8	3.9	5.6	6.7	6.2	5.1	3.3	4.6	7.1	5.5
Withdrawal	3.8	2.3	1.4	2.3	4.0	5.4	3.0	1.6	2.4	4.3	2.3

Source: BDHS 1993–94.

Diamond *et al.* (1997) examined spatial variations in contraceptive use, using a multilevel approach to examine individual, community and district level influences. At the individual level, the use of a modern method was highest among women aged 20–30 and those with a higher educational level. Women who were permitted to go out alone or who demonstrated a high level of autonomy[3] were also found to be more likely to be using a modern method. However, contraceptive use was found to be relatively similar in urban and rural areas.

At the community level, access to the thana headquarters and visits by the family planning worker were both found to be important correlates of modern method use. The study found that while some individual and community variables were important predictors of use, much unexplained community and district level variation in use requires further investigation.

Spatial variations in contraceptive use were also studied by Amin *et al.* (1997), using data from the 1989 BFS. The authors found that, while religious strength[4] did not predict contraceptive use at the individual level, at the district level it was an important predictor. Districts in which religion was very strong showed relatively lower levels of contraceptive use, particularly of modern reversible methods and sterilization. The authors suggest that this finding could be due to problems recruiting women fieldworkers in highly religious areas, and to the fact that, once recruited, these workers often have difficulty moving around freely. The results of this study are also supported by early work by Caldwell (1980), who showed that district literacy was an important predictor of contraceptive use in Bangladesh, and thus argued that mass education was a precursor for the uptake of contraception.

Unmet Need

A high level of unmet need for family planning still exists in Bangladesh. Unmet need is defined as the proportion of currently married fecund women who say they do not want any more children, or that they want to wait two or more years before having another child, but who are not using any method of contraception. The 1993–94 BDHS found that 19 per cent of currently married women had an unmet need for family planning. Levels of unmet need vary across the country, with the highest level found in Chittagong—27.2 per cent—and the lowest in Khulna—13.7 per cent (BDHS 1993–94). At the national level, total demand for family planning services was at 65 per cent of currently married women—45 per cent, current users, and 20 per cent, having an unmet need either for spacing or limiting.

As unmet need is defined in terms of a woman's current status, it is not clear what happens to these women after the survey. Will they adopt a contraceptive

[3] For this analysis, two indicators of autonomy, based on responses to direct questions in the 1989 BFS, were used. The third indicator used was whether or not a woman works for cash.

[4] At the individual level, the religiosity variable was divided into three: strict Muslim (those who pray every day), non-strict Muslim (those who pray less frequently) and Hindu. At the district level, religiosity was measured as the proportion of Muslim women who report praying every day.

Table 7.10. Contraceptive discontinuation rates

Method	12 month discontinuation rate	Mean duration of use	Number of segments of use
Pill	44.6	15.9	3,217
IUD	37.5	19.0	365
Injection	57.2	11.2	794
Condom	72.1	4.5	778
Traditional methods	47.6	13.4	1,302
Total[a]	47.7	13.3	6,670
Total[b]	49.4	12.3	6,456

[a] All methods.
[b] All reversible methods.

method, or will they experience an unplanned pregnancy? The level of unplanned pregnancy is measured by comparing actual TFRs with total wanted fertility rates. In this calculation, unwanted births are excluded from the numerator. The BDHS found a total wanted fertility rate of 2.1 in 1993–94, compared to a TFR of 3.4. This gap between wanted and actual fertility indicates that although the family planning programme has been successful, there remain areas in which it can be improved.

Contraceptive Discontinuation Rates

With the increased maturation of family planning programmes, it is not sufficient to use impact indicators that are primarily output measures, such as number of new acceptors and couple-years of protection. What increasingly needs to be examined is the quality of care that clients receive and their reproductive behaviour after they leave the clinic. On a national level, discontinuation rates and contraceptive switching levels can provide information on the reliability and effectiveness of contraceptive method use, and these are likely to have an increased impact on fertility levels in the future.

The collection of calendar data on contraceptive use allows contraceptive use dynamics to be investigated in the population as a whole, rather than among specific groups, such as the participants in small-scale studies of clinic patients. Because of the specialized nature of these studies, the findings are limited in their applicability to other population groups (Jejeebhoy 1991).

Mitra and Al-Sabir (1997) have examined contraceptive discontinuation in Bangladesh, and some of their findings are presented in Tables 7.10 and 7.11 (Mitra and Al-Sabir 1997). These data are similar to those reported for the late 1980s by Ali and Cleland (1995). Table 7.10 reveals that the discontinuation of reversible methods is high in Bangladesh, with nearly 50 per cent of women stopping the use of a reversible contraceptive method within a year. IUDs have the lowest discontinuation rate,

Table 7.11. First-year contraceptive discontinuation rates

Method	Reason for discontinuation				
	Method failure	To become pregnant	Side effects/ health concerns	All other reasons	All reasons
Pill	1.7	7.1	25.6	10.6	45.0
IUD	0.3	1.8	29.9	5.1	37.1
Injectable	1.1	4.8	40.0	11.7	57.6
Condom	5.9	13.6	13.8	38.8	72.0
Periodic abstinence	8.6	12.3	2.0	21.8	44.7
Withdrawal	8.8	11.5	5.4	29.3	55.0
Other	16.5	3.2	9.1	17.7	46.6
Total	3.5	7.7	20.8	15.8	47.8

Source: BDHS 1993–94.

and condoms, the highest. Table 7.11 shows the reasons for discontinuation by method. Side effects are the main reason for discontinuation among users of the pill, the injectable, and the IUD. Condoms, periodic abstinence, and withdrawal are primarily discontinued for 'other' reasons.

Explaining Fertility Decline in Bangladesh

The fact that Bangladesh has remained one of the poorest countries in the world throughout the entire period of its fertility transition has raised questions about the driving force of this decline. That is, what was it that led couples in Bangladesh to want to reduce their fertility levels, and to adopt contraceptive methods to achieve this.

In 1993, Cleland and Thomas debated the necessary conditions for fertility decline. Thomas argued that fertility would remain high in a society until children ceased to be a source of parental security in times of hardship. Cleland, on the other hand, argues that economic considerations are relatively unimportant to reproductive motivations. He asserts that while improvements in economic and social conditions can aid fertility decline, these are not prerequisites. In populations with historically high mortality rates, a woman would bear around seven children, but an average of only two or three would survive to adulthood. Thus, as mortality conditions improve, adaptation to lower fertility is a reaction to the improved survival of children rather than to a change in their economic value. Cleland also points out that fertility declines in Western Europe occurred before extra-familial mechanisms for insurance against risk were in place (Cleland 1993).

Cleland *et al.* (1994) offer additional evidence to support the fact that certain social and economic conditions are not essential for fertility decline to occur. In Bangladesh, the continuing existence of the following factors—even at the start of the fertility decline—supports this argument: infant and child mortality levels were still high; living standards had not increased markedly; levels of schooling had increased, but at a modest rate; and female age at marriage had increased by only a small amount. These last two measures are commonly used as proxies of women's status—the accurate measurement of which is fraught with difficulty. Balk (1994) points out that commentators are sometimes unaware that while examining 'women's status', they may well be comparing identically named variables that are actually measuring very different entities.

In Bangladesh, additional improvements in women's status are likely to be brought about through the spread of micro-credit organizations. Studies have found that the beneficial impact of these organizations accrues not only directly, to members, but also indirectly, to members of the community in which the programmes operate (Amin *et al.* 1996). Assessing the impact of these organizations on women's status, national fertility levels and trends, and the determinants of the initial fertility decline in Bangladesh, is beyond the scope of this paper. That topic is covered in greater depth elsewhere in this volume (see Hakim and Miller, Chapter 6; Hadi *et al.*, Chapter 12; and Robinson, Chapter 16). Suffice it to say that the fertility decline in Bangladesh is not related to improvements in the level of female schooling, the more commonly used socioeconomic proxy for women's status.

In their study of the relationship between the human development index (HDI)[5] and the fertility transition, Bongaarts and Watkins (1996) have further contested dependence on socioeconomic explanations of fertility decline. The authors, using data from 69 developing countries, found that the development level at the time of the onset of fertility transition, as measured by the HDI, has declined over time. If Bangladesh had waited until it had attained the development level of Hong Kong or Singapore for its fertility transition to occur, the fertility decline is unlikely to have started before the next century.

Cleland *et al.* (1994) have argued that it is ideational change that has brought about the decline in fertility in Bangladesh. Ideational change, according to these authors, creates a national climate of acceptance of fertility regulation, and thus radically changes the societal, economic and psychological context within which the individual can gain access to contraceptive services and regulate his or her childbearing.

Conclusion

While Bangladesh has experienced fertility decline under socioeconomic and cultural circumstances that most commentators would not have predicted as

[5] The HDI is a linear function of life expectancy, literacy and GNP per capita.

conducive to decline, there are still aspects of the current situation that require attention and action. The existing family planning programme needs further strengthening in order to reduce the level of unmet need, currently at 20 per cent. The dominance of the pill as the primary vehicle for the reduction of fertility in Bangladesh should be examined. Finally, since an individual's contraceptive behaviour in terms of continuation rather than adoption is likely to play an increasingly dominant role in fertility levels in Bangladesh, the quality of care provided to clients has to be examined to ensure that if they so wish, individuals are able to switch methods easily, rather than discontinue use completely.

References

Ali, M., and Cleland, J. (1995), 'Contraceptive Discontinuation in Six Developing Countries: A Cause Specific Analysis', *International Family Planning Perspectives*, 21(3): 92–7.

Amin, R., Li Yiping, and Ahmed Ashrad (1996), 'Women's Credit Programs and Family Planning in Rural Bangladesh', *Studies in Family Planning*, 22: 158–62.

Amin, S., Diamond, I., and Steele, F. (1997), 'Contraception and Religiosity in Bangladesh', in G. Jones, R. Douglas, J. Caldwell and R. D'Souza (eds.), *The Continuing Demographic Transition*, Oxford: Oxford University Press, 268–89.

Balk, D. (1994), 'Individual and Community Aspects of Women's Status and Fertility in Rural Bangladesh', *Population Studies*, 48: 21–45.

Bongaarts, J. (1982), 'The Fertility Inhibiting Effects of the Intermediate Fertility Variables', *Studies in Family Planning*, 13(6–7): 179–89.

—— and Amin, S. (1997), 'Prospects for Fertility Decline and Implications for Population Growth in South Asia', Research Division Working Paper No. 94, New York: Population Council.

—— and Watkins, S. C. (1996), 'Social Interactions and Contemporary Fertility Transitions', *Population and Development Review*, 22(4): 639–982.

Caldwell, J. C. (1980), 'Mass Education as a Determinant of the Timing of Fertility Decline', *Population and Development Review*, 6(2): 553–77.

Cleland, J. (1993), 'Equity, Security and Fertility: A Reaction to Thomas', *Population Studies*, 47(3): 345–52.

—— (1996), 'Demographic Data Collection in Less Developed Countries', *Population Studies*, 50(3): 433–50.

—— Phillips, J. F., Amin, S., and Kamal, G. M. (1994), *The Determinants of Reproductive Change in Bangladesh. Success in a Challenging Environment*, Washington, DC: World Bank (World Bank Regional and Sectoral Studies).

Diamond, I., Tonkin, P., Rahman, A. P. M., and Noor, A. (1997), 'Spatial Variation in Contraceptive Method Use in Bangladesh', In A. Kantner, A. Al-Sabir and N. Chakraborty (eds.), *Bangladesh Demographic and Health Survey Extended Analysis*, Dhaka: NIPORT, pp. 136–57.

Huq, N., and Cleland, J. (1990), *Bangladesh Fertility Survey 1989 (Main Report)*, Dhaka: National Institute of Population Research and Training.

Jejeebhoy, S. (1991), 'Measuring Contraceptive Use-Failure and Continuation: An Overview of New Approaches', in *Measuring the Dynamics of Contraceptive Use*, New York: United Nations.

Johnston, H. B. (1997), 'Induced Abortion: Users and Providers in Rural Bangladesh', Paper presented at the 4th Canadian Conference on International Health, Ottawa, 1997.

—— (1998), 'Measuring Induced Abortion: Integrating Qualitative with Quantitative Research Techniques', Paper presented at the Annual Meeting of the Population Association of America, Chicago, 1998.

—— and Hill, K. H. (1996), 'Induced Abortion in the Developing World: Indirect Estimates', *International Family Planning Perspectives*, 22: 108–14, 137.

Mitra, S. N., and Al-Sabir, A. (1996), Contraceptive Use Dynamics in Bangladesh. Demographic and Health Surveys Working Papers No. 21, Macro International Inc.

—— Ali, M. N., Islam, S., Cross, A. R., and Shah, T. (1994), *Bangladesh Demographic and Health Survey 1993–1994*, Calverton, Maryland: National Institute of Population Research and Training (NIPORT), Mitra and Associates, and Macro International Inc.

Report of the 1974 Bangladesh Retrospective Survey of Fertility and Mortality, 1977 Population Bureau, Ministry of Overseas Development, London and Census Commission, Statistics Division, Ministry of Planning, Dacca.

Salway, S. (1996), 'Contraception Following Childbirth in Bangladesh', Ph.D. thesis, London School of Hygiene and Tropical Medicine.

Steele, F., and Diamond, I. (1999), 'Contraceptive Switching in Bangladesh', *Studies in Family Planning*, 30(4): 315–28.

Thomas, N. (1993), 'Economic Security, Culture and Fertility: A Reply to Cleland', *Population Studies*, 47(3): 353–9.

Weis, P. (1993), 'The Contraceptive Potential of Breastfeeding in Bangladesh', *Studies in Family Planning*, 24(2): 100–8.

Part II

Explanations

8 A Cross-Border Comparison of Reproductive Behaviour among the Punjabi and Bengali Communities of South Asia

B. M. RAMESH

Introduction

The Indian subcontinent is often called an 'ethnological museum' because of its huge variety of races, religions and languages. An ethnic group may be defined as a population living in a contiguous geographical area, sharing common history, language, religion and a host of cultural traits including family, marriage, dress and food habits. Language is usually the most important factor defining ethnicity since people speaking the same language but living in different geographical locations or professing different religions are often observed to possess similar cultural traits. For instance, very little or no difference in culture is observed between the Punjabi-speaking populations in Punjab and South India, or between Punjabi-speaking Hindus and Punjabi-speaking Sikhs. Thus, an ethnic group is very often identified in terms of the language it speaks, rather than its geographical location or religion.

Language and ethnicity are also considered important determinants of fertility and contraceptive behaviour, and differences in these factors across communities are often attributed to language and ethnic differences. However, do communities of different nationalities, but living in geographically contiguous areas and sharing the same history, language and culture, behave in similar fashions, or do they behave differently? In other words, what would be the similarities and dissimilarities in reproductive behaviour of a common ethnic group living in two different national settings?

A comparison of a similar ethnic group living on two sides of a national border might also help us to understand the relative importance in determining the level and pattern of fertility transition attributable to culture and ethnicity as compared to the influence of a country's national family planning programme and of possible other regional characteristics.

Conventional explanations of fertility decline, linking culture and various aspects of socioeconomic development, often seem inadequate in explaining the rapid fertility declines observed in Bangladesh and India over the last two or three decades. The degree of commitment to the goal of fertility reduction on the part of the national and local governments, and the efficiency with which health and family planning programmes are implemented, seem to override the effects on increased contraceptive use—and the resultant reduction in fertility—exerted by culture and by socioeconomic development.

Data from a number of recent demographic surveys in Bangladesh, India and Pakistan provide ample scope for analysing the role of ethnicity in explaining fertility transition across national borders. A comparison of the experience of the Punjabi-speaking population of India with that of the Punjabi-speaking population of Pakistan, and a comparison of the experience of the Bengali-speaking population of India with that of the Bengali-speaking population of Bangladesh can be particularly useful on several grounds:

1. Each of the Punjab areas (the state of Punjab in India and Punjab province in Pakistan) and each of the Bengals (the state of West Bengal in India and the Republic of Bangladesh) used to be a single province prior to 1947. Each of the two paired areas also shared a heritage of similar language, institutions, economies and peoples (though not religion).
2. Bangladesh, India and Pakistan differ considerably in terms of their national family planning programmes and strategies.
3. The effects of differences in family planning strategies can therefore be seen more readily by comparing similar ethnic groups across borders than by comparing regions that have little in common.

This chapter, therefore, compares levels, trends and differentials in fertility and its proximate determinants between two Punjabi-speaking and two Bengali-speaking populations living in different national settings.

Punjab is the largest province in Pakistan, covering approximately one-fourth of the country's total land area (205,344 square kilometres) and more than half of the country's total population (around 47 million in 1981, since when there has not been a population census). Thus, Punjab province has a major influence on the overall demographic characteristics of Pakistan. The Indian Punjab is comparatively smaller in area (50,362 square kilometres), and has a relatively smaller population (around 16 million in 1981 and 20 million in 1991).

Although a semi-arid zone, the Punjab region has the largest gravity-fed irrigation system in the world. The irrigation system, developed during and after colonial rule, is based on a large network of canals, minor tributaries and watercourses around the Indus river and its tributaries, carrying water to the farmlands. Agriculture occupies the most important place in the economy of both the Punjabs, and wheat is the major food crop.

The major language of the people in both regions is Punjabi: mostly written in Guru Mukhi script in the Indian Punjab, and mostly written in Perso-Arabic script in the Pakistan Punjab.

Compared to Bangladesh, West Bengal is smaller in area and population: Bangladesh stretches over a land area of 147,570 square kilometres with a

population of 111.4 million. West Bengal has a land area of 88,752 square kilometres and a population of 68.1 million. The two Bengals are located in the delta of
major rivers such as the Ganges and Brahmaputra, and for most part, have similar
topography. The flat and featureless alluvial plain is traversed by the Ganges and the
Brahmaputra rivers and their numerous tributaries. Agriculture plays a pivotal role
in the economy of both Bengals: rice is the major food crop and jute is the major
non-food crop. West Bengal is relatively more industrialized than Bangladesh. The
principal language spoken in both Bengals is Bengali, or Bangla.

Data and Methods

The major data sources for the present paper are: the Pakistan Demographic and
Health Survey (PDHS); the National Family and Health Survey (NFHS) for the
Indian states of Punjab and West Bengal; and the Bangladesh Demographic and
Health Survey (BDHS). For the most part, the three data sources are comparable
because each country survey adopted similar sampling designs, questionnaires and
methods of data collection and analysis. However, the data refer to somewhat
different points in time. The PDHS (December 1990–May 1991) was conducted
nearly two-and-a-half years before the NFHS in Punjab (July 1993–September
1993), and the BDHS (November 1993–March 1994) was conducted nearly 18
months after the NFHS in West Bengal (April–July 1992).

In addition, the age criterion adopted to define eligible women (ever-married
women interviewed using the woman's questionnaire) was different in the three
surveys: ever-married women ages 15–49, 13–49 and 10–49 were defined as eligible
in the PDHS, NFHS and BDHS, respectively. In this paper, however, most comparisons between ethnic groups are restricted to currently married women in the age
range 15–49.

Comparisons of levels, trends and differentials in fertility between each of the two
linguistic groups across national borders are made using simple cross tabulations.
Fertility differences across ethnic groups are further examined in the context of the
differential impact of the proximate determinants of fertility—marriage, postpartum infecundability and contraception. Logistic regression is used on the two
pooled data sets of the Punjabs, to examine the effect of national family planning
programmes on current use of contraception, after controlling for relevant socioeconomic and demographic characteristics.

Table 8.1 presents selected background characteristics of currently married
women in the four study areas. Although the distributions by residence and age do
not differ much between the two Punjabs, the distributions by education, exposure
to mass media, and a measure of standard of living[1] differ considerably. A higher

[1] The standard of living is measured in terms of amenities available in the household. Depending on
the availability of information, the variables used in the construction of the measure differ slightly for the

Table 8.1. Selected background characteristics of currently married women: the Punjabs and the Bengals

Characteristic	The Punjabs		The Bengals	
	Pakistan	India	Bangladesh	India
Age				
15–24	22.7	22.5	36.1	32.4
25–34	40.8	39.5	36.9	36.1
35–49	36.6	38.0	27.0	31.5
Residence				
Urban	28.5	27.8	11.3	27.5
Rural	71.5	72.2	88.7	72.5
Education				
No schooling	76.4	51.0	56.9	49.3
Primary incomplete	3.1	3.6	17.7	16.8
Primary complete	8.7	17.9	9.8	12.8
Secondary/higher	11.7	27.5	15.6	21.1
Religion				
Muslim	—	1.1	87.6	21.4
Hindu	—	38.0	11.8	76.5
Sikh	—	59.1	0.0	0.0
Other	—	1.8	0.6	2.1
Exposure to mass media				
Exposed	40.0	65.8	44.6	60.2
Not exposed	60.0	34.2	55.4	39.8
Standard of living				
Low	57.1	24.4	36.0	30.0
Middle	28.7	57.4	54.1	47.0
High	13.5	18.1	9.9	23.0
Total	100.0	100.0	100.0	100.0
Number	3,678	2,877	8,840	3,970

proportion of women in the Indian Punjab than in the Pakistan Punjab have had some schooling, and a greater proportion have completed secondary education. Similarly, a greater proportion of women in the Indian Punjab either listen to the radio or watch television at least once a week. The standard of living is also

two Punjabs and the two Bengals. In the case of the Punjabs, the measure was based on: source of drinking water, toilet facility, electricity, and household ownership of radio, television, refrigerator, bicycle, motorcycle, car and water pump. In the case of the Bengals, however, the measure excluded the household ownership of refrigerator, motorcycle, car and water pump, but included the household ownership of agricultural land and of a watch or clock.

Table 8.2. Age-specific and total fertility rates: the Punjabs and the Bengals

Age	The Punjabs		The Bengals	
	Pakistan (1985–91)	India (1989–93)	Bangladesh (1991–93)	India (1989–91)
15–19	79	63	140	123
20–24	226	249	196	202
25–29	275	174	158	138
30–34	237	63	105	75
35–39	159	20	56	31
40–44	70	5	19	8
45–49	30	2	14	5
Total fertility rate	5.39	2.88	3.44	2.92
Mean CEB for women aged 40–49	6.3	4.2	6.6	4.7

Source: NIPS and IRD/Macro International (1992), PRC, CRRID and IIPS (1995), NIPORT, Mitra and Associates, and Macro International (1994), IIPS (1995).

comparatively better in the Indian Punjab. The samples in the two Punjabs also differ considerably in terms of religion. Although information on religion of the respondents was not collected in the PDHS, according to the 1981 census, more than 95 per cent of the household heads in the Pakistan Punjab are Muslim (NIPS 1988). In the Indian Punjab, on the other hand, 59 per cent of currently married women are Sikh, 38 per cent are Hindu, 2 per cent are Christian and only 1 per cent are Muslim. Thus, the comparison between the Punjabs is essentially a comparison between Muslim women of the Pakistan Punjab and Sikh and Hindu women of the Indian Punjab.

Comparison of the two Bengals shows that currently married women in West Bengal are relatively older, reflecting a later age at marriage in this area. A larger percentage of women in West Bengal live in urban areas and are exposed to mass media, when compared to Bangladeshi women. In terms of education too, West Bengal fares better than Bangladesh. Fifty-seven per cent of currently married women in Bangladesh have never been to school, compared with 49 per cent of those in West Bengal. Similarly, a greater proportion of women in West Bengal than in Bangladesh have completed secondary school (21 per cent versus 16 per cent). The standard of living also is somewhat better in West Bengal. The two Bengals do not differ much in the proportion of women having a poor standard of living (36 per cent in Bangladesh compared with 30 per cent in West Bengal), but the proportion of women having a high standard of living is much greater in West Bengal than in Bangladesh (23 per cent versus 10 per cent). The Bangladesh sample is predominantly Muslim and the sample in West Bengal is predominantly Hindu. However, 12 per cent of Bangladeshi women are Hindu, and 21 per cent of Bengali-speaking women in West Bengal are Muslim.

Fertility Levels and Trends

The age-specific and total fertility rates (TFR) for the Punjabs and the Bengals are shown in Table 8.2. The rates for the Pakistani and Indian Punjabs correspond roughly to the calendar years 1985–91 and 1988–93, respectively. And the rates refer roughly to the calendar years 1991–93 for Bangladesh and to the calendar years 1989–91 for West Bengal.

The TFR in the Indian Punjab is almost half that in the Pakistan Punjab (2.88 versus 5.39 children per woman). The age pattern of childbearing also differs considerably between the two Punjabs. Fertility peaks in the 20–24 age group in the Indian Punjab, reflecting a pattern of early childbearing; whereas the peak fertility is observed in the next five-year age group (25–29) in the Pakistan Punjab. The age-specific fertility rates are consistently lower in the Indian Punjab than in the Pakistan Punjab, except in the age group 20–24, further substantiating relatively early childbearing in the Indian Punjab. While fertility declines sharply after age 24 in the Indian Punjab, childbearing in the Pakistan Punjab continues until a woman's late thirties, with fertility declining sharply only after age 34. Fertility in the Indian Punjab is highly concentrated in the 20–29 age group; almost three-fourths (73 per cent) of total fertility is concentrated in this age group. In comparison, fertility in the Pakistan Punjab is concentrated over a wider age range: 46 per cent of total fertility is accounted for by births to women ages 20–29, and more than four-fifths (83 per cent) by births to women ages 20–39. Very early childbearing is negligible in both the Punjabs; births to women in the 15–19 age group account for only 11 and 7 per cent of total fertility in the Indian and the Pakistan Punjabs, respectively. The contribution to total fertility of women in the 40–49 age group is negligible in the Indian Punjab (1 per cent), and is relatively higher in the Pakistan Punjab (9 per cent).

Table 8.2 also shows the mean number of children ever born (CEB) among women ages 40–49, that is, women who are approaching the end of their reproductive years. A comparison of this cumulative measure of childbearing with the TFR gives a rough indication of the trend in fertility over the last several decades. Accordingly, fertility decline has been much slower in Pakistan Punjab than in Indian Punjab. While the TFR is 31 per cent lower than the CEB in the Indian Punjab, it is only 14 per cent lower in the Pakistan Punjab.

Similar trends in fertility transition in the two Punjabs are also evident in the past fertility estimates for the two regions. According to surveys conducted over the 1969–85 period, changes in the TFR have been minor in the Pakistan Punjab. The 1975 Pakistan Fertility Survey (PFS) estimated a TFR of 6.28 children per woman for the period 1970–74, and according to the 1979–80 Population, Labour Force and Migration Survey (PLM), the TFR in the Pakistan Punjab for the period 1975–79 was 6.44 children per woman, slightly higher than the PFS estimate (Sathar and Irfan 1984; Shah *et al.* 1986). However, the 1984–85 Contraceptive Prevalence Survey estimated a TFR of 6.17 children per woman for the Pakistan Punjab, which is only about 2 per cent lower than the PFS estimate and only about 4 per cent lower than the PLM estimate. The TFR of 5.39 estimated in the PDHS thus indicates a decline of about 13 per cent in the TFR between 1984–85 and 1985–91. However, the observed rate of decline in fertility is suspected to be an overestimate (Retherford *et al.* 1987). During the same period, fertility decline was more impressive in the Indian Punjab. The TFR in the Indian Punjab declined from 5.2 in 1971 to 4.0 in 1981 and further to 2.9 in 1989–93, a decline of almost 45 per cent during the last two decades (PRC CRRID and IIPS 1995).

The total fertility rate of the two Bengals, however, differs only by about half a child, fertility being lower in West Bengal (2.9 children per woman) than in Bangladesh (3.4 children per woman). Fertility rates are higher in Bangladesh than in West Bengal in every age group except ages 20–24. The age pattern of childbearing suggests that women in both Bengals have children early in their childbearing years: by age 30, a woman in Bangladesh and West Bengal will have given birth to 72 and 79 per cent, respectively, of the children she will ever have. However, women in West Bengal tend to stop childbearing earlier than women in Bangladesh.

A comparison of the total fertility rate and completed fertility suggests that fertility decline has been more rapid in Bangladesh than in West Bengal. Bangladesh experienced a fertility decline of about three children (48 per cent) over the past two decades, from 6.6 to 3.4 births per woman. On the other hand, during the same period, fertility in West Bengal declined by about two children (38 per cent), from 4.7 to 2.9 children per woman.

A steep fertility decline in Bangladesh is also supported by the previous estimates. The fertility estimates in the 1975 and 1989 Bangladesh Fertility Surveys reveal that the TFR declined from 6.3 children per woman in 1971–75 to 5.1 in 1984–88 (MHPC 1978; Huq and Cleland 1990). The 1989 and 1991 Contraceptive Prevalence Surveys estimated a TFR of 4.8 and 4.3 children per woman for the periods 1986–88 and 1989–91, respectively (Mitra *et al.* 1993). Thus the BDHS estimate of TFR of 3.4 children per woman suggests an unlikely drop of 21 per cent in the TFR in a two-year period. On the other hand, West Bengal experienced a more steady decline in fertility during this period. The TFR declined from 4.2 in 1981 to 2.9 in 1989–91, a decline of 31 per cent in a ten-year period (IIPS 1995). The TFR in the early 1980s in West Bengal was lower than the TFR in the mid-1980s in Bangladesh, by exactly 1 child, and by the early 1990s, the difference had narrowed down to half a child.

Fertility Differentials

Differentials in the average number of CEB by background characteristics, shown in Table 8.3, provide further information on fertility patterns in the two ethnic groups. To avoid the confounding influence of age distributions of women in different groups, the mean values for different socioeconomic categories have been age standardized. The age distributions of all currently married women in the Indian

Table 8.3. Age-standardized mean number of children ever born for currently married women ages 15-49, according to selected background characteristics: the Punjabs and the Bengals

Characteristic	The Punjabs		The Bengals	
	Pakistan	India	Bangladesh	India
Age				
15–19	0.67	0.52	0.70	0.66
20–24	1.48	1.30	1.88	1.81
25–29	2.93	2.60	3.04	2.73
30–34	4.57	3.26	4.22	3.51
35–39	5.67	3.82	5.34	4.19
40–44	6.53	4.05	6.62	4.82
45–49	6.46	4.42	7.11	5.06
Residence				
Urban	3.85	2.66	3.16	2.47
Rural	4.18	3.04	3.76	3.25
Education				
No schooling	4.24	3.33	3.88	3.58
Primary incomplete	4.09	2.86	3.79	3.22
Primary complete	3.80	2.78	3.57	2.72
Secondary/higher	3.10	2.27	2.75	1.63
Religion				
Muslim	—	—	3.76	4.03
Hindu	—	2.98	3.24	2.77
Sikh	—	2.88	—	—
Standard of living				
Low	4.20	3.52	3.87	3.57
Middle	4.14	2.92	3.72	3.19
High	3.49	2.32	2.86	2.02
Total	4.08	2.93	3.69	3.00

The means are standardized on the age distribution of all currently married women in the Indian Punjab and West Bengal, respectively, in the case of the Punjabs and the Bengals.

Punjab and West Bengal were used as the standards for the two Punjabs and the two Bengals, respectively.

In every age group, the mean CEB in the Pakistan Punjab is higher than in the Indian Punjab, and the difference between the two Punjabs is greater after age 30 (ranging from a difference of 1 child in the age group 30–34 to around 2 children after age 34), suggesting a greater use of contraception in the Indian Punjab after age 30. The mean CEB to women ages 45–49, which reflects completed family size, is higher by 2.0 children in the Pakistan Punjab.

Within urban and rural areas, the mean CEB is higher by 1 child in the Pakistan Punjab compared with the Indian Punjab. Within the Indian Punjab, however, mean CEB does not differ much between urban and rural areas. Although the mean CEB decreases with increases in women's education in both Punjabs, at every level of schooling, women in Pakistan Punjab have a mean CEB higher by 1 child. A similar pattern is observed with respect to differentials by standard of living. Hindus and Sikhs in the Indian Punjab do not differ in fertility.

Between the two Bengals, the mean CEB is almost the same below age 30, is higher in Bangladesh by about 1 child in the age group 30–39 and by about 2 children for women in their forties. In each socioeconomic category shown in Table 8.3, the mean CEB is lower in West Bengal than in Bangladesh, except among Muslims. The difference in the mean CEB increases with women's increasing educational attainment. For instance, the mean CEB for women with no schooling (the group with the highest fertility in both the Bengals) is lower by 0.3 child in West Bengal than in Bangladesh, but for women with at least a secondary education (the group with the lowest fertility in both the Bengals), it is lower by 1.1 child in West Bengal than in Bangladesh. A similar pattern of fertility differential is observed by the standard of living.

In both the Bengals, fertility is higher in rural than in urban areas and it is higher among women with no formal education than among those with at least a secondary school education. However, these differences are greater in West Bengal than in Bangladesh. The mean CEB in rural Bangladesh is only 19 per cent higher than that in urban Bangladesh, but in West Bengal the mean CEB in rural areas is 32 per cent higher than that in urban areas. Similarly, the difference in the mean CEB between women with no formal education and those with at least some secondary education is 29 per cent in Bangladesh, while it is 54 per cent in West Bengal. The pattern is the same in the case of standard of living. The Hindu–Muslim differential in fertility is also greater in West Bengal than in Bangladesh. While the mean CEB is 16 per cent higher among the Muslims than among the Hindus in Bangladesh, it is 45 per cent higher among the Muslims than the Hindus in West Bengal.

We now examine differences between the two Punjabs and the two Bengals in the proximate determinants of fertility. Because reliable data on induced abortions are not available, the comparison is restricted to age at marriage, postpartum nonsusceptibility and the use of contraception.

Age at Marriage

Table 8.4 presents the median age at first marriage among women ages 20–49, according to current age, for the two ethnic groups. Increased age at marriage has been considered one of the major factors underlying rapid fertility decline in the Indian Punjab (Basu 1988; Das Gupta 1995; Nag 1989; Taylor and Singh 1975;

Table 8.4. Median age at first marriage among women aged 20(25)–49 years, by current age: the Punjabs and the Bengals

Age	The Punjabs		The Bengals	
	Pakistan	India	Bangladesh	India
20–24	nc	19.8	15.3	17.3
25–29	19.4	19.1	14.8	16.6
30–34	18.5	18.8	14.2	16.4
35–39	19.0	18.7	13.9	15.8
40–44	18.9	19.5	13.6	15.2
45–49	19.0	19.0	13.6	14.9
20–49	nc	19.5	14.4	16.3
25–49	19.0	19.0	14.1	16.0

nc: not calculated because less than 50 per cent of the women have married for the first time by age 20.

Source: NIPS and IRD/Macro International (1992), PRC, CRRID and IIPS (1995), NIPORT, Mitra and Associates, and Macro International (1994), IIPS (1995).

Wyon and Gordon 1971). However, the differences in fertility between the two Punjabs cannot be attributed to the differences in age at marriage, because the two areas differ little in this respect. The median age at marriage for women in the age group 25–49 is the same in the two Punjabs, and the median is moderately high at 19 years, even among older cohorts. That the marriage age for females in the two Punjabs has been high is also indicated in the previous estimates of singulate mean age at marriage (SMAM). The SMAM for females in the Pakistan Punjab increased from 20.1 years in 1974–75 to 20.6 years in 1979–80 (Shah *et al.* 1986). In the Indian Punjab, it increased from 20.1 years in 1971 to 21.1 years in 1981 (PRC CRRID and IIPS 1995).

Although early and universal marriage is customary for females in both the Bengals, women in Bangladesh tend to marry earlier than women in West Bengal (Table 8.4). In each age group, women in West Bengal marry later than their counterparts in Bangladesh, with an overall difference of about two years in the median age at marriage among women ages 20–49 (16.3 and 14.4, respectively). There has been a slow and steady increase in the age at marriage over the past 25 years in both the Bengals, and the increase has been somewhat greater in West Bengal (an increase of about 16 per cent, from 14.9 years for women ages 45–49 to 17.3 years for women ages 20–24) than in Bangladesh (an increase of about 13 per cent, from 13.6 years for women ages 45–49 to 15.3 years for women ages 20–24).

During the period 1975–76, the mean age at marriage among all ever-married women in Bangladesh was estimated to be 12.3 years (MHPC 1978), and it increased to 14.8 years in 1989 (Huq and Cleland 1990). The SMAM for females increased from 16.3 years in 1975 to 18 years in 1989. The SMAM for females in

West Bengal estimated from the censuses, on the other hand, indicates that the marriage age was relatively higher in West Bengal even in the 1970s, and that it increased from 18.0 years in 1971 to 19.3 years in 1981 (IIPS 1995). Thus, some of the fertility differences between the two Bengals may be attributed to higher age at marriage for females in West Bengal.

Postpartum Nonsusceptibility

The PDHS and the NFHS data reveal that the duration of postpartum nonsusceptibility (due either to postpartum amenorrhoea or postpartum abstinence) is longer in the Pakistan Punjab (7.7 months) than in the Indian Punjab (4.4 months). While the two Punjabs do not differ much in the median duration of postpartum abstinence (2.4 versus 2.5 months), the median duration of postpartum amenorrhoea is longer in the Pakistan Punjab (6.4 months) than in the Indian Punjab (4.1 months) (NIPS and IRD/Macro International 1992; PRC CRRID and IIPS 1995). Considering that

Table 8.5. Percentage of currently married women aged 15–49 by knowledge of contraceptive method, knowledge of a source, ever use and current use, by specific method: the Punjabs and the Bengals

Method	The Punjabs							
	Pakistan				India			
	Knows method	Knows source[a]	Ever using	Currently using	Knows method	Knows source[a]	Ever using	Currently using
Any method	80.6	47.8	22.9	13.0	99.8	99.5	67.0	58.7
Any modern method	79.9	46.2	17.3	9.8	99.8	99.4	59.3	51.3
Pill	60.0	27.7	4.0	0.6	83.9	82.8	6.2	2.2
IUD	55.4	24.0	4.2	1.5	87.5	86.5	14.1	6.3
Injection	63.0	28.7	3.4	0.8	47.2	45.6	0.3	0.0
Diaphragm	13.3	6.4	0.6	0.0	u	u	u	u
Condom	36.7	18.7	7.8	3.0	82.1	80.6	17.9	8.9
Female sterilization	73.6	38.5	3.8	3.8	99.7	99.0	31.5	31.5
Male sterilization	22.0	11.8	0.1	0.1	99.1	98.0	2.5	2.5
Any traditional method	23.6	na	8.3	3.2	64.1	na	17.9	7.4
Periodic abstinence	15.8	8.4	5.4	1.4	56.0	43.2	12.1	4.4
Withdrawal	14.4	na	4.1	1.5	41.5	na	8.3	2.9
Other	4.1	na	2.4	0.3	1.5	na	0.9	0.1

Table 8.5. *(Contd.)*

Method	The Bengals							
	Bangladesh				India			
	Knows method	Knows source[a]	Ever using	Currently using	Knows method	Knows source[a]	Ever using	Currently using
Any method	99.8	98.2	66.2	44.9	99.1	96.8	70.8	57.7
Any modern method	99.8	98.2	59.5	36.6	98.9	96.0	49.1	37.6
Pill	99.5	96.1	44.5	17.5	85.9	67.3	15.3	3.6
IUD	90.3	79.8	7.8	2.2	68.5	52.1	3.4	1.3
Injection	96.7	89.5	11.8	4.6	42.6	31.7	0.6	0.1
Condom	87.6	79.6	14.8	3.0	67.8	52.9	10.9	1.9
Female sterilization	99.0	93.0	8.2	8.1	98.1	94.0	26.5	26.5
Male sterilization	83.4	75.6	1.4	1.1	85.0	79.4	4.4	4.3
Any traditional method	76.5	na	25.2	8.3	72.8	na	44.6	20.1
Periodic abstinence	65.4	38.3	17.2	4.8	62.3	50.6	33.6	11.3
Withdrawal	50.3	na	10.6	2.4	55.6	na	26.4	8.3
Other	17.6	na	3.7	1.1	5.1	na	1.8	0.5

[a] For modern methods, the source refers to a place that a person could go to get the method. For rhythm/periodic abstinence, the source refers to a source of advice on how to use periodic abstinence; na: not applicable; u: not available.

the duration of postpartum infecundability has a negative effect on fertility, the observed fertility differences between the two Punjabs cannot be attributed to the difference in postpartum nonsusceptibility.

On the other hand, the two Bengals do not differ much in terms of the median duration of postpartum nonsusceptibility, either due to amenorrhoea or abstinence following a birth. The data from the BDHS and the NFHS reveal that, on average, women in the two Bengals remain nonsusceptible for about 12 months after a birth, primarily because of postpartum amenorrhoea. The median duration of postpartum amenorrhoea is 9.5 months in West Bengal and 10.3 months in Bangladesh, and the median duration of postpartum abstinence is 2.3 and 2.0 months, respectively. Interestingly, the median durations of postpartum amenorrhoea, abstinence and total nonsusceptibility do not differ much between the two Bengals in every group of women classified by age, residence and education for which medians could be compared (IIPS 1995, Mitra and Associates, Macro International 1994 and NIPORT).

Knowledge and Use of Family Planning

Differences in contraceptive knowledge and use between the two Punjabs parallel the observed differences in fertility (Table 8.5). Both knowledge and use of specific family planning methods are lower in the Pakistan Punjab, and the difference is greater for use than for knowledge. While knowledge of a modern method of family planning is universal in the Indian Punjab, it is less widespread in the Pakistan Punjab, where only 80 per cent of currently married women know of a modern method of family planning. Except for hormonal injectables, knowledge of every single method of family planning is lower in the Pakistan Punjab than in the Indian Punjab. Knowledge about the source of contraception is also higher in the Indian Punjab, with 99 per cent of currently married women knowing where to obtain at least one modern method of family planning, compared with only 46 per cent in the Pakistan Punjab. While less than one-fifth (17 per cent) of currently married women in the Pakistan Punjab have ever used a modern method of family planning, nearly three-fifths have ever done so in the Indian Punjab. Similarly, almost three-fifths (59 per cent) of currently married women ages 15–49 are currently using a method of family planning in the Indian Punjab, compared with only 13 per cent in the Pakistan Punjab. According to the recent Contraceptive Prevalence Survey in Pakistan, 20.2 per cent of currently married women in the Punjab province were using contraception in 1993–94, 13.6 per cent were using modern methods, and another 6.6 per cent were using traditional methods (Ministry of Population Welfare and Population Council 1995).

Whereas the knowledge of any modern method of family planning is almost universal in both the Bengals, the percentage of women who know of modern temporary methods (pill, IUD, injection and condom) or their source is much lower in West Bengal than in Bangladesh. For instance, between 88 and 100 per cent of currently married women in Bangladesh report the knowledge of these modern temporary methods, while this proportion ranges from 43 to 86 per cent in West Bengal. But knowledge of sterilization and traditional methods (periodic abstinence and withdrawal) and their source are almost equal in the two Bengals.

Although ever use of any method is higher in West Bengal (71 per cent) than in Bangladesh (66 per cent), this measure is higher in Bangladesh (60 per cent) than in West Bengal (49 per cent). Forty-five and 25 per cent of currently married women in West Bengal and Bangladesh, respectively, have ever used any traditional method of family planning. In West Bengal, more women report having used periodic abstinence (34 per cent) than any other method, and ever use of withdrawal (26 per cent) is equal to ever use of female sterilization. Ever use of modern temporary methods is higher in Bangladesh (ranging from 8 per cent for IUDs to 45 per cent for the pill) than in West Bengal (ranging from less than 1 per cent for injectables to 15 per cent for the pill). On the other hand, the ever use of sterilization (both male and female sterilization) is higher in West Bengal (4–27 per cent) than in Bangladesh (1–8 per cent).

A similar method mix is observed with respect to current use of contraception. Fifty-eight per cent of currently married women in West Bengal practise family planning, compared with 45 per cent in Bangladesh. All the difference in contraceptive use is accounted for by differences in the use of traditional methods, given that the use of modern methods is almost the same in the two Bengals. A larger proportion of couples practise traditional methods of family planning in West Bengal (20 per cent) than in Bangladesh (8 per cent). On the other hand, a larger proportion of couples use modern temporary methods in Bangladesh (27 per cent) than in West Bengal (7 per cent), and the reverse is true for current use of terminal methods. More than half (53 per cent) of current use in West Bengal is accounted for by male and female sterilization, another 35 per cent by traditional methods and the remaining 12 per cent by modern temporary methods. In contrast, 20, 18 and 62 per cent of current use in Bangladesh is accounted for by the use of sterilization, traditional methods and modern temporary methods, respectively. The single most popular method of family planning is female sterilization in West Bengal and the pill in Bangladesh.

The increase in contraceptive use rates has been more dramatic in Bangladesh than in West Bengal, as is also true of the decline in fertility. In Bangladesh, the proportion of currently married women using family planning increased from 8 per cent in 1975 to 40 per cent in 1991 (Cleland *et al.* 1994). The use of modern methods increased from 11 per cent of married women in 1981 to 31 per cent in 1991, while the use of traditional methods increased only marginally—from 8 to 9 per cent of married women between 1981 and 1991 (Larson and Mitra 1992; Mitra *et al.* 1993). The share of terminal methods declined from 38 per cent of all contraceptive use in 1983 (Mitra and Kamal 1985) to 32 per cent in 1989 (Huq and Cleland 1990), and to a low of 26 per cent in 1991 (Mitra *et al.* 1993), reflecting the increased emphasis given to modern reversible methods in the Bangladesh family planning programme as well as the increased acceptance of family planning among younger women, who wish to space births.

Differentials in Current Contraceptive Use

Current contraceptive use[2] is lower in the Pakistan than in the Indian Punjab in every group of women classified by current age, residence, education, exposure to mass media and standard of living (Table 8.6). The rate increases with the age of

[2] Because of the very low contraceptive prevalence in the Pakistan Punjab, the comparison of contraceptive use differentials between the two Punjabs is restricted to the current use of any method.

Table 8.6. Percentage of currently married women aged 15–49 who are currently using any contraceptive method, according to selected background characteristics: the Punjabs and the Bengals

Characteristic	The Punjabs		The Bengals					
	Pakistan	India	Bangladesh			India		
	Any method	Any method	Any method	Any modern method	Any modern temporary method	Any method	Any modern method	Any modern temporary method
Age								
15–19	1.6	10.7	24.7	19.6	19.4	27.2	6.5	5.1
20–24	6.4	28.0	37.6	32.0	29.6	44.9	24.1	8.7
25–29	9.9	55.3	50.6	43.5	36.2	63.9	40.7	11.0
30–34	15.1	73.6	57.2	46.1	31.6	72.1	51.5	6.7
35–39	23.9	81.4	58.5	46.7	26.9	76.5	57.1	4.9
40–44	17.4	73.6	51.9	38.2	19.5	66.3	48.0	1.8
45–49	12.9	57.6	29.3	21.3	7.2	47.9	36.6	2.3
Residence								
Urban	28.0	62.7	55.0	45.1	37.9	61.9	36.7	11.2
Rural	7.1	57.2	43.6	35.5	26.0	56.1	37.9	5.0
Education								
No schooling	8.8	56.9	41.2	34.6	22.4	50.2	37.1	2.4
Primary incomplete	16.1	60.2	45.8	37.3	29.2	60.9	42.8	5.2
Primary complete	17.9	60.2	46.6	35.1	30.7	60.8	38.5	10.7
Secondary/higher	35.9	61.0	56.3	44.2	40.2	70.1	34.1	15.7
Religion								
Muslim	—	—	43.7	35.9	27.3	43.2	23.7	6.5
Hindu	—	60.0	54.3	42.3	28.3	61.6	41.4	6.9
Sikh	—	59.1	—	—	—	—	—	—
Standard of living								
Low	5.9	50.3	40.8	35.0	21.7	50.0	36.8	2.5
Middle	16.3	59.9	45.1	35.8	28.5	56.6	37.4	5.8
High	36.5	66.4	59.0	46.9	41.2	69.9	38.9	14.2
Exposure to mass media								
Exposed	22.5	63.1	49.8	40.2	31.9	63.7	39.6	8.8
Not exposed	6.7	50.4	41.0	33.7	23.6	48.5	34.5	3.7
Total	13.0	58.7	44.9	36.6	27.3	57.7	37.6	6.7

Table 8.7. Percentage of currently married women aged 15–49 who are currently using any contraceptive method, according to the number and sex composition of living children: the Punjabs and the Bengals

Number and sex composition of living children	The Punjabs		The Bengals					
	Pakistan	India	Bangladesh			India		
	Any method	Any method	Any method	Any modern method	Any modern temporary method	Any method	Any modern method	Any modern temporary method
None	0.0	2.3	13.3	9.0	7.5	21.3	5.1	3.5
1 child	2.5	28.9	34.6	29.2	26.4	49.0	15.0	10.2
1 son	4.2	31.2	36.5	30.7	27.4	53.7	16.2	10.4
No sons	0.6	26.3	32.6	27.6	25.3	44.5	13.7	10.0
2 children	13.3	61.1	50.1	42.3	33.4	63.3	42.3	10.6
2 sons	12.8	70.2	53.1	45.0	26.3	74.8	55.8	10.5
1 son	14.8	61.5	53.3	45.4	35.0	67.0	41.0	10.8
No sons	10.5	34.8	37.8	30.7	35.0	52.7	26.0	10.2
3 children	10.7	74.1	57.6	48.2	33.8	73.8	60.9	4.3
3 sons	6.9	85.7	60.0	50.4	32.9	82.4	70.7	1.3
2 sons	13.6	82.3	62.0	52.6	35.4	78.0	69.1	3.6
1 son	9.8	65.9	56.0	47.4	34.5	72.0	55.9	4.1
No sons	6.7	29.8	43.7	32.4	26.3	53.3	26.5	12.3
4+ children	20.5	76.1	51.9	40.8	27.6	62.9	48.8	4.1
2+ sons	21.7	80.9	52.2	40.9	27.4	61.4	47.9	3.2
1 son	15.8	61.8	52.3	41.4	28.7	66.7	55.8	7.4
No sons	4.6	29.4	39.9	35.7	25.7	47.3	28.7	5.1

the woman, reaching a peak at ages 35–39 in both the Punjabs. In the age groups with the highest fertility (women 20–24 and 25–29), contraceptive prevalence rates are 28 and 55 per cent, respectively, in the Indian Punjab and 6 and 10 per cent, respectively, in the Pakistan Punjab. Although the contraceptive use differentials by residence, education, exposure to mass media and standard of living in both the Punjabs are in the expected direction, they are greater in magnitude in the Pakistan Punjab than in the Indian Punjab. For instance, in the Pakistan Punjab, the contraceptive use rate is four times higher in urban than in rural areas (28 per cent in urban areas compared with 7 per cent in rural areas) and in the Indian Punjab it is only 10 per cent higher in urban than in rural areas (63 per cent compared with 57 per cent). Similarly, contraceptive use rates do not differ much across different educational categories in the Indian Punjab, but in the Pakistan Punjab the current use rate increases sharply with increased women's education. The percentage of women currently practising family planning in the Pakistan Punjab increases from 9 per cent for women with no schooling to 36 per cent for women with at least a secondary school education.

Differentials in contraceptive method choice in the two Bengals are also presented in Table 8.6. Although the current use of any method and any modern method is higher in West Bengal than in Bangladesh in every group (except the Muslims), the current use of any modern method is lower in West Bengal among women living in urban areas, women with at least a secondary school education, Muslims, and women with a 'high' standard of living. The overall differences in method choice between the two Bengals, observed in Table 8.5, persist in each subgroup of women. In other words, among current users in every group, a higher proportion use traditional methods in West Bengal than in Bangladesh, and a higher proportion of current users of modern methods use temporary methods in Bangladesh than in West Bengal.

The use of any method and of any modern method peak in the age group 35–39 in both Bengals, but the use of any modern temporary method peaks among women ages 25–29 and 30–34 in Bangladesh and West Bengal, respectively. Below age 30, a larger proportion of women use modern temporary methods in Bangladesh, and above age 30, the use of sterilization is greater among women in West Bengal.

By residence, the use of any method, any modern method and any modern temporary method is higher in urban than in rural areas of Bangladesh. In West Bengal, on the other hand, the use of any method and of any modern temporary method is higher in urban than in rural areas, while the use of any modern method is almost the same in the two areas. Thus the urban–rural difference in the current use of any method in West Bengal is almost entirely due to a higher use of traditional methods in urban areas. Educational differences in contraceptive use are large in both the Bengals; and in both areas, current use increases with the increase in women's education.

The prevalence rate for Muslims is almost the same in the two Bengals, but the rate for Hindus is higher in West Bengal (62 per cent) than in Bangladesh (54 per cent). As was the case with fertility, Hindu–Muslim differentials are greater in West Bengal than in Bangladesh.

Table 8.7 shows differences in current use by the number and sex composition of living children. In all the four study areas, a curvilinear relationship is observed between the number of living children and contraceptive use. Between the two Punjabs, a stronger preference for sons exists in the Indian Punjab, where at each parity, the current use of family planning is lowest for women with no sons and highest for women with two or more sons. In the Pakistan Punjab, on the other hand, current use is highest for women with at least one daughter. The data on prevalence rate by sex composition of living children indicate the existence of son preference in both the Bengals. Although the data on use of any method suggests a greater preference for sons in Bangladesh than in West Bengal, the use of any modern method by sex composition of living children indicates a greater preference for sons in West Bengal. At each parity, the use of traditional methods in West Bengal is the highest for women with no sons. Thus, the number of living sons determines the couple's decision to use a modern method of family planning to a greater extent in West Bengal than it does in Bangladesh.

Fertility Preferences, Intention to Use and Unmet Need for Family Planning

The data on fertility preferences, intentions to use family planning in the future and the unmet need for family planning are presented for the two ethnic groups in Table 8.8. In the Pakistan Punjab, the proportion of women who say they want another child at some time in the future is almost twice (47 per cent) that in the Indian Punjab (25 per cent). A total of 72 per cent of currently married women in the Indian Punjab either do not want any more children or are sterilized, and this proportion is only 44 per cent in the Pakistan Punjab. Similarly, a much greater proportion of currently married nonusers do not intend to use contraception in the future in the Pakistan Punjab (68 per cent) than in the Indian Punjab (36 per cent). Only 18 per cent of currently married nonusers in the Pakistan Punjab say that they intend to use family planning in the future.

Thirteen per cent of women in the Indian Punjab have an unmet need for family planning[3] compared with 31 per cent in the Pakistan Punjab. While the unmet need for spacing births and for limiting births is similar in the Indian Punjab, the unmet need for limiting births is greater than the unmet need for spacing births in the Pakistan Punjab. On the other hand, only 44 per cent of currently married women in the Pakistan Punjab have a demand for family planning,[4] compared with 72 per cent in the Indian Punjab. This means that only 30 per cent of the demand for

[3] Currently married women who say that they either do not want any more children or that they want to wait two or more years before having another child, but are not using contraception.
[4] The sum of the met need (current users of family planning methods are considered to have a met need for family planning) and of unmet need for family planning.

Table 8.8. Fertility preferences, intentions to use family planning and unmet need for family planning: the Punjabs and the Bengals

Measure	The Punjabs		The Bengals	
	Pakistan	India	Bangladesh	India
Desire for additional children[a]				
Have another soon[b]	23.3	11.4	13.2	10.0
Have another later[c]	20.2	13.3	21.3	20.5
Have another, undecided when	3.6	0.2	2.0	0.8
Undecided	1.1	1.3	2.4	0.7
Up to God	5.9	0.4	0.0	0.8
Want no more	40.5	37.8	48.6	34.5
Sterilized	3.9	34.0	9.3	30.6
Declared infecund	1.3	1.6	3.2	2.1
Missing	0.2	0.0	0.1	0.0
Number	3,768	2,877	8,840	3,970
Intention to use family planning in the future[d]				
Intends to use	17.7	46.8	67.4	47.0
Unsure	14.6	16.9	4.1	7.1
Does not intend	67.7	36.3	28.5	45.8
Number	3,277	1,188	4,706	1,706
Need for family planning services[d]				
Unmet need for family planning: To space	11.4	6.5	10.9	9.4
To limit	19.0	6.5	9.7	8.0
Total	30.5	13.0	20.6	17.4
Met need—currently using: To space	2.2	5.4	10.8	10.2
To limit	10.9	53.4	34.1	47.2
Total	13.0	58.7	44.9	57.4
Total demand for family planning: To space	13.6	11.8	21.7	19.6
To limit	29.9	59.9	43.8	55.2
Total	43.5	71.7	65.5	74.8
Per cent of need satisfied	29.9	81.9	68.6	76.7
Number	3,768	2,877	8,840	3,970

[a] Among all currently married women aged 15–49.
[b] Wants next birth within two years.
[c] Wants to delay next birth for two or more years.
[d] Among currently married nonusers.

family planning is met by current programmes in the Pakistan Punjab compared with 82 per cent in the Indian Punjab.

Fertility preferences do not differ much between the two Bengals. The proportion of women who say they want another child in the future is almost the same in the two Bengals (37 per cent in Bangladesh and 31 per cent in West Bengal). Similarly, a total of 58 and 65 per cent of currently married women in Bangladesh and West Bengal, respectively, either do not want any more children or are sterilized. However, a greater proportion of currently married nonusers intend to use contraception in the future in Bangladesh (67 per cent) than in West Bengal (47 per cent).. The two Bengals do not differ much in the proportion of currently married women with an unmet need for family planning. But the proportion of women who are current users and do not want additional children within two years or any time in the future (met need) is greater in West Bengal (57 per cent) than in Bangladesh (45 per cent).

Discussion

The Punjabs

The comparisons shown in this analysis suggest that differences in fertility between the two Punjabs can largely be accounted for by the difference in contraceptive use. Why is fertility so much lower and contraceptive use so much higher in the Indian Punjab than in the Pakistan Punjab? Three alternative explanations can be offered. These explanations are only hypotheses and not conclusions, because the relative importance of each of these factors needs to be further determined.

The first explanation relates to major religious differences between the two Punjabs. Although the two populations speak the same language, they profess different religions. While the population of Pakistan Punjab is predominantly Muslim, Sikhs and Hindus form the major two religious groups in the Indian Punjab. Therefore, some of the differences in fertility and contraceptive use be-tween the two Punjabs may be due to the differences in religion. Within the Indian Punjab, however, no major differences in fertility and family planning use are observed between Sikhs and Hindus (Tables 8.3 and 8.6).

It is difficult to determine whether religion *per se* is an important factor affecting differentials in fertility and contraceptive use between the two Punjabs. However, the extent to which women report their religion as a major reason for not using contraception may be considered as an indirect measure of the role of religion in determining contraceptive use. According to the PDHS and the NFHS, less than 1 per cent of the currently married nonusers who do not intend to use family planning in the future gave religion as the main reason in the Indian Punjab, compared with 15 per cent in the Pakistan Punjab. It may also be noted here that during the course of evolution of population control programmes in Pakistan, misperceptions about the Islamic position on family planning have often played a significant role in determining the family planning programme messages and the degree of political support given to the programme (Mahmood and Ringheim 1993; Rosen and Conly 1996).

The two Punjabs have experienced differences in governance for the last half a century or so, and these have resulted in differential developmental inputs. In fact, past research has attributed the rapid fertility decline in the Indian Punjab to various developmental inputs, including the Green Revolution in the state

(Ali 1981; Basu 1988; Das Gupta 1995; Kak 1984; Leaf 1983; Nag 1989; UNESCAP 1975).

Levels of developmental input were considerable in the two Punjabs even before partition in 1947. The united Punjab was a major province of British India, and received huge investments in the agricultural sector under British colonial rule (Calvert 1936; Darling 1947; Das Gupta 1995). Beginning in the 1860s, irrigation was expanded through the construction of canals and the digging of wells; and by the 1930s, improved seeds, agricultural technologies and livestock breeds were brought to the farmers through large-scale agricultural extension programmes. However, when compared to the part that remained in India, the part of the Punjab that became Pakistan in 1947 was larger in area, and was at that time richer in terms of existing agricultural assets, agricultural potential and mineral wealth. The Pakistan Punjab contained important canals, and had about 70 per cent of all the fertile canal-irrigated tracts that had existed in the undivided Punjab. The Indian Punjab was left with only about 34 per cent of the irrigated area (Kak 1984).

The Indian Punjab has benefited from a great deal of developmental input since around 1966, and is today by far the richest state in India. Although agriculture in the Pakistan Punjab has also been flourishing, the relative increase in agricultural outputs and productivity has been greater in the Indian Punjab, particularly in the late 1960s (Papanek 1991). The mid-1960s for the Indian Punjab was also the period when social development infrastructures—such as education, health and family planning—were expanded rapidly. These developmental inputs resulted in increasing standards of living, literacy, health and family planning facilities, and employment opportunities off-farm, which in turn resulted in a further increase in the already increasing age at marriage and the use of contraception in the state. Differential developmental inputs in the two Punjabs are also reflected in better education and standard of living among currently married women in the Indian Punjab (Table 8.1).

The two Punjabs also differ in terms of the planning and implementation of programmes to provide family planning services. Although family planning programmes in India and Pakistan were initiated around the same time, family planning was given greater priority in India. The family planning programme in Pakistan suffered frequent shifts in political commitment as well as in approach and strategy, and this reduced to a considerable extent the overall efficiency of the programme (Rosen and Conly 1996). A recent assessment of the strength of key elements of national family planning programmes by Ross and Mauldin (1996) indicates that the programme of Pakistan is weaker than that of India on all of four components: policy, service, recordkeeping and method availability. Programme-effort scores as a percentage of a maximum were lower for Pakistan than for India in all the four study periods: 1972, 1982, 1989 and 1994.

The vast differences observed in fertility preferences, intentions to use family planning in the future and the unmet need for family planning (Table 8.8) as well as in contraceptive prevalence rates (Table 8.6) between the two Punjabs suggest that both the demand for and supply of family planning methods and services (which are determined to a large extent by the relative strengths of the two family planning programmes) are greater in the Indian Punjab than in the Pakistan Punjab.

Multivariate analysis. In order to examine the extent to which the differences in the socioeconomic and demographic characteristics of women in the two Punjabs explain higher contraceptive use in the Indian Punjab, we use logistic regression on the pooled data set, with the country of residence as one of the predictor variables. The dependent variable is a dichotomous indicator that equals 1 if the woman is currently using contraception and 0 otherwise. The predictor variables included are: one dummy variable to represent two countries (Pakistan and India), one dummy variable to represent two age categories (<30 years and 30+ years), four dummy variables to represent five categories of number of living children (none, 1, 2, 3 and 4+), four dummy variables to represent five categories of number of living sons (none, 1, 2, 3 and 4+), one dummy variable to represent two residence categories (rural and urban), three dummy variables to represent four educational categories (no schooling, primary incomplete, primary complete and secondary/higher), one dummy variable to represent two categories of exposure to mass media (regularly exposed to either radio or television at least once a week; and not exposed and exposed), and two dummy variables to represent three standard of living categories (poor, middle and high). The odds of a woman currently using contraception relative to the reference group in each category of the predictor variable are presented in Table 8.9.

Even after controlling for the selected socioeconomic and demographic characteristics by holding them constant, the effect of country of residence on contraceptive use is very strong. Compared with the women in the Pakistan Punjab, women in the Indian Punjab are 12 times more likely to be currently using contraception. It is assumed here that after controlling for relevant socioeconomic and demographic variables, the effect of country on contraceptive use represents the effect of differences between the two Punjabs in terms of the characteristics of family planning programmes as well as the religious composition of the populations.

The Bengals

Current fertility is slightly lower and the use of family planning and median age at marriage is slightly higher in West Bengal than in Bangladesh, although the two Bengals do not differ much in median duration of postpartum nonsusceptibility. The two areas differ considerably in terms of the choice of methods among current users of family planning: while the use of modern methods of contraception is almost the same in the two areas, the use of traditional methods is higher in West Bengal than in Bangladesh. Thus, most of the difference in fertility between the two Bengals may be attributed to differences in age at marriage and to the use of traditional methods of family planning. (Since the difference in contraceptive use rate is small between the two Bengals and is not the most important variable in explaining

Table 8.9. Logistic regression explaining current use of contraception: the Punjabs

Predictor variables	Odds ratio	Standard error
Country (Reference: Pakistan Punjab)		
Indian Punjab	11.91*	1.13
Current age (Reference: <30 years)		
30+ years	1.41*	0.13
Number of living children (Reference: none)		
1	13.07*	5.37
2	32.38*	13.27
3	48.21*	19.97
4+	55.22*	23.20
Number of living sons (Reference: none)		
1	2.05*	0.29
2	4.10*	0.62
3	5.14*	0.93
4+	4.24	0.85
Residence (Reference: rural)		
Urban	1.20***	0.11
Education (Reference: no schooling)		
Primary incomplete	1.09	0.22
Primary complete	1.37**	0.16
Secondary/higher	2.17*	0.25
Exposure to mass media (Reference: not exposed)		
Exposed	1.78*	0.17
Standard of living (Reference: low)		
Middle	1.54*	0.16
High	1.89*	0.27
Number	4,977	—
Log likelihood	−2,190.91	—
Chi-square	2,356.66*	—

*Significant at 0.000.
**Significant at 0.005.
***Significant at 0.050.

the fertility differences between the two Bengals, a multivariate analysis of contraceptive use between the two Bengals—which was done in the case of the two Punjabs—is not presented here.) Moreover, fertility decline and increase in contraceptive use has been much more rapid in Bangladesh than in West Bengal.

Rapid fertility decline in Bangladesh has been one of the major themes in recent demographic literature, and has been considered a classic example of how an effectively planned and implemented family planning programme can affect fertility decline, even in adverse socioeconomic conditions (Cleland *et al.* 1994). As seen in Table 8.1, women in West Bengal fare better than their counterparts in Bangladesh on almost all aspects of socioeconomic development. However, fertility decline in Bangladesh has been synchronous for all large socioeconomic groups, as indicated by smaller differentials in fertility across residence and education groups compared to those observed in West Bengal. It is well documented in the recent demographic literature that rapid fertility decline in Bangladesh has been possible largely because of its family planning programme.

Summary and Conclusions

In this paper, the role of ethnicity (defined in terms of a population living in geographically contiguous areas, sharing the same language, history and cultural traits) *vis-à-vis* the role of socioeconomic developmental inputs and programmes specific to family planning is examined by comparing fertility and its proximate determinants in the two Punjabi-speaking populations across the India–Pakistan border, and in the two Bengali-speaking populations across the India–Bangladesh border. The major differences and similarities between these two ethnic groups across national borders can be summarized as follows:

1. Fertility is substantially higher and contraceptive use substantially lower in the Pakistan Punjab. However, the two Punjabs do not differ in age at marriage for females. Differences in fertility and contraceptive use between the two Punjabs persist in every socioeconomic category. The two Punjabs also differ considerably in terms of the role of religion in determining the intention to use family planning, socioeconomic development inputs, and the strengths of family planning programmes.

2. West Bengal has a somewhat lower fertility, a somewhat higher contraceptive use rate and a somewhat higher age at marriage than Bangladesh. The two Bengals do not differ in the duration of postpartum nonsusceptibility. Most of the difference in contraceptive use between the Bengals is due to the difference in the use of traditional methods, as the two areas do not differ much in the use of modern methods. Overall, traditional methods are more popular among current users in West Bengal than in Bangladesh, and the modern temporary methods are more popular in Bangladesh than in West Bengal. The two Bengals also differ considerably on various socioeconomic development indicators such as urban residence, education, exposure to mass media and standard of living. However, the decline in fertility and increase in contraceptive use has been much more rapid in Bangladesh than in West Bengal.

There are more differences than similarities in fertility and contraceptive use between similar ethnic groups across national borders. Most of these differences may be attributed to the nature and strengths of respective national family planning programmes. A weak population control programme in Pakistan is reflected in substantially lower contraceptive use in the Pakistan than in the Indian Punjab. The rapid decline in fertility in the Indian Punjab may also be attributed to greater developmental inputs it received during the last three decades. A strong family planning programme has also contributed to a more rapid fertility decline and increase in contraceptive use in Bangladesh than in West Bengal. Religion is possibly an important factor explaining differences in fertility and family planning use between the two Punjabs. However, a comparison between the Pakistani Punjab and Bangladesh, which share a common religion but contrasting fertility levels, suggests that the initiatives and strengths of the national family planning programmes, rather than religion, have to a large extent determined the course of fertility transition. Thus, although the Punjabs and the Bengals are situated in geographically contiguous areas, sharing language, history and several other cultural characteristics, the course of their fertility transition has been shaped by their respective developmental programmes—particularly their family planning programmes.

References

Ali, K. (1981), 'Impact of Agricultural Modernization on Crude Birth Rate in Indian Punjab', *Pakistan Development Review*, 20(2): 247–67.

Basu, Alaka Malwade (1988), 'How Economic Development can Overcome Culture: Demographic Change in Punjab, India', *Population Research and Policy Review*, 7.

Calvert, H. (1936), *The Wealth and Welfare of the Punjab*, Lahore: Civil and Military Gazette Press.

Cleland, J., Phillips, J. F., Amin, S., and Kamal, G. M. (1994), *The Determinants of Reproductive Change in Bangladesh: Success in a Challenging Environment*, Washington, DC: World Bank.

Darling, M. (1947), *The Punjab Peasant in Prosperity and Debt*, Bombay: Oxford University Press.

Das Gupta, M. (1995), 'Fertility Decline in Punjab: Parallels with Historical Europe', *Population Studies*, 49.

Huq, M. N., and Cleland, J. (1990), *Bangladesh Fertility Survey 1989: Main Report*, Dhaka: National Institute of Population Research and Training (NIPORT).

International Institute for Population Sciences (IIPS) (1995), *National Family Health Survey (MCH and Family Planning), West Bengal 1992*, Bombay: IIPS.

Kak, N. (1984), *Determinants of Fertility: A Case Study of Punjab (India)*, Ann Arbor, Michigan: University Microfilms International.

Larson, A., and Mitra, S. N. (1992), 'Family Planning in Bangladesh: An Unlikely Success Story', *International Family Planning Perspectives*, 18(4).

Leaf, M. J. (1983), 'The Green Revolution and Cultural Change in a Punjab Village 1965–1972', *Economic Development and Cultural Change*, 31: 227–70.

Mahmood, N., and Ringheim, K. (1993), 'Five Factors Affecting Family Planning Use in Pakistan: An Analysis of Husbands and Wives', Paper presented to the IUSSP World Conference, Montreal, Canada.

Ministry of Health and Population Control (MHPC) (1978), *Bangladesh Fertility Survey, 1975–1976: First Report*, Dhaka: Government of the People's Republic of Bangladesh and the World Fertility Survey.

Ministry of Population Welfare and Population Council (1995), *Pakistan Contraceptive Prevalence Survey 1994–95, Basic Findings*, Islamabad: Population, Council.

Mitra, S. N., Lerman, C., and Islam, S. (1993), *Bangladesh Contraceptive Prevalence Survey—1991: Final Report*, Dhaka: Mitra and Associates.

—— and Kamal, G. M. (1985), *Bangladesh Contraceptive Prevalence Survey—1983: Final Report*, Dhaka: Mitra and Associates.

Nag, M. (1989), 'Alternative Routes of Fertility and Mortality Decline: A Study of Kerala and Punjab', in M. K. Premi, P. S. Bhatia and Ashish Bose (eds.), *Population Transition in India*, Vol. 1, Delhi: B.R. Publishing, pp. 143–57.

National Institute of Population Research and Training (NIPORT), Mitra and Associates, and Macro International Inc. (1994), *Bangladesh Demographic and Health Survey 1993–1994*, Dhaka: NIPORT, Mitra Associates and Macro International Inc.

National Institute of Population Studies (NIPS) (1988), *The State of Population in Pakistan*, Islamabad: NIPS.

—— and IRD/Macro International (1992), *Pakistan Demographic and Health Survey 1990/1991*, Islamabad: NIPS.

Papanek, G. F. (1991), 'Market or Government: Lessons from a Comparative Analysis of the Experience of Pakistan and India', *The Pakistan Development Review*, 30(4), Part I, 601–39.

Population Research Centre, Centre for Research in Rural and Industrial Development (PRC, CRRID) and International Institute for Population Sciences (IIPS) (1995), *National Family Health Survey (MCH and Family Planning), Punjab 1993*, Bombay: PRC, CRRID and IIPS.

Retherford, R. D., Mirza, G. M., Irfan, M., and Alam, I. (1987), 'Fertility Trends in Pakistan—The Decline that Wasn't', *Asian and Pacific Population Forum*, 1(2): 3–10.

Rosen, J. E., and Conly, S. R. (1996), *Pakistan's Population Program: The Challenge Ahead*, Washington, DC: Population Action International.

Ross, J. A., and Mauldin, W. P. (1996), 'Family Planning Programs: Efforts and Results, 1972–94', *Studies in Family Planning*, 27(3): 137–47.

Sathar, Z. A., and Irfan, M. (1984), 'Reproductive Behaviour in Pakistan: Insights from the Population, Labour Force and Migration Survey 1979–80', *Pakistan Development Review*, 23(2&3): 207–18.

Shah, I. H., Pullum, T. W., and Irfan, M. (1986), 'Fertility in Pakistan during the 1970s', *Journal of Biosocial Science*, 18: 215–29.

Taylor, C. E., and Singh, R. D. (1975), *The Narangwal Population Study: Integrated Health and Family Planning Services*, Narangwal: Rural Health Research Centre.

United Nations Economic and Social Commission for Asia and the Pacific (UNESCAP) (1975), *Comparative Study of Population Growth and Agricultural Change: Case Study of India*, Bangkok: UNESCAP.

Wyon, J. B., and Gordon, J. E. (1971), *The Khanna Study*, Cambridge: Harvard University Press.

9 Synthesizing Diverse Interpretations of Reproductive Change in India

MONICA DAS GUPTA

Introduction

Within the span of a century and a half, monarchies have been replaced by popular governments through most of the world. Anyone reflecting on this fact would consider it meaningless to look in the specific local circumstances of a particular setting for the prime driving force behind these changes. For example, it would make little sense to explain the French Revolution in very different terms from the Communist Chinese Revolution or from the independence movements of colonized countries, simply because these settings differed substantially in their specific economic and other circumstances. It would seem to make more sense to seek the underlying explanation in terms of hypotheses that are more generalizable and can only be reached by a broad comparative approach.

The fertility transition, which has also taken place largely within the span of a century, is very similar to the spread of popular governments in that it, too, involves an enormous shift in ways of thinking across the globe. This shift also took place under very different local conditions: economic, political, social, cultural and demographic. However, most existing explanations of reproductive change tend to be highly embedded in the local circumstances of the setting being discussed. Thus we are given a multiplicity of reasons for the change (or lack thereof), including the role of specific forms of economic development, social development, family planning programmes, mortality decline, female education and women's status, as well as location-specific reasons for changes in the costs and benefits of childrearing. There has been heated debate, for example, on the subject of whether development or family planning programmes is the factor primarily responsible for reproductive change.

Some explanations accounting for fertility decline do highlight the role of changes that are sweeping the globe, such as Notestein's (1953) emphasis on the role of industrialization, urbanization, education and mortality decline. Caldwell (1976, 1978, 1980) has emphasized the changes in intrafamilial relations brought about by the spread of education, Westernization, and the shift to modern occupations. He draws attention to attitudinal shifts which, along with a new need to invest in children's education, led to a reversal of the traditional wealth flows whereby parents benefited economically from their children.

A large study of fertility decline in Europe found considerable uniformity of behaviour within linguistic/cultural groups, leading Coale (1973) to suggest that linguistic boundaries served as 'firebreaks' in the diffusion of new family size norms. More recent works on the diffusion of fertility norms and information about means of fertility control (Cleland and Wilson 1987; Pollack and Watkins 1993) have emphasized the role of exogenous as opposed to endogenous factors. To avoid an excessively particularistic interpretation of reproductive change, it is important to widen the geographical and historical scope of the analysis. As the scope of analysis is extended, it becomes possible to move beyond the immediate local-specific factors and obtain a broader understanding of the factors that speed or hinder fertility decline.

Another important reason why social scientists have come up with very diverse interpretations of the reasons underlying fertility decline is the fact that they use very different approaches and methodologies. Sometimes, the use of multiple approaches can even result in very different explanations for fertility change in the same location. This makes it critical to understand the strengths, limitations and biases of these different methodologies. We will illustrate this problem by using the case of a district in Punjab, in which several different studies have reached quite different conclusions regarding the fertility transition.

We begin by addressing this more mechanical (yet often overlooked) reason for disparate theories of reproductive change, and then move on to exploring some of the more generalizable lessons to be derived from inter-regional comparisons within India.

Different Methodologies Used in One Setting

The strengths and limitations of some approaches commonly used by demographers in studying fertility behaviour are well illustrated by the case of the Khanna Study villages in Ludhiana district of Punjab, localities that have been studied several times using a variety of methodologies. The original study was a carefully designed epidemiological study (Wyon and Gordon 1971) with a followup in 1969. In 1970, a quasi-anthropological study was carried out in one of the villages (Mamdani 1972). In 1982, another brief study was carried out in the same village (Nag and Kak 1984). In 1984–88, I conducted a prospective study in these same villages, collecting demographic survey data along with anthropological data and archival data (Das Gupta 1994, 1995a; Dyson and Das Gupta, forthcoming). Thus the strengths and limitations as well as the results of different methodologies can be compared quite effectively in this setting.

Four commonly used methodologies are discussed here. One is to compare data from different surveys separated by some time interval: if fertility has changed during the intervening period, then other factors that have also changed during that time are analysed, in an effort to understand how they may be related to the change in fertility. A second approach is the purely qualitative one, which involves inter-viewing people to understand their childbearing motivations. The third is that of analysing cross-sectional survey data to look for the statistical correlates of family size, which are assumed to be causally related to fertility differentials. The fourth is a more historical approach, combining demographic and anthropological method-ologies to examine fertility behaviour over a longer sweep of time.

Method 1: Studying Changes between Two Points in Time

Given that demographic data are available from two surveys spaced as much as 30 years apart, one standard analytical approach would be to compare fertility levels at the two points in time. Such an analysis would reveal that fertility was high in the study villages in the 1950s, with a total fertility rate (TFR) of 5.55 in 1957–59. By 1984, this had fallen to 3.26 children per woman. Examination of the events that might have helped bring about such a decline in fertility during this intervening period would reveal that there were, in fact, many factors at work, many of which could be expected to lead to fertility decline.

From the mid-1960s onwards, this region of India underwent rapid economic and social development. One of the most important aspects was the introduction of the new Green Revolution technology in agriculture, which led to a rapid rise in income and wage levels in the agricultural sector. This impetus also transformed employment opportunities in the region. Industries related to the agricultural sector mushroomed, including the production and maintenance of agricultural machinery, food processing, dairying and other agribusiness. Investments in other light and heavy industry also opened up employment opportunities, as did the expansion of the tertiary sector, which sprang up to service the newly transformed primary and secondary sectors. Thus, there was a substantial shift in the occupa-tional structure, with a fall in the proportions employed in agriculture. Nag and Kak (1984: 671) mention, for example, that the proportion of workers employed in the industrial, commercial and government sectors rose from 8 per cent in 1970 to 29 per cent in 1982. Integration between the rural and the urban areas was also fostered by the development of roads and public transportation, as well as by increased communication in the form of radio and television.

The public education system was greatly expanded. The opening of new schools meant that children could go to a school either in their own village or in a nearby village a short walk away. Among all population groups, levels of education rose rapidly as a result. In 1984, the proportion of women with some schooling was 11 per cent among those aged 45–49, compared with 84 per cent among those aged 10–14 (Das Gupta 1994).

The public health system was also expanded, which meant that primary health care changed from being essentially urban-based to being widely available in the rural areas. Primary health centres were opened in villages, and by 1984, every study village had access to a health centre, if not within the village, then within two miles of the village. Mortality rates declined: for example, the infant mortality rate (IMF) in the study villages, which had been 156 per 1,000 live births in 1957–59, fell to 62 per 1,000 by 1979–84. Along with the primary health care system came a totally new effort to spread free family planning information and supplies to the entire population. For the first time, family planning services became available in the rural areas.

This transformation in levels of income, types of occupations available, integration with urban areas, general education and female education in particular, infant mortality decline, combined with the advent of an active family planning programme, all created conditions ideal for fertility decline, in line with Notestein's theory (1953). Thus, the fertility decline in this region would seem merely to confirm the validity of this classical theory.

Method 2: The Quick Qualitative Study

One of the most influential books in terms of shaping academics' and policy makers' views about fertility behaviour also happens to be one of the best examples of how misleading a quick qualitative study can be, especially if imbued with a strong ideological bias (Mamdani 1972). Based on a brief visit to one of the 11 villages included in the Khanna Study, Mamdani set out to explain the apparent failure of an intensive family planning programme carried out in the 1950s in these villages (Wyon and Gordon 1971). The authors of the original study had found that although fertility declined in these villages between the 1950s and their followup in 1969, the reduction did not seem to be related to the intervention in question. Mamdani ignored the fact of fertility decline and focused on the causes of the apparent failure of the family planning programme.

The book's thesis is that people did not want to reduce their fertility, because of the labour value of children. People needed to have many children in order to avoid impoverishment, or to rise out of impoverishment. Despite the fact that the community as a whole was suffering from the effects of rapid population growth, children's labour value to the household was such that individual families did not perceive it to be in their interest to reduce their fertility.

Mamdani argued that high fertility was a necessary survival strategy for all but the few rich farmers who could afford tractors. In the case of agricultural labourers (who, he acknowledged, were underemployed most of the year), Mamdani argued that they needed to have the maximum number of hands available during the peak labour seasons, so that the household earnings at that time could be maximized and savings generated for the lean seasons. 'A larger family means a greater income during the busy season and higher savings for the slow season' (Mamdani 1972: 95).

Mamdani does not substantiate this statement with any evidence that, even though the peak labour seasons are short, the earnings from an extra pair of hands did indeed give rise to *net* savings for the household. This omission is completely at odds with the results of a careful and detailed study carried out in Bangladesh

(Cain 1977), which found that amongst the poorer strata, children's earnings did *not* constitute a net contribution to the household.

The artisan castes in the village had found that their traditional occupations had been rendered obsolete by the advent of new technologies. They were trying to educate their children for employment outside the village, or in the use of new technologies for work within the village. Mamdani argued that in order to do this, they also needed as many children as possible. He said that the adults' earnings were too low to enable them to educate or to retrain their children. Therefore, they needed to have large numbers of children, so that their combined earnings could be used to put one child at a time through the educational process. Once again, he offered no evidence that this was in fact an effective strategy for these families.

In the case of the landowners, Mamdani argued that the costs of hiring labour were crippling, and that if households were to avoid financial ruin, they must generate their own family labour. Only the children of farmers who owned tractors, he said, were likely to be favourable to reducing family size, and this was inapplicable to most farmers because they did not have enough land to justify buying a tractor (1972: 87). This conclusion is misleading, because it has been common practice for smaller landowners to rent tractors from larger landowners.

However, this is one occasion on which Mamdani did provide some corroborative data, so it becomes possible to verify his statement. He used the case of Gurdev Singh (1972: 82–3) to illustrate his point about the ruinous cost of hiring labour. Gurdev Singh, he says, was unfortunate because he had only two sons, both of whom were working outside the village. Thus the farmer had to use hired labour to cultivate his fields. The resultant operating expenses he cited amount to 77 per cent of his farm income. One can only conclude from this that Gurdev Singh understated his income (as is commonly found when collecting income data), because the standard sharecropping terms would have given him at least 50 per cent of the share of the crop, and more if he provided a managerial role.

A major factor in the continuing influence of Mamdani's book is the fact that this thesis held strong appeal for people from both the right and left of the political spectrum, in academic and policy-making circles. The book was very well written and highly persuasive in its conclusion that Indian villagers needed large families in their grim struggle for survival, and that they could not afford to concern themselves with their children's welfare: 'To practice contraception would have meant to wilfully court economic disaster' (Mamdani 1972: 21). He also writes:

The problem of the fragmentation of land is the problem of the next generation, of tomorrow. The farmer's main problem is to make a living off the land in his own lifetime, to meet the costs of production in the present generation. The problem of production costs is the problem of today.   (Mamdani 1972: 74.)

Such powerful writing is clearly appealing to many shades of the political spectrum. However, as will be discussed later in this analysis, fertility decline was already well established amongst all socioeconomic strata of the population decades before

Mamdani's study, so the villagers seem to have disagreed with his conclusions about the powerful need for high fertility. Moreover, even under the circumstances of real poverty prevailing at the turn of the century, households commonly regulated their future growth by having the number of children intended to ensure the welfare of the next generation.

Nag and Kak (1984) visited the same village in 1982, 12 years after Mamdani's study. They conducted a contraceptive use survey, and found that rates had risen since 1970. The new state family planning programme, organized around 1966, began to make modern contraceptive methods available, and programme outreach to the rural areas expanded enormously during the 1970s. Interpreting the rise in contraceptive prevalence as reflecting a new interest in fertility reduction, these researchers sought to understand what happened between 1970 and 1982 to account for people's shift towards lower fertility. They concluded that the new agricultural technology had reduced the labour value of children, and that the growth of female education had also helped bring about the fertility decline. However, the research summarized below showed that fertility had begun to decline long before the 1970s, so their analysis provided at best a partial understanding of the reasons for the decline.

Nag and Kak also interviewed some of the people whom Mamdani had used as case studies, and found that they uniformly favoured fertility reduction. Many had actively encouraged their children to become sterilized and keep their families small, because they felt this to be advantageous from every viewpoint, including economically. This is of considerable interest, because it draws attention to the fact that most of the respondents reported by Mamdani must have had most of their children in the 1940s, as the children were already grown up and employed when Mamdani interviewed them in 1970. Thus the views Mamdani reported the villagers as holding reflect the childbearing logic prevailing in the 1940s, when fertility decline was just beginning. Their contemporary (1970) views about desired family size are better reflected in the advice they gave their grown children in the 1970s, when as Nag and Kak report they were actively encouraging their children to have smaller families.

Method 3: A Cross-Sectional Study of the Statistical Correlates of Family Size

A 1994 study by this author analysed data from a cross-sectional fertility survey in an attempt to investigate how family size was related to various measures of household socioeconomic status, female education and autonomy, desired family size, son preference, child survival and media exposure (Das Gupta 1994). Two variables were used as indices of child survival: the conventional variable of the mother's experience of child loss; and the mother's parents' experience of child loss. This latter variable was incorporated because qualitative investigation suggests that people whose parents suffered from reproductive failure have a strong sense of the pain and insecurity associated with the experience, and are inclined to over-respond by wanting to have more children than their spouses or other peers deem necessary.

The results suggest that per capita income is strongly negatively correlated with fertility. Controlling for per capita income, the size of landholding is positively correlated with fertility, but the size of the coefficient is small, indicating that large increments in land ownership are associated with only small increases in family size. Wealth is different from income, in that it provides insurance against future variations in income, but even the possession of such insurance has only a small effect on raising fertility. Differentials by occupational status are virtually negligible, as people from lower occupational groups do not end up with larger numbers of surviving children.

In India, caste is a good general indicator of socioeconomic status. There appeared to be a strong negative correlation between fertility and belonging to the high landowning caste, even controlling for income, education, and other factors that might generate such caste differentials in fertility. Qualitative data suggest that the landowning caste are motivated to control their fertility to avoid rapid subdivision of their land. The onset of a fertility decline among this group occurred a little earlier than it did among the lower castes, and the resulting differential in fertility levels still persists (Das Gupta 1994, 1995a).

Women's autonomy is negatively related to fertility, and, interestingly, this holds even after controlling for factors normally viewed as causally related to this link, such as education and household socioeconomic status. This finding should not necessarily be interpreted as meaning that men are less motivated than women to control childbearing. Rather, it is likely that poorer communication and coordination of plans between spouses in authoritarian households hinders the realization of family-building goals.

Women's education does not have a significant effect after controlling for per capita income. This finding suggests that much of the effect of education may in fact be that of the higher economic and social status associated with higher education. Introducing infant mortality and desired family size into the calculation further reduces the effect of women's education, confirming that these are some of the pathways through which education influences fertility. As expected, the higher the woman's age at marriage, the lower her fertility. Also as expected, the lower the desired family size, the lower the fertility. The real factor at work here is the number of *sons* desired, rather than the number of children desired, which is consistent with the strong son preference of this society (Das Gupta 1987, 1998).

Infant mortality is associated with a larger number of children ever born, but a *smaller* number surviving. This finding suggests that people have more births if they lose children, but not enough to replace all the children who died. By contrast, if a woman's parents experienced extreme reproductive failure, she has significantly higher numbers of children, surviving as well as ever born. It must be remembered, though, that the indicator used is whether the woman was the only surviving child of her parents, which is an extreme experience of reproductive failure.

Media exposure (ownership of a television) is significantly negatively related to fertility, both children ever born and surviving. This is only slightly mitigated by controlling for per capita income, which suggests that ownership of a television is not simply a proxy for economic status, but that exposure to the media significantly influences behaviour. State-run television channels make considerable effort to design programmes and soap operas that convey a variety of messages conducive to lowering family size. This includes much material that goes well beyond messages about the more attractive lifestyles associated with small families. For example, there is a serious effort to alter women's status: by portraying images of self-confident women in charge of their own lives; by discussing women's legal rights; by portraying the complexities of some of the social problems faced by women; by incorporating into storylines information on sources of subfecundity and letting people know that the majority of cases of childless marriages are due to male rather than female infertility. It is important from a policy perspective to be able to find evidence that these efforts at social engineering have been successful.

Perhaps the most important finding from a policy perspective is the strong confirmation of the impact of the media on fertility (see also Bhat 1998). Another interesting finding is that reproductive failure in one generation results in higher fertility in the next generation, suggesting an inter-generational transmission of insecurity about reaching family size goals. Efforts to reduce the risk of child loss are conducive to fertility decline. Efforts to increase women's autonomy are clearly important as goals in their own right, and will also help accelerate fertility decline. As the next section shows, however, the results of this multivariate analysis do not take us to the heart of the reasons underlying the fertility decline.

Method 4: A Longer Historical Approach

An examination of the historical dimension of demographic change in Ludhiana district (see Fig. 9.1) shows that fertility had already started declining in the 1940s (Dyson and Das Gupta, forthcoming). This was almost a quarter of a century before the spread of universal education, and extension of the health and family planning programmes. At the time fertility began to decline in Punjab, infant mortality was over 150 per thousand, levels of literacy were negligible, and there was effectively no access to modern contraceptive methods. Moreover, though agricultural yields were rising steadily, levels of living in Punjab in the 1940s remained relatively low as compared with the affluence generated by the recent Green Revolution.

What seems to have triggered off this fertility decline is substantial effort by the colonial administration to promote economic development in Punjab (Das Gupta 1995a). In particular, an ambitious effort to construct canals and wells to bring perennial irrigation to this arid region was very successful at raising agricultural productivity. The expansion of transport, marketing infrastructure, and other developmental inputs generated substantial economic growth and raised income levels. Even more important was the fact that these developments *stabilized* yields, putting an end to the epidemics and famines caused by sharp fluctuations in harvests that had earlier generated tremendous insecurity in people's lives. All strata of the population benefited from these dramatic improvements.

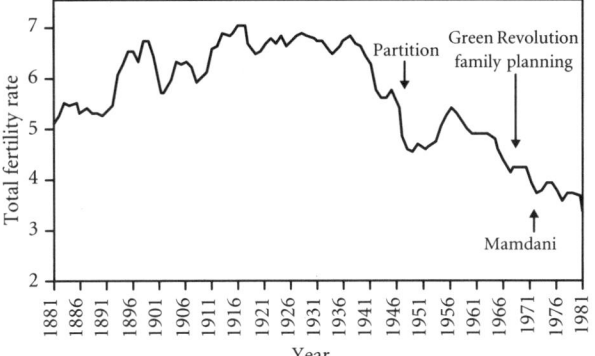

Figure 9.1. Total fertility rate, Ludhiana district, Punjab, 1881–1981 (three-year moving average).

Source: Dyson and Das Gupta, forthcoming.

The newly found security of life and livelihood make it not only possible for people to practise fertility regulation, but also imperative to do so in order to minimize the pressure on resources caused by sustained mortality decline. Traditional practices of population regulation existed (Das Gupta 1995a), notably the practice amongst the landowning caste of regulating marriage in order to avoid rapid subdivision of property and to ensure the household's continued viability over time. Figure 9.2 reveals that these limitations on marriage were practised more commonly amongst those who had smaller landholdings (Census of India 1901: 223, 1911: 65, 260). With the sustained mortality decline, marriage regulation was increased (Table 9.1), the age at marriage was raised, and the age at last birth was lowered by methods such as terminal abstinence. It is probably safe to say, therefore, that the advent of modern contraceptives and family planning outreach has greatly facilitated, but not invented, the transition to low fertility.

This longer historical perspective illustrates some of the pitfalls of the other approaches to understanding reproductive change. Simply looking at changes between two points in time for which data are easily available, with no reference to a longer sweep of time, can clearly be misleading. Qualitative study with no quantitative reference points is dangerous: by the time that Mamdani was arguing that all social classes needed high fertility, the TFR had already fallen substantially (Fig. 9.1). Analysis of cross-sectional fertility survey data points to the contemporary correlates of lower fertility, which, at least in this instance, are not those underlying the decline. Moreover, some of the factors highlighted by such analysis may be more proximate determinants than underlying causes of the process. A combination of historical, anthropological and demographic approaches gives a deeper understanding of the factors underlying reproductive change.

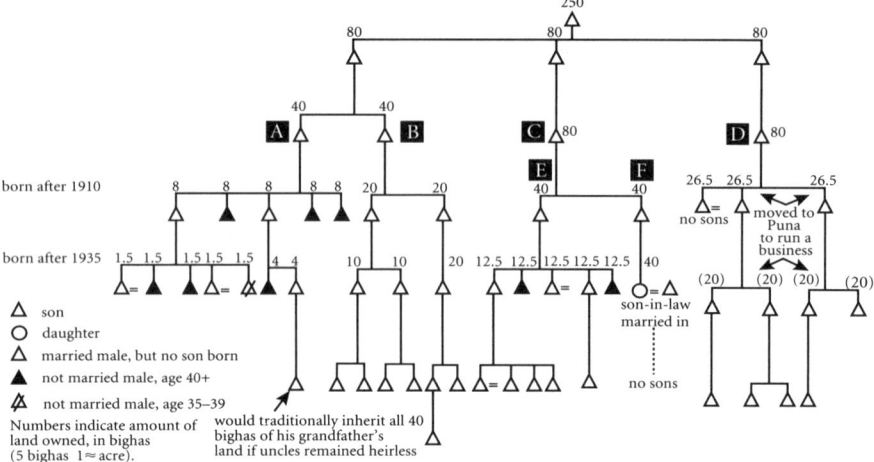

Figure 9.2. Genealogy of a Jat sublineage, Ludhiana district.

Source: Das Gupta (1995a), based on records and interviews.

Regional Comparisons within India

Studying Different Regions of India

If one can obtain such different interpretations of the causes of reproductive change from the study of a single setting, we can expect much more diversity of explanation when looking at different parts of India. In-depth studies of reproductive change in India tend to focus on a particular part of the country rather than the country as a whole, perhaps because it is such a heterogeneous country. The explanations advanced for fertility decline seem at first sight to be quite different for different parts of the country. However, we argue that the underlying causes are similar across the country. Here we discuss the explanations put forward in five different regions of the country—Kerala, Tamil Nadu, Punjab, Maharashtra—and those advanced to explain the slowness of the decline in India's central states.

One of the striking features of reproductive change in India is the wide regional differences in the timing and pace of the transition. By 1991, Kerala and Tamil Nadu in South India had approached replacement-level fertility, and the majority of states had moderate fertility levels of around three children per woman, while the central states continued to have high fertility levels of around 4.5–5.0 children per woman. Compared with the rest of the country, fertility transition in the central states not only began later, but is also proceeding more slowly (Table 9.2).

With total fertility around 1.7 and infant mortality around 16 per 1,000 in 1993, Kerala's demographic indices resemble those of developed countries. This achievement is especially remarkable in view of the state's lack of prosperity, even in comparison with the rest of India, let alone with developed countries. Kerala is,

Table 9.1. Marriage regulation in Punjab: percentage of men age 40+ never married, 1911–1994

Caste	Punjab		Khanna villages	
	1911	1921	1969	1984
Jat (landowners)	12	13	23	18
Chamar (landless labourers)	4	5	5	4

Source: Das Gupta (1995a), based on Census of India 1911, 1921, and surveys in Khanna villages, 1969, 1984.
Note: Table refers to Sikhs only, as the population of the Khanna villages is predominantly Sikh.

therefore, often held up as a model of what can be accomplished in low-income settings given a political commitment to human development.

Fertility decline in Kerala is attributed to efforts to provide universal education and health care by the state. Efforts in this direction began as early as the beginning of the nineteenth century, when the queen of the princely State of Travancore-Cochin proclaimed that universal education and health care were desirable goals and began to set up schools and encourage missionaries to do the same. By the late nineteenth century, quite substantial proportions of the population were educated, mostly amongst the higher castes. In the early decades of the twentieth century, education was spread actively to the lower castes (Krishnan 1995, 1998). The spread of health care also seems to have had some success (Krishnan 1995).

As in the rest of India, Kerala experienced several movements for religious reform in the late nineteenth and early twentieth centuries. These movements gradually accumulated momentum in breaking down the rigidities of the caste system and loosening up traditional hierarchies. The lower castes in Kerala were active in measures such as establishing universal rights of access to temples, and using educational facilities to establish upward social and economic mobility.

Kerala was more specifically influenced by several socialist movements, such as those to keep wage levels high and to protect workers' welfare. The population is almost universally literate, and high proportions read newspapers on a regular basis and use the public libraries available to both urban and rural areas. The population is highly politicized and aware of its rights, and ensures that public services such as health facilities are well run.

While Kerala presents an impressive example of the human development path of demographic transition, Punjab represents the path of economic development. Punjab has by far the highest per capita income amongst Indian states. Much of Punjab's prosperity derives from agriculture, which was given a major impetus by the opening up of canal and well irrigation in the late nineteenth century. Agriculture received another major impetus with the spread of the Green Revolution from the mid-1960s. More recently, growing industry and agribusiness have

Table 9.2. Indices of fertility and development, major states of India

	Total fertility rate, 1991 [a]	% decline in TFR from 1971 to 1991 [a]	Infant mortality rate, 1992 [a]	Female literacy rate, 1991 [b]	% main workers, 1991 [b]		From live births, 1988–1992 [d]			% of women not regularly exposed to any media, 1992–93 [e]
					Primary sector	Tertiary sector	% coverage of birth registration, 1981 [c]	% antenatal care	% deliveries assisted by allopathic doctor or nurse/midwife	
South										
Andhra Pradesh	3.0	34.78	71	32.72	71.25	18.27	65	86.3	49.3	24.8
Karnataka	3.1	29.55	73	44.34	67.37	19.46	71	83.5	50.9	29.9
Kerala	1.8	56.10	17	86.17	48.02	33.81	76	97.3	89.7	20.8
Tamil Nadu	2.2	43.59	58	51.33	61.81	22.01	78	94.2	71.2	22.0
North Centre										
Bihar	4.4	n.a.	73	22.89	82.36	13.00	20	36.8	19.0	70.5
Madhya Pradesh	4.6	17.86	104	28.85	77.54	14.09	58	52.1	30.0	59.0
Rajasthan	4.6	26.98	90	20.44	71.63	18.50	19	31.2	21.8	69.9
Uttar Pradesh	5.1	22.73	98	25.31	73.01	18.01	21	44.7	17.2	64.5
North West										
Haryana	4.0	40.30	75	40.47	58.84	27.98	66	72.7	30.3	39.9
Punjab	3.1	40.38	56	50.41	56.08	29.08	80	87.9	48.3	34.5
West										
Gujarat	3.1	44.64	67	48.64	59.76	22.38	87	75.7	42.5	44.6
Maharashtra	3.0	34.78	59	52.32	61.51	22.69	74	82.7	53.2	37.2
East										
Orissa	3.3	29.79	115	34.68	75.83	16.66	53	61.6	20.5	60.5
West Bengal	3.2	n.a.	65	46.56	56.49	25.69	46	75.3	33.0	38.7
India	3.6	30.77	79	39.19	67.37	20.50	53	62.3	34.2	47.3

Sources: [a] Sample Registration System, 1970–75, 1991, 1992.
[b] Primary Census Abstract of India, Paper 2 of 1992, pp. 57 and 169–74.
[c] Das Gupta (1996b); calculated as birth rate from Vital Registration System, 1981 expressed as a percentage of birth rate from Sample Registration System (three-year moving average, 1980–82).
[d] National Family Health Survey, India, 1992–93, p. 242.
[e] National Family Health Survey, India, 1992–93, p. 71; percentages calculated from ever-married women aged 13–40.

opened up new avenues of industrial employment, and income levels have been rising in the state.

The emphasis in Punjab has always been on economic development, with far less attention paid to social development. Only in recent decades have attempts been made to provide universal education. Mortality levels in Punjab are only a little lower than the rest of the country, and far higher than those of Kerala (Table 9.2). This is quite out of line with the relative affluence of Punjab. Although fertility decline was evidenced in both Punjab and Kerala in the 1940s, the pace of decline has been much more rapid in Kerala. As discussed above, it was not improvement in the measurable indices of human development that were primarily responsible for triggering the fertility decline in Punjab. Instead, greater stability of expectations and security of life and livelihood were critical factors enabling people to reduce fertility in response to a felt need to reduce the growing pressure of people on available landholdings and other resources.

Tamil Nadu, which has the second lowest fertility rate in India, is also close to replacement fertility. There is less consensus about the reasons for fertility decline in Tamil Nadu than in Kerala. This state has pursued the path of social development mixed with economic development (Kishor 1994; Ramasundaram 1995). Levels of education and mortality are not as favourable as in Kerala, but compare favourably with the rest of India. Tamil Nadu underwent steady industrial growth during the 1950s and 1960s, and became one of the more industrialized and urbanized states of the country (Kishor 1994; Ramasundaram 1995). During this period, public irrigation facilities were expanded, raising agricultural productivity and laying the basis for further rapid rise in production when the inputs of the Green Revolution became available.

Despite these efforts, among Indian states, Tamil Nadu ranks below average in per capita income. This has led some to argue that the fertility decline is 'poverty-driven' (Basu 1986; Kishor 1994; Mencher 1980). Kishor, for example, argues that the development of the state has been exclusionary of the poor, which has left them with no choice but to shift over to investing in their children's education to enter the urban job market. Rising aspirations give further impetus to the need to reduce family size. This argument, of course, is premised on the availability of jobs in urban areas, which itself is indicative of economic growth and the spread of economic opportunities. Bhat (1998) finds no evidence that the fertility decline is poverty led. He points out that the electronic media are especially widespread in Tamil Nadu, and that they seem to have an especially strong negative impact on fertility in this state. Another argument sometimes put forward is that the decline is due to an especially active and innovative family planning programme, but this argument has also been dismissed in recent analyses (Ramasundaram 1995).

In his comparison of Maharashtra and Bangladesh in the late 1970s, Cain (1981, 1983) emphasized the contrast between the institutional structures in the two settings. In particular, he drew attention to Maharashtra's efforts to generate employment and provide credit, and the relatively smooth operation of the legal system in protecting property rights. He attributed the more advanced fertility transition in Maharashtra, as compared with Bangladesh, to the security created by these aspects of administrative order, along with the relatively greater autonomy of women.

Analysing why the central Indian states have lagged behind the rest of India in fertility decline, Satia and Jejeebhoy (1991) point to the fact that these states have lower levels of female literacy and poorer health status, and that they lag behind the rest of the country in most aspects of social development. Eastern Uttar Pradesh and Bihar are the greatest outliers on these fronts. These states have also had less success in reducing infant mortality, have the highest maternal mortality, and the poorest performance of the family planning programme. They conclude that these various aspects of underperformance reinforce each other.

Toward a Synthesis Explaining Reproductive Change in India

The evidence from India suggests that the reproductive transition has proceeded earliest in those parts of the country where the administration intervened successfully to promote development efforts and to provide a stable legal order and other impersonal institutional structures (Das Gupta 1999). Before Independence, the administrations of Punjab and Travancore-Cochin (parts of present-day Kerala) were especially active in these spheres, although adopting very different ways to achieve these goals. These are also the parts of the country that show early fertility decline. Where the administration has been less successful in promoting channels of social and economic mobility for people, reproductive behaviour has been slower to change.

The quality of government administration in formulating and implementing state policies affects people's lives profoundly, and thereby influences fertility behaviour through a miscellany of routes. The central states of India are characterized by considerably poorer administration of government programmes than is found in the rest of the country. This is reflected in virtually any indicator one chooses to examine, including education (low), mortality rates (high), fertility decline (slow), utilization of water tables for irrigation (poor), agricultural wages and levels of industrialization (both low).

The states also offer the least personal security: these are the only parts of the country where *dacoits* continue to flourish, frequently supported by or even drawn from local élites, where female health workers have to be careful of their movements, and where local landlords continue to use physical force to keep wages low. These are just a few examples of the striking differences in security of life, sense of optimism and ability to improve one's life between central India on the one hand and Punjab/Haryana and southern India on the other hand. All this is despite the fact that the basic sectors of health, education and legal and administrative institutions are designed to be uniform throughout the country.

Table 9.2 shows some indicators of fertility and socioeconomic development in the central states. There is considerable overlap between states. All register slower fertility transition and poorer child health, poorer reproductive health services, lower literacy, less industrialization and less administrative efficiency (as measured by the coverage of the vital registration system). This is not only because people are less able to control fertility because they have poorer access to health, education and family planning services, but also because their lives are far less secure and amenable to improvement through personal efforts than elsewhere in the country.

This suggests that whether states have placed greater emphasis on economic development or on social development is of far less consequence than whether they have placed emphasis on development at all. Both forms of development have in common the feature that they make for greater security of life and allow people to aspire to improving their living conditions, thus motivating and enabling them to plan under conditions of far less uncertainty about the future. Both social and economic development increase people's control over their lives and, in Ansley Coale's words, bring fertility control 'within the calculus of conscious choice'. It is to be noted that even in Punjab, people did not initiate fertility decline because of increased incomes and income levels, which were still quite low in the 1940s, but because of greater security of life and livelihood.

Nevertheless, emphasis on social development seems to make for more rapid improvements in people's control over their lives than does emphasis on economic development. The parts of the country that have lagged in social as well as economic development are also those that have lagged in their demographic transition, and which continue to have high mortality and fertility rates. These are the parts of the country where the environment of risk in daily life remains far higher than elsewhere, whether it be in terms of earning a living wage or the likelihood that one's child will survive. The slow penetration of some economic and social development has also been accompanied by a slow decline in mortality and fertility.

Conclusion

The use of different approaches to explaining reproductive change can give rise to very different kinds of understanding of the phenomenon. We argue that reliance on qualitative data alone can be problematic, and that quantitative analysis of cross-sectional surveys tends to draw attention to the proximate causes (or correlates) of fertility behaviour, rather than to the underlying causes of the change. Broader analysis combining qualitative and quantitative methodologies is more likely to lead to a more nuanced understanding of the processes underlying reproductive change.

A review of the broad analysis of fertility decline in different parts of India demonstrates an emphasis on local-specific factors. Sometimes these studies seem to arrive at conclusions that seem almost at odds with each other. For example, we read that social development was the key in Kerala, while economic development was the key in Punjab, that modern institutional structures were the key in Maharashtra, but that a combination of some of these—along with media exposure—were the key in Tamil Nadu. Yet these analyses seem to point in the same direction, namely that efficient administrations with well-considered policies to bring security into people's lives enable reproductive change. Whether these policies focus more on social or economic change seems less relevant than whether they succeed in bringing people an enhanced possibility of individual mobility, security and control over life. It is changes such as these that seem to be critical to enabling reproductive change.

The specificities of which social and economic changes help initiate fertility decline can be expected to differ in different settings. In this sense, it seems inappropriate to conclude that Notestein's (1953) view of demographic transition is disproved by the lack of common thresholds of variables such as literacy and urbanization associated with fertility decline in various regions of Europe. We should not logically expect to find specific thresholds common to all settings.

Different combinations of structural changes can make for shifts in desired fertility. There are clear commonalities between regions of India in factors that make for altered fertility behaviour. The demand for children was altered by structural changes, often resulting from the unintended consequences of state policies. Largely as a spinoff of state policies related to economic and social development, people gained increased control over their lives, which enabled them to alter their reproductive behaviour. The state has provided health and education, particularly in the case of Kerala. In some other parts of India, economic development has given people increased control over their lives. The regions that were left behind in the development process were the 'demographic laggers', being the last to experience the onset of fertility decline.

References

Basu, Alaka Malwade (1986), 'Birth Control by Assetless Workers in Kerala: The Possibility of a Poverty-Induced Fertility Transition', *Development and Change*, 17(2): 265–82.

Bhat, P. N. Mari (1998), 'Emerging Regional Differences in Fertility in India: Causes and Correlations', in George Martine, Monica Das Gupta and Lincoln C. Chen (eds.), *Reproductive Change in Brazil and India*, New Delhi: Oxford University Press.

Bongaarts, John, and Watkins, Susan C. (1996), 'Social Interactions and Contemporary Fertility Transitions', *Population and Development Review*, 22(4): 639–82.

Cain, Mead (1977), 'The Economic Activities of Children in a Village in Bangladesh', *Population and Development Review*, 3(3): 201–27.

—— (1981), 'Risk and Insurance: Perspectives on Fertility and Agrarian Change in India and Bangladesh', *Population and Development Review*, 7(3): 435–74.

—— (1983), 'Fertility as an Adjustment to Risk', *Population and Development Review*, 9(4): 688–702.

Caldwell, John C. (1976), 'Toward a Restatement of Demographic Transition Theory', *Population and Development Review*, 2(3/4): 321–66.

Caldwell, John C. (1978), 'A Theory of Fertility: From High Plateau to Destabilization, *Population and Development Review*, 4(4): 553–77.

—— (1980). 'Mass education as a determinant of the timing of fertility decline', *Population and Development Review*, 6(2): 225–55.

Census of India (1901), Punjab, Part I: *Report*.

—— (1911), Punjab, Part I: *Report*, and Part II: *Tables*.

Cleland, John C., and Wilson, Chris (1987), 'Demand Theories of the Fertility Decline: An Iconoclastic View', *Population Studies*, 20: 149–74.

Coale, Ansley J. (1973), 'The Demographic Transition Reconsidered', *Proceedings of the International Population Conference*, Liège, 1: 53–72.

Das Gupta, Monica (1987), 'Selective Discrimination against Female Children in Rural Punjab, India', *Population and Development Review*, 13(1): 77–100.

—— (1994), 'What Motivates Fertility Decline?: A Case Study from Punjab, India', in B. Egero and M. Hammarskjold (eds.), *Understanding Reproductive Change*, Lund, Sweden: Lund University Press.

—— (1995a), 'Fertility Decline in Punjab, India: Parallels with Historical Europe', *Population Studies*, 49(3): 481–500.

—— (1995b), 'Population and Development Policies and Programmes in India', in S. P. Gupta, N. Stern and A. Hussain (eds.), *Development Patterns and Institutional Structures: China and India*, New Delhi: Allied Publishers.

—— (1998), 'Missing Girls' in China, South Korea and India: Causes and Policy Implications, *Harvard University Center for Population and Development Studies Working Paper 98.03*.

—— Martine, George, and Chen, Lincoln C. (1998), 'Reproductive Change in India and Brazil: Implications for Understanding Fertility Decline', in G. Martine, M. Das Gupta and L. C. Chen (eds.), *Reproductive Change in India and Brazil*, New Delhi: Oxford University Press.

—— (1999), 'Liberté, Egalité, Fraternité: Exploring the Role of Modern Governance in Fertility Decline', *Journal of Development Studies*, 35(5): 1–25.

Dyson, Tim (1996), 'Birth Rate Trends in India, Sri Lanka, Bangladesh and Pakistan: A Long, Comparative View', Paper prepared for the IUSSP seminar on Comparative Perspectives on the Fertility Transition in South Asia, Islamabad, 17–20 December 1996.

—— and Das Gupta, Monica (forthcoming), 'Mortality Trends in Ludhiana District, Punjab, 1881–1981', in Ts'ui-jung Liu *et al.* (eds.), *Population History of Asia*, Oxford: Clarendon Press.

International Institute for Population Science (IIPS) (1995), *National Family Health Survey (MCH and Family Planning)*, India 1992–93, Bombay: IIPS.

Kishor, Sunita (1994), 'Fertility Decline in Tamil Nadu, India', in B. Egero and M. Hammarskjold (eds.), *Understanding Reproductive Change*, Lund, Sweden: Lund University Press.

Knodel, John, and van de Walle, Etienne (1986), 'Lessons from the Past: Policy Implications of Historical Fertility Studies', in Ansley Coale and Susan Cotts Watkins (eds.), *The Decline of Fertility in Europe*, Princeton, NJ: Princeton University Press.

Krishnan, T. N. (1995), 'The Route to Social Development in Kerala', Study prepared for the World Summit on Social Development, March 1995.

—— (1998), 'Social Development and Fertility Reduction in Kerala', in George Martine, Monica Das Gupta and Lincoln C. Chen (eds.), *Reproductive Change in Brazil and India*, New Delhi: Oxford University Press.

Lesthaeghe, Ron (1983), 'A Century of Demographic and Cultural Change in Western Europe: An Exploration of Underlying Dimensions', *Population and Development Review*, 9(3): 411–35.

McNicoll, Geoffrey, and Cain, Mead (1989), 'Institutional Effects on Rural Economic and Demographic Change', in G. McNicoll and M. Cain (eds.), *Rural Development and Population: Institutions and Policy*, supplement to *Population and Development Review*, 15: 3–42.

Mamdani, Mahmood (1972), *The Myth of Population Control*, New York and London: Monthly Review Press.

Mencher, Joan P. (1980), 'The Lessons and Non-lessons of Kerala: Agricultural Laborers and Poverty', *Economic and Political Weekly*, 15(41/42/43): 1781–1802.

Nag, Moni, and Kak, Neeraj (1984), 'Demographic transition in a Punjab village', *Population and Development Review*, 10(4): 661–78.

Notestein, Frank (1953), 'Economic Problems of Population Change', in *Proceedings of the Eighth International Conference of Agricultural Economists*, Oxford University Press.

Pollack, Robert A., and Watkins, Susan Cotts (1993), 'Cultural and Economic Approaches to Fertility: Proper Marriage or Mesalliance?' *Population and Development Review*, 19(3): 467–95.

Ramasundaram, S. (1995), 'Causes for the Rapid Fertility Decline in Tamil Nadu: A Policy Planner's Perspective', *Demography India*, 24(1): 13–22.

Registrar-General of India, *Sample Registration System* 1970–93.

—— (1992), *Primary Census Abstract of India*, Paper 2 of 1992.

Satia, J. K., and Jejeebhoy, Shireen (eds.) (1991), *The Demographic Challenge: A Study of Four Large Indian States*, Bombay: Oxford University Press.

Wyon, John M., and Gordon, John E. (1971), *The Khanna Study*, Cambridge, MA: Harvard University Press.

10 Women's Autonomy and Reproductive Behaviour in India

SHIREEN J. JEJEEBHOY

Introduction and Objectives

Regional disparities in reproductive behaviour are well established in India: the recent National Family Health Survey (IIPS 1995) observes a total fertility rate of 3.39 for the country as a whole, ranging from 3.6 to 4.8 in the five large northern states of Bihar, Haryana, Madhya Pradesh, Rajasthan and Uttar Pradesh to between 2.0 and 2.8 in the four southern states of Andhra Pradesh, Karnataka, Kerala and Uttar Pradesh. The total fertility rate is as high as 5.2 in Uttar Pradesh, but as low as 2.5 in Tamil Nadu; age at marriage is 17.9 among rural women in Uttar Pradesh but 20.0 in Tamil Nadu. Likewise, wide differences are observed in rural infant mortality rates (126.5 and 76.2 per 1,000 live births, respectively), current contraceptive use rates (16.7 per cent and 49.2 per cent, respectively) and ideal family size (3.5 and 2.1, respectively).

Not as well established are the factors underlying this huge variation in reproductive behaviour. Over the last decade, however, there has been a growing understanding that gender inequality plays a leading role in regional differences in fertility behaviour (see e.g. Dyson and Moore 1983; Jejeebhoy 1981; Satia and Jejeebhoy 1991). Unfortunately, empirical analyses thus far have suffered from an absence of comparable data on the critical dimensions of women's lives that are held to enhance their autonomy or constitute their status. There is an increasing recognition that such routinely available measures as education or economic activity profiles are inadequate proxies for women's decision-making authority, their freedom of movement, the power relationships within their families, or their control over economic resources. Yet, few studies have measured these dimensions of status, and fewer still have measured them in different cultural contexts. Exceptions include Basu's (1992) study comparing north and south Indian women residing in the same Delhi slum, and Morgan and Niraula's (1995) study in Nepal; both studies observe notable contextual effects on such dimensions of women's autonomy as decision-making, mobility, and control over resources.

This study is part of a larger study of five Asian countries (India, Malaysia, Pakistan, the Philippines and Thailand), and was supported by the Mellon Foundation. I am grateful to Michael Koenig and Zeba Sathar for suggestions, and to Shantha Rajgopal for research assistance.

The objective of this chapter is to explore the dimensions of female autonomy and the linkages of these dimensions to reproductive behaviour in rural India and, more specifically, in two culturally distinct sites, namely, Uttar Pradesh in the north and Tamil Nadu in the south. In so doing, the paper first attempts to operationalize the much-used but difficult-to-measure concept of female empowerment, and describes a range of dimensions of female autonomy and power among rural women. Measures of autonomy include women's decision-making authority, their freedom of movement, the power relationships within their families, and their access to, and control over, economic resources. They also include more traditionally available measures such as education and economic activity status. Finally, the paper explores the ways in which these dimensions of empowerment influence reproductive behaviour—notably recent fertility, contraceptive use, and family size preferences—and the extent to which these relationships are influenced by regional and communal differentials.

Background

Uttar Pradesh and Tamil Nadu lie at two extremes of the social and cultural spectrum in India, although economically they are relatively similar. Both states are poor, with about 37 per cent living below the poverty line in Uttar Pradesh, and 40 per cent in Tamil Nadu (compared with 33 per cent in India). Both states are largely agricultural (Uttar Pradesh 72 per cent, Tamil Nadu 61 per cent, India 70 per cent), yet there are huge differences in social development levels. For example, literacy rates are much higher in Tamil Nadu (63 per cent) than in Uttar Pradesh (42 per cent), and fertility and mortality are much lower—for example, the infant mortality rate is 98 per 1,000 live births in Uttar Pradesh, compared to 58 in Tamil Nadu, and the total fertility rate is 5.1 in Uttar Pradesh, compared to 2.2 in Tamil Nadu. Within each state, Hindu–Muslim disparities are evident in Uttar Pradesh, but not in Tamil Nadu: Muslims experience higher total fertility rates than do Hindus in Uttar Pradesh (4.8 and 5.3, respectively), but identical rates in Tamil Nadu (2.5 each).

Although both states are typically patriarchal and patrilocal, kinship structures and the ways in which kinship norms affect women's lives vary widely. Female powerlessness is much more acute in North than in South India. There is considerable ethnographic evidence, for example, of regional differences in the situation of women (Altekar 1962; Karve 1965). Women in the north have relatively little autonomy or freedom of movement, limited inheritance rights in practice, limited support from their natal family after marriage, and limited opportunities for control over economic resources. The practice of marrying young girls into distant villages—and into families with which previous contact has been limited and subsequent contacts are usually infrequent—is expected to heighten women's powerlessness. Women are perceived traditionally as temporary members in their natal homes (Dube 1988), who, like bottomless pits, can only take from their natal family's resources, not just in the form of huge dowries but also after marriage. And the pattern and flow of resources is strictly one way (Das Gupta 1987).

After marriage, a young woman is expected to remain largely invisible and under the authority of her husband's family. She has little say in domestic decisions and little freedom of movement. About the only avenue available to enhance her prestige and even security in her husband's home is through her fertility, and particularly the number of sons she bears. In contrast, women in South India have relatively more autonomy in all these areas—they have closer natal family ties, and greater decision-making authority; they are less secluded, and more likely to work and to control resources, and less likely to perceive sons as their only source of prestige.

The few available social indicators reflecting gender disparities make these regional differences in women's situation and vulnerability clear. For example, in Uttar Pradesh, life expectancy is about four years higher for males than for females (54 and 49, respectively); in Tamil Nadu, life expectancy for both females and males is 61 years. Moreover, the maternal mortality ratio ranges from 931 in Uttar Pradesh to 319 in Tamil Nadu. And gender disparities in literacy are far wider in Uttar Pradesh (25 per cent for females compared to 56 per cent for males) than in Tamil Nadu (51 per cent for females compared to 74 per cent for males).

Less can be said about Hindu–Muslim differences. On the one hand, Muslim women are more likely than Hindu women to be denied work opportunities, a secular education, control over economic resources, and recourse in case of abandonment or divorce, and hence may be more vulnerable than Hindu women. On the other hand, their marriage patterns, at least in North India, are less alienating from natal kin than those of Hindus—a factor that may enhance aspects of their autonomy.

Data

The data set employed in this study is one of the first to try and operationalize autonomy among rural Indian women—both North and South Indian, and both Hindu and Muslim women. The main objective of the survey, conducted in 1993–94, was to operationalize the concept of autonomy or empowerment, and assess its relationships to reproductive behaviour. The study also inquired, thus, whether measures of autonomy do in fact differ among North and South Indian women, and among Hindu and Muslim women. Similar studies were conducted in four other Asian countries, including Pakistan in South Asia (and Malaysia, the Philippines and Thailand).

Uttar Pradesh in North India and Tamil Nadu in South India were selected deliberately to represent a range of gender and sociocultural conditions. Within each state, similarly, two districts were purposively selected (on the basis of an index of development, measured from such indicators as income, per cent of roads surfaced and other economic criteria) so as to maximize differences in socioeconomic conditions, while at the same time allowing for comparisons of Hindu and Muslim women. From each district, one taluka (subdistrict) was selected similarly. The four sites thus selected include: from Tamil Nadu, Pollachi subdistrict in the district of Coimbatore (ranked 1 of 21) and Mudukulathur subdistrict in the district of Ramnathpuram (ranked 18 to 21); and from Uttar Pradesh, Kunda subdistrict in the district of Meerut (ranked 2 to 63) and Baghpat subdistrict in the district of Pratapgarh (ranked 51 to 63).

From each of the four sites, a cluster of contiguous villages of roughly 1,000–2,000 households was randomly selected, and about 800 currently married women aged 15–39 and their husbands were randomly selected for interview.[1] In each setting, on the assumption that sociocultural norms governing female autonomy vary widely among Hindus and Muslims, about half of all respondents selected were Hindu, and the other half Muslim. As a result, a total of eight communities are covered: four geographical sites, and within each site, two distinct religious groups, Hindus and Muslims. A total of 1,842 women, ages 15–39, constituted the sample.

In the course of interviews, women respondents were asked not only about their education and their work status but also about a variety of dimensions of autonomy within their married lives, including their decision-making authority, their personal freedom of movement, control over economic resources, wife–husband power relations, and other attitudes. The inclusion in this data set of these dimensions of female status allows for a better understanding of women's status and the extent to which education and economic activity are reliable proxies for autonomy more generally.[2]

---

[1] In each selected taluka, village lists were drawn up; these included information on the total number of households in each village by religion and caste. In order to adequately represent Muslims and scheduled caste households, contiguous villages were merged into sampling units of roughly 1,000–2,000 households, in a way that would allow for adequate representation of the different groups in our design. As a result, in Tamil Nadu, where there are generally few Muslims, clusters of villages were much larger than in Uttar Pradesh where Muslims represent a substantial proportion of the population. The PSU included in the sample was then selected randomly.

In Tamil Nadu, the selected PSU contained a total of 12 villages from Pollachi (Coimbatore district) and 15 from Mudukulathur (Ramnathpuram district). The selected PSUs in Uttar Pradesh contained fewer villages: seven from Kunda (Pratapgarh district) and two large villages (with many 'petis' or identifiable clusters) in Baghpat (Meerut district). Each household in the selected cluster of villages was listed and this list constituted the sampling frame. The difference in the number of villages selected in each state is attributed to the following: (1) village sizes tend to be larger in Uttar Pradesh than in Tamil Nadu, and (2) since Muslims constitute less than 10 per cent of the population of Tamil Nadu, a larger number of villages were required in order to reach our target ERs.

A household listing exercise was carried out in each of the selected PSUs prior to data collection. House listing was conducted on every structure in the PSU and comprised: assigning numbers to structures (SWAFNOs), recording the addresses of each structure and listing the names, religion and caste of each household head. Households to be interviewed were selected randomly from the household lists of each religion and caste list.

[2] The survey comprised a household questionnaire, an eligible respondent's questionnaire (ER), and a husband's questionnaire. Also fielded were community questionnaires of each village site and a total of 25 focus group discussions, held among women in different sites and different religion and caste groups, and one among men. A total of six focus groups were conducted per site: two among Muslims, two among the dominant Hindu caste and one each among the high and low caste groups. The group was restricted to women aged up to 39 but was not restricted to respondents to the questionnaire (about 75 per cent were respondents). In Meerut district, one FGD was conducted among Jat men as well.

A profile of the eight communities highlights considerable heterogeneity. In Uttar Pradesh, Pratapgarh, in the east, is a poor, largely wheat-producing area, with few amenities; while theoretically available, health and educational facilities function only sporadically. Brahmins comprise the dominant Hindu caste. In contrast, Meerut district is very well off: its main crop is sugar cane, although wheat, millet and maize are also produced. Sites lie in relatively close proximity to the main town, and less than 100 km from New Delhi. Amenities and services are largely available, and there are a host of private health and educational facilities available as well. Jats comprise the main Hindu caste.

In Tamil Nadu, Ramnathpuram lies on the south-eastern coast. Palmyra is the main crop, and occupations revolve around tending plantations, cutting down and marketing coconuts, and processing fibre. Villages tend to be poorly connected by roads, have huge water problems and are often reduced to depending on rain and river water. School and health facilities exist in, or in walking distance of, most villages, and, by and large, do function regularly.

The other district, Coimbatore, is, in contrast, one of the richest districts of Tamil Nadu: its main crops are cotton and groundnuts. Transport, communication and other amenities are of good quality: piped water is available in a large number of villages. The main Hindu castes of Ramnathpuram and Coimbatore are, respectively, Nadars and Gounders, both from the upper castes.

Table 10.1 highlights socioeconomic differences between the households in the eight communities. Economic status appears to be relatively similar across states, although Meerut Hindus (Uttar Pradesh), followed by Coimbatore Hindus (Tamil Nadu) are typically wealthier than those in other communities. Meerut Hindus, for example, are more likely than other groups to live in more solidly built, large houses, and to have a separate room for cooking; they also own more consumer goods and have larger incomes. While Muslims are clearly worse off than Hindus in Uttar Pradesh, wealth disparities are less evident in the south, partly the result of an influx of wealth among Muslims from Ramnathpuram as a result of Gulf migration.

The occupational profile of the husbands suggests clear differences: Hindu males are, by and large, more likely to be engaged in agriculture than are Muslims, both as cultivators and, to a lesser extent, as labourers. Conversely, Muslim males are more likely to be engaged in non-agricultural activities: as sales-workers, mostly petty, as skilled workers and as unskilled labourers.

Female Autonomy

Traditionally Used Indicators

Studies of female autonomy have usually relied on such available indicators as education, work status, spousal age difference, marital age and family structure. Table 10.2 suggests that, in contrast to their condition in relatively similar

Table 10.1. Socioeconomic characteristics of household

	Uttar Pradesh						Tamil Nadu					
	Total		Pratapgarh		Meerut		Total		Ramnathpuram		Coimbatore	
	Muslim	Hindu	Muslim	Hindu	Muslim	Hindu	Muslim	Hindu	Muslim	Hindu	Muslim	Hindu
1. Husband's occupations												
Business, professional or clerical	14.5	18.5	22.4	18.7	6.3	18.3	26.5	12.4	19.7	11.4	37.7	13.3
Skilled worker	17.8	11.0	22.4	14.0	13.0	8.0	6.6	8.5	3.2	6.6	12.1	10.2
Cultivator	18.5	35.8	9.8	33.6	27.5	38.0	8.8	16.1	10.0	9.5	6.8	22.2
Allied work (fishing, forestry, palmgroves)	10.9	2.1	17.8	2.8	3.9	1.3	5.7	22.3	4.7	33.2	7.3	12.0
Agricultural labourer	18.8	19.6	1.9	17.8	36.2	21.4	31.1	35.1	38.8	35.1	18.4	35.1
Sales	13.1	0.9	18.7	0.9	7.3	0.9	7.1	2.3	5.0	0.0	10.6	4.4
Unskilled worker	5.5	11.2	5.6	10.8	5.3	11.6	12.1	3.2	15.9	4.3	5.8	2.2
2. Land ownership												
% landless	66.3	25.8	69.2	11.7	63.3	39.3	68.9	64.2	59.7	61.6	84.1	66.7
% owning less than 5 acres	30.4	60.1	29.4	74.8	31.4	46.0	28.5	22.9	37.7	30.3	13.5	16.0
% owning 6 or more acres	3.3	14.2	1.4	13.6	5.3	14.7	2.6	12.8	2.6	8.1	2.4	17.3
3. Mean per capita income (Rs)	3,092	4,360	2,729	2,815	3,468	5,837	2,972	3,853	3,077	2,465	2,798	5,514
4. Mean number of items owned: clock, radio, fan, small appliance, sewing machine, stereo, TV, refrigerator or vehicle	1.5	2.3	2.2	1.4	0.7	3.1	2.1	1.9	1.9	1.3	2.4	2.4
5. Size of house: no. of rooms												
Mean no. of rooms	2.5	3.6	2.7	3.4	2.3	3.8	2.4	2.1	2.4	1.9	2.3	2.3
Mean no. of persons per room	3.4	2.6	3.4	2.4	3.3	2.7	3.1	3.0	3.3	3.6	2.9	2.5
6. Building material												
Thatch	2.1	4.3	3.7	8.9	0.5	0.0	6.2	18.1	7.4	33.7	4.4	3.6
Brick/cement	55.3	55.7	47.7	24.8	63.3	86.2	51.0	34.9	50.0	22.8	59.1	46.2
Mud	42.5	40.0	48.6	66.4	36.2	13.8	42.8	47.0	42.7	43.6	42.5	50.2
7. Sanitation facility: none	83.1	87.9	77.1	97.2	89.4	79.0	89.9	90.0	94.7	98.6	82.1	81.8
8. Cooking facility in separate room/bldg	74.4	78.5	68.7	71.0	80.2	85.7	77.3	60.6	81.2	56.9	71.0	64.0
9. Cooking fuel: gas/kerosene	1.2	5.5	2.3	4.2	0.0	6.7	2.2	5.0	1.5	1.9	3.4	8.0
10. Source of drinking water												
Well or handpump	99.3	98.6	99.5	98.1	99.0	99.1	68.9	79.8	77.1	99.5	31.9	61.3
Tap	0.7	0.9	0.5	1.4	1.0	0.5	23.6	19.5	0.3	0.5	61.8	37.3
River/rain	0.0	0.5	0.0	0.5	0.0	0.5	7.5	0.7	22.7	0.0	6.3	1.3
N	421	438	214	214	207	224	547	436	340	211	207	225

Table 10.2. Respondent's background characteristics by community

| | Uttar Pradesh | | | | | | Tamil Nadu | | | | | |
| | Total | | Pratapgarh | | Meerut | | Total | | Ramnathpuram | | Coimbatore | |
	Muslim	Hindu	Muslim	Hindu	Muslim	Hindu	Muslim	Hindu	Muslim	Hindu	Muslim	Hindu
1. Age (mean)	27.5	27.6	28.2	27.1	26.7	28.1	29.0	29.0	28.9	28.9	29.1	29.1
2. Education status												
% with any schooling	18.8	38.8	36.0	35.5	2.4	42.0	70.4	53.9	66.8	46.5	76.3	60.9
Mean year of schooling	2.9	3.7	2.0	2.6	0.1	3.1	30.0	20.2	3.0	1.9	4.2	4.1
3. Exposure to mass media												
% read newspaper in last week	4.5	5.0	8.9	4.2	0.0	5.8	9.14	7.34	6.5	2.4	13.5	12.0
% listened to radio in last week	29.7	55.0	29.0	42.1	27.5	52.2	45.2	54.1	44.1	48.8	41.6	40.9
% watched TV in last week	6.7	27.6	7.5	12.2	5.8	42.4	30.9	31.9	27.7	20.9	36.2	42.2
4. Work status												
% worked in last 12 months	63.9	73.1	58.4	69.6	69.6	76.3	39.9	75.2	39.1	84.8	41.1	66.2
% working for wages (last year)	18.1	13.2	19.6	15.9	16.4	10.7	21.2	56.0	20.6	70.6	22.2	42.2
5. Mean age at marriage	16.3	16.6	16.2	16.0	16.4	17.2	17.3	18.3	17.0	17.9	17.8	18.8
6. Age difference between spouses	5.4	4.8	5.6	4.7	5.2	4.8	6.6	6.0	5.9	4.9	7.3	7.0
7. Co-residence with mother-in-law	40.2	58.8	39.7	54.7	40.6	62.9	31.9	24.5	32.9	23.2	30.9	25.8
N	421	438	214	214	207	224	547	436	340	211	207	225

socioeconomic conditions, based on many of these indicators the situation of women varies consistently between the two regions. First, age distributions are different, with Tamilian women being moderately older than North Indian women, largely as a result of later marital age.

As far as access to education is concerned, large proportions of women in both Tamil Nadu and Uttar Pradesh have never been to school, a few have completed primary school. Attainment levels are, however, higher among Tamilian women than among women from Uttar Pradesh: 70 and 54 per cent among Tamilian Muslims and Hindus, respectively, to 39 and 19 per cent among UP Hindus and Muslims, respectively. On the district level, schooling rates range from as little as 3 per cent among the Muslims of Meerut to 61 and 76 per cent, respectively, among the Hindus and Muslims of Coimbatore. Unexpected is the finding that Muslims in Meerut, the more developed district, are distinctly worse off in terms of educational attainment than are those in Pratapgarh. While the typical Tamilian woman, both Hindu and Muslim, had had over three years of schooling, the typical Hindu woman from Uttar Pradesh had had slightly less than three years, and the Muslim woman no more than one year.

Work histories suggest that well over half of all women were engaged in any work in the last 12 months—about three-quarters of all Hindu women and far fewer Muslim women (two-thirds and two-fifths of northern and southern women, respectively); this measure includes working as unpaid family workers on their own farms or plantations, or tending their own animals. Yet, comparatively few women worked for wages, and here it is largely the Tamilian Hindus who stand out, when compared to the others: 56 per cent were engaged in wage work, compared to a fifth or fewer of the other groups. Almost all working women, irrespective of region or religion, have some say in the disbursal of their income.

There is considerable evidence that suggests that women who delay marriage are more independent and have more autonomy and self-confidence than those who marry early. As Table 10.2 shows, there is not much variation in marital age in Uttar Pradesh, where 90 per cent of all respondents are married between 14 and 18, and the average age at effective marriage is 16. In the south, marital age is somewhat higher: now, about three-quarters of Tamilian Muslims and three-fifths of Tamilian Hindus are married by age 18; the mean age at marriage is 17 among Muslims and 18 among Hindus.

Other indicators occasionally used to capture female autonomy include spousal age difference (Cain *et al.* 1979) and joint family residence. Results suggest that spousal age differences are wider among Tamilian women than among women from Uttar Pradesh, with differences in each setting somewhat wider among Muslims than among Hindus. As far as joint family residence is concerned, Tamilian women are far less likely than women from Uttar Pradesh to co-reside with their mothers-in-law.

Other Indicators of Female Autonomy

Aside from the more usually measured dimensions of women's status—their educational attainment, their work force participation profiles and the difference in age between them and their husbands—women in this survey were asked a battery of questions concerning the distribution of autonomy and power within the household. From these responses, five dimensions of autonomy have been selected, and indices for each created: economic decision-making, mobility, power relations in the household, access to economic resources, and control over economic resources.

1. *Decision-making authority*. Economic decision-making authority is represented by information on the participation of women in three economic decisions: the purchase of food, major household goods and jewellery. The index sums the number of these three types of purchase in which the woman participates, assigning a score of 1 if she only participates in the decision and 2 if she also has the major say. The index thus ranges from 0 to 6.

2. *Mobility*. The mobility index sums the number of five places—the health centre, community centre, the home of a relative or friend, a fair, or the next village—to which the woman can go unescorted. The index thus ranges from 0 if the respondent must be escorted to every place, to 5 if she can move about unescorted to every place.

3. *Power relations between women and their husbands*. The index of husband's power ranges from 0 to 3: a zero is assigned if women neither fear nor suffer beating at the hands of their husbands; 1 if they fear but are not beaten; 2 if they are beaten but do not fear their husbands; and 3 if they both fear their husbands and are beaten.

4. *Access to economic resources*. The index of access to economic resources sums responses to four questions dealing with: (a) the woman's say in how household income is spent; (b) how she obtains cash to spend; (c) her freedom to purchase small items of jewellery; and (d) her freedom to purchase gifts. The index ranges from 0 to 4.

5. *Control over economic resources*. Fewer questions were asked about women's actual control over economic resources. The index ranges from 0 to 2 and includes (a) whether any of the family's valuables (land/jewellery/vessels) belong to the woman and are controlled by her; and (b) whether she expects to support herself in old age through her own savings.

Results presented in Table 10.3 list communities by region and religion, from Muslims of Pratapgarh, hypothesized to be the community with the least autonomy, to Coimbatore Hindus, hypothesized to be the community with the most. Results generally confirm the limited autonomy of women in all spheres of autonomy, but suggest strong regional differences in almost every dimension of autonomy. Women from Uttar Pradesh fall significantly below Tamilian women in almost every measure of autonomy, a finding that strongly supports the argument

Table 10.3. Women's autonomy indices, by community

	Decision-making (0–6)	Mobility (0–5)	Power of husband (0–2)	Access to resources (0–4)	Control over resources (0–2)
1. By district					
Pratapgarh, Muslims	0.89	1.54	1.05	1.91	0.42
Pratapgarh, Hindus	0.74	1.18*	1.56*	1.61*	0.36
Meerut, Muslims	0.59*	1.18	1.71*	1.81	0.42
Meerut, Hindus	0.71	1.76	1.54*	1.89	0.54
Rammathpuram, Muslims	2.58*	1.88*	0.89	2.21*	0.66*
Rammathpuram, Hindus	2.80*	2.75*	1.22*	2.22*	0.57*
Coimbatore, Muslims	2.75*	2.12*	1.25	2.20*	0.74*
Coimbatore, Hindus	3.00*	3.00*	1.06	2.32*	0.76*
2. By state					
UP Muslims	0.74	1.36	1.38	1.86	0.42
UP Hindus	0.73	1.47	1.55	1.75	0.45
TN Muslims	2.67*	2.00*	1.07*	2.21*	0.70*
TN Hindus	2.90*	2.88*	1.14*	2.27*	0.66*
3. Average	1.81	1.93	1.26	2.04	0.56

*Differences in means compared to Pratapgarh Muslims significant ($t > 2.0$).

that the north–south divide powerfully conditions the extent of women's autonomy. Tamilian women have significantly more decision-making authority and
mobility than women from Uttar Pradesh, considerably greater access to and
control over economic resources, and somewhat more balanced power relations
with their husbands.

What is far less clear is the commonly held assumption that Muslim women have
less autonomy than Hindu women, or that within each state, women in the more
developed district exhibit greater autonomy than those in the lesser developed one.
Religious differences, for example, are generally modest, and do not necessarily
support the hypothesis that Muslim women are more constrained than Hindu
women.

Table 10.4 presents the relationships between each indicator of female autonomy
and the two factors most commonly assumed to measure this, namely, education
and work status. Also included are other factors that may affect women's status in
the gender-stratified settings of South Asia: age, economic status as measured by the
number of consumer goods owned, and co-residence with the mother-in-law. Age
difference with spouse is consistently unrelated to any measure of autonomy and
has thus been dropped. Three sets of regressions are presented: all women combined, and women from Uttar Pradesh and Tamil Nadu, in turn, in each case
including communities in the set of explanatory variables.

A look at the relationships for all women (panel 1) suggests that education of the
woman, and particularly a secondary education, consistently and significantly
enhances every indicator of autonomy included. This finding supports other studies
that suggest that the impact of education is not always linear; that whereas modest
amounts of education are unlikely to affect autonomy levels, increasing amounts of
education have a marked impact (Caldwell *et al.* 1982; Jejeebhoy 1995). Wage work
status, in contrast, while also important for such dimensions of autonomy as
decision-making, mobility and access to resources, has no effect on either power
relations or control over resources. Similar effects are observed in the case of age,
and co-residence with the mother-in-law.

A look at the community-level variation once again highlights the fact that, in
every dimension of autonomy, Tamilian women are significantly better off than
women from Uttar Pradesh. Inter-state variation is consistently more powerful than
intra-state variation by district level of development, or religion. District-level
differences suggest, for example, that women residing in the more developed
district have greater mobility and control over resources than other women, but
more inegalitarian relationships with their husbands.

The hypothesis that Muslim women experience greater constraints on their
autonomy than do Hindu women is not borne out in these data. The one area in
which Hindu women have decidedly greater autonomy than Muslim women is
their mobility, a difference that is much more evident in the freer south than in
Uttar Pradesh, where differences are modest. But in one dimension of autonomy—
power relations with husband—it is Muslim women who are better off; it appears

Table 10.4. Correlates of women's autonomy indicators: OLS regression coefficients

	Decision-making (0–6)	Mobility (0–5)	Power of husband (0–2)	Access to resources (0–4)	Control over resources (0–2)
1. All women					
Age	0.04**	0.06**	0.00	0.03**	0.00
Primary schooled	0.09	0.26*	−0.18*	0.08*	−0.01
Secondary schooled	0.29**	0.43**	−0.34**	0.24*	0.11*
Wage work in last 12 months	0.21**	0.72**	0.10	0.28**	−0.01
No. consumer goods owned	0.03[a]	0.00	−0.08**	0.06**	0.08**
Resides with mother-in-law	−0.46**	−0.17*	−0.07	−0.27**	−0.01
State (TN = 1)	1.79**	0.62**	−0.33**	0.23**	0.24**
District (more dev = 1)	0.03	0.26**	0.28**	0.05	0.07
Religion (Hindu = 1)	0.09	0.38**	0.12*	−0.09[a]	−0.03
Constant	−0.27[a]	0.80**	1.57**	1.00**	0.28**
Adjusted R^2	0.47	0.18	0.08	0.12	0.11
2. Uttar Pradesh					
Age	0.02**	0.06*	−0.01	0.03**	0.01
Primary schooled	0.08	0.36*	−0.12	−0.03	−0.04
Secondary schooled	0.03	0.31	−0.39**	0.20	−0.05
Wage work in last 12 months	0.34**	0.92**	0.10	0.41**	0.08
No. consumer goods owned	0.03*	0.02	−0.10**	0.10**	0.09**
Resides with mother-in-law	−0.43**	−0.30*	−0.08	−0.37**	−0.01**
District (more dev = 1)	−0.11[a]	0.23*	0.35**	0.12[a]	0.07[a]
Religion (Hindu =1)	0.05	0.13	0.30**	−0.13[a]	−0.03
Constant	0.16	−0.55[a]	1.62**	0..87**	0.10
Adjusted R^2	0.12	0.10	0.07	0.13	0.08
3. Tamil Nadu					
Age	0.05**	0.07**	0.00	0.02**	−0.01*
Primary schooled	0.14	0.28**	−0.21*	0.14*	0.03
Secondary schooled	0.45**	0.57**	−0.33**	0.31**	0.26**
Wage work in last 12 months	0.14	0.49**	0.17*	0.15*	−0.06[a]
No. consumer goods owned	0.02	−0.03	−0.06**	0.02	0.07**
Resides with mother-in-law	−0.50**	0.01	−0.13	−0.14*	0.02
District (more dev = 1)	0.11	0.23*	0.24**	−0.01	0.03
Religion (Hindu = 1)	0.18[a]	0.74**	−0.04	0.02	0.01
Constant	1.14**	−0.33	1.22**	1.39**	0.69**
R^2	0.10	0.17	0.05	0.04	0.10

Significance levels:
*0.05 level;
**0.01 level;
[a]0.10 level.

that the greater familiarity between natal and post-marital kin experienced by Muslims may have resulted in less domestic violence perpetrated by, and less fear of, the husband among Muslim than among Hindu women.

A look at individual state-level relationships, while generally similar—for example, the positive relationship of participation in wage work and age to autonomy—point to some important differences. First, education is a far stronger predictor of every indicator of autonomy in Tamil Nadu, the setting in which gender relations are more egalitarian, than in Uttar Pradesh, where they are more inegalitarian. Even then, in Tamil Nadu the effect does not always become significant until the woman has attained some secondary education. It is interesting to note that in this more egalitarian setting, co-residence with the mother-in-law does little to restrict mobility or control over resources; it does, however, reduce women's decision-making authority and access to resources.

In Uttar Pradesh, in contrast, education effects are mixed: the familiar empowering effect is infrequently observed. Unlike the significant positive effect of education on mobility seen in Tamil Nadu, effects in Uttar Pradesh are more modest. However, we do not observe, as have other studies in South Asia, inverse (Balk 1994, *Bangladesh*; Mandelbaum 1988, *North India*) or zero relationships (Sathar and Kazi 1996, *Pakistan*) between education and mobility. Also, in Uttar Pradesh, co-residence with the mother-in-law is a strong determinant constraining almost every dimension of autonomy—decision-making, mobility, access to and control over resources, a finding also noted in Pakistan (Sathar and Kazi 1996).

Reproductive Behaviour

Table 10.5 presents measures of reproductive behaviour—cumulative, recent and adolescent fertility, current contraceptive practice, and family-size preferences. Again, the familiar north–south divide is evident in every indicator. Rates fall roughly on the expected continuum, reflecting highest fertility levels and norms among the Muslims of Pratapgarh, and lowest among the Hindus of Coimbatore. For example, the mean number of children ever born, age-standardized, ranges from 3.9 among the Muslims of Pratapgarh to 1.8 among the Hindus of Coimbatore, and births in the last five years, correspondingly, from 1.19 to 0.44. Finally, in most settings, over one in three women has given birth at ages under 18. This proportion ranges from 53 per cent among the Hindus of Pratapgarh to 17 per cent among the Hindus of Coimbatore.

On average, more than three in five women between the ages of 15–39 want no more children: percentages range from a low of 43 per cent among the Muslims of Pratapgarh to a high of 76 per cent among the Muslims of Coimbatore. Contraception is practised, in contrast, by about one-third of all women, ranging, as above, from 13 per cent among the Muslims of Pratapgarh to 59 per cent among the Muslims of Coimbatore. Finally, 21 per cent of women who want no more children and are not infertile or pregnant do not practise contraception: this proportion ranges from 29 per cent among the Muslims of Pratapgarh to 11 per cent among the Hindus of Coimbatore.

Table 10.5. Reproductive behaviour: fertility, choice and contraceptive practice, by community

	Children ever born (age standardized)	Children ever born in last 60 months	% women giving birth at less than 18 years	% women wanting no more births	% women currently using some contraception	% women[a] wanting no more children
1. By district						
Pratapgarh, Muslims	3.9	0.72	50.9	42.5	13.1	29.4
Pratapgarh, Hindus	3.5	0.63	53.3	50.9	26.6*	22.0
Meerut, Muslims	3.8	0.71	42.0	47.8	19.8	26.6
Meerut, Hindus	3.4*	0.63	33.9*	69.6*	48.7*	20.5*
Ramnathpuram, Muslims	3.3*	0.59*	36.8*	68.2*	25.0*	25.0
Ramnathpuram, Hindus	3.2*	0.56*	21.8*	66.8*	37.0*	23.2
Coimbatore, Muslims	2.6*	0.39*	19.8*	75.9*	59.4*	11.6*
Coimbatore, Hindus	1.8*	0.33*	17.3*	71.1*	56.9*	10.7*
2. By state						
UP Muslims	3.9	0.71	46.5	45.2	16.4	28.0
UP Hindus	3.4*	0.63*	43.6	60.3*	37.7*	21.3*
TN Muslims	2.9*	0.51*	28.3*	72.0*	42.2*	18.3*
TN Hindus	2.5*	0.44*	19.6*	69.0*	46.9*	16.9*
3. Average	3.2	0.57	34.6	62.2	35.2	21.3

* Differences in means compared to Pratapgarh Muslims significant ($t > 2.0$).
[a] Non-pregnant, fecund women.

Again, intra-state differentials appear to be less pronounced than inter-state differences. Compared to the Muslims of Pratapgarh, significant declines in fertility appear only among Tamilian women. Differences are evident in the case of contraceptive practice and desire for additional children in Uttar Pradesh, largely the result of lower family-size preferences and greater contraceptive practice among the Hindus of Meerut, the wealthiest and best served community in the sample. In Tamil Nadu, religious differences are uniformly negligible; here, it is district-level development levels that have a more pronounced effect on almost every indicator of reproductive behaviour.

Women's Autonomy and Reproductive Behaviour

To what extent are the differences in reproductive behaviour observed above attributable to disparities in female autonomy? And how do community-level factors influence these effects? Tables 10.6 and 10.7 explore these questions through multivariate analysis.

Table 10.6 presents logistic regressions showing the relationships between women's autonomy and two measures of reproductive behaviour: wanting no more children; and current contraceptive practice. In model 1, independent variables comprise the five autonomy indices, and such sociodemographic factors as age, marital age, and parity. Additional variables in model 2 include other indicators of female autonomy (education and work status), and such sociocultural factors as economic status, and co-residence with the mother-in-law. Finally in model 3, we add controls for state, district and religion.

As model 1 shows, both desire for no additional children and current contraceptive practice are powerfully affected by selected—but not identical—autonomy indices. Decision-making authority, mobility, and control over resources are significant in the case of desire for additional children. In the case of current contraceptive practice, it is access to rather than control over resources that has a powerful influence on contraceptive practice, along with mobility, and decision-making authority. A quite puzzling finding is that women whose husbands exert more power over them appear to be significantly more likely to practise contraception than women in more egalitarian relationships. Also of interest is the expected finding—underscoring widespread son preference—that while parity is important in determining both whether additional children are desired and current contraceptive practice, it is the number of sons, rather than daughters, that is key.

Model 2 shows that the strengths of these indices remain relatively undisturbed by the addition of sociocultural factors, education and work status. As expected, female education, and particularly some secondary schooling, now joins these autonomy indicators as important in determining the desire for no more children, and, to a lesser extent, current contraceptive practice. In contrast, the effects of economic activity, and co-residence with the mother-in-law appear to have little effect.

Table 10.6. How female autonomy indicators affect wanting no more children and current contraceptive practice, currently married women aged < 40, logistic regressions, odds ratios

	Odds ratios					
	No desire for additional children			Current contraceptive practice		
	Model 1	Model 2	Model 3	Model 1	Model 2	Model 3
A. Autonomy indicators						
1. Decision-making authority	1.25**	1.23**	0.99	1.09*	1.11**	0.99
2. Mobility	1.12**	1.12*	1.05	1.11**	1.13**	1.06a
3. Husband's power	1.00	1.03	1.01	1.11*	1.17**	1.10
4. Control over resources	1.35**	1.31*	1.23*	1.15ª	1.02	1.00
5. Access to resources	0.94	0.93	0.97	1.11ª	1.08	1.13*
B. Other autonomy indicators						
6. Education						
Primary		1.67**	1.58*		1.08	1.19
Secondary		2.00*	2.22**		1.17	1.26ª
7. Work status: worked for wages in last 12 months		0.93	0.67*		1.00	0.84
C. Sociodemographic indicators						
8. Age	1.17**	1.18**	1.18**	1.10**	1.10**	1.09**
9. Age at effective marriage	0.97	0.92*	0.82**	1.10**	1.06*	0.97
10. Sons surviving	2.27**	2.28**	2.67**	1.27**	1.28**	1.49**
Daughters surviving	1.40**	1.41**	1.63**	0.97	0.97	1.12*
D. Sociocultural factors						
11. Modern goods owned		1.00	0.96		1.15**	1.11**
12. Co-residence with mother-in-law		0.89	0.94		1.22	1.24
E. Community indicators						
13. State (1 = Tamil Nadu)			4.70**			2.65**
14. District (1 = Meerut, Coimbatore)			2.60**			3.32**
15. Religion (1 = Hindu)			2.42**			2.37**
Log likelihood	−771.76	−763.86	−701.76	−1,049.47	−1,030.71	−946.64
Pseudo *R* squared	0.37	0.38	0.43	0.12	0.14	0.21

**Significant at the 0.01 level.
*Significant at the 0.05 level.
ªSignificant at the 0.1 level.

Table 10.7. Relationships between female autonomy and births in the last five years, currently married women aged <40, Uttar Pradesh and Tamil Nadu, OLS beta coefficient

	Model 1	Model 2	Model 3
A. Autonomy indicators			
1. Decision-making authority	−0.05**	−0.05*	0.01
2. Mobility	−0.01	0.00	0.01
3. Power of husband	0.04*	0.03[a]	0.03*
4. Control over resources	−0.08**	−0.07*	−0.05[a]
5. Access to resources	0.02	0.02	0.01
B. Other autonomy indicators			
6. Education			
Primary		−0.12*	−0.09[a]
Secondary		−0.26**	−0.26**
7. Work status: working for wages in last 12 months		−0.11*	−0.06
C. Sociodemographic indicators			
8. Age	−0.05**	−0.05**	−0.05**
9. Age at effective marriage	0.00	0.05*	0.04*
10. Children ever born till five years ago	0.05*	0.03[a]	0.03[a]
D. Sociocultural indicators			
11. Economic status: ownership of consumer goods		0.00	0.01
12. Co-residence with mother-in-law		−0.01	−0.02
E. Community indicators			
13. State (1 = Tamil Nadu)			−0.33**
14. State (1 = Meerut, Coimbatore)			−0.20**
15. Religion (1 = Hindu)			−0.09*
Constant	2.31**	2.14**	1.93**
Adjusted R squared	0.11	0.12	0.14

**Significant at the 0.01 level.
*Significant at the 0.05 level.
[a]Significant at the 0.10 level.

The inclusion of state, district and religion (model 3), however, changes this picture. In both models, the effect of adding community-level variables sharply reduces the influence of most autonomy indicators. Among the determinants of desire for no additional children, while education remains a strong determinant, the effects of all three of the autonomy indicators that were significant in the earlier models weaken, and only control over resources remains significant. In the case of current contraceptive practice, in contrast, mobility and access to resources remain significant determinants.

These results suggest that much of the effect of the autonomy indicators are captured by community-level factors, notably region, but also level of development
(district), and religion, reinforcing the importance of community norms and values
in influencing women's situation. The fact that the inclusion of community variables has weakened several indicators of women's personal autonomy—particularly
their mobility and decision-making authority—supports the argument that autonomy is powerfully conditioned by context, that is, by region, level of development
and religion. Despite this, however, individual-level effects remain. The finding that
control over economic resources remains strong and significant even after community-level controls are applied suggests the centrality of individual-level resource
control in reducing women's reliance on large numbers of children. And central to
the determinants of contraceptive practice are women's mobility, and access to
resources.

It is interesting to note that, by and large, the effects of the more usually available
indicators of female autonomy in model 2 are largely undisturbed by the inclusion
of community-level controls. Clearly education, and particularly a secondary
education, has an independent effect on both indicators, irrespective of region,
religion or level of development; so also do age and parity, particularly the number
of surviving sons.

Finally, in Table 10.7, we consider the influence of this set of independent variables on recent fertility, that is, births in the last five years. Again, the evidence
strongly suggests the importance of female status indicators in affecting fertility.
Among the usually available indicators, education, and particularly a secondary
education, and current work force participation have a significant inverse effect on
recent fertility. So also, among the autonomy indices, do women's decision-
making authority, control over resources, and more egalitarian spousal relations. A
comparison of models 1 and 2 shows that these three autonomy indicators lose
very little of their power when education, wage work status and sociocultural
factors are added.

Again, when community variables are included (model 3), the effect of adding
community-level variables sharply reduces the influence of most autonomy indicators, and completely erases the effect of decision-making authority on fertility.
While contextual factors clearly account for some of the individual-level variation in
autonomy, the results of model 3 suggest that, even so, some individual-level effects
persist. Recent fertility appears to be strongly determined by a host of indicators of
female autonomy: education and particularly, again, secondary education, as well
as by control over economic resources and egalitarian relations with husbands.

Worth noting from the results of Tables 10.6 and 10.7 is the finding that the effect
of autonomy indices are not necessarily captured by such traditionally available
indicators as education or economic activity. These results tentatively suggest that
empowerment indicators can have an independent net effect on reproductive
behaviour, that is, that such elements of autonomy as control over resources, and
closer spousal relations do in fact reduce women's need for children as their only

support and security; and that such elements of autonomy as mobility, and freedom to spend household economic resources enable greater access to contraception.

The relative contributions of the three community-level variables suggest that, by and large, region (South India) and, to a lesser extent, district-level development (Meerut and Coimbatore, compared to Pratapgarh and Ramnathpuram) have stronger effects on all of the three dependent variables—and particularly fertility—than does religion.

Summary and Conclusions

The objectives of this paper were to explore the dimensions of female autonomy, and the linkages of autonomy to reproductive behaviour in rural India, and, more specifically, in two culturally distinct sites, namely, Uttar Pradesh in the north and Tamil Nadu in the south. Several conclusions can be drawn from this study, some very clear, and others, tentative and suggestive.

Autonomy is powerfully conditioned by social context. There is a clear regional divide in almost every index of autonomy; decision-making authority, mobility, access to and control over resources and, to a lesser extent, power relations between women and their husbands, with Tamilian women experiencing far greater autonomy than their North Indian counterparts. Reproductive behaviour—intentions, contraceptive practice, and cumulative and current fertility—falls roughly on the same continuum, highlighting the well-known regional differences in reproductive behaviour. Intra-state differences—by district development levels and religion—exist, but are more muted.

Correlates of autonomy indices vary both by index and by region. Education, and particularly a secondary education, is consistently and significantly associated with every single index of autonomy. Other factors—wage work, co-residence with the mother-in-law, and economic status—have less consistent effects. Also notable is the finding that, at the regional level, education is far more closely related to autonomy indicators in Tamil Nadu than in Uttar Pradesh and, conversely, co-residence with the mother-in-law, a stronger inhibitor of autonomy in Uttar Pradesh than in Tamil Nadu. Spousal age difference is weakly related to autonomy in all settings. These kinds of findings suggest the conditioning effect of context: education can have a more powerful influence on enhancing autonomy, and, conversely, joint family residence and the presence of the mother-in-law present a far weaker constraint on women's autonomy in a relatively egalitarian setting than in a highly gender-stratified one.

The ways in which these dimensions of empowerment influence reproductive behaviour are far more complex. Results are exploratory and tentative, but suggest that contextual factors—notably region, and less consistently district-level development and religion—powerfully condition the impact of autonomy on all three measures of reproductive behaviour: fertility intentions, contraceptive use, and recent births. Even so, in each case, there is some evidence that individual-level indices of autonomy do independently exert an influence on reproductive behaviour: control over resources in the case of fertility intentions; mobility and access to resources in the case of contraceptive practice; and egalitarian spousal relations and resource control in the case of recent fertility. So also, of course, does education, and particularly a secondary education. These kinds of results suggest that greater gender inequality at the contextual level clearly affects both female autonomy and reproductive behaviour. However, results suggest that indicators of female empowerment do indeed affect reproductive choices, contraceptive practice, and ultimately fertility, although they are less powerful once this conditioning effect is taken into consideration.

References

Altekar, A. S. (1962), *The Position of Women in Hindu Civilization*, Delhi: Motilal Banarasidas.

Balk, Deborah (1994), 'Individual and Community Aspects of Fertility and Women's Status in Rural Bangladesh', *Population Studies*, 48: 21–45.

Basu, A. M. (1992), *Culture, the Status of Women, and Demographic Behaviour: Illustrated with the Case of India*, Oxford: Clarendon Press.

Cain, Mead, Khanam, S. R., and Nahar, S. (1979), 'Class, Patriarchy, and Women's Work in Bangladesh', *Population and Development Review*, 9(1): 405–38.

Caldwell, J. C., Reddy, P. H., and Caldwell, P. (1982), 'The Cause of Demographic Change in Rural South India: A Micro Approach', *Population and Development Review*, 8/4: 689–727 (December).

Das Gupta, Monica (1987), 'Selective Discrimination against Female Children in Rural Punjab, India', *Population and Development Review*, 13/1: 77–100 (March).

Dube, Leela (1988), 'On the Construction of Gender: Hindu Girls in Patrilineal India', *Economic and Political Weekly*, 23: 18.

Dyson, Tim, and Moore, Mick (1983), 'On Kinship Structure, Female Autonomy and Demographic Behaviour in India', *Population and Development Review*, 9: 35–60 (March).

International Institute for Population Sciences (IIPS) (1995), *National Family Health Survey: India 1992–93*, Bombay: International Institute for Population Sciences.

Jejeebhoy, Shireen (1981), 'Status of Women and Fertility: A Sociocultural Analysis of Regional Variations in Fertility in India', in K. Srinivasan and S. Mukerji (eds.), *Dynamics of Population and Family Welfare 1981*, Bombay: Himalaya Publishing House.

—— (1995), *Women's Education, Autonomy, and Reproductive Behaviour: Experience from Developing Countries*, Oxford: Clarendon Press.

Karve, Iravati (1965), *Kinship Organization in India*, Bombay: Asia Publishing House.

Mandelbaum, David, G. (1986), 'Sex Roles and Gender Relations in North India', *Economic and Political Weekly*, 21/46 (15 November).

—— (1988), *Women's Seclusion and Men's Honor: Sex Roles in North India, Bangladesh and Pakistan*, Tucson: University of Arizona Press.

Morgan, S. Philip, and Niraula, Bhanu B. (1995), 'Gender Inequality and Fertility in Two Nepali Villages', *Population and Development Review*, 21/3 (September).

Population Research Centre, Lucknow University, Lucknow, and International Institute for Population Science, Bombay, India (1994), *National Family Health Survey: Uttar Pradesh 1992–93*, Bombay: International Institute for Population Sciences.

—— The Gandhigram Institute of Rural Health and Family Welfare Trust, and International Institute for Population Sciences, Bombay, India (1994), *National Family Health Survey: Tamil Nadu 1992*, Bombay: International Institute for Population Sciences.

Sathar, Zeba, and Kazi, Shahnaz (1996), 'Women's Autonomy and the Onset of Fertility Change in Rural Pakistan: The Significance of Gender Inequality across Communities', Paper presented at the Annual Meeting of the Population Association of America, May.

Satia, J. K., and Jejeebhoy, Shireen J. (1991), *The Demographic Challenge: A Study of Four Large Indian States*, Bombay: Oxford University Press.

11 The Relative Roles of Gender and Development in Explaining Fertility in Rural Punjab

SHAHNAZ KAZI AND ZEBA A. SATHAR

Introduction

Even by South Asian standards, Pakistan is considered a demographic outlier. Only in the last decade has fertility begun to decline somewhat, going from 6.1 in 1991 to 5.5 in 1996, while the most rapid mortality declines occurred about three decades earlier (Sathar 1993). Yet economic development, at least in terms of rising per capita income, has advanced significantly in the last two decades. The question is, therefore, why fertility decline in Pakistan has been so delayed.

Recently, contraceptive prevalence has been shown to reach 18%—a significant increase from earlier levels. This measure is nevertheless low enough to stimulate inquiry into why Pakistan still lags so far behind neighbouring countries in South Asia with higher levels of contraceptive prevalence and much lower levels of fertility.

The most pronounced reductions in fertility levels and the highest levels of contraceptive use are found in urban areas, while similar trends have been slow to emerge in rural areas (Population Council 1995). The 1994–95 Pakistan Contraceptive Prevalence Survey confirms the existence of a wide urban–rural gap in contraceptive prevalence, with levels in large cities being three times higher than those in rural areas. Thus, what little fertility decline has occurred in Pakistan at the national level has been of very recent origin, very gradual, and largely attributable to a reduction in urban fertility rates.

In rural areas, the fertility transition started only within the past five years, while in urban areas, particularly in large cities, the beginnings of a decline could be observed in the mid- and early 1980s (Sathar 1993). In this chapter, we seek to explain the absence of decisive fertility change in rural Pakistan by exploring the relative influences on reproductive behaviour of family structure, migration, urbanization and women's autonomy.

Hypotheses

Other than its ability to predict urban change as an antecedent of fertility change in rural areas, demographic transition theory offers little help in understanding why Pakistan is experiencing a later transition than that of neighbouring countries of

South Asia. Despite Pakistan's moderate economic growth, which places it on a par with—if not more prosperous than—other South Asian countries, this factor has obviously not been sufficient to bring about demographic change. Is it then the case in Pakistan, as has been widely posited in other regions of the world, that social development, particularly educational advances for women, is a more necessary prerequisite for demographic change than economic development?

While no major theory of fertility decline has viewed women's status as the single central force determining fertility, it has been argued that the low status of Pakistani women is a major reason for the country's slow rate of demographic change. The major theoretical underpinnings supporting the importance of women's status are found in Caldwell's theory of fertility transition, based on inter-generational wealth flows (Caldwell 1978). The author argues that high fertility is a function of the upward flows of wealth and other resources in the patriarchal extended family, and that women's disadvantaged position is a subsidiary factor encouraging high fertility in these settings. In fact, the low status of women is also the explanation offered by the present authors (Sathar *et al.* 1988), as well as by others, in explaining both the slow rate of demographic change in some countries of the region (Caldwell 1982) and differences in fertility within the region (Dyson and Moore 1983).

Female education has always emerged as a strong explanatory factor of both fertility and mortality differentials in Pakistan. Seen as a strong proxy for women's general condition, female education is also believed to convey other socioeconomic effects (United Nations 1993). Levels of female employment, on the other hand, have been found to have a more ambivalent relationship with both women's status and fertility (Sathar and Kazi 1989). As far back as the 1980s, women working in the formal sector and educated women were considered to be the forerunners of the fertility transition in urban areas (Sathar and Mason 1993). However, both women's education and women's employment are, at best, proxies for women's broader social and economic status. In the more recent literature, they are seen as factors determining actual measures of women's status (Mason 1984).

The current study uses new data that provide direct measures of various other aspects of women's status to assess the synergies that might exist between gender and development in determining levels of fertility in rural Pakistan. The main aim of this paper is to explore possible routes to higher levels of contraceptive use. It attempts to identify the relative roles of development and of gender relations and women's autonomy in explaining variations in reproductive behaviour within rural Punjab. Differences in the development contexts are depicted through education, migration and urbanization patterns.

Data and Methods

The data used in the core analysis come from ten communities in rural Punjab (Fig. 11.1). As part of a larger comparative study of five Asian countries, 1,036

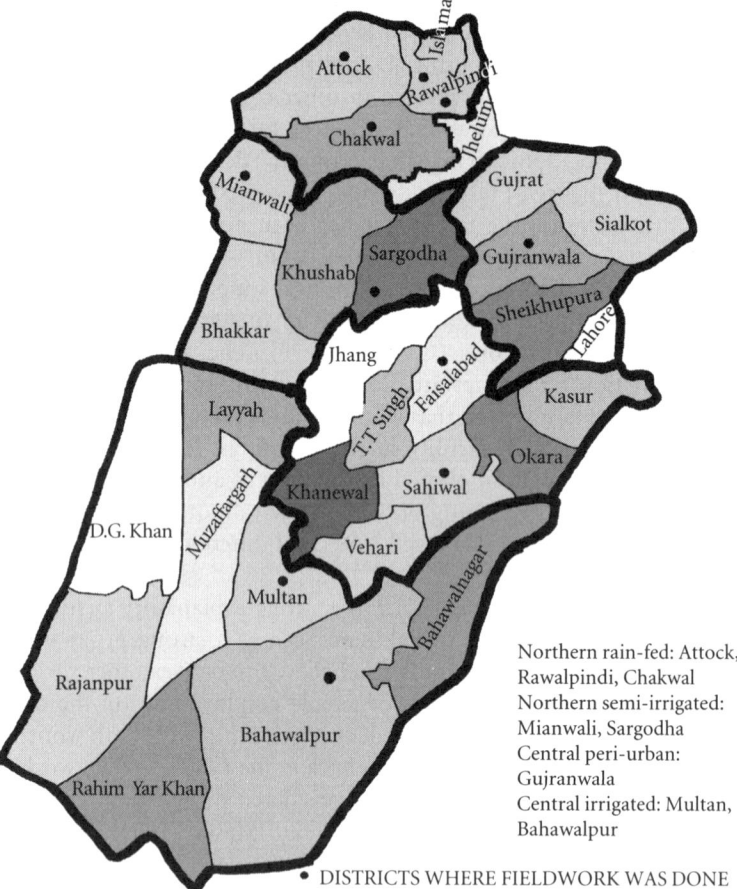

Northern rain-fed: Attock, Rawalpindi, Chakwal
Northern semi-irrigated: Mianwali, Sargodha
Central peri-urban: Gujranwala
Central irrigated: Multan, Bahawalpur

• DISTRICTS WHERE FIELDWORK WAS DONE

Figure 11.1. Map of Punjab.

Pakistani women were interviewed in 1993–94. (The five-country project, led by Karen Mason of the East-West Center, was based on a total of 59 communities, with each country using its own selection criterion.) In Pakistan, the ten communities represent the full range of agro-climatic, ethnic and linguistic conditions in rural Punjab (see map). The ten sites are: Attock, Rawalpindi and Chakwal in the northern rain-fed region; Mianwali and Sargodha in the northern semi-irrigated region; Faisalabad and Sahiwal in the central irrigated region; Multan and Bahawalpur in the south irrigated region; and a central peri-urban region, represented by the community of Gujranwala. The nine rural locations were all roughly of the same size and were selected to be at a considerable distance from any major roads. The one peri-urban community was included for purposes of comparison.

In each village, about 100 currently married women between the ages of 15 and 40 were randomly selected for detailed interviews. The questionnaire for women (the husbands' questionnaire has not yet been analysed) collected household information and was also used to establish the number of currently married women in each household. Only one of the eligible respondents was chosen using a Kish chart. The 42-page questionnaire, which took about an hour to complete, covered background information, a birth history, contraceptive knowledge and use, employment, intra-family decision-making and relations, women's autonomy, mobility, and related issues.

The variables used in the analysis fall into four main areas: community characteristics, women's status, socioeconomic household characteristics and fertility. The communities are distinguishable by their difference in socioeconomic development, cultural norms and agro-climatic zones. Women's status is depicted by its various dimensions of mobility, inter-spousal communication and intra-household decision-making. Socioeconomic characteristics include the education of both spouses, income and land holdings. Reproductive and related measures include children ever born, number of living sons and daughters, current use of contraception, and proportion wanting no more children. Several models are tested to study the various possible routes of influence of these four sets of variables. Special emphasis is placed on incorporating both community-level and individual-level information to fully understand the influences that shape patterns of social and demographic change in rural areas. So far, most analyses on this topic have been based on aggregated data—broad rural and urban divisions of the type available in most surveys. The data set used in the current study allows us to investigate in more detail some community-level dynamics of development, gender and demographic change.

Findings

Development Differences at the Community Level

Punjab province is the most developed in Pakistan in terms of agricultural productivity, road structure, sanitation, communications, and availability of educational and health facilities. However, the rural areas of the province are by no means homogeneous in terms of communications networks and links with the outside world, educational levels, exposure to media, income and, we expect, women's status. All these factors are likely to vary across regions.

Land ownership patterns also vary by region. In the northern rain-fed (barani) regions, land ownership is broad-based, and a large majority of households own small parcel of land (Table 11.1). Agriculture in the rain-fed region is constrained by the uncertainty of the water supply and is mainly geared to subsistence production, the main crops being wheat, maize and millet. Since agriculture does not offer a reliable and adequate source of income, there has been a tradition in these areas of

Table 11.1. Household economic status, by region

	Northern rain-fed	Northern semi-irrigated	Central peri-urban	Central irrigated	Southern irrigated	All areas
Husband's occupation						
Army/Police/Professional	26.1	38.4	8.0	9.9	3.9	18.3
Business/Commercial	8.6	6.3	11.0	10.4	8.2	8.7
Non-agricultural labour	38.4	34.2	52.0	35.9	50.2	41.3
Farmers	20.9	20.5	27.0	42.7	36.2	30.3
Migrants	3.0	0.5	2.0	1.6	0.9	0.5
Ownership of land						
No land	24.7	58.9	87.3	64.0	60.3	53.9
Less than 6 acres	62.0	30.7	9.8	21.2	30.0	35.1
More than 6 acres	13.3	10.4	2.9	14.8	9.7	11.1
Mean per capita income	4,560	3,496	7,144	4,245	4,630	4,563
Husband's educational level						
0	27.4	29.2	47.1	32.5	63.9	39.2
1–8	44.1	33.7	29.4	35.5	25.7	34.7
9+	28.5	36.1	23.5	32.0	10.4	26.2

men seeking employment outside the farm sector. Consequently, a large proportion of the male population is employed in non-agricultural occupations, particularly in the armed forces and in jobs in the nearby urban center. Due to the specific circumstances of these villages, a livelihood system has evolved that provides relatively greater male wage employment in the formal sector combined with subsistence agricultural production managed by women. The northern semi-irrigated villages are very similar to the northern barani areas, except that some cash crops are grown and land ownership is more concentrated.

The nature of farming and agrarian structure is markedly different in the canal-irrigated communities of central and southern Punjab. Agriculture in these regions is market-oriented and provides a good source of income. Farming is the principal occupation of men living in land-owning households. However, the large majority of households in these villages do not have access to land. Among households owning land there are a substantial number of middle-sized farms in the central Punjab sites in comparison to the presence of large farmers and feudal lords in the southern Punjab villages. The more feudal character of southern Punjab is seen in Bohsin, where a family of large landlords owns the entire agricultural and residential area. The communities of south Punjab are also characterized by greater dependence on agriculture and very little employment in urban white-collar jobs. The villages in central Punjab are located near areas of rapid industrial growth; Faisalabad, particularly, is a major industrial centre of the country. The factories in the area are an important source of employment, and there are relatively larger numbers of residents in the army and working in professional jobs, although the representation is much lower that that found in the rain-fed villages.

Education is differentially valued in the five regions: generally it is more highly valued in the northern barani context as a means to gaining better non-agricultural employment opportunities, whereas in the canal-irrigated, agriculturally prosperous areas education is not so directly relevant to the means of livelihood. The greater importance of education in the northern rain-fed regions is reflected in the fact that in the northern barani villages, primary schools for boys were established in the 1920s, decades before the advent of boys' schooling in the central and southern irrigated villages (Sathar and Kazi 1996). The educational level of males in the northern barani regions is considerably higher than average, with a significant proportion who have completed ten years of schooling—a prerequisite to entry into the army and other government employment (Table 11.1). The lowest levels of education for both men and women are found in southern Punjab, which is also the setting in which agriculture is the principal source of livelihood.

Recent trends in female education are quite different for the five subregions. The association between education and the age of female respondents—an indicator of trends in female education—shows considerable variation by region (Table 11.2). The proportion of women who have received some schooling is highest in the northern rain-fed region, although it has not changed much over time. In contrast, in the central peri-urban site and in the central Punjab villages, there seem to have been dramatic improvements in female literacy in more recent years, particularly in central Punjab, where nearly half the women aged 25 years or less have received some education, as compared to only one-fifth of women aged 35–40. In southern Punjab, not only is female illiteracy all-pervasive (94% are illiterate) but there is absolutely no difference by age.

Patterns of female employment also show distinct regional differences (Sathar and Kazi 1996). In the northern rain-fed region, the overwhelming majority of women are engaged in unpaid work on their own farm, while in the irrigated sites, remunerative employment is the more prevalent form of productive activity for women. The sale of livestock products is the major source of earnings for women in the central Punjab villages, while women in the southern Punjab sites are dependent on farm labour.

As would be expected, the most developed site in the sample was the central Punjab peri-urban community, where there was barely any agricultural activity (only 3 per cent of husbands were working as farmers, and only 13 per cent of the households owned land). The residents of this community were not better educated, but they had easier access to the facilities located in the major city of Gujranwala, including secondary schools and hospitals. Exposure to mass media was relatively widespread: more than 43 per cent of the respondents had watched television in the last week. Housing conditions were more typical of a low-income urban neighbourhood than of a rural site. The community also had the highest monthly household income per capita. Its relatively high economic status was also reflected

Table 11.2. Trends in female education, by region and age cohorts

Age (years)	Proportion of women who have received some education		
	< 25	25–35	35+
Regions			
Northern rain-fed	32.1	25.2	27.9
Northern semi-irrigated	19.6	11.6	9.1
Central peri-urban	31.0	22.2	17.1
Central irrigated	47.6	23.5	18.6
Southern irrigated	5.7	5.9	5.9
All areas	24.2	18.4	16.8

in ownership of a range of consumer durables. So in highest to lowest order, the development ranking of the five regions is as follows: central Punjab, peri-urban; central Punjab, irrigated; northern Punjab, barani; northern Punjab, semi-irrigated; and southern Punjab, irrigated belt.

Reproductive Behaviour by Region

In the past there was little documentation of any substantial variation in levels of rural fertility. This is probably because of the largely natural fertility conditions that prevailed until recently, with very little evidence of any modern contraceptive use. Differences in fertility were largely based on factors other than contraception, such as greater spousal separation or higher age at marriage. Thus, the northern belt of Punjab was found to have somewhat lower fertility than the southern belt (World Bank 1995). This is still the case, but not for reasons involving volitional fertility behaviour. The northern Punjab belt, which is mainly made up of barani areas, has already been identified as a major sending area for migrants. Long periods of spousal separation are typical of these areas, in addition to higher levels of infecundity. Advanced age at marriage for women in these areas has been typically attributed to migration patterns and higher levels of education. Fertility has been traditionally lower in these areas.

In the current situation, in which the onset of fertility change is under way in parts of Pakistan, particularly in rural Punjab and the North West Frontier Province (Population Council 1995), across Punjab's rural regions we also start to find variations in fertility brought about by deliberate fertility control, as well as variations in levels of unmet need for family planning.

The five Punjabi regions reveal differences in levels of fertility, desired fertility and the use of contraception to control fertility (see Table 11.3). The total number of children ever born is highest in the central Punjab peri-urban site (4.6 per woman)

Table 11.3. Variations in reproductive outcomes

	Northern rain-fed	Northern semi-irrigated	Central peri-urban	Central irrigated	Southern irrigated	All areas
Mean age at current marriage	18.1	18.9	17.8	19.1	16.4	18.0
Mean no. of children ever born	3.2	3.1	4.5	4.0	4.0	3.6
Mean no. of living children	2.8	2.8	4.0	3.4	3.1	3.1
Proportion of dead children	0.13	0.10	0.11	0.15	0.18	0.14
Mean ideal size of family	3.5	3.6	3.9	3.7	4.1	3.7
Proportion of women who want no more children:						
All	44.4	38.1	52.0	55.2	40.7	45.2
4+ children	85.0	68.4	80.0	88.0	81.1	81.2
% currently using contraception	21.5	20.3	39.2	27.1	17.8	23.4
% ever used contraception	31.7	30.2	55.9	39.9	27.8	34.5
% current users of contraception among those who want no more children	35.2	33.8	47.2	31.3	37.8	16.0

and lowest in the northern semi-irrigated areas (3.1). Interestingly, the average number of living children follows a different pattern: the highest level is found in central Punjab, and differentials by region are much slighter. This finding points to the importance of notable infant child mortality differences across communities. The proportion of children who have died is highest in the southern Punjab, the central Punjab peri-urban region and the central Punjab irrigated regions.

Ideal family size is highest in southern Punjab and lowest in the northern barani villages. Even the central Punjab peri-urban site has a high ideal family size of almost four children. This indicates a continuing demand for large families, though not as high as the prevailing total fertility rate of around 5.5 children per woman would suggest. However, the differences in ideal family size across communities are not huge. Average ideal family size hovers around four, but is slightly lower in northern than in southern Punjab. It is worth noting that in all communities, the number of boys desired exceeds the number of girls (data not shown), reflecting an all-pervasive son preference in Punjab. Furthermore, in all communities the average number of living children is far smaller than the 'ideal' number. This suggests that most of the survey respondents have not yet achieved their complete family size.

We look at the desire for no more additional children as a broad indicator of women's desire to control their fertility. The findings indicate that a little less than half of these relatively young women (women under the age of 40, as compared to the full reproductive range of 15–49) want no more children. This figure is comparable with that found nationally in the Pakistan Contraceptive Prevalence Survey of 1994–95 (Population Council 1995). Furthermore, after controlling for the number of living children, 81 per cent of women with four or more children (that is, women who have attained the ideal family size) have no further desire for children. Certainly these figures are higher than those of earlier findings. They also appear to be indicative of some change in reproductive attitudes. The regions with the highest proportion of women who want to limit fertility are central Punjab and the northern barani areas, and the regions with the lowest are the northern semi-irrigated regions.

Current contraceptive use is highest in the central Punjab peri-urban site. However, the central Punjab irrigated and the northern barani regions, which are definitely rural, also show very high levels of contraception. The lowest levels of contraceptive use are found in southern Punjab. Ever use of contraception is much higher than current use (34 versus 23 per cent). Ever use is highest in the peri-urban sites, followed, again, by central Punjab.

In order to estimate which women are able to act upon their reproductive intentions, we look at those who say they want no more children and are also using contraception. We assume that these women have reached the stage of ensuring that their fertility intentions are implemented. The proportion of users relying on effective contraceptive methods is highest in the peri-urban site, but is at almost equivalent levels in other regions. It is clear that inter-regional variation in fertility is significant and that it is associated with the level of each region's level of socio-economic development.

Variations in the Impact of Development

Migration and the Family

The data also indicate substantial inter-community variation in migration patterns. The rain-fed villages, as was noted earlier, are areas in which a considerable proportion of men (between half and one-fourth) work in nearby urban centres or are enlisted in the armed forces, leaving their families behind in the village. The peri-urban village and the villages of central Punjab, which are located near industrial centres, areas of in-migration, given that a significant proportion of respondents there have moved from a distant village or city. Although women often migrate to marry, we separated women who grew up in a nearby village from those who grew up in a far away village or city. Given high levels of endogamous marriages, the majority of women marry their cousins or relatives and do not migrate long distances after marriage. If they are currently living away from their natal village, women are more likely to have moved as a result of their husbands' migration.

Two major outcomes of the developmental changes described above—migration and increased exposure to urban lifestyles—have direct implications for family structures, living arrangements and, ultimately, for gender and generational relations. The more generalized change that has accompanied development in rural Punjab is a shifting away from traditional farming to non-agricultural based jobs, which are necessarily more likely to be urban-based and to require a minimum education. Education and urbanization are both associated with quite different occupational structures. With an increasing proportion of Pakistanis living in urban areas (32 per cent of the population is now estimated as urban), the increasing nuclearization of households is an additional concomitant social change.

Migration has two types of effect on household living arrangements. The first is to encourage the continuation of extended households. With husbands away, alternate family members (preferably men) are expected to fill their shoes as heads of the household. Also, more importantly, the 'corporate unit of the family' (Cain *et al.* 1993) continues to function, which is the situation in the northern rain-fed sites. Another outcome of migration may be when men migrate with their wives and children and move to a new setting, to form a new, nuclear family. The two situations have very different implications for the family in terms of breakaway from the extended unit, economic links and, in particular, social controls on behaviour and values. Note in Table 11.4 the regional variation in the proportion of nuclear families, a measure that to some degree is based on varying levels of migration. Northern (barani and semi-irrigated) regions having higher proportions of husbands who are living away correspond to regions in which extended families are more predominant. On the other hand, in regions (central Punjab and the peri-urban site) in which higher proportions of women are not natives, a greater proportion of households are nuclear.

The limited evidence available for Pakistan points to the relatively lower economic status of nuclear families (Irfan 1989; Sathar and Kazi 1987). In particular, access to land seems to be an important factor in determining family structures. Income, land tenure and husband's occupational status all have strong associations

Table 11.4. Family structure and migration patterns by region

Regions	% of respondents who have migrated from distant village	% of husbands who are living away from home	% of nuclear households	
			Total	Households where husbands are not at home
Northern rain-fed	16.7	36.8	41.3	34.0
Northern semi-irrigated	16.8	28.7	40.6	36.2
Central peri-urban	48.0	9.8	58.8	40.0
Central irrigated	36.5	18.2	51.7	43.2
Southern irrigated	14.9	11.7	32.4	21.4
All areas	23.3	23.2	42.7	34.6

with nuclear households. Significant social changes are a corollary: the control of the patriarchal head is reduced because his sons are less dependent on their father's land or trade for employment. There is generally less economic rationale to stay in an extended family when it stops being a unified economic unit. The authority wielded by the old over the young is, therefore, diminished.

In Table 11.5 we look at the relationship between family structure and the economic changes described above, mainly migration, the division between the barani and irrigation-fed agriculture, and land holding patterns. A strong association can clearly be seen between the size of land holdings and the proportion of women currently in a non-nuclear living arrangement. Land ownership plays a strong role in keeping families extended and in restraining them from becoming nuclearized. Household income also shows the same positive association with non-nuclear households. We see in Table 11.5 how lower per capita income deciles contain a disproportionately large proportion of nuclear households.

Table 11.5. Association between household income, land size holdings, husband's occupation and family structure

	Proportion of nuclear households		Proportion of nuclear households
Ownership of land		*Total household income*	
Landless	50.4	*quintiles*	
Land owners	34.2	1	57.4
		2	54.5
Size of land holdings		3	45.1
Landless	50.4	4	35.3
Less than 3 acres	43.2	5	20.6
3–6	27.4		
6–12	25.4	*Per capita income*	
12–25	27.6	*quintiles*	
25+	19.2	1	48.8
		2	39.9
Husband's occupation		3	42.6
Army and police	34.2	4	40.9
Professional	26.5	5	41.9
Business and commercial	38.8	All	42.9
Factory workers	43.2		
Casual labourers	50.4		
Agricultural labourers	69.0		
Informal sector workers	56.4		
Farmers	40.3		

Table 11.6. Selected women's autonomy indicators by region

	Northern rain-fed	Northern semi-irrigated	Central peri-urban	Central irrigated	Southern irrigated	All areas
Mobility indicators						
% of women who can go alone to:						
Local market	35.8	26.4	50.6	54.2	20.3	35.4
Health centre	27.1	17.4	41.2	45.3	17.0	27.8
Next village	13.5	7.0	20.6	16.3	5.0	11.5
% of women who observed purdah in village	23.0	46.0	23.5	19.1	36.0	29.8
Percentage of women who have the final say in:						
Major economic decisions						
Sale/purchase of animals	5.2	5.9	5.9	3.5	3.3	4.6
Purchase of major household goods	6.9	3.5	5.9	4.0	2.9	4.6
Women's work for income	14.6	9.9	21.6	16.4	13.7	14.5
Sale/purchase of jewellery	8.3	5.0	15.7	5.5	4.6	7.0
Children-related decisions						
Number of children to have	14.2	19.3	19.6	16.0	12.0	15.6
Level of schooling of children	14.6	14.9	27.5	17.9	16.6	17.3
Care of sick child	31.6	33.2	49.0	31.3	28.6	32.9
Marriage of children	6.3	5.0	14.7	8.0	4.6	6.8

Variations in Women's Status

Gender systems—which ascribe certain forms of male and female behaviour, prescribe a division of labour and responsibilities, and grant the different sexes certain rights and obligations—are the outcome of the various economic and social constructs found in every society. Women's status refers to such dimensions of gender stratification as control of material resources, ability to make decisions, ability to move freely, and the acquisition of social honour or prestige.

The data in Table 11.6, which provide us with information on various aspects of women's lives, including education and means of livelihood, reveal distinct differences across communities in women's mobility, decision-making powers, intra- and extra-household division of responsibilities, and in gender relations. Most notably, they show how circumscribed women's mobility is in rural Pakistan and how limited are their decision-making powers in the household.

Overall, over 70 per cent of rural Punjabi women need permission to leave their homes, only 28 per cent can go alone to a health centre, and fewer than 10 per cent have a major part in deciding who their children will marry. However, there are very significant variations by community in all of these indicators of women's status, pointing to considerable differences in women's mobility and autonomy across rural Punjab. Most significantly, the indicators do not necessarily always move in the same direction, and one can often counteract the effect of another. In particular, the effects of mobility and employment are inextricably related to, but do not necessarily correlate directly with, measures of decision-making.

Mobility is highest in the central Punjab villages and in the central Punjab peri-urban locality, and lowest in the communities of south Punjab. Only 20 per cent of the southern Punjabi women may go unescorted to the local market, as compared to more than half of those in the central Punjab settings. There are also distinct village-level differences in adherence to the custom of purdah. The practice is most common in the northern semi-irrigated region, where 46 per cent of the women observe purdah, compared to 19 per cent in central Punjab.

Regional variations in women's decision-making authority are less pronounced, possibly because mobility is more likely to be conditioned by community norms, while household and individual characteristics might have a greater bearing on family decision-making. Overall, women have a very limited say in major economic decisions, while their authority is considerably greater in decisions related to children's schooling and child sickness, but not in decisions related to who their children will marry. In general, women in the urban locality are most likely to have a say in most decisions, while southern Punjabi respondents are the least empowered. Respondents in the northern barani regions had relatively greater authority in major economic decisions, such as purchase of major household goods or jewellery. This might be partly due to the fact that many husbands in these regions are absent, which leaves women with the responsibility of managing many family decisions. In terms of other indicators of economic autonomy, such as access to cash-earning opportunities, the ranking of women in the northern barani regions, who work largely as unpaid labourers on their farms, would be much lower than that of women in central and southern Punjab, who have greater opportunities for remunerative employment.

Linkages between Development, Gender and Demographic Change

Many have argued that patriarchal family structures are at the core of the gender systems used in South Asia to limit the status of females in the family, both girls and women (Cain et al. 1993; Caldwell 1978; Dyson and Moore 1983; Mason 1984). More recently, Mason (1995) has argued that gender systems may have a conditioning rather than a direct impact on women's status.

Family structures are changing quite dramatically in Pakistan, particularly as a result of migration to urban areas or abroad, but also as an outcome of changes in land size holdings, which are also closely connected with living arrangements. Gender relations and women's status must necessarily change concomitantly, since gender and family hierarchies have numerous interrelationships (Mason and Bulatao 1998). Living in a nuclear family as opposed to an extended family has both positive and negative implications for women. To a large extent, family structure may be a life-course event, with older couples forming their own households. The loss of the social control of the patriarch, or more likely the matriarch, has strong implications for the lives of women. On the positive side, women become more autonomous, and they control resources more directly. On the other hand, they lose something through the removal of buffers between themselves and other household members—conditions that might lead to a greater work load, and sometimes to wife beating (Sathar and Kazi 1996).

By far the most notable finding of this study is the strong correlation found between family structure and all indices of women's relative status. Living in a nuclear family has a strong positive association with being able to go to the market or to a health centre alone. It also has a strong positive and statistically significant association with the woman being the major decision-maker in matters such as children's marriages, household income expenditures and other spheres. It is also associated with much lower levels of purdah outside the home, in the village and outside the village. Findings on the importance of family structure (defined narrowly by us to lend emphasis to some stark comparisons) show that women living in a household where there are no other married couples and no parents-in-law are likely to participate more equally with their husbands in decision-making. On the other hand, women in such households are also found to work longer hours and to do more household tasks because there are no adults to share the burden.

The dilution of the control exercised by other household members has another negative implication: women in nuclear households are much more likely to have been beaten and to have been beaten regularly by their husbands. In a similar situation, in-laws might have acted as a buffer and might have insisted on preserving social propriety.

Older age also offers similar advantages in terms of mobility and decision-making, but it is by no means as strongly linked to women's status as family structure. As women age they are more likely to gain control over decisions and to become free to move about. But this finding is largely related to life-cycle effects, whereby a young blushing bride in her in-laws' home may become a tyrant ruler in her own home 20 or so years later.

The more interesting juncture is the point at which the family decides to nucleate away from a larger unit. Our data show that 90 per cent of young married couples lived with the husband's parents right after marriage. What keeps a married couple tied to the larger family, and what causes it to break away? One natural process is having their own completed family and a large number of children: when that happens, a couple is likely to move away from the larger extended family unit.

Another causal factor may be migration away from the original village, which would necessarily mean the setting up of a new home. Yet another might be land fragmentation or land dispossession, which would induce sons to form their own

Table 11.7. Coefficients of some measures of women's autonomy with their characteristics such as education, age, family structure and work status in the last year

	Education	Age	Family Structure	Working for income in the last year
Mobility				
Able to go alone to market	+	+***	+***	+**
Able to go alone to next village	+	+***	+***	+***
Family decisions				
Decides what food to buy	−*	+***	+***	+**
Decides where to marry children	−	+**	+***	+
Decides how many children to have	−	+**	+***	+***
Has freedom to buy herself a dress	+***	+***	+***	−
Economic decisions				
Decides whether respondent should work	−	+***	+***	+***
Decides whether to purchase major household goods	+**	+*	+**	+
Decides whether to buy animals	−	+**	+***	+***
Has any say in how household income is spent	+*	+***	+***	+
Inter-spousal communication				
Talks about birth control	+	+	+**	+***
Talks about money	+	+***	+***	+***

*Significant at 0.01.
**Significant at 0.00.
***Significant at 0.000.

economic units once the joint holding of the land dissipates. A last but obvious reason that emerged very early in the exploratory field work leading up to the survey is the perennial problem of friction between mothers-in-law and daughters-in-law. There are also clear signs of greater intimacy in nuclear households, where significantly larger proportions of women report that they talk to their husbands about various topics (Table 11.7). This greater intimacy applies in particular to talking about birth control—a factor that emerges as quite important and significant when we move to explanations of reproductive behaviour.

In earlier analyses of these data, almost all indicators of greater involvement in paid employment are negatively associated with changes in fertility behaviour (Sathar and Kazi 1996, table 4.13). The role of employment is likely to be very difficult to decipher because of the diversity in rural women's employment patterns. These vary significantly by ownership of land, by agro-climatic patterns and by social class (Sathar and Desai 1996; Sathar and Kazi 1996). In particular, women's status may be more complexly defined in terms of agrarian structures than in terms of education and employment (particularly since the most common form of employment is on family farms, labour that is often not recognized as employment).

The effects of family structure on fertility, which we found to be at the nexus of synergies between gender and development, are still not clear despite the existence of strong patrilocal, patriarchal and patrilinear family norms and strong male child preferences. Within all societies, fertility behaviour is a reaction to the kinds of economic or social pressures and support that may impact on both the nature and locus of decision-making. Older generations are likely to be more traditional, more pronatalist. Women in these families are less mentally prepared to innovate and are socialized to depend on others to make decisions. Husband–wife communication is greater in nuclear households. Greater autonomy within a socioeconomic system and a stronger position within the household allow women to ensure that their fertility desires will prevail.

An interesting finding from these data is the fact that among women using contraception, those living in nuclear households are much more likely to state that they themselves made that decision than are women living in extended households. Earlier findings for Pakistan regarding the effects of family structure on fertility are ambivalent (Karim 1974; Khan 1981). Generally, studies in other countries have found that fertility seems to be higher in nuclear households: Caldwell's study of Sri Lanka and Bangladesh found higher fertility in nuclear households and contraceptive use to be less common in extended families (Caldwell *et al.* 1982). Our findings show that while fertility in nuclear families is distinctly higher than in other living arrangements, women living in nuclear households are also more likely to use contraception.

One of the main manifestations of inequality in gender relations is an overriding reliance on sons. This reliance is expected to be greater in agricultural communities and lesser (though still strong) in more urbanized communities. In addition, settings in which women lack economic opportunities and where enforced seclusion creates limitations on women's mobility serve to reinforce their economic and social dependence on sons (Cain *et al.* 1993). The significance of the strong and overriding preference for sons in rural Punjab is firmly documented in the much higher number of sons than of daughters that is considered ideal. The study data also provide strong empirical evidence of the almost universal reliance on sons in old age found in every community (Sathar and Kazi 1996). A strong degree of son preference is seen as providing significant support for high fertility (Cain 1979). But in fact, son preference in a society may intensify as fertility begins to fall (KIHASA 1996). An analysis of these data carried out by one of the authors of the five-country study found son preference to be a strong factor influencing contraceptive use across almost all of the communities (Smith *et al.* 1995).

Finally, in an effort to discern the most important influence on changes in fertility behaviour, we present two sets of logistic regressions, using current use of contraception and wanting no more children as dependent variables. The results are

Table 11.8. Logistic regression with current contraceptive use and want no more children as dependent variables

	Want no more children		Current use of contraception (non-pregnant women) odds ratio	
	Odds ratio		Odds ratio	
Socioeconomic status				
Respondent's education	1.05	1.04	1.09**	1.08**
Husband's education	1.01	1.01	1.01	1.02
Total household income	1.00	1.00	1.00	1.00
Demographic variables				
Age	1.06***	1.06***	0.99	0.99
Number of living sons	4.29***	4.43***	1.38***	1.33***
Number of living daughters	1.62***	1.66***	0.96	0.95
Family structure (nuclear = 1, other = 0)	1.33	1.31	1.84**	1.91***
Women's status measures				
Can go alone to health centre	1.11	1.03	1.31*	1.25
Has say in household income	1.11	1.11	0.93*	0.92
Talks to her husband about birth control	1.96***	1.96***	8.42**	8.70***
Has say in decisions about jewellery	1.25	1.18	0.55**	0.52**
Regions (omitted southern irrigated)				
Northern rain-fed		1.51		1.69*
Northern semi-irrigated		0.96		1.16
Central peri-urban		0.83		1.93**
Central irrigated		1.82**		1.27
–2 log likelihood	722.84	714.54	774.91	735.02
Goodness of fit	935.64	941.63	863.04	827.76
Chi squared	680.5	688.8	231.9	237.8
Degrees of freedom	11	15	11	15

*Statistically significant at the 0.10 level.
** Statistically significant at the 0.01 level.
*** Statistically significant at the 0.00 level.

presented in Table 11.8. The first model includes a set of socioeconomic variables (respondent's and husband's education and total household income); demographic variables (age, number of living sons and daughters); family structure (whether the family is nuclear or otherwise); and four indicators of women's autonomy representing mobility (ability to go to the health centre alone), decision-making (whether she has a say in household income matters), inter-spousal communication (whether the respondent talks to her husband about birth control) and control over resources (whether the respondent has a say in decisions about buying and selling jewellery). The second model adds on the effects of four dummy variables covering the four regions of northern barani, northern semi-irrigated, central peri-urban and central irrigated Punjab. The omitted category is the southern irrigated Punjab.

We find that the strongest effects in explaining wanting no more children come from the number of living sons and, to a lesser extent, the number of living daughters. Inter-spousal communication also seems strongly associated with wanting no more children. In the second model, which includes the dummy variables for region, central Punjab emerges as the region with the highest desire for limiting fertility. The findings seem to point towards women's strong desire to control fertility after they have had a certain number of children, particularly sons.

The results explaining current use of contraception are quite different. Respondent's education emerges as a strong and statistically significant explanatory factor. However, husband's education and household income are not significant factors. The number of living sons, but not of daughters, is critical in explaining contraceptive adoption. Family structure emerges as a strongly significant factor explaining the adoption of contraception: women in nuclear families are almost twice as likely as those in extended families to adopt contraception. Among the selected women's status variables, inter-spousal communication is found to be highly significant, with an odds ratio indicating that women who talk to their husbands about birth control are 8.4 times as likely to use contraceptives as those who do not. We interpret this variable with caution. It is ridden with causality issues, and possibly reflects the easier diffusion of information between couples who talk to each other (Mason and Bulatao 1998). Having a say in decisions about household expenditures, though statistically significant, has an unexplained negative coefficient. In the case of contraceptive use, the northern barani regions (odds ratio of 1.69) and the peri-urban site (odds ratio of 1.93) show a significantly higher use of contraception. These are important effects, reflecting actual changes in fertility behaviour in these areas over and above the influences of the number of sons and other individual-level variables.

Conclusions

Explanations for fertility change in rural Pakistan seem to be embodied in both development patterns and gender relations, particularly as these relate to changes in family structures. Strong regional patterns of economic and social change have also been identified as important factors. The levels of gradation in rural Pakistan's transformation from a primarily agrarian society to a more urbanized industrial one are captured in the findings from these ten villages located in five distinct geographical and agro-climatic regions. Increasing shifts away from traditional farming to non-agricultural occupations, which leads families and communities to attach a higher premium to education, have resulted in major changes away from traditional rural settings and more enclosed agrarian systems. The situation in earlier decades, when sons mainly followed their fathers' occupations, is vastly changing. This change is seen in its most exaggerated form in the central Punjab peri-urban and rural sites.

These economic changes are creating concomitant social change. Above all they are associated with migration and changes in family structure. These, in turn, exert influence on families' considerations about the number of children they want to have. In primarily agricultural economies, children contributed significantly to household production, and there was little reward from educating children. The growth of towns and the expansion of non-agricultural employment have increased the importance of schooling. In areas of growing industrialization and urbanization, such as central Punjab, we were able to show a negative association between age and female schooling. This is not the case in southern Punjab, where no trend in female schooling exists.

Family structures are also more prominently nuclear in these last two regions, where women are more likely to have recently in-migrated or to have moved away from their original villages. Changes in family structure tend to weaken the authority of the old over the young, and to some extent they alter gender relations, though not always positively. We present strong evidence of an association between living in a nuclear family and the selected indicators of women's status. Greater mobility among women as well as more say in household decisions—as the locus of decision-making moves away from other relatives to the conjugal couple—are also documented by these data.

Although Pakistan has had an official population program since the 1960s, it is recognized in the Eighth Plan to have had only limited outreach in rural areas (Planning Commission 1993). The newly introduced Village-Based Family Planning Program and the Lady Health Workers program had hardly taken off as of 1993, when the current study was conducted. At that time, the majority of rural women relied on either traditional contraceptive methods (of which there was substantial evidence), on their husbands (using condoms or practising withdrawal), and on family welfare centres and hospitals, which are largely located in towns or cities. Rural outreach has long been a major weakness in Pakistan's population program (Rukanuddin and Hardee-Cleaveland 1992). For all these reasons, women's mobility and their relationship with their spouse acquire even greater importance in the scheme of contraceptive adoption. It is worth pointing out that only two of our sites—the peri-urban site and one of the villages in the central Punjab region—had a family planning facility in the village. These villages happen to be the sites with the highest contraceptive prevalence, which suggests that location of a facility may be associated with a sufficiently high demand for family planning services in a given area.

Reproductive change, first in the form of the desire to regulate family size and then in the desire to adopt contraception, is strongly related to family structures. While the selected indicators of women's status are correlated with these two measures of future fertility change in bivariate analysis, they do not appear to be as important in multivariate analysis. This is not altogether surprising since women's status is found to be closely related to family structure and to the five regions of Punjab, which have distinctly different fertility patterns. The strong need for a minimum number of sons before fertility is controlled is one of the dominant findings of our analysis.

In conclusion, it would seem that in rural Punjab, gender and development are closely associated. Even though no unique predictors of fertility change emerge as especially important, it is clear that fertility change in rural Punjab was well under way in 1993, and may be even more rapid in current times. While proximity to urban centres and access to non-agricultural occupations may be the main factors explaining communities with high proportions practising contraception, women's empowerment, particularly in terms of strong son preference, changes in relations between men and women, and underlying changes in living arrangements, is also found to be a strong conditioning factor.

References

Cain, M. (1979), 'Risk and Insurance: Perspectives on Fertility and Agrarian change in India and Bangladesh, *Population and Development Review*, 7(3): 435–74.

—— Syeda Rokeya Khanum, and Shamsun Nahar (1993), 'Patriarchal Structure and Demographic Change', in Nina Fredirici, Karen Mason and Solvi Sogner (eds.), *Women's Position and Demographic Change*, Oxford: Clarendon Press, pp. 43–60.

Caldwell, J. C. (1978), 'A Theory of Fertility from High Plateau to Destabilization', *Population and Development Review*, 4(4): 553–77.

—— (1982), *Theory of Fertility Decline*, London: Academic Press.

—— Immerwahr, G, and Ruzicka, L. T. (1982), *Illustrative Analysis: Family Structure and Fertility*, World Fertility Survey Scientific Report, Voorburg: International Statistical Institute.

Dyson, T., and Moore, M. (1983), 'On Kinship Structure, Female Autonomy and Demographic Behaviour in India', *Population and Development Review*, 9(1): 35–60.

Irfan, M. (1989), 'Poverty, Class Structure and Household Demographic Behaviour in Rural Pakistan', in Gerry Rodgers (ed.), *Population Growth and Poverty in Rural South Asia*, New Delhi: Sage Publications, pp. 76–120.

Karim, M. (1974), 'Fertility Differentials by Family Type', *Pakistan Development Review*, 13(2): 129–44.

Khan, J. (1981), 'Contraceptive Usage, Fertility and Family Structure in Pakistan', *Population Sciences*, (2): 47–55.

KIHASA (1996), *Sex Preference for Children and Gender Discrimination in Asia*, Seoul: Korea Institute for Health and Social Affairs.

Mason, K. (1984), *Status of Women: A Review of its Relationship to Fertility and Mortality*, New York: The Rockefeller Foundation.

—— (1995), *Gender and Demographic Change: What Do We Know?*, Liège: IUSSP.

Mason, Karen O., and Bulatao, Rodolfo A. (1998), 'Gender and Family Systems in the Fertility Transition', Paper presented at the Rockefeller Foundation's Conference on the Global Fertility Transition, Bellagio, Italy, 18–22 May.

Planning Commission (1993), *The Eighth Five Year Plan*, Islamabad.

Population Council (1995), *The Pakistan Contraceptive Prevalence Survey 1994–95*, Islamabad.

Rukanuddin, R. and Hardee-Cleaveland, K. (1992), 'Can the Pakistan Program Suceed'? *International Family Planning Perspectives*, 18(3): 109–115.

Sathar, Z. (1993), 'The Much Awaited Fertility Decline in Pakistan: Wishful Thinking or Reality'? *International Family Planning Perspectives*, 19(4): 142–6.

—— and Desai, S. (1996), 'Work Patterns in Rural Pakistan: Intersections between Gender, Family and Class', *Population Council Working Paper*.

—— and Kazi, S. (1987), 'Variations in Demographic Behaviour by Levels of Living in Pakistan', *GENUS*, XLIII(3, 4).

—— and Kazi, S. (1989), 'Female Employment and Fertility: Further Investigation of an Ambivalent Relationship', *Population and Development Review*, 28(3).

—— and Kazi, S. (1996), '*Women's Autonomy, Livelihood and Fertility in Rural Punjab: First Report*', Islamabad: PIDE.

—— and Mason, K. (1993), 'How Female Education affects Reproductive Behaviour in Urban Pakistan?', *Asia and Pacific Forum*, 6(4).

—— Crook, N., Callum, C., and Kazi, S. (1988), 'Women's Status and Fertility Change in Pakistan', *Population and Development Review*, 14(3).

Smith, H., *et al.* (1995), 'The Impact of Women's Status on the Unmet Need for Contraception in Five Asia Countries', Paper presented at the PAA annual meeting, San Francisco.

United Nations (1993), '*Women's Status and Fertility Change in Pakistan: The Most Recent Evidence*', United Nations Population Division.

World Bank (1995), '*Fertility and Human Resources: Investing in the Future*', Paper prepared for the World Bank Poverty Assessment Study.

12 The Effect of Micro-Credit Programmes on the Reproductive Behaviour of Women in Rural Areas of Bangladesh

ABDULLAHEL HADI, SAMIR R. NATH, AND
A. M. R. CHOWDHURY

Background

An extensive literature is now available on the social, economic and cultural determinants of contraceptive use and fertility in developing countries (Dharmalingam and Morgan 1996; Koenig and Simmons 1992; Lapham and Simmons 1987; Schuler *et al.* 1997). However, evidence of the specific mechanisms and pathways through which societal and development factors influence reproductive behaviour is still limited (Koenig and Simmons 1992). Many studies examining the relationship between social and economic development and changing fertility aspirations still do not clearly demonstrate how women's empowerment, which can depend on many factors and assume multiple dimensions, affects their reproductive behaviour (Mason 1995). Nevertheless, it is widely understood that the major keys to improvements in women's status are education and paid employment.

Focusing on the particular role of education in influencing reproductive behaviour, Caldwell (1982) suggests that education helps women to understand the options available to them, re-think traditional cultural values, and challenge the authority and domination of men over women. A number of researchers argue that education influences reproductive outcome by reducing the number of children that women want, by stimulating their aspirations to attain a higher standard of living, by exposing women to new knowledge and practices regarding contraceptive use, by increasing husband–wife communication, and by enhancing women's knowledge and access to birth control (Cochrane *et al.* 1982; Le Vine *et al.* 1991; Schuler *et al.* 1997). Poor female education has also been found to be an important impediment to contraceptive use (Koenig and Simmons 1992).

Female education is also believed to operate by creating value changes in the community. Longer schooling increases husband–wife communication and knowledge, modifies attitudes to contraception, changes the balance in the couple's reproductive decision-making process (Cochrane *et al.* 1982; Jejeebhoy 1995), and encourages the rejection of traditional values that foster the low status of women. In and of itself, school attendance encourages girls to modify their individual attitudes and to be more free in moving around the community (Cleland *et al.* 1996; Lindenbaum 1983).

As with the relationship between education and fertility, the link between female employment and women's contraceptive and childbearing behaviour has attracted the attention of a number of social scientists (Amin and Pebley 1990; Cain 1981). In many impoverished rural settings, children, especially male children, are expected to provide their parents with security in their old age. It is argued that women who gain economic and psychosocial independence from their children, and increased self-reliance—through their ability to earn money for themselves—acquire the motivation to practise contraception and have smaller families (Cain 1981; Dyson and Moore 1983). Similar views are also reflected in a study conducted in Pakistan, which finds that female labour force participation modifies reproductive behaviour through enhancing women's status (Govindasamy and Malhotra 1996; Sathar *et al.* 1988).

The relationship between women's work and their reproductive behaviour depends on such additional factors as the type of work a woman does, the amount of control she has over her earning, and her place of work (Mahmud and Johnston 1994). It is clear that employment for women and their ability to earn their own money help reduce women's dependency on their husbands. This affects traditional gender relations within the household, creates opportunities to exercise some degree of autonomy, and enhances women's participation in household decision-making—including limiting or spacing births (Amin *et al.* 1994; Dharmalingam and Morgan 1996; Dixon-Mueller 1978; Mahmud and Johnston 1994; Safilios-Rothschild 1982). However, no significant association between female employment and contraception is found when women are below subsistence level, forced to take employment for their survival, or when they suffer from gender-based inequalities in the household (Bruce and Dwyer 1988; Mahmud and Johnston 1994).

Conceptualizing and Measuring Women's Autonomy

The need to conceptualize women's status, female autonomy, women's rights (and the differences between these various terms) has been emphasized in many recent demographic discourses (Mahmud and Johnston 1994; Mason 1984). While women's status is defined as 'the esteem in which she is held by different individuals and groups who come in contact with her' (Epstein 1982), women's autonomy is usually regarded as the ability to make their own decisions about what to do without external influence (Visaria 1993). Some components of women's autonomy that have been identified are: control over material resources; knowledge; economic opportunities available to women; decision-making role; and freedom of movement (Jejeebhoy 1996; Visaria 1993). Women may rise to higher status levels as producers, as reproducers of labour, as mothers-in-law or in other social roles, but high status does not automatically provide autonomy as long as their subordination to men is not eliminated (Mahmud and Johnston 1994; Safilios-Rothschild 1982). Mason (1984) identified gender inequality in prestige, power and access to or control over resources as the three most common dimensions of subordination. However, there is no consensus regarding the concept of women's autonomy that can be measured cross-culturally (Govindasamy and Malhotra 1996) because of variation in its indices with differing social context and with life cycle.

Women's autonomy, or decision-making ability in personal affairs, is determined by both social custom and tradition (Dyson and Moore 1983). A clear understanding of the power relations between women and men within the household is, therefore, needed to understand the role of women's increased autonomy on reproductive decision-making (Jejeebhoy 1996; Mahmud and Johnston 1994). Employment and control over resources help create women's self-respect and perception of self-worth that can subsequently enhance a sense of identity and reduce their dependence on men. Such an environment, in turn, helps reduce gender inequalities and enhance women's decision-making role.

In this study, female empowerment is conceptualized as the process whereby women gain access to a new world of knowledge and can begin to make new, informed choices in their life (Batliwala 1994). In traditional structural contexts that tend to perpetuate the oppression and exploitation of poor women (Moser 1989), empowerment involves enhancing women's awareness of, and readiness to act against, such subordination and inequality (Young 1988).

The relationship between women's autonomy and their reproductive behaviour has been well documented (Cleland *et al.* 1996; Mason 1984; Schuler *et al.* 1997). Women in patriarchal settings are forced to be dependent upon men for protection and economic support, and to assume a subordinate role in familial decision-making. They are thus limited in their ability to adopt such innovative behaviour as contraception (Cain 1984; Dyson and Moore 1983; Mason 1984). Women's subordinate status and their dependency upon men limit their mobility, requiring them to spend most of their time inside the household (Koenig and Simmons 1992).

Micro-Credit Programmes

Collateral-free micro-credit programmes—designed primarily to involve poor rural women in income-generating and education projects—typically offer women a wide array of support services: training in how to form an income-generating group; advice on setting up mechanisms for group savings; and special skills training in areas of commerce that will give women the opportunity to earn by themselves and contribute financially to their family. Several earlier studies have assessed how women's participation in credit-based income-generating activities affects their decision-making capacity or reproductive behaviour (Amin *et al.* 1993; Schuler and Hashemi 1994).

Most of these studies have been insufficiently attentive to the issue of endogeneity and self-selection (Pitt *et al.* 1999). While numerous studies have found that the beneficiaries of micro-credit development programmes are more likely than nonbeneficiaries to use contraceptives (Amin *et al.* 1996; Khan *et al.* 1997; Mahmud 1991; Schuler and Hashemi 1994), it has also been shown that this relationship can be a result of the self-selection bias: that is, women who participate in credit programmes were often better off than nonparticipants before entering the programme, or represented an especially motivated group of women (Pitt *et al.* 1999). This study has attempted to reduce such errors by employing a longitudinal approach.

Data and Methods

The data used in this chapter come from a demographic registration system (WATCH) covering 87 villages in Manikganj district of Bangladesh in which private voluntary development agencies—such as BRAC, Grameen Bank, Proshika, and others—have been operating intensive credit-based income-generating programmes since the mid-1970s. The registration system was designed to document the possible demographic changes associated with this array of income-generating activities and development programmes for women in the area.

In the 1986 benchmark survey, 11,011 married women aged between 15 and 49 were interviewed about their participation in income-generating activities, and their reproductive and contraceptive history. A followup survey was conducted eight years later, in 1994, when 1,535 married women in the same age range were randomly selected. The two samples—from 1986 and from 1994—were comparable in the sense that the women were residing in the same villages with nearly similar demographic characteristics. But they were different in terms of their literacy rate, land ownership and level of exposure to a development programme.

In this study, we look at the effect on various measures of women's reproductive behaviour exerted by four dimensions of their autonomy, independently of the effect of the usual demographic and background characteristics. The four dimensions of female autonomy are: women's mobility within their locality; their ability to manage their households; their role in the decision-making process within the household; and their freedom from control by husbands.

Physical mobility: Women's mobility outside the home has been used as a key indicator of autonomy in many studies (Hashemi *et al.* 1996; Jejeebhoy 1996; Khan *et al.* 1997), where mobility means the freedom to move within and between villages (Dharmalingam and Morgan 1996), visiting the local market and clinic alone or with their minor children (Amin *et al.* 1996; Schuler and Hashemi 1994).

In constructing an index of physical mobility for this study, four items were used: a woman's ability to move *within* her village; *outside* her village; to a local *market*; and to a *clinic*. A woman received zero if the response was negative. One point was given if the response was positive, and two points if she ever went out of the home alone or with minor children. All items were added to construct the index.

Purchasing power: Women's involvement in paid employment enhances their economic independence, raises their ability to buy essential household items, and determines their position within the households (Amin *et al.* 1996; Dharmalingam and Morgan 1996). A woman's purchasing power defines the degree of control she has over at least a part of the household resources, regardless of whether or not she earns some small income of her own. However, the capacity to make purchases may be a misleading indicator of autonomy if it must be permitted or granted by the husband (Khan *et al.* 1997; Schuler and Hashemi 1994).

The index of purchasing power used here is based on whether a woman has the capacity to buy such items as daily food, grocery, utensils, snacks and apparels for children, clothing for herself, cosmetics, and medicines, without her husband's support (Amin *et al.* 1996; Schuler and Hashemi 1994). One point was given if the response was positive, and zero if negative. The points were then added together to create the index.

Decision-making: The capacity of women to make decisions for themselves, or the degree to which women can actively participate in the decision-making processes within the household, is the most commonly used indicator of women's autonomy (Dharmalingam and Morgan 1996; Dyson and Moore 1983). Major decision issues are education of the children, the type of medical treatment she or her children receive, whether or when to visit the natal home or other places, the amount of money to be spent by family members during festivals, and whether or how much money should be lent to or borrowed from others.

Items used in the construction of this index include: decisions about education for a woman's children; the type of medical treatment she or her children can obtain; when to visit her natal home and other places; the amount of money to be spent during festivals; and how much money should be lent to or borrowed from others. One point is given for a positive response, and zero for a negative response in each of the eight decision issues.

Spousal relations: The way in which husbands and wives interact when making decisions about family spending, women's ability to bargain with their husbands about the control of household resources, and women's relative freedom from spousal domination are some of the various dimensions of power relationships among couples (Dharmalingam and Morgan 1996; Schuler and Hashemi 1994).

The indicator of spousal relations used here is based on women's answers to four items of behaviour. The respondent was asked to assess herself on a five-point scale (ranging from 0 to 4) where zero was considered negative and four was given for positive responses in constructing this variable. The items were: whether her husband always consulted with her about family finances; whether she participated in controlling household resources; whether she could bargain with her husband about household affairs; and whether she had ever been physically or verbally abused by her husband within the past year.

The internal consistency and reliability of the indices of autonomy are examined using reliability analysis[1] that provides correlation coefficients and an overall index of the repeatability or internal consistency of the scale as a whole. The analysis indicates that only the spousal relations variable is fairly correlated with buying capacity (with a value of correlation matrix of 0.204). The estimates of common inter-item correlation and reliability of scale are within acceptable limits.

In estimating the effect of credit programmes on contraceptive behaviour, most studies have used data from multiple sources that were pooled together if the sample proportion of credit programme participants was not equal to the population proportion of the participants (Pitt *et al.* 1999). This combined, choice-based, sample may lead to inconsistent estimates of the impact of credit programmes. In this study, samples were randomly chosen, and both credit participants and non-participants were proportionately represented.

As found in many other studies, cross-sectional data that does not randomly assign women between participants and nonparticipants in credit programmes may have generated biased estimates, because women who are more likely to use contraceptives may also be more likely than others to join the credit programmes (Amin *et al.* 1996; Hashemi *et al.* 1996; Pitt *et al.* 1999). The problem of possible self-selection is addressed in this study by using retrospective data that permit a before-and-after group framework of analysis (Rahman and De Vanzo 1997). Women who were nonusers of the contraceptive method in 1986 were followed until 1994. Of the 1,535 randomly selected women interviewed in 1994, 707 women were identified who had not used any contraceptive method before 1986. The reason why so many cases had dropped out was that a significant proportion of women 42 years or older in 1986 were no longer eligible to be in the sample in 1994, by virtue of their age. For the same reason, women aged 23 years or less were excluded from the sample because they were not eligible (< 15 years old) in 1986. Thus, the sample forms a cohort of women aged between 23 and 49 in 1994 who had never used a contraceptive method before 1986. This approach (i) helps establish a causal link between credit-based income-generating activity and its subsequent impact on autonomy indices and contraceptive use, and (ii) largely reduces the probability of selection bias (Pitt *et al.* 1999).

However, since NGOs generally operate in relatively poorer villages, the study suffers from the problem of the nonrandom placement of credit programmes. In many studies, the unobserved village attributes were not controlled in the statistical analysis. This omission might lead to upward or downward bias in the estimated effect of programme participation on contraceptive behaviour (Pitt *et al.* 1999).

The hypothesis to be examined in this study is that the participation of poor rural women in organized credit-based income-generating programmes improves

---

[1] Women who had not used contraception until 1986 ($N = 707$); estimated common inter-item correlation: 0.0945; unbiased estimate of reliability: 0.2964; full sample of all women surveyed in 1996 ($N = 1,534$); estimated common inter-item correlation: 0.2269; unbiased estimate of reliability: 0.5406.

women's autonomy in ways that subsequently modify their relationship with their husbands and lead to increased contraceptive use. Ordinary least-squares regression models are employed when women's autonomy indices are considered as the outcome variables (Jejeebhoy 1996). On the other hand, in assessing the impact of participation in a micro-credit programme on contraceptive use, a logit regression approach is followed, by modelling a dichotomous dependent variable, contraceptive use, which is coded 1 if a woman has accepted any method after 1986, and 0 otherwise. The logit model is considered appropriate because the dependent variable is dichotomous (Aldrich and Nelson 1984; Hanushek and Jackson 1977). The main independent variables are credit programme participation during the study period and the four indices of women's autonomy.

In addition, other variables included in the analytical framework are women's age, years of attendance in school, number of living children, husband's occupation, and amount of land owned by the household. These variables are assumed to modify the impact of our main hypothesis: that participation in a credit programme leads to enhanced autonomy, which leads to increased contraceptive use. The measurement of these variables is shown below:

Definition and measurement of variables

Variable	Category
Contraception	Prevalence of any contraceptive method (no = 0, yes = 1)
Autonomy indices	
Physical mobility	Women's physical mobility score within the community (range: 0–8)
Buying capacity	Buying capacity of usual household items (range: 0–9)
Decision-making	Decision-making role of women in the household (range: 0–8)
Spousal relations	Level of bargaining capacity with the husband and freedom from domination (range: 0–6)
Credit programme	Participation in micro-credit programme (never participated = 1, participated = 2)
Other variables	
Age	Age of eligible women (in years)
Living children	Number of living children
Years of schooling	Years of schooling completed by a woman
Land	Household ownership of land (in dec.)
Agri-labour	Husband is agricultural labourer (no = 1, agricultural labour = 2)

Results

The background characteristics of the study women in 1986 and 1994, shown in Table 12.1, indicate that differences in mean age and parity are minor, although significant differences in years of schooling, literacy rate, land ownership and

Table 12.1. Background characteristics of sample women, 1986 and 1994

Background characteristics	Married women ages (15–49)	
	1986	1994
Mean age (in years)	29.8	31.1
Mean no. of living children	2.6	2.5
Mean years of schooling	0.8	1.7
% literate	11.5	30.2
% of husbands labourers	39.9	47.7
% landless	38.7	47.7
Mean land (in dec.)	142	126
N	11,011	1,535

husband's occupation are evident. The increase in literacy may reflect the general increase of female education in Bangladesh and the efforts of NGOs to raise female literacy. The size of land holding has decreased, and both landlessness and the proportion of husbands employed as labourers are on the rise, trends that have also been found elsewhere (Cleland and Phillips 1994).

Table 12.2 shows differentials in contraceptive use by participation in credit programme and sociodemographic variables among all randomly selected women in 1994. Older women—both participants and nonparticipants in the credit programme—are less likely than younger women to use contraceptives, a finding similar to that of other studies (Mitra 1992; Mitra *et al.* 1994). This is probably because many older women become infertile as a result of menopause or from chronic illnesses. It is also likely that it is more difficult to convince older women to accept contraception, given their relatively shorter exposure to the family planning programme. Furthermore, a positive association is found between women belonging to a credit programme and their utilization of a contraceptive method, even after controlling for sociodemographic categories.

Various dimensions of women's autonomy are regressed, controlling for the amount of land owned by the household and husband's occupation (Table 12.3). Participation in credit programmes appears to have a positive association with each of the autonomy indexes. As participants of credit schemes, women are required to go outside their homes to attend meetings with other women and men. Moving beyond their homes and attending meetings has provided women with wider exposure to the outside world, and strengthens their self-confidence (Egero and Hammarskjold 1996). Access to credit and the income earned from the investment of that credit raise their buying capacity. Increasing self-confidence and earning opportunities not only have raised their decision-making capacity but also have increased their bargaining power capacity within the household— particularly with their spouses. For all equations, R^2 values are low, suggesting that

Table 12.2. Estimated contraceptive acceptance rates among women in 1994 by sociodemographic characteristics and involvement in credit programme ($N = 1,535$)

Sociodemographic characteristics	Credit programme	
	Did not participate	Participated
All	45.4	61.6
Age		
15–29	39.7	49.6
30–39	54.4	66.1
40–49	19.0	62.6
Significance	$p < 0.01$	$p < 0.01$
Living children		
2 or less	42.3	48.1
3–4	47.8	70.0
5 or more	46.8	61.3
Significance	ns	$p < 0.01$
Years of schooling		
None	46.2	62.9
I–V	43.2	54.0
VI+	43.0	61.9
Significance	ns	ns
Occupation of husband		
Labourer	47.4	64.1
Agriculture	41.3	56.5
Business	52.5	59.4
Service	37.5	55.0
Significance	ns	ns
Land ownership		
Landless	48.4	64.1
1–199 dec.	45.4	59.3
200+ dec.	40.8	52.5
Significance	ns	ns
N	904	631

other factors not included in the model significantly influence autonomy indices. Despite the low R^2 values, the regression equations for most indices are statistically significant.

The impact on contraceptive use of credit programme participation, women's autonomy indices and selected sociodemographic variables is examined using logit regression analysis (Table 12.4). Model I indicates that credit programme participants are 40 per cent more likely to use contraceptives ($p < 0.01$) than nonparticipants, controlling for age and living children. When autonomy indices are added to model II, the credit programme effect on contraceptive use declines ($p < 0.05$), indicating that women's autonomy indices also explain a part of that effect. The effects of the autonomy indices on contraceptive use—controlling for age and

Table 12.3. Correlates of women's autonomy: OLS regression coefficients controlling for amount of land owned by the household, and occupation of husband ($N = 1,535$)

Explanatory variable	Autonomy indices			
	Physical mobility (0–8)	Buying capacity	Decision-making (0–8)	Spousal relations (0–16)
Credit taken (rc = no)	0.50***	0.15	0.42***	0.44***
Age of women	0.04***	0.02***	0.01	0.07***
Years of schooling	0.07***	0.01	0.08***	0.17***
Constant	1.18***	3.30***	1.37***	6.25***
R^2	0.11	0.04	0.05	0.09

***$p < 0.01$, two-tailed test.

living children—are estimated in model III. No indicator except spousal relations ($p < 0.01$) is found to be significant. In model IV, the effects of both credit programme participation and the autonomy indices are estimated after controlling for the sociodemographic variables. Among the autonomy indices, only the spousal relations variable is found to have a statistically significant impact on contraceptive use. Overall, it appears that both raising women's autonomy, by empowering them in their relationships with their husbands, and participation in credit programmes have a positive impact on contraceptive use, even when demographic and socio-economic differences are controlled. This finding was also the case in studies in other parts of South Asia (Dharmalingam and Morgan 1996; Visaria 1993).

Longitudinal Analysis

The analysis based on data from 1994 indicates possible associations between credit programme participation, women's autonomy and contraception. In this section, an attempt has been made to establish a causal link between credit programme participation and contraceptive use. We are working here with a subsample of women who had not used contraceptives until 1986. Influences on women's autonomy for this group are shown in Table 12.5. Although much of the influence on autonomy remains unexplained, the data clearly suggest that programme participation raises the scores of physical mobility ($p < 0.01$), decision-making capacity ($p < 0.01$), and relations with husband ($p < 0.05$). The role of credit programme participation in raising the buying capacity of women is not statistically significant. The role of age in increasing women's autonomy is negligible, while education seems to have visible and statistically significant effects on decision-making and women's relationships with their husbands.

Table 12.4. Log odds ratios of selected explanatory variables to predict contraceptive use among women in 1994 ($N = 1,535$)

Explanatory variable	Model I	Model II	Model III	Model IV
Credit programme				
Not involved	1.0	1.0		1.0
Taken credit	1.40***	1.33**		1.27**
Autonomy indices				
Physical mobility		0.98	0.99 ·	0.98
Buying capacity		1.04	1.04	1.04
Decision-making		1.05	1.06	1.06
Spousal relations		1.07***	1.07***	1.06***
Other indicators				
Age of women	1.02	1.01	1.01	1.01
Living children	1.15***	1.17***	1.17**	1.17***
Years of schooling				1.00
Amount of land owned				1.00
Agri-labour (rc = no)				0.68***

***$p < 0.01$, two-tailed test.

Among the group of women who never used any contraceptive method until 1986, the sociodemographic differentials in contraceptive use are very wide, and statistically significant, regardless of their participation in credit programmes (Table 12.6). Across all subgroups, involvement with a credit programme significantly raises a woman's chances of accepting contraceptives. Land ownership is associated negatively with contraceptive use, although the differences are small and not statistically significant among nonrecipients of credit programmes. Other variables such as age, years of schooling, living children and occupational status do not show any consistent or significant association with contraceptive use.

The logit regression estimates, shown in Table 12.7, provide a clearer picture of the linkages between credit programmes, women's autonomy indices and their contraceptive behaviour. The models show that the impact of women's participation in credit programmes on contraceptive use is strong, positive and significant, regardless of women's sociodemographic characteristics. Model I indicates that women's participation in credit programmes after 1986 means they were 65 per cent more likely ($p < 0.01$) to use any method of contraceptives when compared to women who never received any credit, even after controlling for age and the number of living children. The effect on contraceptive use exerted by participation in a credit programme remains nearly unchanged in model II, where the autonomy variables are added to model I. This analysis indicates that the effect of women's autonomy indices (except for the spousal relation variable) on contraceptive use is

Table 12.5. Correlates of women's autonomy: OLS regression coefficients controlling for amount of land owned by the household, occupation of husband and religion ($N = 707$)

Explanatory variable	Autonomy indices			
	Physical mobility (0–8)	Buying capacity (0–9)	Decision-making (0–8)	Spousal relations (0–16)
Credit taken (rc = no)	0.78***	0.03	0.55***	0.52**
Age of women	0.02***	0.02	0.00	0.03*
Years of schooling	0.06**	0.05	0.11***	0.17***
Constant	1.25***	2.88	1.83***	6.70***
R^2	0.09	0.05	0.07	0.05

** $p < 0.05$, two-tailed test.
*** $p < 0.01$, two-tailed test.

minimal. The role of female autonomy in explaining increased contraceptive use is more clearly shown in model III, when age and the number of living children are controlled. The data also suggest that older women are less likely to practice contraception. However, contraceptive use among women with a large number of living children is more likely ($p < 0.01$). In model IV, the linkage between participation in a credit programme and contraceptive use weakens when autonomy indices and the socioeconomic variables are controlled. This weaker relationship can be explained by the different acceptability of contraception across socioeconomic groups (as we reported earlier). The effects of women's relations with their husbands on contraceptive use remain consistently strong in all estimated models. This indicates that differences in power relations with husband by sociodemographic groups are minimal.

Discussion

Evidence from this study reveals several major points of interest concerning the relationship between credit programme participation and reproductive behaviour. Participation in a micro-credit programme appears to improve women's position in the household. Although involvement in the programme enhances most dimensions of women's autonomy, the programme's influence on women's autonomy is conditioned by many other contextual factors. As a result, the changes in women's status are reflected only partially in modifying reproductive behaviours. With certain caveats, the study largely supports the hypothesis linking participation in a credit programme to women's increased autonomy and changed reproductive behaviour.

Table 12.6. Estimated contraceptive acceptance rates among women in 1994 who did not borrow credit or use contraception until 1986, by sociodemographic characteristics and involvement in the credit programme ($N = 707$)

Sociodemographic characteristics	Credit programme	
	Did not participate	Participated
All	44.1	56.1
Age		
15–29	58.8	53.8
30–39	49.0	64.9
40–49	27.0	35.5
Significance	$p < 0.01$	$p < 0.01$
Living children		
2 or less	58.1	44.7
3–4	43.1	65.5
5 or more	34.5	48.6
Significance	$p < 0.01$	$p < 0.10$
Years of schooling		
No school	42.8	58.5
I–V	50.8	38.5
VI+	44.1	66.7
Significance	ns	$p < 0.10$
Occupation of husband		
Labourer	46.1	62.9
Agriculture	38.9	41.3
Business	53.6	53.2
Service	34.6	28.6
Significance	ns	$p < 0.01$
Land ownership		
Landless	48.1	62.8
1–199 dec.	45.1	49.6
200+ dec.	36.7	38.9
Significance	ns	$p < 0.05$
N	404	303

These findings are consistent with those of other recent studies (Amin *et al.* 1996; Dharmalingam and Morgan 1996; Schuler and Hashemi 1994).

Over the last two decades, a number of NGOs in Bangladesh have introduced programmes offering collateral-free credit to rural poor women. These programmes

Table 12.7. Log odds ratios of selected explanatory variables to predict contraceptive use among sample women in 1994 who did not borrow credit or use contraception until 1986 (*N* = 707)

Explanatory variable	Model I	Model II	Model III	Model IV
Credit programme				
No	1.0	1.0		1.0
Yes	1.65***	1.66***		1.50**
Autonomy indices				
Physical mobility		0.88	0.99	0.88
Buying capacity		1.08	1.06	1.07
Decision-making		0.95	1.01	1.00
Spousal relations		1.10**	1.12**	1.10**
Other indicators				
Age of women	0.90***	0.90***	0.89***	0.90***
Living children	1.20***	1.22***	1.23***	1.22***
Years of schooling				1.01
Amount of land owned				1.00
Agri-labour (rc = no)				0.91

* $p < 0.10$, two-tailed test.
** $p < 0.05$, two-tailed test.
*** $p < 0.01$, two-tailed test.

have also provided skills training, adult education and reproductive health services. Bringing poor rural women together to collaborate in income-generating projects has created a kind of group solidarity among the members that serves to reduce their physical and social isolation in the home. By providing women with opportunities to earn and financially contribute to the family, the credit programme has played an important part in reducing gender inequality within the household. Involvement in credit programme activities increases women's outside contacts and helps widen their knowledge and skills. It forces women to move outside the home and thus modifies their traditional role of housewife into becoming a household provider.

The apparent success of self-employed women in our study villages in gaining greater autonomy should also be viewed from within a structural context. Given the cultural context, the expected role of the husband as sole provider is challenged when his wife engages in economic activities and is able to contribute financially to the household. Through this process, women's decision-making capacity increases because they become responsible not just for their traditional domestic activities, but also for a new productive role. Their participation in income-generating projects increases women's mobility, exposes them to new ideas, and enhances their ability to interact in the public sphere (Schuler and Hashemi 1994)—including the ability to demand and receive services available in the public sector. Participation in credit programme activities gives women the opportunity to regulate their fertility, by choosing their own method of contraception. This happens, in part at least, by a strengthening of their bargaining position within the household, either as a result of their ability to financially contribute to the family, or by their new-found ability to move beyond traditional values and beyond confinement within the household.

By organizing poor rural women into strongly bonded social groups, and by providing them opportunities to become involved in self-reliant economic activities, micro-credit programmes in rural Bangladesh have created a dramatically new situation for many women. While credit programmes alone are not sufficient to change women's position in a traditional community, the sustained and wider involvement of poor women in such programmes clearly enhances their reproductive choices. The apparently increased demand for fertility regulation and the increased contraceptive prevalence found among women involved in income-generating activities provide a clear message that family planning programmes should become a more integrated part of overall development efforts in Bangladesh.

References

Aldrich, J. H., and Nelson, F. D. (1994), *Linear Probability, Logit and Probit Models,* Beverly Hills: Sage Publications.

Amin, R. *et al.* (1993), 'Increased Contraceptive Use in an Impoverished Society: The Case of Bangladesh', Paper presented to the 1993 Annual Meeting of the Population Association of America, April 1993, Cincinnati.

—— Ahmed, A. U., Chowdhury, J., and Ahmed, M. (1994), 'Poor Women's Participation in Income Generating Projects and their Fertility Regulation in Rural Bangladesh: Evidence from a Recent Survey', *World Development,* 22: 555–65.

—— Li, Y., and Ahmed, A. U. (1996), 'Women's Credit Programs and Family Planning in Rural Bangladesh', *International Family Planning Perspectives,* 22(4): 158–62.

Amin, S., and Pebley, A. R. (1990), 'Gender Inequality within Households: The Impact of a Women's Development Programme in 36 Bangladesh Villages', Princeton University OPR Working Paper No. 91–6, Princeton.

Batliwala, S. (1994), 'The Meaning of Women's Empowerment: New Concepts from Action', in G. Sen, A. Germain and L. Chen (eds.), *Population Policies Reconsidered. Health, Empowerment, and Rights.* Boston: Harvard University Press.

Bruce, J., and Dwyer, D. (1988), 'Introduction', in D. Dwyer and J. Bruce (eds.), *A Home Divided: Women and Income in the Third World,* Stanford: Stanford University Press.

Cain, M. (1981), 'Risk and Insurance: Perspective on Fertility and Agrarian Change in India and Bangladesh', *Population and Development Review,* 7(3): 435–74.

—— (1984), 'Women Status and Fertility in Developing Countries: Son Preference and Economic Security', Center for Population Studies, Working Paper No. 110, New York: The Population Council.

Caldwell, J. C. (1979), 'Education as a Factor in Mortality Decline: An Examination of Nigerian Data', *Population Studies,* 33(3): 395–413.

—— *et al.* (1982), 'Education and Fertility: An Expanded Examination of the Evidence', in G. P. Kelly and C. M. Elliot (eds.), *Women's Education in the Third World: Comparative Perspectives,* Albany: SUNY Press.

Chaudhury, R. H. (1983), 'Female Labour Force Status and Fertility Behaviour in Bangladesh: Search for Policy Intervention', *Bangladesh Development Studies,* 11(3): 59–102.

Cleland, J., Phillips, J. F., Amin, S., and Kamal, G. M. (1994), *Bangladesh: The Determinants of Reproductive Change,* New York: Oxford University Press.

—— Kamal, N., and Sloggett, A. (1996), 'Links between Fertility Regulation and the Schooling and Autonomy of Women in Bangladesh', in R. Jeffery and A. M. Basu (eds.), *Girls' Schooling, Women's Autonomy and Fertility Change in South Asia,* New Delhi: Sage Publications.

Cochrane, S. H., Leslie, J., and O'Hara, D. J. (1982), 'Parental Education and Child Health: Intracountry Evidence', *Health Policy and Education,* 2(3–4): 213–50.

Dharmalingam, A., and Morgan, S. P. (1996), 'Women's Work, Autonomy, and Birth Control: Evidence from Two South Indian Villages', *Population Studies,* 50(2): 187–201.

Dixon, R. B. (1976), 'The Role of Rural Women: Female Seclusion, Economic Production, and Reproductive Choice', in R. Ridker (ed.), *Population and Development,* Baltimore: Johns Hopkins University Press.

Dixon-Mueller, R. (1978), *Rural Women at Work: Strategies for Development in South Asia,* Baltimore: Johns Hopkins University Press.

Dyson, T., and Moore, M. (1983), 'On Kinship Structure, Female Autonomy and Demographic Behaviour in India', *Population and Development Review,* 9(1): 35–6.

Egero, B., and Hammarskjold, M. (1996), 'Poverty and Fertility: Reproductive Change under Persistent Poverty', Lund University Programme on Population and Development Working Paper No. 5, Lund.

Epstein, T. S. (1982), 'A Social Anthropological Approach to Women's Roles and Status in Developing Countries: The Domestic Cycle', in R. Anker, M. Buvinic, and N. H. Youssef (eds.), *Women's Roles and Population Trends in the Third World,* London and Sydney: Croom Helm.

Fuglesang, A., and Chandler, D. (1988), *Participation As a Process: What We Can Learn from Grameen Bank, Bangladesh,* Dhaka: Pearl Printing and Packaging.

Govindasamy, P., and Malhotra, A. (1996), 'Women's Position and Family Planning in Egypt', *Studies in Family Planning,* 27(6): 328–40.

Hanushek, E. A., and Jackson, J. E. (1977), *Statistical Methods for Social Sciences,* New York: Academic Press.

Hashemi, S., Schuler, S. R., and Riley, A. P. (1996), 'Rural Credit Programs and Women's Empowerment in Bangladesh', *World Development,* 24(4): 635–53.

Hossain, M. (1984), *Credit for the Rural Poor: The Grameen Bank in Bangladesh,* Dhaka: Bangladesh Institute for Development Studies.

—— (1988), *Credit for Alleviation of Rural Poverty: The Grameen Bank in Bangladesh,* Washington, DC: International Food Policy Research Institute Research Report No. 65.

Jejeebhoy, S. J. (1995), 'Women's Education, Autonomy and Reproductive Behaviour: Assessing What We Have Learned', East-West Center Working Paper, Honolulu.

—— (1996), 'Women's Autonomy and Reproductive Behaviour in India: Linkages and Influence of Sociocultural Context', Paper presented at the Seminar on Comparative Perspectives on Fertility Transition in South Asia, Islamabad, Pakistan, 17–20 December.

Khan, S. R., Chowdhury, A. M. R., and Bhuiya, A. (1997), 'Women's Status vs Reproductive Behaviour: Does BRAC Have any Role Through its Development Programs?', Paper presented at the Population Association of America, March 1997, Washington, DC.

Khandker, S. R., and Latif, M. A. (1994), 'The Role of Family Planning and Targeted Credit Programs in Demographic Change in Bangladesh', The World Bank and Bangladesh Institute of Development Studies (unpublished report), Dhaka.

Koenig, M., and Simmons, R. (1992), 'Constraints on Supply and Demand for Family Planning', in J. Phillips and J. Ross (eds.), *Family Planning Programmes and Fertility*, Oxford: Oxford University Press.

Korten, D. C. (1991), *Bangladesh Rural Advancement Committee. Strategy for the 1990s*, New York: PACT.

Lapham, R. J., and Simmons, G. B. (1987), *Organizing for Effective Family Planning Programs*, Washington, DC: National Academy Press.

Le Vine, R. A. *et al.* (1991), 'Schooling and Survival: The Impact of Maternal Education on Health and Reproduction in the Third World', Harvard School of Public Health Working Paper No. 3, Cambridge.

Lindenbaum, S. (1983), 'The Impact of Female Education on Maternal and Child Health in Bangladesh', ICDDR,B Research Monograph, Dhaka.

Mabud, M. A. (1992), 'Population Growth, Women's Status, and Development Programmes', in M. A. Mabud (ed.), *Bangladesh's Population Problem and Programme Dynamics*, Dhaka: Sheba Printing Press.

Mahmud, S. (1991), 'Current Contraception among Programme Beneficiaries', *Bangladesh Development Studies*, 19(3): 35–62.

—— and Johnston, A. M. (1994), 'Women's Status, Empowerment, and Reproductive Outcomes', in G. Sen, A. Germain and L. Chen (eds.), *Population Policies Reconsidered. Health, Empowerment, and Rights.* Boston: Harvard University Press.

Maloney, V., and Ahmed, A. B. (1988), *Rural Savings and Credit in Bangladesh*, Dhaka: The University Press Ltd.

Marum, E. (1982), *Women in Food for Work in Bangladesh*, Dhaka: USAID.

Mason, K. O. (1984), *The Status of Women: A Review of its Relationships to Fertility and Mortality*, New York: The Rockefeller Foundation.

—— (1995), 'Gender and Demographic Change: What Do We Know?', International Union for the Scientific Study of Population Paper, Liège, Belgium.

Mitra, S. N. (1992), 'Bangladesh Contraceptive Prevalence Survey, 1991. Preliminary Report', Mitra & Associates (unpublished report), Dhaka.

—— *et al.* (1994), *Bangladesh Demographic and Health Survey, 1993–1994*, Dhaka: National Institute of Population Research and Training (NIPORT).

Moser, C. (1989), 'Gender Planning in the Third World: Meeting Practical and Strategic Needs', *World Development*, 17: 1799–825.

Pitt, M. M., Khandker, S. R., McKernan, S., and Latif, M. A. (1999), 'Credit Programs for the Poor and Reproductive Behavior in Low Income Countries: Are the Reported Causal Relationships the Result of Heterogeneity Bias?', *Demography*, 36(1): 1–21.

Rahman, A. (1986), 'Consciousness Raising Efforts of Grameen Bank', Grameen Bank Evaluation Project Working Paper No. 3, Bangladesh Institute of Development Studies, Agriculture and Rural Development Division, Dhaka.

Rahman, M., and De Vanzo, J. (1997), 'Influence of the Grameen Bank on Contraceptive Use in Bangladesh', unpublished manuscript, Rand Corporation.

Safilios-Rothschild, C. (1982), 'Female Power, Autonomy and Demographic Change in the Third World', in R. Anker, M. Buvinic and N. H. Youssef (eds.), *Women's Roles and Population Trends in the Third World*, London and Sydney: Croom Helm.

Sathar, N., Crook, N., Callum, C., and Kazi, S. (1988), 'Women's Status and Fertility Change in Pakistan', *Population and Development Review,* 14(2): 415–32.

Schuler, S. R., and Hashemi, S. M. (1994), 'Credit Programs Women's Empowerment and Contraceptive Use in Rural Bangladesh', *Studies in Family Planning,* 25(2): 65–76.

—— Hashemi, S. M., and Riley, A. P. (1997), 'The Influence of Women's Changing Roles and Status in Bangladesh's Fertility Transition: Evidence from a Study of Credit Programs and Contraceptive Use', *World Development,* 25(4): 563–75.

Visaria, L. (1993), 'Female Autonomy and Fertility Behaviour: An Exploration of Gujrat Data', *International Population Conference, 24 August–1 September 1993,* Vol. 4, International Union for the Scientific Study of Population, Montreal.

Young, K. (1988), *Gender and Development: A Relational Approach,* Oxford: Oxford University Press.

13 Son Preference in South Asia

FRED ARNOLD

Introduction

The preference of parents for sons has been observed to be unusually strong in the South Asian region, as well as in East Asia, the Middle East and North Africa (Arnold 1997; United Nations 1985). Virtually every study in Bangladesh, India, Nepal, Pakistan and Sri Lanka (at both the national and local levels) has found son preference to be both pervasive and largely resistant to change. Sons are valued above daughters for their economic value in providing help on the family farm or in the family business, in providing security for their parents in old age, and in carrying on the family line. In some South Asian cultures, other important reasons for wanting sons include the receipt of dowry payments at the time of marriage and the need for sons to perform certain religious duties. For example, according to Hindu tradition, sons are needed to light the funeral pyre when their deceased parents are cremated. By performing *pind daan* (making offerings to Brahmins and the poor), sons can also help in the salvation of their parents' souls.

Despite a strong desire for sons, in many parts of the region there is increasing evidence that parents also want to have at least one girl (Kabir *et al.* 1994; Muhuri and Preston 1991; Niraula and Morgan 1995; Visaria 1994). The desire for at least one girl is particularly strong among Hindus because of the duty of *kanya daan* (selflessly giving away a daughter at the time of marriage without the expectation of receiving anything in return). Fulfilling this duty is one way for parents to attain *punya* (religious merit) and make sure that they have a place in heaven. Daughters may also be considered as a source of wealth (*laxmi*) and good fortune.

A substantial literature exists documenting both the pervasiveness of son preference and various types of discriminatory treatment of daughters in South Asian countries (Ali 1989; Basu 1989; Booth and Verma 1992; Chen *et al.* 1981; Das 1987; Das Gupta and Mari Bhat 1996; Karki 1988; Kishor 1995; Levine 1987; Miller 1984; Murthi *et al.* 1995; Nadarajah 1983; Nag 1991; Niraula and Morgan 1995; Sathar 1987; Stash 1996; Vlasoff 1990). The effect of son preference on demographic behaviour, however, is not as well established. Some studies find the effect to be substantial, but other have been able to demonstrate only weak or negligible effects

The author gratefully acknowledges excellent data processing assistance from Martin Wulfe and Trevor Croft, and research assistance from Andrea Piani.

(Bairagi and Langsten 1986; Das 1989; De Silva 1992; De Tray 1984; Koenig and Foo 1992; Rajaretnam 1995; Raju and Bhat 1995; Repetto 1972; Sarma and Jain 1974; Talwar 1975).

Most available studies on gender preferences in South Asia are based on local data sources, largely individual villages, or hospitals in some cases. The sample populations are rarely representative of the country as a whole. In recent years, however, large-scale, nationally representative sample surveys of ever-married women in their childbearing years have been carried out in Bangladesh, Pakistan, Sri Lanka, India and Nepal. These Demographic and Health Surveys (DHS) were carried out in the first three countries between 1987 and 1994; the remaining two countries conducted similar surveys in 1991 and 1993.[1] Although they did not focus specifically on gender preferences or sex discrimination, the surveys provide a rich source of data that can be used to shed light on these issues.

This analysis compares findings from these national-level surveys as they relate to preferences for male children. In particular, the study examines three types of measure:

1. expressed gender preferences;
2. the effect of expressed gender preference on reproductive behaviour; and
3. differential treatment of daughters and sons.

Gender Preferences

The surveys in all five countries asked currently married women whether or not they wanted to have a child (or another child) at any time in the future. Table 13.1 presents the responses according to the sex of women's living children. Pregnant women are excluded because they were asked only whether they wanted another child after the one they are expecting, and the sex of that child is usually not known.

In every country, at least 85 per cent of women with no children say they want to have a child. Many of the remaining women either cite infecundity as the reason for not wanting children or say that such matters are up to God. A large majority of women with one living child also say they want to continue childbearing. However, in India, Nepal and Pakistan women with one child already are more likely to want another if the first is a girl. By the second parity, strong influences of the living children's sex emerge in every country. In each case, women without a son are by far the most likely to say they want to continue childbearing.

India and Nepal exhibit the strongest form of son preference: the percentage of women wanting another child declines steadily as the number of sons increases. This finding suggests that many women do not consider one son to be sufficient. Women in Bangladesh and Sri Lanka also have a strong son preference at the

---

[1] A Demographic and Health Survey (the Nepal Family Health Survey) was also conducted in Nepal in 1996, but the data were not available in time to be included in this chapter.

Table 13.1. Percentage of currently married, non-pregnant women aged 15–49 who want another child, by number and sex composition of living children

Number and sex of living children	Bangladesh	India	Nepal	Pakistan	Sri Lanka
No children	94	85	90	89	94
One child					
No sons	88	79	89	85	80
One son	88	74	79	81	80
Two children					
No sons	65	57	77	77	47
One son	25	27	39	60	26
Two sons	39	22	25	61	36
Three children					
No sons	48	50	66	79	18
One son	15	19	29	56	11
Two sons	8	6	7	28	6
Three sons	20	11	10	33	16
Four children					
No sons	(52)	37	63	(72)	(20)
One son	13	14	18	43	6
Two sons	3	4	3	18	3
Three sons	3	3	4	17	5
Four sons	7	11	6	(31)	(12)
Five or more children					
More daughters than sons	3	5	6	15	1
Daughters = sons	2	3	2	2	2
More sons than daughters	2	2	2	7	1

( ) Based on 25–49 unweighted cases.

second parity, but they appear most satisfied with their current family composition if they have one child of each sex. It is interesting to note that in these four countries, as long as they already have at least one son only a minority of women with two children say they want another child. The situation in Pakistan is characterized by unusually high fertility desires even after women have at least one son, and by no difference in the desire for more children between women with two sons and those with one child of each sex.

For women who already have three children, the pattern of differentials is the same in all five countries. The proportion of women wanting more children declines rapidly up to two sons, but increases for women with all sons. This pattern provides clear evidence that throughout South Asia, many women do have an interest in having one daughter. Once again, Pakistani women are much more

Table 13.2. Percentage of pregnant women aged 15–49 whose pregnancy was unwanted, by number and sex composition of living children

Number and sex of living children	Bangladesh	India	Nepal	Pakistan
No children	0	1	1	0
One child				
No sons	1	2	1	2
One son	0	1	4	1
Two children				
No sons	(4)	5	5	(11)
One son	22	13	18	7
Two sons	(21)	14	16	(0)
Three children				
No sons	†	5	14	(0)
One son	(36)	19	30	6
Two sons	†	31	44	(11)
Three sons	†	20	(30)	†
Four children				
No sons	†	(6)	†	†
One son	†	26	40	†
Two sons	†	34	60	22
Three sons	†	40	(59)	(26)
Four sons	†	†	†	†
Five or more children				
More daughters than sons	†	32	53	37
Daughters = sons	†	(58)	†	(43)
More sons than daughters	(86)	44	64	33

( ) Based on 25–49 unweighted cases.
† Percentage not shown; based on fewer than 25 unweighted cases.

likely than women from any other country to express a desire for more children, regardless of the sex composition of their living children. A similar pattern can be seen for women with four children. At the fifth and higher parities, very few women want to continue childbearing, but women with more daughters than sons are still generally slightly more likely than other women to want another child.

Another way of gauging the extent of gender preferences is to examine the responses given by pregnant women who are asked whether at the time they got pregnant, their current pregnancy was wanted, wanted at a later time, or not wanted at all. The percentages of women who classify their pregnancy as unwanted at the time they conceived are shown for four countries in Table 13.2. At every parity, women who do not have any sons are very unlikely to say that their current pregnancy is unwanted. Women with three or four children are much more likely

Table 13.3. Per cent distribution of preferred sex for the next child among currently married, non-pregnant women who want another child

Country	Female	Male	Doesn't matter/ up to God	Total
India	11	49	40	100
Pakistan	5	49	46	100

to have an unwanted pregnancy if they have at least two sons than if they have one son or no sons. Once again, a reversal in the trend is sometimes seen for women who have only sons, suggesting that daughters retain at least some importance in South Asian families.

Additional information on gender preference attitudes is available from questions on the ideal number of daughters and sons that women would like and on the preferred sex of the next child (for women who want another child). However, again, these questions were not asked in all five countries. The average number of sons in the ideal family exceeds the average number of daughters by 26 per cent in Bangladesh, 43 per cent in Pakistan and 49 per cent in India (not shown). In India and Pakistan, the desire for sons is very pronounced with respect to the preferred sex of the next child (see Table 13.3). Among women who specify the preferred sex of the next child, sons are preferred to daughters by almost 5 to 1 in India and by nearly 10 to 1 in Pakistan. Despite these lopsided results, nearly half of the women said that the sex of the child does not matter, or that it is up to God.

Effect of Gender Preference on Reproductive Behaviour

An important question for both academic and policy purposes is whether son preference actually affects parents' reproductive behaviour. Several survey measures can be used to assess the demographic impact of son preference. One constellation of measures deals with contraceptive prevalence, the contraceptive method mix, the contraceptive discontinuation rate and the effectiveness of contraception (estimated by the contraceptive failure rate). Questions on intentions to use contraception in the future are also included in the surveys. These may be considered attitudinal measures, but, if predictive of future behaviour, they will ultimately affect reproduction.

Other measures of reproductive behaviour—such as pregnancy rates, birth intervals and sex ratios of children—more directly measure fertility. In some cases, son preference may indirectly affect reproduction by influencing marriage patterns (for

Table 13.4. Percentage of currently married women aged 15–49 who are currently using contraception, by number and sex composition of living children

Number and sex of living children	Bangladesh	India	Nepal	Pakistan	Sri Lanka
No children	13	4	1	0	6
One child					
No sons	33	17	4	3	44
One son	36	21	7	3	44
Two children					
No sons	38	31	6	9	65
One son	53	46	19	12	64
Two sons	53	55	31	10	64
Three children					
No sons	44	32	8	10	76
One son	56	51	22	9	80
Two sons	62	68	45	14	78
Three sons	60	65	45	9	71
Four children					
No sons	(38)	36	8	(7)	(79)
One son	50	52	27	12	81
Two sons	60	62	41	19	77
Three sons	61	63	44	21	81
Four sons	58	62	39	15	(67)
Five or more children					
More daughters than sons	51	48	29	18	77
Daughters = sons	50	43	32	21	69
More sons than daughters	47	46	33	18	73

( ) Based on 25–49 unweighted cases.

example, if divorce or polygyny are more common among couples without sons). Because of space constraints, this chapter discusses only some of these measures.

Table 13.4 shows the pattern of current contraceptive use in relation to the sex composition of living children. Gender preference has the least effect on contraceptive prevalence in countries with the highest and lowest overall level of contraceptive use (Sri Lanka and Pakistan, respectively). In the remaining countries, the influence of son preference begins to emerge at the first parity and is most

Table 13.5. Sex ratios of living children by current contraceptive use, for currently married, non-pregnant women

Country	Sex ratio		
	Female or male sterilization	Any other method	Not currently using
Bangladesh	119.0	109.3	102.5
India	125.4	102.0	97.1
Nepal	134.6	108.9	95.2
Pakistan	118.1	101.2	106.6
Sri Lanka	103.2	101.1	110.4

Note: Sex ratio is the number of male children per 100 female children.

prominent for women with 2–4 children. In every case, contraceptive use rates are lowest for women with no sons, demonstrating the importance of having at least one son. In India and Nepal, there is strong evidence that even one son is not considered sufficient. Contraceptive use rates are considerably higher for women with two or more sons than for women with one son. The slight decline in contraceptive use rates for third- and fourth-parity women with no daughters indicates that some couples do want to have a daughter, but the differentials are not large enough to be very convincing. In fact, contraceptive use rates (for women with 2–4 children) are typically 1–1/2 times as large for women with no daughters as for women with no sons in Bangladesh, and 2–5 times as large in India and Nepal.

Cross tabulations similar to those in Table 13.4 could be constructed for each different method of contraception, but analysis of such detailed tables would be cumbersome. The analysis can be simplified by combining contraceptive methods and examining sex ratios of living children (see Table 13.5). In every country, sex ratios are higher among women using sterilization than among those using other methods of contraception. This pattern indicates that couples are much less reluctant to adopt terminal methods of family planning when the number of boys they have exceeds the number of girls. The sex ratio differentials by type of contraception are particularly pronounced in the case of India and Nepal.

The death of a child after a sterilization operation may cause a woman to reassess her decision to become sterilized. Although it is unusual for a woman to say that she regrets having been sterilized, the death of a male child is more likely than the death of a female child to trigger regret (data not shown). In the case of India, for

Table 13.6. Percentage of currently married women aged 15–49 who were pregnant at the time of the interview, by number and sex composition of living children

Number and sex of living children	Bangladesh	India	Nepal	Pakistan	Sri Lanka
No children	22	21	18	26	34
One child					
No sons	15	14	15	20	10
One son	12	13	13	19	10
Two children					
No sons	10	11	15	21	5
One son	7	7	10	19	5
Two sons	6	6	10	12	6
Three children					
No sons	11	11	12	22	3
One son	7	6	9	18	3
Two sons	4	3	5	12	3
Three sons	3	3	5	19	0
Four children					
No sons	(12)	10	9	(15)	(3)
One son	6	4	7	8	1
Two sons	5	3	5	17	2
Three sons	4	3	5	17	0
Four sons	4	3	5	4	(5)
Five or more children					
More daughters than sons	2	3	4	11	1
Daughters = sons	3	4	4	12	1
More sons than daughters	3	3	4	8	1

( ) Based on 25–49 unweighted cases.

example, among women who regret sterilization because of the death of a child, 64 per cent of their children who had died since the sterilization were male.

Because contraceptive methods may be used ineffectively, or may fail, the current fertility impact of son preference can best be seen by analysing pregnancy rates at the time of the survey in relation to the number and sex of living children (see Table 13.6). There does not seem to be any impact of gender preference on reproduction in Sri Lanka, but son preference has a strong impact on fertility in all of the remaining countries, including Pakistan, where contraceptive prevalence rates are quite low.

Table 13.7. Mean closed and open birth intervals, by sex of preceding child

Country	Mean closed birth interval		Mean open birth interval	
	Female child	Male child	Female child	Male child
Bangladesh	33.7*	34.7*	63.3*	67.3*
India	31.5*	32.4*	78.2*	83.7*
Nepal	32.5*	33.3*	55.3*	60.8*
Pakistan	27.5	28.0	49.5	48.3
Sri Lanka	33.0*	34.1*	79.6*	73.4*

* $p < 0.05$ for difference between females and males.

In countries where son preference is widespread, in the hope of having a boy couples may try to have another child sooner after the birth of a girl than after the birth of a boy. They may try to hasten the birth of the next child by shortening the period of postpartum abstinence or the duration of breastfeeding (to reduce the overall length of postpartum amenorrhoea), or by avoiding the use of contraceptives. Table 13.7 shows differentials in birth intervals according to the sex of the preceding child. The open birth intervals are an indicator of recent reproductive behaviour, whereas the closed birth intervals measure the impact of reproductive behaviour over the course of the childbearing career. Thus, it is not surprising that differentials in birth intervals are smaller in the case of closed birth intervals, which include a time period when contraceptive prevalence was lower in all of the South Asian countries. In every country, the mean closed birth interval is about one month shorter after the birth of a female child than after the birth of a male child, and the differentials, while small, are statistically significant in every country except Pakistan. In Bangladesh, India and Nepal, the mean open birth interval is 4–5 months shorter after the birth of a daughter, but the reverse pattern is evident in Sri Lanka.

If, depending on the sex of previous children, couples employ different rules to determine when to stop childbearing, then eventually sex ratios of children at different parities will become skewed. In general, if couples are more likely to discontinue or delay childbearing after having a son, sex ratios at birth will be abnormally high for last births and abnormally low for all previous births. Of course, the overall sex ratio at birth will not be affected by such differential rules unless couples use sex pre-selection techniques, such as sex-selective abortion. Table 13.8 reveals that the sex ratio at birth for all births is in the normal range in all the South Asian countries, varying narrowly between 105.6 in Pakistan and 107.0 in

Table 13.8. Sex ratio at birth for last births and all other births

Type of birth	Bangladesh	India	Nepal	Pakistan	Sri Lanka
Last birth	110.4	119.4	119.1	106.7	109.2
All except last births	105.1	102.4	101.5	105.3	104.5
All births	106.5	107.0	105.7	105.6	105.9

Note: Sex ratio is the number of male births per 100 female births.

India. In every country, however, sex ratios of last births are substantially higher than sex ratios of previous births. The differentials are particularly pronounced for India and Nepal, where the sex ratio is 119 for last births and 102 for all previous births. Another consequence of this type of fertility behaviour is that girls will tend to grow up in disproportionately large families, in which they will have to share limited family resources with a larger number of siblings.

The impact of sex-selective stopping rules can also be seen in the number of women with various numbers of living daughters and sons. Sex differentials in the survival of children also affect this measure, so the outcome is not based solely on stopping rules. Based on average sex ratios at birth alone, without considering differential mortality or stopping rules, we would expect there to be about 13 per cent more women with exactly two sons than exactly two daughters.[2] The survey results for second-parity women show that the excess of two-son families over two-daughter families is 55 per cent in India, 48 per cent in Nepal, 41 per cent in Bangladesh, 32 per cent in Pakistan, and 29 per cent in Sri Lanka (not shown). These abnormal distributions provide yet another indication of the demographic effects of son preference in South Asia.

Quantitative Estimates of the Effect of Gender Preference

The effect of gender preference differs depending on the number and sex of children a woman has. The overall impact of gender preference, therefore, depends not only on the strength of such preferences but also on the percentage of couples with each combination of children. For example, women with four daughters and no sons may have a strong desire to have a son (and consequently may be very reluctant to use contraception), but the chances of having four children all of whom are daughters are very small, so the overall impact of this group on reproductive

---

[2] This calculation assumes an average sex ratio of 106, which implies that 51.5 per cent of all births are male.

Table 13.9. Effect of gender preference on the desire for another child, current pregnancy, and current contraceptive use

Measure/effect	Bangladesh	India	Nepal	Pakistan	Sri Lanka
Percentage wanting another child [a]					
Actual	36.4	32.5	36.3	41.6	30.3
In absence of gender preference	31.7	27.4	28.9	34.6	27.3
Absolute decrease	4.7	5.1	7.4	7.0	3.0
Per cent decrease	12.9	15.7	20.4	16.8	9.9
Percentage pregnant [b]					
Actual	8.7	8.5	9.5	15.5	6.9
In absence of gender preference	7.4	7.5	8.5	12.3	6.1
Absolute decrease	1.3	1.0	1.0	3.2	0.8
Per cent decrease	14.5	11.0	10.3	20.6	11.6
Percent currently using contraception [b]					
Actual	44.9	40.7	22.7	11.8	61.7
In absence of gender preference	47.6	45.5	28.4	13.9	63.1
Absolute increase	2.7	4.8	5.7	2.1	1.4
Per cent increase	5.9	11.8	24.8	17.3	2.3

[a] Based on currently married, non-pregnant women aged 15–49.
[b] Based on currently married women aged 15–49.

behaviour is likely to be minimal. Arnold (1985) developed a measure for quantifying the effect of gender preference, taking these considerations into account. The measure can be used to determine what would happen if all gender preferences were to disappear suddenly. The measure assumes that in the absence of gender preference, all couples at each parity would behave in the same way as couples at the same parity who are currently most satisfied with the sex composition of their children. For example, Table 13.1 shows that at the second parity the desire to have another child in Bangladesh is lowest for women with one son and one daughter (25 per cent). The measure assumes that in the absence of gender preference the entire group of second-parity women, no matter how many sons and daughters they have, would be subject to the same 25 per cent figure. A similar assumption is made at every other parity.[3]

The results of this calculation are shown in Table 13.9 for three variables: the percentage of women who want another child, the percentage who were pregnant at

[3] This method of measuring the impact of gender preferences is most reliable in countries where there is considerable homogeneity in gender preferences, such as the South Asian countries. The influence of gender preferences on reproductive behaviour might be underestimated by this measure under conditions of heterogeneity in gender preferences.

the time of the survey, and the percentage currently using contraception. In each panel the third row shows the absolute amount by which the percentage would decrease or increase in the absence of gender preference, and the fourth row shows the percentage change. Bairagi (1993) calls the latter measure the Sex Preference Effect Measure (SPEM). The calculations show that in the absence of gender preference the percentage of women who would want another child would decrease modestly (between 3 and 7 percentage points). The percentage decrease is much higher, however, ranging from 10 per cent in Sri Lanka to 20 per cent in Nepal. Although the absolute differences are much smaller in the case of pregnancy (because only a small proportion of women are pregnant at any time to begin with), the percentage differences are of roughly the same magnitude (10–21 per cent). The contraceptive prevalence rate would increase by 1–6 percentage points in the absence of gender preference, corresponding to increases of between 2 per cent in Sri Lanka and 25 per cent in Nepal. Overall, Sri Lanka appears to be least affected by gender preferences, whereas Nepal and Pakistan are the most affected. Thus, there is a gradient whereby the impact of gender preference is weakest in the country with the highest level of contraceptive prevalence (and the lowest level of fertility) and strongest in the countries with the lowest levels of prevalence (and the highest fertility rates).

Although gender preferences clearly have an impact on reproductive attitudes and behaviour in South Asia, the effects are generally modest considering the strength of son preference attitudes in these countries. Even the complete disappearance of gender preferences would have only a modest effect on the variables measured in Table 13.9, and such a radical change in deeply imbedded cultural traditions is unlikely in the short run.

Differential Treatment of Daughters and Sons

It seems intuitively obvious that in societies in which son preference is strong, daughters may be faced with discrimination and with neglect of many kinds, particularly with respect to medical care and feeding practices. Nevertheless, evidence from a large variety of countries suggests that preferences for children of a particular sex do not necessarily result in this type of discrimination, at least for young children (Arnold 1992). In South Asia, however, as indicated earlier, there is ample evidence that girls often receive unfavourable treatment even when they are young. In this section, the analysis focuses on mortality levels for infants and young children, preventive and curative medical care, and nutritional status.

In most countries throughout the world, males have higher mortality than females in nearly every age group. In South Asia, on the other hand, female mortality has typically been higher than male mortality from early childhood through the early childbearing years (Tabutin and Willems 1995). Table 13.10 shows the relative risks of mortality for males and females up through age five. During the neonatal

Table 13.10. Relative risk of neonatal, postneonatal, infant, child and under-five mortality by sex of child, for the ten-year period preceding the survey

Period	Bangladesh	India	Nepal	Pakistan	Sri Lanka
Neonatal	1.27*	1.18*	1.27*	1.30*	1.74*
Postneonatal[a]	0.97	0.88*	1.01	1.07	1.36
Infant	1.15*	1.06*	1.16*	1.19*	1.59*
Child	0.75*	0.70*	0.89*	0.60*	1.03
Under-five	0.99	0.94*	1.05	1.03	1.43*

* $p < 0.05$ for difference between females and males.
[a]Computed as the difference between the infant and neonatal mortality rates.

Note: Relative risk is the probability of dying for male children divided by the probability of dying for female children during each period.

period, when biological factors predominate, male mortality is much higher than female mortality in every country, as expected. By the postneonatal period, girls in Bangladesh, and particularly in India, are already at a disadvantage when it comes to the probability of survival. The female disadvantage comes to the fore for children aged 1–4 years. Except in Sri Lanka, female mortality at that age exceeds male mortality by amounts ranging from 12 per cent in Nepal to 67 per cent in Pakistan. The severity of the female disadvantage is striking when compared to the average situation in all countries having had DHS surveys. In those countries, female child mortality exceeds male child mortality by an average of only 2–3 per cent (Arnold 1997). The situation in Pakistan, India and Bangladesh is, therefore, virtually unique in the world. Egypt is the only other country with a DHS survey in which girls suffer a similar survival disadvantage.

A complete analysis of the reasons for disproportionately high child mortality for girls is beyond the scope of this chapter. However, discrimination against girls in a variety of areas is undoubtedly a contributing factor. Table 13.11 provides one indicator of preventive care for children, i.e. the percentage of children aged 12–23 months who are fully vaccinated or have received no vaccinations at all. Children who are fully vaccinated have received all eight of the recommended vaccinations against vaccine-preventable childhood diseases. In every country, boys are more likely to be fully vaccinated than girls, with differences ranging from 3 to 8 percentage points. Similarly, in every country except Sri Lanka, girls are more likely than boys to have been completely missed by immunization programmes.

Information on the prevalence and treatment of common childhood illnesses is shown in Table 13.12. The prevalence of these conditions varies little by the sex of the child, and where there are significant differentials, boys are more likely to be sick. It might be argued that parents are less likely to recognize an illness in a

Table 13.11. Percentage of children 12–23 months old who are fully vaccinated or who have not received any vaccinations

Country	Fully vaccinated[a]		Received no vaccinations	
	Female child	Male child	Female child	Male child
Bangladesh	56*	62*	17*	11*
India	34*	37*	32*	28*
Nepal	36*	39*	26*	22*
Pakistan	31	39	31	25
Sri Lanka	63	66	0*	2*

* $p < 0.05$ for difference between females and males.

[a] Children who are fully vaccinated have received vaccinations for BCG and measles, plus three doses each of DPT and polio vaccines, not including polio vaccine administered at the time of birth (Polio 0).

daughter until the illness reaches a more serious stage, but through those surveys there is no way of assessing how perceptions of illness are formed. In Bangladesh and India, boys are significantly more likely than girls to be treated with oral rehydration therapy (ORT) when they are sick. In most cases, boys are also more likely than girls to be taken to a health facility or health provider when they are sick.[4] In India, for example, the treatment differentials are significant for each illness and they range as high as 10 percentage points for the treatment of acute respiratory infection (ARI).

Frequent untreated illness and the lack of proper nutrition can have serious consequences for a child's nutritional status and ultimately for its probability of survival. The surveys in India, Pakistan and Sri Lanka measured the height and weight of children, and the results are shown in Table 13.13 for children aged 3–35 months and for children aged 24–35 months (an age at which girls seem to be particularly vulnerable relative to boys). Height-for-age is an indicator of chronic undernutrition over a long period of time; weight-for-height can be used to measure acute undernutrition; and weight-for-age is a combined measure of chronic and acute undernutrition. By international standards, overall levels of undernutrition are high in all three countries. At 3–35 months of age, levels of undernutrition are similar for girls and boys and the differential is significant only in the case of wasting in India (where boys are *more* likely to be wasted than girls).[5] Two-year-old girls are more likely to be undernourished than two-year-old boys in seven of the nine comparisons, but the differences are usually small. At that age, girls are significantly more

[4] The 1996 Nepal Family Health Survey found no sex difference in the treatment of ARI for children under three years of age and a slight advantage for boys in the use of oral rehydration therapy for the treatment of diarrhoea (Pradan *et al.* 1997).

[5] According to the 1996 Nepal Family Health Survey, girls are more likely than boys to be stunted and underweight in the first three years of life (by 4 percentage points and 2 percentage points, respectively), but boys are more likely to be wasted (by 2 percentage points) (Pradan *et al.* 1997).

Table 13.12. Percentage of children under five years of age with diarrhoea, fever, and symptoms of acute respiratory infection during the two weeks preceding the survey, and treatment of these conditions, by sex of child

Prevalence and treatment/ sex of child	Bangladesh	India[a]	Nepal	Pakistan	Sri Lanka
Prevalence of diarrhoea					
Female child	13	10	15*	14	6
Male child	12	10	17*	15	7
Prevalence of fever					
Female child	NA	19*	20	30	NA
Male child	NA	21*	21	30	NA
Prevalence of ARI					
Female child	21*	6*	16*	16	NA
Male child	26*	7*	18*	16	NA
Treatment of diarrhoea[b]					
Female child	21	59*	NA	54*	68
Male child	20	63*	NA	43*	75
Treatment of fever[b]					
Female child	NA	65*	NA	63	NA
Male child	NA	72*	NA	66	NA
Treatment of ARI[b]					
Female child	25	63*	NA	65	NA
Male child	30	73*	NA	68	NA
Use of ORT for diarrhoea					
Female child	54*	29*	35	42	34
Male child	63*	32*	34	41	36

ARI: symptoms of acute respiratory infection; NA: not available; ORT: oral rehydration therapy.
*$p < 0.05$ for difference between females and males.
[a] Limited to children under four years of age.
[b] Percentage taken to a health facility or health provider.

likely to be undernourished than boys only for the degree of stunting and under-weight in Sri Lanka.

Conclusion

Information available from recent large-scale national surveys in Bangladesh, India, Nepal, Pakistan and Sri Lanka confirms the strength of parents' preferences for sons

Table 13.13. Percentage of children who are undernourished, by type of nutritional status index, age and sex of child

Nutritional status index/age/sex of child	India[a]	Pakistan	Sri Lanka
Height-for-age (stunting)			
Age 3–35 months			
Female child	49	45	29
Male child	50	47	26
Age 24–35 months			
Female child	62	57	40*
Male child	59	56	29*
Weight-for-age (underweight)			
Age 3–35 months			
Female child	54	38	38
Male child	55	41	37
Age 24–35 months			
Female child	63	47	54*
Male child	62	45	42*
Weight-for-height (wasting)			
Age 3–35 months			
Female child	18*	9	12
Male child	22*	11	12
Age 24–35 months			
Female child	15*	10	11
Male child	18*	10	9

* $p < 0.05$ for difference between females and males.
[a] In India, height-for-age and weight-for-height cover only 21 of the 26 states included in the survey since children's height was not measured in the first phase of the survey.

Note: The table shows the percentage of children who are undernourished (i.e. children who are more than two standard deviations below the median of the International Reference Population). Children with imputed dates of birth and children whose z-score was improbably high or low are excluded from the table.

throughout the South Asian region. Son preference is clearly evident in the reproductive attitudes of parents, as well as in their demographic behaviour. The preference for sons, however, is tempered in some cases by a desire to have at least one daughter in the family. These patterns of gender preference are deeply rooted in the cultural and religious traditions of the region. A strong preference for sons is also evident in measures of discrimination against daughters. In every country except Sri Lanka, sons are more likely to have received vaccinations against common childhood diseases, and in many cases sons are more likely than daughters to be taken for medical treatment if they do become ill. In addition, girls are sometimes nutritionally disadvantaged around the typical age of weaning. The most serious consequence of differential treatment by sex is evident in the data on excess female child mortality. In Bangladesh, India and Pakistan, girls have a 33–67 per cent higher probability than boys of dying between their first and fifth birthdays.

On almost every measure, women in Sri Lanka are the least likely to exhibit a strong preference for sons, and it is in that country that the fertility transition is nearing completion. Overall, son preference is most pronounced in Nepal and India. Moreover, the preference for sons is much stronger and more influential in North India (where much of the previous research on gender preference has taken place) than in South India (Arnold et al. 1996).

A quantitative assessment of the impact of gender preference demonstrates that contraceptive use, fertility, and reproductive preferences are all influenced by gender preference for children, but the effects are not as large as might be expected. Although the complete elimination of gender preferences in South Asia would undoubtedly increase contraceptive use and reduce the level of fertility, the impact of such a change is estimated to be fairly modest.

The strong preference for sons in South Asia serves some cultural and religious purposes, but it has many serious adverse consequences. Female children and adult women are discriminated against in a variety of ways and are not allowed to reach their full potential. In the worst case, their very survival in the early childhood years is jeopardized. Moreover, son preference leads to inflated levels of fertility, as well as unwanted births. A major concern for the future is the increasing use of sex-selective abortion techniques, which could ultimately skew the sex composition of the population, as has happened in Korea and China (Park and Cho 1995). The spread of sex-selective abortion has so far been fairly limited in many parts of South Asia, and even in India there is a substantial debate about the degree to which sex-selective abortions are having a measurable impact (Arnold et al. 1996; Das Gupta and Mari Bhat 1996). But there is no question that the abortion of female foetuses could become a more serious problem throughout South Asia if clear legal prohibitions and reasonable enforcement procedures are not in place to contain the problem. In addition, educational programmes in support of the girl child need to be strengthened to curb the demand for sex-selective abortions and to reduce the overall impact of son preference on South Asian societies.

References

Ali, S. M. (1989), 'Does Son Preference Matter?', *Journal of Biosocial Science*, 21(4): 399–408.

Arnold, F. (1985), 'Measuring the Effect of Sex Preference on Fertility: The Case of Korea', *Demography*, 22(2): 280–8.

Arnold, F. (1992), 'Sex Preference and its Demographic and Health Implications', *International Family Planning Perspectives*, 18(3): 93–101.

—— (1997), 'Gender Preferences for Children: Findings from the Demographic and Health Surveys', Paper presented at the 23rd General Population Conference of the International Union for the Scientific Study of Population, 11–17 October 1997, Beijing.

—— Choe, M. K., and Roy, T. K. (1996), 'Son Preference, the Family-Building Process and Child Mortality in India', East-West Center Working Paper No. 85, Population Series, Honolulu, Hawaii.

Bairagi, R. (1993), 'Is Gender Preference an Obstacle to the Success of Family Planning Programmes in Rural Bangladesh?', in International Union for the Scientific Study of Population, *International Population Conference, Montreal 1993*, Vol. 1, Liège: IUSSP, 121–34.

—— and Langsten, R. L. (1986), 'Sex Preference for Children and its Implications for Fertility in Rural Bangladesh', *Studies in Family Planning*, 17(6): 302–7.

Basu, A. M. (1989), 'Is Discrimination in Food Really Necessary for Explaining Sex Differentials in Childhood Mortality?', *Population Studies*, 43(2): 193–210.

Booth, B. E., and Verma, M. (1992), 'Decreased Access to Medical Care for Girls in Punjab, India: The Roles of Age, Religion and Distance', *American Journal of Public Health*, 82(8): 1155–7.

Chen, L. C., Huq, E., and D'Souza, S. (1981), 'Sex Bias in the Allocation of Food and Health Care in Rural Bangladesh', *Population and Development Review*, 7(1): 55–70.

Das, N. (1987), 'Sex Preference and Fertility Behaviour: A Study of Recent Indian Data', *Demography*, 24(4): 517–30.

—— (1989), 'A Simulation Model to Study the Effect of Sex Preference on Current Fertility', *Demography India*, 18(1, 2): 49–72.

Das Gupta, M., and Mari Bhat, P. N. (1996), 'Intensified Gender Bias in India: A Consequence of Fertility Decline', Paper presented at the Annual Meeting of the Population Association of America, 9–11 May 1996, New Orleans.

De Silva, W. I. (1992), 'Relationship of Desire for No More Children and Socioeconomic and Demographic Factors in Sri Lankan Women', *Journal of Biosocial Science*, 24(2): 185–99.

De Tray, D. (1984), 'Son Preference in Pakistan: An Analysis of Intentions vs. Behaviour', *Research in Population Economics*, 5: 185–200.

Kabir, M., Amin, R., Ahmed, A. U., and Chowdhury, J. (1994), 'Factors Affecting Desired Family Size in Bangladesh', *Journal of Biosocial Science*, 26(3): 369–75.

Karki, Y. B. (1988), 'Sex Preference and the Value of Sons and Daughters in Nepal', *Studies in Family Planning*, 19(3): 169–78.

Kishor, S. (1995), 'Gender Differentials in Child Mortality: A Review of the Evidence', in M. Das Gupta, L. C. Chen and T. N. Krishnan (eds.), *Women's Health in India: Risk and Vulnerability*, Bombay: Oxford University Press, 19–54.

Koenig, M. A., and Foo, G. H. C. (1992), 'Patriarchy, Women's Status, and Reproductive Behaviour in Rural North India', *Demography India*, 21(2): 145–66.

Levine, N. E. (1987), 'Differential Child Care in Three Tibetan Communities: Beyond Son Preference', *Population and Development Review*, 13(2): 281–304.

Miller, B. D. (1984), 'Daughter Neglect, Women's Work and Marriage: Pakistan and Bangladesh Compared', *Medical Anthropology*, 8(2): 109–26.

Muhuri, P. K., and Preston, S. H. (1991), 'Effects of Family Composition on Mortality Differentials by Sex among Children in Matlab, Bangladesh', *Population and Development Review*, 17(3): 415–34.

Murthi, M., Guio, A.-C., and Drèze, J. (1995), 'Mortality, Fertility, and Gender Bias in India', *Population and Development Review*, 21(4): 745–82.

Nadarajah, T. (1983), 'The Transition from Higher Female to Higher Male Mortality in Sri Lanka', *Population and Development Review*, 9(2): 317–25.

Nag, M. (1991), 'Sex Preference in Bangladesh, India and Pakistan and its Effect on Fertility', *Demography India*, 20: 163–85.

Niraula, B. B., and Morgan, S. P. (1995), 'Preference for Sons and Daughters in Benighat, Nepal: Implications for Fertility Transition', *Social Biology*, 42(3–4): 256–73.

Park, C.-B., and Cho, N.-H. (1995), 'Consequences of Son Preference in a Low-Fertility Society: Imbalance of the Sex Ratio at Birth in Korea', *Population and Development Review*, 21(1): 59–84.

Pradan, A., Aryal, R. H., Regmi, G., Ban, B., and Govindasamy, P. (1997), *Nepal Family Health Survey 1996*, Kathmandu, Nepal and Calverton, Maryland: Ministry of Health [Nepal], New ERA, and Macro International Inc.

Rajaretnam, T. (1995), 'Family Size Desire, Sex Preference, Socio-economic Condition and Contraceptive Use in Rural Karnataka, India', *Demography India*, 24(2): 275–90.

Raju, K. N. M., and Bhat, T. N. (1995), 'Sex Composition of Living Children against Socio-economic Variables while Accepting Family Planning Methods', *Demography India*, 24(1): 87–99.

Repetto, R. (1972), 'Son Preference and Fertility Behaviour in Developing Countries', *Studies in Family Planning*, 3(4): 70–6.

Sarma, D. V. N., and Jain, A. K. (1974), 'Preference about Sex of Children and Use of Contraception among Women Wanting No More Children in India', *Demography India*, 3(1): 81–101.

Sathar, Z. A. (1987), 'Sex Differentials in Mortality: A Corollary of Son Preference?', *Pakistan Development Review*, 26(4): 555–68.

Stash, S. (1996), 'Ideal-Family-Size and Sex-Composition Preferences among Wives and Husbands in Nepal', *Studies in Family Planning*, 27(2): 107–18.

Tabutin, D., and Willems, M. (1995), 'Excess Female Child Mortality in the Developing World during the 1970s and 1980s', *Population Bulletin of the United Nations*, 39: 45–78.

Talwar, P. P. (1975), 'Effect of Desired Sex Composition in Families on the Birth Rate', *Journal of Biosocial Science*, 7(2): 133–9.

United Nations (1985), *Fertility Preferences: Selected Findings from the World Fertility Survey Data*, New York: United Nations.

Visaria, L. (1994), 'Deficit of Women, Son Preference and Demographic Transitions in India', Paper presented at the International Symposium on Issues Related to Sex Preference for Children in the Rapidly Changing Dynamics in Asia, 21–24 November 1994, Seoul.

Vlasoff, C. (1990), 'The Value of Sons in an Indian Village: How Widows See It', *Population Studies*, 44(1): 5–20.

14 Son Preference and the Dynamics of Fertility Decision-Making among Wives and Their Husbands in Rural Nepal

SHARON STASH

'Euta ankha ke ankha? Euta chhora ke chhora?'

What good is just one eye? What good is just one son?

Introduction

Within the demographic literature, or at least that which pertains to western countries, there exists a concept that certain parities are 'discretionary'—implying that there are certain parities at which couples' fertility decision-making processes are likely to be more evident than others. This concept is evident in the very title of Westoff, Potter and Sagi's seminal book *The Third Child* (1963). As in other studies done during the same period of time, this study examines the relative contributions of various factors that predict a third birth among couples with two children. Such investigations of fertility decision-making benefit from a focus on spousal dynamics occurring at key decision-making junctures.

Westoff's book is typical of the sociological literature on fertility decline, which has tended to phrase its arguments in terms of parity—or numbers of births. The types of decisions couples face, however, depend upon cultural systems of valuation that frame the decision-making context, and that place priority on certain outcomes in relation to others. In societies that place a high value on sons, decisions about the birth of additional children are augmented by decisions about the birth of additional sons—and there is no reason to believe that family size considerations always predominate (Stash 1996). As such, failure to take into account son preference can confound an understanding of the relationship between desired family size and fertility (Anderson and Silver 1995), particularly in societies in which peoples' decisions are more likely to reflect their desire for sons rather than for children of either sex.

In Nepal, as in broader South Asia, the importance of sons and the centrality of decisions regarding the birth of sons are well-established concepts in the literature on son preference (Karki 1988). Son preference has deep roots in the structure of

Nepalese households, and in cultural rules that define the relative responsibilities and expected behaviours of boy and girl children, both before and after marriage. Son preference in Nepal hinges upon a patriarchal family structure, in which daughters marry out to other households at young ages, and in which sons and their wives reside with parents after marriage, inherit family property, assume responsibility for the maintenance of the household economy, and care for their parents in old age. Sons enhance the power, prestige and (hopefully) wealth of the patrilineage, while daughters, by definition, are lost to other households after marriage.[1]

There now exists considerable evidence that son preference has been perpetuated and reinterpreted throughout the current period of rapid social change in Asia (Nizamuddin 1996). There is also evidence in certain countries, for example Taiwan and China, that a shift in the modal preference from two toward one son is part of this reinterpretation (Greenhalgh 1992). For example, Greenhalgh observes that, with social change accompanying decollectivization and economic reform in China, preexisting motivations for having more than one son have been weakened, although the birth of one son remains essential. This shift between a minimum of two toward a minimum of one son is, therefore, consistent with a continued preference for sons.

Son preference is also more likely to affect fertility when the birth of more than one son is desired, because the birth of a second son, on average, would be expected to require the additional births of more than one child. In his study on fertility decision-making in Nepal, the author writes, 'The need for a second son stands apart from the need for the first.' (Folmar 1992)

With social change and technological advances, couples can manipulate the balance between desired family size and its composition through an increasing array of behaviours, including resorting to a range of permanent and temporary contraceptive methods, ultrasound and selective abortion, child fostering and adoption practices, differential child care, child neglect and infanticide. The mechanisms employed within a given context have bearing on the social and demographic

---

[1] The argument regarding the role of sons in providing risk insurance is consonant with aspects of studies conducted by Mead Cain in Bangladesh (1989, 1984, 1979). However, Cain's argument is tailored specifically to fit the context of rural Bangladesh, just as the current argument fits the observations of contemporary rural Nepal. Both approaches share a focus on aspects of patriarchal social systems that promote the value of sons (over daughters) as security assets for parents.

Cain further builds a hypothesis of 'patriarchal risk' that is specific to the structural position of women within strongly patriarchal households and social systems governing female seclusion in Bangladesh. He explains why security gained through the birth of sons is also of extreme importance to women because of their overt economic dependence on men. Women experience precipitous declines in their well-being if they live in the absence of sons' social and economic protectorateship. However, this argument is not specifically relevant in the context of Nepal.

In Nepal, high fertility may well persist because men want it as much as women do, even if for different reasons. Although the survey data demonstrate considerable disagreement between spouses in their desire for sons, neither spouse was found to be consistently more pronatalist, or to consistently prefer a greater number of sons (Stash 1997). Husbands, however, were found to be more likely than wives to pursue the birth of sons at the cost of an increasingly large family size (Stash 1996), perhaps because of women's greater level of involvement in the work of giving birth to and raising children.

consequences of son preference. Further research on son preference in Asia will benefit from an increased understanding of the precise behavioural mechanisms through which couples actualize their preferences for male children.

In this study of reproductive strategies prevailing in a rural district of Nepal, multivariate analysis is used to examine the effects of son preference on contraceptive adoptions after births that occurred during a ten-year period, 1981 to 1990. Regression analysis is used to examine the extent to which birth intervals are prolonged through the adoption of temporary contraceptive methods, or closed through the use of permanent methods or by additional births. A final set of analyses explores the relative influence of husbands and wives in decisions that govern the balance between the desire for sons and the perceived benefits of a small family size. This analysis provides indirect evidence of whose preferences, husbands' or wives', are likely to predominate—at least, when the birth of sons is at issue.

Data

The current project involves data collected during an extensive period of fieldwork, from August 1993 to August 1994, in Chitwan district of Nepal. Among other rural districts in Nepal, Chitwan stands out as a region with an unusually high level of social and economic development. Two major roads transect the district, the Prithivi Highway and the Mahendra Highway. Some industrial development has occurred in the district along these highways, but households in the district remain predominantly agricultural. People do, however, have improved access to roads, schools and health services. This is reflected in higher than average levels of education, health care utilization, and family planning acceptance.

Fieldwork for the project consisted of three consecutive stages: (1) initial exploratory qualitative interviews, pre-tests of survey questions, and the development of an interview guideline for subsequent in-depth interviews; (2) a standardized fertility survey questionnaire administered to a cluster sample, representative of Chitwan district, including a total of 801 ever-married women and their 601 co-resident husbands (absence of all but five husbands was due to temporary migration or travel); and (3) qualitative in-depth re-interviews with samples of wives and husbands. The principal investigator was resident in the field site throughout fieldwork and was actively involved in all stages of study design, data collection and supervision. The survey team achieved a response rate of 99.5 per cent.

Chitwan district was selected as the site for the research because it is unusually well equipped with access to permanent and temporary methods of contraceptives. This permitted an investigation of variables affecting the demand for contraception, assuming that supply of contraceptives is reasonably constant. Moreover, the three clusters for in-depth interviews were selected to have roughly equivalent access to contraceptives. All three communities were located within 20 minutes' access to government health posts that provide family planning services. All three had roughly equivalent access to secondary roads, and they were all within 2–2½ hours of the district centre by local transport. In the district centre, two clinics provide permanent sterilization operations to men and women.

Statement of Hypotheses

The initial analysis tests the hypothesis that, holding parity constant, (1) couples' number of sons, and (2) husbands' and wives' attitudes regarding the desirability of additional sons predict additional births or the adoption of permanent and temporary methods of family planning. The first set of analyses examines the propensity of couples to adopt permanent methods of family planning after all births occurring between April 1981 and 1990 ($N = 1,035$ births).[2] This period of observation encompasses years during which contraceptive use increased rapidly. A subsequent analysis examines couples' decisions to (1) have another child, (2) prolong a birth interval through the use of temporary methods, or (3) close a birth interval through the adoption of permanent methods of family planning. The dependent variable constructed for this analysis also takes into account birth intervals that remain open throughout the period of observation (i.e. no additional birth, no contraceptive use) (John *et al.* 1988). Here the sample is restricted to births occurring during a five-year period of time in which information on temporary and permanent method use can be used to construct a dependent variable.[3]

The primary independent variable in the initial analyses is a set of indicator variables describing women's number of sons (1, 2, 3+ sons). Because each case in the analysis represents a birth, and because women can contribute more than one birth to this sample, this variable represents the total number of sons at the time of each birth (or case) under consideration. Other variables that vary across a woman's births are similarly constructed to represent the value of the variable at each birth *i*.

Because permanent methods terminate childbearing, the two-son norm is expected to be actualized in a strong relationship between the birth of two sons and the adoption of permanent methods. The use of temporary methods usually does not preclude the birth of additional children (or sons) if they are subsequently

[2] The period of observation was purposely lagged four years prior to the date of interview so that the occurrence of contraceptive events could be observed in a standard four-year interval following each birth included in the sample.

[3] Although the date of sterilization operations is known, similarly complete data are not available regarding the adoption of temporary methods. Data are not available on previous adoptions of temporary methods among women who used more than one method of family planning. Fortunately, these women constitute only 14 per cent of contraceptive users, or approximately 4 per cent of the sample of currently married women giving birth during the period of observation. Missed temporary contraceptive events would result in birth intervals that were prolonged for a period of time no greater than a couple of years on average (because, within the five-year period, women would have had to use temporary methods both prior and subsequent to a birth). Missing information on these previous temporary contraceptive events would bias the dependent variable to capture temporary use at higher parities and greater numbers of sons than in actuality.

desired. Because temporary methods allow couples to have smaller families while preserving their ability to have another son, it is predictable that couples will be more willing to adopt temporary methods (as versus permanent methods) after the birth of one son.

According to the theoretical framework employed in this analysis, fertility-related attitudes[4] of both wives and husbands are likely to affect fertility behaviour. A second major independent variable summarizes the fertility preferences of husbands and wives.

The extent to which husbands and wives share similar preferences (or the interaction of wives' and husbands' preferences) could have an impact on their process of fertility decision-making. In Nepal there is considerable utilization of both male and female methods; therefore, it is likely that men's attitudes may be as (or more) important than their wives' in decisions to adopt male or female family planning methods (Axinn 1992). Couple disagreement over the adoption of family planning methods after the birth of children may occur as a result of differences in the desire for sons among husbands and wives. A previous analysis (Stash 1996) indicated that, although husbands and wives expressed similar desires for children and sons, husbands were more willing than their wives to pursue the birth of sons at the cost of an increasingly large completed family size. This finding is consistent with suggestions in the literature (Caldwell 1981; Folbre 1983) that, within patriarchal family structures, many of the benefits of children accrue to men, while women shoulder a disproportionate share of work involved in the bearing and rearing of children. By contrasting the responses of wives and husbands, we can examine contraceptive use when the birth of sons is at issue.

A variable was designed to summarize husbands' and wives' joint preferences for sons in relation to their respective ideal number of sons. This variable was constructed by contrasting wives' and husbands' responses to questions on their ideal number of sons in relation to their actual number of sons (both spouses have fewer than their ideal number of sons, husband only has fewer sons than ideal, wife only has fewer sons than ideal, both spouses have more sons than their ideal) (see also Anderson 1991). To formulate this variable, husbands' and wives' sons from all unions are included—present, previous, polygynous,[5] formal or informal.

Because the use of family planning often (but not always) involves the participation of both spouses, couple agreement over preferences for sons is expected to be positively associated with use of contraception. In cases of couple agreement, couples will be least likely to use permanent or temporary methods when both

---

[4] Fertility preference variables are potentially endogenous to other attitudinal variables that similarly affect the use of contraception. For example, some underlying propensity to be 'modern' could simultaneously affect the preference for sons and the use of modern contraception, thereby biasing the model estimates. The difficulty of identifying appropriate instrumental variables of modernity (or other broader attitudinal variables) precludes the estimation of models that could address this type of endogeneity, at least in the context of this analysis.

[5] In total, 17 of 601 unions were polygynous. Thus, 12.3 per cent of women and 25.3 per cent of men had more than one formal or informal union.

husband and wife have fewer than their respective ideal number of sons, including husbands' and wives' sons from other unions. Conversely, couples will be most likely to use family planning when both husband and wife have their respective ideal number of sons, or more.

Among couples who disagree in their preferences for sons, patterns can emerge that provide indirect evidence of spousal dynamics in fertility decision-making. Thus, it is expected that the less powerful spouse is likely to adopt or behaviourally comply with the attitudes and values of the more powerful spouse (Beckman *et al.* 1983). Individuals' willingness to assert authority in fertility decision-making, particularly when their spouse is not in agreement with them, is further conditional on how strongly husbands or wives are motivated to achieve their desired end. At first glance, a hypothesis of 'patriarchal authority' seems applicable. By merit of patriarchal family structures and relatively low status of women, one would expect that, in cases of couple disagreement, husbands' preferences would predominate. This hypothesis may be all the more relevant when the birth of sons is at issue. Whereas daughters marry out to other households, men expect their sons to inherit household property, and promote the prosperity, prestige and continuation of the patrilineage. A strong motivation to have sons, coupled with men's power in patriarchal households, suggests that spousal disagreement over the desire for sons is likely to be resolved in favour of the husbands' wishes.

A second hypothesis also appears to have some relevance in the context of Nepal, based on the concept of 'women's power in the reproductive realm'. Women clearly played the major role in the biological and social reproduction of children in the study area. This hypothesis suggests that, because of their importance in the reproductive realm, women may wield power in fertility decision-making, even where they have lesser power in other realms of household decision-making (e.g. major purchases). Analysis of in-depth interview data reveals competing motivations among women with regard to the birth of sons. Women, throughout their lives, are expected to remain dependent upon male relatives for economic support. Because women are, on average, five years younger than their husbands, women expect to be dependent upon sons at some point in their lives. Women also look forward to the assistance of sons' wives, or their daughters-in-law, in their households. However, it was apparent in my interviews that women also had greater experience with the direct and indirect costs of children. A previous analysis demonstrated that women are more likely than men to sacrifice desired sons in the interest of a smaller completed family size (Stash 1996). The balance between these competing interests may mitigate women's otherwise strong motivations to have sons.

Dependent Variables

The dependent variables used in this chapter include two measures: (1) a dichotomous variable representing the adoption of permanent methods after all births, 1980 to 1990 (1 = sterilization operation after birth i; 0 = otherwise), and

(2) a multinomial measure of the adoption of temporary or permanent methods after births, 1986 to 1990 (1 = had another birth; 2 = adopted a temporary method; 3 = adopted a permanent method; 0 = no birth, no contraception).[6] The construction of each of these dependent variables accounts only for cases of contraceptive adoption occurring within a four-year period following each birth—between 1981 and 1994 and 1986 to 1994, respectively. Available information on the timing of contraceptive events suggests that this four-year interval captures the vast majority of contraceptive events.[7]

Sterilization is the most commonly used method of family planning, at present and throughout the history of the programme in Nepal (NIV 1993). Sterilization precludes the births of additional children, and, as such, the adoption of permanent methods of family planning constitutes stopping behaviour. The use of temporary methods can denote a desire to postpone (or prevent) additional births. There is reason to believe that factors that predict stopping as versus spacing behaviour might be substantively different, or that factors predictive of both behaviours would at least be given differential weights in peoples' fertility decision-making processes. Permanent and temporary use, though conceptually distinct, are implicitly interrelated, because once couples are sterilized, they are no longer eligible to adopt temporary methods of family planning. Moreover, women can go on to have another birth, or the birth interval can remain open throughout the period of observation even in the absence of contraception. This dependency between the two contraceptive (permanent and temporary) and fertility (another birth, no birth in the absence of contraception) outcomes influenced the design of models used in the analyses that follow.

Control Variables

The construction of variables used in this analysis is presented in Table 14.1, along with their per cent distributions or means. Complexity in this analysis stems from the simultaneous use of data from both wives and their husbands. This complexity, however, provides theoretical depth, and allows an investigation of spousal dynamics in fertility decision-making using direct measures formulated from the responses of wives and their husbands.

---

[6] This multinomial construction of the dependent variable assumes that the events (1 = had another birth; 2 = adopted a temporary method; 3 = adopted a permanent method; 0 = no birth, no contraception) are independent. It is reasonable to conclude in this context that permanent and temporary outcomes are independent. Qualitative analysis suggests that women specifically use temporary methods in order to prevent additional births while still preserving their reproductive capacity. As such, permanent methods are not an equivalent substitute for temporary methods or vice versa.

[7] The age of women at birth and the age of women at contraceptive adoption are closely related, i.e. for permanent use (mean difference = 1 year and 6 months) and for temporary use (mean difference = 2 years and 1 month). The present formulation of the dependent variable was considered to be more robust than similar variables defined on the basis of the timing of contraceptive events.

Table 14.1. Variable definitions and per cent distributions of individual characteristics of co-resident wives and their husbands, and joint characteristics of couples

Variables/definitions	Variable type	Per cent/ mean	Per cent/ mean	Per cent/ mean
a. Dependent variables				
Permanent method use after birth i [a]	Dichotomous	0.49	0.15	NA
Additional births, and permanent or temporary method use after birth i	Multinomial			
Another birth		NA	NA	0.68
Temporary methods		NA	NA	0.08
Permanent methods		NA	NA	0.14
No birth, no contraception		NA	NA	0.11
b. Independent variables	Indicator			
Couples' sons at birth i				
No sons		0.11	0.19	0.20
1 son		0.25	0.43	0.35
2 sons		0.35	0.28	0.26
3+ sons		0.29	0.10	0.19
Sons by INS at birth i	Indicator			
Both spouses have fewer sons than INS		0.19	NA	0.31
Husband only has fewer sons than INS		0.14	NA	0.09
Wife only has fewer sons than INS		0.07	NA	0.09
Both spouses have more sons than INS		0.65	NA	0.82
c. Control variables				
Wives' parity at birth i	Continuous, and indicator			
1 child		0.11	0.24	0.23
2 children		0.16	0.32	0.33
3 children		0.21	0.24	0.22
4+ children		0.52	0.20	0.22
Mean				Mean = 3.4
Husbands' children	Indicator	0.21	0.07	0.07
Child deaths	Continuous	Mean = 0.53	Mean = 0.68	Mean = 0.65
Residence	Indicator			
Hill region		0.09	0.10	0.12
Eastern Chitwan		0.40	0.43	0.43
Western Chitwan		0.29	0.28	0.26
Municipality		0.21	0.19	0.19
Couples' ethnicity	Indicator			
High caste		0.52	0.48	0.46
Hill ethnic group		0.23	0.23	0.24
Terrai		0.25	0.29	0.30
Wives' education	Indicator			
Some primary		0.15	0.13	0.14
Some secondary		0.12	0.08	0.10
No schooling or higher		0.74	0.80	0.76
Spousal difference in education	Continuous	Mean = 2.84	Mean = 2.76	Mean = 2.76
Household SES	Indicator			
Business/service		0.27	0.07	0.07
Day labour		0.19	0.12	0.10
Agricultural		0.54	0.81	0.84
Total		512 couples	1,037 births 1981–90	588 births 1986–90

INS = ideal number of sons.

[a] Represents the value of variable X at each birth i across multiple births per woman.

Although the current analyses give primacy to couples' numbers of sons as a determinant of contraceptive use, no doubt numbers of children are also important. The theoretical perspective evolving from in-depth interviews recognizes an implicit tradeoff between peoples' desires for certain numbers of sons and desires for smaller families. To control for parity while examining the effects of sons, a set of indicator variables to represent wives' parities at the time of each birth i is used. An indicator variable, husbands' children from other wives, is used to control for husbands' children in addition to those listed in the context of complete birth histories that were done with women (mean number of husbands' children from other wives = 0.53).[8] Initial analyses (not presented here) also tested variables representing couples' numbers of daughters. Variables denoting the birth of daughters consistently failed to contribute to the models. On the basis of this evidence, we conclude that couples' desires for daughter(s), in the majority of cases, do not drive their decisions regarding additional births, or the adoption of temporary or permanent contraceptive methods.

The death of children not only affects the extent to which couples have their desired number of sons (or children), but may increase couples' sense of risk, and thereby their desire to insure against the negative effects associated with their loss. Therefore, implicit in the construction of this variable is the assumption that couples' experiences with child death(s) have additional effects above and beyond the net loss of children (or sons) they represent. Although ever-married women, 15–49, in the study area reported an average of 3.5 children ever born, their mean number of living children was only 3.0. The mean number of child deaths among couples with children in the sample is 0.53. A continuous variable representing the number of child deaths experienced by couples at each birth i is used as a control.

A strong set of variables accounting for variation in programme factors is necessary, in order to clear the path for an analysis of individual-level behavioural and attitudinal factors that affect contraceptive use. A continuous measure, year of birth i, is used to control for increased family planning presence and efforts in Chitwan across the ten-year period of observation. A set of residence variables controls for, among other things, variation in the intensity of the family planning programme and the availability of contraceptive technologies across the district. This set of variables divides Chitwan district into four regions (municipality, western Chitwan, eastern Chitwan, and a hill region).[9] Family planning services, and particularly

[8] A continuous variable representing the number of husbands' births from other wives at each birth i is preferable to the indicator variable used in these analyses. However, because complete birth histories were not collected from husbands, the birth dates of husbands' children from other wives were not known.

[9] Community-level data on local infrastructure were collected in all survey clusters, including access to health and family planning services, schools, roads, transportation, water, electricity, irrigation, etc. Data collection activities included visits to local clinics within the vicinity of the survey clusters, and discussions with local health providers. These data were used to divide the district into the four regions described above.

temporary methods, are more readily available through clinics in the western region of Chitwan than elsewhere in the district. Access to contraceptive methods is also reasonably good in eastern Chitwan, although this region has less infrastructural development, including all-weather roads and thereby access to clinics. The steep topography of the hill region results in lesser access to and availability of health and family planning services. Finally, although the municipality includes the residents of a prosperous bazaar and a government office district, a substantial number of people also live in dense squatters' settlements that are not particularly well served with community resources.

A continuous variable, women's age at birth i, is used to control for individual-level variation in reproductive capacity and motivation to use family planning across women's reproductive careers. In addition a quadratic term, age squared, was tested for inclusion in the various models, although it achieved significance and is presented only in the models in Tables 14.3 and 14.5. This term accounts for a curvilinear relationship between age and contraceptive or fertility outcomes, with the greatest probability of additional births or contraceptive adoptions occurring during mid-reproductive years.

The population of Chitwan is quite mixed, and includes a variety of indigenous people and ethnic groups who migrated into the district from the hill regions to the north. The various caste and ethnic groups have been divided into three major groups, i.e. indigenous people of the *terai* or plains region (Tharu, Kumal, Darai, Chepang, and other terai castes), migrants from hill ethnic groups (Tamang, Gurung, Magar), and high caste people (Brahmins, Chhetris and Newars). As elsewhere in Nepal, high caste people occupy many positions of wealth, power and prestige throughout the district. This advantaged group is expected to utilize family planning services to a greater extent than hill or terai ethnic groups. Indigenous terai ethnic groups, although until the last 50 years the majority population in the study area, have a recent history of domination by hill and high caste ethnic groups. People from terai ethnic groups were among the poorest in the sample, and they are expected to be less well integrated with government programmes, including family planning services, than are people from hill ethnic or high caste groups.

Increasing levels of schooling among Nepalese women has been shown to affect their fertility and use of family planning services. A recent study in Nepal found that men's schooling also directly affects couples' use of family planning, in part because a major portion of contraceptive use in Nepal is by men (Axinn 1992). A set of indicator variables representing wives' exposure to schooling (some primary, some secondary or higher, and no schooling) captures the direct effects of women's schooling on contraceptive use. In addition, a variable representing the difference in years of schooling between wives and their husbands was formulated for use in the various models. Higher education among men than their wives is expected to result in higher levels of contraceptive use, and men's greater power in reproductive decision-making.

Finally, a set of indicator variables was formulated to represent three household occupational[10] structures, thereby attempting to account for major socioeconomic strata in contemporary terai society (business or service, agricultural, and day-labour households). Although there are some wealthy farmers, there is typically not much reported variation in average landholdings in the terai (Central Bureau of Statistics 1993), and agricultural households can be grouped into a middle socioeconomic strata. Because child labour is valued, and sons are needed for inheritance, farmers are expected to have moderate levels of fertility and contraceptive use. People in households whose landholdings are too small to support a family are likely to seek temporary day-labour jobs. As such, day labour is a marker for households of lower socioeconomic status. Poverty in these day-labour households can limit integration with health and family planning services; however, it can also increase their need to limit fertility. Chitwan district also has a fair number of people involved in small-scale businesses in roadside bazaars, or civil-service occupations in governmental offices. Households involved in business or service occupations are expected to make more frequent use of family planning services, because they are better integrated with the modern and governmental service sector.

Sons and Decision-Making about Fertility

Figure 14.1 represents current use of permanent and temporary methods by women's parity and number of sons. These frequency distributions demonstrate at what parity and at what number of sons couples use temporary and permanent methods. A large peak in the use of permanent methods occurs among women with two sons (46 per cent of permanent methods). A peak in temporary use occurs among women with one son (35 per cent of temporary use), although a fairly substantial proportion of respondents also use temporary methods after two sons (approximately 27 per cent of temporary use).[11] Figure 14.1 provides some indication that parity and sons differentially affect the adoption of permanent as versus temporary methods of family planning, and that a greater number of sons appears

---

[10] Occupational variables are sometimes considered to be endogenous with fertility behaviour among women. The assumption that women cannot rear children while simultaneously engaged in productive activities is questionable for many women in third world countries. As Mason (1987) argues, rural women in the third world often have child care help available to them, or they engage in productive activities that accommodate their child care responsibilities. In the present case, women's involvement in day labour, cottage industries, or small businesses is most likely compatible with their child care and reproductive roles.

[11] About 13 per cent of currently married women who are using contraception used other temporary methods prior to their current (permanent or temporary) method. Because data on the timing of prior contraceptive events are not available, the measure of temporary method use in Fig. 14.1 under-represents the extent to which temporary methods are adopted by women at lower parities and with fewer sons.

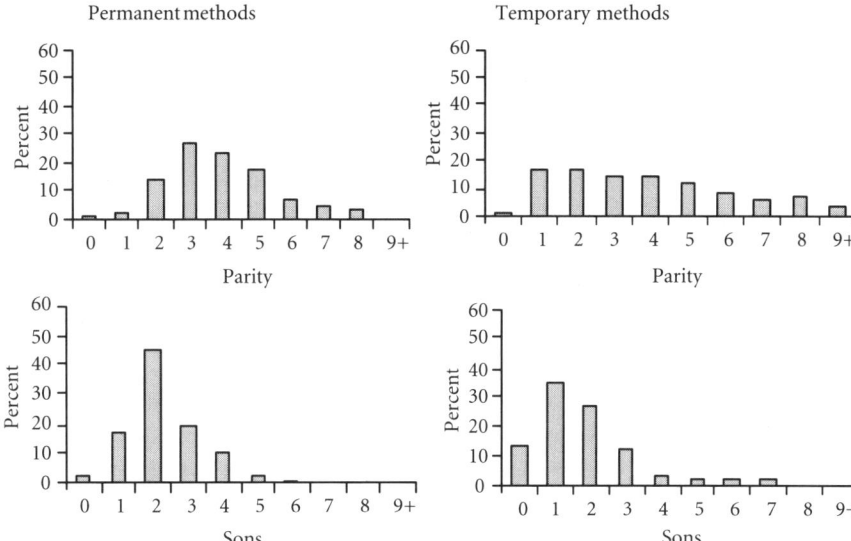

Figure 14. 1. Per cent distribution of current use of permanent and temporary methods by parity and sons among couples.

to be requisite for couples to adopt methods that terminate their ability to have additional children.

As is shown in Table 14.2, a series of models tests the extent to which sets of indicator variables representing parity and sons contribute to the model (see the Appendix for a detailed explanation of how these models were constructed).[12] The inclusion of variables representing women's parity, when added to the base model that includes control variables only (M1), makes a significant contribution to the model. Variables representing sons improve the overall fit of the model, as evident in likelihood ratio chi-square tests calculated between models M2 and M3. The set of variables representing women's parity no longer improves the overall fit of the model when the variables for sons are included. The variable defining husbands' children from other wives does little in the model. However, the inclusion of variables for parity and husbands' children from other wives is justifiable because their inclusion allows an examination of the effects of sons on contraceptive use, holding parity and husbands' additional children constant.

When parity is held constant (Table 14.3), the birth of sons is highly predictive of the adoption of permanent methods of family planning. The model suggests that couples with only one son are more likely to use permanent methods of family planning than are couples with no sons, and the effect of one son is significant.

---

[12] Only main effect terms are presented in this and subsequent models. Although a wide range of theoretically relevant interaction terms were tested for inclusion in this and subsequent models, none were found to be significant.

Table 14.2. Logistic regression of parity and sons on the adoption of permanent methods after births, 1981–1990

Variables/models	M1 coef	M1 s.e.	M2 coef	M2 s.e.	M3 coef	M3 s.e.
Wives' parity at birth (X^2 = 3.78, d.f. = 3, p = 0.2862)[a]						
1 child			−1.96	0.869**	−1.162	0.940
2 children			−0.116	0.457	0.286	0.515
3 children			0.065	0.408	0.193	0.445
(ref. 4+ children)						
Husbands' children (X^2 = 0.01, d.f. = 1, p = 0.9249)			0.043	0.217	0.011	0.233
Couples' sons at birth i (X^2 = 20.02, d.f. = 3, p = 0.0002)						
1 son					1.553	1.068
2 sons					2.543	1.064**
3+ sons					3.297	1.125**
(ref. no sons)						
Year of birth i (X^2 = 24.95, d.f. = 1, p = 0.0000)	−0.352	0.063**	−0.337	0.069**	−0.329	0.071**
Wives' age at birth i (X^2 = 43.82, d.f. = 1, p = 0.0000)[a]	−0.384	0.055**	−0.358	0.057**	−0.325	0.058**
Child deaths (X^2 = 7.69, d.f. = 1, p = 0.0056)	−0.504	0.262**	−0.569	0.275**	−0.757	0.300**
Residence (X^2 = 6.09, d.f. = 3, p = 0.1073)						
Hill region	−1.67	1.09	−1.10	1.90	−1.11	1.08
Eastern Chitwan	0.361	0.405	0.305	0.410	0.342	0.430
Western Chitwan	0.050	0.455	−0.51	0.466	−0.034	0.495
(ref. municipality)						
Couples' ethnicity (X^2 = 0.6950, d.f. = 2, p = 0.7065)						
High caste	−0.020	0.419	0.009	0.423	0.193	0.439
Hill ethnic group	−0.558	0.573	−0.516	0.577	−0.227	0.599
(ref. Terai)						
Wives' education (X^2 = 8.91, d.f. = 2, p = 0.0116)						
Some primary	0.804	0.402**	0.880	0.415**	0.866	0.433**
Some secondary or higher	1.295	0.530**	1.328	0.533**	1.553	0.557**
(ref. no schooling)						
Spousal difference in education (X^2 = 4.54, d.f. = 1, p = 0.0330)[a]	0.076	0.045*	0.086	0.046*	0.102	0.048**
Household SES (X^2 = 8.56, d.f.=2, p=0.0139)						
Business/service	0.765	0.357**	0.842	0.369**	1.066	0.394**
Day labour	0.718	0.457*	0.747	0.469	0.854	0.482**
(ref. agriculture)						
Constant	315.8	2.877	18.015	3.073	14.391	3.342
−2LLR	315.8		306.573		286.559	
No. parameters	13		17		20	

* Significant at an alpha level of 0.10.
** Significant at an alpha level of 0.05.
coef = coefficients, s.e. = standard error.
Reference categories are in parentheses. Goodness-of-fit chi-square is 315 with 13 d.f., $p < 0.0000$ for model M1, 206 with 16 d.f., $p < 0.0000$ for model M2, and 210 with 20 d.f., $p < 0.0000$ for model M3
[a] Likelihood ratio chi-square test of the difference between the full model and the model without the set of variables.
Note: The total number of records examined was 1.035.

Table 14.3. Multinomial logistic regression of parity and sons on the adoption of contraceptive methods after births, 1986–1990

Variables/model	Another birth		Temporary		Permanent	
	coef	s.e.	coef	s.e.	coef	s.e.
Wife's parity at birth i	−0.105	0.088	0.232	0.121**	0.299	0.107**
Husband's children	−0.161	0.388	0.305	0.499	0.580	0.432
Couple's sons at birth i						
1 son	0.303	0.264	0.881	0.412**	1.708	0.535**
2 sons	−0.478	0.296*	0.670	0.449	2.564	0.537**
3 sons	−0.173	0.377	0.567	0.547**	2.982	0.595**
(ref. 0 sons)						
Year of birth i	−0.483	0.032**	0.062	0.051	−0.377	0.034**
Wife's age at birth i	0.122	0.133	−0.012	0.173	0.715	0.190**
Wife's age at birth i squared	−0.004	0.002*	−0.001	0.003	−0.016	0.003**
Child deaths at birth i	0.420	0.119**	−0.094	0.183	−0.421	0.150**
Residence						
Municipality	−0.410	0.362	0.977	0.740	0.934	0.598
East	−0.001	0.317	1.989	0.676**	1.217	0.554**
West	0.112	0.339	2.513	0.670**	1.341	0.571**
(ref. hill)						
Ethnicity						
High caste	−0.163	0.257	0.204	0.376	0.244	0.306
Hill ethnic group	0.131	0.273	0.636	0.397*	0.065	0.352
(ref. terai ethnic group)						
Wife's schooling						
Some primary	−0.566	0.296**	−0.545	0.445	0.105	0.341
Some secondary	−0.011	0.372	1.086	0.488**	0.820	0.446**
(ref. no school)						
Spousal difference in education	−0.008	0.030	0.083	0.040**	0.058	0.034**
Household SES						
Business/service	−0.290	0.410	−0.043	0.584	0.385	0.456
Day labour	−0.261	0.339	0.257	0.474	0.621	0.389*
(ref. agriculture)						
Constant	23.110	2.238**	−4.784	3.292	5.884	2.902**

*Significant at an alpha level of 0.10.
** Significant at an alpha level of 0.05.
coef = coefficients, s.e. = standard error.
Reference categories are in parentheses. Goodness-of-fit chi-square is 1,358 with 57 d.f., $p < 0.0000$.
[a] Log-likelihood ratio chi-square test of the difference between the full model and the model without each set of variables above confirms that all variables make significant contributions to the model.
Note: The total number of records examined was 584.

Couples with two sons are about 13 times more likely to use permanent methods of family planning than are couples with no sons, and the effect is significant. Couples with three or more sons are even more likely to adopt permanent methods. The magnitude of these effects is inflated because, although there were a few cases in which permanent methods were used prior to the birth of sons, these cases were infrequent.

Table 14.4. Predicted probabilities of adoption of temporary and permanent methods after births, 1986–1990, by sons, and by select social and demographic characteristics of wives, husbands and couples

Variables/outcomes	No birth, no method	Another birth	Temporary methods	Permanent methods
Couples' sons at birth i[a]				
0 sons	0.12	0.83	0.03	0.01
1 son	0.09	0.80	0.05	0.05
2 sons	0.12	0.66	0.05	0.17
3 sons	0.10	0.67	0.04	0.19
Wives' parity at birth i[a]				
1 child	0.11	0.81	0.03	0.05
2 children	0.11	0.79	0.04	0.07
3 children	0.11	0.76	0.04	0.09
4 children	0.11	0.73	0.05	0.12
5 children	0.10	0.69	0.06	0.15
Child deaths[a]				
0 deaths	0.11	0.68	0.05	0.15
1 death	0.10	0.76	0.04	0.09
2 deaths	0.09	0.83	0.03	0.05
3 deaths	0.07	0.87	0.03	0.03
Residence				
Hill region	0.13	0.82	0.01	0.04
Municipality	0.13	0.73	0.03	0.11
Eastern Chitwan	0.10	0.74	0.05	0.11
Western Chitwan	0.08	0.74	0.07	0.11
Wives' education				
No schooling	0.10	0.76	0.04	0.10
Some primary	0.13	0.69	0.03	0.14
Some secondary or higher	0.08	0.68	0.08	0.15
Household SES				
Agriculture	0.11	0.76	0.04	0.09
Business/service	0.11	0.70	0.04	0.14
Day labour	0.10	0.68	0.05	0.16

[a] Listed categories are a subset of all possible values for the continuous variable.

Note: Adjusted results are mean predicted probabilities derived through logistic regression using the model presented in Table 14.3.

The coefficient for a variable representing the year of birth i is negative and significant. This coefficient masks a curvilinear relationship between year of birth i and permanent method use, with sterilizations first increasing and then decreasing among eligible couples over the ten-year period of observation. Residence variables appear to contribute to the model, although the effect of their inclusion is not significant. The coefficients for residence suggest that households in the hills are less likely to use contraceptive methods than those in the municipality. Moreover, residence in either eastern or western Chitwan results in a higher likelihood of permanent method use in comparison to the municipality, perhaps because the urban sample includes households from both prosperous bazaar areas and squatters' settlements.

The continuous variable representing women's age at birth i is less than 1 and significant. It reflects a curvilinear relationship between age and permanent method use, with both younger and older women less likely to use permanent methods than are women in their mid-reproductive careers (although a quadratic term tested for inclusion in the model did not achieve significance). The mean age at sterilization (26.0 years) suggests that fairly young women are willing to use terminal methods of family planning. The deaths of children significantly reduce the likelihood of permanent method use.

Women's exposure to primary and secondary schooling has positive effects on the adoption of permanent methods, and their effects are significant (Table 14.4). The variable for household SES captures socioeconomic differentials in the population, with business/service households significantly more likely to use permanent methods than are purely agricultural households. Interestingly, household economies that are dependent to some extent upon day labour to augment their income are also more likely to use permanent methods than are farming households. This may indicate a poverty push that encourages contraceptive use among poorer couples in Chitwan. Similarly, this finding could be indicative of the high value of child labour in agrarian households (Nag 1978).

To examine the effects of sons on the adoption of permanent and temporary methods, analysis is restricted to the sample of births during the five-year period of observation. Although a comprehensive set of theoretically relevant interaction terms was tested for inclusion in this model, no interaction terms achieved significance.

Comparison of model coefficients suggests that, in addition to parity, sons are strongly predictive of contraceptive use. However, although variables representing the birth of two and three sons are significantly related to the adoption of permanent methods, the birth of one son most strongly predicts the adoption of temporary methods. With regard to the likelihood of another birth, the dummy variable representing two and three sons has a negative coefficient, a finding which is confirmed in predicted probabilities that demonstrate that, whereas the probability of having another birth during the five-year period of observation is 80 per cent among couples with one son, it drops to 66 per cent among couples with two sons.

Variables for year of birth, women's age at birth and the quadratic term, and child deaths are significant. Among the other control variables, residence in eastern and western Chitwan has significant effects on the adoption of temporary and permanent methods, as does women's participation in some secondary schooling or higher. In contrast, primary schooling of women has a significant effect on the likelihood of another birth. The variable representing spousal differences in education also significantly affects the adoption of both temporary and permanent methods, but it is not significantly related to the likelihood of couples having another birth. Membership in a hill ethnic group has a significant effect on the adoption of temporary methods. The variable representing households of lower socioeconomic status (i.e. day-labour households) has a significant effect on the adoption of permanent methods.

Examination of predicted probabilities of having another birth, adopting temporary or permanent methods, reveals the direction and magnitude of effects. Table 14.5 presents select predicted probabilities derived through logistic regression using the model presented in Table 14.3.[13] The adoption of temporary methods is nearly equally likely to occur after the birth of 1, 2 and 3 sons. Permanent use is clearly more likely to occur after the birth of 2 or 3 sons than it is after the birth of 0 or 1 son. With increasing parity, women are increasingly likely to adopt permanent methods. There is also some suggestion that the probability of adopting temporary methods also increases with parity. The probability of couples having another birth bears little relationship to parity although, as mentioned earlier, the birth of 2 sons clearly reduces the probability that couples bear another child during the period of observation. The prior death of children suppresses the adoption of both temporary and permanent methods, and child death(s) increase(s) the probability that couples go on to have additional births.

The two variables controlling for programme differences over time and across the district capture meaningful differentials in contraceptive use. Year of birth is negatively associated with the adoption of permanent methods, although it does not appear to affect the adoption of temporary methods. Examination of predicted probabilities (not shown here) suggests that couples in the sample were more likely to adopt permanent methods earlier and temporary methods later during the ten-year period of observation. This multinomial model provides some indication that the decrease in the adoption of permanent methods during recent years may represent, in part, a substitution effect, that registers the increasing use of temporary methods among couples that, at an earlier point in time, may have opted for sterilization operations. This finding is consistent with the history of family planning programme efforts in Nepal, that began in widespread efforts to promote permanent methods, and that only recently began to more effectively promote the use of temporary ones.

Residence in western Chitwan is positively related to the adoption of temporary methods, reflecting their more consistent availability here than elsewhere in the district. Not only are services more available here, our fieldwork suggested that

---

[13] In these models, categories representing 0 and 1 son have been collapsed because there were no couples who, in the absence of sons, adopted permanent methods after a birth.

Table 14.5. Multinomial logistic regression of couples' joint preferences for sons on the adoption of contraceptive methods after births, 1986–1990

Variables/model	Another birth		Temporary method		Permanent method	
	coef	s.e.	coef	s.e.	coef	s.e.
Wife's parity at birth i	−0.105	0.085	0.204	0.116*	0.391	0.101**
Husband's children	−0.152	0.390	0.256	0.501	0.485	0.428
Couple's joint preferences for sons						
Both spouses have fewer sons than INS	0.709	0.230**	−0.644	0.366*	−1.546	0.347**
Wives only have fewer sons than INS	0.310	0.397	0.611	0.519**	−0.919	0.500**
Husband only has fewer sons than INS	0.510	0.328*	−0.757	0.573	−0.825	0.449**
(ref. both spouses have INS or more sons)						
Year of birth i	−0.475	0.032**	0.064	0.051	−0.387	0.034**
Wife's age at birth i	0.103	0.129	0.004	0.169	0.754	0.187**
Wife's age at birth i squared	−0.004	0.002*	−0.001	0.003	−0.016	0.003**
Child deaths at birth i	0.426	0.118**	−0.107	0.183	−0.428	0.149**
Residence						
Municipality	−0.326	0.363	0.936	0.745	0.592	0.602
East	0.068	0.319	1.902	0.676**	0.938	0.558*
West (ref. hill)	0.197	0.339	2.482	0.670**	1.047	0.573*
Ethnicity						
High caste	−0.187	0.257	0.112	0.379	0.195	0.306
Hill ethnic group	0.107	0.272	0.476	0.400	−0.102	0.351
(ref. terai ethnic group)						
Wife's schooling						
Some primary	−0.505	0.296*	−0.530	0.448	0.128	0.340
Some secondary	0.029	0.371	1.032	0.485**	0.648	0.438
(ref. no school)						
Spousal difference in education	−0.004	0.029	0.076	0.040**	0.048	0.034
Household SES						
Business/service	−0.230	0.419	0.196	0.587	0.325	0.460
Day labour (ref. agriculture)	−0.221	0.338	0.203	0.477	0.637	0.390*
Constant	22.490	2.301**	−6.032	3.432*	7.107	2.968**

* Significant at an alpha level of 0.05.
** Significant at an alpha level of 0.10.
Coef = coefficients, s.e. = standard error.
Reference categories are in parentheses. Goodness-of-fit chi-square is 1,274 with 57 d.f., $p < 0.0000$.
Notes: The total number of records examined was 584.
INS = ideal number of sons.

Table 14.6. Predicted probabilities of adopting temporary and permanent methods after births, 1986–1990, by couples' joint-preferences for sons (sons by ideal number of sons)

Couples' joint preferences for sons	No birth, no contraception	Another birth	Temporary methods	Permanent methods
Both spouses have INS or more sons	0.11	0.68	0.05	0.15
Wife only has fewer sons than INS	0.10	0.77	0.14	0.06
Husband only has fewer sons than INS	0.11	0.80	0.03	0.06
Both spouses have fewer sons than INS	0.10	0.84	0.03	0.03

INS = ideal number of sons.
Note: Adjusted results are mean predicted probabilities derived through logistic regression using the model presented in Table 14.5.

the quality of care provided in clinics in western Chitwan appears to be higher, and there is a model health clinic with family planning services that was constructed by returned Gurkha soldiers. Temporary methods are somewhat less likely to be adopted in eastern Chitwan and in the municipality, and they are least as likely to be adopted by couples in the remote hill regions. The probability of couples adopting temporary methods in the district municipal centre is moderate, perhaps because the municipality encompasses prosperous bazaar areas that are well served with access to a range of health and contraceptive services, and dense squatters' settlements where, despite the presence of a new satellite clinic, couples are less likely to use contraceptive services. Permanent methods are equally likely to be adopted by couples in the district municipal centre, and in eastern and western Chitwan, and they are less likely to be adopted by couples in the more remote hill region.

The probability of open birth intervals (no additional birth in the absence of contraception) appears to vary little across categories of the independent variables in the model. Breastfeeding, a practice expected to prolong birth intervals, is virtually universal in the study population and tends to be long term. Interestingly, residence in the hill region and the municipality is slightly more predictive of open birth intervals. Survey data show that these hill and municipality residences are also subject to higher levels of long-term labour migration by husbands than are the richer agricultural regions of eastern and western Chitwan, perhaps accounting for longer birth intervals in these parts of the district.[14]

---

[14] Temporary, circular labour migration to a location within Nepal and neighbouring countries is quite high. The survey included a series of questions regarding migration of men and women. A previous analysis suggests that estimates of unmet need (the proportion of women who want no more children and are not using family planning, adjusting for pregnancy, fecundity, postpartum infecundity status) in the district are substantially reduced when women whose husbands have been away for 12 of the previous 12 months are accounted for (Stash 1997).

Of the various control variables, variables for women's schooling demonstrate the largest effects on contraceptive adoption. The pattern of effects appears to be somewhat different for temporary and permanent use. The probability of adopting a temporary method increases slightly from 0.03 to 0.08 as women's exposure to schooling increases from some primary to some secondary schooling. Permanent use is equally as likely to occur among women at both of these levels of education. As husbands have increasingly higher levels of schooling than their wives, couples are more likely to adopt permanent methods.

Finally, agricultural households are the least likely to use either temporary or permanent methods of family planning. Business/service and day-labour households are more likely to adopt permanent methods than are agricultural households. The adoption of temporary methods varies little across the measure of household socioeconomic status.

In summary, it is only among more highly educated couples, and couples who live in better-served western Chitwan, that increases in the probability of adopting temporary methods were observed. This finding is consistent with the history of the family planning programme in the district. Access to a wider array of temporary methods is a relatively recent occurrence in the district in comparison to permanent methods. The adoption of temporary methods here, where their overall prevalence remains low, constitutes an innovative behaviour—a behaviour more likely adopted by better educated women, in regions within the district that have better access to family planning services. Finally, the sustained use of temporary methods by couples requires more and better interactions with family planning service providers than do one-time sterilization operations. The supply of methods must also be consistent. Availability of services and quality of available care create notable variations in couples' use of temporary methods within Chitwan district.

Desire for Sons among Husbands vs Wives

This final set of analyses seeks evidence that disagreement in the desire for sons among husbands and wives results in differential levels of contraceptive adoption after births. In this analysis, a variable is used to represent couples' joint preferences for sons. When this variable is introduced in a multivariate model, it is possible to examine the relative effects of husbands' and wives' desires for sons on the probability of additional births, or the adoption of temporary and permanent methods—once again, subsequent to births during the five-year period of observation employed in the previous analysis. The formulation of the independent variable takes into account the number of sons husbands and wives already have, as well as their relative preferences for sons. As in the previous models this variable is time-varying, and compares respondents' ideal number of sons (assumed to be fixed across people's reproductive careers[15]) with the number of sons they have already given birth to at any given birth.

The set of indicator variables representing spouses' joint preferences for sons does contribute toward explaining variation in the model, as indicated by the results of a likelihood ratio chi-square test between the model in Table 14.5 and the model without this set of variables. Coefficients representing couples in which one or more spouse has yet to achieve their desired number of sons positively predict the likelihood of additional births, and the coefficients tend to be significant. Coefficients for couples in which one or more spouse has yet to achieve their desired number of sons tend to be negatively and significantly related to the adoption of permanent and temporary methods, with one exception. The coefficient representing couples in which wives only have fewer than their ideal number of sons is positively related to the adoption of temporary methods, and the effect is significant.

Selected predicted probabilities estimated using the model in Table 14.5 are presented in Table 14.6. Because the results of this model differ little from those of previous models, only the effect of variables denoting couples' joint preferences for sons is discussed. Apparently a higher level of agreement between spouses is necessary for couples to adopt permanent methods. Couples in which both spouses said they had their ideal number of sons or more were most likely to adopt permanent methods, and couples in which both spouses had fewer sons than they wanted were least likely to adopt permanent methods. Couples in which one spouse had yet to achieve their desired number of sons were significantly less likely to adopt permanent methods and there is no indication that, in the case of permanent methods, either spouse's preferences tend to predominate.

The most interesting observations emerge in relation to the adoption of temporary methods. Couples in which wives only have fewer sons than they ideally would like to have are most likely to adopt temporary methods subsequent to a birth, and the probability of these couples adopting temporary methods is far greater than among all other couples. The probability of adopting a temporary method is smaller among couples in which husbands only have fewer than their ideal number of sons. In fact, couples in which husbands only have fewer than their ideal number of sons are no more likely to use temporary methods than are couples in which neither spouse has their ideal number of sons. Finally, the probability of adopting temporary methods among couples in which both spouses have their ideal number of sons is also low, presumably because these couples are more likely to adopt permanent methods, and adoption of permanent methods is indeed highest among this group.

---

[15] This formulation of the joint-preference variable does not take into account the extent to which people modify their reproductive preferences according to their reproductive experiences. This measure, therefore, may be biased in the direction of respondents saying they gave birth to the number of sons they wanted, versus that they did not. This bias would result in a more conservative estimate of the effects of the joint-preference variable on decisions to use contraception.

These findings lead to the conclusion that temporary methods are one mechanism through which women assert power in reproductive decision-making. Cases in which wives only have fewer sons than they want do not result in an inflated use of permanent methods, but they do result in an increased use of temporary methods. A substantial proportion of temporary method use is composed of female methods (62 per cent female method), and temporary method use is most common among younger women. (The mean age of women currently using a temporary method is 22 years, and the mean age of women using permanent methods is 26.) Earlier evidence indicated that couples view temporary methods as one way to insure against risk in the eventuality that an only son should die or otherwise fall short in their expected contributions toward the household. Temporary methods may be one way in which women preserve their reproductive capacity,[16] further their reproductive goals, and insure against risk, while appeasing their husbands.

The same story, however, does not appear to apply to couples in which husbands only have fewer sons than they want. These couples are no more likely to adopt temporary methods than are couples in which neither spouse has the sons they want. Husbands' preferences appear to predominate, at least in situations where husbands express an interest for more sons than they have. This finding supports previous evidence of husbands' overriding interest in the continuation and prosperity of the patrilineage, an eventuality that can only be achieved through the successful social and biological reproduction of sons. These findings offer evidence of women's power in the reproductive realm, but they similarly demonstrate a tendency for husbands' preferences to prevail over those of their wives—at least when husbands have fewer sons than they want.

Summary of Findings

In this chapter, a theoretical perspective, evolving from in-depth interviews, was pursued in a series of logistic regression equations, using data from a district-wide sample of wives and their co-resident husbands. The purpose was to ground a quantitative analysis in an in-depth, and culturally specific, understanding of the

---

[16] Bledsoe *et al.* (1994) similarly argues that young women in sub-Saharan Africa use traditional methods of family planning in an effort to achieve culturally desired longer birth intervals (of two and a half years), while preserving their reproductive potential. More effective Western contraceptives tend to be used by women at higher parities, who are less motivated to have additional births. The Bledsoe study also parallels a concept that is implicit in the approach used in this paper—the observation that women use different types of contraceptive methods in sophisticated attempts to pursue different reproductive goals. In another study, Bledsoe *et al.* (forthcoming) similarly argues that women who have experienced reproductive mishaps (the loss of a foetus or child before it reaches maturity) use contraception in an attempt to enhance their ability to have additional births. Bledsoe's work is similar to the approach taken in this study, in its focus on local cultural perceptions garnered through observation of and discussions with women.

fertility decision-making process among couples in rural Nepal. By delineating the decision-making context to decisions about sons, the analysis explores differing motivations of wives and husbands, how, and under what situations men and women are able to enact them.

In the area of southern Nepal in which the current study was conducted, there was not only evidence of a strong preference for sons, but also a well-defined cultural rationale promoting the merits of a two-son over a one-son family. Within this system, two sons insure against the risks that one son might become ill or die, fail to economically support the household, or care for his parents in old age. The risk of child mortality is real, because mortality levels remain high. Further, mean age at marriage and women's ages at childbearing are quite young (15.3 years in the study area), and couples have ample time to adjust their childbearing strategies, should they fail to achieve their goals through sons born early in their reproductive careers.

The study reveals the cultural rationale supporting the desire for a minimum of two sons in Nepal. However, a substantial minority of respondents were willing to space or stop future pregnancies after the birth of one son. These respondents tended to define themselves in opposition to the two-son norm, championing the perceived benefits of smaller family size. This willingness to contracept after one son is indicative of impending change in the social construction of family and fertility in Nepal. The accumulation of such decisions ultimately changes the context of fertility decision-making by setting examples of alternative fertility and contraceptive behaviours, thereby lowering the cost to any one individual of adopting the new behaviour (Knodel and van de Walle 1979). Decisions to contracept after one son inspire a redefinition of values that define the balance between family size and composition, and generate demand for the methods through which couples regulate, rather than terminate, their fertility.

In qualitative interviews, the reasons given for having two sons were often expressed as a desire to insure against risk—the risks that sons might become ill or die, or fail to support their parents and promote the economic interests of the family. However, a minority of respondents expressed a willingness to reject the two-son norm in the interest of a smaller family. These respondents tended to state their preference in opposition to the two-son norm, explaining the perceived benefits of having fewer children. This observation is quite optimistic, because it demonstrates change in fertility-related attitudes in favour of smaller families, and a willingness to regulate fertility even at the cost of a second son. Further quantitative analyses suggest that, although couples tend to use permanent methods after the birth of two sons, use of temporary methods is likely to begin even after the birth of only one. Temporary methods are also used by young women. The decision to have a sterilization operation terminates fertility while temporary methods allow the potential for additional births and sons, if need be. This is particularly true in Chitwan, where mean ages at marriage and childbearing remain quite young. These findings indicate that, although couples are less willing to *terminate* fertility before they have their second son, they are willing to *regulate* their fertility after the birth of only one.

The findings seem to support the conclusion that son preference and its effects on fertility behaviour are undergoing reinterpretation in contemporary Nepal. Although decisions regarding the birth of sons remain central in peoples' fertility decision-making processes, the decision to try for a second son has become discretionary. In the context of in-depth interviews, it was quite apparent that the cultural priority placed on a minimum of two sons is currently being challenged in the interest of the perceived benefits of smaller families. Changes in couples' ability to regulate their fertility through the use of temporary methods permit a reinterpretation of the two-son norm. If a major purpose of having a second son is to insure against risk, couples' ability to use temporary methods permits them to postpone additional births—while leaving the potential for additional sons (or children) open. Temporary method use after one son, therefore, amounts to risk insurance, that enhances couples' ability to achieve their desired sons, while keeping family size reasonably small.

Husbands and wives are apt to disagree in their preferences for sons, and the last section of analysis includes a set of models that captures the differential effects of son preference among husbands and wives on the use of temporary and permanent methods after births. Indirect evidence of spousal dynamics in decision-making suggests that both spouses assert authority in fertility decision-making, although through slightly different mechanisms, and in light of their own competing motivations. There is some initial evidence that women are apt to use temporary methods after the birth of one son, particularly in situations where women want more sons, but their husbands already have reached (or exceeded) their desired number. Temporary methods allow women to address their husbands' concerns, while preserving their capacity to have more children, thereby insuring themselves and their family against the risks associated with a one-son family. Men's preferences, however, appear to predominate when they do not have the number of sons they desire, but their wives do. The tendency for men's preferences to prevail when their desire for sons is at issue is indicative of men's overriding interest in promoting the prosperity and continuation of the patrilineage, in the face of the many uncertainties and economic contingencies of life in rural Nepal.

On a final note, in Nepal, the use of temporary methods for spacing pregnancies remains at a minimum. However, Caldwell *et al.*'s (1992) work in sub-Saharan Africa suggests that spacing behaviour can be an important component of contemporary fertility declines. Research in Bangladesh (Phillips *et al.* 1988) demonstrates that family planning programmes offering temporary contraceptive methods can be successful, even in traditional settings where a high value is placed on the birth of children and sons. As this paper demonstrates, temporary methods provide a means through which husbands and wives can regulate the changing balance between family size and composition preferences, in a society that places a high value on the birth of sons. It is instructive, for example, that temporary method use is higher in the survey district, Chitwan (10.1 per cent of currently married women), than nearly any other rural district (NIV 1993).

These findings support a growing body of criticism on the family planning programme in Nepal (Gonzalez 1990; Thapa 1989; USAID 1993) for its over-reliance on permanent methods. A redefinition of the balance between the desire for sons and the desire for smaller family sizes, coupled with increasing access to contraceptive counselling and methods, has the potential to facilitate fertility decline in Nepal, as women's capacity to space or prevent additional births is increased. Thus, there remains considerable scope to promote the use of temporary methods in Nepal.

Appendix

Estimation Techniques

A series of logistic regression equations were developed to model couples' decisions to use temporary and permanent methods of family planning subsequent to the birth of certain numbers of sons and children. Each case represents a birth that occurred during recent periods of time, 1981 to 1990 and 1986 to 1990.

An initial analysis uses logistic regression to model the effects of 1, 2 and 3 or more sons on the adoption of permanent methods of family planning after all births between 1981 and 1990, controlling for parity and a variety of background social and demographic characteristics of wives, husbands and couples. As such, this model is conceptually similar to an event-history model, although the timing of contraceptive events is measured in births (as versus a standard unit of time, for example, months). By definition, the covariates developed to represent sons and children at birth i precede the adoption of permanent methods; therefore, measurement of these independent variables precedes the contraceptive outcomes (although by an interval of no more than four years). Other control variables are either similarly expressed at the time of each birth i (represented by the subscript i below), or represent characteristics that did not vary across births to women.

$$\ln (q_i/(1 - q_i)) = \alpha + \beta_1 \chi_i + \beta_2 \gamma_i^h + \beta_3 \gamma_i^w + \beta_4 \lambda_i + \varepsilon, \qquad (1)$$

where β_1 represents the value of the covariates for each birth i, for example, year of birth i, women's age at birth i, wives' sons at birth i, or wives' parity at birth i; γ_i^h (γ_i^h) represents characteristics of husbands (or wives) that are assumed to be invariant across women's child-bearing years, for example, wives' schooling; λ_i represents couples' characteristics that are assumed to be invariant across women's childbearing years, for example, residence and ethnicity; and where q_i represents the probability of using permanent methods of family planning, β_{1-4} are coefficients, and α is the intercept. To note, although theoretically relevant interaction terms were tested for inclusion in this and subsequent models, they were not found to be significant. The dependent variable is the log odds ratio of permanent method use among couples, denoting the probability of permanent use (as versus no use of permanent methods). The exponentiated coefficients (e^β) presented in the text represent the odds of permanent method use given variable $x = 1$ (versus variable $x = 0$) for the dichotomous variables used in the models. For continuous variables, the exponentiated coefficients represent the associated change in the odds of permanent method use (versus no use) given a one-unit change in the variable. The results of model 1 are presented in Table 14.2.

A second series of models uses a multinomial logistic regression to estimate the effects of sons on the likelihood of additional births, and the adoption of permanent or temporary methods of family planning (versus no additional birth in the absence of contraception), 1986 to 1990. This multinomial model addresses a dependency between the likelihood of additional births and the adoption of permanent or temporary methods (John $et\ al.$ 1988). This model includes all covariates that were justified from a theoretical perspective, and that were used in the model of permanent use after all births during the ten-year period of observation. Although the sample size for these births is considerably smaller, all variables were shown to make significant contributions to the model. Variables were included in the model on the basis of log-likelihood ratio chi-square tests.

Let q_{ij} represent the probabilities of three outcomes for the birth interval subsequent to the index birth (the couple had another birth, adopted temporary methods, or adopted permanent methods), i.e. $\Pr(y_i = j$, where $j = 1, 2, 3)$, and q_{i0} is the probability that couples did not have an additional birth or adopt contraception subsequent to the index birth, i.e. $\Pr(y_i = 0)$. The multinomial model used in this analysis is

$$\ln(q_{ij}/q_{i0}) = \alpha + \beta_{1ij}\gamma_i^h + \beta_{2ij}\gamma_i^w + \beta_{3ij}\lambda_i + \varepsilon_{ij},\qquad(2)$$

where γ_i^h (γ_i^w) and λ_i are defined as they were in model 1, β_{1-3} are coefficients, and α is the intercept. The results of this analysis are presented in Tables 14.3 and 14.4. Because coefficients for multinomial models are not directly interpretable, the mean predicted probabilities of additional births and contraceptive use (permanent and temporary) are predicted for each category of key independent variables, holding all other variables at their actual value. Mean predicted probabilities will represent the average contraceptive response, given the actual characteristics assigned to each birth, and given a designated value of the independent variable of interest.

A last set of models demonstrates the differential effects of wives' and husbands' preferences for sons on the likelihood of additional births, or the adoption of temporary or permanent methods of family planning, after births to women occurring between 1986 and 1990. The principal independent variable used in this analysis is an attitudinal measure of husbands' and wives' ideal number of sons, in relation to their actual number of sons.[17] Model 2 (above) with the addition of one set of variables is used to capture couples' preferences for sons. The results of this analysis appear in Tables 14.5 and 14.6.

References

Anderson, B. A. (1991), 'The Role of Abortion in Fertility Decision in the Soviet Union: Results from Analysis of Data from Soviet Émigrés', Research Report 91–231, Population Studies Centre, University of Michigan.

---

[17] Particularly in the case of permanent methods, the potential exists for reciprocal effects between attitudes measured at the time of the survey and the contraceptive events that preceded them. However, these reciprocal effects are likely to suppress the effects on couples' use of permanent methods of sons by ideal number of sons, rather than inflate them.

Anderson, B. A. and Silver, B. (1995), 'Ethnic Differences in Fertility and Sex Ratios at Birth in China', *Population Studies*, 49(2): 211–26.

Axinn, W. G. (1992), 'Family Organization and Fertility Limitation in Nepal', *Demography*, 29(4): 503–21.

Beckman, L. J., Aizenberg, R., Forsythe, A. B., and Day, T. (1983), 'A Theoretical Analysis of Antecedents of Young Couples' Fertility Decisions and Outcomes', *Demography*, 20(4): 519–33.

Bledsoe, C., Hill, A. G., Alessandro, U. D., Langerock, (1994), 'Constructing Natural Fertility: the Use of Western Contraceptive Technologies in Rural Gambi'. *Population and Development Review*, 20(1): 81–113.

—— Banja, F., and Hill, A. G., 'Reproductive Mishaps and Western Contraception: Tiny Numbers, Far-Reaching Challenges to Western Theories of Fertility and Aging', *Population and Development Review*, forthcoming.

Cain, M. (1984), 'Women's Status and Fertility in Developing Countries: Son Preference and Economic Security', Working Paper No. 110, The Population Council, Centre for Policy Studies, New York.

—— (1989), 'Family Structure, Women's Status and Fertility Change', in *International Population Conference/Congres International de la Population, New Delhi, September/septembre 20–27, 1989, Vol. 1*, Liège, Belgium: International Union for the Scientific Study of Population (IUSSP), 181–88.

—— Khanam, S. R., and Nahar, S. (1979), 'Class, Patriarchy and Women's Work in Rural Bangladesh', *Population and Development Review*, 5(3): 405–38.

Caldwell, J. C. (1981), 'The Mechanisms of Demographic Change in Historical Perspective', *Population Studies*, 35(1): 5–27.

—— Orubuloye, I. O., and Caldwell, P. (1992), 'Fertility Decline in Africa: A New Type of Transition?', *Population and Development Review*, 18(2): 211–42, 392–4.

Central Bureau of Statistics (1993), *Statistical Yearbook of Nepal 1993*, Kathmandu: Central Bureau of Statistics.

Folbre, N. (1983), 'Of Patriarchy Born: The Political Economy of Fertility Decisions', *Feminist Studies*, 9(2): 261–84.

Folmar, S. (1992), 'Wives' Roles in Fertility Decision-Making Among Nepalese Caste-Hindus', *Central Issues in Anthropology*, 10: 39–50.

Giddens, A. (1990), *Central Problems in Social Theory: Action, Structure and Contradiction in Social Analysis*, Berkeley: University of California Press.

Gonzalez, G. (1990), 'Toward a Comprehensive Population Strategy for Nepal', *Asia-Pacific Population Journal*, 5(3): 3–28.

Greenhalgh, S. (1992), 'The Changing Value of Children in the Transition from Socialism: The View from Three Chinese Villages', Working Paper No. 43, The Population Council, New York.

John, A. M., Menken, J. A., and Trussell, J. (1988), 'Estimating the Distribution of Onterval Length: Current Status and Retrospective History Data', *Population Studies*, 42(1): 115–127.

Karki, Y. B. (1988), 'Sex Preference and the Value of Sons and Daughters in Nepal', *Studies in Family Planning*, 19(3): 169–78.

Knodel, J., and van de Walle, E. (1979), 'Lessons from the Past: Policy Implications of Historical Fertility Studies', *Population and Development Review*, 5(2): 217–45.

Mason, K. O. (1987), 'The Impact of Women's Social Position on Fertility in Developing Countries', *Sociological Forum*, 2(4): 718–45.

Nag, M. (1978), 'An Anthropological Approach to the Study of the Economic Value of Children in Java and Nepal', *Current Anthropology*, 19(2): 293–306.

NIV Joint Ventures (1993), *Nepal Fertility and Family Planning and Health Survey 1991: Main Report*, Kathmandu: HMG/FP/MCH Planning, Research and Evaluation Section.

Nizamuddin, Alam, I. (1996), 'Nature of Sex Preference for Children and Gender Discrimination in Asia', Korean Institute for Health and Social Affairs, Research Monograph 96–2.

Phillips, J. F., Simmons, R., Koenig, M. A., and Chakraborty, J. (1988), 'Determinants of Reproductive Change in a Traditional Society: Evidence from Matlab, Bangladesh', *Studies in Family Planning*, 19(6): 313–34.

Stash, S. (1996), 'Ideal-Family-Size and Sex-Composition Preferences Among Wives and Husbands in Rural Nepal', *Studies in Family Planning*, 27(2): 107–18.

—— (1997), 'The Dynamics of Fertility Decision-Making Among Wives and their Husbands in Chitwan, Nepal'. Unpublished dissertation thesis, Department of Sociology, University of Michigan.

Thapa, S. (1989), 'A Decade of Nepal's Family Planning Programme: Achievements and Prospects', *Studies in Family Planning*, 20(1): 38–52.

USAID (1993), 'Nepal. Priority Country Population Strategy', Office of Health and Family Planning, Kathmandu.

Westoff, C. F., Potter, R. G., and Sagi, P. C. (1963), *The Third Child. A Study in the Prediction of Fertility*, Princeton: Princeton University Press.

Part III

The Role of Policy

15 Intellectual Origins of Post-World War II Population Policies in South Asia

PAUL DEMENY

No manifestation of what Gunnar Myrdal called the Asian Drama—essentially with the subcontinent in mind—has been more striking than the growth of its human population. Between 1950—just a few years after partition—and 1995, the populations of the three largest countries of South Asia went from 358 million to 929 million in India, from 40 million to 136 million in Pakistan, and from 42 million to 118 million in Bangladesh. The two main demographic factors underlying that growth—mortality and fertility—each exhibited major changes. Between the first quinquennium of the period, 1950–55, and the last, 1990–95, life expectancy at birth rose from 39 years to 61 years in India. In Pakistan and in Bangladesh the corresponding figures were 39 and 62, and 37 and 56, respectively. During the same period, the total fertility rate declined from 6.0 to 3.4 in India, from 6.5 to 5.5 in Pakistan, and from 6.7 to 3.4 in Bangladesh. (United Nations 1996.)

Of the three demographic indicators just cited, the one relating to mortality is, without qualification, documentation of a great human achievement. Although it escapes the more conventional welfare measure used by economists—income per capita—extension of the average life span signals a gain that must be valued high on any ordinary scale of human preferences.

But even though it is largely a result of declines in mortality, population growth lends itself to a more qualified interpretation. Half a century ago, well before the start of the great acceleration in rates of growth, observers commonly felt that the population of the subcontinent, when considered in relation to its existing and potential resources, was already too large.

In his monumental study of pre-partition India, published in 1951, Kingsley Davis opined that population growth in that country could not long continue. In 1944, Jawaharlal Nehru, in his *Discovery of India*, written during his internment in Ahmednagar Fort, saw the expected acceleration of population growth in Asia as less than a blessing. The 'eastward sweep of technology, accompanied by education, sanitation, and better public health, is continuing and will cover many countries in Asia', he predicted. He then stated: 'Some of these countries, like India, far from needing a bigger population, would be better off with fewer people.' (Nehru 1946.)

Even though the gains in mortality reduction were welcome, fewer people, or, more realistically, less rapid population growth, also meant reducing fertility. Reduction of fertility indeed emerged as an avowed major objective of public policy in the successor states of the former British India, and did so very shortly following Independence. The main form that policy took—the launching of government-organized family planning programs, providing information about and access to methods of birth control, combined with varying doses of exhortation and pressure to persuade potential clients to make use of such services—represented a radical institutional innovation in the history of modern statecraft.

In India the programme was launched as early as 1952; in the ensuing years, similar state actions became ubiquitous throughout the developing world. The large demographic weight of the subcontinent's population, and the fact that India played a pioneering role in conceptualizing and giving substance to a new institution to address the population problem, makes an examination of the intellectual background of this policy innovation especially interesting. This paper, within the limits imposed by its brevity, explores the theoretical-ideological antecedents of the policy choices adopted first in India and then in the rest of the subcontinent, assesses the rationale of those choices, and elucidates the reasons that led to the rejection of alternative policy approaches aimed at influencing fertility.

Probing such issues may, at first blush, appear to be looking for puzzles where none exist. The pervasiveness of family planning programmes in the contemporary developing world would certainly seem to constitute compelling, even if indirect, proof of the ability of these programmes to survive and sometimes flourish, thus providing a Darwinian proof of their fitness. Yet, upon reflection, history does pose a riddle. Before governments actively sought to reduce aggregate fertility, fertility reduction did in fact occur in many countries. It led, often over a relatively short period of time, to levels that by any standard would be considered low—in many instances, levels inadequate for the long-run maintenance of population size.

Clearly, factors not involving explicit government intervention, but which could achieve the same end that governments meant to accomplish through family planning programmes, have also been in operation. Logically, awareness of this fact should have generated strong interest in understanding what were those forces that created this desired aggregate effect before and without the introduction of new institutions, institutions whose operation added costly and organizationally demanding tasks to the agenda of often inexperienced, weak, and already overburdened governments.

Such understanding did exist, at least in rudimentary form, but it was dismissed as not relevant to the circumstances developing countries found themselves in after the end of World War II. The ultimate population policy choices that were made then may have been mandated by those circumstances. But it is legitimate to pose the retrospective question of whether this was indeed the case. Moreover, trying to answer the question, however tentatively, is potentially instructive.

Early Perceptions of the Population Problem

In the present context, early is taken to mean in the period before family planning programmes. Nehru's lapidary 1944 judgment on India's population just cited—the country 'would be better off with fewer people'—was part of an extended commentary by him on the population question. It appeared as a separate section in the closing chapter of his book, *The Discovery of India*, under the intriguing title 'The Problem of Population: Falling Birth Rates and National Decay'. Given Nehru's standing as a knowledgeable observer of the Indian as well as the global scene, and his subsequent prominence as the leader of newly independent India, the passage is of more than routine interest.

Remarkably, the observations Nehru made specifically about the population of India, or even of Asia in general, were quite cursory. His preoccupations concerning the subject were rather those of a weary Western intellectual. He was worried about the falling birth rate. The passage cited above, imbued with Oswald Spenglerian gloom, continues:

Meanwhile in western Europe a reverse process [to that in Asia] has set in as regards population, and the problem of a falling birth rate is growing in importance. This tendency appears to be widespread and affects most countries in the world, with some notable exceptions like China, India, Java, and the U.S.S.R. It is most marked in the industrially advanced countries. The population of France ceased to grow many years ago and is now slowly declining. In England a steady fall in the fertility rate has been noticeable since the eighties of the last century, and it is the lowest now in Europe except for France. ...

What is the cause of this widespread phenomenon of falling birth rates? The increasing use of contraceptives and the desire to have small, regulated families may have produced some effect, but it is generally recognized that this has not made any great difference. ...

It would seem that the kind of modern civilization that developed first in the West and spread elsewhere, and especially the metropolitan life that has been its chief feature, produces an unstable society which gradually loses its vitality. ...

What is wrong with modern civilization which produces at the roots these signs of sterility and racial decadence? ... Modern industrialism and the capitalist structure of society cannot be the sole causes, for decadence has often occurred without them. It is probable, however, that in their present forms they do create an environment, a physical and mental climate, which is favorable for the functioning of those causes.

Nehru thus clearly perceived a path toward low fertility—one that would permit low mortality without leading to the increase of a population that he deemed already too numerous for its own good. But he contemplated that recipe with distaste, and his commentary veers off in the direction of a murky Gandhian utopianism. 'One fact seems to stand out', wrote Nehru, 'a divorce from the soil, from the good earth, is bad for the individual and the race ... If we keep away from them for long, life begins to ebb away.' What to do, then? The prescription

Nehru offered was rather elusive:

The competitive and acquisitive characteristics of modern capitalist society, the enthrone-
ment of wealth above everything else, and the continuous strain and lack of security for
many, add to the ill health of the mind and produce neurotic states. A saner and more
balanced economic structure would lead to an improvement of these conditions. Even so it
will be necessary to have greater and more living contacts with the land and nature ... It
should be possible to organize modern industry in such a way as to keep man and women,
as far as possible, in touch with the land, and to raise the cultural level of rural areas. The
village and the city should approach each other in regard to life's amenities, so that in both
there should be full opportunities for bodily and mental development and a full, all-
rounded life.

Nehru's reading of the record in parts leaves much to be desired. Contraceptive
use—more broadly, deliberate birth control—of course had more than 'some
effects'. As a proximate variable—that is to say, as the means through which control
is exercised—it was the dominant cause of fertility decline. And control *was* exercised because there *was* a desire by most couples to have 'small, regulated families'.
But Nehru's reluctance to accept the structural factors—the 'competitive and
acquisitive' characteristics of capitalist society—which, he realized, spawned such a
desire, transpires clearly enough. He yearned, instead, for a solution that would
dispense with the need to accept those, to him, repellent characteristics of capitalism that had lowered fertility in the more developed world. There must be, he felt, a
special Indian way to achieve demographic stability. Attitudes of this sort reflected a
frame of mind that was receptive to Western advice on social and economic policy,
but which at the same time rejected market solutions as inappropriate in the Asian
setting.

Alternative Diagnoses of the Causes of 'Classic' Fertility Transitions

Nehru was a patriot and a politician, not a social scientist. What was the then
prevailing social scientific view of fertility change, on which debates about post-war,
post-Independence discussions of policy choices could have relied? Much of what
existed was inevitably and predominantly Western, both because the observed
record of fertility decline was Western and because social analysis was then still
largely a Western specialty. However, elaboration of a systematic theory of fertility
decline left much to be desired. Not surprisingly, present-day retrospective accounts
of classic fertility theory tend to start with post-war formulations—those, above all,
of Frank Notestein and Kingsley Davis. There existed, nevertheless, a well-formed
quasi social-scientific understanding of the factors that explained what Adolphe
Landry called the 'fertility revolution' in his eponymously titled book, published in

1934. Two competing formulations may be distinguished, both with antecedents going back to at least the early nineteenth century.

The first, and by far the dominant, interpretation saw fertility control as a rational adjustment of couples' behaviour to changing social and economic circumstances. Consider, for example, a late nineteenth century view of the causes of the American fertility decline, a decline which by then was well advanced. The author is John Billings (1893), a physician, who also served as chief librarian of the New York Public Library. What are the factors that explain 'the deliberate and voluntary avoidance or prevention of childbearing on the part of a steadily increasing number of married people'? asked Billings. It is, he answered in part,

[T]he great increase in the use of things which were formerly considered as luxuries, but which now have become almost necessities. The greater temptations to expenditure for the purpose of securing or maintaining social position, and the corresponding greater cost of family life in what may be called the lower middle classes, lead to the desire to have fewer children in order that they may be each better provided for, or perhaps, in some cases, from the purely selfish motive of desire to avoid care and trouble and of having more to spend on social pleasures.

In the struggle for what is deemed a desirable mode of existence at the present day, marriage is held less desirable, and its bonds less sacred, than they were forty years ago. Young women are gradually being imbued with the idea that marriage and motherhood are not to be their chief objects in life, or the sole methods of obtaining subsistence; that they should aim at being independent of possible or actual husbands, and should fit themselves to earn their own living in some one of the many ways in which females are beginning to find increasing sources of remunerative employment; that housekeeping is a sort of domestic slavery, and that it is best to remain unmarried until someone offers who has the means to gratify their educated tastes. They desire to take a more active part than women have hitherto done in the management of the affairs of the community, to have wider interests, and to live broader lives than their mothers and grandmothers have done.

This changing utility calculus by individuals explained changing fertility desires—a process reinforced, Billings noted, by 'the growth of opinion that the abstaining from having children on the part of a married couple is not only not in itself sinful, or contrary to the usual forms of religious creeds, but that it may even be under certain circumstances commendable'. He also noted, true to his profession, the 'diffusion of information ... on physiology and hygiene'—the means of birth control—by modern terminology. '[M]arried women are much better informed as to the means by which the number of children may be limited than were those of thirty years ago.' But he clearly put motivation over means as the crucial element in the equation.

This view was articulated by many later observers. A particularly clear example is a 1932 discussion—cast in terms intended to reach a popular audience—by the noted economist and historian of economic thought, Joseph Spengler.

The immediate cause of [the rapid decline of western fertility] is the rapid and widespread dissemination of birth control information. The *underlying* causes, however, are not birth control but the social and economic forces which lead modern men and women to practise birth control.

What factors have contributed to this recent spread of birth control practice? To answer this question would be to define the growth and the spirit of modernity, of megalopolitan civilization ... Among the factors which undoubtedly have accelerated the adoption of birth control are the gradual emancipation of women, increased knowledge of physiology, the spread of the desire for comfort and luxury, the disappearance of the frontier as an escape from poverty or as the possible source of wealth, the increased education of all classes, and the movement of population to cities, where the child becomes largely a non-earning liability. ...

Human unwillingness to bear children thus seems to be the result largely of the discrepancy between what the individual considers essential to his welfare and happiness and what the contents of his weekly pay envelope enable him to buy. Competitive capitalism thus far has been marked by wide variations in income. The ten-hundred-dollar-a-year man learns in the schools and sees in the rotogravure sections and in the advertising columns of newspapers and magazines what the ten-thousand and the hundred-thousand-dollar a year men buy. Billboards make the expenditures of the wealthy common knowledge among the beggars.

Given a thousand dollars a year and a taste for things that can be purchased only with a three-thousand-dollar-a-year income, one whom our competitive economic system has taught to calculate may resort to two courses of action. He may endeavor to increase his income, but until he achieves this increase he must omit expenditures for every value except those which, in light of his new set of tastes, yield him the greatest immediate satisfaction per dollar spent. Placed in this predicament from which there is no escape except through winning a fortune, the average person, if he marries at all, finds himself unable to afford the expense of more than one or two children, if that many. In short the cost of the child is so great relative to the pleasure and satisfaction yielded by a child, that parenthood is viewed as a bad bargain. So reason the American, the Frenchman, the Englishman, the German, the Swede, and others.

And, three decades before Gary Becker, Spengler commented:

Children are economic commodities even as are books, dogs, or automobiles. The production of commodities, such as automobiles, occasion pain to the producers. Men produce automobiles only when the price obtained for the automobiles offsets the pain of producing them. So with children. Four out of every five couples who become parents do so because they feel that the joy and pleasure of rearing the children will more than balance the money cost and pain cost of parenthood. Couples who refuse to become parents or who raise but one child are of the opinion that the money cost of raising one or more children greatly exceeds the money value of any pleasure the child may bring to the parents.

These somewhat lengthy quotations from long defunct writers are merely illustrative. Any reader of the pre-World War II demographic literature in general and, in particular, of social science commentaries on why birth rates fell would be well aware that the central mechanism explaining the fall of fertility was well understood and agreed upon. The explanation centred on the role of changing structural conditions of the market economy, conditions to which micro-level units in society tended to respond with alacrity and flexibility, in demographic as well as other matters. The *means* by which this was done were not entirely ignored in this main-stream understanding—there was always a bow in the direction of the importance of the spread of knowledge about 'physiology', or 'hygiene'. All observers, and especially economists—firm believers in utility calculus as the governor of family planning decision—took it for granted that lowering the cost of birth control (costs broadly interpreted) would have facilitated birth control's actual practice. But for all practical purposes the matter of 'how to' was left buried in a black box. Family planning was something families did, in the privacy of their home.

Contraceptive technology by all accounts was primitive at best, what later came to be called modern methods being virtually nonexistent save the lowly condom, and the birth control technology that existed was mostly illegal and hard to obtain. But as observed fertility rates showed, couples—then mostly husbands and wives—somehow managed, presumably using their newfangled knowledge of 'physiology', to have few children. Where there was a will, there was a way. What mattered was not technology—most people knew how babies came about. Hence, a totally reliable way of preventing their arrival was always there as a means of last resort. And these ways did not necessarily deny the enjoyment of that commonly and strongly sought good, sexual gratification.

The crucial change was not in the domain of physiology but located in peoples' heads: in the ideas they formed about their interests and those of their potential children, given the obligations, responsibilities, and opportunities hammered into their consciousness by their everyday experience. The results—the output of a myriad of black boxes—spoke for themselves. Fertility became controlled. So much so, in fact, that the challenge Western policy-makers came to be concerned about, to the extent that they paid any attention at all to the birth rate, was not how to keep it down but how to raise it.

Remarkably, after World War II, this record was declared irrelevant to solving what became popularly known as the problem of Third World population explosion. The spontaneous and uncoordinated—indeed, by governments, often vigorously resisted—process of fertility decline that had occurred in the West was deemed far too slow to be relied upon in situations that demanded speedier results.

Yet the historical record gave at best tenuous support to this contention. If perhaps not 'socially optimal' in speed or pattern (concepts, in any case, hard to substantiate when speaking of a process being governed by optimization on the micro-level), the Western process was nevertheless more accurately describable as one that reflected actual pressures toward family limitation, when and as those pressures arose. In the paradigmatic 'original' cases of France and the United States, the process was indeed slow. But this was hardly surprising. France was a relatively thinly populated country, fairly comfortably off: French couples could afford to take their time. As to the United States, it had an open frontier that offered plentiful economic opportunities. Nevertheless, by the end of the nineteenth century, the native white urban population of the eastern United States had below-replacement fertility. Elsewhere, the process was anything but slow by the standards of history.

In Western Europe, the downward trend started about 1880, more or less, and by 1900 it was a general movement. By the 1920s, fertility was at or near replacement everywhere in that region.

The process was also generating speed and momentum as it spread. For example, between 1920 and 1939, Bulgaria's birth rate dropped by 50 per cent. That country was economically backward by any definition: poor, agricultural, and at the margin of the European cultural sphere. In comparison to what became common after World War II, there was at best modest exposure to the flow of mind-shaping international communications—such as those products created by rotogravure presses. But what little there was, combined with domestic economic pressures, sufficed to generate at a dramatic speed, among a basically peasant society, the adjustment of long-term patterns of fertility behaviour. Nor did theory or observation support the view that such adjustments were somehow natural when effected by European peoples but could not be expected from non-Europeans under similar socioeconomic conditions. Immigrant groups, for example, whatever their cultural background, adopted new patterns of fertility behaviour with remarkable speed.

The historical record thus provided a recipe for fertility transition that could reasonably be interpreted as universally valid. The transition presupposed changing fertility preferences, and such preferences were the general and inevitable outcome of the natural evolution of capitalist market societies. Should a polity be dissatisfied with the speed of fertility decline that this pattern of development spontaneously generated (and in the West there were no apparent reasons to be so dissatisfied), the particular motivational forces behind it could presumably have been isolated and used to shape government policy.

There existed, however, an alternative interpretation of the driving force of the Western fertility transition. For brevity's sake, I will describe that interpretation with reference to just one writer, the economist Sir William Beveridge, later Lord Beveridge, widely regarded as the intellectual father of the post-World War II British welfare state. In a 1925 article, 'The Fall of Fertility Among the European Races', Beveridge sought to offer an explanation for that fall. He looked for evidence supporting the standard explanation—namely, that the evolution of the birth rate in Europe reflected changing economic circumstances—and, he said, he failed to find it. He concluded that the explanation was elsewhere, and was in fact quite obvious:

The divergence between economic and vital movements [in Europe] could hardly be more complete. It leaves only one answer to our question. The practice of birth control, that is to say the deliberate prevention of fertilisation, suddenly increased about 1880, not because there was then any change of economic conditions making restriction of families suddenly more desirable than before, but because the means of birth control were perfected and the knowledge of them was spread, both by those interested in their sale and by disinterested propagandists ... From the facts briefly recited we have to infer that shortly before 1875 means of preventing fertilisation, more effective and more easily used, were brought to the stage of practical exploitation. We have to infer an invention, like that of chloroform or motor cars, but an invention driven underground by public opinion and the law. We may and must make the inference from the indirect evidence of the course of economic and vital movements, as surely as the planet Neptune was inferred by mathematicians from the movement of Uranus, before ever it was seen and recognised by observers.

This exalted picture of 'perfected' means of birth control may strike today's reader as rather quaint. Since, Sir William's inference notwithstanding, we know that the birth control technology by means of which Europe's fertility transition was effected was, by today's standard, anything but efficient, the more obvious inference would be that the intrinsic effectiveness of that technology was a secondary matter, dwarfed in importance by the vigour and determination with which it was applied. Yet the Beveridgian interpretation was destined to exert a dominating influence on Western official attitudes and on action toward population policy in the developing world adopted just a few decades later.

But the interpretation was not adopted whole. Beveridge had no trouble in surmising that those perfected means of birth control could find their way to their users thanks to the exertions of those 'interested in their sale'. Indeed, these interested persons could find potential users even when the products had been 'driven underground by public opinion and the law'. But, according to the judgment of mid-century Western observers, in South Asia this mechanism of spreading birth control technology was out of the question: it seemed obvious that it just could not work.

Amusing—and perhaps condescending, or somewhat racist or culturally prejudiced—as this sounds today, Western elite opinion took it for granted that 'Asiatics' were not cut out for the rigours of the market, whether as suppliers seeking to make a penny, or as customers allocating resources, however modest, to secure utility. If there was a need for technology transfer, that was to be effected not through markets, but through the ministrations of 'disinterested propagandists'. That presumably could not mean Mother Teresa. But there was always Margaret Sanger. Or, if need be, the government could take over and hire, by the tens of thousands, cadres of disinterested propagandists.

Such a conclusion was ironic. During the preceding 150 years, Western economic and social progress was based on the recognition that although disinterestedness does play some role in social interaction, that role is necessarily narrow and constrained. And further, Western experience demonstrated that in delivering personal services, information, or products, government's ability as a supplier, good intentions notwithstanding, is vastly inferior to the ability of markets to do the job.

Policy Alternatives for Lowering Fertility in the Developing World

Thus, beginning some 50 years ago, Beveridge's answer, *sans* market, was wholeheartedly embraced by Westerners giving advice to the Third World on matters of population policy. That advice—which in contemporary American political parlance might be summarized as 'it is the technology, stupid' and 'you need this technology, even if you don't know it, and I am the one who will satisfy your need'—has dominated the population activities of private foundations (the first actors in the field) and, from the 1960s onward, the population activities of bilateral and international aid agencies. The advice given—with varying degree of enthusiasm—was in due course embraced by and internalized in the agenda of most Third World governments. In some instances, however, there was a major supplement: the addition of administrative muscle. In other words, circa 1950, what in the judgment of most social scientists was still identified as the key to the Western fertility decline—structural transformation in a particular institutional context— was deemed irrelevant for shaping the policy response to the sudden post-war acceleration of population growth in the developing world. Why this was so may be explained by the confluence of several factors.

First, the explanation for the sudden acceleration of population growth *was* largely technological. The transfer of the devices and methods of Western medicine was chiefly responsible for the extraordinarily rapid fall in mortality that sparked rapid population growth. It seemed symmetrically proper, therefore, that the remedy for high fertility would have to be the transfer of something equally tangible: this time, the transfer of birth control technology. Such reasoning was flawed, *prima facie*, since the motivational underpinnings of the two interventions bore no resemblance to one another. Death and disease are seldom welcome, babies generally are. Eager acceptance of technology to control the former foreshadowed no similarly ready receptivity to devices for controlling the latter. The argument advocating a medicine-based solution for the problem of high fertility seemed, nevertheless, compelling to decision-makers in Washington and elsewhere.

Second, Western intellectual opinion in the immediate post-war years gloried in economic *dirigisme*. Political leaders in the newly independent states, and in India especially, reciprocated the sentiment: with rare exceptions they were strong believers in the magic of economic planning and of five-year plans. Markets as a coordinating device and reconciler of conflicting interests—thus, as an institution simultaneously serving both the individual and the common good—had a distinctly bad reputation at the time, and were dismissed as irrelevant, or rather as something to be reined in, if not outright suppressed. In the West, in particular, the memory of the Great Depression, a calamity blamed on the market, was still fresh, and so were the government-organized triumphs of the collective planned effort that won the war. The historical lessons of how the West grew rich were not simply ignored but largely forgotten.

Furthermore, the shadow of the Soviet Union, offering policy recipes that seemed to provide a short cut to rapid economic development, loomed large. Those recipes, stressing the need for central planning, sometimes interpreted through the more moderated social-democratic versions of economic *dirigisme*, were admired and copied in many countries of the less developed world. This was especially the case in South Asia. Foreign aid, a new institution, was largely invented as a device to counter this socialist influence. Paradoxically, from its inception, the actual conse-quences of foreign aid tended to be anti-market, in part by intent and wholly *de facto*. Foreign aid channelled resources from government to government, thus inevitably favouring centralization and bureaucratic organization. Spending the money of tax payers, few of whom considered themselves rich, required that aid givers disburse it responsibly. This meant entrusting it to government officials in the receiving countries: presumably they could be counted on to be responsible for spending the money wisely.

Foreign aid also meant, by its very conception, *spending*. Spending presupposes tangibles. When, with a delay of almost two decades, the objective of reducing population growth was added to the many other objectives of post-war economic aid, it was a natural expectation that population aid, too, had to have at least a modicum of budgetary heft. But what could population money buy that would register as a perhaps relatively small, yet respectably sized, line item in an aid budget, and that would require a respectably sized bureaucratic apparatus to administer it? Sending foreign officials worried about their countries' 'uncontrolled' fertility books authored by the classics of the Scottish enlightenment could have been a good idea, and may have done a lot of good, but it would not have made a dent in any aid budget. Birth control technology, and the machinery needed for its deployment and distribution, provided the welcome answer. In the fourth year of USAID and the first year of UNFPA's existence Gunnar Myrdal outlined what was to be done. His account was essentially a summary of ideas that had been developed and rehearsed, in good part as a result of initiatives by American private founda-tions, over the preceding 20 years:

What underdeveloped countries are in dire need of accomplishing is something as unprecedented in the world as the rapid fall in mortality and the ensuing population explosion have been.

The reason why such a task should not, offhand, be deemed impossible springs from two very important advantages in the initial situation of underdeveloped countries when facing the birth control issue, as compared with the situation of the developed countries when starting a similar movement.

For one thing, *underdeveloped countries today can make the spread of birth control public policy.* ...

The second advantage of the underdeveloped countries today is that *they can from the beginning distribute technical contraceptives.*

The technical solution Myrdal endorsed was to be no easy task:

The government of an underdeveloped country must accomplish tremendous things in order to carry out an effective policy of spreading birth control.

First, it must realize the overwhelming importance for its development planning of bringing down fertility ... and it must make *a firm decision to take action by instituting a vigorous public policy to spread birth control.* ...

To effectuate a decision when taken, the government must, secondly, *build up an adminis-trative apparatus for the purpose.* The distance is long between the bureaucracy in the capital and the individual families in the villages or the urban slums. This is particularly true in large countries like India and Pakistan, which just because of their population size weigh so heavily.

Administration, particularly on the lower level, is not the strong side in underdeveloped countries, which are all 'soft states'. When, as in India and Pakistan, goals of bringing down fertility have not been reached, this is often due to the fact that the administrative apparatus has been faltering.

Implied in this second requirement of a sufficient and effective administrative apparatus is, thirdly, *the need to deploy a large staff of medical and paramedical personnel.* (Emphases in the original.)

The main beneficiaries of assistance supporting such a programme were to be India and Pakistan (then comprising also today's Bangladesh)—countries in which local private as well as government initiatives, financed in part through American foundation grants, created a hospitable milieu. Given its huge population and limited financial and administrative resources, the burdens imposed by having to execute the ambitious agenda outlined by Myrdal were obviously very high in the subcontinent. More significant, however, was the implied commitment to a course of action that, by its conceptual framing, foreclosed the kind of alternative development policy options that foreign aid might have otherwise encouraged.

The weakness of lower-level administration noted by Myrdal is especially relevant in this regard. In virtually all poor countries, strengthening lower-level structures of government, or, as the case may be, creating them from scratch, *was* a key requirement for setting the stage for a sound long-term process of economic and social development. Satisfying that requirement was, arguably, a condition for the proper functioning of any state intent on performing the essential tasks of government and anxious to provide a framework for the protection and development of the economy and of civil society.

The list of these essential tasks is familiar from successful Western historical experience. The list is short, yet by any measure difficult and demanding. It is centred on what in shorthand may be called law and order—establishment of the basic institutions of participatory democracy, safeguarding public safety, guaranteeing the impartial administration of justice, the enforcement of contracts, the establishment of reliable records in land and other real property rights, setting up local membership lists, and maintaining full registration of births, deaths, and marriages. Around these core functions—some of them seemingly humdrum, yet each essential—there is a range of tasks for government to tackle, at the appropriate level. The latter criterion is best approached by applying the principle of subsidiarity: the performance of functions at the lowest feasible level.

The most important among these broader tasks of government at the local administrative level are primary education, and the provision of basic measures of public health, including matters that may need collective action, such as securing supplies of clean drinking water, sanitation, and local environmental management. The establishment of basic health services and a basic social safety net are logical early additions to such a list, epitomized by maternal and child care services and by measures of support for the indigent old.

Around such tasks, local-level action, initially gently prodded from above, can be plausibly organized, since the aims of such action, the benefits of which are tangible and widely distributed, can command early popular support. Activities promoting family planning would have been, by all odds, expected to become a relatively divisive and controversial matter, hence would have been an unlikely early candidate for addition to the core list. Social policy concerning birth control could have been envisaged along two main approaches.

As development progressed, one might have replicated the classic Western pattern, in which reliance on the emergence of strong micro-level motivation to control fertility could confidently have been expected. By the evidence of the historical record, such confidence would have been warranted if a stable market-based economic and social order—open to international trade and to the cultural and social contacts with the outside world—were successfully established. Whenever and wherever such conditions obtained in the developing world after World War II, rapid economic growth ensued, thanks to the exceptionally favourable international environment for economic growth in the early post-war decades. Then, given the conditions just stated, there would be strong reason to expect a rapid shift in micro-level incentive structures, fostering desires for lower fertility even if economic development were sluggish, at least as conventionally measured in terms of per capita incomes.

It is totally mistaken to consider a situation characterized by both rapid economic growth and unchanging levels of income per capita as a situation of economic stagnation. A Bangladesh of 120 million people would be radically different in terms of economic structure and capacity, and in terms of the micro-level incentive structure that such changes inevitably entail, from a Bangladesh of 40 million, even if income per capita remained unchanged—which of course it did not. In such situations, along the classic pattern, lowered fertility desires would have been expected to generate a mixture of birth control activity, partly home produced—requiring cooperation between husband and wife—and partly acquired, through the market. The latter would be more flexible than that divined by Beveridge; not hampered by legal restriction and disapproving public opinion; and benefiting from a far larger and better armamentarium than was the case a century or even fifty years ago.

In a second variant, under circumstances of less readily developing demand for birth control and less responsive markets responding to it, as administrative prowess developed and as the local-level connections between the burdens imposed by rapid population growth became explicit, family planning services would be plausibly added to the core functions of local-level activities. The centre could readily find channels through which local endeavours to provide family planning services could be helped and stimulated.

The Myrdalian recipe—typical of the Western developmental advice given to recipients of foreign aid and typical of other kinds of international assistance—short circuits this process of orderly 'development from below'. It fosters a centralized model of administration, organized around competing specialized tasks, each with its top-down structure, and presided over by a ministry in the capital issuing commands and providing cadres, equipment, and finance. Such a model has a close resemblance to the administrative arrangements that came to characterize the Western welfare state following World War II. In fact, it is largely inspired by it. But it also reflects the sectoral organization of functions along which, if only as a matter of sheer convenience and administrative tidiness, Western aid came to be packaged. The model has little resemblance to the arrangements which, by the evidence of the West's own history, sound development of government would have required in the developing world in the post-war, post-Independence period.

Quite apart from the narrower domain of population policy, the extent to which foreign aid and advice-giving ignored the lessons of the West's own successful development experience was remarkably complete. Consider, as an example, the goal of rapidly expanding elementary education as an early and high-priority task in development. Achievement of that goal is valuable in its own right, but it also yields multiple side benefits for development (including, notably, with respect to fertility behaviour). This was quickly recognized and paid constant lip service to by all partners in development. Many new countries even enshrined the right to universal primary education as a constitutional right.

The United States and also most European states already had a successful historical recipe for creating universal primary education. It was something to be done locally, by local resources, under local supervision. Carrying out such a task did not just educate children. It was also an ideal training ground for local-level democracy or, at any rate, for concerted local-level action; a prerequisite for the development of a sound system of local-level taxation for the financing of local projects; and *pari passu*, a tangible reminder that children are costly not only to parents but also for the immediate community, and that in raising them choices must be made between quantity and quality. Decentralized decision-making also provided wide scope for experimentation and comparison of alternative local solutions—a Darwinian weeding out of the unworkable and propagation of the viable.

The notion that adoption of this successful Western approach, or appropriately adapted variants thereof, might be something to be considered by the developing countries was, however, never entertained. The matter was seen as too important to be left to locals, ignorant folks as they are. Besides, aid givers' convenience and the vested interests of local élites favoured centralized decision-making. Furthermore, the potential inequalities that the alternative model, decentralized and market-based, would have entailed—the prospect that some inevitably will do better than others—was ideologically distasteful. The latter consideration—equality—was especially cogent. The importance of a just, meaning equal, distribution of the benefits of government programmes, or indeed one favouring the poor, was invariably emphasized both by aid givers and by recipients. In practice, and pre-dictably, the centralized decision-making process tended to benefit the more privileged—those closest to the seats of political and economic power.

Admittedly, practical considerations were also at work in advice-giving. The cen-tral government existed everywhere and was convenient to deal with. Local gov-ernment was weak or nonexistent, and, in any case, distant from aid givers and inconveniently decentralized. Time was also short: strengthening or creating a new institutional framework for government seemed to be a detour, and recommending it was a politically troublesome intrusion into local affairs. Drawing on models taken from an earlier phase of Western development—however appropriate that model might have been, given the existing circumstances of the developing coun-tries—also seemed inappropriate, as this would have been at variance with the best modern practices of social policy—those of the contemporary Western welfare state. Unfortunately the financial resources that made that model plausible, for example, in Sweden or, in a more rudimentary variant, in the United States, were entirely absent.

What sociologists might call a bad case of cognitive dissonance in post-World War II Western advice-giving to developing countries was especially acute in the field of population. Rapid population growth, hence high fertility, was perceived as a menace: it had to be reduced. But by the inter-war years fertility in the West *was* everywhere below replacement level, a level that some decades ago, even by the most sanguine calculation, was only a distant prospect in the developing world. Even halfway progress toward such a goal would have been welcome as a great achievement in countries of high fertility. Logically, therefore, there should have been intense interest in understanding how such a reduction came about, and in identifying the policies that could foster the conditions that would best replicate those that had so effectively generated a pervasive fertility reduction in the West. On the practical political level, such an interest seems to have been entirely missing, and on the academic level it was at best cursory. The recommended policy settled upon was, instead, entirely novel: the launching of government-organized family planning programmes. The West ignored its own proven record, offering, instead, something in which it had no experience whatsoever. 'Do not what I did (and in which I succeeded), but try something I never tried (and in which perhaps you will succeed)' sums up the guiding principle of post-war Western advice to the develop-ing world.

Conclusion

Monday morning quarterbacking is easy. Still, it is worth to look back from time to time, and ask if there are some lessons to be learned from hindsight. What would we want to do differently if only we could go back to some time around 1950 and start again? And given where we are now, how should we proceed? Addressing these questions is beyond the purview of the present paper. It is clear, however, that answering them should reflect the realization that history cannot be undone. Reform is necessarily path-dependent. Devolution of the present system of population policy has to take into account the consequences of policies pursued during the past four decades.

In a recent commentary, John Caldwell observed that 'in rural India, the people assume that fertility control cannot be practiced without a government family planning program'. This reminds one of the ex-Soviet citizen, who, after 70 years of experience, assumes that groceries will no longer be there once the government quits the grocery business. If Caldwell is correct—even though his comment was offered in praise, not as criticism—one would have to conclude that the Indian programme followed a profoundly ill-chosen path. Creating relationships of dependency on government when no dependency could be justified is a classic demonstration of the law of unintended consequences. But as the said citizen will eventually discover, government as a universal grocer is not the only solution, or the best one. Transition from one model to another, even if the latter is clearly a better one, is necessarily difficult and fraught with problems. But a path can be found and taking it should be rewarding.

References

Beveridge, Sir William (1925), 'The Fall of Fertility Among European Races', *Economica*, pp. 10–27 (March).

Billings, John (1893), 'The Diminished Birth-Rate in the United States', *Forum*, Vol. 15. Reprinted in part in *Population and Development Review*, 2: 279–82 (June 1976).

Myrdal, Gunnar (1970), *The Challenge of World Poverty*, New York: Pantheon Books.

Nehru, Jawaharlal (1946), *The Discovery of India*, New York: Harper & Row.

Spengler, Joseph J. (1932), 'The Birth Rate—Potential Dynamite', *Scribner's Magazine*, Vol. 92 (July). Reprinted in *Population and Development Review*, 17: 157–69 (March 1991).

United Nations (1996), *World Population Prospects: The 1996 Revision, Annex I, Demographic Indicators*, New York: United Nations, Department for Economic and Social Information and Policy Analysis, Population Division, 24 October 1996 (mimeographed).

16 Common Beginnings but Different Outcomes: The Family Planning Programmes of Pakistan and Bangladesh

WARREN C. ROBINSON

Introduction

When the previously undivided union of British India achieved independence in 1947, Bangladesh and Pakistan began their national existence as two wings of the same country—East and West Pakistan. The two territories inherited an administrative and governance structure from the colonial period, but they quickly developed their own political and economic systems and began to shape their own development plans and programmes. The two wings were bound together by their common religion—Islam—but from the very outset, language and other cultural differences created internal tensions. Nonetheless, East and West Pakistan shared a common social and economic development until 1971, when a political dispute erupted into civil war, leading to the intervention of India and the creation of the new state of Bangladesh in what had been East Pakistan.

Pakistan was a poor, predominantly rural and agricultural country, with low levels of income per capita, poor social infrastructure and virtually no industrial capacity. Only Lahore, in West Pakistan, could claim status as a major city in the old pre-partition India. Both wings lay on the periphery of the Indian subcontinent and had functioned as frontier areas supplying raw materials to the economic centres in North and Central India and, in turn, drawing on these centres for most manufactures and technical services. This economic marginality was reflected in social and demographic characteristics as well. In 1947 Pakistan had lower literacy and higher mortality, on the average, than did India, as well as higher fertility and lower levels of contraceptive practice.

Formal economic planning was launched in Pakistan in 1955 with the first five-year plan. The second plan (1960–65), very far-sightedly for the times, called attention to the fact that the prevailing rapid rate of population growth posed a threat to the economic future of the nation and allocated a modest sum for policy and programme interventions through the Ministry of Health. Pakistan was receiving substantial technical assistance from the Ford Foundation, the Harvard

Development Advisory Service and other international donor groups, and an awareness and concern over the population explosion was growing in such circles.

In the third five-year plan (1965–70), population policy became a major objective and a priority programme. The then president, Mohammed Ayub Khan, was a firm supporter of the programme. A detailed operational scheme was developed for both wings, top-flight civil service administrators were assigned to the task, and the programme moved into high gear. Donor groups, including by then the United States Agency for International Development (USAID), were deeply involved in financial and technical ways, but direction of the programme was distinctly under the control of Pakistan nationals. The director of Pakistan's first family planning programme, Enver Adil, was fond of saying that he took orders only from the president, and most who knew him believed this to be true.

Conservative Islamic groups were troubled by the notion of family planning and, while this never seems to have seriously hindered any programme activities, it was a constant background factor, and one that probably influenced some policy decisions. Such anti-programme sentiment was probably greater in the West than in the East, but this issue was not part of the continuing quarrels that led to the break between the parts of the continent in 1971. For the crucial first five years of the plan, 1965 to 1970, the two wings thus had a common population policy and family planning programme structure.

Differences in practice did emerge, but, generally speaking, the approach was the same and so was the experience flowing from these efforts. The fact is that neither wing had much to show for their efforts by the end of the five-year plan period. Contraceptive practice had not risen appreciably, and fertility had not fallen. The creation of Bangladesh did not change this picture. Family planning continued to be both a policy and a programme in the two countries, but the programmes languished. Both countries seemed to provide excellent case studies of why family planning programmes in poor Third World nations were a hopeless, foolish or even wicked idea.

In their eagerness to explain this failure, most commentators failed to note that by the mid-1980s the situation was changing. Pakistan and Bangladesh had begun to follow sharply divergent demographic paths. In Bangladesh, contraceptive prevalence rose and fertility fell, slowly but steadily, whereas in Pakistan, contraceptive prevalence remained static, at very low levels, and fertility actually appeared to be rising. This divergence between the two former twins continued to intensify in the 1990s. Bangladesh is now viewed as a particularly interesting success story—a desperately poor country with falling fertility; and Pakistan, as a puzzling failure— a country that has experienced considerable economic and social change, accompanied by little or no impact on contraceptive prevalence or fertility, that is, until almost the end of the 1990s.

These facts are now well known to all students of the South Asian population scene, and many earlier authors have grappled with the fascinating problem they pose. The present paper makes one more such effort, focusing, in particular, on the actual process of programme implementation in both countries. The key issue, it seems, is what caused the divergence in demographic trends that emerged between Bangladesh and Pakistan in the 1980s? The question generates three possible responses:

- Differences in the social and cultural structures of the two countries have led to different outcomes.
- The two countries have followed different paths of socioeconomic development, one leading to lower fertility, the other to static fertility.
- The Bangladesh family planning programme did things that the Pakistan programme did not.

Subsidiary questions are: Could the 1965–70 Pakistan programme have succeeded if it had adopted a different approach? And can Pakistan ever follow the same path as Bangladesh? A further question on which this review also touches is whether the prevailing demand–supply analytical paradigm is actually helpful in understanding real-world programme experiences.

Pakistan's First Family Planning Programme

It is important to recall the context in which the first Pakistan government family planning programme was launched. The year was 1965, an era of strong commitment to development planning by Third World governments, of generous international and private donor support for such efforts, and of boundless enthusiasm and optimism for the tasks that lay ahead. Only a few dissenters questioned that a development plan, based on a macroeconomic model and representing a variety of different development projects, was the correct approach to transforming a stagnant traditional economy like that of Pakistan (Lewis 1969). Coale and Hoover (1958) had shown how the population factor could be made part of such planning, and their model had been applied to Pakistan (Hoover and Perlman 1966).

Thus, the family planning programme initiative in Pakistan was based on the best available technical advice and seemed an eminently sensible idea. This conventional wisdom was not seriously challenged from any quarter. Most considered family planning an absolutely vital programme, well worth trying, even if a bit of a gamble. Other development interventions in the health area had worked—the eradication of malaria and smallpox, for example. Why not family planning? What was required was a sound plan, strong leadership and adequate resources.

An important point to remember is that 1965 was still at a very early point in many of the developments in contraceptive technology that were to fully take hold in the 1970s and 1980s. It is true that even in 1965 there was much talk about the cafeteria approach in family planning, which recommended that clients should have several methods of birth control among which to choose. But, in Pakistan, this position largely reflected talk, not action. At that time, there were five methods officially available: female or male surgical contraception; the IUD; the oral pill; female barrier and spermicidal methods; and the condom.

In Pakistan, as elsewhere, the first two methods were considered clinical methods, requiring an appropriate medical setting for proper use. Thus, these methods were generally only available in clinics in urban areas. Moreover, the IUD was a relatively new method at that time, and responsible medical opinion in Pakistan was opposed to the use of paramedics or field workers to insert IUDs, even if such workers had been available.

The oral pill was still in its first-generation formulation, and side effects were common. Mini-dosage types of pill had not yet been developed, and many trained medical people were extremely suspicious of this powerful, new hormonal intervention. The traditional barrier methods had proven very difficult for village women to use effectively, since they lacked privacy and a sound knowledge of their own bodies. Hence, barrier methods were never popular. What these considerations added up to was that in 1965, the Pakistan programme offered most rural couples the condom, and little else. Couples who were very strongly motivated could obtain an IUD or the pill, but followup for possible complications or even for re-supply was not reliable. Obtaining surgical contraception required an even greater effort by the client, and involved genuine health risks for many.

Family planning was viewed in a simpler fashion in those days. Leibenstein had already laid the foundations for what was to become, at the hands of Becker and others, the microeconomic theory of fertility. But, in 1965, it was still assumed that couples had children because they enjoyed having sex, and that many, if not all, of them would have fewer children if they were offered the means of continuing their marital pleasures while also avoiding pregnancies. There was modest support for this belief from early field trials and action-research projects, most notably in Comilla, East Pakistan, and Lulliana, West Pakistan, where respectable levels of contraceptive practice among rural women were obtained by well-designed experimental programmes. The year 1965 was also long before the revolutions in survey data collection techniques, data processing and nearly instantaneous publication of results. Evaluation of a programme took special effort and considerable time and money. Frequently, it was an afterthought.

Main Features of the 1965 Programme

The third-plan family planning scheme created a new administrative entity, the Family Planning Council, and outlined a detailed programme by which it proposed to reach 20 million couples in 36 districts of the West and 16 districts of the East, the goal being a reduction of 20 per cent in fertility by 1970. The scheme operated mostly through the existing political and administrative structure of government— provinces, districts, Thanas (Talukhas in the East), and village-union councils—by attaching family planning staff at each level, or by adding family planning to their functions on a part-time basis. The scheme aimed at nationwide coverage and represented, for the most part, an effort to distribute conventional contraceptives through village midwives and other local agents. Clients wanting a clinical method were to be referred to clinics, most of which were in existing urban hospitals and rural health centres. However, the scheme was explicitly not clinic-oriented. Day-to-day supervision and control were decentralized, and the key managers were the district executive officer and the Thana family planning supervisor. Publicity was a responsibility at the province level, and only evaluation, research and training were central government functions (Robinson 1966).

The time schedule for launching the plan was extremely ambitious, but it was met. Much of the early training of programme workers was conducted by expatriate staff drawn from the Population Council, the Ford Foundation, USAID, the Pakistan–Sweden Family Welfare Project and other groups. By 1966 the scheme was under way and apparently making real progress. The programme was one of the first generation of such government family planning efforts, along with those of Taiwan, India, Egypt and one or two other countries. A steady stream of visitors came from other countries to see what was being called a model programme. Articles were written explaining why family planning had succeeded in Pakistan and had failed in India (Finkle 1971). A substantial volume of high-quality research was generated, and the famous couple-year-of-protection (CYP) measure was developed by Wishik as an evaluation tool for the Pakistan programme (Wishik and Chen 1973). Pakistan, in fact, proved a fertile training ground, and its graduates have become the cadre for numerous international family planning organizations since then.

The service statistics generated by the programme indicated that success was indeed being achieved. That is, the supplies were being distributed and CYP measures rose steadily. However, no independent surveys of prevalence or fertility were undertaken to validate these apparent achievements, and concern and doubt about actual results slowly grew. Finally, in 1968–69, the programme itself sponsored a National Impact Survey in both wings of the country. This showed conclusively that the contraceptive prevalence rate (CPR) was only 6 per cent of currently married women, and that fertility remained unchanged. The good news was that most women had heard of family planning and knew of at least one method, and that a majority approved of the idea. The bad news was that very few were currently actually using any method. The CPR was only slightly higher in urban than in rural areas, a still more discouraging finding.

The programme did seem to have modestly more success in East than in West Pakistan. In particular, the use of clinic methods was twice as high. And although the government programme did not emphasize surgical contraception, this proved a more popular method in East than in West Pakistan.

In 1969 the top leadership of the programme was replaced, and much soul searching occurred. What came to be considered the 1965–70 debacle effectively discredited the programme in the eyes of other government ministries and demoralized the family planning staff and many of its donor friends. The new official in charge of the family planning programme, correctly deciding that the use of village midwives as part-time fieldworkers had not worked very well, announced a new approach, the continuous motivation system (CMS), under which full-time male–female teams (typically, it was hoped, a husband and wife) would be permanently assigned to a given area, in which they were to make continuous rounds of all prospective clients for motivation and supply. Most other aspects of the programme were left much as before.

CMS had hardly been introduced when the civil war in the East broke out, followed by full-scale international war between Pakistan and India. The hostilities resulted in a near-complete suspension of all programme activities in both wings of the country. After 1972, East and West Pakistan become two separate countries: Bangladesh and Pakistan.

Pakistan's Family Planning Programme after 1972

Many political changes followed from the events of 1971–72, but in the new Pakistan, the population policy remained in place, as did much of its organizational structure. Some among the donor community, in particular, were reluctant to accept that the previous effort had really failed. Instead, they argued that it simply had not been pushed hard enough or long enough.

The response to programme failure was the famous inundation scheme, which by now has entered into the folklore of family planning. The logic behind the inundation approach was that the 1965–70 plan had simply failed to do what it set out to do, namely, make contraceptives instantly available to all prospective clients throughout the country. If this could still be accomplished, it was argued, success might still follow. This required more outlets and more supplies. The programme was to be expanded, and the country truly 'inundated' with contraceptives.

The results of this dogged return to a lost cause are well known. Millions of condoms—for it was still mostly a condom-based programme—and millions of pills were imported and distributed. The CYP rose, but actual contraceptive prevalence and fertility remained virtually static. The 1974–75 Pakistan Fertility Survey showed a TFR of nearly 7.0, up slightly from the estimate of the Impact Survey in 1968–69. Contraceptive prevalence remained under 10 per cent, with only modest inter-provincial or rural–urban differences (Robinson 1978). Another profound period of disillusionment followed, but the next step was not clear.

In 1978, responsibility for the family planning programme shifted briefly to the health ministry. In 1981, it shifted yet again to the Ministry of Planning and Development, where it became part of the Population Welfare Division (PWD). There, as Hakim and Miller elaborate in Chapter 6, a newly created agency was charged with operating a network of multipurpose Family Welfare Centres, which would provide family planning motivation and distribute supplies. The new family planning strategy also gave somewhat greater formal recognition to the role of the NGOs and to the private sector, creating a contraceptive social marketing programme to subsidize sales in the private sector (Robinson 1987). The family welfare division was given independent ministerial status in 1990. However, this move, along with a number of other organizational changes made in the 1980s and 1990s, has not made any fundamental change in the family planning programme's approach or structure.

The record outlined above is not a particularly happy one. The expenditure of considerable resources, plus the time and hard work of many dedicated persons over the course of an entire generation, has still not achieved the goals the plan hoped to reach 25 years ago. Yet, as Hakim and Miller in this same volume concur, the most recent survey data from Pakistan perhaps offers some hope that future prospects are not altogether bleak.

The 1990–91 PDHS showed a modest increase in the CPR, to 12 per cent. The most recent survey (the PFFPS in 1996–97) indicates a CPR of 24 per cent and a TFR of 5.3, putting the TFR below 6.0 for the first time in the history of such data. Pakistan appears to be preparing to turn a corner at last. Yet if family planning now seems on the verge of succeeding, it may be in spite of government programmes, not because of them.

Family Planning Policy and Programmes in Bangladesh

Bangladesh's war for independence cost the country heavily in terms of human lives and physical infrastructure. The impact of these losses on the family planning programme sector has been described as follows: 'The devastation of the war was particularly debilitating to the health and social services sectors of the government. The bureaucracy had collapsed, universities and training institutes were decimated, and many of the critically needed health facilities were destroyed. Basic communication was disrupted, further straining capacities to organize effective government, ... mechanisms for coordinating complex tasks at the periphery, where family planning services would have their effect, simply did not exist.' (Cleland *et al.* 1994: 107.)

The new government committed itself to essentially the same policy and programme that had been in place under Pakistan rule. The first five-year plan of the new nation (1973–78) gave population a high priority, and government moved quickly to replace lost staff and to rebuild its organization and facilities. The reconstituted programme was placed in a Ministry of Health and Family Planning, thus eliminating the separate family planning council framework that had existed in the earlier period. The new plan also sketched out an ambitious multisectoral approach, which assigned some family planning functions and responsibilities to eight different ministries. By 1975 the programme was certainly up and running again.

For a time, the history of Bangladesh's programme after independence threatened to follow a course similar to that of Pakistan. In the period between 1975 and 1985, there was, at best, slow progress. The existence in several ministries of overlapping, parallel structures engaged in family planning work led to bureaucratic in-fighting over budgets. The health bureaucracy seemed particularly resistant to new methods, or to the kinds of field structures already in use by the NGOs that were being proposed by donors. The bureaucracy continued to operate with the old procedures and operating rules that had been laid down in 1965, without questioning their usefulness for the 1980s.

But modest increases in the CPR did occur, dating from about 1975 (Cleland *et al.* 1994). According to findings from a highly reliable series of fertility and contraceptive prevalence surveys carried out in Bangladesh in the 1980s and 1990s, prevalence rose slowly—from 8 per cent in 1975, to 13 per cent in 1979, to 18 per cent in 1981, and to 19 per cent in 1983.

The programme was for a time haunted by an unfortunate legacy of the Pakistan days: namely, the accusation that family planning was a coercive scheme being forced on the helpless peasants of Bangladesh by 'outsiders' (Warwick 1982). The continued use of incentive payments—'bribes' to the critics—and the important role played by surgical contraception—'castration' to the critics—were part of the reason for this negative impression. Also, some representatives of the international women's movement found the male-dominated family planning programme in Bangladesh a particularly inviting target (Hartmann and Standing 1983), as did the equally militant Christian and Muslim groups who were opposed to any kind of birth limitation (O'Reilly 1985). For a time in the early 1980s, the programme was very much on the defensive, particularly in international donor circles.

At the same time, several important positive elements helped to strengthen the programme and point it in the right direction. Well before independence, there existed in Dhaka a major international epidemiological research centre, then called the Pakistan-SEATO Cholera Research Laboratory. This laboratory operated an epidemiological surveillance area in Matlab Thana, in the rural area south of Dhaka, collecting birth, death and morbidity statistics. After independence, this laboratory was reconstituted as the International Centre for Diarrhoeal Disease Research, Bangladesh (ICDDR,B), and beginning in 1975 it used the test area and field staff in place to conduct a series of carefully designed family planning interventions and experiments. With support from the Population Council and USAID, these studies generated an enormous volume of high-quality research, nearly all of it highly pertinent to programme improvement. The research showed conclusively that when services were delivered in a high-quality fashion, contraceptive prevalence in a rural setting rose sharply and fertility fell.

From 1983 onwards, the Matlab-based work was extended to several other rural areas in Bangladesh, in an attempt to investigate whether the same approach and procedures would work when applied in regular government facilities whose staff had been retrained to deliver higher-quality services. (This was the extension project, which continues in a different form today.) The answer to this new question was a resounding yes. When properly delivered, family planning services seemed to find clients nearly everywhere in Bangladesh.

The second favourable, if exogenous, factor affecting the Bangladesh programme was the presence of a very large number of non-governmental organizations (NGOs) operating in the rural areas of the country. Some 7,000 such organizations are registered with the Ministry of Social Welfare. They are involved in everything from agricultural improvement to women's education and employment. Some 400 engage in family planning and MCH activities, typically with linkages to and support from international donor organizations such as Pathfinder, the Asia Foundation, Ford Foundation and others. Other larger rural development groups, such as the Bangladesh Rural Advancement Committee (BRAC) and the Grameen Bank, also started over time to include family planning and other social welfare components in their programmes (Cleland *et al.* 1994: 154–67). Most of these NGOs provided family planning in conjunction with programmes aimed at empowering women through education, employment and income-generation schemes.

By the mid-1980s, a very significant and increasingly visible non-governmental family planning success story was emerging in Bangladesh. Services provided through the private sector came to represent as much as one-quarter of all contraceptive use, and they were highly cost-effective. Many of the NGOs aimed at bettering the situation of women in general, and success in these other development programmes interacted with the contraceptive delivery efforts. To this was added a highly effective contraceptive social marketing programme (SMP), which distributed condoms and pills through thousands of private sector outlets. While sanctioned by the government, the SMP was completely independent in its operations, and the level of use it accounted for came to represent another one-quarter of total prevalence.

Initially, ministry officials reacted to reports of rising contraceptive prevalence achieved through nonofficial sources by ignoring or even attempting to discredit them, probably because the success of the private sector represented an implicit criticism of the official family planning programme. By the mid-1980s, a behind-the-scenes struggle over the role of NGOs and other private-sector entities reached a crisis point. The ministry made a bid to take over and 'regularize' all NGO operations. This would have meant that all budget and administrative control would pass into the hands of the ministry.

The NGOs, with strong donor support, resisted this attempted takeover. The donors paying for the overwhelming share of all Bangladesh development activities, had, indeed, been unhappy with the progress of the official programme for some time. At one point, the donor consultative group, chaired by UNDP, had even commissioned its own review of the situation, producing a set of rather sweeping proposals for change, the so-called donors plan of 1983. Many of these proposals would have moved the official programme in the directions that NGOs were already taking.

Probably due to the growing importance of nonofficial participants in pro-gramme activities, by the late 1980s the CPR in Bangladesh had begun to rise even more sharply. It reached 25 per cent in 1986, 30 per cent in 1989, and 40 per cent by 1991. Success is hard to fight, and the ministry officials came to see that it was in everyone's best interest to cooperate and build on the approaches and the structures that were leading to such irrefutable results.

Fertility levels also changed substantially within those years. A definitive recent review of contraceptive and fertility trends in Bangladesh states: 'The decline probably started in the late 1970s and accelerated in the mid-1980s ... In 1975, the total fertility rate was about seven births per woman. By 1988, it had fallen to five births per woman, equivalent to a 30 per cent drop ... Fertility in 1990 was almost certainly well below five births.' (Cleland et al. 1994: 131.) This same review also notes that the decline in fertility has been pervasive, and has touched nearly all socioeconomic strata and all geographical regions of the country. The most recent data suggest a slight levelling off, but most observers predict that the trend will continue.

What Explains the Different Outcomes?

At the outset of this paper we suggested three possible explanations for the diver-gent paths followed by family planning in Pakistan and Bangladesh since 1972: (1) Different sociocultural structures in the two regions made family planning more acceptable to one society than to the other. (2) The two regions experienced quite different degrees of modernization and socioeconomic change following separation in 1972. (3) Differences in the family planning programme approaches followed by authorities in the two nations led to different outcomes.

The first two of these considerations might, using the conventional terminology, be considered demand factors, whereas the third might be considered a supply factor. But they lead to further questions. For example, are there structural sociocultural factors that have made children more valuable in Pakistan than in Bangladesh?

Historically, natural fertility was higher in East Pakistan than in West Pakistan—a TFR of 7.0 compared to one of 6.0–6.5. And nearly all descriptions of traditional Bengali values, family structure and village life paint a picture of an enormously pro-natalist setting (Maloney et al. 1981). The custom that girls should marry soon after puberty, the *purdah* system, the social opprobrium accorded childless women, and the fact that a woman's entire social status and security are dependent upon her husband and sons, are all factors that hardly make Bangladesh a promising setting for family planning to succeed.

It is, of course, true that at the time the programmes were getting started, rural West Pakistan presented a very similar picture. But that is not the issue. Rather, it is that some authors, presumed close students of village life in Bangladesh, constructed convincing sociocultural arguments showing why family planning would be at least as difficult to introduce in Bangladesh as anywhere else in the developing world, and why, therefore, the programme would not work. One particularly careful review concluded: 'We would not look for a major decline in fertility in Bangladesh in the next ten to fifteen years'. (Arthur and McNicoll 1978: 63; see also Demeny 1975.)

These estimations of the structural difficulties initially facing a family planning programme in Bangladesh turned out to be wrong, or at least exaggerated. But, in all fairness, it must be noted that after independence, the concerted NGO and donor programme efforts to empower women probably resulted in a more favourable environment for family planning. As a result of these efforts, the traditionally negative sociocultural setting probably became more neutral or even mildly positive.

Secondly, conventional socioeconomic theory suggests that fertility falls with economic development or modernization. In fact, an examination of the development experience of Pakistan and Bangladesh supports an exactly opposite conclusion. As Cleland *et al.* (1994) asserted:

Economically, Pakistan has done better than Bangladesh in the past 15 years, with a much higher growth in per capita income, a larger industrial base, more modernized agriculture and a larger urban population. (p. 136.)

Per capita income doubled in Pakistan between 1975 and 1985, whereas it increased by about one-third in Bangladesh. The gap in per capita income between the two nations widened over time. Poverty in Bangladesh has been a constant, but, remarkably, the population has managed to maintain itself. Dire predictions about a sharp increase in poverty do not seem to have materialized. This leads Cleland *et al.* to reject the notion of a poverty-led economic mechanism driving fertility reduction. In their judgment, economic factors do not appear to have been controlling the changes observed. This proposition remains unproven. Nevertheless, the evidence does not support the belief that rising levels of economic development invariably are either necessary or sufficient for fertility decline.

Pakistan's economic growth has been due less to wise economic policy by government than to favourable but fortuitous outside events. Pakistan benefited enormously from the boom in the oil-producing state of the Persian Gulf. The great demand for labour of all types produced a flow of remittances to Pakistan that exceeded all other sources of foreign exchange for nearly a decade. The war in neighbouring Afghanistan, while it no doubt caused many social problems, also led to an inflow of foreign funds and an economic boom in the northwest that spread to the rest of the country.

In terms of social influences, the picture is somewhat different. Social welfare indicators for the two countries are dissimilar, but they go in opposite directions. In Pakistan, the percentage of school-age children enrolled in school has been static—at 40 per cent—for the last two decades, whereas in Bangladesh it has risen, and is now over 50 per cent. Infant mortality has fallen appreciably in both countries, but it is still around 100 per 1,000 live births in Pakistan and well below this level in

Bangladesh. Female school enrolment is significantly higher in Bangladesh than in Pakistan, but both are well below male rates, and only a small fraction of students in secondary school are girls. As measured by female employment, legal rights to divorce or child support, and personal freedom, the status of women is deplorably low in both countries, although in some qualitative sense, the situation is slightly better in Bangladesh than in Pakistan. The influence of conservative religious leaders on such issues appears to be greater in Pakistan and to have affected policy in the last decade. But it is possible to overestimate the importance of this factor.

Where does this review lead us? In terms of the economic factors usually thought to be associated with falling fertility, Bangladesh is worse off than Pakistan and even more so now than was true 30 years ago. In terms of the social indicators usually associated with lower fertility, there are real, if modest, differences between the two countries. Perhaps, in some indefinable qualitative sense the climate for great equality between the sexes and the attitude of policy towards such a goal is more favourable in Bangladesh than in Pakistan. In any case, socioeconomic changes in the two countries cannot explain all the differences between the family planning and fertility experiences of the two states since 1972.

A last remaining possibility is that somehow since 1972 Bangladesh has created a family planning supply programme that has met whatever latent demand for family limitation already existed, and has also created new demand on the part of other couples. Our reading of the evolution of the family planning programmes of Pakistan and Bangladesh over the past several decades supports the view that this is exactly what has happened.

As late as the early 1980s, both programmes still seemed mired in the same bureaucratic and administrative morass. Then several changes began to occur in Bangladesh:

- The family planning programme had become a health programme, and this was important. The health bureaucracy was no longer threatened by the programme but came to accept it as legitimate.
- There was active debate about the programme, and a growing body of local research about what worked and what did not work. Over time, this debate resulted in the programme becoming a less monolithic supply network and adopting more pragmatic, programme-focused, problem-solving approaches.
- NGOs grew and prospered in Bangladesh and they became the cutting edge for programme improvement. The government, albeit reluctantly, was willing to learn from these organizations.
- The international donor community—bilateral and multilateral—was allowed to play an important role in Bangladesh, providing technical assistance as well as financial support. This element provided another force for change and for critical review of the programme.
- Even while its measured income per capita was lagging, what development did occur in Bangladesh was *social development*, with an emphasis on education

and health. (The thrust of the recent criticisms of the Cleland *et al.*/World Bank study of Bangladesh (Caldwell *et al.* 1999) seems to be that the authors fail to note this distinction, a point which has some modest merit.)

The elements of *social development* have been largely absent from the Pakistan programme. In a very real sense, Pakistan has not yet managed to escape the legacy of her first programme mistakes. The programme continues to operate in comparative isolation from its natural setting of health care delivery. It continues to view family planning as essentially an administrative problem. The private sector and NGOs are tolerated but not allowed to lead. The modest success that had been occurring in urban areas, and the successful experimental use of TV commercials, should point the way. But it is not clear that this is happening.

Put bluntly, our subjective reading of the history and the data is that Bangladesh has been successful because it has found a way to deliver services that attract clients. This has meant a wider and better supplied system of delivering services, and that clients have been given a wider choice of contraceptive methods. Family planning has also been integrated into broader women-oriented social and economic programmes. Pakistan has been less successful because it has only recently begun to do these things.

Could the 1965 Pakistan Programme Have Succeeded?

If the family planning programme planners in Pakistan in 1965 had known what we now know, thanks to Matlab and its research findings, could they have designed and implemented a programme that would have been successful? To answer this, we must first return to Pakistan's family planning programme, as it was actually implemented in 1965, and summarize what, in our judgment, went wrong:

The programme was overambitious. Putting a new programme in place all over the country—in fact, all over two countries—was an administrative *tour de force* but a logistical nightmare. A more manageable strategy might have been to start the programme in districts centred around a large urban centre and then to move outward in a phased way, so as to reach most districts by the end of five years. But, this gradualist approach was explicitly rejected as being politically unacceptable.

The decision to make family planning an administrative rather than a health task was a mistake, even if it was understandable in the context. The Pakistan Ministry of Health in those days was full of old Indian Army doctors who barely believed in public health, much less family planning. Bypassing these professionals must have seemed easier than fighting them. But, it meant that the programme limited itself to mostly nonclinical methods, since it really did not control the facilities in which clinical methods were supplied. This made it harder to bring new contraceptive methods into the programme as they were being developed and to meet the clients' actual desires, which were (and still are) mainly for long-term methods.

Inadequate attention was given to the IEC function. Even in 1965 radio was a major medium of communication in Pakistan, and TV appeared on the scene before the end of the first plan. Too much attention was given to brochures and posters, which impressed visitors but were meaningless to illiterate rural women. This approach followed partly from an unstated decision that the programme should keep a relatively low profile, which was counterproductive. In practice, a low profile meant no profile.

Insufficient attention was given to programme evaluation and to the detailed monitoring of results. The rapid feedback now possible with DHS-type techniques was obviously not possible at that time. But even small-scale local surveys could have been planned and undertaken. Findings from such studies might have given a more realistic sense of the programme's performance, even if the results ran counter to service statistics and the optimism of the programme advisors and officials. The National Research Institute for Family Planning, attached to the central secretariat, was intended to perform such tasks. However, because of weak leadership and inadequate staffing it never became a real resource. Numerous training and research centres were also established at the provincial level, but these also quickly lost their edge.

To some extent, this failure to evaluate the programme arose from an initial misunderstanding on the part of programme leaders about a then ongoing vital statistics registration project, the famous PGE (later the PGS). It came as a distinct shock to the top administrators when they learned that PGE sample design produced only estimates of the birth and death rates for the two wings and for the nation as a whole. Strenuous efforts by the programme to get PGE to produce estimates below the provincial level were stoutly, and correctly, resisted by the PGE staff. Thus, it was relatively late in the programme that the managers came to realize that they had no way of estimating fertility or contraceptive prevalence aside from their own service statistics.

The private sector was not enlisted or made use of to the extent it should have been. Most private physicians knew nothing about the programme, and those who knew of it realized it was not a medical programme and hence were deeply suspicious. The NGOs also were not made full partners, nor was their experience drawn upon for programme tactics. There tended to be a feeling that only government could take on the really big jobs. And the private sector would merely get in the way.

Linking the programme to the apparatus of political governance—union councils, district councils, and so on—meant that there was inevitable pressure on the programme to meet the normal demands of political patronage and largesse. There is no real evidence of excessive levels of corruption. However, identification of a family planning programme with a country's power structure is unfortunate in situations in which that power structure is already suspect in the eyes of the masses.

In the end, the answer to the question posed at the outset of this section is, probably, yes. If there had been a newly created division in the Ministry of Health, and if this division had begun work through existing hospitals and clinics, including the

NGOs, had undertaken educational work with private physicians and other health care providers, and had slowly moved out into rural areas in a phased manner, bringing new methods on line as soon as they became available, it is possible that beginning in 1965, a family planning programme organized in this way could have had a perceptible impact on prevalence and fertility within 5–10 years. This strategy would not have satisfied the demands for a crash programme but it would have avoided the enormous waste of time, money and talent that has characterized the Pakistan programme. If this seems a harsh judgment, it comes from one who, in a small way, contributed to some of the mistakes made all those years ago.

Recent data suggest that Pakistan has finally learned the lessons of its original failure. The current programme is addressing several of the key factors contributing to the debacle of the 1965–70 programme, including: making family planning a responsibility of the health ministry and emphasizing modern, long-term methods; launching an effective, mass media IEC campaign; mobilizing a contraceptive social marketing scheme in the private sector; and undertaking relatively frequent surveys so as to give programme planners reliable, objective data on performance. Further steps need to be taken, including allowing greater freedom for the NGOs; more legal, social and economic measures to empower women; and improvement of the quality of services at all levels. But, these needs are now recognized and discussed. There is reason to hope that change will follow. Pakistan now seems destined to follow the same path as Bangladesh (Sathar and Casterline 1998).

Obiter Dicta

This paper, like much of the other recent literature, has used the demand–supply paradigm as an organizing framework. We conclude that the demand factors, as these are usually understood—economic and social growth, modernization, improvements in the status of women—cannot explain all the difference in the fertility and family planning experience since 1972 of the birth twins, Bangladesh and Pakistan. We argue instead that it is the supply factor that provides the rest of the explanation. Bangladesh has supplied a rising quantity and quality of family planning services, and this supply has created its own demand, in a setting which most people had judged to be especially challenging for a programme. To a consid-erable degree *social development* (education, health) probably has stimulated demand, but the family planning service programme has been a part of this social development. It is, therefore, poor logic to argue that demand factors can be clearly separated from supply factors.

The other element in the simple demand–supply interaction is price. We now understand that in reality, the price, or cost, of obtaining contraceptive services in countries like Bangladesh and Pakistan is, for most prospective clients, made up of mostly sociopsychological factors. Consideration of sheer physical accessibility, or distance to the nearest clinic, does not address most of the real concerns (DeGraff 1991).

The list of elements involved in the 'quality paradigm' (Bruce 1990) does address these concerns, and this realization leads to the interesting conclusion that price is not a separate variable that somehow equates demand and supply, but is itself mostly controlled by the supply factors. Quality, in fact, helps set the subjective price perceived by the client. Put in noneconomic terms, if quality of services is high enough, a programme can overcome the sociopsychological fears and concerns of prospective clients, while also making the services physically available and accessible. Sophisticated, educated clients probably have fewer such fears and concerns and can even learn to manage on their own. But, a well-managed, high-quality programme can go a long way towards substituting for the slow process of education and modernization that produces such clients. And service programmes that work closely with schemes for female empowerment move more rapidly than do others. This is what family planning programmes are (or should be) all about. The family planning staff of NGOs knew this long before the economists arrived on the scene and started confusing the issue with notions of demand and supply.

References

Arthur, Brian, and McNicoll, Geoffrey (1978), 'An Analytical Survey of Population and Development in Bangladesh', *Population and Development Review*, 4(1): 23–80.

Bruce, Judith (1990), 'Fundamental Elements of Quality of Care: A Simple Framework', *Studies in Family Planning*, 21(2): 61–91.

Caldwell, John C., Barkat-e-Khuda, Caldwell, Bruce, Pieris, Indrani, and Caldwell, Pat (1999), 'The Bangladesh Fertility Decline: An Interpretation', *Population and Development Review*, 25(1): 67–84.

Cleland, John, Phillips, James F., Amin, Sajeda, and Kamal, G. M. (1994), *The Determinants of Reproductive Change in Bangladesh: Success in a Challenging Environment*, Washington, DC: The World Bank, World Bank Regional and Sector Studies.

Coale, Ansley, and Hoover, Edgar (1958), *Population Growth and Economic Development in Low-Income Countries*, Princeton: Princeton University Press.

Conly, Shanti R., and Rosen, James E. (1996), *Pakistan's Population Programme: The Challenge Ahead*, Population Action International, Country Study Series No. 3.

DeGraff, Deborah S. (1991), 'Increasing Contraceptive Use in Bangladesh: The Role of Demand and Supply Factors', *Demography*, 28(1): 65–82.

Demeny, Paul (1975), 'Observations on Population Policy and Population Programme in Bangladesh', *Population and Development Review*, 1(2): 307–21.

Finkle, Jason (1971), 'Policies, Development Strategies and Family Planning Programmes in India and Pakistan', *Journal of Comparative Administration*, 3: 135–52.

Harbison, Sarah F., Robinson, Warren C., and Khalique, Kibraul (1989), 'Female Autonomy and Fertility—The Case of the Garo of Northcentral Bangladesh', *The American Anthropologist*, 91(4): 1000–7.

Hartmann, Betsy, and Standing, H. (1983), *A Quiet Violence*, London: Zed Press.

Hoover, Edgar, and Perlman, Mark (1966), 'Measuring the Effects of Population Control on Economic Development: a Case-study of Pakistan', *Pakistan Development Review*, 6(4): 541–66.

Koenig, M. A., Phillips, J. F., and Simmons, R. (1987), 'Trends in Family Size Preferences and Contraceptive Use in Matlab, Bangladesh', *Studies in Family Planning*, 18(3): 117–27.

Lewis, Stephen R., Jr., (1969), *Economic Policy and Industrial Growth in Pakistan*, London: George Allen and Unwin.

Maloney, Clarence, Aziz, K. M. A., and Sarkar, P. C. (1981), *Beliefs and Fertility in Bangladesh*, Monograph No. 2, Bangladesh: International Center for Diarrhoeal Disease Research.

O'Reilly, W. M. (1985), *The Deadly Neo-Colonialism*, Washington, DC: Human Life International.

Pakistan, Government of, Ministry of Population Welfare (with the Population Council) (1996), *Pakistan Contraceptive Prevalence Survey, 1994–95, Basic Findings*, Islamabad.

Phillips, James F., Hossain, Mian Bazle, and Arends-Keu (1996), 'The Long-Term Demographic Role of Community-Based Family Planning in Rural Bangladesh', *Studies in Family Planning*, 27(4): 204–19.

Robinson, Warren C. (1966), 'Family Planning in Pakistan's Third Five-Year Plan', *Pakistan Development Review*, 6(2): 6–281.

—— (1978), 'Family Planning in Pakistan, 1955–1977: A Review', *Pakistan Development Review*, 17(2): 233–47.

—— (1987), 'The "New Beginning" in Pakistan's Family Planning Programme', *Pakistan Development Review*, 26(1): 107–18.

Sathar, Zeba (1993), 'The Much Awaited Fertility Decline in Pakistan: Wishful Thinking or Reality?', *International Family Planning Perspectives*, 19(4): 142–6.

—— Casterline, John B. (1998), 'The Onset of Fertility Transition in Pakistan', *Population and Development Review*, 24(4): 773–96.

Tsui, Amy Ong (1996), *Family Planning in Asia; Approaching a Half-Century of Effort*, East-West Center, Programme on Population, Hawaii, Asia-Pacific Population Research Reports, No. 8, April 1996.

Warwick, Donald P. (1982), *Bitter Pills*, New York: Cambridge University Press.

Wishik, Samuel, and Chen, Kwan-hwa (1973), *Couple-Year of Protection: A Measure of Family Planning Programme Output*, Family Planning and Population Programme Manuals No. 7, New York, International Institute for the Study of Human Reproduction, Columbia University.

World Bank (1994), *Staff Appraisal Report, Islamic Republic of Pakistan, Social Action Programme Project*, Washington, DC, Country Department III, Population and Human Resources Division, South Asia Region, Report No. 12588-Pak.

17   Determinants of the Fertility Transition in Bangladesh

BARKAT-E-KHUDA, JOHN C. CALDWELL,
BRUCE K. CALDWELL, INDRANI PIERIS,
PAT CALDWELL, AND SHAMEEM AHMED

Introduction

Demographic theory has failed to keep up with the spread of fertility transition to most parts of the world. There is still a tendency to exclude the role of national family planning programmes and to regard their activities as extraneous or artificial, lying outside the scope of the socioeconomic theory of demographic transition. This paper will argue that the programmes are indeed a social phenomenon and an integral part of the larger social process that constitutes the fertility transition.

Most social scientists suffer from a strong attraction to almost pure theories of socioeconomic determination, with no ideational component. It is, after all, their craft. They welcomed the discovery made by the world's first major household fertility investigation, the 1941 Indianapolis Survey, that there were in American society marked fertility differentials by social status, while psychosocial measures had little explanatory power. Yet, as in the case of other social change, the truth is almost certainly not only that social and behavioural change with regard to fertility control led to ideologies justifying that control, but that the ideologies, as they crystallized, reinforced and shaped the tendencies towards control (Caldwell 1994). Cleland (1985) wrote of the importance of aspirations and ideas regarding fertility control and saw evidence of this in the World Fertility Survey data.

The nineteenth century fertility decline in the West inevitably found its champions and theorists, and there is a direct descent from them to the twentieth century family planning movement and the growth of the discipline of demography. It was inevitable, too, that theories which explained fertility control should foresee its spread, and the need for that spread, especially when population growth accelerated. Technical aid programmes in the Third World after World War II, carried out in a context of the Cold War and burgeoning population growth, and by societies influenced by the American New Deal of the 1930s or the erection of social welfare states in Europe from the late 1940s, were destined sooner or later to add a family planning component to such other mainstream programmes as health, agriculture and education (Caldwell and Caldwell 1986). Certainly the process was accelerated by the advancement of demographic theory at Princeton's Office of Population

Research during World War II and by Frank Notestein's high profile in policy circles, by John D. Rockefeller 3rd's promotion of the cause and the establishment of the Population Council, by the activities of the Ford Foundation, and by the growth of demographic studies. But there was no possibility that rapid post-war population growth in the developing world would have continued indefinitely without the contrast between low population growth rates and high per capita incomes in the First World and high population growth rates and poverty in the Third World being noted, given explanatory power, and ultimately influencing governmental and aid policies.

These policies were promoted at a particular time in the world's history. The vast economic growth of the second half of the twentieth century and the resulting creation of a global economy led to an equally important transformation, the movement towards a global society. This was largely the product of the spread of mass education, a huge increase in the global media—print, radio and now satellite and cable television—and the greater movement of people. The arguments that small families have social and economic advantages and that rapidly growing populations press upon resources are now known not only to the élites of the world but to the great majority of ordinary men and women. Furthermore, the élites and governments know what their regional neighbours are doing. Nothing else will fully explain the degree of regional homogeneity in population trends and policies. It is these global and regional parallels in fertility trends which make any attempt to analyse the factors leading to fertility decline in a single country, while ignoring the larger picture, so self-defeating. And the social and ideational change did not exist in a sphere of its own. It was driven directly by a reaction to accelerating population growth and hence, ultimately, by declining death rates, and it also interacted with unprecedented economic growth.

Neither population policies nor national family planning programmes met equal acceptance or success everywhere. In hindsight it is now apparent that, given their per capita income levels, the policies were more warmly embraced and the pro-grammes achieved earlier and with greater success than might have been predicted in an arc of countries from India through Bangladesh to Southeast Asia and up East Asia to China and South Korea (Caldwell 1993; Leete and Alam 1993). The reasons seem to be: a tradition of national élites providing not only political but moral leadership; dense populations and their consequences on land–man ratio, high unemployment and underemployment; and, in many, but not all of those settings, an absence of religious or cultural traditions strongly opposed to either birth control or artificial contraceptives.

A good test of these propositions is provided by the experience of Bangladesh, the poorest country in this arc of Asian countries with fertility decline, and indeed the poorest country in the world with declining fertility. In Bangladesh, sustained fertility decline was apparently catalysed by the activities of a national family planning programme. Furthermore, the causes of fertility decline in Bangladesh have recently been analysed in a World Bank report (Cleland *et al.* 1994). In addition, the authors of the present paper have had direct experience of population policies and programmes and their effects in Pakistan during the 1960s, and of the institution of a research programme to investigate the onset of fertility decline in one of the areas in Bangladesh in which that onset had been longest delayed, Mirsarai *thana* in Chittagong district on the eastern border of the country.[1] Chittagong division, of which Chittagong district is part, has the lowest contraceptive prevalence and highest total fertility rate in Bangladesh.

Bangladesh also has other claims to interest. It has no ancient national élite identifying with the country—one of the preconditions for declining fertility (Caldwell 1993). The pre-1947 élite was largely Hindu in composition: most of its members left the country at or during the years following partition from India, and those remaining are no longer part of the national leadership. Bangladesh and Indonesia are the only predominantly Muslim countries in the arc from India to Korea, and village Muslim clerics have been identified as often having doubts as to whether the control of family numbers was good Islamic behaviour.

Before examining the explanation for Bangladesh's fertility decline put forward in the World Bank report, we shall pause to place that decline in perspective. This is helped by an unusual number of World Fertility, Contraceptive Prevalence and Demographic Health Surveys, decennial censuses and an analysis of trends by the US National Academy of Sciences (1979). When taken together—and ignoring some apparently spurious indications of steeper fertility decline in retrospective reports—these sources appear to show a total fertility rate of 7.0 until at least the mid-1970s, and possibly the late 1970s, thereafter declining moderately until about 1985, and subsequently more steeply to a level perhaps as low as 3.4 in 1993–94 (Cleland and Streatfield 1992: 12ff.; Cleland *et al.* 1994: 10ff., 56–7; Haider *et al.* 1995: 10; National Academy of Sciences 1979).[2] At the same time, and largely providing the mechanism for controlling births—for changing age at marriage

[1] The main fieldwork was delayed because of the prevailing political situation in Bangladesh during the first quarter of 1996. The study is part of a collaborative research programme between the Health Transition Centre, Australian National University, and the Extension Project (Rural), International Centre for Diarrhoeal Disease Research, Bangladesh, funded by the Rockefeller Foundation. Principal Investigators are Barkat-e-Khuda, Shameem Ahmed, John Caldwell and Pat Caldwell; Research Co-ordinator is Indrani Pieris. This paper is based on preliminary and training fieldwork, carried out especially by Bruce Caldwell and Indrani Pieris, on preliminary experimental fieldwork, on focus groups, and on archival and other documentary research by the authors. The paper has benefited from: insights from Syed Shamim Ahsan; the Bangladesh field experience of Barkat-e-Khuda; a 1969 interview by John Caldwell with President Ayub Khan; a 1968–69 research project by the Caldwells on leadership in Third World family planning programmes, which included West and East Pakistan; the Impact Survey and the Comilla family planning project (funded by the Population Council); and a 1986 project on the effect of Ford Foundation and other expenditure on Third World family planning (funded by the Ford Foundation). The latter projects are reported in Caldwell and Caldwell (1986). The paper also benefits from interviews conducted by the Caldwells with Indian Administrative Service officers since 1963.

[2] Das Gupta and Narayana (1996) cast doubt on this description of the fertility decline, pointing out that the earlier figures were very substantially adjusted upward, while the later ones were not. However, the earlier high levels of fertility and the recent much lower levels receive support from the Matlab Demographic Surveillance System and from early research around Comilla (Stoeckel and Chowdhury 1973).

played little part—contraceptive prevalence rose from 4 per cent in 1970 to 45 per cent in 1993–94. A halving of the birth rate over 15 years certainly suggests that there is something to explain.

The Explanation for Fertility Decline Offered by the 1994 World Bank Report

The argument in the report is fundamentally the Cleland thesis, documented and focused through a series of publications. Cleland and Wilson (1987) treat both historical and contemporary societies, concluding that 'the key to the control of family size has been ideas concerning the means of fertility reduction, rather than ideas that provide the motive' (p. 29). Cleland and Streatfield (1992) gave considerable emphasis to necessary preceding demographic and social change, but concluded that by the 1970s, '[a]ll that was now required for fertility decline was a program that would legitimate the idea of birth control and make the means accessible', adding '[p]opulation theorists typically underestimate the magnitude of this task' (p. 20). Shah and Cleland (1993) compared Bangladesh, Nepal and Pakistan, concluding that, although long-term change required structural and attitudinal changes in the society, '[i]n the short-term, governmental attitudes and programs may be a crucial influence on the climate of opinion and acceptance of the new outlook implied by family planning' (p. 207).

The World Bank report (Cleland *et al.* 1994) is an important and insightful work. It rightly gives a major place to government actions in moving the onset of fertility decline forward in time and in steepening that decline. It opens the way to making government policies and programmes part of a sociologically based demographic transition theory. It is full of concessions to underlying longer-term social and economic forces. It is a subtle document. Yet, we have two sets of problems with it.

The first is a tendency to credit the national family planning programme with nearly all responsibility for fertility decline, as is brought out most clearly by a summarizing document published the year before the report by the Population Reference Bureau (Carty *et al.* 1993), presumably with the agreement of the report's authors. This bulletin has undoubtedly had a far greater readership than the report. It states boldly what appear to be the report's central themes, without its protective afterthoughts and qualifications. The authors identify two key points:

- 'the critical importance of sustained political commitment to an effective family planning program, adopted and pursued at the highest levels of government', and
- 'the necessity of adapting service delivery to cultural realities, which, in Bangladesh, include a patriarchal system with limited female mobility' (pp. 3–4).

The authors get to the nub of the issue in concluding that Bangladesh challenges the conventional wisdom that fertility will fall only when there are shifts in the social or economic structure (p. 5). The bulletin concludes in its summary: 'In the absence of other compelling explanations, analysis of Bangladesh's recent fertility reduction must focus on the government's unremitting commitment to the family planning program as the key to its success.' (p. 16.) They then point to the ingredients of this successful package, including some doubtful assertions, such as that rural women travel to the market and become acquainted with contraception, for 'every market has outlets where contraceptives are advertized and sold at subsidized prices', and that family planning workers take their message not only to young wives but also to their husbands. The World Bank report itself states, although it is apparently refer- ring only to the period of the fertility decline and not to the longer period:

The crucial change that has taken place concerns acceptability of and access to birth control and not structural change that has driven down the demand for children. Economic and social change, with concomitant shifts in ideas and outlook, may have been an important facilitating factor, just as contraceptive availability is seen as a facilitating factor in demand theories.   (Cleland *et al.* 1994: 134.)

The major stress is on shifts in ideas and outlook. There is an extraordinary unwillingness in both Cleland and Streatfield (1992) and Cleland *et al.* (1994) to give sufficient attention to very significant rises in the level of female education, as is demonstrated by the fact that little space or statistical information is devoted to the issue, and by the fact that this increase is at other times blurred into discussions of literacy or child labour. Yet, between 1973 and 1992, primary school enrolment more than doubled for girls—from 2,698,000 female children to 6,245,000—and girls' secondary enrolment increased threefold (Khuda and Hossain 1996: 6). Moreover, primary school enrolment of girls as a proportion of the age group increased from 35 per cent in 1970 to 71 per cent in 1992 (World Bank 1995).

Our second set of problems lies in the fact that the report's analysis is carried out from a standpoint that makes its contribution to demographic transition theory much less than might at first be implied (admittedly the authors may not be aiming at such a contribution, but this is unclear). There are at least four reasons for this.

- The report treats the Bangladesh fertility decline almost as *sui generis*. Activi- ties within Bangladesh are taken as the sole cause of fertility decline, while the truth is that such a decline would have been most unlikely indeed if it had not been part of a global movement with global explanations.
- Partly as a result, the report, in contrast with what would be required from any plausible demographic transition theory, takes the fertility control attitudes of government and the élites as a given, and addresses only the position of the mass of the people.
- The report places itself outside the sphere of social enquiry by employing, sometimes explicitly and sometimes less so, an Easterlin framework

(Easterlin 1975). The Easterlin framework meets the needs of family planning programmes by treating as costs not only monetary costs but religious and ethical views, social structures and aesthetic attitudes to coitus. But any study of historical change that greeted social trends as an increase or reduction in costs from the point of view of any social engineering programme would be untenable. The attempt by Bulatao *et al.* (1983) to achieve both objectives clearly failed.

- In order to demonstrate the prime role of the national family planning programme, the report consistently plays down the substantial social change that has taken place in Bangladesh. It often does this by pointing only to economic change, as if this is the sole form of socioeconomic change. Yet there have been substantial changes not just in female education (Khuda and Barkat 1992) but also in women's mobility and in their limited economic activity, associated most strikingly with the garment industry but also with the involvement of women in NGO-sponsored activities.

The report has been subject to criticism from other stances, notably Das Gupta and Narayana (1996), who presented data to show that Bangladesh's socioeconomic, family planning and demographic trends were not unique but were similar over time to such Indian states as Madhya Pradesh and Uttar Pradesh, and possibly Bihar, states with experiences often used to characterize the family planning programme there as near-failures. From our point of view, the value of the Das Gupta and Narayana paper is its demonstration that these fertility transitions are explained not only by local events but very largely by happenings on a much larger scale.

We shall now attempt, through an effort to reconstruct the history and nature of the Bangladesh fertility transition, to show how this global phenomenon impinged on Bangladesh.

Revisiting the Bangladesh Fertility Transition

As noted above, the attitudes and practices of political leaders and social élites are an important element in demographic transition, and cannot be taken as a given. Over the long run they may not be as important in determining fertility transition as mortality decline or economic change, but in the perspective of the last few decades they are an essential element in explaining the establishment of the Asian fertility programmes, and the fact that only a few years span the period covering the onset of the various Asian fertility declines, despite substantial differences in social and economic indices.

Ideas about curbing population growth began to form long ago when Bangladesh was part of British India, which in turn, at least for the élites, was part of the English-speaking world. Even in the nineteenth century, much of that world was Malthusian, in that it suspected that densely populated lands would not benefit from rapid population growth, and that such growth was the cause of periodic famine. Malthus's message of self-restraint and moderation appealed to one strain in the Protestant makeup of Britain and the United States, as it was later to do to Hindu and Confucianist elements in Asia.

Malthus (1959 [1798]) was himself a product of the dawn of the European fertility transition, deeply conscious of the effect of delayed female marriage on Western Europe's population growth-rate, aware—even if disapproving—that forms of birth control were already being used, and convinced that India and China faced potentially disastrous population problems (Malthus 1959: 46). Most of his working life was spent teaching economics and population theory at the East India Company's training school for young Britons going out to rule India. The British officials in India, and with time their growing number of Indian colleagues, appeared to take the Malthusian diagnosis for granted. The introductions to the census volumes do so from their beginning in the 1880s, and the 1911 volume sought statistical proof of a Malthusian situation in Bengal and other parts of India. The very influential Bhore Report (Government of India 1946) on health (which advocated government intervention in family planning) and the Casey Report (Government of India 1945) on the 1944 Bengal famine (mostly located in present-day Bangladesh)—the two reports which together with the preliminary results of the 1951 census led to India's 1952 decision to create the world's first national family planning programme—had Malthusian elements and were deeply conscious of the pressure of population growth on resources. There was little in Hinduism, as there was little in Confucianism, at odds with family planning, and clearly it was preferable to infanticide, which had a long history in both India and China. The important point is that the pre-Independence Indian Civil Service, and most of the non-British officers, were deeply imbued with a Malthusian outlook, and this carried over into the public services of India and Pakistan (and eventually Bangladesh). There were few problems of conscience, and much support among higher ranks of government officials, when India opted for a national family planning programme in 1952 (in 1952, Nehru had the 1944 Bengal famine in mind), and Pakistan, in 1956. This support continued in Bangladesh when it started its own family planning programme after independence in 1971.

During the next four decades, that support was to intensify, most clearly in Bangladesh and India. It might not have done so if these officials had found themselves out of step with the rest of the world, but, as time passed, they found themselves supported by the existence of other national family planning programmes in Asia, and by increasing interest in this field, first from American foundations and subsequently from the international agencies. Two forces stand out clearly in the memories of senior public servants: the increasing belief in the world's media of the existence of a population problem; and the same beliefs encountered when they took higher degrees or shorter training or familiarization courses overseas. This was especially true when these courses took place, as most did, in English-speaking countries, or in Scandinavia or the Netherlands. In terms of the media, university education and technical aid, the world was a unit as never before. Because the subject no longer had to be discussed surreptitiously, as had been the case in an older Europe, it no longer encountered the same language barriers as the Princeton project had identified there (Coale and Watkins 1986), although language and culture areas were by no means insignificant (Caldwell 1966: 164–8 on Africa).

The international and national identification of a population problem was important, as the need to control population became embedded in the views of lower-level bureaucrats, the élite generally—including such opinion-makers as newspaper editors (Khuda *et al.* 1994)—and, finally, the great mass of the people. Recent studies in Bangladesh have shown almost all officials and 80–90 per cent of the ordinary people believing that there is a population crisis (Khuda *et al.* 1992: 35). What should be noted is just how Malthusian the argument in South Asia has been.

In the 1960s, Ayub Khan saw the need for family planning mostly as a race between food production and population growth, and he stressed this theme in his communications with the administration of East Pakistan. In present-day Bangladesh villagers explain the need for family planning in terms of the increasing problems of feeding the nation as well as their own families, and of the problem of increasing land subdivision, with its implications for both food and employment. It is impossible to overestimate the role of population ideologies in driving South Asia's family planning programmes and, indeed, in explaining the near-simultaneity of the establishment of family planning programmes around the Third World and the onset of fertility decline in very different economic and social circumstances only a few years apart.

Other and more specific messages came to the Bangladeshi administrative élite. From 1952 in India, and from the 1955–60 First Five-Year Development Plan in Pakistan, population control became the established policy of the government. In the 1960s, President Ayub Khan made it even clearer that population control was the policy of the country. In 1959 Pakistan, with the help of USAID and the Ford Foundation, had set up administrative training colleges, as India had done, in Peshawar and Comilla (the former was the less successful) to train recruits to the administrative division (separately recruited and organized, as in the British Civil Service) of the public service in rural development.

Until 1971, all recruits into the senior ranks of the Pakistan public service were sent for training to the Civil Service Training College in Lahore, where, among other themes, they were taught the need to control population growth. Then the East Pakistanis among them (like the Bangladesh public servants after 1971) were sent for further rural development training to the Academy of Rural Development (ARD, later BARD) at Comilla, where, from 1960, the first director, Dr Akhtar Hameed Khan, trained every new cohort of recruits to the administrative level of the East Pakistan public service in family planning. And from 1961 on, the Academy developed a family planning component to its development projects (Stoeckel and Chowdhury 1973: 1–8). Not only were the administrative and other urban élites converted to population control, but their numbers increased after 1971 in a way that occurred under neither the British nor the Pakistanis (Hartmann and Boyce 1983: 269–70).

Nevertheless, to a greater extent in Bangladesh than in India, and to a much greater extent than in Pakistan, another factor played a role—a factor that goes far toward explaining why there has been no political opposition to Bangladesh's family planning programme, and why even Marxist or Islamic opposition has at the most been extremely half-hearted. This is that Bangladesh, an almost entirely deltaic country with the world's highest rural population density, seems so obviously the classic example of Malthusian pressures (even though mortality is in fact now falling consistently). This interpretation does not come unless bidden by theories and ideologies. Past observers of similar population densities and high production per unit (although much lower densities than now, still relative to neighbouring areas very high) marvelled at such fruitfulness (Hartmann and Boyce 1983: 11 on 'Golden Bengal', citing Ibn Battuta, the fourteenth century Arab traveller). In contrast, a 1990 study of both urban and rural community leaders showed that 96 per cent considered population to be a national problem, and 94 per cent supported the family planning programme (Khuda *et al.* 1992: 35). The succeeding image of population outstripping the food supply, although not statistically a correct picture of modern Bangladesh, was given additional emphasis by the 1974 flood and the ensuing famine. Bangladeshis also increasingly thought of population outstripping land, as subdivision for inheritance left sons with too little land to support them.

This was the context in which a national family planning programme was planned and implemented, first in the 1955–59 Pakistan First Five-Year Plan and then more forcibly by Ayub Khan in the Second and Third Plans during the 1960s. This early family planning activity is now regarded as largely a failure, partly because the 1969 Impact Survey found lower contracepting levels than the service statistics had indicated (Huber and Khan 1979: 246). The survey may have understated the situation, for Green (1969) analysed the East Pakistani data to suggest that attitudes of traditional respectability led to women understating their contraceptive practice by 26–35 per cent, and men doing so by 13–22 per cent. Certainly, at the time, some of the world's highest levels of vasectomy were reported from East Pakistan.

In any case, it was this programme—receiving assistance in its design and implementation from the Population Council, Sweden and the University of California—that nurtured the future leaders of the Bangladesh programme, and which accumulated experience of what a family planning programme would have to do to be successful. The government official directing the programme, Enver Adil (1966: 128), was able at a 1965 conference to outline measures that from 1977 on ICDDR,B—and subsequently the Bangladesh government—was to adopt: separate female family planning workers, preferably drawn from the village where they worked, individual motivation, and a rural emphasis. It was probably also true that, while radio was extensively employed, it was used more to spread the message about the availability of contraception than to provide an ethic justifying its use.

The family planning programme, like many other development programmes, was temporarily eclipsed during the 1971 War of Liberation from Pakistan and the political infighting of the next three years. Although the Awami League Government of 1972–75 dismissed thousands of public servants for alleged wartime collaboration, and the Zia administration brought military officers into the higher ranks of the public service (Ahmed 1985: 39; Haque 1985: 6), the service retained many of its pre-war and pre-partition characteristics. Indeed the administrators, during subsequent decades of political instability, tended to take the view that they were a more continuing and stable force than politicians, and that, anyway, development programmes were technical in nature and hence predominantly their concern (Rahman 1989: 127). This view was strengthened by the arrival in early 1972 of United Nations Development Programme personnel, followed by the World Bank and the American foundations, all fostering plans and offering funding for family planning, and all talking more to civil servants than to politicians.

The result was that family planning was given emphasis in the 1975–80 First Five-Year Plan of Bangladesh and greater emphasis still—with World Bank and other powerful support—in all subsequent plans. Fertility probably began to fall from the second half of the 1970s but did so more steeply from about 1985. This may have owed much to the efficiency of the programme and to the impact of female family planning workers at the household level (Mita and Simmons 1995; Simmons *et al.* 1988), but there were probably many other elements: a pre-existing demand, snowballing contraceptive use, as familiarity with contraception increased in society; ideational shifts; and social and economic change. These are matters that we will now address.

Pre-transitional Society and its Erosion

In the decades immediately before fertility decline, society does not appear to have favoured high fertility but, rather, thought it to be inevitable. In a 1975 village study, Hartmann and Boyce (1983: 115ff.) found that '[m]ost of the older women were tired of having children and dreaded the thought of another pregnancy'. Both men and women worried about feeding large families and about their implications for further land division. Most women with several children felt that every extra pregnancy, birth and period of breastfeeding drained their strength. This is not surprising, given that the international fertility surveys of the 1970s and 1980s showed Bangladeshi women to have the longest average breastfeeding periods in the world, averaging three years and usually not terminating until well into the next pregnancy, presumably a testimony to food shortage and the value of mother's milk. A similar situation—where fertility would have been controlled if there had been the means—had been reported the previous year in another rural anthropological study (Arens and van Beurden 1977: 67–8). A village survey carried out as early as 1960 had arrived at a similar conclusion (Zaidi 1961: 82). By 1985, a national survey could report that most married women over 30 years of age wanted no more children (Khuda and Howlader 1990: 106).

There seems little doubt that this desire for only moderate fertility has existed for at least the last 35 years. Why, then, were methods for controlling fertility not worked out? Or was the situation relatively new, and, if so, was it the product of demographic or socioeconomic change? Or, even in the 1960s, was the cause ideational, as the first attempts to propagate family planning were encountered? Why did research in the 1970s appear to indicate that high fertility was economically rational?

Third World research seems to show that the last generation to pass through their reproductive years before the advent of family planning programmes are still incredulous that anyone could believe that before access to modern contraception, they could have controlled their fertility (Caldwell and Caldwell 1984: 123). It has been pointed out that this is in contrast to the situation in historic Europe, where marital fertility was constrained in France from the late eighteenth century—and more widely elsewhere in the nineteenth century—by the practice of *coitus interruptus* and other methods of 'natural' contraception (Demeny 1988: 458–9; van de Walle and Muhsam 1995; Weir 1994). It appears that Europe learnt these methods over a long period, during which children were becoming an increasing burden (Caldwell 1994). Sauvy (1969: 362) has even argued that it required the licentious way of life of the aristocracy of the *ancien régime* for such methods to evolve. Bangladesh was typical of the contemporary Third World. Adil (1966: 129) reported on a study of an East Pakistan village in the early 1960s showing that no one believed fertility could be controlled. And Hartmann and Boyce (1983: 225–6) interpreted the situation in a 1975 Bangladesh village:

The recognition of alternatives is one of the first steps towards overcoming fatalism. For instance, when the villagers learnt that birth control was possible, many readily shed the belief that only Allah controls reproduction. The obstacle quickly became the failure of the government services to reach the poor, rather than so-called peasant conservatism.

The above evidence suggests that Bengalis did not have centuries or even generations to learn how to control fertility. Cleland *et al.* (1994: 61) plausibly argue that mortality was so high at the beginning of the present century that most parents, even with uncontrolled fertility, were lucky to reach old age with two surviving sons and one daughter—the Bengali minimum for meeting security needs and social obligations (Bairagi and Langsten 1986; Muhuri and Preston 1991). These same authors are on less sure ground when they concede that infant and child mortality declined steeply in the late 1980s, but regard this as being too late to have played a significant role in the fertility decline (Cleland *et al.* 1994: 61). It might be noted that most of the fertility decline has taken place since 1985, and that contraceptive acceptance may well be strongly affected by parents' impressions of the current level of child mortality risk.

The Passing of Traditional Society

Bengali society has been eroding, or at least changing, for a long while. Traditional Bengali Muslim rural society itself is the product of the last few centuries, replacing a Hindu society that was probably dissimilar to modern, mainstream, largely urban Hinduism. Nevertheless, we shall concentrate here on largely illiterate, village-based society, in which the Muslims received moral leadership from the *imams* and teachers in Koranic schools (*madrassahs*).

This traditional society has long been under assault. There has been a leavening educated minority, not wholly urban, for at least a century. Some of it has been oriented toward the English-speaking world. There was a tremendous growth of private, fee-paying, mostly English-medium, tertiary-level colleges in Bengal in the nineteenth century, a surprising number being in East Bengal. Feeding into them were secondary schools: 3,000 in all of India, and nearly half of these in Bengal (Ahmad 1992: 123–5). Although the majority of students were Hindus, educated persons of any religious persuasion helped in all kinds of ways to weaken traditional society.

Villages in Bangladesh are geographically almost indefinable. Compounds of households or *baris* stretch across the countryside, often forming nucleated groups above flood level. Researchers have found village boundaries to be 'elusive' (Adnan 1990: 35). Politically, this is even more the case. The *panchayat* form of village government, already decaying under the Moghuls, was destroyed by the East India Company's Permanent Settlement Act of 1793 which created the *zamindars*, equivalent to large land owners, who collected taxes and were encouraged to keep law and order. Later British legislation established the *union* as the smallest administrative unit (Barman 1989: 100ff.).

Apart from planned changes during the Zia administration of the late 1970s, the village has never since been a political entity. All that was left was a kind of village court, which dealt mostly with moral matters such as sexual and religious indiscretions (Adnan 1993: 293–4). The British Acts created a system of top-down administration, which has not differed greatly between British, Pakistani and Bangladeshi administrations (Rahman 1989: 127ff.). It has meant rule by bureaucrats, with political factions in the countryside aiming to secure for their villages the maximum gain from each new government programme, rather than changing or challenging the programme itself.

Demeny (1975) and Arthur and McNicoll (1978) believed that rather in the spirit of Alma Ata, neither family planning programmes nor local government in other fields could work efficiently without grassroots power and mobilization. In fact, the top-down system has furthered family planning fairly effectively in Bangladesh, though it may be responsible for quality-of-service concerns such as poor client counselling on side effects that have contributed to worryingly high contraceptive discontinuation rates. Askew and Khan (1990) have concluded that it is precisely this type of administrative system that has allowed the Asian governmental élites to implement such successful family planning programmes. The villages have also lost their role as bastions of traditional culture because successive political crises, especially the 1971 elections and the subsequent independence war, have politicized them along national lines.

The real bastion of tradition has probably been the conservative interpretation of religion by local Muslim religious leaders, although it might be noted that most such leaders in rural areas are self-selected, little educated and not very politically or theologically sure of themselves. They are not a priesthood. As village attitudes and reactions to governments change, so do they. Every survey has shown that religion, as interpreted by women, their husbands or their parents-in-law, is almost the only argument against family planning (apart from apprehension about the health effect of contraception or the side effects of specific methods), though the overall impact on contraceptive acceptance of this influence appears to have greatly declined. Amin *et al.* (1995) found that community religiosity is a powerful determinant of the level of family planning acceptance, and suspected that religious meetings, even when there is no mosque, can be 'an influential forum for the dissemination of ideas and the dissemination of values'. Rob (1988: 69) concluded, when comparing two Bangladesh districts, that the higher concentration of religious institutions and schools in one could be the reason for lower levels of family planning. Amin and colleagues (1995: 15) went further:

[T]he effect of community religiosity reported here highlights the importance of cultural factors in shaping the process of fertility decline triggered by family planning programs. It also supports the view that program influence has indeed been responsible for triggering fertility decline in Bangladesh. One would not expect a strong impact of religiosity of the community when fertility change is demand-led. ...

Our experience of Bangladesh suggests a somewhat different interpretation. There has not been aggressive religious leadership, and there are no paramount Muslim figures or institutions in Bangladesh accustomed to making national moral pronouncements. Village religious leadership is respected but not revered. That leadership does not, and has not been in a position to, oppose government collectively, even on moral issues. Most imams were distressed in 1971 at the breakup of Pakistan, which they saw as a Muslim entity, in contrast to their followers, who saw East Pakistan as a Bengali entity. Nationalism won decisively, and the Awami League Government declared Bangladesh to be a secular state. Later governments reintroduced some religious symbolism but not much substance.

The truth seems to be that religion, as elsewhere, supported the ancient *status quo*. To a large extent, religion was the *status quo*. Most village imams interpret religion largely as maintaining the old ways, respecting the patriarchy and ensuring the acceptability of female sexual behaviour. (Thus, the description by Hartmann and Boyce (1983: 89–90) of the madrassah teacher ill-treating his wives gives the impression that he felt that this followed from his position rather than conflicted with it.) The old men also regarded the patriarchal rural family as being almost a religious creation, but as being unstable once they could not provide their sons with land and had to let them seek jobs elsewhere. These elders rightly suspected that a decline in control of their sons would imply some decline in control of their wives too, as the family destabilized, and they regarded both developments as a sign of religious decay. Contraception did not conflict with specific tenets of Islam, but it was startlingly new, brought women's sexual activities into the open, seemed to take from Allah his decision about the ultimate family size, and to question his ability to provide for the future. Inevitably, contraception seemed sinful both to individuals and their religious leaders.

To some extent, there were things that were God's and those that were Caesar's, although this precept should not be taken too far because Allah makes no great distinction here. Much, however, was clearly in the secular realm, including politics. What was needed was an ethic that both justified contraception and firmly placed it in the secular sphere. The government provided that ethic, although not dishonestly, since the bureaucratic élite had long since been converted. Government leaders said that a reduction in the population growth rate was both a national and a personal necessity so that population would not outstrip food production, so that farms would not be made impossibly small, and so that families could educate their children.

The new ethic provided a justification for some, and a rationalization for others, including apparently the individual behaviour of a significant number of imams: a parallel here to the fall in fertility in late nineteenth century Britain among Anglican clergy, at a time when the Church of England's official position was strongly opposed to contraception. The situation is more complex than this, because, at least in this transition period, a surprising number of women who have adopted family planning still believe that they are personally sinning by using a contraceptive method, but have little alternative other than to do so for the future earthly good of their family and themselves: here the Christian parallel of the ordinary person forced to remain a sinner is probably better known to Catholics than Protestants.

Other women, and their husbands, solve the ethical problem by using temporary rather than permanent methods of contraception so that it will ultimately be Allah, rather than themselves, who will be deciding their final family size. This is one reason why temporary methods constitute such a large segment of Bangladeshi family planning, with sterilization accounting for only 10 per cent, and the IUD another 6 per cent.

Parents often took the view that they were restricting family size not for their own benefit but for their children's good, and such unselfish behaviour seemed less sinful. The new ethic was easier for those in the earlier stage of family building to accept than for older women, who had long equated family planning with sin. In the part of our research area—Chittagong division—that had low levels of family planning before a recent intensive programme effort, most women under 35 years of age have accepted contraception, in contrast to the majority of older women who have refused.

We may also speculate on the effect of differences in women's and men's understanding of Islam. To a large degree, the imams belong to the world of men, from which women are secluded by the institution of purdah. Rural women's understanding of Islam—and particularly its implications in terms of fertility behaviour—is influenced by pre-Islamic beliefs. Such beliefs may once have encouraged high fertility, but appear currently to be retreating under the influence of modernization.

The Bangladesh family planning programme has taken no chances with the spread of the new ethic. The Information, Education and Motivation Unit of the Directorate of Family Planning has had information courses for leaders at every level, including imams. In fact, imams have regularly been paid lecture fees for making statements about family planning at the Friday mosque. Since 1975, Radio Bangladesh has assigned 65 minutes daily to population and family planning issues on its national service, and 30 minutes on its regional programmes, while television currently allocates 120 minutes weekly (Haider *et al.* 1995: 67; Khuda *et al.* 1994: 6). The radio sessions are heard throughout the community.

An obvious question is why the family planning programme has been so effective, given the number of research projects demonstrating the degree of security that children provide their parents (Cain 1978, 1981, 1983), and the usefulness of child labour (Cain 1977; Caldwell *et al.* 1984; Khuda 1978, 1988). In terms of security the answer is probably that all the cited research was carried out in Bangladesh during a period of unusual insecurity, only a few years after the 1971 war, shortly after the vast erosion of land caused by the 1974 floods, and during the famine that followed those floods.

In subsequent years, rural security increased, as governments more successfully intervened and as 'food for work' and credit schemes made their appearance. Hydrologically, the 1988 flood was worse than the 1974 one, but few villagers think so. In any case, the most common way that land is lost is to creditors—with an enforceable agreement—or to relatives, especially women's brothers (Jansen 1987: 62ff., 127–31), both circumstances against which children provide little protection. The security value of sons has also declined, with falling land–man ratios as the overall population increases, and with increasing nucleation of households, associated with a declining proportion of the workforce working on family land and new ideas of family relations.

Children's labour is undoubtedly still of value, especially in rural areas. Caldwell *et al.* (1984) showed that this value was greater to the landed and better-off, a situation that Cleland *et al.* (1994: 70–2) believe to be at odds with the insignificant economic differential in family planning. In fact, child labour partly explains the meagre differential, since elsewhere contraceptive use is higher among the better-off, who have greater and more expensive aspirations for their children. Children are still a guarantee in old age, but parents feel that assistance from this source is less certain than it was 20 years ago (Rob 1988: 65). But some parents feel that strict patrilineality, in which only sons are able to give help to sick or aged parents, is part of the old rural system, and that daughters with urban jobs may be able to assist them. Where the poor can use the labour of their children and do not have aspirations to educate them, as among the rickshaw drivers of Dhaka, they are much less receptive to family planning (Siddiqui *et al.* 1990: 235, 174).

Socioeconomic Change

The 1994 World Bank report on Bangladesh (Cleland *et al.* 1994) has been accorded so much interest because it appears to say that very substantial fertility decline can be achieved by an efficient family planning programme in the absence of significant socioeconomic change. The report is not wholly constant on this point. Sometimes it appears to restrict the qualification solely to economic change.

There is a problem here. The respondents in our study in Chittagong division nearly all talk of great changes over the last two decades, and so did the focus groups organized by Duza and Nag (1993: 73–4). Most think their children have opportunities that they lacked. Some of this change is difficult to quantify. Village society is now much more open to the outside world. The 1971 war and ever greater politicization have seen to that. So has public transport. The roads have improved, and the few buses that travelled them before 1971 have since multiplied repeatedly. Most villagers are even more impressed by the vast increase in rural areas of bicycle rickshaws and rickshaw vans, which can take people and their goods between the roads and villages along pathways mostly built in the last 30 years.

Water transport has been revolutionized by the use of motors in the large 'country boats'. These processes have accelerated the monetization of the economy so that there is more selling of crops and subsequent buying of food from the market than used to be the case. The agricultural workforce has ceased to grow, and all new jobs are outside the primary sector, many of them in off-farm rural occupations, which are changing the nature of the villages. Dhaka has grown from a provincial city with a million people to a metropolis of eight million, jammed with traffic. Poverty may have been little mitigated, but life has changed, especially as many of the new jobs are in the informal sector and are often subject to extreme exploitation (Khuda and Alam 1993). All kinds of things have increased much faster than the population. In the decade up to 1986 (when fertility began to fall more steeply), the number of electrified villages multiplied by four, the number of doctors trebled, and the number of nurses increased fivefold. Even tube wells increased by 53 per cent (Khuda and Howlader 1990: 95–6).

The World Bank report seems also to underestimate other quantifiable change. Both it, and the preceding Cleland and Streatfield (1992) report, place very little emphasis on educational change, and treat it as if its only importance is whether or not it alters children's work inputs. In the 13 years from 1973 to 1986, there was a substantial increase in the number of schools. The number of primary school pupils rose by 39 per cent, admittedly not much faster than the total number of children in that age group, and secondary students increased by 50 per cent. Of greater social significance was the rise in the numbers of girls at school: 70 per cent in primary schools, and 61 per cent in secondary schools (Khuda and Barkat 1992; Khuda and Howlader 1990: 95–6).

It is the mothers in Chittagong division, and not only the educated ones, who repeatedly tell interviewers, as did those involved in discussions with Duza and Nag

(1993: 74ff.), that they want their children to become educated, so that they can become part of the new world and seize its opportunities. Parents want their children educated because they cannot offer them sufficient land or agricultural work. Parents also feel that their own futures are bound up with the ability of their children to secure nonfarming employment.

As early as 1975, Hartmann and Boyce (1983: 109–10) were reporting that villagers of a remote village knew that literacy was the key that unlocked the door between their village and the outside world; that although parents worried about the potential moral dangers to girls attending school, many mothers nevertheless wanted their daughters to be educated; and that all parents were aware of the additional expenses they would incur in schooling their children.

This is precisely the situation reported by Caldwell *et al.* (1982) in South India, where farming parents hope education will lead their children to nonfarming jobs, both for the children's own sake and so that parents may have access to nonrural income during agricultural disasters. Furthermore, as the village can no longer easily support deserted or divorced wives, in a society where divorce is fairly common, parents feel that educated girls are more likely to be able to support themselves. But so as to be able to support successive children at school, parents must have a limited number, with substantial gaps between each one. Most Bangladeshi rural respondents speak in similar terms. In addition, education and an urban job can do much more to free a girl from village purdah restrictions than to change a boy's way of life. Even Bangladeshi rural society is now willing to countenance female employment if the women are very poor, or if they are educated and can gain a white-collar position (Rob 1988: 66; White 1992: 84).

Almost certainly, Bangladeshi parents, like South Indian ones, are overoptimistic about schooling leading to such employment. Some of these rising expectations have been taught by the family planning programme itself. Such aspirations to keep children in school fit best with contraception used to achieve long intervals between births, precisely the pattern aimed at in Bangladesh.

Women's ability to earn money and to work outside the house is slowly increasing in Bangladesh. In rural areas, the Bangladesh Rural Advancement Committee (BRAC) and the Grameen Bank lend money to women to start small productive enterprises, like poultry-raising, which does appear to be related to greater contraceptive use (Schuler and Hashemi 1994). But the most significant change in women's economic status is probably attributable to the large numbers of young women going out to work in Dhaka's new garment industries. Typically, these women are young (over 90 per cent under 35 years of age), married (52 per cent currently married, and 18 per cent never married), with children to support (mostly 1–3), uneducated (52 per cent with no schooling at all), and poor (a monthly family income of under Taka 1,500—or US$60—in 1990), and most with rural parents who are either landless or have very little land (Hossain *et al.* 1990, in their examination of women workers in all Dhaka factories, even though females are mostly employed in the garment industry). Most of these women workers live in shanty towns, where poor rural–urban migrants are largely found, and most of the married women practise family planning. Khuda *et al.* (1990) found that Save the Children's SAVE program members' families were significantly more likely to use contraception and had lower fertility—as well as lower infant and child mortality, itself often associated with lower fertility (see also Barkat *et al.* 1994).

The other persistent themes expressed by both the study respondents in Chittagong division and by those participating in other studies are of changes to the family and changes in the practice of family planning. There is evidence of increased nuclear family residence (arising partly from the reduced size of land holdings—but a difficult concept in a land of baris or small houses owned by related people and grouped around a courtyard) of the husband's parents having a lesser role in decision-making (Adnan 1993: 291; Arens and van Beurden 1977: 89–93). In the case of family planning, this change has been accelerated by the fact that women family planning workers go directly to the home of the young wife, even though the mother-in-law is present at most interviews, if only to participate in an event of interest for women that is happening at the house (A. Nosaka, personal communication, 1996).

Duza and Nag (1993: 79) attribute the stronger position of the wife to later age at marriage. Age at marriage among women has risen, on average, from 14 to 17 years over the last 20 years. The operation of the family planning programme, the practice of contraception, and the restriction of family size have undoubtedly all changed the nature of the family and the position of women within it. In summary, it is difficult, and perhaps undesirable, to distinguish between social and economic change. But there have been vast social changes since 1970—all occurring in the context of continuing levels of very great poverty. It would be foolish to underrate the effect of this last factor on family planning acceptance.

References

Adil, E. (1966), 'Pakistan', in B. Berelson *et al.* (eds.), *Family Planning and Population Programs: A Review of World Developments*, Chicago: University of Chicago Press.

Adnan, S. (1990), *Annotation of Village Studies in Bangladesh and West Bengal. A Review of Socio-Economic Trends over 1942–88*, Kothari Comilla: Bangladesh Academy for Rural Development.

—— (1993), 'Birds in a Cage': Institutional Change and Women's Position in Bangladesh', in N. Federici, K. O. Mason and S. Sogner (eds.), *Women's Position and Demographic Change*, Oxford: Clarendon Press.

Ahmad, Z. (1992), 'State and Education', in S. Islam (ed.), *History of Bangladesh, 1704–1971*, Dhaka: Asiatic Society of Bangladesh.

Ahmed, S. G. (1985), 'Public Personnel Administration in Bangladesh: An Overview of its Formal and Informal Operations', in M. M. Khan and S. A. Husain (eds.), *Bangladesh Studies: Politics, Administration, Rural Development and Foreign Policy*, Dhaka: University of Dhaka.

Amin, S., Diamond, I., and Steele, F. (1997), 'Contraception and Religiosity in Bangladesh'.

Arens, J., and van Beurden, J. (1977), *Jhagrapur: Poor Peasants and Women in a Village in Bangladesh*, Birmingham: Third World Publications.

Arthur, W. B., and McNicoll, G. (1978), 'An Analytical Survey of Population and Development in Bangladesh', *Population and Development Review*, 4: 1.

Askew, I., and Khan, A. R. (1990), 'Community Participation in National Family Planning Programs: Some Organizational Issues'. *Studies in Family Planning*, 21: 3.

Bairagi, R., and Langsten, R. L. (1986), 'Sex Preference for Children and Implications for Fertility in Rural Bangladesh'. *Studies in Family Planning*, 17: 6, Pt. 1.

Barkat, A., Khuda, B.-e, and Rahman, A. (1994), *Women's Employment in Nasiragairthana: A Large-Scale Sample Survey*, Dhaka: University Research Corporation.

Barman, D. C. (1989), 'Political Institutions and Processes in a Village in Historical Perspective', in E. Ahamed (ed.), *Society and Politics in Bangladesh*, Dhaka: Academic Publishers.

Bulatao, R. A., Lee, R. D., Hollerbach, P. E., and Bongaarts, J. (1983), *Determinants of Fertility in Developing Countries*, New York: Academic Press.

Cain, M. (1977), 'The Economic Activities of Children in a Village in Bangladesh', *Population and Development Review*, 3: 3.

—— (1978), 'The Household Life Cycle and Economic Mobility in Rural Bangladesh', *Population and Development Review*, 4: 3.

—— (1981), 'Risk and Insurance: Perspectives on Fertility and Agrarian Change in India and Bangladesh', *Population and Development Review*, 7: 3.

—— (1983), 'Fertility as an Adjustment to Risk', *Population and Development Review*, 9: 4.

Caldwell, J. C. (1966), 'Africa', in B. Berelson *et al.* (eds.), *Family Planning and Population Programs: A Review of World Developments*, Chicago: University of Chicago Press.

—— (1993), 'The Asian Fertility Revolution: Its Implications for Transition Theories', in R. Leete and I. Alam (eds.), *The Revolution in Asian Fertility: Dimensions, Causes and Implications*, Oxford: Clarendon Press.

—— (1994), 'The Course and Causes of Fertility Decline', IUSSP Distinguished Lecture, International Conference on Population and Development, September 1994, Cairo.

—— and Caldwell, P. (1984), 'The Family Planning Programme at the Local Level', in G. W. Jones (ed.), *The Demographic Transition in Asia*, Singapore: Maruzen Asia.

—— and Caldwell, P. (1986), *Limiting Population Growth, and the Ford Foundation Contribution*, London: Frances Pinter.

—— Reddy, P. H., and Caldwell, P. (1982), 'The Causes of Demographic Change in Rural South India', *Population and Development Review*, 8: 4.

—— Jalaluddin, A. K. M., Caldwell, P., and Cosford, W. (1984), 'The Changing Nature of Family Labour in Rural and Urban Bangladesh: Implications for Fertility Transition', *Canadian Studies in Population*, 11: 2.

Carty, W. P., Yinger, N. V., and Rosov, A. (1993), *Success in a Challenging Environment: Fertility Decline in Bangladesh*, Washington, DC: Population Reference Bureau.

Cleland, J. (1985), 'Marital Fertility Decline in Developing Countries: Theories and Evidence', in J. Cleland and J. Hobcraft (eds.), *Reproductive Change in Developing Countries: Insights from the World Fertility Survey*, New York: Oxford University Press.

—— and Streatfield, K. (1992), *The Demographic Transition: Bangladesh*, Dhaka: UNICEF.

Cleland, J. and Wilson, C. (1987), 'Demand Theories of the Fertility Transition: An Iconoclastic View', *Population Studies*, 41: 1.

—— Phillips, J. F., Amin, S., and Kamal, G. M. (1994), *The Determinants of Reproductive Change in Bangladesh: Success in a Challenging Environment*, Washington DC: World Bank.

Coale, A. J., and Watkins, S. C. (1986), *The Decline of Fertility in Europe*, Princeton: Princeton University Press.

Das Gupta, M., and Narayana, D. (1997), 'Bangladesh's Fertility Decline from a Regional Perspective', *Genus*, 53: 3–4.

Demeny, P. (1975), 'Observations on Population Policy and the Population Program in Bangladesh', *Population and Development Review*, 1: 2.

—— (1988), 'Social Science and Population Policy', *Population and Development Review*, 14: 3.

Duza, M. B., and Nag, M. (1993), 'High Contraceptive Prevalence in Matlab, Bangladesh: Underlying Processes and Implications', in R. Leete and I. Alam (eds.), *The Revolution in Asian Fertility: Dimensions, Causes and Implications*, Oxford: Clarendon Press.

Easterlin, R. A. (1975), 'An Economic Framework for Fertility Analysis', *Studies in Family Planning*, 6: 3.

Government of India (Casey Report) (1945), *Famine Inquiry Commission, Final Report*. Madras: Government Press.

—— (Bhore Report) (1946), *Report of the Health Survey and Development Committee, 2, Recommendations*, Delhi: Government of India Press.

Green, L. W. (1969), 'East Pakistan: Knowledge and use of Contraceptives', *Studies in Family Planning*, 39.

Haider, S. J., Streatfield, K., and Karim, M. A. (1995), *Comprehensive Guidebook to the Bangladesh Family Planning Program*, Dhaka: Population Council.

Haque, A. (1985). 'Politics in Bangladesh: Conflict and Confusion', in M. M. Khan and S. A. Husain (eds.), *Bangladesh Studies: Politics, Administration, Rural Development and Foreign Policy*, Dhaka: University Press.

Hartmann, B., and Boyce, J. C. (1983), *A Quiet Violence: View from a Bangladesh Village*, Dhaka: University Press.

Hossain, H., Jahan, R., and Sobhan, S. (1990), *No Better Option? Industrial Women Workers in Bangladesh*, Dhaka: University Press.

Huber, D. H., and Khan, A. R. (1979), 'Contraceptive Distribution in Bangladesh Villages: The Initial Impact', *Studies in Family Planning*, 10: 8/9.

Jansen, E. G. (1987), *Rural Bangladesh: Competition for Scarce Resources*, Dhaka: University Press.

Khuda, B.-e (1978), 'Labour Utilization in a Village Economy in Bangladesh', Ph.D. thesis, Australian National University, Canberra.

—— (1988), *Rural Development and Change: A Case Study of a Bangladesh Village*, Dhaka: University Press.

—— and Alam, M. M. (1993), *Informal Sector Manufacturing Activities in Dhaka City: Some Empirical Evidence from the Metal Subsector*, Dhaka: Bureau of Economic Research, Dhaka University.

—— and Barkat, A. (1992), *An Impact Study of the Female Education Scholarship Program in Bangladesh*, Dhaka: University Research Corporation.

—— and Hossain, M. B. (1996), 'Fertility Decline in Bangladesh: An Investigation of the Major Factors', ICDDR,B Working Paper No. 48, International Centre for Diarrhoeal Disease Research, Bangladesh, Dhaka.

Khuda, B.-e and Howlader, S. (1990), 'Demand Aspects of Fertility and Family Planning', in M. B. Duza (ed.), *South Asia Study of Population Policy and Programmes: Bangladesh*, Dhaka: UNFPA.

—— Hadi, A., and Barkat, A. (1990), *Women's Savings Groups and Contraceptive Use under the SAVE Program*, Dhaka: University Research Corporation.

—— Barkat, A., Helali, J., Shahzadi, N., Akhter, R., and Mannan, M. A. (1992), *Literature Review for the Development of the National FP-MCH IEC Strategy, Bangladesh*, Dhaka: University Research Corporation.

—— Barkat, A., Robey, B., Mannam, M. A., Helali, J., Sultana, A., and Salam, S. A. (1994), *Bangladesh Journalists Reporting on Population and Family Planning: Study Results*, Baltimore: Center for Communication Programs, Johns Hopkins School of Public Health.

Leete, R., and Alam, I. (eds.) (1993), *The Revolution in Asian Fertility: Dimensions, Causes and Implications*, Oxford: Clarendon Press.

Malthus, T. R. (1959 [1798]), *Population: The First Essay*, Ann Arbor: University of Michigan Press.

Mita, R., and Simmons, R. (1995), 'Diffusion of the Culture of Contraception: Program Effects on Young Women in Bangladesh', *Studies in Family Planning*, 26: 1.

Muhuri, P. K., and Preston, S. H. (1991), 'Mortality Differentials by Sex in Bangladesh', *Population and Development Review*, 17: 3.

National Academy of Sciences (1979), *Estimation of Recent Trends in Fertility and Mortality in Bangladesh*, Washington, DC.

Rahman, A. H. M. A. (1989), 'Politico-administrative Relationships in Development', in E. Ahamed (ed.), *Society and Politics in Bangladesh*, Dhaka: Academic Publishers.

Rob, A. K. U. (1988), 'Community Characteristics, Leaders, Fertility and Contraception in Bangladesh', *Asia-Pacific Population Journal*, 3: 2.

Robinson, W. C., and Rachapaetayakom, J. (1993), 'The Role of Government Planning in Thailand's Fertility Decline', in R. Leete and I. Alam (eds.), *The Revolution in Asian Fertility: Dimensions, Causes and Implications*, Oxford: Clarendon Press.

Sauvy, A. (1969), *General Theory of Population*, London: Weidenfeld and Nicolson.

Schuler, S. R. and Hashemi, S. M. (1994), 'Credit Programs, Women's Empowerment and Contraceptive Use in Rural Bangladesh', *Studies in Family Planning*, 25: 2.

Shah, I. H., and Cleland, J. G. (1993), 'High Fertility in Bangladesh, Nepal and Pakistan: Motives vs Means', in R. Leete and I. Alam (eds.), *The Revolution in Asian Fertility: Dimensions, Causes and Implications*, Oxford: Clarendon Press.

Siddiqui, K., Qadir, S. R., Alamgir, S., and Huq, S. (1990), *Social Formation in Dhaka City: A Study in Third World Urban Sociology*, Dhaka: University Press.

Simmons, R., Bagee, L., Koenig, M. A., and Phillips, J. F. (1988), 'Beyond Supply: The Importance of Female Family Planning Workers in Rural Bangladesh', *Studies in Family Planning*, 19: 1.

Stoeckel, J., and Chowdhury, M. A. (1973), *Fertility, Infant Mortality and Family Planning in Rural Bangladesh*, Dhaka: Oxford University Press.

Van de Walle, E., and Muhsam, H. (1995), 'Fatal Secrets and the French Fertility Transition', *Population and Development Review*, 21: 2.

Weir, D. R. (1994), 'New Estimates of Nuptiality and Marital Fertility in France, 1740–1911', *Population Studies*, 48: 2.

White, S. C. (1992), *Arguing with the Crocodile: Gender and Class in Bangladesh*, Dhaka: University Press.

World Bank (1995), *World Development Report 1995*, New York: Oxford University Press.

Zaidi, W. (1961), *A Survey of the Attitude of Rural Population towards Family Planning*, Pakistan Academy for Rural Development.

18 Population Policy Implications of the 1994 International Conference on Population and Development (ICPD)

ANRUDH JAIN

Background

With greater or lesser clarity and emphasis, two major themes, or rationales—the individual's right to control his/her fertility, and a nation's interest in regulating its rate of population growth—have guided the evolution of population policies and family planning programmes in developing countries (see Dixon-Mueller (1993) for a detailed discussion and historical account of these two themes). The dilemma posed by the conjunction of these two themes is that the means adopted to reduce the rate of population growth are not always consistent with individual well-being, while, obversely, there is scepticism that efforts guided by concern for the well-being of individuals may not solve the aggregate problem of rapid population growth.[1] Indeed, the conflict in some cases has appeared to become more explicit, even while, paradoxically, an increasing proportion of individuals are seeking to regulate their fertility voluntarily.

This paper is not about demographers. Neither is it about demographic research, nor about research findings on a particular population issue. Rather, it is about public policies and programmes designed especially to address population issues. Admittedly, demographers and demographic research focus upon wide-ranging issues related to the characteristics of human populations. Similarly, public policies also focus on improving various facets of people's lives. Nevertheless, a reduction in population growth in developing countries has become the main population issue that has been the focus of most public policies labelled as 'population' policies around the world. Interest in reducing population growth can be said to go as far back as Thomas Malthus; but a global interest in simply doing something about

---

This chapter draws heavily from work done by the author on a project on population policies in four developing countries (Jain 1995, 1998).

[1] For example, the Taichung experiment in Taiwan was started in the early 1960s with the purpose of delivering contraceptive services and information to those who wanted them (Freedman and Takeshita 1969). The approach was criticized then. There was scepticism as to whether efforts focused solely on satisfying individual desires could solve the aggregate problem. Davis (1967) argued that population policies should include strategies to reduce people's desired family size by altering institutional arrangements. (For a recent articulation of similar reasoning, see Pritchett (1994) and McNicoll (1997).)

rapid population growth in developing countries is of relatively recent origin. India was the first developing country to take note in 1952 of the adverse consequences of rapid population growth for its socioeconomic development.

While some have always argued against government involvement in population matters, that position is now generally moot because most developing countries already have well-developed policies in this area, and these policies often take the form of government interventions to reduce rapid growth.

Population policy as a statement of government intention must be distinguished from population policy operationalized through government actions. While a population policy that states a government's intentions to reduce its country's population growth or stabilize its population size is an important first step, such declarations tend to be fairly benign and often ineffective measures, whether or not the stated policy includes time-bound demographic targets.[2] The content of such a population policy would probably require very little public debate, except, perhaps, about the need for and desirability of having time-bound targets.

At the operational (or programme) level, things start getting murky and somewhat more contentious. Before the International Conference on Population and Development (ICPD), held in 1994 in Cairo, population policies in many developing countries were often synonymous with family planning programmes. This was because the only intervention to reduce population growth usually took the form of an organized family planning programme. The actual structure of those programmes, and their success in reducing population growth or the total fertility rate, varied by country, and sometimes between different geographic areas of the same country. However, at the ICPD, arguments were advanced calling for the expansion of the scope of services provided through family planning programmes to incorporate broader reproductive health services. Emphasis was also placed on programmes to improve gender equality in health, education, and economic opportunity. The implementation of such a broader policy would blur the distinction between 'population' and 'development'. The ICPD thus revolutionized to some extent the whole concept of population policy. We are still trying to deal with the implications of that revolution.

The purpose of this paper, therefore, is to examine the need for, and the possible contents of, population policy in the light of the broader recommendations made at ICPD. The paper is divided into four sections. The first describes the situation prior to ICPD, the second considers the main recommendations of ICPD, the third examines the implications of these recommendations for population policies, and the last makes some concluding remarks about the future course of population policies in developing countries.

---

[2] The implementation of a policy with time-bound targets, however, has turned out to be counterproductive in India, because of the unrealistic nature of these targets and the way the policy was implemented.

Population Policy before ICPD

Population Policy and its Rationale

In this paper, policy is defined as a formal statement issued by a government. Such a declaration would usually include a rationale, goals and objectives, and an implementation plan to achieve those objectives. Prior to ICPD, most countries' major population policy goal was usually to reduce the growth rate, and sometimes to achieve better population distribution.[3] The rationale for seeking such an objective was usually expressed in terms of aggregates at different levels. Policy makers claimed that slower population growth would be advantageous both for the planet and for the social and economic development of a particular country.

The definition of a population problem at the global level—in terms of the planet's carrying capacity and the global environment—has long been a useful strategy to attract funds for population activities. However, the definition of the population problem as a global issue of resource depletion also creates a divide between developed and developing countries, because the world is not one unified political unit. The division becomes especially obvious when the debate focuses on the relative impact on the global environment of high per capita consumption in the developed countries as compared to the impact of a large and growing number of people living in developing countries. For example, if in China, which is believed to have solved its population growth problem, per capita consumption were to rise to the same level as in the United States, the adverse implications for the global environment could be enormous.

By rights, therefore, a search for solutions to the global population problem should include not just the achievement of replacement fertility in developing countries, but also goals to achieve an optimal range (and perhaps more equalization) of consumption per capita in both developed and developing countries. The difficulty is that in pursuit of global objectives, effective and appropriate plans must be made for actions to be taken by individuals. This means that population problems must first be defined at the national, community, family, and individual level.

---

[3] According to the Population Policy Data Bank maintained by the UN Population Division, out of 131 developing countries surveyed in 1990, only 69 considered their growth rate to be too high, 17 perceived it to be too low, and 45 perceived it to be satisfactory. These three groups constitute 86, 3, and 12 per cent, respectively, of the people living in developing countries. Of the 69 countries that considered their growth rates to be too high, only 61 have policies and programmes to reduce their growth rates. These 61 countries constitute 82 per cent of the population of the developing countries and 63 per cent of the population of the world (see United Nations 1992: 39).

In terms of fertility, 74 developing countries considered their fertility level to be too high, 9 perceived it to be too low, and 48 perceived it to be satisfactory. These three groups constitute 85, 1, and 14 per cent of the people living in developing countries. Out of the 74 developing countries that considered their fertility to be too high, only 64 have policies and programmes to reduce their fertility rate. These 64 countries constitute 82 per cent of the population of the developing countries and 63 per cent of the world's population (see United Nations 1992: 76).

At the national level, Coale and Hoover (1958) illustrated the negative consequences of rapid population growth for economic development in India and
Mexico. A report prepared in 1986 under the auspices of the National Academy of
Sciences (NAS), however, did not find convincing empirical evidence concerning
the negative consequences of rapid population growth (National Research Council
1986), even though there has been some reassessment of the NAS conclusions since
then. Despite these uncertainties, it is difficult for policy makers to believe that the
sheer size of a country (let us say, Bangladesh or India) does not have adverse
consequences for its ability to address issues of human rights and human well-being
effectively. Most population policies, therefore, were primarily articulated to
address the single issue of rapid population in developing countries.

The Inadequacy of Much Population Policy

Population growth is determined by three components: fertility, mortality, and
migration (internal and international). While a formal population policy statement
may express concern about these dimensions of growth, it rarely specifies means to
modify all three. A typical developing country population policy prior to ICPD
usually specified the means to modify only one component—fertility—and that,
too, through organized family planning programmes. It would neither specify the
means to reduce mortality and morbidity nor deal with internal and international
migration. Measures of this kind were, and continue to be, specified in a country's
health policy, in its urban or rural development policy, or in its immigration policy.
In other words, national policies in health, urban planning, rural development, and
immigration—though each addressing important issues of population growth—
were rarely classified under a country's population policy. Population policy had
concerned itself only with reducing a country's rate of population growth, which, in
the absence of mass international migration and high mortality, can occur only
through fertility reduction.

Fertility is determined by intervening, or proximate, factors and by various background factors (see Davis and Blake 1956). While contraceptive use and fertility are
highly correlated, other important proximate factors include age at marriage,
postpartum infecundability associated with breastfeeding and abstinence, and
abortion (Bongaarts 1978). The background factors that affect a woman's desire for
childbearing and her ability or power to implement these desires include existing
levels of infant and child mortality, female education, employment, and empowerment in general (see Bulatao and Lee 1983). Yet policies and means to influence
these various background factors still tend to be addressed in a country's development and health policies and programmes. Thus, even from a narrow perspective of
fertility reduction, population policies prior to ICPD did not fully take into account
the knowledge created by demographers about fertility determinants (see Mason
(1997) for a recent review of various theories of fertility decline). Instead they

focused on increasing the use of contraception through the organization of family planning programmes.[4] The usual sequence of arguments assumed the following simple path: a family planning programme increases contraceptive use; this, in turn, reduces fertility; which, in turn, reduces the population growth rate.

At the 1974 World Population Conference in Bucharest, developing country delegates emphasized the role of development as 'the best contraceptive'. At the 1984 conference in Mexico, the United States delegates emphasized the role of economic development in slowing the rate of population growth. While many of those involved in these earlier international forums subsequently changed their positions, the emphasis on development as a means to reduce the rate of population growth persisted. Nevertheless, the contents of population policies did not change.

The fact that a country's population problem was generally defined in terms of aggregates has also affected the nature and scope of the family planning programmes implemented to reduce the rate of population growth. Initially, family planning programmes were designed to provide contraceptive information and services to women who wanted to regulate their fertility. These efforts showed promise in raising levels of contraceptive use and reducing unwanted childbearing. Following the initial successes of those family planning programmes, high hopes were placed on their ability to reduce fertility under all circumstances—even under conditions of high desired fertility. With varying degrees of success, the scope of service provision programmes changed over time, and the range of activities included within the family planning programmes of various countries began to vary widely. In some programmes, any approach that successfully reduced fertility—including cash incentives to clients and providers, and even coercion and compulsion—was deemed acceptable. In others, despite public statements expressing interest in government support for family planning, services actually providing contraceptives remained limited. The wide differences in the scope of family planning programmes found from one country to another make it extremely difficult to draw any valid conclusions about the effectiveness of 'voluntary' programmes in reducing fertility (see Jain and Bruce 1994).

In sum, a tendency to equate population policy narrowly with family planning programmes was the result of: an interpretation of population policy as a policy to reduce fertility; use of the label 'family planning programme' to encompass all means to induce fertility decline, ranging from voluntary contraceptive services to community-wide incentives and coercion; and little or no effort made to influence investment patterns in other sectors of development as a means of achieving fertility reduction.

[4] A distinction is made between family planning and family planning programmes. The former refers to actions taken by individuals to plan their families, whereas the latter refers to an organized effort by governmental and non-governmental organizations to provide services and information.

How ICPD Has Changed the Concept of Population Policy

Undoubtedly, a paradigm shift occurred at ICPD. However, there is some confusion about the nature of this shift. Has there been a shift in the overall goal of population policies—away from reducing population growth and ensuring population stabilization and toward improvements in individual well-being? If so, this shift would suggest that certain means cannot legitimately be used to reduce rapid rates of population growth. Rather, the means now to be used for this end must fully respect human rights and must be just in and of themselves. In which case, governments signatory to the ICPD document should not use means to reduce population growth that do not respect human rights. In this sense the paradigm shift includes both a shift in the stated goal—from population stabilization to individual well-being—and a shift in the means used to achieve the intermediary goal of population stabilization. A reduction in population growth and the achievement of population stabilization are now both seen as factors contributing to the improvement of individual well-being. At the programme level, the means rejected by this paradigm shift would include incentives/disincentives, targets, coercion, and compulsion.

The Programme of Action adopted at the Cairo conference is a comprehensive document. However, the main message consists of two elements: provide contraceptive methods within a broader type of reproductive health service; and improve women's equality in education, health, and economic opportunity. These two elements are consonant with the known determinants of both unwanted and wanted fertility. Thus, the provision of contraceptive services within the context of reproductive health is expected to reduce unwanted fertility, and improvements in gender equality are expected to create conditions favourable to smaller families.

However, these two messages are nowhere specifically linked to the reduction of population growth in the Cairo Programme of Action (United Nations 1994). The message about gender equality is imbedded in chapter IV, and the message about family planning and reproductive health, in chapter VII. The issue of population growth is discussed in chapter VI, which does not refer either to chapter IV or to chapter VII—the two chapters which, taken on their own, are sufficient to form the basis of any government action to reduce fertility.

It is not necessary to justify improvements in reproductive health and gender equality on the basis of their effects on population growth. These ends of public policies are justified in and of themselves. For example, paragraph 4.1 states that '[t]he empowerment and autonomy of women and the improvement of their political, social, economic, and health status is a highly important end in itself'. Those interested in women's well-being or social justice would naturally be interested in these elements, irrespective of their effects on population growth. While fertility has declined under the conditions of poor reproductive health and extreme gender disparities, adopting strategies that would help reduce fertility in a more humane way implies the adoption of public policies that pay attention to these two elements.

In brief, there is a good match between the women's agenda and the agenda of those interested in reducing population growth. However, there is one major caveat. The women's agenda treats reproductive health and gender equality as ends of public policy, whereas the population agenda could treat them as means to achieve population stabilization and as a desirable consequence of population stabilization.

Implications of ICPD for Population Policy

Whether to improve gender equality is not an issue. Similarly, whether to provide reproductive health services is not an issue. The issues are: What are the implications of ICPD's main message for a country's population policy? Who should do what to implement policy? And who should pay for the required actions, and why?

A broadened population policy cognizant of the need to reduce gender disparities in education, health, and economic opportunity (and thus to create conditions conducive to small families) becomes synonymous with a general development policy oriented to the removal of those disparities and to improvements in human well-being. The implementation of such public policies—and thus the implementation of the ICPD's main message—would, therefore, require ideological transformation of both the population and the development establishments. It would also require realignment of the missions and mandates of various ministries/offices in national and international bureaucracies, which are used to working within narrow sectoral areas. Moreover, new institutional mechanisms would be needed to ensure that the policies and programmes of all the various sectors involved are consistent with regard to the objective of individual well-being and to the reduction of gender and other disparities.

Redefining the Term 'Population Problem'

The usual objective of a population policy is to address a population problem. Traditionally, population problem has been defined in terms of numbers—a high population growth rate, a high fertility rate, and the size of the population. Should the goals and objectives of a population policy post-ICPD continue to be defined in terms of reducing population growth and achieving a stable population size in a country? Or should the goal be defined in terms of improving individual well-being, reducing gender and other disparities, and improving the regional balance between population distribution and the use of the country's resources? To incorporate the central tenets of ICPD, the population problem itself needs to be redefined not in terms of numbers but in terms of improving existing conditions of poor reproductive health and of gender and other disparities. The main objective of a population policy, therefore, needs to be redefined explicitly in terms of enhancement of individual well-being through the modification of population growth.

Moving Family Planning Programmes Toward Reproductive Health Programmes

There has been a tendency to replace the phrase family planning by the term reproductive health, or to use the blanket term reproductive health/family planning in official documents, without making any changes in the nature and scope of the services offered. The ICPD Programme of Action defines reproductive health as 'a state of complete physical, mental, and social well-being and not merely the absence of disease or infirmity, in all matters related to the reproductive system and to its functions and processes' (United Nations 1994: para 7.2). There is little consensus on the type of services needed in order to improve reproductive health, as defined in the ICPD document. A comprehensive reproductive health package, according to Pachauri (1996), includes services to prevent and manage unwanted pregnancies; promote safe motherhood; promote child survival; prevent and treat reproductive tract infections, sexually transmitted infections, and gynaecological problems; and screen and treat breast cancer. This package also includes nutritional services for vulnerable groups; reproductive health services for adolescents; health, sexuality and gender information, education, and counselling; and establishment of an effective referral system.

Who should provide and pay for such reproductive health services, and why? Should family planning programmes be equated or replaced with reproductive health programmes? And should reproductive health be incorporated within the health sector? The answer to some of these questions depends on whether reproductive health services are provided as an end in themselves or as means to reduce fertility.

It can be argued that contraceptive services are subsumed within reproductive health, which in turn is subsumed within broader health services. The problem with this scenario is that both reproductive health and contraceptive services would have to compete for resources with other health issues, such as malaria eradication. We know that the allocation of health resources in many countries is biased toward urban areas and hospital-based curative care. Primary health care in rural areas is relatively neglected. Reproductive health including contraception, thus, may not receive as high a priority among all health issues as it deserves, and as the advocates of reproductive health or of population growth reduction would want.

Contraceptive services and health services each have their own separate constituency and budget; reproductive health, on the other hand, has some constituency but, so far, very little independent budget. Thus, in order for all the recommended reproductive health services to be delivered, donors and national governments would have to allocate additional resources (independent budgets) for reproductive health services similar to those allocated for family planning, child survival or safe motherhood programmes. In such a case, all reproductive health services could be delivered either as another vertical programme or integrated within health or family planning services.

In practice, if all the recommended reproductive health services are to be made available, reproductive health advocates must work with both family planning and general health departments. Some reproductive health services would be delivered through family planning programmes, and others through general primary health care programmes. To make this a reality, additional resources for reproductive health services would still be required.

With regard to family planning programmes, a reproductive health approach to family planning implies that these programmes cannot be simply reclassified as reproductive health programmes. Rather, at a minimum, the safe and voluntary use of contraceptives must be guaranteed. Implementation along these lines would require the main objective of a family planning programme to be redefined in terms of empowering individuals and couples to achieve their own reproductive intentions in a healthful manner, rather than in terms of reducing population growth and total fertility. The first part of this objective maintains the link with the current objective of fertility reduction by focusing on unwanted childbearing. The second part extends the link with reproductive health by ensuring that the use of contraception is made safe and voluntary. Thus, a practical strategy would be for reproductive health services that interact directly with the reduction of unwanted childbearing to be paid for and delivered through the family planning programmes, and for other issues of reproductive health to become the responsibility of other health programmes.

Population professionals should not have a problem with this objective. It is consistent with the ICPD's Programme of Action. Moreover, survey data indicate the existence of substantial levels of unmet need for contraception, as well as high levels of unwanted fertility. Acceptance of this objective would, however, have profound implications for the design of services, their costs, and evaluation of programme performance.

Redefining the Objectives of Sector-Specific Policies

The bureaucracies of national governments and other donor agencies are divided into various sectors, each with its own mandate and a separate budget. The part of population policy that is concerned with the reduction of population growth and fertility is implemented mainly through a single government department or ministry.

In terms of gender equality, the ICPD Programme of Action states that '[c]ountries should act to empower women and should take steps to eliminate inequalities between men and women as soon as possible' (United Nations 1994: para 4.4). A reduction in gender disparities in education, health, and economic opportunity would require the implementation of gender-sensitive social and economic policies. However, this task is outside the purview of any government department now considered responsible for implementing population policy, even though such actions are precisely what the entire development sector is supposed to do. About 98 per cent of the funds allocated for all developmental activities is spent on programmes other than family planning. The efficiency of these expenditures, therefore, must be improved in order to promote women's equality. Progress made by each sector toward the achievement of its objective of reducing gender disparities is also expected to create conditions conducive to low fertility desires.

In brief, in order to be consistent with ICPD recommendations, the mainstream development process must incorporate the reduction of gender disparities as its primary goal. The objective of each sector of development must be redefined in terms of improving gender equality.[5] For example, the objective of the education sector should be defined in terms of reducing gender disparities in education; that of the health sector, in terms of improving gender equality in health; and that of the other economic sectors, in terms of improving gender equality in economic opportunity. This is not to deny the importance of reducing other disparities in society, or to deny the fact that development policies are oriented to improve economic growth in the same way as health policies are designed to reduce mortality. These policies do not pay adequate attention to existing gender, race, or class disparities. This discussion simply illustrates the implications of ICPD recommendations for sector-specific policies.

A New Accountability Mechanism

At present, there is no bureaucratic mechanism to ensure that development policies adhere to the goal of reducing gender and other disparities in the society. Such a mechanism did not exist 20 years ago. Consequently, very little progress has been made since the Bucharest conference in 1974 in bringing development policies into line with population policy.

It is clear that a government department assigned to implement a family planning programme cannot implement a broader population policy. That is, it cannot ensure that development policies pay adequate attention to the reduction of gender disparities, or that they allocate the resources needed to improve female education and economic opportunity for women. Similar bureaucratic problems exist within the UN system and other major donor agencies. Most of the developmental expenditures required to reduce gender disparities are not controlled by UNFPA, the agency responsible for helping governments to implement the broad ICPD Programme of Action.

The implementation of a broader population policy would require a watchdog organization within national and international agencies to ensure that other

---

[5] The concept of equality implies being equal, whereas the concept of equity implies being just or fair. It is not clear whether government policies should focus on providing equal opportunities or ensuring equal outcome. I have used the term gender equality to denote lack of discrimination based on gender. For education and health, the focus is on equal outcome, whereas for the economic sector, the focus is on equal opportunities.

ministries modify their policies and programmes, and that they examine the effects of their programmes on gender equality and family size preferences. It is not known whether any existing organization within most national and international bureaucracies could play this role. It is also not clear whether a new bureaucratic structure would be more effective than existing ones—Planning Commissions or Finance Ministries within national governments, for example, or UNDP within the UN system. It is possible that community-level mechanisms—including participation by women's groups—could be shaped into powerful watchdog institutions at the grassroots level to ensure accountability in public policies and expenditures.

Role of the Research Community

The research community can contribute to the process of implementing a broader population policy and to monitoring and evaluating such a policy. Four research issues that need to be addressed—not including the research required to move family planning programmes more rapidly and effectively toward becoming reproductive health programmes—are identified.

Gender equality and economic development: While there is some agreement about the shift toward gender equality in the goal of economic development, the widespread adoption of this objective by development professionals, who control financial resources, would be made easier by empirical evidence linking a reduction in gender disparity to economic growth.

Gender equality and fertility reduction: While there is some agreement that improvements in gender equality will create conditions conducive to small families, the widespread adoption of this objective by population professionals would be made easier if it could be shown that improvements in gender equality will contribute to fertility reduction.[6]

Examination of the effect of sector-specific policies on gender disparity: While investment in development sectors can be justified on the basis of their non-demographic objectives alone (for example, improved education or improved health), the effect of these policies and programmes on the reduction of gender disparity needs to be examined in order for them to be modified.

Monitor the progress made in terms of improving gender equality: The effect on gender equality in education, health, and economic conditions that is brought about by sector-specific policies and programmes needs to be regularly monitored in order for these programmes to be accountable for improving gender equality. This function is similar to that being performed by population professionals in regard to the evaluation and monitoring the effect of family planning programmes.

---

[6] The desire for large families may also decline with an increase in women's education, without decreasing societal gender disparities in education. It is for this reason that empirical evidence is required.

Conclusion

In this paper I have argued that implementation of a broader population policy—as it is now imbedded in the ICPD Programme of Action and as unanimously approved by all participating countries—would have the effect of blurring any distinction between population and development. Under such circumstances, the need for a population policy, separate from an overall development policy for a country, would be highly questionable.

The broadest interpretation of the ICPD Programme of Action implies that there is no dramatic difference between a population policy and a development policy. Both must be attentive to reducing gender and other disparities. In effect, population policy will eventually be subsumed within a good, strong social and economic development policy; and family planning will be subsumed within reproductive health, which in turn will be subsumed within health.

Under such circumstances, the contents of a population policy as both government intention and as government programme would have to change. While it may be easier to modify the statement of a population policy to reflect the ICPD's main message, the implementation of that message will continue to present bureaucratic challenges. Public funds will continue to be assigned to the population sector for some time to come, because in a number of countries it is assumed to be legitimate for public policies to address the issue of population size and growth. This assumption is necessary, because in the absence of a clearly perceived population problem, there is no need for a separate population policy or a population sector.

The relationship between a population policy and family planning and reproductive health can be examined under three scenarios. The first scenario is to continue using the narrow interpretation of population policy as fertility reduction through family planning programmes. The second is to equate population policy with a reproductive health policy, and to expand the scope of family planning programmes to incorporate all reproductive health services. The third scenario is to equate population policy with a development policy, and to further expand the arena of population activities to influence all sectors of development.

How far the population sector of any developing country will move away from its pre-ICPD configuration will depend upon two factors: the basis on which resources for the population sector are mobilized; and the way these funds are allocated.

In allocating funds to family planning programmes, the overriding intent of national governments and international donors has been to reduce societal fertility and population growth. If that continues to be the case, it would be difficult for country programmes to move beyond the situation they found themselves in before the ICPD. Family planning programmes would then only be able to pay lip service to the issues of reproductive health, but ignore any modification of contraceptive services required by a genuine reproductive health perspective. Moreover, some family planning programmes may continue to rely on coercive means to reduce fertility, which could be justified on the basis of the common good. Under such regrettable circumstances, the individual rights of a certain class of people may be compromised in the name of fertility reduction.

Equating population policy with a reproductive health policy is likely to run into serious problems of resource mobilization and allocation. The reproductive health approach focuses on individual rights and well-being, and there is a growing constituency for the provision of reproductive health services (Pachauri 1996). However, some managers of, and donors (internal as well as external) to, family planning programmes are concerned that governments are unlikely to allocate funds on the basis of individual well-being. In other words, a focus on individual well-being alone may reduce the availability of funds for family planning programmes (Caldwell 1997). Managers and international donors are also concerned that adopting a reproductive health approach might divert funds from contraceptive to reproductive health services. Under these circumstances, they are likely to implement a reproductive health approach only if it can be justified as a cost-effective way to reduce total fertility and population growth.

Where services for safe abortions are concerned, the interests of reproductive health advocates and of family planning programme managers easily converge because such services reduce fertility, expand choice, and reduce maternal morbidity and mortality. The issue of abortion, however, is so politically charged that the expansion of abortion services is often limited, even in countries where the procedure is legal. There is no empirical evidence in support of the cost-effectiveness in reducing fertility to be derived from adding other reproductive health services, such as the treatment of reproductive tract infections (RTIs) and sexually transmitted diseases (STDs). Efforts to gather such evidence are unlikely to be productive. For example, empirical research might reveal that adding services to diagnose and treat RTIs and STDs is not as cost-effective in reducing fertility as giving cash incentives to providers and clients. Moreover, judging their effectiveness on the basis of their impact on fertility reduction could not be justified in terms of equity and human well-being.

Equating population policy with a development policy assumes that either population becomes subsumed within development, or development becomes subsumed within population. The first alternative would not be acceptable to population professionals, who would fear the loss of funds. The second alternative assumes that the population problem is a country's primary problem, and that, therefore, development can be subsumed within population. This premise is unlikely to be acceptable to those who control resources for development, especially since fertility has declined and can decline under various conditions, including economic hardship, extreme gender disparity, and adverse reproductive health.

What is a practical strategy for the population field? First, we need to avoid semantic problems by making a distinction between a policy and a programme, and by making the two consistent.[7] At the policy level, we need to distinguish between a

---

[7] Prior to ICPD, the problem, in part, was semantic because the word 'population' at the policy level was replaced by the term 'family planning' at the programme level.

population policy, a 'fertility reduction' policy, a 'reproductive health' policy, and a 'family planning' policy. We need to recognize that a family planning policy can be implemented through a family planning programme, but a population policy or a fertility reduction policy cannot.

Second, we need to distinguish between wanted and unwanted fertility and stop burdening the family planning programme with the responsibility of reducing both. We need to explicitly recognize the role of other sectors of development in reducing desired family size. Third, we need to redefine the main objective of the family planning programmes in terms of reducing unwanted childbearing in a healthful manner; and we must advocate for the redefinition of the objectives of sector-specific policies in terms of reduction in gender and other disparities, instead of asking these sectors to become involved in the delivery of contraceptive services.

References

Bongaarts, John (1978), 'A Framework for Analyzing the Proximate Determinants of Fertility', *Population and Development Review*, 4(1): 105–32.

Bulatao, Rodolfo, and Lee, Ronald (1983). *Determinants of Fertility in Developing Countries*, New York: Academic Press.

Caldwell, Jack (1997), 'Reaching a Stationary Global Population: What we Have Learnt, and What we Must Do. Where is the International Population Movement Going? Cairo's Legacy', *Health Transition Review*, Supplement 7 (4).

Coale, Ansley, and Hoover, Edgar M. (1958), *Population Growth and Economic Development in Low-Income Countries*, Princeton: Princeton University Press.

Davis, Kingsley (1967), 'Population Policy: Will Current Programmes Succeed?', *Science*, 158(3802): 30–739.

—— and Blake, Judith, (1956). 'Social Structure and Fertility: An Analytical Framework', *Economic Development and Cultural Change*, 4(3): 211–35.

Dixon-Mueller, Ruth (1993), *Population Policy and Women's Rights: Transforming Reproductive Choice*, Westport: Praeger Press.

Freedman, Ronald, and Takeshita, John Y. (1969) *Family Planning in Taiwan: An Experiment in Social Change*, Princeton: Princeton University Press.

Jain, Anrudh (1995), 'Commentary: Implementing the ICPD's Message', *Studies in Family Planning*, 26(5).

—— (1998), *Do Population Policies Matter? Fertility and Politics in Egypt, India, Kenya, and Mexico*, NY: The Population Council.

—— and Bruce, Judith (1994), 'A Reproductive Health Approach to the Objectives and Assessment of Family Planning Programs', in Gita Sen, Adrienne Germain and Lincoln Chen (eds.), *Population Policies Reconsidered: Health, Empowerment, and Rights*, Boston: Harvard University Press.

McNicoll, Geoffrey (1997). 'The Governance of Fertility Transition: Reflections on the Asian Experience', in G. W. Jones *et al.* (eds.), *The Continuing Demographic Transition*, Oxford: Clarendon Press, 365–82.

Mason, Karen Oppenheim (1997), 'Explaining Fertility Transitions', *Demography*, 34(4): 443–54.

National Research Council (1986), *Population Growth and Economic Development: Policy Questions*, Washington, DC: National Academy Press.

Pachauri, Saroj (1996), 'Defining a Reproductive Health Package for India: A Proposed Framework', *South & East Asia Regional Working Paper* No. 4, New Delhi: Population Council.

Pritchett, Lant H. (1994), 'Desired Fertility and the Impact of Population Policies', *Population and Development Review*, 20(1): 1–55.

United Nations (1987–90), *World Population Policies*, 3 vols, New York.

—— (1992), *World Population Monitoring*, 1991, New York.

—— (1994), Programme of Action adopted at the International Conference on Population and Development, Cairo, 5–13 September 1994, Vol. 1.

19 Prospects for Fertility Decline and Implications for Population Growth in South Asia

JOHN BONGAARTS AND SAJEDA AMIN

Despite relatively low levels of development, South Asia is moving rapidly through the demographic transition. Since 1950 the crude death rate has dropped from 25 to 9 per 1,000, and the birth rate, which remained at about 40 per 1,000 until the early 1970s, has since declined to below 30 per 1,000. As a consequence, the annual population growth rate rose from 2.0 to 2.4 per cent per year between 1950 and 1970 and then declined slowly, reaching 1.9 per cent in 1995. The overall population size of the region has grown from 0.5 billion in 1950 to 1.37 billion in 1995, a 174 per cent increase (United Nations 1996).

Population projections by the UN and the World Bank anticipate that all countries in the region will complete the demographic transition over the next several decades, thus ending a period of historically unprecedented population growth. Since death rates will see only minor further declines (improvements in life expectancy will be offset in part by changes in the population age structure), future reductions in population growth will largely be the result of further declines in birth rates. We begin our discussion of these issues by assessing prospects for fertility decline in a number of countries in the region. Next, we review factors affecting post-transitional fertility, a crucial factor in long-range population growth. We conclude with an overview of population projections and policy options for reducing population growth.

Completing the Fertility Transition

An obvious place to start a discussion of future fertility trends is with the assumptions regarding fertility that were incorporated into the most recent long-range projections made by the United Nations (1996) and the World Bank (Bos *et al.* 1994). Figure 19.1 plots UN estimates of the total fertility rate (TFR) for selected South Asian countries from 1950 to 1995, as well as projections until 2050 for the medium variant. In the 1950s, fertility was high in all countries in the region, and the limited available data from the earliest surveys in these countries suggest that only a small proportion of couples practised contraception at the time. The estimated total

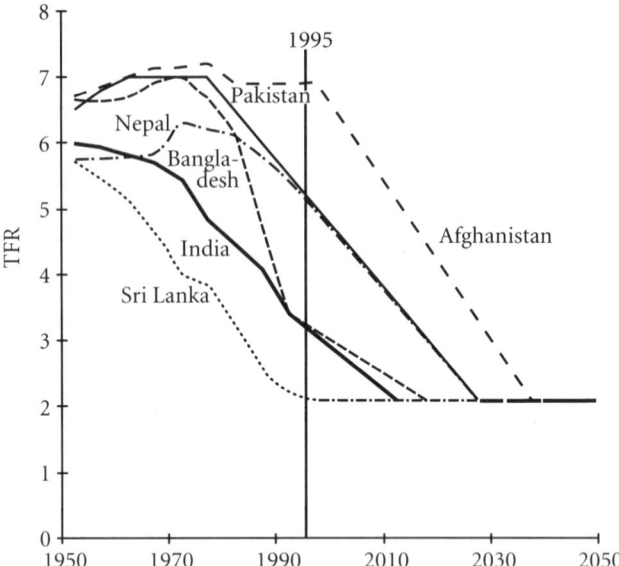

Figure 19.1. Total fertility rate (TFR) for six South Asian countries: estimates (1950–1995) and projections (1995–2050).

Source: United Nations (1996).

fertility rate in 1950–55 varied from a high of 6.7 births per woman in Afghanistan to a low of 5.7 in Sri Lanka. Most of this modest variation between countries was due to differences in marriage patterns, breastfeeding, and postpartum abstinence, rather than to the practice of deliberate birth control. Between 1950 and 1995 fertility remained initially quite stable, but was then followed in most countries by an abrupt decline. The timing of the onset of this transition (as measured by a 10 per cent decline from the pre-transitional level) ranged between the late 1950s in Sri Lanka to around 1990 in Nepal and Pakistan. Only in Afghanistan is there still no evidence of a fertility transition.

In the future, the UN projects a linear decline in fertility, with the pace of change varying only modestly among countries. As a consequence, countries that currently have the highest fertility will reach replacement the latest (e.g. Afghanistan in 2035), while Sri Lanka, with a TFR of 2.2 in 1990–95, was expected to reach replacement by 1995. Once fertility reaches the replacement level, it is assumed to remain invariant until at least 2050.[1]

---

[1] The UN actually assumes that post-transitional fertility equals 2.1 births per woman. In most countries this is very close to a net reproduction rate of 1.0, but, depending on the level of mortality and the sex ratio at birth, the actual level of replacement fertility might be slightly different.

Table 19.1. Total fertility rate in 1990–1995 and year in which replacement fertility is reached, as projected by the United Nations and the World Bank

Country	Total fertility rate 1990–95		Year in which replacement fertility is reached	
	UN	World Bank	UN	World Bank
Afghanistan	6.9	6.9	2,030	2,050
Bangladesh	3.4	4.0	2,015	2,010
India	3.4	3.7	2,010	2,010
Nepal	5.4	5.5	2,025	2,030
Pakistan	5.5	5.6	2,025	2,030
Sri Lanka	2.2	2.5	1,995	2,000

Sources: UN (1996); Bos *et al.* (1994).

The World Bank's assumptions regarding future fertility trends are broadly similar to those of the UN: fertility declines to replacement level over the next few decades in all South Asian countries. Table 19.1 compares UN and World Bank estimates of the TFR for 1990–95 and for the year in which replacement fertility is expected to be reached. For most countries, fertility in 1990–95 differs little between the two estimates. The UN estimates for India and Bangladesh are in agreement with the findings from the most recent surveys in these countries (IIPS 1995; Mitra *et al.* 1994), but these survey results were apparently not available when the latest published projections of the World Bank were prepared, leading to slightly higher fertility projections for these two countries.

The assumptions about the years in which replacement fertility is reached are also generally similar (Table 19.1, last two columns), with one notable exception: in Afghanistan the World Bank assumes replacement to be reached 20 years later than the UN (2050 versus 2030). Before commenting on the plausibility of these projections, we briefly summarize the key features of the projection methodologies employed by the UN and the World Bank.

The UN's methodology for projecting fertility in developing countries consists of three steps. First, available data from surveys, censuses, and other sources are analysed to obtain an estimate of the most recent five-year period before the beginning of the projection period (i.e. 1990–95 for the 1996 revision). Next, the year in which fertility reaches replacement is determined. Finally, linear interpolation between 1990–95 and the replacement year yields a complete trajectory for the TFR. Countries that were still pre-transitional in 1990–95 are assumed to initiate a decline after 1995. Once the initial fertility level has been determined, the entire future trajectory of fertility is established by the timing of the onset of replacement fertility. The procedure to determine this year is described as follows:

The assumed target period at which fertility will stabilize is determined by taking into account a range of socio-economic factors, such as population policies and programmes, adult literacy, school enrolment levels, economic conditions (gross domestic product or gross national product per capita), infant mortality and nuptiality, as well as historical, cultural and political factors. No attempt is made to use mathematical equations to estimate the dates because of the non-quantitative nature of some of the variables, and the uneven quality and availability of data. (UN 1995: 146.)

No further methodological details are provided, and it is therefore difficult to evaluate this approach. In addition to the medium projection, which is summarized in Fig. 19.1 and Table 19.1, the UN also published 'high' and 'low' variants in which fertility levels off above and below the replacement level.

The World Bank's procedures consist of a complex and explicit set of rules and equations, described in detail in Bos *et al.* (1994). The most important of these rules are:

- in pre-transitional countries, the fertility decline begins in the first quinquennium after life expectancy reaches 50 years, until after 2005, when all countries are assumed to be in transition;
- the pace of fertility decline in any five-year period is country-specific and is a linear function of the rate of decline in the preceding quinquennium;[2] and
- once the TFR drops below three births per woman, the remainder of the transition takes 15 years along a geometrically decelerating path to the replacement level.

How reliable are these procedures, and how plausible are the resulting forecasts? Unfortunately, little can be said with confidence to answer this question. This is in part due to the difficulty in projecting socioeconomic conditions, changes in population policies, and new efforts to introduce or strengthen family planning programmes, all of which presumably would affect fertility trends. However, the most important problem is the absence of an agreed-upon theory of fertility linking various determinants to reproductive behaviour. In the absence of such a theoretical framework, it is difficult to fault analysts at the UN and the World Bank for resorting to a set of mechanical heuristic rules to obtain fertility projections.

Some insights into what is and is not reasonable to assume about future fertility can be gained from a recent study by Bongaarts and Watkins (1996). This study examines trends in fertility and socioeconomic variables in 69 developing countries between 1960 and 1985 in an attempt to find empirical regularities in the relationship between these variables. A key finding from this analysis is that the level of development at the time of the onset of transitions varies systematically among

---

[2] To avoid exceptionally slow and rapid transitions, upper and lower limits for the pace of decline are set. The rates of decline in the first and second quinquennium after the onset of the transition are set at 0.3 and 0.6 births per woman, respectively.

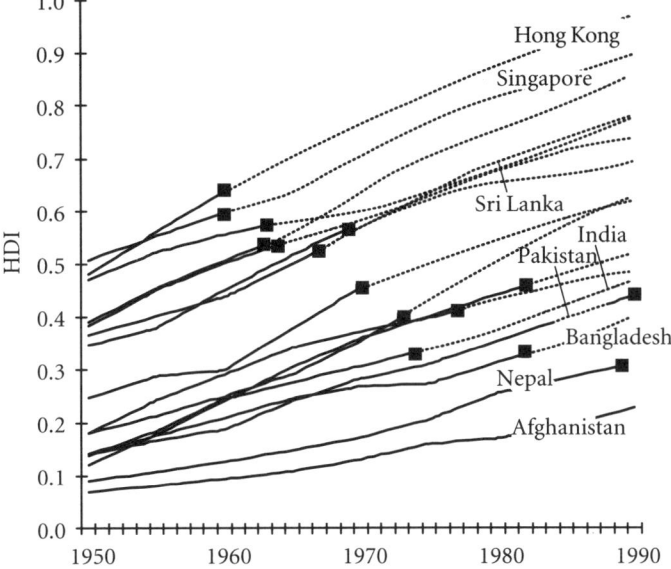

Figure 19.2. Trends in development level (HDI) and fertility transition status for 16 Asian countries.

Note: The solid part of each line indicates that a country is pretransitional; the following dashed line represents the transitional phase. The square marker represents the transition point.

Source: Bongaarts and Watkins (1996).

countries and has declined over time. This pattern is demonstrated for selected Asian countries in Fig. 19.2, which plots the trend in the human development index (HDI) over time for 16 Asian countries (HDI is calculated as a linear function of life expectancy, literacy, and GDP per capita (UNDP 1990)). Each line represents one country, and the upward slope of these lines indicates that countries have generally experienced a steady improvement in development since the 1950s. The solid part represents the pre-transitional phase, and the square marker represents the transition point. The first countries to enter the transition (around 1960) were Hong Kong, Singapore, Korea, and Sri Lanka, while Pakistan and Nepal were the latest (circa 1990).

The most interesting finding in Fig. 19.2 is a clear decline over time in the level of development associated with the onset of the transition. The first Asian countries to begin a sustained decline did so after attaining relatively high levels of development. Once a few countries entered the transition, the development threshold dropped for the remaining countries, and the last countries to enter the transition had much lower levels of development than the region's 'leaders'. The most important implication of this moving threshold is that the difference in the timing of transitions between countries in Asia has been reduced from many decades to just a few. For example, Bangladesh's transition would have been delayed well into the next century if it had had to wait until it achieved the same level of development as Hong Kong or Singapore had in 1960. This finding lends support to assumptions by both the UN and the World Bank that countries that are currently pre-transitional will initiate a fertility decline in the near future. It is, however, unlikely that all pre-transitional countries will have begun a decline in 1995, as the UN projects.

A second finding by Bongaarts and Watkins (1996) is that the pace of fertility decline is not systematically related to the pace of development. Instead, the rate of fertility decline was found to depend on the level of development at the onset of the transition. Countries that had reached a relatively high level of development when the transition began (e.g. Hong Kong and Singapore) experienced relatively swift declines to the replacement level, while countries that started the transition early in the development process (e.g. India) tended to have a slower pace of fertility decline. This empirical relationship lends support to the World Bank's assumption about the relationship between the rate of change in one quinquennium and the rate in the next.

On the whole, the general shape of the future fertility trajectories incorporated in the UN and World Bank projections is plausible (although actual trends could turn out differently). One of the most critical assumptions made in all projections is that a fertility decline, once under way, will continue until replacement is reached. This is a pattern observed in other developing countries that have completed the transition. It is reasonable to assume that a similar future trend will be observed in countries that are currently in transition. Although there are a few instances of brief stalling in fertility declines (e.g. in Korea and Costa Rica), such events are sufficiently rare to be considered unlikely to recur in the future.

The most critical issue for long-range trends in population size is whether fertility levels are at, below, or above the replacement level of about 2.1 births per woman. The World Bank and the UN medium projections assume that fertility remains permanently at replacement. This has the benefit of resulting eventually in a stationary population rather than one in which growth is permanently positive or negative, but it is likely that many countries will deviate significantly from this simple assumption. The effects on population growth of such deviations, if they are maintained for long periods, are very large. This is well demonstrated by the differences between the high, medium, and low projections of the UN (1996). These projections differ in the level of fertility after the fertility transition is completed: 0.5 births per woman above the replacement level of 2.1 for the high variant and 0.5 below replacement for the low variant. For example, the high projection for India yields a population of 1.89 billion in 2050, compared to 1.23 billion for the low variant, a difference of 0.66 billion. By 2100 the high variant reaches 3.1 billion, fully 2.2 billion more than the low variant estimate of 0.9 billion (UN 1992). Clearly, minor changes in post-transitional fertility have huge consequences for population size in 2100. Since the

Table 19.2. Estimates of wanted and unwanted components
of the total fertility rate (TFR) for four South-Asian countries

Country	Wanted TFR	Unwanted TFR	TFR
Bangladesh (1993–94)	2.1	1.2	3.3
India (1992–93)	2.6	0.8	3.4
Pakistan (1990–91)	4.7	0.7	5.4
Sri Lanka (1987)	2.2	0.4	2.6

Sources: Mitra *et al.* (1994); IIPS (1995); NIPS and IRD/Macro (1992);
DCS/MPI and IRD/Westinghouse (1988).

level of post-transitional fertility is of such critical importance for future population trends, we discuss in greater detail the factors that may influence it.

Post-transitional Fertility

The level of overall fertility at any time in the future equals the sum of the corresponding levels of wanted and unwanted fertility. Estimates of recent unwanted fertility levels range from 1.2 births per woman in Bangladesh to 0.4 in Sri Lanka (see Table 19.2). These levels are likely to decline in future decades as family planning programmes improve, new contraceptive and abortion technologies become available, and levels of education rise (there will be more discussion on this point later). As a consequence, the main determinant of future trends in fertility will be trends in wanted fertility, and wanted fertility is, in turn, largely determined by desired family size. We first discuss factors affecting trends in desired family size in the region, and then briefly summarize the various reasons why wanted fertility differs from desired family size.

Levels and Trends in Desired Family Size

There is strong evidence of a global trend toward smaller desired family size. Data from surveys conducted in the past 20 years reflect this trend (see Table 19.3). Desired family size has fallen by as much as 39 per cent in Bangladesh, between the WFS surveys in the mid-1970s and the DHS surveys in the early 1990s. However, the other countries of South Asia vary considerably in terms of decline in ideal family size.

In Bangladesh, evidence from a series of fertility surveys conducted over the past 20 years indicates that changes in desired family size have paralleled declines in actual fertility (see Fig. 19.3). These changes have happened over a relatively short time when campaigns to promote the ideal of small families were intense. The official population programme included an information, education, and communication strategy that explicitly articulated the objective of promoting such

Table 19.3. Trends in wanted fertility rates and desired family size in seven Asian countries

Region and country	Wanted fertility rate		Number of children desired	
	WFS	DHS-II or III	WFS	DHS-II or III
Asia				
Bangladesh	4.6	2.1	4.1	2.5
India	u	2.6	u	2.9
Indonesia	4.0	2.5	4.1	3.1
Pakistan	4.3	4.4	4.2	4.1
Philippines	4.1	2.8	4.4	3.5
Sri Lanka	2.9	2.2	3.8	3.0
Thailand	3.2	1.8	3.7	2.8

u = unknown.

Sources: Bankole and Westoff (1995); Westoff (1991).

an ideal (Duza 1990). The low level of development at which Bangladesh's fertility decline occurred has attracted the attention of demographers because it suggests that family planning programmes can play a part. It is likely that rapid fertility decline occurred in Bangladesh as a result of a family planning programme that was introduced at a time of increasing openness to and expansion of social development innovations in the country in general and rural areas in particular (Amin *et al.* 1995).

Regionally disaggregated data from the 1993 India National Family Health Survey (NFHS) show considerable evidence of preference for small families as well as variation across states in measures of desired family. Very low levels of ideal family size, ranging from 2.1 to 2.6, are reported in 11 out of the 25 Indian states and territories (see Table 19.4). Although patriarchal family structure has been identified as a key factor in maintaining high fertility (Dyson and Moore 1983), low family size ideals appear to exist in the North where patriarchal structure and level of development are strong, as well as in the South where they are relatively weak. Kerala and Tamil Nadu in the South have family size ideals similar to those of Haryana and Punjab in the North. A common characteristic of all four states is historically high levels of migration within and outside India. Such patterns of migration may have resulted in greater openness that creates opportunities for social interaction and the spread of new ideas, including ideas about family size.

It is also striking that the highest desired family sizes are reported for relatively remote and isolated states and territories of Northeast India. This region is little known to demographers because prior to the NFHS they were excluded from analyses owing to lack of data (Malhotra, *et al.* 1995; Murthi *et al.* 1995). Years of political unrest and physical remoteness have heightened the region's isolation: special permission is required for travel to or data collection in the region. Although there is reason to believe that the available data need to be interpreted with caution (IIPS 1995), it is

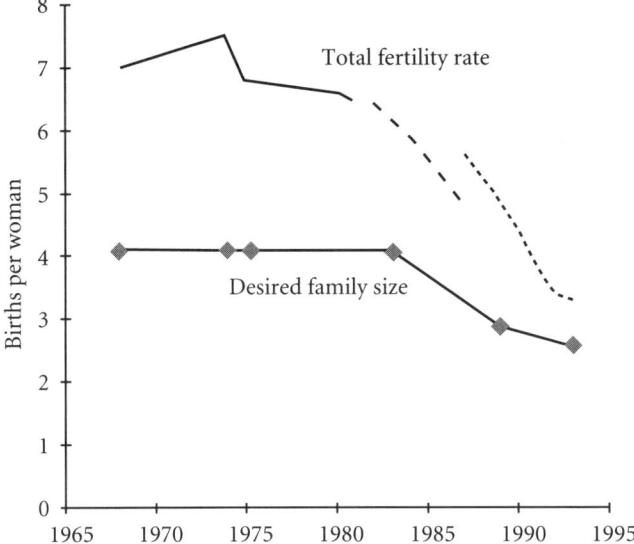

Figure 19.3. Trends in desired family size and actual fertility in Bangladesh, 1996–1993.

Source: Cleland *et al.* (1994); Mitra *et al.* (1994).

interesting that most of the Northeastern states have high levels of ideal family size despite low mortality, high female labour force participation, and high literacy. While these positive characteristics may be a product of the traditionally high status of women, there is no obvious explanation for higher pronatalism in these societies. The isolation of these states may in part explain the relatively high level of desired family size observed relative to the rest of India and to neighbouring Bangladesh.

Although desired family size is currently at very different levels throughout South Asia, it is likely that fertility preferences in the rest of South Asia will eventually reach the low levels evident in Bangladesh and states such as Kerala and Tamil Nadu. The course of change and the factors behind it may vary by context, but a number of factors will contribute to this trend. First, there is an increasing tendency toward replicating successful elements of health and family planning programmes, with particular attention focused on regions that are lagging behind. An intense programme of exchange at the intergovernmental level between Bangladesh and Pakistan is underway. Such exchanges occur at many policy levels, including small-scale grassroots development efforts in family planning, health, and other social-sector programmes that can serve as examples. Replication of successful programmes is promoted by international development organizations such as the World Bank and UNICEF, leading to increasing similarities in programmatic style and outreach.

Second, a similarly homogenizing trend within South Asia is attributable to the rising influence of the electronic media, with satellite television playing a particularly important role in propagating ideas. Finally, the broad similarity in cultures within the region will play a part in the rapid diffusion and acceptance of ideas that are spread by the media. As a consequence, it is reasonable to assume that the ideal of small families that has already taken root in parts of the subcontinent will diffuse across religious and political boundaries, leading to a convergence in social trends.

Most of the strongest correlates of ideal family size are also moving in a direction that will reinforce the preference for smaller families. Education levels, urbanization, and development more broadly all lead to lower family size preferences (Bankole and Westoff 1995). Advances in all three factors are occurring in South Asia, albeit at different paces, reinforcing the trend toward smaller families. However, these factors do not appear to be necessary conditions, as is evident in Bangladesh where fertility preferences have declined rapidly without the benefit of dramatic changes in urbanization, education, or the expansion of mass media (Cleland *et al.* 1994).

Son Preference

Although desired family size is the most commonly used measure of fertility preference, it does not capture the potential impact of son preference. Son preference is usually associated with strongly patriarchal societies commonly found in South Asia (Williamson 1976). The questions on ideal family size that are asked in fertility surveys are usually framed so that the response is unlikely to allow for any effects of the current or desired composition of offspring. Indirect procedures based on survey questions about the proportion wanting additional children are therefore used to estimate the effect of son preference on fertility.

One such estimate using data from the Matlab area in Bangladesh concludes that the elimination of all son preference would reduce fertility levels by 8 per cent, that is, son preference has a modest impact on propping up fertility (Chowdhury and Bairagi 1990). However, this, like most other estimates of the impact of son preference on fertility, refers to a time when fertility was well above replacement level. Cleland *et al.* (1983) showed a moderate impact of son preference on fertility for Nepal and Pakistan and a statistically insignificant association for Bangladesh from World Fertility Survey data when all three countries were still pre-transitional.

For an assessment of the impact of son preference on post-transitional fertility, we use examples from countries outside the region that have similarly strong son preference but are further along in the fertility transition. Evidence from China, Taiwan, and Korea suggests that son preference indeed does not prevent fertility from declining to below replacement levels (Westley 1995). This is the case despite evidence of intensified parental efforts to implement the desire to produce at least one son. Part of their strategy is to employ sex-selective abortion and contraceptive methods, which were widely available first in Korea and now also in China and

Table 19.4. Ideal family size and wanted fertility rates
by state, India, 1993

State	Ideal family size	Total wanted fertility rate
All India	2.9	2.6
North		
Delhi	2.5	2.2
Haryana	2.6	2.8
Himachal Pradesh	2.4	2.0
Jammu Region of J & K	2.8	2.2
Punjab	2.6	2.2
Rajasthan	3.0	2.8
Central		
Madhya Pradesh	3.1	3.2
Uttar Pradesh	3.4	3.8
East		
Bihar	3.4	3.2
Orissa	3.0	2.3
West Bengal	2.6	2.2
Northeast		
Arunachal Pradesh	4.7	3.8
Assam	3.2	2.5
Manipur	3.7	2.3
Meghalaya	4.6	3.4
Mizoram	4.3	2.1
Nagaland	4.0	3.0
Tripura	2.6	2.0
West		
Goa	2.7	1.6
Gujarat	2.6	2.3
Maharashtra	2.5	2.1
South		
Andhra Pradesh	2.7	2.1
Karnataka	2.5	2.2
Kerala	2.6	1.8
Tamil Nadu	2.1	1.8

Source: IIPS (1995).

India. Although illegal and costly, sex-selective abortion of foetuses is on the rise and has led to increasingly masculine sex ratios in all three settings (Zeng *et al.* 1993).

There is increasing evidence from India of an alarming rise in the incidence of sex-selective abortion. As may be expected, these rates are particularly high in states that combine a strong patriarchal structure with low desired family size. The soundest evidence of sex selection exists in the form of increasing sex ratios at birth that rise with parity (Westley 1995). Das Gupta and Bhat (1995) attribute intensification of gender bias to rapid fertility decline.

Traditional son preference in South Asia may persist because of cultural characteristics, but there are other reasons also:

- The traditional role of the family in caring for the elderly is expected to remain strong. Knodel and Debavalya (1992) project, based on a review of the situation of the elderly in Asia, that a shift of responsibility for the elderly from the family to the state is unlikely to occur because the financial implications exceed the capacity of governments. Thus son preference may be reinforced by the needs of the elderly.
- The overall level of development at which fertility decline began is lower in South Asia than elsewhere in Asia. Thus, the fertility transition is occurring in these countries in an otherwise more traditional context than in countries where son preference has not prevented fertility from reaching replacement level, such as Korea or Taiwan.
- Development in general has taken a different, less modern, course. This in part is manifest in the rising influence of religion in economic and political life, which argues, among other things, for the preservation of traditional family structures and support systems.
- Cross-cultural comparisons that included Bangladesh, India, and Pakistan rate these countries as having some of the highest levels of son preference and strongest patriarchal structures, even though there is considerable variation in these indicators within South Asia (Williamson 1976).
- Adverse social trends such as the rising practice of dowry throughout South Asia, even in communities that did not traditionally practise dowry, reinforce the preference for sons as daughters become a greater financial burden for parents (Amin and Cain 1995).

A recent analysis of family structure in the context of rapid fertility decline in Bangladesh shows how traditional rules of interaction persist despite widespread challenges to the integrity of the family in the form of economic change and increasing landlessness (Amin 1996). Indeed, the pattern of persistence in family systems has similarities with the course societies have taken in much of East Asia, where much more rapid economic and social change has taken place.

Taken together, the evidence on family size ideals and sex-composition preferences suggests that these factors are not likely to prevent fertility from falling to levels assumed by the UN and World Bank projections. The persistence of son preference has potentially important implications for women's status that have to be addressed by direct policies for support of the elderly and education, as suggested by Mason (1992).

Wanted Fertility and Desired Family Size

A comparison of estimates of desired family size and wanted fertility from seven recent surveys (Table 19.3) indicates that the former exceeds the latter in virtually all countries. The difference between these two preference measures averages 0.5 births per woman. Measurement errors and problems such as rationalization and non-numerical responses are one source for these differences, but even in the absence of such errors, desired family size would still differ from wanted fertility for the following reasons (Bongaarts 1990):

- *Inability to implement preferences*: A couple may want a certain number of children, but if one of the partners becomes infecund or the marriage ends early due to divorce or death, then the desired family size may not be achieved. In addition, a small proportion of individuals never marry or are permanently infecund. When such involuntary limitation of fertility occurs, it reduces wanted fertility below the desired family size. This effect is largest in populations with late age at marriage, high proportions of nonmarriage, wide spacing of births, large desired family size, and high levels of sterility.

- *Infant and child mortality*: Desired family size is measured in terms of surviving children, while wanted fertility refers to all births. Other things being equal, the latter will exceed the former to the extent that deceased children are replaced with additional births. In other words, child deaths that are replaced are counted once in measures of family size and twice in measures of wanted fertility.

- *Compositional preference*: Fertility surveys such as the WFS and DHS typically do not inquire about preferences for the gender composition of offspring. If, in specifying a family size preference, a woman also has a particular composition in mind, then her wanted fertility may exceed her desired family size. For example, if a woman wants a two-child family, including at least one son, she may decide to have a third (wanted) child if her first two children are girls.

- *Changes in the timing of childbearing*: The wanted total fertility rate is a period measure, while desired family size is a cohort indicator. Changes in the average age at childbearing therefore affect the former but not the latter. A trend toward later age at marriage or first birth would tend to reduce period fertility (both wanted and unwanted), independent of the level of desired family size.

The observed differences between desired family size and wanted fertility in Table 19.3 are the net results of these four effects (and measurement errors). Involuntary childbearing limitation and an increase in the average age at childbearing lead to a wanted fertility level below the desired family size, while child mortality and compositional preferences have the opposite effect. The fact that in most countries wanted fertility is lower than desired family size implies that the impact of involuntary childbearing limitation and a shift in the timing of fertility together usually outweigh the effects of child mortality and compositional preferences.

The future trend in wanted fertility relative to desired family size will depend on trends in each of the above factors, and they will vary among countries. No attempt will be made here to project these trends, but our assumptions for South Asia are as follows:

- *Inability to implement preferences*: This factor will probably increase, as the average age at marriage and the proportion never marrying are likely to rise from the low levels that currently prevail in most of the subcontinent, except in Sri Lanka.
- *Infant and child mortality*: While high at present, declines are expected to low levels over the next few decades, thus minimizing the impact of this factor.
- *Compositional preference*: Son preference is likely to remain important, but probably less so than in the past. The role of this factor will also be reduced as the practice of abortion for achieving gender preferences spreads.
- *Changes in the timing of childbearing*: In the long run this effect will average to zero.

Overall, these trends suggest that the difference between desired family size and wanted fertility will increase somewhat in the future. In other words, India and Bangladesh, with relatively small differences in the order of 0.3–0.4 births per woman at present, may well move in the direction of Sri Lanka and Thailand, which have much larger differences (0.8–1.0 births per woman). (The large gap between desired family size and wanted fertility in Sri Lanka and Thailand is probably in part due to ongoing shifts in the timing of childbearing.) The implication of this conclusion is that, if the desired number of children reaches two in the future, then wanted fertility will probably be somewhat lower. If, in addition, unwanted fertility is reduced to less than 0.5 births per woman, the total fertility rate could drop slightly below the replacement level of 2.1. This will in turn have important implications for future population growth.

Population Projections

Country-specific projections to 2050 are available from the UN (1996) in three variants: high, medium, and low. These variants differ only in their assumptions regarding future fertility. In the medium variant, fertility declines over time to the replacement level of 2.1 births per woman and is held constant thereafter. In the high and low variants, fertility also declines, but levels off at 2.6 and 1.6 births per woman, respectively, in the same year as the medium variant reaches replacement. The World Bank makes projections to 2150, but publishes only one variant.

The key results from the most recent UN and World Bank projections for South Asian countries are summarized in Table 19.5. In all six countries, population size is expected to increase substantially between 1995 and 2050, but the amount of growth over this period varies widely among countries. According to the UN, the largest proportional increase will occur in Afghanistan (212 per cent) and the smallest in Sri Lanka (51 per cent). Pakistan and Nepal are also expected to more than double in size. While India's relative growth is among the smallest in the region (65 per cent), it amounts to a large absolute rise of 604 million (from 929 to 1,533 million). In general, there is a strong positive correlation between the current level of fertility and the projected increase in population between 1995 and 2050.

A comparison of the UN variants shows only very modest differences among them in 2000. Even by 2020 the high and low variants stray on average only 6 per cent from the medium variant. Over the next quarter-century, population growth will therefore likely remain within a fairly narrow growth path. However, in the long run the variants deviate increasingly from one another. In 2050, the differences are about three times as large as in 2020, and by 2100 they become very large indeed. The high variant for India in 2100 cited earlier (3.1 billion) is more than 60 per cent above, and the low variant (0.9 billion) is 50 per cent below the medium variant of 1.9 billion.

It should be noted that all projection variants of the UN and the World Bank rely on a single trajectory for mortality in each country. An assessment of the plausibility of country trends in future mortality is beyond the scope of this paper, but a brief comment on the potential role of the AIDS epidemic is appropriate. The epidemic is spreading rapidly in India, with an estimated 3 million persons infected with HIV in 1996 (UNAIDS and WHO 1996). Reliable data for other countries are not available, but it may be assumed that the virus is spreading elsewhere in South Asia as well, although presumably levels of infection are lower than in India. The UN projections make adjustments to account for the mortality impact of AIDS only in countries in which HIV prevalence exceeds 1 per cent of the adult population. In 1994 this adjustment was made in 16 countries worldwide—15 in sub-Saharan Africa and 1 in Asia (Thailand). In other countries (including South Asia) 'the impact of AIDS on the demographic picture at the national level is insignificant' (UN 1995: 40). This conclusion is supported by a recent study (Bongaarts 1996), which found that, as a first approximation, the increase in the death rate attributable to AIDS equals about half the HIV prevalence rate. For example, in India the HIV prevalence rate of about 0.5 per cent among adults (aged 15–65) implies a rise in the death rate of 0.25 per 1,000. While this effect may be small enough for the moment to justify ignoring it for the purposes of making long-range projections, the epidemic could well grow much larger in the future. If that happens, the epidemic becomes an even larger public health problem than it already is, and it then can no longer be ignored in population projections.

The long-range projections of the World Bank for 2050 are broadly similar to those of the UN in that they foresee continued growth in all countries of roughly the same magnitude as the UN's projections. In a few countries the estimates for 2050 are close (e.g. Bangladesh and Sri Lanka), while in other countries the differences are quite large (e.g. India and Pakistan). These are the result of differences in assumptions about future trends in fertility and mortality.

Table 19.5. Projections of population size from the UN to 2050 and the World Bank to 2100 for South Asian countries

Country	United Nations					World Bank	
	Population size (millions)				Per cent change	Population size (millions)	
	1995	2000	2020	2050	1995–2050	2050	2100
Afghanistan							
Medium	19.7	25.6	41.0	61.4	212	79.1	113.0
High		25.6	43.1	72.6			
Low		25.2	38.4	50.6			
Bangladesh							
Medium	118.2	128.3	171.4	218.2	85	217.8	247.5
High		128.8	181.1	264.7			
Low		127.8	161.7	178.2			
India							
Medium	929.0	1,006.80	1,271.60	1,532.70	65	1,622.9	1,813.3
High		1,011.00	1,349.90	1,885.40			
Low		1,002.50	1,192.70	1,230.50			
Nepal							
Medium	21.5	24.3	37.5	53.6	149	49.8	61.1
High		24.4	38.7	62.2			
Low		24.3	36.3	45.7			
Pakistan							
Medium	136.2	156.0	247.8	357.4	162	316.4	379.9
High		156.3	255.4	412.8			
Low		155.7	240.2	306.3			
Sri Lanka							
Medium	17.9	18.8	23.1	27.0	51	26.6	28.3
High		19.2	25.1	34.3			
Low		18.4	21.0	20.8			

Source: United Nations (1996).

The most notable finding in the projections from 2050 to 2100 is that they are based on expectations of continued population growth, despite the fact that fertility will have reached replacement earlier in the twenty-first century in all countries. The tendency of population size to increase for decades after a two-child family has been reached is due to population momentum. It is primarily the consequence of a young population age structure. Estimates of momentum and its contribution to future population growth in South Asian countries are presented in Fig. 19.4, which compares the standard World Bank projections from 1995 to 2100 with projections in which fertility is set at the replacement level from 1995 onward. Momentum accounts for nearly all of future growth in Sri Lanka, but only for one-fifth in Afghanistan. Momentum is, on average, responsible for well over half of the projected population growth in India (74 per cent) and Bangladesh (82 per cent).

Policy Options for Reducing Future Population Growth

The expected large increases in population size over the next several decades in South Asian countries will complicate the already difficult task of reducing poverty and bringing about sustainable development. Efforts to slow this population expansion cannot include increases in mortality, and they therefore have to focus on further reduction of fertility. Three broad policy options for accelerating fertility decline can be pursued (Bongaarts 1994):

Reduce the unmet need for contraception and abortion by strengthening family planning programmes: The most direct way to bring about further fertility declines is to implement comprehensive and high-quality family planning programmes in all countries. The aim of these programmes is to assist couples in achieving their reproductive goals by providing services and information. Although past programme investments have been substantial in some countries (e.g. Bangladesh and India), there are others where services are poor (e.g. Afghanistan), and improvements are desirable everywhere. It is therefore not surprising that recent surveys reveal that many women who wish to delay or stop childbearing are not using contraception. For example, total unmet need in Bangladesh is 18.0 per cent among married women, in India it is 19.5 per cent, and in Pakistan, 31.7 per cent. The causes of this unmet need for contraception include:

- lack of knowledge of contraceptive methods and/or sources of supply;
- limited access to and low quality of family planning services;
- side effects and inconvenience of contraceptive methods;
- disapproval of husbands, family members, and others; and
- the prohibitive cost of contraceptive commodities and travel.

Most of these problems can be addressed if family planning programmes are strengthened by the expansion of coverage to unserved or underserved areas, by improving service quality, and providing more understandable contraceptive information and ready access to a wider variety of birth control methods, including abortion.

As a consequence of the unmet need for contraception, a substantial proportion of women bear more children than they want. Available estimates of wanted and unwanted fertility are summarized in Table 19.2. Within this group of four countries, unwanted childbearing is highest in Bangladesh and lowest in Sri Lanka (1.2 versus 0.4 births per woman). In addition, a substantial number of abortions are performed in these countries—many of them unsafe. Most unintended pregnancies

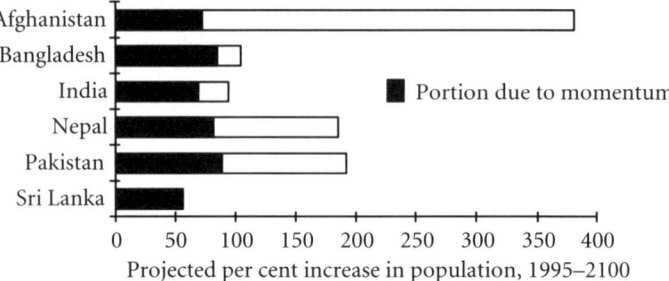

Figure 19.4. Per cent increase in population size between 1995 and 2100, based on World Bank projection, and portion of that increase due to population momentum.

Source: Bos *et al.* (1994) and author's estimates.

and abortions can be prevented if women are given greater control over their sexual and reproductive lives.

The contribution of unwanted fertility to future population growth can be estimated by comparing a country's standard population projection with a hypothetical projection in which all unwanted fertility is eliminated from 1995 onward. For example, for the developing world as a whole, with the inclusion of unwanted fertility population, growth over the next century is estimated to total 5.7 billion (i.e. population size will go from 4.5 billion in 1995 to 10.2 billion in 2100) according to the standard projection. However, in the absence of unwanted fertility this increase would be only 3.8 billion (Bongaarts 1994). These two projections differ by 1.9 billion (i.e. 33 per cent of the projected growth), the amount that is attributable to unwanted childbearing. A similar set of projections was made for India by Visaria and Visaria (1996). According to their standard projection, India would grow from 0.93 to 1.59 billion between 1996 and 2051. If unwanted fertility were eliminated after 1995, the population total in 2050 would be reduced to 1.48 billion. Unwanted fertility would therefore be responsible for approximately 17 per cent of future population growth in India.

Such estimates provide an upper estimate of the reduction in unwanted fertility and population growth that can be achieved by voluntary family planning programmes. In reality, resource constraints, imperfect technology, human error, social obstacles, and the reluctance of governments to take appropriate actions all limit the impact of family planning programmes. As a consequence, unwanted childbearing can be reduced but not eliminated, even in countries with the strongest contemporary family planning programmes (e.g. Indonesia and Thailand). There is, however, no doubt that improvements in the reach and quality of family planning and reproductive health programmes throughout South Asia can bring about substantial further reductions in fertility and in population growth. In addition, such programmes would have substantial health benefits for women and children.

Reduce the demand for large families through investments in human development: Although family planning programmes now claim most of the attention of population policy makers and most of the resources at their disposal, the potential effect of these initiatives is largely limited to reducing the unmet need for contraception. Since such programmes are voluntary, they cannot reduce fertility below the level wanted by couples, and they cannot bring about population stabilization in countries where wanted fertility still exceeds replacement level. This is the case in South Asian countries except Bangladesh and Sri Lanka (see Table 19.2). Preferences for high fertility therefore remain one of the key causes of high birth rates and rapid population growth in the region.

The demand for large families can be reduced through affirmative social and economic policies. Their effect is to change the costs and benefits of child rearing so that more parents will recognize the value of smaller families, while simultaneously increasing the investment they make in their children. Examples of factors potentially under government control include the expansion of educational opportunities (especially for girls), empowering women in their personal and economic lives, and reducing child mortality. Most governments already pursue these socially desirable objectives for reasons other than their potential role in lowering the rate of childbearing. The demographic benefits simply strengthen the rationale for intensifying these social policies. Media campaigns to encourage couples to want fewer children probably also have some effect on desired fertility.

Address the momentum of population growth: Even if fertility could immediately be reduced to the replacement level of two surviving children per woman, population growth would continue for many years, as a result of population momentum (see Fig. 19.4). In the past, discussions of population policy options neglected the key role of momentum, in part because it was thought to be impossible to change. Fortunately, an option to offset momentum is available that has received little attention. Further reductions in population growth can be achieved through raising the average age at which women begin childbearing (by delaying the first birth) and through wider spacing between births. Research has demonstrated that fertility levels in any given year are significantly affected by shifts in the timing of births (Ryder 1980). If successive age cohorts of women start their childbearing earlier and space their births closer together, for example, fertility for that period rises temporarily. Conversely, a delay in the onset of childbearing and wider spacing of births lead to a decline in period fertility and, hence, in the population growth rate. The amount of reduction in momentum obtained by a given increase in the age at first birth will vary among countries, but for the developing world as a whole a future increase of five years has been estimated to reduce momentum by 43 per cent (Bongaarts 1994).

Governments that want to encourage later childbearing have several options at their disposal. National legislation to raise the age at marriage has been moderately effective in a few countries, such as China and Tunisia. The drawback of legislation, however, is that it attempts to force rather than encourage changes in social customs that involve not only young people but also their families. Indirect approaches are likely to be more effective. An example is greater investment in the education of girls, particularly at the secondary level. The longer girls stay in school, the later they marry and the greater the delay in their becoming mothers. Increased employment opportunities for young women can similarly induce later marriage and childbearing. These and other social changes already under way will necessitate a focus on the reproductive health needs of young women as they spend more of their fecund years in unmarried status. As changes in marriage patterns take place, an increased need will emerge for interventions that directly address the issues of adolescent childbearing and sexuality.

Conclusion

This analysis suggests that it is plausible to assume fairly rapid fertility declines over the next few decades in South Asia. The fertility transition is already well under way in Bangladesh, India, and Sri Lanka, and these countries are likely to reach near-replacement fertility within two decades. While high fertility still prevails in Afghanistan, Nepal, and Pakistan, these countries can also be expected to move through the transition before 2050.

We are somewhat less comfortable with the assumption incorporated in the long-range projection of the UN (medium variant) and the World Bank that post-transitional fertility will remain indefinitely at the replacement level of 2.1 births per woman. Most contemporary post-transitional countries (e.g. in Europe and East Asia) now have below-replacement fertility. South Asian fertility could possibly follow a similar trajectory and drop slightly below the replacement level, even if, as seems likely, son preference remains strong.

Despite the expected rapid completion of fertility transitions, the population of all countries in South Asia will grow substantially in size. According to the UN medium variant, the smallest increase between 1995 and 2050 will occur in Sri Lanka (51 per cent) and the largest (212 per cent) in Afghanistan. Total population for the region is projected to rise from 1.37 billion in 1995 to 2.52 billion in 2050. While population projections are robust in the short run (i.e. in the next one or two decades), in the long run they are very sensitive to small deviations from the replacement level. For example, if India's fertility stabilizes at about half a birth below replacement, population size would be 0.9 instead of 1.9 billion in 2100. Conversely, if fertility remains half a birth above replacement, India's population in 2100 could reach 3.1 billion. This finding implies that even modest efforts to reduce fertility could have large effects on future population growth. Several desirable options are available to governments that wish to reduce fertility:

- reduce the unmet need for contraception and abortion by strengthening family planning programmes;

- reduce the demand for large families through investments in human development; and
- reduce the momentum of population growth by encouraging later marriage and childbearing.

Designing policies and programmes to reduce population momentum clearly poses the greatest challenge, but, as we have shown in this paper, it also holds the most promise.

References

Amin, S. (1995), 'The Differentiated Impact of the Expanded Programme on Immunization in Bangladesh', in H. Rashad, R. Gray and T. Boerma (eds.), *Evaluation of the Impact of Health Interventions*, Liège: Derouaux Ordina Editions, 397–414.

—— (1996), 'Family Structure and Change in Rural Bangladesh', Research Division Working Paper No. 87, Population Council.

—— and Cain, M. (1995), 'The Rise of Dowry in Bangladesh', Paper presented at a seminar on the Continuing Demographic Transition, honouring John C. Caldwell, 14–17 August, Canberra, Australia.

—— Cleland, J., Phillips, J. F., and Kamal, G. M. (1995), 'Socioeconomic Change and the Demand for Children in Rural Bangladesh', Research Division Working Paper No. 70, Population Council.

Bankole, A., and Westoff, C. F. (1995), 'Childbearing Attitudes and Intentions', Demographic and Health Surveys Comparative Studies, No. 17, Macro International.

Bongaarts, J. (1990), 'The Measurement of Wanted Fertility', *Population and Development Review*, 16(3): 487–506.

—— (1994), 'Population Policy Options in the Developing World', *Science*, 263: 771–6.

—— (1996), 'Global Trends in AIDS Mortality', *Population and Development Review*, 22(1): 21–45.

—— and Watkins, S. C. (1996), 'Social Interactions and Contemporary Fertility Transitions', *Population and Development Review*, 22(4): 639–82.

Bos, E., Vu, M. T., Massiah, E., and Bulatao, R. A. (1994), *World Population Projections 1994–95 Edition: Estimates and Projections with Related Demographic Statistics*, Baltimore: Johns Hopkins University Press for the World Bank.

Brass, W., Juarez, F., and Sathar, Z. (1996), 'Changing Patterns of Family Limitation: Evidence of Fertility Fall in Pakistan?', unpublished manuscript.

Chowdhury, M. K., and Bairagi, R. (1990), 'Son Preference and Fertility in Bangladesh', *Population and Development Review*, 16(4): 749–57.

Cleland, J., Verall, J., and Vaessen, M. (1983), 'Preferences for the Sex of Children and their Influence on Reproductive Behaviour', World Fertility Surveys Comparative Studies, No. 27, Voorburg, Netherlands: International Statistical Institute.

—— Phillips, J. F., Amin, S., and Kamal, G. M. (1994), *The Determinants of Reproductive Change in Bangladesh: Success in a Challenging Environment*, Washington, DC: World Bank.

Das Gupta, M., and Mari Bhat, P. N. (1995), 'Intensification of Gender Bias in India: A Consequence of Fertility Decline', Center for Population and Development Studies, Working Paper No. 95-03, Cambridge, MA: Harvard University.

Department of Census and Statistics/Ministry of Plan Implementation (DCS/MPI) and Institute for Resource Development (IRD)/Westinghouse (1988), *Sri Lanka Demographic and Health Survey 1987*, Colombo, Sri Lanka, and Columbia, MD.

Duza, M. B. (1990). 'Demand Creation and Crystallization for Family Planning', in M. B. Duza, (ed.), *South Asia Study of Population Policy and Programmes: Bangladesh*, Dhaka: United Nations Population Fund.

Dyson, T., and Moore, M. (1983), 'On Kinship Structure, Female Autonomy, and Demographic Behavior in India', *Population and Development Review*, 9(1): 35–60.

International Institute for Population Sciences (IIPS) (1995), *National Family Health Survey (MCH and Family Planning), India 1992–93*, Bombay.

Knodel, J., and Debavalya, N. (1992), 'Social and Economic Support Systems for the Elderly in Asia: An Introduction', *Asia-Pacific Population Journal*, 7(3): 5–13.

Malhotra, A., Vanneman, R., and Kishor, S. (1995), 'Fertility, Dimensions of Patriarchy, and Development in India', *Population and Development Review*, 21(2): 281–305.

Mason, K. (1992), 'Family Change and Support for the Elderly in South Asia: What Do We Know?', *Asia-Pacific Population Journal*, 7(3): 13–32.

Mitra, S. N., Ali, M. N., Islam, S., Cross, A. R., and Saha, T. (1994), *Bangladesh Demographic and Health Survey 1993–94*, Calverton, MD: National Institute of Population Research and Training (NIPORT), Mitra and Associates, and Macro International.

Murthi, M., Guio, A.-C., and Drèze, J. (1995), 'Mortality, Fertility, and Gender Bias in India: A District-Level Analysis', *Population and Development Review*, 21(4): 745–82.

National Institute of Population Studies (NIPS) and IRD/Macro International (1992), *Pakistan Demographic and Health Survey 1990/1991*, Islamabad, Pakistan, and Columbia, MD.

Ryder, N. B. (1980), 'Components of Temporal Variations in American fertility', in R. W. Hiorns, (ed.), *Demographic Patterns in Developed Societies*, London: Taylor & Francis, 15–54.

United Nations (1992), *Long-Range World Population Projections: Two Centuries of Population Growth 1950–2150*, New York.

—— (1995), *World Population Prospects: The 1994 Revision*, New York.

—— (1996), *World Population Prospects: The 1996 Revision, Annex I*, New York, preprint.

United Nations Development Programme (UNDP) (1990), *Human Development Report 1990*, New York: Oxford University Press.

United Nations Programme on HIV/AIDS (UNAIDS) and World Health Organization (WHO) (1996), 'The HIV/AIDS Situation in mid 1996', HTML document, http://gpawww.who.ch/highband/press/situat96.html, Geneva, WHO.

Visaria, L., and Visaria, P. (1996), *Prospective Population Growth and Policy Options for India, 1991–2101*, New York: Population Council.

Westley, S. (1995), 'Evidence Mounts for Sex-Selective Abortion in Asia', Asia-Pacific Population and Policy, No. 34, East-West Center.

Williamson, N. E. (1976), *Sons or Daughters: A Cross-Cultural Survey of Parental Preferences*, Beverly Hills: Sage Publications.

Zeng, Y., Tu, P., Gu, B., Xu, Y., Li, B., and Li, Y. (1993), 'Causes and Implications of the Recent Increase In the Reported Sex Ratio at Birth in China', *Population and Development Review*, 19(2): 283–302.

Index